Individual Taxes

WORLDWIDE SUMMARIES
2002–2003

Individual Taxes

WORLDWIDE SUMMARIES
2002–2003

PRICEWATERHOUSECOOPERS

John Wiley & Sons, Inc.

This book is printed on acid-free paper. ♾

Published by John Wiley & Sons, Inc., Hoboken, New Jersey.
Published simultaneously in Canada.

PricewaterhouseCoopers refers to the member firms of the worldwide PricewaterhouseCoopers organization.

This document is provided by PricewaterhouseCoopers LLP for general guidance only, and does not constitute the provision of legal advice, accounting services, investment advice, or professional consulting of any kind. The information provided herein should not be used as a substitute for consultation with professional tax, accounting, legal, or other component advisers. Before making any decision or taking any action, you should consult a professional adviser who has been provided with all pertinent facts relevant to your particular situation.

The information is provided "as is," with no assurance or guarantee of completeness, accuracy, or timeliness of the information, and without warranty of any kind, express or implied, including but not limited to warranties of performance, merchantability, and fitness for a particular purpose.

For general information on our other products and services, or technical support, please contact our Customer Care Department within the United States at 800-762-2974, outside the United States at 317-572-3993 or fax 317-572-4002.

Wiley also publishes its books in a variety of electronic formats. Some content that appears in print may not be available in electronic books.

ISBN 0-471-23676-4 (Set)
ISBN 0-471-23677-2 (Corporate Taxes)
ISBN 0-471-23675-6 (Individual Taxes)

Printed in the United States of America

10 9 8 7 6 5 4 3 2 1

Information Guide Series

This Guide is one of a series on business conditions in the countries in which PricewaterhouseCoopers firms have offices or carry out work, and is based on the latest available information from these offices. The Guide series is published by PricewaterhouseCoopers LLP.

Director

Mark Friedlich

Production Coordination

Brenda Dickerson

To obtain a copy of a title in the Information Guide series, contact your local PricewaterhouseCoopers office, or call (800) 579-1646.

This series is available in print, on CD-ROM and on the Internet at *www.pwcglobal.com*

This Guide, *Individual Taxes—Worldwide Summaries*, supersedes the 2001–2002 edition.

PricewaterhouseCoopers Organization—Practice Firms Worldwide

I take great pleasure and pride in releasing the 2002–2003 edition of the PricewaterhouseCoopers annual Information Guide *Individual Taxes—Worldwide Summaries.* This edition has information on 125 countries and territories. All entries, unless otherwise indicated, present the tax rates and rules in effect at January 1, 2002.

As part of the PricewaterhouseCoopers Information Guide series, which also includes another annual Worldwide Summary—*Corporate Taxes,* it is an example of the continuing and expanding service the PricewaterhouseCoopers organization and individual practice firms can offer worldwide. It is a service particularly well adapted to meet the ever-changing needs of the international business community.

PricewaterhouseCoopers (*www.pwcglobal.com*), the world's largest professional services organization, helps its clients build value, manage risk, and improve performance.

Drawing on the talents of approximately 150,000 people in over 150 countries, PricewaterhouseCoopers provides a full range of business services to leading global, national, and local companies and to public institutions. These services include audit, accounting, financial advisory services and tax, as well as legal services provided through a global network of correspondent law firms.

PricewaterhouseCoopers refers to the individual member firms of the worldwide PricewaterhouseCoopers organization.

I speak for all the PricewaterhouseCoopers practice firms in saying that they stand ready to serve you with regard to international taxation problems or other matters relating to your international activities, wherever in the world you might need assistance. Do not hesitate to call on us.

Yours very truly,

Paul JM van Leent
Global Tax & Legal Services Leader

Foreword

This Guide has been prepared to provide a summary of basic information about individual taxes in 125 countries and territories. It is designed to outline briefly the individual tax rates and certain major features of the tax laws that affect individual taxation in the countries covered. For most countries, the tax summary is supplemented by a sample individual tax calculation to illustrate the basic rules.

In a guide of this nature it is not possible to provide detailed rules on which to base specific action. When more detailed information is required on a country, reference should be made to the specific laws, regulations and tax treaties of the country; and/or to tax advisers.

Unless otherwise indicated, the tax rates and rules in effect at January 1, 2002 have been used.

Table of Contents

PwC contact

For additional information on taxation in Antigua and Barbuda, contact:

Donald B. Ward
PricewaterhouseCoopers
11 Old Parham Road
P.O. Box 1531
St. Johns
Antigua, W.I.
Telephone: (1) (268) 462 3000
Fax: (1) (268) 462 1902
e-mail: donald.ward@ag.pwcglobal.com

Significant developments

The 25% tax on business profits has been replaced with a 2% tax on gross revenue.

Territoriality and residence

Income from employment and investment income is tax free for individuals who are resident in Antigua. Individuals are generally resident if their permanent place of abode is Antigua and they are physically present in Antigua for not less than 183 days in the income (calendar) year.

Temporary residents are taxed only on income arising in Antigua.

Permanent Residence Scheme/The purpose of this scheme is to offer permanent residence status to high net worth individuals wishing to establish residence and eventually domicile, for tax purposes, in a country that has no personal income tax, no capital gains tax and no inheritance tax.

Successful applicants will be issued with Permanent Residence Certificates that will enable them and their spouses to freely enter and leave Antigua without restriction. Applicants will not be granted an Antiguan passport, but could be considered for citizenship after seven years' residence.

Where a pension arises in a country with which Antigua has a double taxation treaty, that pension will be taxed at 5% and foreign tax deducted at source from the pension will be reclaimable.

Individuals who have been granted residence under the Permanent Residence Scheme pay an annual levy of US$20,000.

PricewaterhouseCoopers can act as agent for people wishing to take advantage of this scheme and will handle the application from start to finish.

Gross income

Employee gross income/Nonresidents and temporary residents are taxed on income arising in Antigua, including the value of benefits (i.e., houses, cars, and other benefits or allowances) received locally, whether or not in money.

Capital gains and investment income/There is no separate capital gains tax, and capital gains are not included in or taxed as ordinary income. Nonresidents and temporary residents are taxable on investment income arising in Antigua.

Deductions

Personal allowances/Nonresidents and temporary residents are not entitled to claim any allowances in arriving at taxable income.

Tax credits

Relief from double taxation is given on Commonwealth income or in accordance with the provisions of a relevant treaty.

Other taxes

Unincorporated businesses and individuals carrying on any economic activity are required to pay tax monthly on gross income therefrom at the rate of 2% on income in excess of EC$4,167 per month. This does not apply to income received by an individual from employment.

Commission agents, estate agents and persons disbursing clients' funds pay the 2% tax on that portion belonging to the agent only.

Statutory payroll deductions/Statutory payroll deductions are as follows.

1. Social security:
   a. Employee portion—3% of chargeable income up to $4,500 per month;
   b. Employer portion—5% of chargeable income up to $4,500 per month.
2. Medical benefits:
   a. Employee portion—3.5% of chargeable income;
   b. Employer portion—3.5% of chargeable income.

   Chargeable income for the purpose of calculating social security and medical benefits amounts does not include most allowances.
3. Education levy:
   a. On the first EC$6,500 of chargeable income per annum—No deduction;
   b. On chargeable income between EC$6,500 to EC$60,000/year—2.5% deduction;
   c. On chargeable income for amounts in excess of EC$60,000/year—5% deduction.

   Chargeable income for the purpose of calculating the education levy does not include most allowances.

Tax administration

Returns/Individuals who are temporary residents are required to file a tax return for income arising in Antigua. The tax year for individuals is the calendar year.

Payment of tax/Withholding tax is applicable on payments to nonresidents that may be regarded as income arising in Antigua, such as those listed below.

	%
Interest, rent, and annuities and other annual payments	20
Payments of a nature other than interest, rent or annuities	25

At the time of writing, the Commissioner of Inland Revenue is seeking to assess withholding tax on dividends at a rate of 20%. This is the subject of an appeal.

Tax rates

There is a provision for tax on temporary residents of Antigua and Barbuda (defined as living in Antigua and Barbuda for less than 183 days). This tax is calculated on annual chargeable income using a sliding scale as follows:

Annual chargeable income		Rate
From	To	%
0	EC$ 500	2.5
EC$ 501	1,000	5.0
1,001	1,500	7.5
1,501	2,000	10.0
2,001	2,500	12.5
2,500	3,000	15.0
3,001	4,000	20.0
4,001	5,000	25.0
5,001	7,500	30.0
7,501	10,000	35.0
10,001	15,000	40.0
15,001	20,000	45.0
20,001	30,000	50.0
30,001		55.0

The tax is to be withheld by the employer from payment to the employee.

Exchange rate

Exchange rate of the Eastern Caribbean dollar is officially pegged at US$1 = EC$2.70.

Argentina

PwC contacts

For additional information on taxation in Argentina, contact:

Jorge San Martín, Partner
Lilian Falcon, Manager
Price Waterhouse
(Member Firm of PricewaterhouseCoopers)
Cerrito 268
1010 Buenos Aires, Argentina
Telephone: (54) (11) 4370 6700, 4381 8181/7373/7282
Fax: (54) (11) 4370 6800, 4383 6339, 4382 2793
e-mail: jorge.a.san.martin@ar.pwcglobal.com
lilian.falcon@ar.pwcglobal.com

Significant developments

Public Emergency Law No. 25.561 (Official Gazette January 7, 2002) and regulatory decrees have introduced important reforms to the exchange rate system, including exchange restrictions (restrictions for certain transactions in foreign currency and transferring funds abroad) and the abolition of the Convertibility Law (end of parity of the peso with the U.S. dollar) in favor of the establishment of a floating exchange rate for the peso in relation to the U.S. dollar. These measures will have an impact on the tax system.

Territoriality and residence

Individuals resident in Argentina pay tax on worldwide income.

Residence rules for income tax purposes are set out in the tax reform that was published in the Official Gazette on December 30, 1998 and are effective from fiscal year 1998. The definitions are as follows.

1. Residents:
   a. Argentine nationals living in Argentina;
   b. Argentine nationals working abroad during the first 12 months of living abroad (tax residence status is lost as from the first day of the 14th month), if they have not obtained a permanent residence in a country other than Argentina;
   c. Foreign nationals assigned to work in Argentina for more than five years;
   d. Foreign individuals—in general—residing in Argentina for more than 12 months.
2. Nonresidents:
   Foreign nationals assigned to work in Argentina for less than five years.
3. Foreign beneficiaries:
   a. Individuals working in Argentina for less than six months in a calendar year;
   b. Argentine nationals working abroad who do not qualify as residents.

Except for the earned-income allowance, personal and family allowances are applicable only when the taxpayers and their families, if eligible, have been resident in Argentina for over six months of the tax year under consideration.

Foreign beneficiaries who earn income in Argentina through art or a profession are subject to income tax on these earnings at the rate of 24.5% (35% on assumed profit of 70% of gross income) to be withheld by the local payer.

Gross income

Employee gross income/All remuneration paid in cash or in kind, including allowances, reimbursements or paid expenses (e.g., housing and cost-of-living allowances, school fees, tax reimbursements), is taxable without regard to length of residence or source of income.

Capital gains and investment income/There is no special tax on capital gains.

Except as described below, interest, rents, royalties, pensions, and annuities from Argentine and foreign sources are subject to income tax.

Interest on savings bank accounts and term deposits in Argentine banks, as well as government bonds, is exempt from income tax.

Dividends paid by foreign companies are treated as foreign-source income. They are taxable if distributed to residents, but are not taxable if the beneficiary is a nonresident.

As from fiscal year 2001 the gain resulting from the sale of nonlisted shares is taxable.

Deductions

Business deductions/All losses and expenses incurred in obtaining and preserving taxable income are deductible, but living, personal and family expenses are not deductible, except for Pension Fund and other social security contributions. In cases where fringe benefits include lump-sum allowances for travel, entertaining, and so on, only actual expenses incurred, supported by third-party vouchers, may be deducted from the related fringe benefit includable in taxable income.

Nonbusiness expenses/Mortgage and all other interest is not deductible, unless it relates to taxable income. Pension and other social security contributions; donations to tax-exempt charitable institutions up to a maximum of 5% of net income; local life and retirement insurance premiums and funeral expenses, up to a maximum established annually by the tax authorities; and contributions to third-party medical schemes, up to a maximum of 5% of net income, are deductible. Other medical expenses may be deducted up to a maximum of 40% of all corresponding invoices of the fiscal year, provided the deduction does not exceed 5% of net income.

Personal allowances/Allowances in force for the year 2001 are shown below.

	Annual
Basic	AR$ 4,020
Spouse	2,040
Child (each)	1,020
Other admissible dependents (each)	1,020
Earned income allowance:	
Employees	13,500
Self-employed workers	4,500

The allowances are reduced in relation to the net income as follows:

Net income		% by which allowance is reduced
Over	Not over	
0	AR$ 39,000	0
AR$ 39,000	65,000	10
65,000	91,000	30
91,000	130,000	50
130,000	195,000	70
195,000	221,000	90
221,000		100

Tax credits

Tax credits are possible for income taxes paid abroad on foreign-source income.

Other taxes

Social security taxes/Withholdings and contributions assessable on employee gross remuneration are as follows.

	Employer %	Employee %
Pension Fund	10.17 or 12.71	5 or 11
Family Allowance Fund	4.44 or 5.56	—
Social Health	5	3
Social Services	1.39 or 1.73	3
Total social tax	21 or 25	11 or 17

The total employer social security rate of 25% is required from companies whose main activity consists of commerce or rendering services, provided their annual sales exceed AR$48,000,000. All other companies are subject to the 21% rate.

Decree 1676 (published on December 20, 2001) reduced the employee contribution to the pension fund from 11% to 5% for those employees who contribute to the individual capitalization account system administered by authorized private entities (AFJP). The reduction is valid for one year and may be extended for another year.

The Family Allowance Fund entitles an employee to receive a tax-free monthly allowance for his or her spouse and children, including the education of the latter, provided the employee's salary is not higher than AR$1,500.00. Self-employed persons are subject to pension fund contributions; the monthly payments range from AR$99.84 to AR$1,536.00. These contributions are adjusted annually.

The maximum remuneration subject to both employee and employer contribution is AR$4,800 per month. This amount is adjusted annually.

Depending on the location of the employee, a specific percentage of the social tax basis of the employer's contributions can be offset against the value-added tax (VAT) liability in its monthly VAT return. In Buenos Aires City the creditable percentage amounts to 1.30%, so that the final social tax burden would amount to 19.7% or 23.7%, respectively.

Professionals, researchers, scientists, and technicians contracted abroad to render services in Argentina for a term not exceeding two years and on a once-only basis may be excluded from the system at their own or their employers' request, provided the corresponding requirements are fulfilled.

Gross income tax/Gross income tax is a provincial tax applicable to self-employed individuals on gross earnings. The general tax rate is 3% in the Federal Capital, and similar rates are applicable in the different provinces. Professionals are exempt in the Federal Capital.

Tax on personal assets (wealth tax)/Individuals domiciled in Argentina are subject to an annual tax of 0.5% on their worldwide personal assets valued from AR$102,300 to AR$302,300 as at December 31, without consideration of liabilities. On assets with a total value of more than AR$302,300, the applicable tax rate is 0.75%. These taxable assets include, among other items, real estate, cars, shares, and bank accounts. However, savings accounts at Argentine banks are exempt, as is the stock of Argentine corporations valued to up to AR$100,000 if quoted on the Argentine stock exchange. Individuals domiciled abroad and working in Argentina for reasons duly proved for a period no longer than five years are assessable only on personal assets located in Argentina.

All taxpayers must file an annual tax return and pay the tax liability in April or May of every year, depending on whether they have or do not have shares in nonlisted corporations whose financial year-end is December, respectively.

Individuals living abroad who own assets located in Argentina must pay the corresponding tax in full and final settlement through a local representative. The tax rate is 0.75% on all assets. Tax is not levied where the total value of the assets does not exceed approximately AR$34,000.

Tax on bank account debits and credits/Debits and credits from bank accounts are subject to a new tax at 0.6% on the amount of the transaction. However the deposit and disposal of employment compensation and pension payments are tax exempt.

Local taxes on income/There are no local taxes on income payable in addition to the taxes mentioned above.

Tax administration

Returns/The earnings of each spouse (i.e., from employment, business activities, etc.) are assessable separately and individually.

Tax is assessable on individuals on a calendar-year basis. The general due date for filing is during the second week of April of each year.

Individual income tax returns are not required to be filed by employees who have no sources of income other than payroll compensation, since the tax should be duly withheld at source by the employer. However, the company should prepare an annual tax return reporting the annual remuneration, deductions and withholdings of each fiscal year; this is filed only if the total tax liability has not been withheld. In addition, when annual net income is over AR$40,000, the employee is required to report his or her annual opening and closing net worth (locally and abroad) in a separate personal tax return, which must be filed by the company.

Self-employed workers (including members of boards of directors) must register with the tax authorities and file an annual income tax return. In addition, they are required to make advance payments on account of their income tax liability of the current year based on their income tax liability of the prior fiscal year.

Payment of tax/There is income tax withholding from salaries. Employers are required to withhold tax at the appropriate personal rates applied to the net taxable remuneration of each employee. Self-employed workers must pay the tax balance due subsequent to the filing of the respective tax return at the authorized banks.

Tax rates

The following individual income tax rates are as from January 1, 2000.

Taxable income		Tax on	Percentage
Over (Column 1)	Not over	Column 1	on excess
0	AR$ 10,000	—	9
AR$ 10,000	20,000	AR$ 900	14
20,000	30,000	2,300	19
30,000	60,000	4,200	23
60,000	90,000	11,100	27
90,000	120,000	19,200	31
120,000		28,500	35

INDIVIDUAL TAX CALCULATION

Calendar year 2001

Assumptions

Resident husband and wife, two children; one spouse earns all the income and is included on a local payroll; subject to Pension Fund contributions.

Tax computation

Gross income:		
Salary (including 13th salary)		AR$ 79,840.00
Interest income—Taxable (other than from bank time deposits, etc.)		8,500.00
Capital gain		1,800.00
Total gross income		90,140.00
Less—Capital gain (not subject to tax)		1,800.00
		88,340.00
Less—Deductions:		
Taxes on salary (social security taxes—17% up to a cap of 4,800 per month)	10,608.00	
Charitable contributions	1,200.00	
Medical scheme contributions (up to a maximum of 5% of net income) and other medical expenses (1)	3,886.60	15,694.60
		72,645.40
Less—Personal allowances:		
Spouse	1,428.00	
Children (two)	1,428.00	
Basic allowance	2,814.00	
Earned-income allowance	9,450.00	15,120.00
Taxable income		AR$ 57,525.40
Income tax		AR$ 10,530.84

Notes:

1. Maximum of 40% of invoices up to 5% of net income.
2. Exchange rate of the peso at December 31, 2001: US$1 = AR$1.00.
   For fiscal year 2002 onward this exchange rate is no longer applicable.

PwC contact

For additional information on taxation in Australia, contact:

Ann M. Previtera
PricewaterhouseCoopers
201 Sussex Street
Sydney, New South Wales 2000
Australia
Telephone: (61) (2) 8266 2946
Fax: (61) (2) 8266 5658
e-mail: ann.previtera@au.pwcglobal.com

Significant developments

On October 15, 2001 the federal government announced that from July 1, 2002 it would enhance the tax exemption for certain foreign-source income of expatriates resident in Australia for less than four years. These enhancements include an exemption for their foreign-source income from assets, regardless of when acquired, and for interest withholding tax on interest payments for liabilities, regardless of when incurred. (Further details are discussed under "Capital gains and investment income.")

On November 5, 2001 the federal government announced changes to the taxation of superannuation (see "Superannuation and retirement taxation").

Territoriality and residence

Australia taxes its resident individuals on a worldwide basis. Resident individuals are liable to Australian tax on income derived from all foreign sources, except for salary and wages derived in performing duties overseas for a continuous period of at least 91 days, provided these earnings are not exempt from tax in the foreign country in which they are earned. A tax credit is allowed for foreign taxes paid on taxable income derived from foreign sources (see "Tax credits" below).

Certain income is taxed as it accumulates in the case of investments in certain foreign entities (see "Tax credits").

Individuals are residents of Australia if they reside in Australia, and this includes the following.

1. Individuals whose domicile and permanent place of abode is in Australia.
2. Individuals who have actually been in Australia during more than one-half of the income year, unless the individual's usual place of abode is outside Australia and the individual does not intend to reside in Australia.

Persons coming to Australia to take up a contract of employment may be regarded as residents even if they are to be in the country for a short term of, say, two or four years. Citizenship and nationality do not determine liability to Australian income tax.

A nonresident individual is liable to Australian income tax only on income (other than interest, royalties and dividends) derived from sources in Australia. Nonresidents are subject to withholding tax on (1) interest income paid to them by a resident, (2) dividend income from resident corporations, and (3) Australian-source royalties.

Under the Australian dividend imputation system, dividends paid out of Australian-taxed corporate income (franked dividends) entitle resident individuals to a rebate (and in some cases a refund) of the corporate tax and nonresidents to an exemption from dividend withholding tax (see "Capital gains and investment income").

Gross income

Employee gross income/Gross income of an employee includes cash remuneration arising from employment. Cash remuneration includes salaries, wages, commissions, bonuses, and allowances paid to employees. Employers are liable for a fringe benefits tax levied at 48.5% of the taxable value multiplied by a gross-up factor of the fringe benefits granted to employees. The gross-up factor is 2.1292 for "type 1 aggregate fringe benefits," broadly being fringe benefits where, subject to certain exceptions, the employer was entitled to an input tax credit for GST. The gross-up factor is 1.9417 for other fringe benefits, which are referred to as "type 2 aggregate fringe benefits." Fringe benefits tax is deductible by the employer for income tax purposes. Benefits subject to fringe benefits tax are excluded from the employee's taxable income, but may be taken into account (reportable fringe benefits) when determining the employee's liability for tax surcharges such as the Medicare levy surcharge and the superannuation contributions surcharge and income-related obligations such as child support.

Foreign nationals are generally taxable on salary and allowances relating to services performed in Australia, regardless of where payment is made and whether the income is remitted to Australia. Nonemployee resident taxpayers are subject to tax on noncash business benefits.

Resident individuals are subject to Australian tax on their overseas employment income, unless special exemption requirements are met (see "Tax credits"). However, tax treaties are in force with various countries, and provisions in those treaties may require a different tax treatment of certain employment income.

Capital gains and investment income/Capital gains tax applies to assets acquired on or after September 20, 1985. Capital gains made upon the realization of such assets are included in assessable income and are taxed at ordinary rates of tax. If the asset was acquired before 11:45 a.m. AEST on September 21, 1999 and was held for at least 12 months, the individual has a choice of including in taxable income 50% of the nominal gain (gross proceeds less costs not indexed for inflation) or 100% of the gain, allowing for the inflation indexing of costs up to September 30, 1999, but not beyond that date. If the asset was acquired on or after 11:45 a.m. AEST on September 21, 1999 and has been held for at least 12 months, 50% of the nominal gain (with no indexing of costs for inflation) is included in the individual's taxable income. Capital losses are allowable as deductions only against capital gains and cannot be offset against other income. In calculating capital losses, there is no indexation of the cost base.

Residents of Australia, including short-term residents, are liable for the tax on gains from the disposal of assets wherever situated, subject to a credit for foreign tax paid. Nonresidents are liable for tax on gains on the disposal of assets having a "necessary connection with Australia," defined broadly as including land or buildings situated in Australia, assets used in carrying on a business through a permanent establishment in Australia, shares in Australian private companies, interests in resident trusts, interests owned in partnership assets that are taxable Australian assets, and shareholdings of 10% or more in the issued capital of Australian public companies.

Where a nonresident becomes an Australian resident, capital assets owned by the nonresident (other than assets acquired before September 20, 1985 and assets having a "necessary connection with Australia") are deemed to have been acquired by the nonresident for a consideration equal to the market value of the assets at the time residence is achieved. Special provisions also apply where a resident individual ceases to be a resident, so that non-Australian assets can be deemed to be disposed of, unless an election to the contrary is made.

The government has announced that from July 1, 2002 there will be a tax exemption for certain foreign-source income of expatriates resident in Australia for less than four years. The exemption will be available for foreign-source income of eligible temporary residents from assets, regardless of when they were acquired, and interest withholding tax for liabilities, regardless of when they were incurred. No capital gain or loss will arise on the disposal by such a resident of assets not having the necessary connection with Australia, other than portfolio interests in Australian publicly listed companies. Periods of residence terminated more than ten years before the current period of tax residence will be ignored when determining if an individual is tax-resident for the first time. Where the period of the temporary visa exceeds four years, the exemption will be available for up to four years. Special conditions apply for expatriates who are New Zealand citizens.

Resident individuals are taxable on foreign-source dividend, interest and royalty income but are eligible for a credit for foreign taxes paid on such income (see "Tax credits" below).

A dividend imputation system designed to prevent the double taxation of Australian corporate profits distributed to individual shareholders applies to dividends paid out of Australian-taxed profits of resident corporations (franked dividends). Resident individual shareholders receiving franked dividends are entitled to a rebate of Australian corporate tax paid on the dividends. From July 1, 2000, if a franking rebate exceeds the tax payable by an resident individual, the excess is refundable to the individual. Nonresident individuals receiving franked dividends are not entitled to a rebate but are exempt from withholding tax on the dividends, and they are exempt from withholding tax on unfranked dividends to the extent that the dividends are paid out of certain foreign-source dividend income and the company has specified an "FDA declaration percentage" in relation to the dividend.

Nonresidents are not taxable on income from sources outside Australia. Australian-source unfranked dividend income, interest income and royalty income are normally subject only to withholding tax. Other Australian-source income is taxable at personal rates applicable to nonresidents.

Deductions

Business deductions/To the extent these are not reimbursed, residents and nonresidents can deduct properly substantiated business expenses incurred in earning employment and other income, for example, business-connected travel expenses, automobile expenses, subscriptions to professional or trade organizations, and tax-agent fees. Expenses of a private or domestic nature are generally not deductible. Entertainment expenses are not allowable deductions, except for entertainment benefits provided by employers to employees, which are subject to fringe benefits tax.

Living-away-from-home allowances are subject to fringe benefits tax that is payable by the employer. A portion of living-away-from-home allowances in relation to the provision of accommodation and excess food costs is exempt from fringe benefits tax.

Certain relocation fringe benefits are exempt from fringe benefits tax. To the extent that a fringe benefit is exempt from fringe benefits tax, it will also usually be exempt from income tax. Employer-provided cars are taxed concessionally under fringe benefits tax rules.

Nonbusiness expenses/Gifts of A$2 or more to specified charities, cultural organizations, environmental organizations, and public institutions are deductible. A tax rebate is available at the rate of 20% of the excess of qualifying medical expenses over A$1,250. A 30% tax rebate is available for the cost of private health insurance premiums.

Personal allowances/Residents receive the first segment of taxable income tax free. The tax-free threshold for the year ending June 30, 2001 is A$6,000 (see "Tax rates"). Provided family income is below certain thresholds, a resident individual (or an individual in Australia with a temporary visa for social security purposes) is entitled to family tax benefit Part A if he or she has a dependent child under 21 or a dependent full-time student aged 21 to 24 (who is not in receipt of youth allowance or a similar payment). If a couple are both eligible, only one may claim. Where family income is A$29,857 or less, the maximum family tax benefit Part A is payable, and reduces by 30 cents for each dollar above A$29,857 until the base rate for this benefit is reached. The base rate reduces by 30 cents for each dollar of family income over A$77,234 (plus $3,139 for each family tax benefit child after the first) until the payment cuts out. The annual family income limits at which the family tax benefit Part A cuts out are: A$80,665 for a recipient with a dependent child under 18; A$81,846 for a recipient with a dependent child aged 18 to 24. These limits increase by A$6,570 for each additional family tax benefit child under 18 and A$7,750 for each additional family tax benefit child aged 18 to 24. These limits may be higher in certain cases for larger families.

The maximum annual rates of family tax benefit Part A are: for each child under 13—A$3,204.70; for each child 13 to 15—A$4,062.45; for each child 16 to 17—A$1,029.30; for each child 18 to 24—A$1,383.35.

The annual base rate of family tax benefit Part A is: for each child under 18—A$1,029.30; for each child 18 to 24—A$1,383.35.

In determining entitlement for the family tax benefit Part A, family income, known as "adjusted taxable income", includes taxable income, reportable fringe benefits, tax-free pensions and benefits, foreign income not taxed in Australia, certain net rental property losses less 50% of payments to support a child from a previous relationship, rising to 100% of such payments from July 1, 2001.

Where all or most of family income is earned by one person, family tax benefit Part B may be payable in addition to Part A. If the secondary earner's adjusted taxable income is A$1,679 or less, the maximum family tax benefit Part B is paid, regardless of the income of the primary earner. For each dollar above that limit, the payment reduces by 30 cents, cutting out when the secondary earner's annual income reaches: A$10,853 if the youngest child is under 5; A$8,079 if the youngest child is between 5 and 18. Regardless of their income, sole parents receive the maximum family tax benefit Part B.

Maximum annual rates of family tax payment Part B are: if the youngest child is under 5—A$2,752.10; if the youngest child is 5 to 15 or a full-time student of 16 to 18—A$1,919.90.

There are three choices as to the way in which the family tax benefit may be paid. There is also a childcare benefit to help low income families with childcare costs.

Residents are entitled to specified rebates of tax, including a rebate set at a maximum of A$1,437 for 2001/2002 for a dependent resident spouse. The spouse rebate is subject to abatement for separate net income of the spouse, cutting out if this exceeded A$6,029 (in 2001/2002). In general, the dependent spouse rebate is not available to couples with children who are entitled to the family tax benefit Part B.

If a spouse's assessable income does not exceed A$10,800, a resident may make a maximum rebatable contribution of A$3,000 for the spouse (including a de facto) to a complying superannuation fund or retirement savings account (RSA) and obtain a maximum tax rebate of A$540 (the rebate is the amount of the contribution x 18%). The rebate is subject to abatement if the spouse's assessable income exceeds A$10,800, cutting out if this exceeds A$13,799. Other rebates include those for residence in isolated areas and certain lump sums received in arrears.

Nonresidents generally do not benefit from a tax-free threshold, nor do they qualify for the various rebates.

Tax credits

Australian-resident individuals are subject to Australian tax on their worldwide income, with credit allowed for foreign taxes paid on foreign-source income to the extent of Australian tax payable. However, an Australian resident deriving foreign salary and wage income from overseas employment during a continuous period of at least 91 days is exempt from Australian tax on this income, provided these earnings are not exempt from tax in the foreign country in which they are earned. For those taxpayers with exempt foreign-source income, a notional average rate of tax payable on the sum of exempt and nonexempt income is to be applied to the nonexempt component. For the purpose of calculating foreign tax credits, exempt foreign earnings are not to be aggregated with foreign income other than earnings.

Certain foreign noncomparably taxed income, which is generally sheltered in low-tax countries through foreign companies controlled by Australian residents and through trusts, may be attributed to Australian-resident controllers and taxed in Australia. Any income subject to taxation on attribution will be exempt from Australian tax when repatriated to Australia.

There are also measures to deal with passive foreign investment funds (FIFs), including interests in foreign companies, foreign trusts and foreign life insurance policies. Essentially, and subject to important qualifications, the FIF rules tax increases or deemed increases in value and distributions from interests in offshore entities (wherever located), except for some categories that are specifically exempted. Investments in foreign companies listed on approved stock exchanges that are principally engaged in certain active businesses are exempt.

There are several other exemptions, including an exemption for life insurance policies held by natural persons giving life or life and disability coverage only. It has been announced that taxpayers holding temporary residents visas will from July 1, 2002 be exempt from FIF rules, regardless of the length of time for which the visa is held. Special rules will apply to New Zealand citizens.

Other significant items/Nonresidents are exempt from Australian tax on foreign-source income; therefore, no foreign tax credit is applicable.

Personal allowances (see above) generally take the form of tax rebates, which are available only to residents.

Other taxes

Social security taxes/There are no social security taxes; a 1.5% levy on taxable income is imposed on residents for the funding of a National Health Scheme (Medicare). A surcharge of 1% applies to high income taxpayers where the taxpayer and his or her dependants are not covered by private health insurance.

Superannuation and retirement taxation/Employer supported and self-employed contributions to more than 100,000 complying superannuation entities and retirement savings accounts (RSAs) have a role in Australia similar to that of social security levies. The retirement benefits provided by these superannuation entities (which are independent of government, but have to comply with regulations so they are "complying") are in addition to the age pension which is provided by the federal government and is means tested. The rules regarding the taxation of superannuation are extremely complex and what follows is a brief summary of some highlights. For 2001/2002 employers must contribute on behalf of their employees' superannuation an amount broadly equal to not less than 8% of their payroll, (9% in 2002/2003) subject to exceptions, or be liable to a superannuation guarantee charge. It is usually tax effective, subject to certain limits, for employees to "sacrifice" salary to allow employer superannuation contributions on their behalf above this minimum. The maximum annual deductible contributions for employers per employee (for the 2001/2002 income year) are, based on the age of the employee: age 0 to 34—A$11,912; age 35 to 49—$A33,087; age 50 and over—$82,054. The superannuation entity receiving employer contributions pays contributions tax of 15% on the amount of the contribution. In addition it is liable to a "surcharge" tax of an additional 15% for contributions on behalf of employees whose adjusted taxable income for the 2001/2002 year equals at least A$103,507. Shading in applies if the employee's income is less than this amount and not less than A$85,242 The government has announced that starting from July 1, 2002 the surcharge will be reduced by a tenth of its current level each year over the next three years (by 1.5 percentage points per year).

Complying superannuation funds pay tax of 15% on their earnings, except for venture capital franked dividends from a pooled development fund (PDF) which are not taxed, and tax on capital gains on assets acquired after 11:45 am AEST on September 21, 1999 and held for more than 12 months, which are effectively taxed at 10%. A similar treatment is available for capital gains on assets acquired before that time, or the fund may choose to pay tax of 15% on the capital gain less indexation for inflation to the earlier of the disposal date or September 30, 1999. For 2001/2002 the reasonable benefit limit (RBL) that an individual may accumulate for withdrawal as a lump sum in superannuation benefits (without paying excess benefits tax) is $A529,373, and the RBL is A$1,058,742 if at least half of the benefits are taken as a complying pension. Provided the individual is over 55, there is no tax on withdrawals from superannuation funds up to the first A$105,843 for components accumulated since June 1983. This is a lifetime threshold, indexed annually. Lump-sum withdrawals above this threshold, subject to the lifetime RBL, made by taxpayers over age 55 are taxed at 15%. More concessional tax rules apply for components deemed to be pre-June 1983. A tax rebate of 15% applies for certain superannuation pensions and qualifying annuities paid to recipients over age 55.

Local taxes on income/There are no state or city income taxes.

Stamp tax (including Financial Institutions Duty)/All the states and territories of Australia impose stamp taxes at various rates on documents, such as mortgages and other secured interests, insurance policies, leasing transactions, and contracts effecting the transfer of shares or real estate or interest therein. Because stamp tax is levied by the states and territories, the rates vary, depending on where the transactions are carried into effect.

Debits tax/The state governments impose a tax on most debits made to checking accounts kept with a bank. Certain debits and accounts are exempt from the tax. The tax is to be repealed on July 1, 2005. In New South Wales debits tax ceased on January 1, 2002.

Tax administration

Returns/A resident individual is required to file an income tax return where gross income exceeds the tax-free threshold (for the 2000/2001 income year, A$6,000—see rate table below). A nonresident earning A$1 or more salary or wage income must file a return. There is no joint assessment or joint filing in Australia.

Employees and holders of certain investments must quote their income tax file number to their employer and/or relevant financial institution if they wish to prevent tax from being withheld (at the top marginal rate) on income paid to them.

Returns for individuals are filed on the basis of a fiscal year ending June 30; they are due for filing by the following October 31, unless an extension is approved.

Payment of tax/When salaries are paid by an Australian company or by a nonresident company from a base in Australia, pay-as-you-go (PAYG) tax installments must be withheld. PAYG tax must also withheld from payments to contractors if an Australian Business Number (ABN) is not provided by the contractor and the payment amount disregarding GST exceeds A$50.

PAYG quarterly installments of tax calculated on certain income derived during the previous quarter are payable by certain individuals. The due dates for these quarterly payments are October 28, February 28, April 28, and July 28. The tax installments are based on the total of certain gross income such as fees for services, sales in carrying on a business, interest, dividends, and royalties derived during the previous quarter (but not salary or wages) multiplied by an installment rate provided by the Commissioner of Taxation to determine the tax payable. The individual may vary this installment rate, but if this is less than 85% of the rate that should have applied, a general interest charge will be payable. Individuals may choose to pay quarterly installments based on their "GDP-adjusted notional tax" if they are not registered for GST, nor a partner of a partnership registered for GST, and if their most recent "notional tax" is $8,000 or more. Individuals, and companies and funds with an annual turnover of under A$1,000,000, may also adopt this method. If this method is chosen the installment payable will be based on the tax of a previous year adjusted for movements in Australia's GDP. Individuals whose notional tax amount is less than A$8,000 pay a single annual installment. It has been indicated that if the balance of an individual's last assessment was less than A$250, the individual will be not subject to PAYG installment tax and need only pay tax on such income upon annual assessment.

Tax rates

For the year ending June 30, 2002/The following rates of tax apply to resident and nonresident individuals for the year ending June 30, 2002.

Residents

Taxable income			
Over (Column 1)	**Not over**	**Tax on Column 1**	**Percentage on excess**
0	A$ 6,000	—	0
A$ 6,000	20,000	—	17
20,000	50,000	A$ 2,380	30
50,000	60,000	11,380	42
60,000		15,580	47

Note:

Resident rates apply to a person who has been an Australian resident for tax purposes at any time during the income year and also to any nonresident in receipt of taxable Australian social security pensions.

Nonresidents

Taxable income			
Over (Column 1)	**Not over**	**Tax on Column 1**	**Percentage on excess**
0	A$ 20,000	—	29
A$ 20,000	50,000	A$ 5,800	30
50,000	60,000	14,800	42
60,000		19,000	47

INDIVIDUAL TAX CALCULATION

Year ending June 30, 2002 (current as at January 1, 2002)

Assumptions

Resident husband and wife; two children, one aged 4, the other aged 7. Neither the wife nor the children have any separate income. The husband and wife agree that the family tax benefit Part B is claimed through the tax system. Income includes salary of A$93,600, interest of A$5,000, long-term capital gain of A$2,000 (not taxable because asset was acquired prior to September 20, 1985), and gross foreign dividends of A$1,000 (on which foreign tax of A$150 is paid). The husband pays an annual premium of A$2,000 for private health insurance and seeks to claim the relevant rebate through the tax system.

Tax computation

Assessable income:		
Salary		A$ 93,600
Interest		5,000
Foreign dividend		1,000
		99,600
Less—Deductions:		
Gifts to qualifying charities	500	
Employment-related expenses (e.g., professional body subscriptions)	80	580
Taxable income		A$ 99,020
Tax thereon		A$ 33,919
Add—Medicare levy		1,485
		35,404
Less:		
Credit for foreign tax on dividends		(150)
Tax offset for private health insurance premium		(2,752)
Family tax benefit Part B		(600)
Tax payable		A$ 31,902

Note:

Exchange rate of the Australian dollar at December 31, 2001: US$1 = A$1.9704.

PwC contact

For additional information on taxation in Austria, contact:

Friedrich Rödler
PricewaterhouseCoopers
Prinz-Eugen-Strasse 72
A–1040 Vienna, Austria
Telephone: (43) (1) 501 88 0
Fax: (43) (1) 501 88 9
e-mail: friedrich.roedler@at.pwcglobal.com

Significant developments

There have been no significant tax or regulatory developments as regards individual taxation in the past year.

Territoriality and residence

All persons resident in Austria are subject to Austrian income tax on their worldwide income, including income from trade or business, profession, employment, investments, and property. Nonresidents are taxed on income from certain sources in Austria only.

A person is generally regarded as resident with the establishment of an abode or, in any event, after a six-month stay in Austria.

Nationality is not in itself a criterion for determining residence or tax liability. However, it may serve as an indicator of residence in cases of doubt.

Gross income

Employee gross income/Income from employment includes all benefits in cash or in kind received by an individual from an employer and from third parties. Benefits in kind are valued according to specific rules, with some cases of global allocations (mainly cars). Company-provided housing is valued at 75% of the actual gross rent paid by the company; reimbursement for privately paid housing is fully taxable. Certain minor benefits-in-kind are tax exempt (e.g., the granting of company stock up to an annual limit of €1,460 per employee). Further tax-free amounts are available for nontransferable options exercised within seven years after grant. Reimbursement of an employee's actual relocation costs is tax exempt; lump-sum relocation allowances are tax exempt within certain limits. Reimbursement of tax costs is fully taxable.

Bonus payments (e.g., 13th- and 14th-month salaries, i.e., vacation and Christmas pay) up to an annual amount equal to two average monthly salaries are taxed at a flat rate of 6%; the first €620 is tax free. Bonus amounts exceeding this ceiling are taxed at normal rates.

Nonresidents are subject to income tax on Austrian-source income at normal rates.

Special ruling for expatriates/With the aim of reducing taxes and facilitating payroll accounting for the rising number of foreign executives assigned to Austria, expatriates are granted a global allowance to cover housing allowances in the current payroll accounting.

For the purposes of the directive, "expatriates" are individuals who have not been resident in Austria for the past ten years and who work temporarily for an Austrian employer (group company or permanent establishment for wage tax purposes) in Austria on behalf of a foreign employer. The work in Austria must not be planned to last more than five years, and employees must keep their residence in the home country.

Under the directive, the following foreign allowances paid to the expatriate by the employer can be considered tax-free directly in the current payroll accounting.

1. Expenses for moving:
   Lump-sum payments for moves due to assignments are tax-free up to 1/15 of annual gross salary.
2. Expenses for double household:
   Reasonable rental costs for a residence in Austria for the employee and family are tax deductible up to a monthly amount of €2,200.
3. Expenses for home leaves:
   If expatriates visit their foreign employer while on home leave, it is assumed that these costs represent expenses for a business trip and remain tax-free. No per diem allowances for travel to the parent enterprise and home leave can be claimed.

   In addition, home leave for the maintenance of the permanent residence is tax-free up to a monthly amount of €175 for the employee.
4. Expenses for education of children (school fees):
   If children of expatriates accompany their parents to Austria and must attend a private international school instead of a public school to continue their education, a monthly amount of €110 per child is tax deductible.

Additional special expenditures, business expenses and extraordinary financial burdens can be considered in the annual tax return.

The employer must forward a written notification to the appropriate tax office at the beginning of the assignment and thereafter at the beginning of every calendar year, stating the names of the employees for whom the beneficial tax treatment is claimed, and must inform the tax authorities of their personal data, including addresses in Austria and in the foreign country.

Capital gains and investment income/In general, capital gains arising from nonbusiness activities are not taxed, subject to the following two exceptions.

1. Short-term capital gains—Profits on the sale of both Austrian and non-Austrian assets are considered "speculative" transactions and are subject to income tax at normal rates where the period between purchase and sale is not more than one year (real estate—10 years, in some cases 15 years; specific rules apply for sale of principal residence). Such profits totaling less than €440 are not taxable (tax exemption limit). Nonresidents are liable to tax only on "short-term" profits (ten years) from sales of Austrian real estate. Short term capital gains are taxed at normal income tax rates.
2. Sale of participations—Profits on the sale of holdings in corporations (in particular, AGs or Ges.m.b.H.s) are subject to income tax at reduced rates where the vendor has held at least 1% of issued share capital at any time within a period of five years preceding the date of sale. Nonresidents are liable to tax on such profits if the company has its head office or a place of management in Austria.

Investment income comprises mainly dividends, profits from shares in silent partnerships and interest and income from investment funds.

Bank interest and interest on certain securities from Austrian sources received by Austrian residents are subject to withholding tax of 25%. Withholding tax settles the income tax liability on interest as well as inheritance tax on the source of interest. If an individual's average income tax rate is lower than 25%, a tax refund is available. Interest not subject to withholding tax (e.g., withholding-tax-exempt interest from abroad) is to be declared in the income tax return and is taxed at ordinary rates; in the case of inheritance, inheritance tax is applied. Nonresidents are taxed on interest (except interest on bonds) if the underlying loan is secured by Austrian real estate.

Dividends received by Austrian residents and nonresidents are subject to a withholding tax of 25%, which settles the income tax liability; inheritance tax on the source of dividends is covered if less than 1% of issued share capital was held as participation. A refund is available if an individual's average tax rate, divided by two, is below 25%. Dividends from abroad are to be declared in the income tax return and are taxed at normal rates. For nonresidents, withholding tax on dividends represents the final tax burden. The provisions of applicable double taxation treaties must be observed.

For income from foreign investment funds special provisions and lump-sum taxation may apply (minimum taxation). If income from capital gains and investments is received from abroad, the relevant double taxation treaty is to be observed. As a general rule these treaties provide for taxation in Austria with tax credit for corresponding foreign taxes, if any.

Deductions

Business deductions/Expenses incurred in "acquiring, securing and maintaining" income are deductible from the taxable income of the particular source of income concerned. All employees are entitled to a standard allowance of €132. Expenses in excess of this amount will be allowed if supported by receipts (e.g., office in home, continuing education; also, for short-term residents see the new directive described under "Gross income").

Nonbusiness expenses/Employee portions of mandatory contributions to Austrian and/or foreign social security are tax deductible.

Relief allowances are also available against taxable income if annual income does not exceed €50,900. This allowance includes sickness, life and accident insurance premiums; voluntary contributions to employer pension plans and/or state social security; expenses for the construction of a new house/apartment or renovation of housing space in Austria; and the purchase of certain shares and bonds. For these types of expenses, a standard allowance of €60 per year is granted, unless higher payments are substantiated. In the latter case, the deductible amount is limited to 25% of expenses up to €2,900 per year for single taxpayers and €5,800 per year for the sole earner of a married couple. For taxpayers with at least three children, earnings are increased to €4,400 for single taxpayers and €7,300 for sole earners. Taxpayers who earn between €36,400 and €50,900 per year can claim only part of this allowance.

Church tax is deductible up to €75, and charitable contributions to certain institutions are deductible up to 10% of the previous year's taxable income. Austrian tax adviser fees are fully deductible.

Exceptionally heavy financial burdens relief/Where taxpayers unavoidably incur exceptionally heavy financial burdens, they may claim an allowance against taxable income. Depending on the type of burden, this allowance may be claimed either in the amount of actual expenses (e.g., damage due to disaster) or to the extent that such expenses exceed a retention, i.e., a certain percentage of income up to which no deduction is allowed (e.g., medical costs, funeral costs).

The retention percentage depends on the taxpayer's income and personal status, as follows.

Annual income		Retention
Over	Not over	%
0	€ 7,300	6
€ 7,300	14,600	8
14,600	36,400	10
36,400		12

The percentage is reduced by 1% for sole earners and for each dependent child.

Personal allowances/Personal allowances are available as follows.

	€
Basic—All taxpayers (1)	887.00
Employee (general)	54.00
Employee transportation	291.00
Sole earners of married couples or, in case of at least one dependent child, single taxpayers and sole earners of unmarried couples	364.00
Children (2):	
For the first dependent child	610.80
For the second dependent child	610.80
For each additional dependent child	610.80
Pensioners	400.00

*Will be pro rata reduced to zero for income between €16,715 and €21,802 p.a.

Notes:

1. The basic allowance of €887 is granted pro rata for income up to an income of €35,421 p.a. For income exceeding €35,421 p.a. no basic allowance is available.
2. To be prorated according to months of eligibility.

Generally, personal allowances take the form of tax credits, i.e., deductions from tax payable. By contrast, children's allowances are paid to the taxpayer in cash, together with the family allowance.

Tax credits

Austria has entered into double taxation treaties with all major trading countries. Some of the treaties provide for elimination or partial elimination of double taxation by foreign tax credit (e.g., Canada, Japan, United Kingdom, United States). Under the majority of treaties, however, double taxation is avoided or partially avoided by an exemption-with-saving clause as to progression. As an exception to the rule, dividends and interest are usually fully taxable with a foreign tax credit.

Other taxes

Social security taxes/Monthly rates of compulsory (pretax) contributions in effect as of January 1, 2002 are shown below.

1. Pensions, sickness, unemployment, accident insurance, and certain minor contributions:

	Employer %	Employee %	Total %
Social security contribution rates (total)	21.65*	17.65*	39.30*
Social security categories:			
Sickness	3.50	3.40	6.90
Unemployment	3.00	3.00	6.00
Pension	12.55	10.25	22.80
Accident	1.40	—	1.40
Miscellaneous	1.20	1.00	2.20
Total	21.65	17.65	39.30

*On a maximum assessment basis (gross salary) of €3,270 per month and €6,540 p.a. for special payments.

2. In addition, the employer is liable to the Family Burdens Equalization Levy at the rate of 4.5%, the municipal tax on payroll at the rate of 3% of monthly gross salaries and wages and, in the city of Vienna, a public transportation levy of €0.75 per week per employee. In addition, a contribution to the Chamber of Commerce is levied at a rate of approximately 0.44% of gross salaries paid.
3. Social security contributions are levied on bonus payments (e.g., 13th- and 14th-month salaries) up to €6,540 per annum at a total rate of 37.8% (employer 21.15%, employee 16.65%).

   For certain family members (mainly spouses who are not educating or have not educated children for at least four years), an additional insurance contribution of 3.4% within the above-mentioned limits must be paid.

Austria has entered into agreements on social security with its major trading partners, under which, in most cases, it is possible for expatriates on temporary secondment from non-EU (European Union) countries to apply for exemption from Austrian social security contributions for a certain period of time, provided home country social insurance continues. The Austrian social security authorities will ask for a home country certificate of coverage. For EU citizens, different rules apply (form E101).

Local taxes on income/There are no local income taxes for individuals.

Tax administration

Returns/Joint filing of income tax returns is not permitted. The tax year for individuals is always the calendar year.

Payment of tax/In general, income tax is withheld from salaries/wages, interest and dividends (see "Investment income" above). Income tax on other types of income is payable quarterly, with an annual return filing requirement.

Tax rates

Income tax/Tax rates in force as of January 1, 2002 are as follows.

Annual taxable income				
Over	Not over		Percentage	Deduct progression
(Column 1)				
0	€ 3,640	....	0	0
€ 3,640	7,270	....	21	764.40
7,270	21,800	....	31	1,491.40
21,800	50,870	....	41	3,671.40
50,870		....	50	8,249.70

Notes:

1. Total income tax is reduced by the basic personal allowance of €887 (reduced by pro rata computation for certain categories—see above under "Allowances, Note 1").
2. If the taxpayer is the sole earner of a married couple, income tax is reduced by another €364.

Payroll withholding tax/Assuming Austrian social security applies, wage tax and social security contributions are withheld as follows.

(In Euros)

Annual taxable salary		1/14th annual salary	Pretax monthly social security withholding	Monthly wage tax withholding
29,000	....	2,071.43	365.61	317.28
36,000	....	2,571.43	453.86	488.68
54,000	....	3,857.14	577.16	1,003.54
72,000	....	5,142.86	577.16	1,558.63

Notes:

1. Persons having employment income only are not obliged to file income tax returns. However, where such persons have incurred deductible business or nonbusiness expenses or did not have a constant salary for 12 months, a partial refund of taxes may be obtained by filing an income tax return.
2. The basic personal allowance has been considered in the above table.
3. For the sole earner of a married couple, monthly tax amount withheld is reduced by €30.34.
4. Tax rates applicable to monthly salaries are based on the above-listed income tax rates.
5. For children, there is a tax-free subsidy p.a. ("family allowance") as follows:
   a. For children below the age of 10:

	€
First child	1,264.80
Second child	1,418.40
Third and each additional child	1,570.80

b. For children between the ages of 10 and 18:

	€
First child	1,483.20
Second child	1,636.80
Third and each additional child	1,789.20

c. For children between the ages of 19 and 27:

	€
First studying child	1,744.80
Second studying child	1,898.40
Third and each additional studying child	2,050.80

The family allowance for two children is increased by €18.20 per month; the increase is shown in each age level of but is only payable one time.

In addition, for each child the amount of €610.80 p.a. is provided. These family allowances are granted even in the case where no income tax is payable.

As of January 1, 2002 *"Kinderbetreuungsgeld"* (maternity pay) is granted for all children born on or after January 1, 2002. A taxpayer entitled to the family allowance is eligible for maternity pay. This benefit, which amounts to €14.53 per day, is paid up to a maximum of 36 months, in general for 30 months. There is a limit for additional income, currently €14,600 per year, for the beneficiary.

An additional allowance for three or more children is granted, but only when the family allowance for children has been obtained and the household income for the calendar year does not exceed the annual maximum basis of the mandatory social security for the previous year. The additional allowance amounts to €36.40 per month €436.80 per year for the third and each additional dependent child.

Family allowance is paid by the tax office in cash along with the children's allowances (see "Personal allowances" above).

6. The 13th- and 14th-month salaries are subject to social security deductions as described above (see "Social security taxes"). The first €620 is tax exempt (see "Employee gross income" above); from the remaining amount, tax is withheld at a flat rate of 6%.

INDIVIDUAL TAX CALCULATION

Based on the law and tax rates in effect on January 1, 2002

Assumptions

Resident husband and wife, two dependent children; one spouse earns all the income; employment in Austria; Austrian social security applies; interest from Austrian sources—€11,250; dividends from abroad (double taxation treaty country)—€7,030; life insurance premiums of €7,300 per year.

Tax computation

Salary		€ 65,400
Less—Tax-free income		620
		64,780
Less:		
Tax-favored portion (13th- and 14th-month salaries)	8,723	
((65,400 ÷ 14) x 2) – 620		
Social insurance contributions	6,926	
(12 x 577.15 for current salaries)		
Standard allowance—business expenses	132	15,781
		48,999
Interest income from Austrian bank deposits and bonds (gross): 11,250—withholding tax of 25% (see below)		
Add—Dividends from double taxation agreement (DTA) country (gross)		7,030
Taxable income		€ 56,029
Tax thereon at 50%	28,014	
Less—Progression	(8,249)	€ 19,764
Less—Personal allowances:		
Basic (1)	0	
Sole earner	364	
Employee	54	
Transportation	291	(709)
Income tax		€ 19,056
Less—Tax credit according to DTA for foreign withholding tax on dividends (Assumption: 10% of 7,030)		(703)
		18,353
Add—Income tax on the 13th- and 14th-month salaries		458
(6% of (8,723 – 1,089 social security))		
Add—Withholding tax on interest (25%)		2,813
Total income tax payable		€ 21,624

Notes:

1. Basic allowance of €887 after pro rata reductions for employees.
2. Exchange rate of the Euro at January 3, 2002: US$1 = €1.106.

PwC contact

For additional information on taxation in Azerbaijan, contact:

Zaid S. Sethi
PricewaterhouseCoopers
The Landmark Building
96 Nizami str, 5th Floor
370010, Baku
Azerbaijan
Telephone: (994 12) 97 25 15
Fax: (994 12) 97 74 11
e-mail: zaid.sethi@az.pwcglobal.com

Significant developments

A new Tax Code has been introduced into the legislation, completely changing the concept of the calculation, payment and reporting of individual taxes. Thresholds for the calculation of income taxes have been changed effective from January 1, 2002, resulting in the reduction of tax payable.

The Social and Employment Funds have been merged. Effective from January 1, 2002, social security taxes is payable at the rate of 29% (employers) and 1.5% (employees).

Territoriality and residence

Persons actually staying in the territory of the Azerbaijan Republic for more than 182 cumulative days (regardless the duration of stay within a day) during any consecutive 12-month period ended in the taxable calendar year, and those working for a state service of the Azerbaijan Republic in a foreign country during a calendar year or within one calendar year are considered resident. The stay in the territory of the Azerbaijan Republic of officials with a diplomatic or consular status, employees of international organizations or foreign nationals engaged in state service of foreign states, as well as their family members, will not be regarded as a period of stay in the territory of the Azerbaijan Republic, unless such persons are engaged in entrepreneurial activities in Azerbaijan.

A physical person who stays either in the territory of the Azerbaijan Republic or in a foreign country for less than 182 days will be considered a resident of the Azerbaijan Republic according to the criteria outlined below (in order of consideration).

1. Place of permanent residence.
2. Center of vital interests.
3. Regular place of residence.
4. Citizenship of the Azerbaijan Republic.

Taxable income of a resident consists of worldwide income, i.e., income generated in and outside the Azerbaijan Republic. A nonresident's taxable income is that income generated solely from sources in the Azerbaijan Republic.

Gross income

The taxable base of residents is determined as the difference between gross income for a calendar year and expenses (or deductions).

Where income from dependent employment has been taxed at source, no further income tax or deductions are calculated.

The taxable base for a nonresident physical persons engaged in activity in the Azerbaijan Republic through a permanent establishment is the difference between gross income generated in a specific period from Azerbaijan sources with regard to the permanent establishment and the amount of expenses (or deductions) with respect to the generation of income during that period.

For nonresident physical persons engaged in activity in the Azerbaijan Republic without a permanent establishment, the taxable base is the income received from Azerbaijan sources.

Capital gains and investment income/Dividends and interest received by physical persons and taxed at source are not subject to further taxation.

Taxable benefits/The value of any of the following payments or benefits received in connection with employment is treated as taxable income.

1. Loans granted to a physical person at an interest rate that is lower than the interest rate at the interbank credit auction. The difference between the amount that would be paid under the interbank credit auction rate and the amount to be paid at the lower rate is taxable.
2. The assignment of goods (works, services) or gratuitous transfer thereof by an employer to an employee. Tax is levied on the difference between the value of these goods (works, services) based on their fair market value and the amount paid by the employee.
3. Any reimbursement of expenses to an employee—the amount of reimbursement.
4. Where an employee's debt or obligation to the employer is written off—the amount of such debt or obligation.
5. Cumulative life insurance premiums and other similar amounts paid by an employer, except for the difference between insurance premiums and insurance payments—the insurance payments received by the insured are taxable. If life and health insurance is obtained through an insurer in a foreign country, the cost to the employer of the premiums and amounts is considered taxable.
6. Other benefits—unless otherwise stipulated in normative acts, the market value of a benefit.

Tax exempt incomes/The following income is exempt from income tax.

1. Income from a diplomatic or consular employee who is not a citizen of the Azerbaijan Republic.
2. Income from the workplace of a person who is not a resident or citizen of the Azerbaijan Republic and who has lived less than 182 cumulative days in the territory of the Azerbaijan Republic during the tax year. To be exempt, this income must be paid by an employer or in the name of an employer who is not a resident of the Azerbaijan Republic and for activity not relating to a permanent establishment of such a nonresident.
3. The value of gifts and financial aid received within a calendar year that is less than 50 times the nontaxable amount of a monthly salary (currently AZM5 million); inheritances received within a calendar year amounting to less than 1,000 times the nontaxable amount of a monthly salary (currently AZM100 million); and the full value of gifts, financial aid and inheritances received from relatives.

4. State allowances (except for allowances in cases of temporary loss of labor capability), nonrefundable state fund transfers, state pensions, and state stipends.
5. Individual lump-sum payments and material assistance from budget funds made on the decision of the respective executive authority.
6. Income derived from the sale of immovable property that has been the taxpayer's place of permanent residence for the last three years.
7. Income from the sale of movable tangible assets, except for precious stones and metals, precious stone and metal products, fine art, and antique items, as well as property used in the entrepreneurial activity of the taxpayer.
8. Compensation received in respect of payment for damages.
9. Income received directly from the manufacturing of agricultural products.
10. Income of physical persons engaged as professional coppersmiths and tinsmiths or engaged in the making of household equipment, gardening tools, instruments of national music, toys, souvenirs, cane and reed domestic articles, artistic ceramic items, decorative sewing, and wooden domestic items.
11. Alimony.
12. Payments of compensation nature, including monetary or in-kind allowance, of military servants.
13. Other exemptions as provided.

Deductions

The reimbursement of actual business expenses or other business expenses is not included in income.

Dividends and interest received by physical persons and previously taxed at the source of payment in the Azerbaijan Republic are excluded from gross income.

Entertainment and meals, employee's accommodation and other expenses of social nature incurred by the employer for employee are not included in taxable income of employees.

Other taxes

Social security taxes/The Social and Employment Funds have been merged. Effective from January 1, 2002, social security taxes at rate of 29% is payable by the employer from the gross income of the employees. Also, a 1.5% social security contribution is withheld from employees. Entrepreneurs who are physical persons are liable to the social taxes at various rates based on activity type.

Withholding tax and rates/Withholding tax at the following rates is withheld from specified payments.

1. Dividends paid by resident enterprises—10%.
2. Interest paid by a permanent establishment of a resident or nonresident (or on behalf of such permanent establishment)—10%.
3. From the rental fees for movable and immovable property, as well as from royalties paid by a permanent establishment of a resident or nonresident (or on behalf of such permanent establishment)—10%. This tax does not apply to the amounts paid to resident enterprises or permanent establishments of nonresidents.

4. Payments to a permanent establishment of a resident or nonresident (or on behalf of such permanent establishment) or the payments to physical persons employed by entrepreneurs—at monthly income tax rates (12%–35%).
5. Physical persons who receive pretaxed rental fees and royalties—no further tax on the pretaxed amount.
6. Taxes deducted from incomes of nonresident physical persons not attributed to a permanent establishment (base) in Azerbaijan:
   a. Payments in respect of leasing operations of resident enterprises, permanent establishments of nonresident enterprises (or on behalf of such establishment) or entrepreneurs, including financial leasing operations, as well as insurance payments under risk insurance or reinsurance agreements—4%;
   b. Payments by a resident enterprise or a permanent establishment of nonresident enterprise for telecommunication or transport services during international communications or shipments between the Azerbaijan Republic or other states—6%;
   c. Payments by a resident enterprise, permanent establishment of nonresident enterprise (or on behalf of such permanent establishment) or entrepreneur in connection with Azerbaijan source and the above-outlined other income (income from the assignment of goods, performance of works and provision of services, rental fees; income from immovable property in Azerbaijan, including income from the assignment of a participating share in such a property; income from the lease of movable property used in Azerbaijan; other income attributable to an activity in Azerbaijan)—10%.

Oil consortia tax regime

The other type of tax regime applicable in Azerbaijan is the oil consortia tax regime. This regime applies to all foreign investors involved in a Product Sharing Agreement ("PSA"), including foreign oil companies functioning as contractor parties and foreign-service companies providing services to the contracting parties or the operating company.

Expatriate employees that are tax resident in Azerbaijan are taxed only on income earned in connection with their employment in Azerbaijan. PSAs also generally exempt nonresidents from tax in Azerbaijan and define tax residents as those who spent more than 30 consecutive days or 90 cumulative days during a calendar year in Azerbaijan.

Azerbaijan citizen employees are taxed in accordance with the statutory legislation of Azerbaijan.

Tax credits

The amount of income tax paid outside the Azerbaijan Republic on income not connected with an Azerbaijan source is accounted for at the time of payment of Azerbaijan income tax. The accounted amount may not exceed the tax amount computed under the effective tax rates on such income in Azerbaijan.

Tax administration

Tax returns/The taxpayers listed below are liable for the filing of tax returns with tax authorities.

1. Resident physical persons having income that is not taxable at the source of payment, and having income from the granting of royalty, as well as those deriving

income outside the borders of the Azerbaijan Republic, must file a return by April 15 of the year following the reporting one.

2. Nonresidents engaged in activity through a permanent establishment (base) must file by April 1 of the year following the reporting year or, if ownership activity has ceased, within 30 days of cessation.
3. Nonresidents with Azerbaijan-source taxable income that has not been taxed at source must file by April 1 of the year following the reporting year.

A nonresident taxpayer who has no permanent establishment (base) in the Republic of Azerbaijan is entitled to a tax refund, obtainable by filing a declaration about such income before April 1 of the year following the reporting year according to the regulations envisioned for nonresidents engaged in activity through a permanent establishment (base).

A taxpayer may apply for an extension of the filing prior to the expiration of the filing date and at the same time settle the full tax amount to be paid. In this case, the filing date will be deemed to be prolonged for up to three months. The prolongation of the terms for filing of returns does not modify the terms of tax payment.

Payment of tax/Employer should transfer the withheld taxes on the same day of payment of income to its employee. Entrepreneurs shall be obliged to make current payments no later than the 15th day of the month following each quarter.

Loss carryforward/The portion of expenses deductible from gross income generated from the entrepreneurial economic activity, which exceed said gross income, shall be carried forward for a period of up to five years and shall be covered at the expense of the gross income generated from entrepreneurial economic activity of future periods.

Tax rates

Taxable monthly income	Yearly taxable income	Tax Rate
Less than AZM100,000	Less than AZM1,200,000	Nil
AZM 100,001–AZM1,000,000	AZM1,200,000–AZM12,000,000	12%
AZM 1,000,001–AZM5,000,000	AZM12,000,001–AZM60,000,000	25%
More than AZM5,000,000	More than AZM 60,000,000	35%

Note:

Exchange rate of the Azerbaijan Manat at April 1, 2002: US$1 = AZM4,828.

Bahamas

PwC contact

For additional information on taxation in the Bahamas, contact:

Kevin D. Seymour
PricewaterhouseCoopers
P.O. Box N. 3910
Nassau, The Bahamas
Telephone: (1) (242) 302-5300
Fax: (1) (242) 302-5350
e-mail: kevin.d.seymour@bs.pwcglobal.com

Absence of taxation

Income tax is not imposed on individuals or corporations in the Commonwealth of the Bahamas.

Note

The Bahamian dollar (Bah$1.00) is at parity with the U.S. dollar.

PwC contact

For additional information on Bahrain, contact:

Elham Hassan, Country Senior Partner
PricewaterhouseCoopers
BMB Centre, 5th floor
Diplomatic Area
P.O. Box 21144
Manama, Bahrain
Telephone: (973) 540554
Fax: (973) 540556
e-mail: elham.hassan@ae.pwcglobal.com

Absence of taxation

Income tax is not imposed on individuals in Bahrain.

Note

Exchange rate (selling) of the dinar at December 31, 2001: US$1 = BD0.377.

PwC contact

For additional information on taxation in Barbados, contact:

Maria E. Robinson
PricewaterhouseCoopers
The Financial Services Centre
P.O. Box 111
St. Michael, Bridgetown, Barbados, W.I.
Telephone: (1) (246) 431 2700, 436 7000
Fax: (1) (246) 431 1275, 429 3747, 430 9231
e-mail: maria.robinson@bb.pwcglobal.com

Significant developments

There have been no significant tax or regulatory developments in the last year.

Territoriality and residence

An individual who is both resident and domiciled in Barbados is taxed on worldwide income.

Individuals who are resident but not domiciled in Barbados are taxed on income derived from Barbados and on income from any other sources outside Barbados, to the extent that a benefit is received in Barbados.

An individual becomes resident by spending in the aggregate more than 182 days in Barbados in an income (calendar) year or by being ordinarily resident in Barbados in the relevant income year. An individual is considered to be ordinarily resident who has permanent accommodation available for personal use in Barbados and gives notice to the Commissioner of Inland Revenue of intent to reside in Barbados for a period of at least two consecutive income years. In calculating the number of days, the days of departure and arrival are included. Domicile is a question of intention, and long-term residence does not necessarily determine domicile. In general, a nonresident individual is not entitled to personal deductions against income and is taxed only on income arising in or remitted to Barbados.

Gross income

Employee gross income/Income includes salary, bonuses, commissions, and the value of all other benefits, whether or not in money, including housing. Cash housing allowances are treated as salary. The provision of rent-free accommodation gives rise to a taxable benefit to the employee up to a maximum of Bds$14,400 per year. There are special concessions for appropriately qualified foreign employees of corporations engaged in the international financial services sector, whereby up to 35% of their remuneration may be exempt from tax, if approved by the relevant government minister.

Capital gains and investment income/Barbados does not have a capital gains tax. Interest, dividends (except dividends received from local companies and those resident in certain other CARICOM countries), rents, royalties, professional fees, business profits, and annuities are all subject to tax, as is any type of investment income brought into Barbados by short-term residents. One-half of amounts received as royalties is exempt from tax.

Deductions

Business deductions/Where an individual is carrying on a trade, business, profession, or vocation, expenses are generally deductible if they are incurred for the purpose of producing assessable income for the enterprise. Employees may deduct only unreimbursed expenditures incurred for travel and entertainment in the performance of their duties. Depreciation of a motor vehicle is not deductible. Moving expenses to or from Barbados paid by an employer are not taxed.

Nonbusiness expenses/Deductions are allowed for the following.

1. Savings with a cooperative society (up to Bds$3,000 per annum after an initial period of two years).
2. Bonuses converted into shares of the employing company (up to a limit of the lesser of Bds$7,500 or 75% of the value of the bonus payable).
3. Bonuses paid by companies which do not offer shares to those employees converted into bonds, debentures, or stock of the Government of Barbados or invested in mutual funds (up to a limit of the lesser of Bds$7,500 or 75% of the value of the bonus payable).
4. Payments under deed of covenant (up to a limit of 10% of assessable income where payments are to a benevolent organization and 5% of assessable income where payments are to minors or incapacitated individuals).
5. Contributions to a registered retirement plan (up to a limit of the lesser of Bds$4,000 or 15% of assessable income); contributions to a registered retirement plan savings plan (up to a limit of the lesser of Bds$4,000 or 15% of assessable income). Where contributions are made to both a registered retirement plan and a registered retirement savings plan the combined contributions are limited to a maximum of Bds$6,000 or 15% of assessable income.
6. A housing allowance of Bds$3,500 for repairs, renovations, mortgage interest, and water- and energy-saving devices for residents of owner-occupied houses.
7. Purchase of new shares in a public company and/or a mutual fund (up to a limit of Bds$10,000); and contributions to a venture capital fund (up to a limit of Bds$10,000).

Personal allowances/Residents of Barbados can claim the following allowances.

	Bds$
Individuals (Note)	15,000
Individuals over age 60 and in receipt of a pension (Note)	30,000
Individuals whose spouse had no income and who either fully supported or habitually lived with the spouse	3,000
Children (maximum of two)	1,000 each

Note:

No income tax is payable where a resident receives assessable income of less than Bds$15,000 (if a pensioner over age 60, Bds$30,000). Nonresidents are precluded from claiming any allowances or deductions in arriving at taxable income.

Tax credits

Relief for double taxation is given on Commonwealth income or in accordance with the provisions of any relevant double taxation treaty.

Full credit is given for tax withheld at source on dividends from preferred shares issued before January 1, 1975. Dividends on ordinary shares or preferred shares issued to individuals after January 1, 1975, paid to individuals out of pre-July 1992 retained earnings are grossed up by 15% and included in taxable income. A 15% dividend tax credit is permitted on this income. Those paid from post-July 1992 profits are subject to a final tax of 12.5%.

A credit for net foreign currency earnings is available on earnings from construction projects or professional services undertaken outside of the Caribbean Community (CARICOM). The credit varies depending on the percentage of foreign currency earnings to total earnings, but ranges from 35% to 93% of tax otherwise payable on such foreign currency earnings.

Local interest income is subject to a final tax of 12.5% when paid to resident individuals (15% when paid to nonresident individuals). Interest paid to pensioners aged 60 years and over is not subject to tax.

A reverse tax credit of Bds$500 per annum has been granted to any employed individual who is resident in Barbados and earns less than Bds$13,000 annually but not more than Bds $1,084 monthly.

Other taxes

National insurance and social security/The employee's share is 8% on earnings of up to a maximum of Bds$3,100 per month, with the employer paying 9.25%. Self-employed individuals make contributions quarterly of 12% on earnings of up to a maximum of Bds$3,100 per month.

Local taxes on income/There are no local taxes on income.

Tax administration

Returns/All individuals who carry on business (whether or not assessable income has been derived during the income year) or earn assessable income in excess of Bds$15,000 (in the case of pensioners over age 60, Bds$30,000) are required to file a separate income tax return. The tax year for individuals is the calendar year, and returns are filed by the following April 30.

Payment of tax/Income tax is normally withheld from salaries under the pay-as-you-earn (PAYE) system, and interest is payable to the taxpayer on overdue tax refunds. Individuals who have income from business or rents in excess of 25% of their total assessable income are required to make three prepayments of tax on June 15, September 15 and December 15, each representing 25% of the income tax payable on the proportion of such income to total assessable income for the previous income year.

Tax rates

Individual income tax rates are shown below.

Taxable income			
Over (Column 1)	Not over	Tax on Column 1	Percentage on excess
0	Bds$ 24,200	—	25
Bds$ 24,200		Bds$ 6,050	40

INDIVIDUAL TAX CALCULATION

Calendar year 2001

Assumptions

Resident husband (employed in the international financial services sector) and wife; one child aged 12 educated in Barbados, and one child aged 17 educated abroad; one spouse earns all the income; company provides rent-free accommodation and car.

Income tax computation

Salary (gross salary of 160,000 less 35%)		Bds$ 104,000
Car benefit (vehicle with value of 100,000)		10,000
Housing benefit (annual rental of 60,000, say)		14,400
		128,400
Less—Entertainment allowance (1)		7,800
Net employment income and total assessable income		120,600
Deductions:		
Pension contribution	4,000	
Donation under covenant	5,000	9,000
		111,600
Personal deductions:		
Personal	15,000	
Spouse	3,000	
Child (aged 12)	1,000	
Child (aged 17)	1,000	20,000
Taxable income		Bds$ 91,600
Income tax thereon		Bds$ 33,010
Less—Tax withheld from salary (PAYE)		(34,000)
Income tax refund		Bds$ 990

Notes:

1. The deduction of Bds$7,800 would not necessarily be automatically allowed. The taxpayer may be required to substantiate that the amount was expended on business entertainment.
2. Exchange rate of the Barbados dollar officially pegged at US$1 = Bds$2.00.

PwC contact

For additional information on taxation in Belgium, contact:

Anne Murrath
PricewaterhouseCoopers Tax Consultants SCCRL-BCBVA
Woluwedal 18
B-1932 Sint-Stevens-Woluwe, Belgium
Telephone: (32) (2) 710 42 11, 710 31 01 (direct)
Fax: (33) (2) 710 42 99
e-mail: anne.murrath@be.pwcglobal.com

Significant developments

The information in this entry relates to tax year 2003 (calendar year 2002).

There have been no significant tax regulatory developments regarding individual taxation in the past year.

Territoriality and residence

Belgium taxes its residents on their worldwide income irrespective of their nationality. Residents of Belgium are those who have established their domicile or their economic base in Belgium. Persons deemed to have done this are those who have registered in the population register of a commune in Belgium. The fiscal residence of married couples is determined by the place where the family is located. Nonresidents of Belgium are subject to income tax only on their income earned or collected in Belgium.

Within Belgium, nonresident status is granted to non-Belgian executives or specialists who "temporarily" work in Belgium for an international group. Those persons deemed to be nonresident are allowed tax concessions on the payment of certain allowances, which are not taxable on the employee and are tax deductible for the employer. Also they are taxed on their Belgian-source income only.

Gross income

Employee gross income/Foreign executives or specialists working temporarily in Belgium and qualifying for nonresident tax status do not have to include in their gross taxable income reimbursements for additional expenses incurred from their transfer to or employment in Belgium. The additional expenses listed below may be reimbursed on the basis of actual amounts or by means of lump-sum allowances.

1. One-time moving expenses and the costs of setting up a house in Belgium.
2. Ongoing expenses, e.g., cost-of-living, housing allowances, school fees, home leave allowance, travel expenses of children studying outside Belgium, exchange losses, and tax equalization.

Such additional expenses will be, within certain limits, exempt from tax to the extent that the total annual amount (excluding school fees and one-time expenses) does not exceed €11,250 (€29,750 in the case of executives working at a control and coordination office, research center or scientific laboratory). Duties performed outside Belgium are proportionately exempted, but declaration must be made for total worldwide income earned within the employer's group.

Stock options are taxable at the time they are granted. The value of a stock option listed on a stock exchange is determined as the closing market price of the day preceding the offer of the option.

The value of a stock option not listed on a stock exchange is determined on a lump-sum basis and amounts to a certain percentage of the fair market value of the underlying shares increased by the discount, if any. This basic percentage is set at 15%, to be increased by 1% per year of option period exceeding five years.

Under certain conditions, the above percentages are reduced by 50%.

Capital gains and investment income/Capital gains and foreign-source investment income cashed outside the country are not taxable for nonresidents working in Belgium. Residents and nonresidents are, under certain conditions, taxed on capital gains realized on the sale of land as well as on the sale of buildings located in Belgium. Depending on the situation, this tax is levied either by means of a special levy (33%/16.5%) or through the application of professional withholding tax.

Deductions

Business deductions/Social security taxes are deductible. Employment-related expenses are deductible, provided they are substantiated; alternatively, standard deductions may be claimed up to a maximum of €2,950.

Nonbusiness expenses/The following nonbusiness expenses are deductible.

1. 80% of the support payments to near relatives or a separated spouse (nonresidents can deduct only payments made to residents of Belgium; however, there are some tax treaty exceptions).
2. Interest resulting from mortgage loans for real estate.
3. Charitable contributions to certain institutions to the extent of 10% of taxable income, with a maximum of €294,930 for tax year 2003.
4. 50% of the remuneration costs of domestic personnel.
5. 100% of children's custody expenses, up to a maximum of €11.20 per day.

The following nonbusiness expenses give rise to a tax reduction, which is calculated on the basis of the average tax rate on the jointly taxable income, with a minimum of 30% and a maximum of 40%. (In some cases, it is calculated on the basis of the marginal tax rates.)

1. Life insurance premiums, with a maximum of €1,770.
2. Capital repayments of a mortgage loan, with a maximum of €1,770 (applicable together with the life insurance premiums).
3. "*Monory-bis*" deduction (acquisition of shares in employer company), with a maximum of €590.
4. Pension-savings contributions, with a maximum of €590.
5. Employee's contributions to group insurance.
6. Purchases (up to €2,140) of checks to be spent with local employment agencies.

To the extent that the tax reduction has been calculated in the way described above, and if certain other conditions are met, the proceeds of individual and group insurance and of the pension-saving plan will be taxed at a flat rate of 10%.

Personal allowances/Allowances deductible in determining taxable income are shown below. The earned incomes of a husband and wife are taxed separately.

Exempt income/The net taxable income of a taxpayer (in the case of married taxpayers, the amount of the income allocated to each spouse) will be taxed at the rates detailed below (Tax rates applicable for income year 2002). However, the following personal exemptions and exemptions for dependent children and other persons are granted.

1. €4,350 for husband and wife.
2. €5,480 for single persons.
3. For dependent children:

Number	Increase	Accumulated
	€	€
1	1,160	1,160
2	1,840	3,000
3	3,720	6,720
4	4,140	10,860

   For each dependent child above the fourth child, an additional €4,150 is deductible. A handicapped child is counted as two dependency deductions. For each child less than three years old on January 1 of the tax year, the above amounts are increased by €430, provided no children's custody expenses are deducted (see "Nonbusiness expenses" above).
4. For any other dependent person, an amount of €1,160 is deductible.

It must be stressed that the exemption takes place on the lowest part of income (at the lowest marginal tax rates).

The earned income of each spouse is taxed separately. For calculation purposes, the other income of the family is attributed to the spouse who has the highest amount of earned income. Special rules exist when one spouse has no or low earned income, as noted below.

1. Only one spouse receives earned income:

   A splitting is applicable—An income equal to 30% of the net earnings of the spouse will be attributed to the spouse without earnings and taxed in that spouse's own name. Income that may be attributed to the non-earning spouse cannot exceed €7,900.

   If one of the spouses is self-employed or is engaged in a liberal profession and is effectively assisted by the other, an income equal to a maximum of 30% of the earning spouse's net earnings will be attributed to the assisting spouse if the net earnings of the latter do not exceed €10,260. The maximum of 30% can be exceeded, provided sufficient evidence of the real assistance of the helping spouse is given.
2. Both spouses receive earned income:

   The above regulations also apply where both spouses receive earned income if the earnings of one spouse exceed 70% of total earnings and the earnings of the other spouse do not reach €7,900. In this case, income may be attributed to the spouse earning less until 30% of total earnings and without exceeding the maximum of €7,900 is reached.

The exempt income, personal deductions and the attribution of income to the spouse are in principle applicable to residents and nonresidents, although for nonresidents these exemptions and deductions will be applicable only when they have a permanent home in Belgium during the entire taxable period to which the income relates, or when they receive earned income taxable in Belgium that represents at least 75% of their worldwide earnings.

Tax credits

Income from Belgian real estate and from a house that is occupied by and is the principal residence of the taxpayer is subject to a tax credit of 12.5% on the deemed rental value of the property owned.

Self-employed individuals earning business income or exercising a profession generating profits subject to the resident income tax can claim a tax credit of 10% of the difference between current year's equity (fiscal value of assets less debts) and highest equity of the three preceding tax years, up to a maximum of €3,750 per financial year.

Other taxes

Social security taxes/The employee's share of social security taxes is 13.07% of the total gross compensation; the employer's share varies around 34%. Social security taxes are deductible in determining taxable income. For foreign employees with short-term assignments in Belgium who continue to be subject to the social security schemes of their home country, an exemption from social security may be granted, depending on the nationality of the claimant. For foreign employees who are transferred to Belgium by a U.S. employer for a period not exceeding five years and who remain covered by the U.S. social security scheme, the Belgium/U.S. social security agreement provides for full exemption from Belgian social security taxes.

According to recent Supreme Court decisions, additional expenses reimbursed to foreign executives or specialists working temporarily in Belgium (see "Employee gross income") will be, within certain limits, exempt from social security taxes.

Special social security contribution/A special social security contribution is due from April 1, 1994, the amount varying between €9.30 and €60.94 per month. This contribution is collected by means of monthly deductions from net salary, although the final amount due will be determined through the tax return process on the basis of actual net taxable family income. The special social security contribution is not tax deductible. The maximum amount due by a family on a yearly basis amounts to €731.28.

Local taxes on income/For residents of Belgium, communal taxes are levied at rates varying from 0% to 8.5% of the income tax due. For nonresidents, a flat surcharge of 6% is due.

Tax administration

Returns/Spouses must file a joint tax return on their aggregated income (an exception is made for the year of marriage or divorce). The tax year relates to the income of the preceding calendar year.

Payment of tax/There is a compulsory income tax withholding from salaries (also for directors, now called "key men").

Professional withholding tax is indeed due under the following circumstances.

1. When remuneration is paid or attributed by Belgian residents, in Belgium or abroad, to Belgian residents or nonresidents.
2. When remuneration is paid or attributed by Belgian nonresidents if the remuneration concerned can be classified as professional expenses, that is, relating to income of the nonresident employer that is taxable in Belgium.

3. To calculate the withholding tax, employers may, on their own responsibility, take into account the special regulations that pertain to the taxation of both foreign executives and specialists working temporarily in Belgium (see "Territoriality and residence").

Tax rates

The minimum abatement is €4,350 for each married taxpayer and €5,480 for single persons. This minimum abatement is increased for dependent children (see "Exempt income"). The tax rate varies from 25% to 52%, excluding the communal tax. Tax rates for tax year 2003 are shown below.

Taxable income				
Over	**Not over**		**Tax on Column 1**	**Percentage on excess**
(Column 1)			(Note)	
0	€ 6,730	....	—	25.0
€ 6,730	8,920	....	€ 1,682.50	30.0
8,920	12,720	....	2,339.50	40.0
12,720	29,260	....	3,859.50	45.0
29,260	43,870	....	11,302.50	50.0
43,870		....	18,607.50	52.0

Note:

The tax in the third column (not taking into account the crisis tax) must be increased by the additional communal tax (see "Local taxes on income" above).

For income year 2002, a special crisis contribution of 1% of the total income tax payable is also due if the total taxable income exceeds €30,986.70. If the taxable income falls between €29,747.25 and €30,986.70, the special crisis contribution rate varies between 0% and 1%. No special crisis contributions is due if the total taxable amount does not exceed €29,747.24.

INDIVIDUAL TAX CALCULATION

Assumptions

1. Foreign executive working temporarily in Belgium and fulfilling the required conditions to benefit from the special tax regime; married with two children; one spouse earns all the income.
2. Owner of a house in which the family is living; deemed net annual rental income has been fixed at €3,750. Since the taxpayer occupies the house, an abatement of €3,953 (increased by €329 for each dependent) is available. Since the income will be offset by the deduction of mortgage interest, the abatement will not be applied.
3. Gross compensation is deemed to include the reimbursement by the employer of certain exceptional expenses as provided for under the special tax regime and limited to €11,250, as well as the reimbursement of school fees for an amount of €6,500.
4. Services performed in Belgium during the year represent 75% of the total working days of the taxable period.
5. Deductible charitable gifts: €750.

Tax computation

Determination of taxable income

Real estate income		€ 3,750.00
Less—Mortgage interest		3,750.00
Net real estate income		€ 0.00
Total gross compensation		€ 70,000.00
Less:		
Nontaxable allowances	11,250.00	
School fees	6,500.00	17,750.00
Gross salary		52,250.00
Less—Social security taxes (13.07%) (1)		6,829.08
		45,420.92
Less:		
Exempt portion of salary for services performed outside Belgium (25% x 45,420.92)	11,355.23	
Standard deduction for business expenses	2,328.67	13,683.90
Taxable earned income		€ 31,737.02

Calculation of tax

	Taxpayer	Spouse
Taxable earned income	€ 31,737.02	
Attribution to spouse (30%, limited to 7,900)	—	€ 7,900.00
Less—Attribution to spouse	7,900.00	
Less—Itemized deductions (charitable contributions)	563.31	186.69
Net taxable income (2)	€ 23,273.71	€ 7,713.31
Income tax thereon	€ 8,608.67	€ 1,977.49
Less—Income tax on exempt income (3)	(1,668.50)	(1,087.50)
Income tax due	€ 6,940.17	€ 889.99

		Together
Total income tax		€ 7,830.16
Add:		
Communal tax of 6%	469.81	
Crisis tax of 1%	78.30	548.11
		8378.27
Less—Creditable part of real estate tax		(468.75)
Income tax liability		€ 7,909.52

Notes:

1. Social security taxes have been calculated on the gross salary after deduction of the nontaxable allowances and school fees.
2. On the basis of a net taxable family income of €30,987.02 (€23,273.71 for the taxpayer and €7,713.71 for the taxpayer's spouse) the special social security contribution amounts to €352.01 (yearly basis).
3. Calculation of income tax on exempt income is as follows:

	Taxpayer	Spouse
	€	€
Exempt income:		
Exemption for married persons	4,350.00	4,350.00
Exemption for dependent children	3,000.00	—
Total exempt income	7,350.00	4,350.00
Income tax	1,868.50*	1,087.50**

*6,730 at 25% and 620 at 30%.

**4,350 at 25%.

4. Exchange rate of the Euro at January 3, 2002: US$1 = €1.106.

PwC contact

For additional information on Bermuda, contact:

Richard E. Irvine
Director, Tax and Legal Services
PricewaterhouseCoopers
P.O. Box HM 1171
Hamilton HMEX
Bermuda
Telephone: [1] (441) 295 7136
Fax: [1] (441) 295 1242
e-mail: richard.e.irvine@bm.pwcglobal.com

Absence of taxation

Income tax, taxes on capital gains are not imposed on individuals in Bermuda.

Note

Exchange rate of the Bermuda dollar at December 31, 2001: US$1 = Bd$1.00.

Bolivia

PwC contact

For additional information on taxation in Bolivia, contact:

Rosa Talavera
PricewaterhouseCoopers S.R.L.
Avenida Mariscal
Santa Cruz & Yanacocha
Edificio Hansa, 19th Floor
La Paz, Bolivia
Telephone: (591) (2) 2408181
Fax: (591) (2) 211 2752
e-mail: rosa.talavera@bo.pwcglobal.com

Significant developments

The rate for pension funds contributions has been reduced from 12.5% to 12.21%. The Housing Fund employee's contribution is no longer in force, effective November 2000.

Territoriality and residence

Bolivia taxes its citizens and residents on their Bolivian-source income only. Foreign-source income is not taxable in Bolivia. The Bolivian-source income of nonresident aliens is subject to Bolivian tax. Domicile and citizenship do not affect the tax base.

Gross income

Employee gross income/A resident is taxed on salaries, bonuses (except obligatory year-end bonus), profit participation, living allowances, housing allowances, tax reimbursements, benefits-in-kind, and any other form of income earned as an employee for work carried out in Bolivia. There are no concessions to short-term foreign residents. A nonresident is taxed on Bolivian-source earnings at the rate of 12.5% of gross income.

Capital gains and investment income/Investment income from a Bolivian source (except dividends paid to residents) is taxed as ordinary income. Capital gains are not subject to tax. Interest, dividends, etc., earned in Bolivia by nonresidents are subject to a withholding tax of 12.5% when remitted or credited to a personal account. Investment income from outside Bolivia is not taxed in Bolivia.

Deductions

Business deductions/No business expenses may be deducted from income.

Nonbusiness expenses/A resident may deduct social security taxes paid. No other expenses are deductible.

Personal allowances/Residents are entitled to a basic deduction of two minimum salaries per month. As of December 31, 2001 the minimum salary was Bs400 per month.

Tax credits

All value-added tax paid by individuals as part of the price of items for personal consumption is deductible from the personal income tax payable, provided the purchases are properly documented.

In addition to the tax credit for value-added tax (VAT), the law allows an additional tax credit equivalent to 13% of two minimum salaries per month.

Other taxes

Social security taxes/Pension funds are administered privately, and only employees contribute toward their retirement pension. The contribution rate is 12.21% of salary, with a ceiling of approximately US$3,478 per month (12.21% of 60 minimum salaries). This payment is registered under individual account. As from November 2000, there is no longer an employee contribution to the official Housing Fund.

Local taxes on income/Other than the tax on salaries, there are no local taxes on income earned by employees. However, income earned for independent activities as well as that arising from local investments is subject to a 12.5% annual income tax.

Tax administration

Returns/The employer submits a global tax return and withholds the tax on an employee's salary. No further tax-filing requirement exists for this tax. Individual taxpayers must submit tax returns on a monthly basis for value-added tax and transactions tax, and on an annual basis for income tax. There is no joint filing for husband and wife.

Payment of tax/Employers file and pay taxes withheld on behalf of their personnel. Investment and other income must be declared on an individual basis, and the related tax liability is paid by the taxpayer on an annual basis.

Tax rates

The tax rate is a flat 13% on salaries and 12.5% on other income.

INDIVIDUAL TAX CALCULATION

Income year 2001

(Taxes are liquidated on a monthly basis)

Gross income:		
Salary		Bs 336,000
Profit participation (one month's salary)		28,000
Investment income		6,000
		370,000
Less—Nonbusiness deductions:		
Social security taxes—12.21% x 288,000 (60 x 400 x 12)		35,165
		334,835
Less—Personal deductions (Basic deduction, 12 x 800)		9,600
Taxable income		Bs 325,235
Tax payable—13% of 325,235		Bs 42,281
Less:		
Tax credit for value-added tax included in purchases (estimated)	29,000	
Tax credit—13% of two minimum salaries per month (13% x (12 x 800))	1,248	(30,248)
		Bs 12,033

Notes:

1. The year-end bonus, equivalent to one month's salary, is not subject to tax and therefore has not been included in the above computation.
2. Exchange rate of the boliviano at December 31, 2001: US$1 = Bs6.83.

PwC contact

For additional information on taxation in Botswana, contact:

Mr. D.K.U. Corea
Price Waterhouse
P.O. Box 1453
Gaborone, Botswana
Telephone: (267) 584222
Fax: (267) 584300

Significant developments

There have been no significant tax or regulatory developments regarding individual taxation in the past year.

Territoriality and residence

The Botswana tax system operates on a territorial basis, and income is taxable in Botswana if the source is within Botswana. Income for services performed outside Botswana is deemed to be from a Botswana source if the services are incidental to employment in Botswana.

To be a resident of Botswana for a tax year normally means the individual has a permanent place of abode in Botswana and is physically present in Botswana for not less than 183 days in that tax year or the previous tax year.

A resident is taxable on all income from a Botswana source in accordance with the tax rates. A nonresident is taxable on earned income in accordance with the tax rates, but pays withholding tax only at the rate of 15% for interest, dividends, commercial royalties, and management and consultancy fees, and at the rate of 10% on entertainment fees, where such income is of Botswana origin.

Gross income

***Employee gross income*/**Expatriate employees are taxable on salary and on any overseas allowances, wherever payment is made. Living and housing allowances, tax reimbursements and the value of benefits, such as free accommodation and the use of motor vehicles, are included in taxable income. However, airfares and medical costs borne by the employer for the employee, spouse and dependent children and provided in the terms of the employee's contract are not taxable.

For individuals' contracts of employment signed on or after July 1, 1999, any gratuities paid are taxable to the extent of two-thirds of such gratuity. The remaining one-third is tax free. The percentage parameters are still 25% of gross salary for the first contract, 27.5% for the second contract and 30% for the third and subsequent contracts. Contracts normally run two to three years.

The gross income of a resident citizen individual includes any interest or dividend income from an investment made outside Botswana. Interest income in such cases is included in the individuals' gross income and taxed accordingly. Dividend income from foreign source is taxes at 15%.

***Capital gains and investment income*/**Capital gains on the disposal of immovable property and marketable securities (including shares in private companies) are taxable in Botswana if the source is in Botswana. For capital gains purposes, the cost of immovable property is adjusted to take account of inflation. For other gains, no inflation allowances are granted, but the taxable gain is set at one-half of the total gain. Capital gains for individuals are considered to be from a separate source and are taxed on the basis of Table VI of the Act (shown as Tax Rate Table III in this entry).

Interest income for any resident individual, accruing from any banking institution or building society in Botswana is exempt from tax up to a limit of P2,500.

Interest, dividends, commercial royalties, and management and consultancy fees payable by a Botswana resident to a nonresident are subject to withholding taxes of 15%. Similarly, entertainment fees are subject to a withholding tax of 10%. However, the double taxation agreements with the United Kingdom and South Africa exempt management and consultancy fees from the requirement to withhold taxes.

Deductions

Business deductions/No business-related expenses are deductible unless they are incurred as a condition of employment or for the purpose of producing the employee's income, such as in circumstances in which the expenditure can be shown to influence the level of the employee's income. An employee who is employed on a commission basis could be in this position. There are no standard or blanket deductions.

Nonbusiness expenses/Where a gratuity is not provided to the employee, contributions to an approved retirement benefit scheme are allowable up to a maximum of 15% of earned income.

Personal allowances/There are no personal allowances granted. All individual taxpayers are taxed under one of two tax tables (see "Tax rates").

Tax credits

A tax credit is granted unilaterally where amounts received by a Botswana resident have been subject to taxation in a foreign country and in cases where a double taxation agreement has been concluded. Botswana has double taxation agreements with Mauritius, South Africa, Sweden, and the United Kingdom. A tax credit is also granted where income from a source within Botswana has been subject to a withholding tax. The amount of the relief is limited to the lesser of the tax paid by deduction and that normally paid in Botswana on such income.

Other taxes

Social security taxes/There are no social security taxes or contributions.

Local taxes on income/There are no income taxes in addition to central government taxes.

Tax administration

Returns/All individuals are separately taxed, and separate filing of returns by husband and wife is required. The fiscal year, which ends on June 30, must be followed.

Payment of tax/A pay-as-you-earn (PAYE) system, under which income tax is withheld from remuneration payable to employees, is in operation.

Tax rates

For 2001/2002, as shown below.

Table I—Resident individual taxpayers

Taxable income Over (Column 1)	Not over	Tax on Column 1	Percentage on excess
0	P 25,000	—	0
P 25,000	43,750	—	5
43,750	62,500	P 938	10
62,500	81,250	2,813	15
81,250	100,000	5,625	20
100,000		9,375	25

Table II—Nonresident taxpayers

Taxable income Over (Column 1)	Not over	Tax on Column 1	Percentage on excess
0	P 43,750	—	5
P 43,750	62,500	P 2,188	10
62,500	81,250	4,063	15
81,250	100,000	6,876	20
100,000		10,625	25

Table III—Individuals in respect of net aggregate capital gains

Taxable income Over (Column 1)	Not over	Tax on Column 1	Percentage on excess
0	P 12,500	—	0
P 12,500	43,750	—	5
43,750	62,500	P 1,563	10
62,500	81,250	3,438	15
81,250	100,000	6,250	20
100,000		10,000	25

INDIVIDUAL TAX CALCULATION

For fiscal year ending June 30, 2002

Assumptions

Taxpayer is an expatriate employee who is resident in Botswana (tax rates from Table I).

Tax computation

Income tax

Salary		P 160,000
Overseas allowance		12,000
Interest received from South African source (excess over 2,500)		3,000
Motor vehicle benefit		2,750
Housing benefit		3,600
Taxable income		P 181,350
Income tax thereon		P 29,712
Less:		
PAYE paid	28,963	
Withheld from interest from South Africa	550	(29,513)
Balance of income tax payable		P 199

Capital gains tax

Income from sale of Botswana shares (50% of gain is taxable)	P 15,000
Capital gains tax payable	P 125

Note:

Exchange rate of the pula at December 31, 2001: US$1 = P7.1.

PwC contacts

For additional information on taxation in Brazil, contact:

Edmar A. Perfetto, Tax Partner
PricewaterhouseCoopers Auditores Independentes
Centro Empresarial Água Branca
Avenida Francisco Matarazzo, 1400
Torre Torino
São Paulo, SP
Brazil
CEP 05001-400
Telephone: (55) (11) 3674 3722
Fax: (55) (11) 3674 2080
e-mail: edmar.perfetto@br.pwcglobal.com

Significant developments

The most significant tax development in this year was the creation of a new tax rate table, which will be applicable from January 1, 2002.

Territoriality and residence

Residents of Brazil are taxed on their worldwide income, and nonresidents are taxed exclusively at source on their Brazilian-source income. The source of income is determined by the place where the income payer is located, irrespective of where the work is performed.

Work permits and special visas are required for any alien intending to live and/or work in Brazil, whether for a short or a long period. Two types of visa may be granted in connection with work permits.

1. Permanent visas—Holders of permanent visas are considered residents as from the date of arrival in Brazil.
2. Temporary visas (valid only for up to two years)—Holders of temporary visas are also considered residents as from the date of arrival in Brazil, as long as they have an employment contract in Brazil. Otherwise, they will become tax residents as of their 184th day of presence in Brazil within any given 12 month period.

Gross income

Employee gross income/Taxable compensation includes everything that is either directly or indirectly connected with the work and/or assignment remuneration package, including salary, premiums, bonuses, allowances of any kind, tax reimbursements, club dues, and company-owned car.

Capital gains and investment income/In general, capital gains and investment income are computed as taxable income. However, in some circumstances certain transactions are tax-free or are taxed exclusively at source at lower rates.

Nontaxable income/Among other items of less importance, the following are free from any income tax:

1. Board, transportation and special work uniforms or clothing supplied by the employer free of any charge or the difference between the amount charged and their market values.

2. Per diem allowances to cover room and board for working outside the county in which the company or office is based or in which the work is normally performed.
3. Labor indemnities, limited to the legal amounts, including indemnities for labor accidents.
4. Contributions made by the employer to private social security programs in favor of the employee.
5. Reimbursement of relocation costs when moving to a different county at the request of the employer.

Deductions

Business deductions/Business expenses are not deductible.

Nonbusiness expenses/The following may be deducted from taxable income.

1. Alimony payments and/or pension contributions.
2. Medical, dental and hospital expenses, as well as payments to recognized Brazilian health insurance/medical-cost coverage programs.
3. Schooling expenses up to an annual limit of R$1,998 (approximately US$832.50) per student.
4. Social security contributions.
5. Contributions to Brazilian private pension funds (deduction subject to limitations).
6. Annual income up to R$12,696 relating to retirement or military pensions as from the year in which the taxpayer reaches 65 years of age.
7. Expenses of lawsuits and lawyers' fees relating to gross income earned, if paid by the taxpayer and not refunded.

Personal allowances/The taxpayer may deduct a flat allowance for each dependent in computing net taxable income. The allowance is R$1,272 (approximately US$530) per annum per dependent in 2002.

Tax credits

Tax credits are available (within certain limits) with respect to income tax paid to countries with which Brazil has a ratified tax treaty or to countries that would render reciprocal treatment in relation to income taxes paid to the Brazilian government.

Other taxes

Social security taxes/Social security taxes are payable monthly at the rate of 7.65% to 11% of Brazilian-source salary income. However, the total contribution may not exceed US$65.54 per month (based on January 2002 amounts).

Other taxes/Minor amounts are payable annually to applicable unions.

Tax administration

Returns/Residents must file a tax return annually. Since individual income tax is due and payable monthly, this return will account for only minor tax adjustments and will serve to list assets and liabilities.

Individuals receiving income or gains not subject to Brazilian withholding tax (i.e., alimony and/or pensions, rental income received from individuals, non–Brazilian-source income, capital gains on the sale of personal property, etc.) are subject to a special monthly income tax payment, which should be made by the last working day of the subsequent month. The tax is calculated on the basis of the normal tax table.

Spouses may elect to file tax returns jointly or separately. If filed separately, returns must allocate to each spouse income received jointly. Also, in the section pertaining to assets and liabilities, each spouse must show the corresponding items held individually. The value of jointly held assets/liabilities should be allocated according to ownership percentage or shown only on one spouse's return. The spouse not listing the jointly held assets/liabilities must declare that the items will be listed on the other spouse's tax return.

The head of a household may not treat as a dependent a spouse or any dependent who receives taxable income and pays tax accordingly.

Payment of tax/Income tax is normally withheld at source, at rates varying from 0% to 27.5%, depending on the income bracket. The final liability is determined upon filing the tax return. Any difference between the amount as determined by the tax return and that withheld at source must be paid (see Note 7 in the tax calculation below) or is refunded to the taxpayer.

Tax rates

The following tax table is applicable to income tax payable in 2003 with respect to annual income earned during calendar year 2002.

Net taxable income (1)		Tax rate (2)	Amount to be deducted from (1) times (2)
Over	Not over	%	
0	R$ 12,696	—*	—
R$ 12,696	25,380	15.0	R$ 1,904
25,380		27.5	5,077

*Exempt.

Note:

These rates apply to all types of tax returns, i.e., married individuals filing jointly or separately and single taxpayers.

INDIVIDUAL TAX CALCULATION

Fiscal year ending December 31, 2002

Assumptions

1. Resident, married with two children (three dependents; wife takes classes); pays alimony to first spouse.
2. Income and gains in 2002 are as follows:

Brazilian-source salary income	R$ 110,000
Brazilian payroll withholding tax	20,854
Foreign-source income	80,000
Income tax paid to a foreign tax jurisdiction on foreign-source income	15,000
Short-term money market income—Brazilian-source	5,000
Withholding tax on short-term money market income	1,000
Capital gain—Profit on sale of property	5,000
Income tax on capital gain	750

Tax computation

Brazilian-source salary income		R$ 110,000
Foreign-source income		80,000
Short-term money market income—Brazilian source		5,000
Capital gain—Profit on sale of property		5,000
Gross income		200,000
Less—Income taxed only at source:		
Short-term money market income	5,000	
Capital gain subject to special taxation (1)	5,000	10,000
Net taxable income before allowances and deductions		190,000
Less—Allowances and deductions:		
Social security contributions	1,887	
Dependents (three)	3,816	
Medical expenses	1,500	
Alimony payments	10,000	
Schooling expenses	5,994	23,197
Net taxable income		R$ 166,803
Income tax at 27.5%		R$ 45,871
Less—Amount deductible relating to lower tax brackets		(5,077)
		40,794
Less—Tax paid at source:		
On Brazilian-source salary income	20,854	
On foreign-source income	15,000	(35,854)
Net tax payable (2)		R$ 4,940

Notes:

1. Capital gains are taxed at the rate of 15%, payable by the taxpayer up to the last working day of the subsequent month.
2. Balance due is payable in full at the time of filing or, at the taxpayer's option, in up to six installments from April 30. Each installment may not be less than R$50. However, should the return show a balance due of less than R$100, this amount should be paid in one installment.
3. Exchange rate of the real for January 1, 2002: US$1 = R$2.40.

British Virgin Islands

PwC contact

For additional information on taxation in the British Virgin Islands, contact:

Meade Malone
PricewaterhouseCoopers
Geneva Place, 2nd Floor
333 Waterfront Drive
P.O. Box 3339
Road Town, Tortola
British Virgin Islands
Telephone: (1) (284) 494 4388, (1) (284) 494 4727 (direct)
Fax: (1) (284) 494 3088
e-mail: pwcabacus@caribsurf.com

Significant developments

There have been no significant tax or regulatory developments regarding individual taxation in the past year. For subsequent developments consult the contact listed above.

Territoriality and residence

A British Virgin Islands (BVI) resident is liable to income tax on worldwide income. A nonresident is liable for BVI income tax on BVI-source income only. The BVI Income Tax Ordinance defines a resident as "an individual resident in the Territory." There are no established criteria to determine whether a person is resident for this purpose. Factors taken into consideration in determining residency include the following.

1. An individual's immigration status.
2. How many days per year the individual is physically present in the BVI.
3. Where the individual's main place of residence can reasonably be said to be located.

Capital gains and investment income

Capital gains/There are no taxes on capital gains.

Dividends and interest/No withholding taxes are applied to dividends or interest, regardless of whether the taxpayer is resident or nonresident. Dividend and interest income is taxable to resident taxpayers as ordinary income, except dividends earned from companies in the BVI and bank deposit interest from banks registered in the BVI.

Deductions

Costs and expenses incurred in the production of income are deductible, but no personal allowances are granted.

Other taxes

There are no taxes on wealth, inheritance, or gifts.

Social security taxes/The employee and employer are taxed at 4% and 4.5%, respectively, on employee earnings up to a maximum of $23,400.

Withholding tax on rents and royalties/A withholding tax of 14% is payable on any rent, annuity or other annual payment made to nonresidents, whether they are individuals or companies. This requirement also extends to royalties.

Tax administration

Payment of tax/Employers must deduct income tax from employees' wages in accordance with the tax tables on a pay-as-you-earn (PAYE) basis. The tax withheld must be paid to Inland Revenue not later than 15 days after the end of the month in which the wages were paid. Late payments are subject to penalties ranging from 5% to 30%.

Tax rates

Resident individuals are subject to BVI income tax on their taxable income at the following rates.

Taxable income		Tax on	Percentage
Over	Not over	Column 1	on excess
(Column 1)			
0	$ 3,000	—	—
$ 3,000	7,500	—	6
7,500	15,000	$ 270	10
15,000	22,500	1,020	15
22,500		2,145	20

Nonresident individuals are taxed on BVI-source income at the normal sliding-scale rates.

Note

The monetary unit is the U.S. dollar.

Brunei Darussalam

PwC contact

For additional information on taxation in Brunei Darussalam, contact:

Kin C. Lee
PricewaterhouseCoopers
No: 1: 4th Floor
Wisma Setia, Jalan Pemancha
Bandar Seri Begawan
Negara Brunei Darussalam
Telephone: (673) (2) 228593, 228595
Fax: (673) (2) 228594
e-mail: kin.chee.lee@bn.pwcglobal.com

Absence of taxation

Legislation for the collection of personal income tax exists in Brunei, but at present this tax is waived.

Note

Exchange rate of the Brunei dollar at December 31, 2001: US$1 = B$1.859.

The Brunei dollar (B$) is interchangeable with the Singapore dollar (S$).

PwC contact

For additional information on taxation in Bulgaria, contact:

Irina Tsvetkova, Partner
PricewaterhouseCoopers Legal and Tax Consultants
2A, Saborna Street
1000 Sofia, Bulgaria
Telephone: (359) (2) 91 003
Fax: (359) (2) 98 03 228
e-mail: irina.tsvetkova@bg.pwcglobal.com

Territoriality and residence

Taxation of individuals' income in Bulgaria is based on their residence status. Bulgarian tax residents are taxed on their worldwide income. Nonresidents are taxed on their income from Bulgarian sources.

Irrespective of their citizenship, individuals are considered Bulgarian tax residents if they have a permanent domicile in the country (i.e., personal links such as a family or permanent home) or reside in the country for more than 183 days in any 365-day period, in which case the individual becomes a Bulgarian tax resident for the calendar year in which the 183rd day has expired.

If a double taxation treaty (DTT) is in place, the 183-day residency principle is applicable in accordance with the provisions of the treaty.

A foreign tax resident is any individual who is not a Bulgarian tax resident.

The law gives a broad definition of Bulgarian-source income. Generally, income from a Bulgarian source is all income received by an individual as a result of business activities performed in the country. Activities performed in the country are considered business activities if the individual either has a permanent establishment or a base in the country, or assigns or performs services in Bulgaria directly or through a procurator, a dependent agent or otherwise.

Any income derived as a result of performing work or rendering services in the country is deemed Bulgarian-source income, no matter where and by whom it is paid.

Investment income and professional income other than employment income are considered Bulgarian-source income if paid by a resident or by a permanent establishment of a nonresident entity in Bulgaria.

To be allowed to work in the country, expatriates need a work permit, which necessitates following a time-consuming procedure and submitting various documents to the labor authorities. On the grounds of the work permit, a residence permit is issued to the expatriate. No work permits are required for expatriates who are registered with Bulgarian courts as shareholders, directors, managers, or controllers of Bulgarian companies or registered with the Bulgarian Chamber of Commerce and Industry as heads of representative offices of foreign entities. Such individuals need a residence permit only.

Gross income

Individuals must pay personal income tax in accordance with the level of gross income.

Employee gross income/Taxable income from work on the basis of an employment contract includes the following.

1. Salary, wages or any other remuneration for work performed, as well as any additional compensation for, for example, years of service, unhealthy work conditions, higher professional qualifications, cost-of-living adjustments, bonuses and premiums, and overtime pay.
2. All fringe benefits/benefits in kind provided by the employer or on the account of the employer.
3. Certain compensations received by the employee on the basis of the Labor Code (in general, for some cases of termination of the employment contract, unutilized paid leave, etc.).

The following employees' income is not subject to taxation:

1. The value of free preventive food, antidotes and personal protection devices provided by the employer pursuant to the Labor Code and other laws.
2. The value of special work clothes, free work clothes and uniforms provided by the employer pursuant to the Labor Code and other laws.
3. Business trip allowances and compensation for moving to another workplace, reassignment due to health reasons, noncompletion of work due to force majeure circumstances, and redundancy as provided under the Labor Code.
4. The value of any commuting fares provided by the employer free of charge.
5. Social expenses borne by the employer that are subject to taxation under the Corporate Income Tax Act.
6. Compensations for temporary work incapacity under the Mandatory Social Insurance Code.

The loss carryforward facility is not applicable for individuals.

No special concessions are granted to foreigners.

Capital gains and investment income/The concept of income globalization was introduced in Bulgaria as from January 1, 1998. Bulgarian tax residents (including expatriates who are considered Bulgarian tax residents) are taxed on capital gains and investment income realized from all sources during their period of residence. Foreign tax residents are taxed only on the capital gains and investment income derived from sources in Bulgaria.

Capital gains on the disposal or exchange of immovable and movable property as well as on the transfer of sole traders' enterprises are taxable on an annual basis (see the respective table). An exemption provided in respect to capital gains is discussed under "Tax exempt income."

The taxable base in the case of disposal or exchange of immovable property and means of transportation is the difference between the sale price and the higher of the actual and the adjusted purchase price of the property. For immovable property, the adjusted price is equal to the evaluation made for tax purposes; for cars, buses, trucks, and seat traction-engine vehicles, the adjusted price is their price in new condition adjusted by a depreciation coefficient; for other means of transportation, the adjusted price is their insurance value. The taxable base in all other cases of disposal or exchange of movable property is the difference between the sale price and the purchase price adjusted by the general index of consumer goods prices announced by the National Institute of Statistics.

The taxable base in transfers of sole traders' enterprises is the difference between the sale price specified in the purchase agreement and the balancesheet value of the assets.

Income from rent, annuities and leases (except for rent from agricultural land) is subject to advance personal income tax at 20% and final tax on an annual basis. For tax purposes a statutory deduction of 20% of the gross income is available.

Personal income tax is not levied on dividends and liquidation quotas, which are taxed at 15% at source. The withholding tax is final.

Interest on deposits and accounts in local commercial banks and branch offices of foreign banks, mutual benefit funds, and savings and credit cooperatives; interest and discounts on state, municipal and corporate securities; moratorium interest on bond relations; income from investing insurance reserves of life insurance, marriage and child insurance; life insurance if related to an investment fund; and interest on court-established receivables are exempt from taxation. Other interest income is taxable at 20% final tax.

Royalties are taxed on an annual basis at the rates for taxation of nonemployment income (shown below).

Tax-exempt income/The most important kinds of tax-exempt income, in addition to the kinds of income already mentioned, are listed below.

1. Capital gains on the sale or exchange of an apartment, house or villa, including the adjacent land, if it has been the principal residence of the seller for at least three years before the sale or the exchange.
2. Capital gains on the sale or exchange of up to two real estate properties that are not the principal residence of the seller, as well as agricultural and forest estates (no limit on number), if the period between the acquisition and the sale is more than five years.
3. Capital gains on vehicles acquired by the seller not less than one year before the sale.
4. Any other capital gains except those realized from sale of shares and share participation in companies, partnerships and other forms of joint ventures.
5. Amounts received as a result of making compulsory pension, health and social security contributions.
6. Compensation and other similar payments for physical injuries, death and occupational disease; property insurance; alienation of rights; losses; life insurance compensations and compensations from other personal insurance made in the country when the insurance event occurs.
7. Income in cash or in-kind received in accordance with the law as a social aid, and compensation for unemployment.
8. Aid received from social funds and organizations.
9. Stipends granted to Bulgarian tax resident individuals for education in Bulgaria and abroad.
10. Profits distributed in the form of new shares and company stock or in the form of an increase of the nominal value of already issued shares or stock.
11. Profits used for increasing the share capital of a company.
12. Inheritances and donations.
13. Gains from state lotteries, gambling and other games of fortune.

14. Capital gains from shares in public companies and tradable rights in such shares realized on the regulated Bulgarian securities market.

Business income of individuals who perform certain business activities listed in the law and have a turnover for the previous year of not more than BGL75,000 (approximately US$34,658) is also exempt from personal income taxation (see "Business tax").

Tax regulations on specific types of income/The following basic types of income are also subject to personal income taxation (the list, however, is not comprehensive).

1. Income received by sole traders.
2. Income received by freelancers, individuals supplying personal services and artisans.
3. Income of managers, controllers and members of management and supervisory boards.
4. Rental income.
5. Bonuses payable to managers or directors of companies in proportion to realized post-taxable profit, income or turnover.

Certain types of income, such as monetary and in-kind prizes from various competition events, compensations for lost profits and damages, taxable interest, sums received from voluntary pension, health, unemployment and life insurance coverage and income from incidental transactions are taxed at a flat rate of 20%. The tax is final.

Deductions

Business deductions/Individuals earning income other than employment income deduct pre-estimated expenses (not differentiated into business and other expenses) in calculating standard taxable income. For example, freelancers and civil contractors may deduct 35% of their gross income before taxation; and managers and members of management bodies may deduct 10% of their gross income realized from management and supervisory activities. Sole traders determine their taxable base in accordance with the corporate profit tax regulations. Notary officers and privately working physicians and dentists can choose to determine their taxable base either by deducting 35% of the gross income or in accordance with the corporate profit tax regulations, that is, business expenses will be recognized if supported by relevant documents.

Nonbusiness expenses/Compulsory and voluntary health, pension, unemployment, and other related contributions borne by individuals are tax deductible in full. Contributions paid by the employee under life insurance contracts and life insurance, if related to an investment fund, are deductible. Personal income taxpayers, except for employees, may also deduct up to 10% of their taxable income for donations to various nonprofit organizations.

Personal allowances/There are no tax deductions for personal allowances for spouses or dependants. However, standard allowances for children, which are paid from the state budget, are not subject to personal income taxation.

Tax credits

Bilateral tax relief is granted in accordance with the provisions of the DTTs in force. Where no treaty protection is available, unilateral ordinary tax credit is granted, with the credit amount calculated separately for each source country ("per-country limitation").

Other taxes

Business tax/Individuals and legal entities who carry out certain commercial activities and have a total annual turnover of less than BGL75,000 (approximately US$34,658) for the previous year are liable for the so called "final license tax." The tax amount does not depend on realized income, but is a lump sum determined by law for each activity for different regions.

Social security contributions/The general rate of social security contributions is 32.7%, of which 24.7% is payable by the employer and 8% by the employee. Unemployment fund contributions are imposed at the rate of 4%, of which 3% is payable by the employer and 1% by the employee. The general rate of health insurance contributions is 6%, of which 4.5% is payable by the employer and 1.5% by the employee. The base on which the above compulsory contributions are calculated is the employee's gross monthly remuneration, including benefits in kind. The maximum base, however, cannot exceed the amount fixed each year in the Mandatory National Insurance Budget Act. For 2002 this amount is BGL850.For freelancers there is a minimum monthly insurance base amounting to BGL170.

Local taxes on income/There are no local taxes on income.

Tax administration

Returns/In general taxpayers have to submit annual tax returns. Employees who work on the basis of an employment contract are not obliged to submit tax returns if all their income is from employment only. However, tax resident individuals who have received only employment income from non-resident employers have to file an annual tax return. For tax purposes, spouses are treated as separate taxpayers. No income splitting is allowed. The tax year is, without exception, the calendar year. Income is declared in the year in which it is received regardless of the year to which it relates.

The deadline for submission of tax returns is April 15 of the following year and the tax must be paid not later than 30 days as from the date of submission of the tax return. Individuals who file the tax return and pay the annual tax by January 31 of the following year are entitled to 5% discount of the outstanding annual tax. Individuals and legal entities liable to final license tax have to file an annual tax return by January 14 of the following year. The license tax is payable in four equal installments.

Payment of tax/Personal income tax for employees is withheld by the employer from the gross remuneration on a monthly basis. The employer acts as an agent of the revenue authorities and transfers the tax due to the budget. Certain taxpayers who are not employees, such as sole traders, freelancers, managers, and controllers, must pay advance tax, either regularly (monthly/quarterly) or whenever income is received; where the income is paid by a Bulgarian entity, the advance tax must be withheld from the remuneration by the payer.

Tax rates

Employment income/The following tax rates, effective from January 1, 2002, apply to the monthly employment income.

Monthly taxable income				
Over (Column 1)	Not over		Tax on Column 1	Percentage on excess
0	BGL 110		—	0
BGL 110	140		—	18
140	400		BGL 5.40	24
400	1,000		67.80	28
1,000			235.80	29

Nonemployment income/The following tax rates, effective from January 1, 2002, apply to the annual taxable income.

Annual taxable income				
Over (Column 1)	Not over		Tax on Column 1	Percentage on excess
0	BGL 1,320		—	0
BGL 1,320	1,680		—	18
1,680	4,800		BGL 64.80	24
4,800	12,000		813.60	28
12,000			2,829.60	29

INDIVIDUAL TAX CALCULATION

Calendar year 2002

Assumptions

The taxpayer is a foreign citizen who has a work permit and works on the basis of an employment contract with a Bulgarian employer. He/she receives a gross salary of US$3,000 per month (approximately BGL6,000) as well as benefits-in-kind of US$1,500 (approximately BGL3,000).

Tax computation

	(Monthly basis)
Monthly salary	BGL 6,000.00
Monthly benefit in kind (accommodation)	3,000.00
Monthly gross income	9,000.00
Compulsory health, pension and unemployment contributions	89.25
Taxable base	BGL 8,910.75
Tax	BGL 2,529.92
Net monthly income	BGL 6,380.83*

*Approximately US$2,948.61.

Note:

Exchange rate of the lev at January 2, 2002 was US$1 = BGL2.16401; €1 = BGL1.95583.

PwC contact

For additional information on taxation in Cambodia, contact:

David Fitzgerald
PricewaterhouseCoopers (Cambodia) Ltd.
124 Norodom Boulevard
Phnom Penh, Cambodia
Telephone: 855-23-218 086
Fax: 855-23-211 594
e-mail: david.b.fitzgerald@vn.pwcglobal.com

Significant developments

There have been no significant tax or regulatory developments in individual taxation in the past year.

Territoriality and residence

There is no personal income tax per se in Cambodia. Instead, a monthly salary tax is imposed on individuals who derive income from employment. General consulting income is excluded from salary tax but is subject to tax on profit (although rules exist that may deem certain consultants as employees).

Cambodian salary tax rules follow internationally familiar residency and source principles. A Cambodian resident's worldwide salary is subject to Cambodia salary tax, while nonresidents are taxed on Cambodian-source salary.

Residents are persons domiciled in or having a principal place of abode in Cambodia or present in Cambodia for more than 182 days in a calendar year.

Gross income

Employee gross income/A distinction is made between cash salary and fringe benefits.

Cash salary includes remuneration, wages, bonuses, overtime and compensation paid for fulfilling employment activities. Employer-provided loans and advances are also considered cash salary.

Fringe benefits include the following.

1. Accommodation support, including payment of utilitles and domestic helpers.
2. Education assistance (unless employment-related).
3. Provision of motor vehicles (presumably for private use).
4. Low-interest loans and discounted sales.
5. "Excessive or unnecessary" cash allowances, social welfare and pension contributions.
6. Certain insurance support.
7. Entertainment or recreational expenditures (which may additionally be nondeductible to the provider for tax-on-profit purposes).

Exempt salary includes the following.

1. Certain redundancy payments.
2. Reimbursement of employment-related expenses.
3. Certain uniform entitlements.

4. Certain travel allowances.
5. Salaries of employees of approved diplomatic, international and aid organizations.
6. Salaries of nonresidents where the salary cost is not deducted in Cambodia for tax-on-profit purposes.

Deductions

These are limited to small amounts for employee dependents and for repayment of employer loans or advances.

Tax credits

Taxes paid by resident taxpayers on foreign-source salary will be allowed as a credit against Cambodian salary tax on presentation of documentation confirming payment. The credit allowed is the lower of foreign tax paid or the proportion of salary tax on salary from all sources attributable to the foreign-source income.

Other taxes

Social security taxes and local taxes on income/There are no such taxes at present.

Tax administration

Returns/Employers must submit to the tax authorities, together with the payment of tax withheld, a monthly tax declaration for the withholding tax on salary. There is no employee annual return.

Payment of tax/Employers must deduct salary tax from employees' salaries in accordance with the tax tables on a pay-as-you-earn basis. The tax withheld must be paid to the tax authorities not later than 15 days after the end of the month in which the salaries were paid. Late payments are subject to penalties.

Tax rates

The monthly cash salary of residents is taxed at the following rates.

Taxable income		Tax on	Percentage
Over	**Not over**	**Column 1**	**on excess**
(Column 1)			
0	CR 500,000	—	0
CR 500,000	1,250,000	—	5
1,250,000	8,500,000	CR 37,500	10
8,500,000	12,500,000	762,500	15
12,500,000		1,362,500	20

Nonresidents are taxed at a flat rate of 15%, which also constitutes a final tax.

Fringe benefits are taxable to the employer at a flat rate of 20% of the market value of the benefit.

INDIVIDUAL TAX CALCULATION

Assumptions

1. Resident alien and spouse, two school-age children; husband earns all the income.
2. Annual gross salary of US$80,000; employer pays US$3,000 per month for accommodations. Calculations are in local currency.

Tax computation

Gross monthly income:	
Salary	CR 26,000,000
Allowable deductions:	
Wife and children	225,000
Net monthly taxable income	CR 25,775,000
Income tax assessment:	
Tax on first 12,500,000	CR 1,362,500
Tax on remaining 13,275,000	2,655,000
	4,017,500
Salary tax on fringe benefits:	
Accommodation (11,700,000 ÷ 0.8) x 20%	2,925,000
Monthly salary tax payable	CR 6,942,500

Note:

Exchange rate of the riel at December 31, 2001: US$1 = CR3,900.

Cameroon, Republic of

PwC contact

For additional information on taxation in the Republic of Cameroon, contact:

Hampo Ghazarossian
Price Waterhouse Afrique
Tour AIG—Cedex 105
34, place des Corolles
92908 Paris—La Défense 2
France
Telephone: (33) (1) 41 26 40 00
Fax: (33) (1) 41 26 41 26
e-mail: hampo.ghazarossian@fr.pwcglobal.com

General note

This entry is repeated from the 2001/2002 edition. For more up-to-date information, consult the contact listed above or Mark Friedlich at mark.friedlich@us.pwcglobal.com.

Significant developments

There have been no significant tax or regulatory developments regarding individual taxation in the past year.

Territoriality and residence

Cameroon tax residents are subject to personal income tax on their worldwide income unless excluded by a tax treaty. Nonresidents are taxable on their Cameroon-source income.

All persons who have any of the following in Cameroon are considered tax residents.

1. Place of abode as owner, tenant, or life tenant.
2. Principal place of residence.
3. Center of their economic interests or business affairs.

Gross income

Employee gross income/Taxable income includes all cash remuneration, including living and housing allowances and bonuses. It also includes in-kind benefits such as housing, electricity and water, car, domestics, and food. In-kind benefits are valued as follows (as a percentage of gross income): housing—15%; electricity—4%; water—2%; per car—10%; per domestic servant—5%; and food—25% per person, up to a maximum of CFAF50,000 per month, children under 15 counting for one-half. Special allowances inherent to employment function or duties are nontaxable if they genuinely serve their purpose and are not exaggerated.

Capital gains and investment income/Capital gains are taxable only if the recipient or the recipient's spouse, ascendants, or descendants exercise or have exercised during the last five years preceding the transfer a management function in the company whose shares are transferred and if, during the same period, the rights of said persons have exceeded 25% of the profit earned. Such capital gains are liable to a deemed tax at a rate of 20%.

Capital gains resulting from the transfer of developed or undeveloped property that are realized by individuals off balance sheet are subject to a lump-sum tax withheld by the notary.

Dividend income is subject to proportional tax on income from securities (*taxe proportionelle sur les revenus de capitaux mobiliers*—TPRCM) at 16.5% for recipients resident in Cameroon, 15% for French residents, or 25% for nonresident recipients. Interest income is subject to a 16.5% withholding tax, except if paid to a nonresident, in which case it is not taxable.

The net income from dividends and interest is subject to a graduated surtax. The amount withheld is deductible from the income liable to graduated surtax.

Deductions

Business deductions/Professional expenses are deemed to be 20% of gross income and are deductible for proportional tax calculation purposes.

Nonbusiness expenses/For the graduated surtax calculation, the following are deductible: loan interest, financing costs for the purchase in Cameroon of one's personal domicile and of stocks in newly set up businesses, mandatory annuity payments, insurance premiums (under certain conditions), contributions to pension funds (limited to 10% of taxable salary), social security contributions to the National Social Insurance Fund, business expense reimbursements, and all taxes paid by the taxpayer except the graduated surtax.

Personal allowances/The number of a taxpayer's dependents does not affect proportional tax on salaries but is taken into account for graduated surtax calculation purposes.

Tax credits

No specific tax credits are available to short-term residents.

Residents are entitled to tax credits for withholding tax paid in Cameroon and tax treaty countries. Cameroon has tax treaties with Canada, France, and the Central Africa Customs Union (UDEAC) countries.

Other tax credits/A 5% credit is withheld on purchases. Any purchase made by a manufacturer, importer, wholesaler, or forester is decreased by 5% of the amount of the purchase. The total amount of 5% on purchases paid during the fiscal year by the purchaser constitutes an advance payment of income tax for persons with commercial businesses.

Cameroon radio/television allowance either is paid annually, simultaneously with business license tax for persons with commercial businesses, or is withheld by the employer from employees. This is not a tax burden but an advance payment of individual tax to be deducted from the final individual tax due for the fiscal year.

Other taxes

Housing fund tax/Employers must pay housing fund tax (crédit foncier) at a rate of 1.5% on the items of income paid to employees, excluding in-kind benefits. Employees contribute to housing fund tax at a rate of 1% of their taxable income.

Employment fund tax/Employers must pay employment fund tax *(fonds national pour l'emploi)* at a rate of 1% on the items of income paid to employees, including real amounts of in-kind benefits.

Television allowance/Employees contribute to finance Cameroon television according to a fixed scale, depending on monthly taxable income. This allowance should not be considered a tax burden, since the payments may be offset against the final income tax due (i.e., a tax credit).

Social security taxes/Employers must pay social insurance taxes on the following items of income.

1. Family allowances—7% of gross salary, limited to CFAF3,600,000 per annum.
2. Workmen's compensation fund—At rates ranging from 1.75% to 5% on gross salary.
3. Retirement fund—4.2% of gross salary, limited to CFAF3,600,000 per annum.

Employees contribute to the retirement fund at the rate of 2.8% of their gross salary, limited to CFAF3,600,000 per annum.

Local taxes on income/Municipal taxes are withheld monthly by the employer. Their amount is insignificant.

Tax administration

Tax returns/Employers must file monthly salary tax returns showing for each employee the amount of tax withheld. An adjusting declaration must be filed by the employee for self, spouse, and, if applicable, minor working children and must be returned before September 30 of each year. The tax year runs from July 1 to June 30.

Payment of taxes/Employers withhold monthly at source the amount of tax due by the employee and remit it to the Treasury within the first 15 days of the following month.

In case supplementary tax is due according to the annual tax return, the administration recovers this amount through an additional assessment to the taxpayer.

Tax rates

Proportional tax on salary/The rate is 6% plus 10% additional council tax, less 20% professional expenses. Thus, the effective rate is 5.28%.

Graduated surtax/Rates apply on a progressive scale, depending on tax brackets and number of dependents.

Taxable income		Tax on	Percentage
Over	**Not over**	**Column 1**	**on excess**
(Column 1)			
0	CFAF 500,000	—	—
CFAF 500,000	700,000	—	10
700,000	1,000,000	CFAF 20,000	15
1,000,000	1,500,000	65,000	20
1,500,000	2,000,000	165,000	25
2,000,000	2,750,000	290,000	30
2,750,000	3,500,000	515,000	35
3,500,000	4,500,000	777,500	40
4,500,000	5,500,000	1,177,500	45
5,500,000	6,500,000	1,627,500	50
6,500,000	7,500,000	2,127,500	55
7,500,000		2,677,500	60

Note:

This is a graduated scale applicable to one share. Final tax due (proportional tax on salary plus graduated surtax) is increased by 10% for additional council taxes.

INDIVIDUAL TAX CALCULATION

Fiscal year 2000/2001

Assumptions

Resident alien, married with two children.

Withholding tax computation

Annual basic salary		CFAF 30,000,000
In-kind benefits		4,500,000
Total gross taxable income		34,500,000
Taxes withheld from salary (i.e., 30,000,000):		
Social security	100,800	
Crédit foncier	345,000	
Proportional tax on salary (1)	1,821,600	
Graduated surtax	10,916,551	
Communal tax	30,240	
Television allowance	156,000	13,370,191
Net paid to employee		CFAF 16,629,809

Annual tax return

Gross taxable income:		
Salary and in-kind benefits		CFAF 34,500,000
Interest		3,500,000
Long-term capital gains on stocks		6,750,000
		44,750,000
Deductions:		
Professional expenses	6,900,000	
Social security contributions	100,800	
Crédit foncier contribution	345,000	
Proportional tax on salary (1)	1,821,600	
Proportional tax on interest (3,500,000 at 16.5%)	577,500	
Communal tax	30,240	
Loan interest paid	200,000	9,975,140
Net taxable income		CFAF 34,774,860
Income (rounded) per share (34,774,860 ÷ 3)		CFAF 11,591,620
Graduated surtax:		
On first 7,500,000		CFAF 2,677,500
On excess at 60%		2,454,972
Graduated tax per share		CFAF 5,132,472
For three shares (5,132,472 x 3)		CFAF 15,397,416
Additional centimes (10%)		1,485,372
		16,937,158
Less—Graduated surtax withheld		(10,916,551)
		6,020,607
Less—Television allowance (tax credit)		(156,000)
Net amount due on graduated surtax		CFAF 5,864,607

Notes:

1. Determined as follows:

	CFAF
Total gross taxable income	34,500,000
Less—Professional expenses (34,500,000 x 20%)	6,900,000
Net taxable income	27,600,000
Tax at 6%	1,656,000
Plus additional centimes (1,656,000 x 10%)	165,600
Proportional tax	1,821,600

2. Exchange rate at January 1, 2001: US$1 = CFAF699.260.

   Parity remains fixed between the CFA franc, used in 14 French-speaking African countries, and the French franc. The rate is CFAF100 = FF1. The convertibility of the CFA franc continues to be assured, as long as transfers are made through banking channels.

PwC contact

For additional information on taxation in Canada, contact:

Dave Black
PricewaterhouseCoopers LLP
Royal Trust Tower
Suite 3000, Box 82
Toronto Dominion Centre
Toronto, ON M5K 1G8 Canada
Telephone: (416) 365-2706
e-mail: dave.black@ca.pwcglobal.com

Significant developments

Until 2000, all provinces and territories, except Quebec, computed provincial income taxes as a percentage of basic federal tax ("tax on tax" systems). By 2001, all ten provinces and three territories switched to "tax on income" personal tax systems. The change allows the provinces and territories to set their own rates, brackets and credits. Personal taxes decreased in 2001.

General note

The following information is based on actual and proposed legislation as of January 1, 2002. It is assumed the proposed legislation will become law.

Territoriality and residence

Individuals resident in Canada are subject to Canadian income tax on their worldwide income. Relief from double taxation is provided through Canada's international tax treaties and foreign tax credits and deductions for foreign taxes paid on income derived from non-Canadian sources. Nonresident individuals are subject to Canadian income tax on income from employment in Canada, income from carrying on a business in Canada and capital gains from the disposition of taxable Canadian property. Taxable Canadian property includes, among other things, real estate situated in Canada, capital property used in carrying on a business in Canada and shares in Canadian-resident corporations that are not listed on a stock exchange. In certain circumstances, shares in Canadian-resident corporations that are listed on a stock exchange, shares in nonresident corporations and interests in nonresident trusts will be considered taxable Canadian property. Legislation that applies after October 1, 1996 extends the definition of taxable Canadian property.

Individuals resident in Canada for only part of a year are taxable in Canada on their worldwide income only for the period during which they were resident.

Generally, an individual is resident in Canada for tax purposes if there is a continuing relationship between the individual and Canada. In determining an individual's residence, all of the relevant facts must be considered, such as the maintenance of a dwelling suitable for year-round occupancy, credit cards, bank accounts, social and business ties, and personal property. Citizenship, domicile and residency under the tax laws of another country are not relevant. Ordinarily, individuals are considered to be resident where they maintain a fixed abode for themselves and their families. If an individual who, as a matter of fact, is considered not resident of Canada sojourns (i.e., is temporarily resident) in Canada for 183 days or more in a calendar year, the individual is deemed to be resident in Canada for that entire year.

Gross income

Employee gross income/Salaries, wages, commissions, directors' fees, and all other remuneration received by an officer or employee are included in income from employment. Canadian residents are taxable on worldwide income whether or not the income is remitted to Canada. Most fringe benefits received or enjoyed in connection with employment are also taxed as employment income. New federal rules increase the attractiveness of employee stock options to acquire certain publicly traded shares. Foreigners working temporarily or permanently in Canada are eligible for special concessions for employment at a special work site or remote location. The rules may exempt from tax most amounts received as allowances for board and lodging, as well as transportation between the special work site and the employee's principal place of residence.

Capital gains and investment income/No special concessions are available to short-term residents with respect to the taxation of capital gains and investment income. Dividends from Canadian corporations are grossed up by one-quarter for inclusion in income. A tax credit may then be claimed for 16.67% of the dividend before the gross-up, which results in a net tax saving. Accrued interest income on most debt obligations must be reported annually.

Draft legislation that applies to taxation years beginning after 2002 will change the tax treatment of interests held in foreign investment entities (FIEs). In general, taxpayers subject to the new rules must include in income either their share of the income of the FIE or any change in the fair market value of the interest in the FIE from the previous year.

One-half of capital gains are included in net income. When capital property is sold at a profit in the year or a prior year, a reserve may be claimed on any proceeds that are not due until after the year-end. The reserve represents the portion of the gain related to the sale proceeds that are not due until after the end of the year. However, the reserve mechanism cannot be used to postpone gains for more than five years on most types of capital property. Amounts brought into income each year under the reserve mechanism are treated as capital gains. A reserve may not be claimed if the taxpayer was not resident in Canada at the end of the year or at any time in the immediately preceding year.

A lifetime capital gains exemption allows a Canadian resident individual to realize, tax-free, up to Can$500,000 in capital gains on the disposition of qualified farm property and shares of a qualifying small business corporation. An individual resident in Canada for only part of the year may be eligible to claim the exemption if that individual was a resident of Canada throughout the immediately preceding or following year. The federal government has indicated that the rules governing the Can$500,000 exemption will be the subject of a review.

A nonresident's Canadian-source passive income, such as interest, dividends, rents, and royalties, is subject to withholding tax of 25% (unless reduced by a treaty); such income is not subject to graduated rates. Alternatively, a nonresident can elect to be taxed at graduated rates on timber royalties or rental income from real property in Canada net of expenses.

Deductions

Business deductions/In computing income from employment, an individual may claim only very limited, specified deductions. Taxes and interest (except interest related to the earning of business and property income), most life insurance premiums, and casualty losses are not deductible. Allowable deductions in computing employment income include traveling and certain other expenses of officers or employees required as a condition of employment, as well as contributions to a registered pension plan of the employer, within certain limits.

Nonbusiness expenses/Deductible nonbusiness expenses include contributions to various registered savings plans, certain child care expenses, alimony and maintenance payments (if taxable to the recipient), eligible moving expenses for relocation within Canada (usually in connection with a change of employment), and carrying charges on investment income.

Personal allowances/Personal allowances take the form of tax credits. The following credits apply for 2001.

Personal tax credits (1, 2)	**Can$**
Basic personal	1,186
Married (3)	1,007
Infirm dependents and caregivers (3)	560
Disability (4)	960
Age—Persons age 65 and over (3, 4)	579

Other credits (2)	
Pension income	16% of eligible pension income (maximum credit is Can$160) (4).
Tuition fees	16% of eligible fees (minimum Can$100 per institution) (4).
Education	Can$64 per month (4).
Interest on student loans	16% of the interest paid on loans under the Canada Student Loans Act and provincial student loan programs. Unused credits may be carried forward five years.
Medical expenses	16% of amount by which eligible expenses exceed lesser of Can$1,678 and 3% of net income (5).
Charitable donations	16% of the first Can$200 and 29% of the excess. Eligible donations are limited to 75% of net income. Unused donations may be carried forward five years (5).
Government pension plan and employment insurance plan contributions	16% of the lesser of the amount payable and the required premiums for the year (maximum credit is Can$379).

Notes:

1. Personal credits are fully indexed for inflation.
2. Any unused portion of the tax credits is not refundable.
3. The credit is reduced if the income of the individual, spouse or dependent exceeds a threshold amount.

4. In some circumstances, the unused portion of the credit may be transferred to a spouse, parent, grandparent, child, or grandchild, sibling, aunt, uncle, niece, or nephew.
5. One spouse may claim the other's medical expenses and/or charitable donations.

Tax credits

Personal allowances take the form of tax credits (see above).

Relief for foreign taxes in the Canadian system is accomplished through a tax credit and income deduction mechanism. If foreign taxes paid on property income (other than income from real property) exceed 15% of the income, the excess foreign taxes are not eligible for a Canadian foreign tax credit but rather become deductible from the property income. (This provision may have adverse implications for foreign citizens who have foreign property income and live in Canada.)

The overseas employment tax credit allows Canadian-resident individuals working abroad for more than six consecutive months to claim a tax credit if the overseas employment is for a specified employer in connection with contracts for certain defined activities (such as an engineering project). This maximum credit is equal to the employee's Canadian tax on Can$100,000 of qualifying overseas employment income.

Other taxes

Provincial taxes on income/In addition to the federal income tax, an individual who resides in or has income earned in any of the provinces or territories is also subject to provincial or territorial income tax. Except in Quebec, provincial and territorial taxes are calculated on the federal return and collected by the federal government. Rates vary among the jurisdictions and most provinces also impose surtaxes that may increase the provincial taxes payable. Provincial taxes are not deductible in computing taxable income.

Minimum income tax/In addition to the normal tax computation, individuals are required to compute an adjusted taxable income figure and include certain "tax preference" items that are otherwise deductible or exempt in the calculation of regular taxable income. If the adjusted taxable income exceeds the minimum-tax exemption of Can$40,000, a combined federal and provincial tax rate of 22.16% to 25.2%, depending on the province of residence, is applied to the excess, yielding the Alternative Minimum Tax (AMT). The taxpayer then pays the greater of regular tax or the AMT. Taxpayers required to pay the AMT are entitled to a credit in future years when their regular tax liability exceeds their alternative minimum tax level for that year.

Social security taxes/For 2001 Canadian resident employees are required to pay government pension plan contributions up to Can$1,496.40 a year and employment insurance premiums up to Can$878 a year. A credit equal to 16% of the lesser of the amount payable and the required premiums for the year is allowed in computing the individual's federal taxes payable.

Gift and inheritance taxes/There are no federal or provincial gift or inheritance taxes.

Federal goods and services tax/The federal goods and services tax (GST) is levied at a rate of 7%. It is a value-added tax applied at each level in the manufacturing and marketing chain and applies to most goods and services. However, the tax does not apply to sales of zero-rated goods or tax-exempt supplies, such as basic groceries, healthcare services, educational services, and certain services provided by financial institutions.

Harmonized sales tax/New Brunswick, Newfoundland and Nova Scotia have adopted a single sales tax rate of 15% in order to harmonize their sales tax systems with the GST. The 15% rate includes a provincial sales tax rate of 8% and the 7% GST. It is imposed on essentially the same base as the GST.

Other provincial and local taxes/British Columbia, Manitoba, Ontario, Prince Edward Island and Saskatchewan levy retail sales tax, at rates ranging from 6% to 10%, on most purchases. Alberta and the territories do not impose a retail sales tax. Quebec imposes a Quebec sales tax that is similar to the federal GST. The general rate of 7.5% applies to all taxable goods and services. Only Prince Edward Island and Quebec levy retail sales tax on prices that include the GST. As mentioned above, New Brunswick, Newfoundland and Nova Scotia levy a harmonized sales tax. Municipalities throughout Canada also levy property taxes.

Tax administration

Returns/In most cases, taxpayers must file tax returns on a calendar-year basis by April 30 of the following year. Married taxpayers file separately; joint returns are not allowed.

Payment of tax/Income tax is withheld from salaries. Any balance of tax owing is due April 30 of the following year. Individuals are required to pay quarterly installments if their tax payable exceeds amounts withheld at source by more than Can$2,000 in both the current and either of the two prior years.

Tax rates

Federal income tax/Federal rates are applied to taxable income. Personal tax credits, miscellaneous tax credits and the dividend tax credit are subtracted from the result to determine basic federal tax. The following tables assume that only the basic personal tax credit is available.

2001 federal tax rates are given below:

Federal taxable income		Tax on Column 1	Percentage on excess
Over (Column 1)	Not over		
0	Can$ 7,412	—	—
Can$ 7,412	30,754	—	16
30,754	61,509	Can$ 3,735	22
61,509	100,000	10,501	26
100,000		20,509	29

The 5% federal surtax was eliminated after 2000. The tax payable, including surtaxes, may be reduced for creditable foreign taxes (see "Tax computation").

2002 federal tax rates are given below:

Taxable income				
Over (Column 1)	Not over		Tax on Column 1	Percentage on excess
0	Can$ 7,634	....	—	—
Can$ 7,634	31,677	....	—	16
31,677	63,354	....	Can$ 3,847	22
63,354	103,000	....	10,816	26
103,000		....	21,124	29

Provincial income taxes/Until 2000, all provinces and territories, except Quebec, computed provincial income taxes as a percentage of basic federal tax ("tax on tax" systems). By 2001, all ten provinces and three territories switched to "tax on income" personal tax systems. The change allows the provinces to set their own rates, brackets and credits. However, the federal definition of taxable income should continue to apply for provincial purposes.

The following rates apply to interest and ordinary income. They reflect 2001 budgets (provincial budgets are usually introduced in the spring of each year). Lower effective rates apply to capital gains and dividends. In some cases, provincial tax reductions reduce or eliminate provincial tax at low income levels.

Province	Highest federal/ provincial tax rate (1)	
	2001	2002
	%	%
Alberta (2)	39.0	39.0
British Columbia (3)	45.7	43.7
Manitoba (4)	46.4	46.4
New Brunswick (5)	46.8	46.8
Newfoundland and Labrador (6)	48.6	48.6
Northwest Territories & Nunavut (7)	42.1	42.1
Nova Scotia (8)	47.3	47.3
Ontario (9)	46.4	46.4
Prince Edward Island (10)	47.3	47.3
Quebec (11)	48.7	48.2
Saskatchewan (12)	45.0	44.5
Yukon (13)	43.0	42.4
Nonresident	42.9	42.9

Notes:

1. The rates represent the highest combined federal and provincial marginal tax rates, including federal surtaxes (see above) and provincial surtaxes.
2. Commencing 2001, Alberta adopted a "tax on income" personal tax system. For 2001 and 2002, Alberta's tax rate is 10%.
3. The highest British Columbia tax rate, which is 16.7%, applies to taxable income exceeding Can$85,000. This rate will drop to 14.7% for 2002. In 2001, personal surtaxes were eliminated and incorporated into the tax bracket thresholds and rates.
4. The highest Manitoba tax rate, which is 17.4%, applies to taxable income exceeding Can$61,089. In 2001, Manitoba eliminated its 2% surtax and 2% flat

tax, but raised its basic rates. The net effect was a small decrease in effective rates.

5. The highest New Brunswick tax rate, which is 17.84%, applies to taxable income exceeding Can$100,000. In 2001, the 8% surtax was eliminated and replaced by a new tax bracket. The rates dropped slightly as a result.
6. Commencing 2001, Newfoundland and Labrador adopted a “tax on income” personal tax system. The highest Newfoundland tax rate is 18.02% applicable to taxable income exceeding Can$59,180. A surtax of 9% applies where provincial tax exceeds Can$7,032.
7. Commencing in 2001, the Northwest Territories and Nunavut adopted a “tax on income” personal tax system. The highest rate, which is 13.05%, applies to taxable income exceeding Can$100,000. The effective tax rates did not change as a result of the change to the “tax on income” system.
8. The highest Nova Scotia tax rate, which is 16.67%, applies to taxable income exceeding Can$59,180. Nova Scotia also levies a 10% surtax on provincial tax exceeding Can$10,000.
9. The highest Ontario tax rate, which is 11.16%, applies to taxable income exceeding Can$61,629. Ontario also levies a 20% surtax on provincial tax exceeding Can$3,560 and a 36% surtax on provincial tax exceeding Can$4,491. After 2001, the surtax brackets will be indexed.
10. Commencing 2001, Prince Edward Island adopted a “tax on income” personal tax system. The highest Prince Edward Island rate, which is 16.7%, applies to taxable income exceeding Can$61,509. A 10% surtax applies on provincial tax exceeding Can$5,200.
11. Quebec has its own personal tax system, which requires a separate calculation of taxable Income. Tax rates range from 17% to 24.5% for 2001 and will be reduced to 16% to 24% for 2002. In recognition of the fact that Quebec collects its own tax, for Quebec residents federal income tax is reduced by 16.5% of basic federal tax.
12. Commencing 2001, Saskatchewan adopted a “tax on income” personal tax system. The highest Saskatchewan tax rate, which is 16% applies to taxable income exceeding Can$60,000. The flat tax and surtax was eliminated with the introduction of the new system. The highest effective marginal rate dropped from 19.28% in 2000 to 16% in 2001 and will drop to 15.5% in 2002.
13. Commencing in 2001, Yukon adopted a “tax on income” personal tax system. The highest Yukon rate, which is 13.34%, applies to taxable income exceeding Can$100,000. This rate will decrease to 12.76% for 2002. A 5% surtax applies on provincial tax in excess of Can$6,000.

INDIVIDUAL TAX CALCULATION

Calendar year ending December 31, 2001

Assumptions

1. Resident husband and wife living in Ontario; two children (under 18); one spouse earns all the income.
2. Total remuneration of Can$110,000.
3. Capital gains of Can$16,000.
4. Foreign interest income of Can$5,000, from which Can$750 withholding has been deducted. Other interest income of Can$6,000.
5. All amounts are in Canadian dollars.

Tax computation

Income:		
Salary		Can$ 110,000
Interest		11,000
Taxable capital gain (one half of actual gain) (1)		8,000
Net income/Taxable income		Can$ 129,000
Income tax (see table above):		
Federal tax before credits		Can$ 30,104
Less—Personal credits:		
Basic	1,186	
Spouse	1,007	(2,193)
Less—Other credits:		
Canada Pension Plan	239	
Employment insurance	140	(379)
Basic federal tax (BFT)		27,532
Less—Foreign tax credit		(750)
Lesser of (5,000 ÷ 129,000) x 27,532 = 1,067 or 750		
Federal income tax		26,782
Provincial (Ontario) income tax (2):		
Ontario tax	12,258	
Less—Personal credits:		
Basic and spouse	(845)	
Canada Pension Plan and Employment Insurance	(147)	
Basic Ontario tax	11,266	
20% surtax (20% x (11,266 – 3,560))	1,541	
36% surtax (36% x (11,266 – 4,491))	2,439	15,246
Total income tax (3)		Can$ 42,028

Notes:

1. Also, assuming the capital gains are not in respect of qualified farm property or shares of a small business corporation, a capital gains deduction is not available.
2. The following rates apply to taxable income in Ontario:

Taxable income			
Over	**Not over**	**Tax on Column 1**	**Percentage on excess**
(Column 1)			
0	Can$ 30,814	—	6.16
Can$ 30,814	61,629	Can$ 1,898	9.22
61,629		4,739	11.16

Personal tax credits, miscellaneous tax credits and the dividend tax credit are subtracted from the result to determine basic Ontario tax. Ontario personal tax credits for 2001 include the following:

Basic	Can$457
Married	Can$388
Government pension plan and employment insurance premiums	6.16% (maximum credit is Can$146) of the lesser of the amounts payable and the required premiums for the year

Ontario surtaxes are not reflected in the Ontario tax rates and are added to basic Ontario tax. Ontario levies a 20% surtax on provincial tax exceeding Can$3,560 and a 36% surtax on provincial tax exceeding Can$4,491.

3. The taxpayer does not have sufficient tax preference items to be liable for the minimum income tax.
4. Exchange rate of the Canadian dollar at December 31, 2001: US$1 = Can$1.5928.

Cayman Islands

PwC contact

For additional information on the Cayman Islands, contact:

Richard W. Harris
PricewaterhouseCoopers
P.O. Box 258 GT
Grand Cayman, B.W.I.
Telephone: (1) (345) 949 7000
Fax: (1) (345) 949 7352
e-mail: richard.w.harris@ky.pwcglobal.com

Absence of taxation

Income tax is not imposed on individuals in the Cayman Islands.

Note

Exchange rate of the Cayman Islands dollar at January 1, 2002: US$1 = CI$0.83 (fixed rate).

PwC contact

For additional information on taxation in Guernsey, contact:

Tom Birley
PricewaterhouseCoopers
P.O. Box 321
Le Truchot
St. Peter Port
Guernsey
Channel Islands, GY1 4ND
Telephone: (44) (1481) 727777
Fax: (44) (1481) 711075
e-mail: tom.birley@uk.pwcglobal.com

Significant developments

For all years up to and including the year of charge 2001, income from sources within Guernsey has been assessed on a preceding-year basis, while income from outside the island has been assessed on an actual basis. Where a taxpayer was in receipt of unearned income from both Guernsey and non-Guernsey sources, the convention was for *all* investment income to be assessed on an actual basis. However, with effect from the year of charge 2003 all income (other than trading profits arising to companies, individuals or partnerships) will be assessed on a current-year basis. The year of charge 2002 is to be a transitional year, for which the final assessable income from all sources previously assessed on a preceding-year basis (other than trading profits) will be the average of the income from those sources during the calendar years 2001 and 2002.

Territoriality and residence

Individuals who are solely or principally resident in Guernsey are liable to tax on their worldwide income, while individuals who are resident but not solely or principally resident are taxable on Guernsey-source income and overseas income remitted to the Island. A person who is not resident in Guernsey is liable to tax on Guernsey-source income except bank-deposit interest, which by concession is exempt. Income from Guernsey exempt companies is not considered Guernsey-source income. Generally, a person who is on the Island for a period of 182 days or more in total in any year is resident for tax purposes.

Persons will be treated as principally resident if they are not solely resident but maintain their only residence on the Island. Becoming resident or principally resident can also be established in several other particular circumstances.

Gross income

Employee gross income/While treated solely or principally as a resident of Guernsey, an individual is assessable on the full amount of the emoluments of employment, no matter where the duties are performed. This will include certain benefits. Where a nonresident carries out any duties in Guernsey, the emoluments attaching to these duties are assessable in Guernsey.

Capital gains and investment income/There is no assessment on capital gains unless such gains result from a venture in the nature of a trade, in which case they are treated as income and liable to income tax at the rate of 20%.

A "dwellings profits tax" seeks to tax speculative short-term profits from property used for human habitation. The profit on disposal of any such property sold within 12 months of purchase is liable to tax at the rate of 100%.

Individuals who are treated as solely or principally resident are liable to tax at the rate of 20% on their worldwide investment income no matter where that income is paid. Nonresidents are liable to tax at 20% of their investment income arising in Guernsey. Guernsey bank deposit interest is by concession exempt from tax in the hands of nonresidents.

Deductions

Business deductions/There are no significant deductions allowable to the individual.

Nonbusiness expenses/Deductible nonbusiness expenses are listed below.

1. Interest paid to banks and similar financial institutions.
2. One half of life insurance premiums paid is allowable as a deduction, provided the following conditions are met:
   a. The premiums do not in aggregate exceed one-sixth of assessable income;
   b. The premium on each policy must be no more than 7% of the sum insured.
3. Pension contributions paid to approved schemes, subject to restrictions.
4. Certain annual payments.

Personal allowances/Nonresidents are not entitled to Guernsey personal allowances. However, a resident of the United Kingdom or the other Channel Island can claim proportional allowances. Allowances for 2002 are as follows.

	£
Married allowance (Note)	14,000
Single allowance	7,000
Spouse's earned income allowance (maximum)	1,400

Note:

The married couples allowance is simply twice the personal allowance. There are no additional allowances available to married couples in Guernsey that are not available to two single individuals. The married allowance is reduced by the amount of the spouse's earned income allowance.

Other allowances exist for persons over age 65 and certain dependent relatives.

Tax credits

Foreign taxes on income, except income from a Jersey source or income from a U.K. source other than dividends or debenture interest, are not available as credits against the Guernsey tax liability. However, unilateral relief is given at either the rate of foreign tax or three-quarters of the effective rate of Guernsey tax, whichever is lower.

Other taxes

Social security taxes/Employees are subject to social security tax at the rate of 4.5% of their gross earnings up to a monthly earnings limit of £2,444.00. A self-employed person pays at the maximum rate of £50.20 per week.

Other taxes on income/No other taxes are levied on income.

Tax administration

Returns/The tax year is the calendar year.

The income of a married woman who is living with her husband is deemed to be the income of the husband, subject to an election for separate assessment that does not affect total tax payable. A married woman is treated as living with her husband unless there is a permanent separation.

Payment of tax/Tax is due on June 30 and December 31 in the "year of charge" and is normally based on the previous year's income. However, tax is deducted from employee salaries and accounted for by the employer.

Tax rates

Tax is payable at the rate of 20% on net income after allowances.

INDIVIDUAL TAX CALCULATION

Assumptions

Resident husband and wife, two children; one spouse earns all the income.

Personal tax computation

Salary		£ 70,000
Bank interest		10,000
Capital gain of 10,000—Exempt from tax in Guernsey		—
		80,000
Less—Charges on income		5,000
		75,000
Less—Allowances:		
Married couples allowance	14,000	
Life insurance premiums	750	(14,750)
Taxable income		£ 60,250
Tax payable—60,250 x 20%		£ 12,050

Note:

Exchange rate of the pound sterling at December 31, 2001: US$1 = £0.6905

Channel Islands, Jersey

PwC contact

For additional information on taxation in Jersey, contact:

Jane Stubbs
Pricewaterhouse Coopers
Twenty Two Colomberie
St. Helier, Jersey
Channel Islands
Telephone: (44) (1534) 838200
Fax: (44) (1534) 767556
e-mail: jane.stubbs@uk.pwcglobal.com

Significant developments

There have been no significant tax developments in the last year.

Territoriality and residence

Individuals who are resident and ordinarily resident in Jersey are liable to tax on their worldwide income, while individuals who are resident but not ordinarily resident in Jersey are taxed only on Jersey-source income and overseas income that is remitted to Jersey.

A person who is not resident in Jersey is liable to tax on Jersey sources of income, except bank-deposit interest, which by concession is exempt. Income from Jersey exempt companies is not considered Jersey-source income.

Generally, the following establish an individual's residence for tax purposes.

1. Residence for a period of six months or more in total in any year.
2. Residence for more than three months per year on average over a period of four years.
3. Having accommodation available for that individual's use and visits to the Island for any length of time.

The concept of ordinarily resident is similar to that in the United Kingdom and is related, inter alia, to the place where the person is habitually resident.

Gross income

Employee gross income/While a resident of Jersey, an individual is assessable on the full amount of the emoluments of employment no matter where the duties are performed. Benefits are generally not taxable unless they can be converted to money or money's worth. Where a nonresident carries out any duties in Jersey, the emoluments attaching to these duties may be assessable in Jersey.

Capital gains and investment income/There is no assessment on capital gains unless they result from a venture in the nature of a trade, in which case they are liable to income tax at the rate of 20%.

Residents are liable to tax at the rate of 20% on their worldwide investment income, no matter where that income is paid. Nonresidents are liable to tax at 20% on their investment income arising in Jersey, unless their only Jersey source of investment income is bank-deposit interest, which by concession is exempt.

Deductions

Business deductions/There are no significant deductions allowable to individuals not engaged in a trade. Travel to and from work is not regarded as a business expense, nor are moving, motor or entertainment expenses unless they were incurred wholly and exclusively for the purpose of the employment, trade or profession.

Nonbusiness expenses/Deductible expenses are shown below.

1. Interest paid to banks and similar financial institutions.
2. Premiums paid on a qualifying life insurance policy, subject to certain restrictions.
3. Pension contributions paid to approved schemes, subject to restrictions.
4. Annual payments.

Personal allowance/Nonresidents are not entitled to Jersey personal allowances. However, proportional allowances are available to Commonwealth or European Union (EU) citizens in receipt of Jersey-source income.

Allowances for 2001 include the following items.

	£
Earned income allowance—One-quarter of earned income (maximum) (1)	3,400
Married allowance	5,200
Single allowance	2,600
Child allowance (for each child)	2,500
Wife's earned income allowance (maximum) (2)	4,500
Higher child allowance for children in full-time further education	5,000
Additional child allowance for widow(er)s, etc.	4,500
Exempt income:	
Single person—Nil liability, up to	10,750
Married person—Nil liability, up to	17,250

Notes:

1. Joint income in cases of husband and wife.
2. In addition to earned income allowance.

Other allowances exist for persons over the age of 65 and certain dependent relatives. From 1998, tax relief for the cost of childcare has been introduced

Tax credits

Foreign taxes on income are not available as credits against the Jersey tax liability unless the income is Guernsey- or U.K.-source. (Tax on U.K. dividends and debentures is not creditable.) However, limited relief is given for foreign income taxes, which are deductible from the gross income as an expense.

Other taxes

Social security taxes/Employees are subject to social security tax at the rate of 6% of their gross earnings up to a monthly earnings limit of £2,644 for 2002 (maximum contribution per month £158.64). A self-employed person pays at the rate of 12.50% (subject to maximum monthly contribution of £330.50).

Other taxes on income/None.

Tax administration

Returns/The tax year is the calendar year.

The income of a married woman living with her husband is deemed to be the income of the husband. A married woman is treated as living with her husband unless there is a permanent separation. A concessionary form of separate assessment may be applied if both parties request this treatment in writing, explaining the reason for the request.

Payment of tax/Tax is due and payable on assessment, which is usually issued in the following year. There is no statutory withholding from payroll.

Surcharge/A surcharge of 10% may be applied if tax is not paid on a timely basis.

Tax rates

Tax is payable at the rate of 20% on net income after allowances.

Alternative tax calculation/In Jersey, an alternative means of computing tax liability by reference to a marginal rate is undertaken automatically by the tax authorities. The taxpayer's liability is based on the lower of the tax paid at the 20% rate and tax calculated using the marginal rate. The method of computation is shown in the tax calculation below.

INDIVIDUAL TAX CALCULATION

Assumptions

Resident husband and wife, two children; husband earns all the income.

Tax computation

Salary		£ 70,000
Bank interest (1)		10,000
Long-term capital gain—Not assessable		—
		80,000
Less:		
Mortgage interest	5,000	
Life insurance premiums	1,500	6,500
		73,500
Less:		
Earned income relief—Maximum	3,400	
Married allowance	5,200	
Child allowance (x 2)	5,000	13,600
Taxable income		£ 59,900
Tax thereon—59,900 x 20%		£ 11,980

Alternative tax calculation

Total gross income	A
(Including gross amount of Jersey income taxed at source—X)	
Less—Charges (e.g., loan/bank interest paid)	(B)
(Including gross amount of interest paid under deduction of Jersey tax—Y)	
Total net income	C
Exemption limit (2)	(D)
Excess income	E
Tax payable (E x marginal fraction) (3)	F
Less—Tax on income at source (X x 20%)	(G)
	H
Add—Retainable charges (Y x 20%)	I
Maximum tax payable (4)	J

Notes:

1. Interest is assumed to be received gross, which is the same as net of withheld tax where no tax credit is applicable. If a tax credit is applicable, it is restricted to the individual's net effective rate.
2. 2001 figures—Single, £10,750 (aged over 63, £12,000); married, £17,250 (aged over 63, £19,750). Wife's earned income relief, child allowance, higher child allowance, additional personal allowance and child care relief should be added to exemption limits where appropriate.
3. Marginal fraction is 27% for 2000 and 2001.
4. If the result above (J) is lower than the tax levied at 20% on income after allowances (see income tax computation above), then a relief is due.
5. Exchange rate of the pound sterling at December 31, 2001: US$1 = £0.6905.

PwC contact

For additional information on taxation in Chile, contact:

Julio Pereira G.
PricewaterhouseCoopers
Avda. Andrés Bello 2711
Cuarto Piso
Santiago, Chile
Telephone: (56) (2) 9400152
Fax: (56) (2) 9400503
e-mail: julio.pereira@cl.pwcglobal.com

Significant developments

During 2001 a reduction of personal income taxes was approved. The marginal rate will be reduced from 45 to 40%.

Territoriality and residence

Chile taxes its citizens resident or domiciled in Chile on worldwide income. Domicile is defined as physical presence with the intent to remain in the country. Residence is mere physical presence.

Foreigners working in Chile are subject to taxation only on their Chilean-source income during their first three years in Chile, after which worldwide income is taxed. In special cases, the three-year period can be extended.

Residence for tax purposes is acquired upon remaining six consecutive months in the country in one calendar year, or more than six months, whether consecutive or not, in two consecutive calendar years. If domicile is acquired before residence and the intention is to stay in Chile permanently or for a significant period of time, normal taxation applies as of the date of entry into the country. While residence is being acquired, when applicable, a flat 20% tax normally is levied.

Gross income

Employee gross income/Resident or nonresident foreigners are taxed on their salary, deducting social security contributions.

Such items as reimbursement of travel expenses and housing provided in the employer's interest, moving expenses and a reasonable relocation allowance are considered nontaxable income and are excluded from the tax calculation.

Such items as cost-of-living allowance, area allowances, car allowance, vacation travel expenses, and utilities are taxable.

Capital gains and investment income/There is no capital gains tax in Chile. Capital gains are taxed as normal income unless qualified by the law as being nontaxable income.

Investment income is also taxed as normal income. However, in the case of interest, only "real interest" is taxed, that is, interest effectively paid less cost-of-living increase.

Deductions

Business deductions/In general, all expenses incurred that are in the employer's interest, provided they are duly documented, are deductible. Among these are travel and lodging expenses and documented entertainment. No blanket or standard deductions, such as representation allowances, are allowed.

Nonbusiness expenses/Except for social security contributions and a percentage of certain investments in shares and time deposits, no nonbusiness deductions are allowed.

Tax credits

The Income Tax Law allows a tax credit for taxes paid abroad by individuals domiciled or resident in Chile, provided there is a tax treaty in force with the foreign country. Personal allowances are in the form of a tax credit. No other tax credit is available.

Other taxes

Social security taxes/Foreign individuals may be exempt from local social security payments, provided they belong to a foreign social security entity covering at least pension, disability, illness, and death. Salaries are subject to social security contribution of 20%, up to an approximate amount of US$1,450 per month. The excess is not subject to contributions.

In practice, nonresidents normally would not be subject to social security contributions in Chile. However, if they were, the same description as for a resident foreigner would apply.

As noted above, social security contributions are deductible in determining taxable income.

Local taxes on income/There are no local income taxes to be paid, only central government taxes.

Tax administration

Returns/Yearly tax returns need not be filed if the employee receives only salary income. If taxable income from another source is received, such as interest income, a yearly return must be filed.

Husband and wife must file separate returns if each has separate income. The tax year and calendar year coincide. The calendar year is the period of 12 months that ends at December 31. The tax year is that in which taxes or part of them must be paid.

Payment of tax/In the case of employees, there is mandatory monthly withholding by the employer.

Tax rates

Second category tax rates/Tax rates applied to this category are shown below.

Tax units (1)				
Over	To		Factor	Deduction (2)
0	C$ 385,074	....	0.00	—
C$ 385,074	855,720	....	0.05	C$ 19,253.70
855,720	1,426,200	....	0.10	62,039.70
1,426,200	1,996,680	....	0.15	133,349.70
1,996,680	2,567,160	....	0.25	333,017.70
2,567,160	3,422,880	....	0.33	538,390.50
3,422,881	4,278,600	....	0.39	743,763.30
4,278,601		....	0.43	914,907.30

Notes:

1. The tax rates indicated are those for January 2002. The brackets in tax units vary monthly according to the cost-of-living variation. It is important to bear in mind that some rates for the Second Category Tax have changed. For calendar year 2002, the income from 90 to 120 monthly tax units will be subject to tax at a rate of 33%. Amounts from 120 to 150 tax units will be taxed at 39%, and the income that exceeds 150 monthly tax units will be subject to tax at a rate of 43%. As of calendar year 2003 these latter percentages will be 37% and 40%, respectively.
2. As at January 1, 2002, the exchange rate was US$1 = C$654.79. A sample calculation for a monthly salary of US$4,000 for a single individual is shown below.

US$4,000 x 654.79	C$ 2,619,160
Less—Social security	194,736
Taxable income	C$ 2,424,424
2,424,424 x 0.25	C$ 606,106
Less—Fixed deduction	333,017
Income	C$ 273,088

Surtax/Surtax applies on a yearly basis when there has been no income subject to the monthly mandatory withholding tax or when part of the yearly income has not been subject to such withholding. To calculate the surtax, the rates for the second category tax are used.

Nonresidents/While nondomiciled persons are acquiring residence in Chile for tax purposes (physical presence for six consecutive months), they are subject to a sole withholding tax of 20% in lieu of personal income taxes.

INDIVIDUAL TAX CALCULATION

Fiscal year 2002

Assumptions

Resident foreigner plus spouse and two children.

	C$
Gross compensation	40,000,000
Interest income	1,200,000

Tax computation

Second category tax

Salary per year	C$ 40,000,000
Monthly salary (40,000,000 ÷ 12)	C$ 3,333,333
Less—Social security (January 2002)	194,736
Taxable income	C$ 3,138,597
Income tax (3,138,597 x 0.33)	C$ 1,035,737
Less—Fixed deduction	(538,390)
Monthly income tax	C$ 497,347
Yearly income tax	C$ 5,968,164

Surtax

Second category income	C$ 37,663,164
Interest income	1,200,000
Surtax taxable income	C$ 38,863,164
Monthly surtax income (39,009,168 ÷ 12)	C$ 3,238,597
Surtax (3,250,7644 x 33%)	C$ 1,068,737
Less—Fixed deduction	(538,390)
Monthly surtax	C$ 530,347
Yearly surtax (600,867 x 12)	C$ 6,364,164
Less—Second category tax	(5,968,164)
Surtax payable	C$ 396,000

Note:

Exchange rate of the peso at January 1, 2002: US$1 = C$654.79.

China, People's Republic of

PwC contact

For additional information on taxation in the People's Republic of China, contact:

Paul L. Gillis
PricewaterhouseCoopers
18th floor, Beijing Kerry Centre
1 Guang Hua Lu
Chao Yang District
Beijing 100020
People's Republic of China
Telephone: (86) (10) 6561 2233
Fax: (86) (10) 8529 9000
e-mail: paul.l.gillis@cn.pwcglobal.com

Significant developments

Since the implementation of the current Individual Income Tax Law (IIT) in 1994, expatriates have been entitled to a tax-free home leave exemption benefit. The tax authorities have now strengthened the IIT, and only two trips per year are allowed.

Additionally, under the IIT, tax reviews are now being performed regularly. In particular, sole proprietors, marketing personnel, contractors, management executives, actors, and professionals, and so on, are under the spotlight.

Territoriality and residence

Individuals who have a "place of abode" in China are subject to individual income tax on their worldwide income. For this purpose, "individuals having a place of abode" in China means those who maintain a place of residence in China because of their legal residence status, family or economic ties.

Individuals who do not have a "place of abode" in China are taxed in accordance with their length of residency in China, as follows.

1. Nonresidents or resident foreign expatriates who reside in China for less than one year will be taxed only on their China-source income.
2. Foreign expatriates who reside in China for more than one year but not more than five years will be subject to tax on both their China-source income and their foreign-source income. However, upon application to and approval from the tax authorities, the taxation of foreign-source income can be limited to that received from Chinese enterprises, Chinese establishments, Chinese economic organizations, and Chinese individuals.
3. Foreign expatriates who reside in China for more than five consecutive years will be subject to tax on their worldwide income from the sixth year onward.
4. Foreign expatriates who travel in China and derive income from an overseas employer with no permanent establishment in China will be tax exempt if they do not physically stay in China, consecutively or cumulatively, for more than 90 days in a calendar year. The 90-day test is extended to 183 days if the individual is a tax resident of a country that has executed a taxation treaty with China.

Gross income

Employee gross income/Salaries or wages of an individual include basic salary, bonus, foreign service premium, area allowance, cost-of-living allowance, housing allowance in excess of actual rental, local tax reimbursement, insurance and pension contributions, and stock benefits.

Other individual income/Taxable income also includes compensation for personal services, income from the publication of articles, royalties, interest, dividends, incidental income, and rentals.

Capital gains/Capital gains are treated as "other income" (see above) and are subject to tax in the same manner.

Real property gains tax/In addition to income tax, taxpayers are subject to a real property gains tax levied on gains from the transfer of real property. The rate of this tax ranges from 30% to 60%, depending on the size of the gain. This tax is in addition to any applicable income tax on such transfers. However, where an individual transfers the home (ordinary residential apartment), the gain is exempt.

Deductions

Business deductions and nonbusiness expenses/In calculating taxable income for wages and salaries, there are no allowances for actual business expenses. Specific deductions are given for income from compensation for personal services, that is, that of independent contractors; income from the publication of articles; royalties; or income from the lease of property.

1. If the amount received in a single payment is less than RMB4,000, a standard deduction of RMB800 is given.
2. If the amount received from a single economic transaction exceeds RMB4,000, a deduction equal to 20% of the payment is allowed.

Interest and dividends are taxed on the gross amounts received without deductions. For sales of property, the original value of the property and reasonable expenses incurred are deductible from the sales proceeds to arrive at the taxable income.

Personal allowances/All individuals are allowed a standard deduction of RMB800 per month from wages and salaries. The standard deduction for local Chinese individuals may be increased up to RMB1,600, depending on their place of work and return filed. Foreign expatriates, who include Hong Kong, Macau, and Taiwan residents, are given an additional allowance of RMB3,200 per month. Accordingly, the monthly deduction from wages and salaries available to such a foreign expatriate is RMB4,000.

Tax credits

Income tax paid to foreign countries for income earned abroad is allowed as a credit against China tax liability. The credit is limited to the amount of China tax on the foreign income. Documentary evidence of the tax payment to substantiate claims for foreign tax credits is required by the Chinese tax authorities.

Other taxes

Social security taxes/Social contributions to retirement funds, housing funds, etc., which are mandatory for local employees, are usually not applicable to expatriates.

Local taxes on income/The local governments do not impose any tax on individual income.

Tax administration

Returns/Individuals are required to submit individual income tax returns to the Chinese tax authorities on a monthly basis and to make tax payments within seven days after the end of each month.

Payment of tax/The tax liability is assessed on income computed in renminbi (RMB). Foreign currencies are converted to renminbi according to the exchange rate quoted by the People's Bank of China.

Tax returns must be filed on a timely basis. Extensions to file may be granted under "special circumstances." A surcharge of 0.05% per day for all taxes, including individual income tax, will be assessed on delinquent payments pursuant to the law on the administration of tax collection that came into effect on May 1, 2001.

Withholding/When paying taxable income to an individual, the employer, unit or person making the payment is required, as the withholding agent, to withhold the individual income tax due.

Tax rates

Wages and salaries

Monthly taxable income				
Not grossed up	**Grossed up**		**Tax rate**	**Quick deduction**
RMB	RMB		%	RMB
0–500	0–475	....	5	0
501–2,000	476–1,825	....	10	25
2,001–5,000	1,826–4,375	....	15	125
5,001–20,000	4,376–16,375	....	20	375
20,001–40,000	16,376–31,375	....	25	1,375
40,001–60,000	31,376–45,375	....	30	3,375
60,001–80,000	45,376–58,375	....	35	6,375
80,001–100,000	58,376–70,735	....	40	10,375
Over 100,000	Over 70,735	....	45	15,375

Where an individual's income tax liability is borne by the employer, the tax liability is calculated on an infinite gross-up basis (i.e., tax on tax).

Other income categories/A flat rate of 20% is applied on all other categories of income, that is, those included under "Other individual income" and "Capital gains." For independent contractors, if the income received for services performed is deemed to be too high, an additional tax will be assessed. For this purpose, a quantitative test will apply. In addition, a 30% tax reduction will be applicable to income from the publication of articles.

INDIVIDUAL TAX CALCULATION

Calendar year 2001

Assumptions

The individual is a foreign expatriate for income tax purposes. Monthly salary is US$7,000, and the income tax liability is not borne by the employer.

Tax computation

Monthly salary	US$ 7,000
	RMB
Monthly income	58,100
Less—Personal allowance	4,000
Monthly taxable income	54,100
Tax at applicable rate of 30%	16,230
Less—Quick deduction	(3,375)
Monthly tax payable	12,855

Note:

Average exchange rate of the renminbi for 2001: US$1 = RMB8.3.

Colombia

PwC contacts

For additional information on individual taxation in Colombia, contact:

María Helena Díaz Méndez
Carlos Miguel Chaparro
Calle 100 No. 11-A-35, Piso Tercero
Bogotá, Colombia
Telephone: (57) (1) 6340555
Fax: (57) (1) 6104626
e-mail: maria.helena.diaz@co.pwcglobal.com
carlos.chaparro@co.pwcglobal.com

Significant developments

There have been no significant tax or regulatory developments regarding individual taxation in the past year. The information in this entry is current as of March 2002. For subsequent developments consult the contact listed above.

Territoriality and residence

Colombia taxes its nationals and aliens as follows.

1. Alien residents are taxed on Colombian-source income. As from their sixth year of residence, alien residents are taxed on worldwide income.
2. Nonresident nationals and aliens are taxed on Colombian-source income.

For tax purposes, aliens become resident when they remain in Colombia for more than six months continuously or discontinuously within a tax year or when they complete this time period in the calendar year.

Nationals are considered residents if they maintain their family or their principal business site in Colombia.

Gross income

Employee gross income/An alien resident is taxed on salary earned for services provided in Colombia no matter where payment is made. Salary includes bonuses, living allowances, housing allowances, tax reimbursements, benefits in kind, and certain payments that must be made under Colombian labor law. All employees, including those who opt to receive an integral salary, i.e., without the social benefits of a legal bonus and severance compensation, can treat at least 30% of the total annual labor payments or salary as exempt income. Although some payments derived from a labor relationship may be agreed as not being salary, they are deemed to be taxable for income tax purposes.

Capital gains and investment income/An individual in Colombia for less than six years is taxed on Colombian-source capital gains and investment income. Thereafter, the alien resident is taxed on worldwide capital gains and investment income.

Capital gains are taxed separately from ordinary income, but are taxed on the basis of the individual tax rates.

“Monetary correction” on savings accounts (an adjustment that savings and loan institutions credit to clients placed in certain types of savings or term-deposit accounts in order to compensate for inflation) is free of tax. The correction must be certified by the institution. Any additional yield recognized as interest is, however, taxable.

The inflation component of interest received on certain bonds by individuals not required to keep books of account, is not subject to income tax.

Domestic shareholders and individual foreign shareholders resident in Colombia are not subject to income tax on dividends or participations received from Colombian companies whose income has been taxed.

Contributions to pension system/Mandatory contributions made to the Colombian pension system funds by an employee are not deemed to constitute income or capital gains for the employee, and are therefore not part of the withholding tax base.

Similarly, voluntary contributions made by either the employee or the employer to these funds are not considered income or capital gains for the employee and are therefore not part of the withholding tax base, provided they, added to the mandatory contributions, do not exceed 30% of the employee's labor income. Notwithstanding the above, voluntary contributions will become taxable if they are withdrawn by the employee within five years of having been deposited in the fund.

Contributions made to foreign pension systems are deemed to be taxable for the expatriate or employee and are therefore part of the withholding income tax base.

Also, deposits made to savings accounts to support the construction of housing are considered as nontaxable income, provided they do not exceed 30% of the employee's labor income and that the employee does not withdraw them before five years from the date of deposit. However, even if the deposit is withdrawn before five years, it would continue to be treated as nontaxable income if it is used to pay for new housing.

Deductions

Business deductions/Employees are not entitled to deduct business-related expenses from their compensation income.

Nonbusiness expenses/A resident alien can deduct from compensation mortgage interest paid in Colombia, up to a maximum of COP19,500,000 annually. Employees with annual income less than COP73,300,000 may choose to deduct either mortgage interest or prepaid medical assistance and educational expenses.

Some donations are allowed as deductions, provided they are made to certain institutions dedicated to development of health, education, culture, religion, sports, scientific and technological research, ecology and the protection of the environment, or to social development programs of general interest. Most of these donations are limited with respect to their deduction.

Personal allowances/There are no personal allowances.

Tax credits

A resident alien is not entitled to foreign tax credits.

Other taxes

Social security tax/Nonresident aliens should be affiliated with the Colombian Retirement Pension Funds if they are not covered in their native countries with a system equal to or better than Colombia's. The rate of employee contribution to these funds is 3.375% of monthly salary for those assignees whose salary does not exceed four minimum wages and 4.375% for those assignees who receive more than four minimum wages. It is mandatory to be affiliated with the Welfare Security System, to which a supplemental 4% must be contributed.

Local taxes on income/There are no local taxes on individual income.

Tax administration

Returns/Any salaried taxpayer meeting the filing requirements for calendar year 2002 of income (COP95,100,000) or gross assets (COP183,200,000) must file a return. Taxpayers with only passive income must file a return for 2002 when income exceeds COP23,800,000 or gross assets exceed COP183,200,000. Joint returns are not permitted. Income splitting is not allowed.

No taxable year other than the calendar year is permitted.

Payment of tax/There is income tax withholding from salaries. If a balance is payable by the taxpayer, it must be paid on the date for filing the return. Tax-filing season usually starts in April and ends in early June.

Tax rates

Individual income tax rates are voluminous; sample rates for calendar year 2002 are as follows.

Taxable income		
Over	**Not over**	**Income tax**
COP 19,000,000	COP 19,200,000	COP 140,000
41,000,001	41,200,000	5,764,000
83,200,000		18,426,000

The excess over COP83,200,000 is taxed at the rate of 35%.

INDIVIDUAL TAX CALCULATION

Calendar year 2002

Tax computation

Total salary	COP	140,000,000
Less—Contributions made to a pension system that do not constitute income or occasional gain (1)		10,000,000
Net salary		130,000,000
Less—Exempt portion (30%)		39,000,000
Taxable salary		91,000,000
Less—Deductible interest income paid on mortgage (2)		4,000,000
	COP	87,000,000
Income tax:		
On 83,200,000	COP	18,426,000
35% on the excess of 3,800,000 x 35%		1,330,000
	COP	19,756,000
Capital gain obtained in the alienation of fixed assets held for more than two years	COP	9,800,000
Capital gains tax	COP	260,000

Notes:

1. This is the maximum mandatory contribution that would be made by the employee.
2. The maximum monthly amount allowed to be deducted corresponding to mortgage interest is COP19,500,000.
3. Exchange rate of the Colombian peso at January 1, 2002: US$1 = COP2,372.20.

Congo, Democratic Republic of

PwC contact

For additional information on taxation in the Democratic Republic of Congo, contact:

Benjamin Nzailu Basinsa
PricewaterhouseCoopers
B.P. 10195
Kinshasa 1, D.R.C.
Telephone: MCI cardholders (243) (88) 44435, 40239
Fax: (243) (88) 00075
e-mail: bnzailu.pricewat@ic.cd

General note

This entry is repeated from the 2001/2002 edition. For more up-to-date information, consult the contact listed above or Mark Friedlich at mark.friedlich@us.pwcglobal.com.

Significant developments

Since February 18, 1998, the government has established a kind of levy or withholding on individual and corporate income tax (*precompte sur la contribution sur les benefices ou précompte B.I.C*).

Territoriality and residence

Congo applies the rules of the territoriality of income. It taxes its citizens and aliens (residents and nonresidents) on income derived from professional, commercial, and employment activities carried out in Congo; from rental of real estate located in Congo; and from domestic investments. Foreign-source income is not taxable. The tax system is schedular.

Gross income

Employee gross income/The following items are included in taxable compensation: salary, living allowance, tax reimbursements, benefits-in-kind, and any other reimbursement of personal expenses, except medical expenses and reasonable housing and transportation allowances. Company-owned or company-leased housing may be provided to employees without being considered a taxable benefit, provided housing allowances or benefits-in-kind do not exceed 30% of gross salary. Nontaxable transportation allowances are fixed by reference to official public transportation prices.

The private use of company-owned or -leased vehicles is taxable. Moving and home-leave transportation expenses are nontaxable.

Family allowances are nontaxable to the extent that they do not exceed the legal limits. These are at present negligible. There are no special concessions for foreigners.

Capital gains and investment income/Capital gains are taxable at 40%.

Dividends and other profit distributions by domestic companies are subject to a final tax at the rate of 20%, which is withheld at source.

Rental income from real estate is subject to tax at 22% on gross income *(contribution sur les revenus locatifs)*. The main tax amount is withheld by the tenant when paying his or her rent (20% of the rent paid).

Deductions

Business deductions**/**Reimbursement of genuine business expenses is generally nontaxable.

Nonbusiness expenses**/**Expenses deductible by an employee are listed below.

1. Medical expenses for employees and their dependents to the extent not reimbursed by the employer.
2. Pension and health plan contributions to a recognized scheme, provided these are payable under the terms of the employee's work contract.
3. Social security contributions.

Personal allowances**/**There are no personal allowances available, except for the family allowances mentioned above (see "Gross income"). Tax reductions are negligible.

Tax credits

No tax credits are available.

Other taxes

Social security taxes**/**All employees must contribute to a national pension scheme. Since August 20, 1992, the contributions have been fixed at 8.5% of the total gross remuneration; 5% is paid by the employer and 3.5% by the employee, based on gross remuneration less transport allocation, family allowance, and housing allowance. These contributions are deductible in determining taxable income.

Local taxes on income**/**There are no income taxes payable in addition to central government taxes.

Tax administration

Tax returns and payment**/**Salaries and wages are subject to tax withholding at source, and employers are required to make annual tax returns for their employees prior to January 10 following the end of the fiscal year (December 31). Individuals with no sources of income other than wages and salaries need not file a tax return; this is the employer's responsibility. In all cases, income of spouses is combined.

Tax rates

The annual taxable income is subject to tax at graduated rates. For annual taxable income up to CDF78,000, the tax payable at graduated rate is CDF26,269.95. The excess over CDF78,000 is taxed at 60%. However, the total tax payable is limited to 35% of total taxable income.

End-of-career indemnities and indemnities paid by the employer (contractual or otherwise) following cessation of employment or on breaking a contract of employment are taxed separately at 10%.

For occasions workers, the rate for the calculation of tax on remuneration is fixed at 15%.

INDIVIDUAL TAX CALCULATION

Assumptions

Resident alien husband and wife, two children; one spouse earns all the income. The employer furnishes housing and a car and also reimburses medical expenses.

Tax computation

Basic salary		CDF 2,400,000
Overtime		200,000
Bonus		100,000
Compensation for inflation		200,000
Taxable salary		2,900,000
Add:		
Transport allowance	170,000	
Housing allowance	300,000	
Family allowance	80,000	550,000
Gross remuneration		3,450,000
Less:		
Transport allowance	170,000	
Housing allowance	300,000	
Family allowance	80,000	
Social security contribution (1)	101,500	
Legal family allowances	80,000	
Contributions to an outside recognized pension scheme	360,000	
Total deduction		1,011,500
Taxable income		CDF 2,438,500
Tax thereon:		
First 78,000 at graduated rates	26,270	
Remainder of 2,360,500 at 60%	1,416,300	CDF 1,442,570
Maximum tax payable (2)		CDF 853,475
Deduction for family expenses (6% on CDF7,034.40) (3)		(422)
Maximum tax payable		CDF 853,053

Notes:

1. 3.5% of gross remuneration less transport allocation, family allowance, and housing allowance.
2. The maximum tax payable is 35% of taxable income, or NZ 853,475,000 in this calculation.
3. Deductions for family expense are calculated on the amount of tax on income between CDF0 and CDF33,600. The rate is fixed at 2% per person, limited to nine persons.
4. Exchange rate of the Congolese franc at December 31, 2000: US$1 = CDF52.

PwC contact

For additional information on taxation in Costa Rica, contact:

Gerardo Cásares Alvarado
PricewaterhouseCoopers
Edificio Price Waterhouse
Barrio Los Yoses
San José, Costa Rica
Telephone: (506) 224 15 55
Fax: (506) 253 4053
e-mail: gerardo.casares@cr.pwcglobal.com

Significant developments

There have been no significant developments regarding individual taxation in the past year. The information in this entry is current as of January 2002. For subsequent developments consult the contact listed above.

Territoriality and residence

Income taxes on individuals in Costa Rica are levied on local income irrespective of nationality and resident status. For individuals domiciled in Costa Rica, any income obtained within the boundaries of Costa Rica is considered local income. For nonresidents in Costa Rica, any income derived from business, capital invested goods sold or services rendered within Costa Rica is considered of local source and therefore taxable. However, nonresidents are liable only for the applicable withholding taxes, depending on the nature of the local income.

Independent of nationality, an individual who is self-employed and has been living in Costa Rica more than six months of a taxable year and must file a regular income tax return is considered resident. This period may be shorter if the person is employed and subject to payroll withholding taxes.

Gross income

Employee gross income/Individuals domiciled in Costa Rica are taxed on salaries, commissions, fees, royalties, and any other form of remuneration for services rendered, plus any interest and rental income received from local sources. Any income earned abroad while in residence in Costa Rica is not taxable, as indicated above.

Individuals with a monthly salary of less than CRC270,000, and self employed individuals with annual income of less than CRC1,200,000 are exempt from income taxes.

The reimbursement of personal living expenses and travel expenses for individuals not formally domiciled is not subject to taxes. This would include the reimbursement of similar expenses for the taxpayer's family. Certain expense allowances at the discretion of the tax authorities are not subject to taxation, nor are they deductible for the payer.

Capital gains and investment income/At present there is no capital gains tax on the sale of real estate or securities (Paragraph f) article 8 of the Costa Rican Income Tax Law).

Gains on the transfer of real estate are taxed at 1.51%.

Domiciled individuals are subject to a 15% tax on interest on bearer documents except for those bearer documents registered at the local stock exchange, in which case the tax is 8%. This tax is withheld at source of payment. Income on investments from a foreign source is not taxable.

Foreign-domiciled individuals are subject to withholding taxes at the rates shown below.

	%
Interest	15
Dividends	15
Directors' fees, etc.	15
Salaries	10
Fees	15

Because rental income denotes a permanent physical establishment in Costa Rica, the landlord must file a regular tax return indicating total income less permitted expenses; the net income is subject to tax at regular individual graduated rates.

Deductions

Business deductions/A domiciled individual, whether or not a national, whose only source of income is a salary for personal services cannot deduct business expenses, regardless of whether they are reimbursed or not. However, self-employed individuals and those whose source of income is from commissions (sales), fees, etc., may deduct up to 25% of the gross income as a deduction without itemizing the expenses or may elect to itemize the expenses incurred in producing the gross income. Itemized deductions must be substantiated to the authorities upon request.

Nonbusiness expenses/The amount of legal annual bonus (Christmas bonus) that does not exceed one-twelfth of net salary (which is one-thirteenth of gross salary) is exempt from income taxes.

Personal allowances/Individuals are permitted the tax credits shown below.

	Monthly	Annual
	CRC	CRC
Spouse	760	9,120
Child (each)	510	6,120

The child allowance is permissible only if the child is a minor, is unable to work or is a university student under 25 years of age.

Tax credits

In accordance with Costa Rican legislation, there are no tax credits allowed to individuals for taxes paid to foreign governments.

Personal allowances take the form of tax credits (see above).

Other taxes

Social security taxes/An individual's share of social security taxes is 9% on total remuneration, which in the case of salary is deducted from the individual's payroll payment. Self-employed individuals' participation in the social security system can range from 9% to 15% tax on income.

Other taxes on income/None of the provinces or municipalities imposes any income taxes on individuals within its jurisdiction.

Tax administration

Returns/Only self-employed individuals who receive commissions, fees, royalties, or other forms of income for services rendered and those who receive interest or rental income from local sources must file a tax return that corresponds to a 12-month period ended on September 30. If both spouses earn income they must submit individual returns, in which case the personal child credit can be taken by only one of the spouses. The present legislation does not contemplate joint filing.

Payment of tax/Employees who receive salaries and other similar or complementary remunerations or benefits must pay a monthly income tax that is withheld by the employer from the monthly payroll. Individuals need not file an annual tax return for this type of income.

Self-employed individuals are required to make quarterly payments of estimated taxes, which are computed on the average of the last three fiscal years, and a final payment two and a half months after the end of the fiscal year.

Tax rates

Tax rates for self-employed individuals, based on annual taxable income, are as follows.

Annual taxable income		Tax on	Percentage
Over	Not over	Column 1	on excess
(Column 1)			
0	CRC 1,200,000	—	0
CRC 1,200,000	1,792,000	—	10
1,792,000	2,989,000	CRC 59,200	15
2,989,000	5,990,000	238,750	20
5,990,000		838,950	25

Tax rates for employed individuals, based on monthly salary, are shown in the table below. Individuals who are both self-employed and employees may not take the CRC1,200,000 deduction.

Monthly taxable income		Tax on	Percentage
Over	Not over	Column 1	on excess
0	CRC 270,000	—	0
CRC 270,000	405,800	—	10
405,800		CRC 13,580	15

INDIVIDUAL TAX CALCULATION

Income year 2002

Gross income:		
Salary		CRC 12,220,000
Interest		300,000
Long-term capital gain		400,000
Total gross income		12,920,000
Less:		
100% of interest on which 8% is withheld at source	300,000	
Capital gain	400,000	
Legal annual bonus (Christmas bonus)	940,000	1,640,000
Taxable income		CRC 11,280,000
Monthly taxable salary		CRC 940,000
Monthly income tax		CRC 93,750
Less—Personal credits:		
Spouse	760	
Children (two)	1,020	(1,780)
Net monthly income tax		CRC 91,970
Annual income tax		CRC 1,103,640

Note:

Exchange rate of the colon at January 31, 2002: US$1 = CRC343.

PwC contact

For additional information on taxation in Croatia, contact:

Iain McGuire
PricewaterhouseCoopers d.o.o.
Alexandera von Humboldta 4
10000 Zagreb, Croatia
Telephone: (385) (1) 63 28 888
Fax: (385) (1) 6111 556
e-mail: iain.mcguire@hr.pwcglobal.com

Significant developments

The new General Tax Law, which sets a general legal framework for the tax system in Croatia, was introduced on January 1, 2001.

The Tax Advisory Law, which sets the framework for providing tax advisory services, was introduced on January 1, 2001.

The new Personal Income Tax Law was introduced on January 1, 2001.

The new Profit Tax Act was introduced on January 1, 2001.

Territoriality and residence

Every domestic or foreign individual deriving income in the Republic of Croatia is defined as a taxpayer. In principle, all residents and persons temporarily resident or with their usual place of residence (over 183 days per year) within Croatia must pay tax in Croatia on their worldwide income. Individuals who are only temporarily resident in Croatia, or whose usual place of abode is abroad (foreign taxpayers) are liable to pay tax in Croatia on Croatian-source income.

When income is received from abroad, the recipient is required to self-assess tax, make a payment to the tax authorities within seven days of receipt and file a tax return at year-end.

Gross income

Tax is assessed on income derived by a taxpayer (salaries and pensions), income from independent activities (freelance work, crafts, agriculture, and forestry), income from property rights (e.g., rent or trade in real estate and certain intellectual property rights), and income from capital. In relation to rental income, expenses up to 30% of realized rent income is tax deductible. In the case of rooms, beds and flats rented to travelers for whom a tourist charge is paid, expenses incidental to realizing the income are determined to the value of 50% of realized revenue.

Compulsory social care contributions are not subject to income tax.

Tax concessions are provided to residents of special-interest regions. These reduce the tax rate applicable to residents living in these areas through higher personal allowances; income tax exemptions on income derived from agriculture and forestry; and higher depreciation rates for long-term capital invested in property.

Fringe benefits/Employers may give employees certain benefits that qualify as nontaxable. The following are the most significant.

1. Reimbursement of travel expenses (the real cost of traveling to work using public transportation).

2. Daily allowance for business trips in Croatia—Up to HRK170 per diem, plus travel and accommodation expenses.
3. Daily allowance for business trips abroad—The allowed sums as defined by a special decision (depending on the country), plus travel and accommodation expenses.
4. Reimbursement for use of employee's personal car for business purposes—Up to 30% of the price of gasoline per kilometer.
5. Cash granted to employees upon retirement—HRK8,000.
6. Disability benefit, death benefit (upon the death of an employee or a member of his or her immediate family)—HRK2,500 and HRK7,500 respectively.
7. Bonuses (e.g., Christmas bonus) up to HRK1,000 p.a.
8. Loyalty bonuses to employees with 10 and 40 years of service—HRK1,500 to HRK5,000.

If any of these benefits exceeds the quoted limit, the difference is considered to be salary and is taxable (employee and employer contributions, personal income tax, surtax).

Capital gains and investment income/The following gains are not subject to income tax.

1. Income in the form of interest on kuna or foreign currency savings accounts.
2. Interest from securities issued in accordance with a separate act.
3. Profit earned from the sale of financial property.
4. Profit shares from foreign companies that would, if they were resident taxpayers, be liable to pay profit tax.
5. Income realized from a joint business activity that is liable to profit tax abroad.

Profit tax election

Certain self employed individuals may elect to pay profit tax and keep accounts in accordance with accounting standards instead of paying personal income tax.

Deductions

Business deductions/Certain business expenses paid to employees are not taxable (see above). Self-employed individuals can deduct business expenses that are necessary and connected to conducting their business activities. The list of nondeductible expenses is similar to that for profit tax purposes and includes entertainment expenses, excess travel allowances and 30% of the cost of business transport.

Nonbusiness expenses/These expenses are dealt with by the system of personal deductions set out below as well as within the corporate profit tax regime.

Personal allowances/An individual's taxable income is reduced by the following allowances.

1. Personal allowance (HRK1,250 per month).
2. Allowance for supporting a spouse and children—The taxpayer's personal allowance corresponds to a factor of 1. For every dependent, personal deductions are increased as follows.

	HRK per month
Dependent spouse (factor of 0.5)	625
First child (factor of 0.5)	625
Second child (factor of 0.7)	875
Third child (factor of 1.0)	1,250
Fourth child (factor of 1.40)	1,750
Fifth child (factor of 1.90)	2,375
Sixth child (factor of 2.5)	3,125

For every additional child the factor is progressively increased for 0.7, 0.8, 0.9, 1.0, and so on based on the personal allowance for the previous child.

3. Allowance for supporting disabled family members—If the taxpayer or a family member is disabled, the personal allowance factor is increased by 0.3.
4. Allowance for losses can be carried forward for up to five successive years.

Tax credits

Insofar as domestic tax rules give rise to double taxation, Croatia grants unilateral relief on a credit basis. Under the terms of an applicable treaty, relief is granted on the exemption basis in the case of the old Yugoslav double taxation treaties that are still in force and on a credit basis for new Croatian double taxation treaties.

Other taxes

Social security taxes/In the case of income tax on salary from a full-time job, the following contributions are deducted from the tax base. The following rates are effective from June 1, 2000.

	%
Pension and disability funds	10.75
Health care	9.00
Employment funds	0.85
Total	20.60

In addition to this, an employer must make contributions to pension and disability funds of 8.75%, health care fund contributions of 7%, employment fund contributions of 0.85%, and work health insurance contributions of 0.47%. These contributions do not affect the tax base.

Foreigners employed by non-Croatian employers may be exempt from social security contributions, depending on whether Croatia has reciprocal social security agreements with the host country.

Local taxes on income/Towns may levy surtax. For employees who live in towns where surtax is levied, the employer applies the surtax rate to the employees' income tax and deducts it from their salary. The majority of cities levy a surtax ranging from 1 to 18%.

Tax administration

The obligation to pay income tax arises when the taxpayer receives income. Payment is made either through payroll deductions or by advance tax payments.

Deduction of tax on payment of salaries and pensions/On making every salary or pension payment, the employer (or pension payer) is obliged to calculate the amount of tax for each employee (recipient) and pay this into the prescribed accounts. The recipient receives a net salary payment (or pension).

Advance tax payments/Self-employed persons and craftsmen make advance tax payments in accordance with their latest tax assessment. Persons engaged in agricultural activity pay tax quarterly on assessed cadastral income.

Returns/At the end of the year, every taxpayer is obliged to submit a tax return to the appropriate branch of the tax administration. The tax return shows the difference between their tax liability and the amount of tax prepayments made in respect of the tax year. The taxpayer will be either entitled to a tax refund or will be required to make an additional tax payment.

A tax return is not required where the individual's only taxable income is from one employer.

Tax rates

The tax base is defined as gross salary less contributions and the employee's personal allowance. Income tax of 15% on income in the range of HRK1,250 to HRK2,500 per month, 25% is charged on income in the range of HRK2,500 to HRK6,250 and tax of 35% is charged on income exceeding HRK6,250 per month.

INDIVIDUAL TAX CALCULATION

Calendar year 2002

Assumptions

Employee with a gross annual salary of HRK150,300, living in Zagreb with no dependents. This calculation uses the contribution rates effective from January 2002.

Employee tax computation

Gross annual salary		HRK 150,300.00
Less—Employee's contributions from gross salary:		
Pension (10.75%)	16,157.00	
Health (9.00%)	13,527.00	
Employment (0.85%)	1,278.00	30,962.00
Gross salary reduced by contributions		119,338.00
Less—Personal allowance		15,000.00
Taxable base		HRK 104,338.00
Total tax payable		HRK 26,018.30
Surtax on tax payable (at 18%)		HRK 4,683.29
Net salary		HRK 88,636.41

Employer's contributions from gross salary

Pension (8.75%)	HRK 13,151
Health (7.00%)	10,521
Insurance against accidents on work (0.47%)	706
Employment (0.85%)	1,278
Total employer's contributions	HRK 25,656

Note:

Exchange rate of the kuna at February 14, 2002: US$1 = HRK8.5635.

PwC contact

For additional information on taxation in Cyprus, contact:

Panikos N. Tsiailis, Senior Tax Partner, Territory Service Leader
PricewaterhouseCoopers Cyprus
Julia House
3 Themistoclis Dervis Street
CY–1066 Nicosia, Cyprus
P.O. Box 21612, CY–1591 Nicosia, Cyprus
Telephone: (357) 22555000
Fax: (357) 22555001
e-mail: panikos.n.tsiailis@cy.pwcglobal.com

Significant developments

The government has submitted to the House of Representatives its proposals for a reform of the tax system. With the proposed tax reform the government is aiming to conform with European Union law and the EU Code of Conduct as well as to abide by its commitment to the OECD to eliminate harmful tax practices.

Under the government proposals all Cyprus residents will be taxed in the same way and the distinction between locals and expatriates will be abolished. All residents will be taxed at rates up to 28%. There are no details available regarding allowances.

Territoriality and residence

In general, Cyprus income tax is imposed on income accrued, derived or received in Cyprus.

Gross income

Employee gross income/An alien employee is taxed in Cyprus on all remuneration derived from or received in Cyprus, including benefits in kind, such as free accommodation.

An employee is not taxed on reimbursements for travel and entertainment expenses.

Capital gains and investment income/Capital gains other than those from immovable property are not taxed in Cyprus. A 20% tax is imposed on gains arising from the disposal of immovable property in Cyprus or the disposal of shares of companies, other than public, that own immovable property. In the case of disposal of company shares, the gain is calculated exclusively on the basis of the gain from the immovable property. The value of the immovable property will be its market value at the time the shares were sold.

The taxable gain is the difference between the sale proceeds and the original cost of the property plus improvements as adjusted for inflation up to the date of disposal on the basis of the consumer price index in Cyprus. In the case of property acquired before January 1, 1980 the original cost is deemed to be the value of the property as at January 1, 1980 on the basis of the general valuation conducted by the Land Registry Office under the Immovable Property Law.

Only to the extent it exceeds C£2,000, foreign investment income remitted to Cyprus to an individual who is not a citizen and is not a permanent resident of Cyprus is taxed at a fixed rate of 5%. Pensions received from abroad up to C£2,000 are exempt. Any excess over C£2,000 is taxed separately at a fixed rate of 5%.

Cyprus-source investment income is taxed in the normal way, subject to deductions of C£600 for interest on bank deposits (together with debenture interest received from a public company) and C£1,200 for dividends from public companies. Interest receivable from Cyprus government securities, Government Savings Certificates and deposits to the Housing Finance Corporation is totally exempt from tax, without any limitation.

Deductions

Business deductions/In general, any business-related expense (including contributions to trade unions or other professional bodies and professional tax) is deductible, unless reimbursed. Expenses of traveling to and from work are not deductible unless the employee lives in a village involving a return trip to work of at least 30 kilometers, in which case the bus fare actually paid is deductible.

Nonbusiness expenses/Subject to limitations, interest on housing loans, other interest, rent, charitable contributions, social security contributions, and insurance premiums are deductible.

In addition, subject to certain restrictions, 30% of the amount paid by an individual to acquire first-issue shares floated on the Cyprus Stock Exchange is tax deductible.

Personal allowances/All residents are allowed a tax deduction of C£500 for each child under 16 or receiving secondary education or serving in the National Guard and C£1,500 with a maximum tax benefit of C£300 for each child receiving higher education. A C£500 spouse deduction is also available. These allowances are apportioned between spouses according to their income.

Persons over 65 years of age are allowed a tax deduction of C£1,500, with maximum tax benefit of C£300.

Tax credits

Either through double taxation treaty or Cyprus unilateral relief, residents with foreign-source income are entitled to a credit equal to the income tax levied on that income in the foreign country. This credit cannot exceed the Cyprus income tax imposed on the same income.

Special grants/The following three categories of grants are exempt from income tax.

1. A grant of up to C£1,500 per academic year granted to families that have a child receiving higher education abroad.
2. An annual grant of C£40 for each child granted to families with many children.
3. An annual grant to families of C£200 for every blind child under 18 years of age.

Other taxes

Social security taxes/For 2001 the taxpayer's share of social security taxes is 6.3% of the first C£21,424 of salary.

Other taxes on income/Professional tax is imposed by municipal authorities on the income of salaried persons. The tax is based on a graduated scale, and the maximum tax is C£220.50 (on salaries in excess of C£30,000). The tax is deductible in determining taxable income for income tax purposes.

A contribution of 3% for the Defense of Cyprus is also imposed on salaries and pensions (pensions of up to C£3,000 are exempt) under a law that will be in force up to March 31, 2002 but may be extended for a further period by the House of Representatives. This contribution is not deductible in determining taxable income for income tax purposes.

Tax administration

Returns/Husbands and wives cannot file joint returns. Separate returns must be filed on a calendar-year basis.

Payment of tax/There is income tax withholding from salaries under the pay-as-you-earn system (PAYE). If a taxpayer has other income not subject to withholding, payments of estimated tax must be made in three equal installments on August 1, September 30, and December 31.

Tax rates

The following table lists the normal rates of taxation applicable to individuals.

Taxable income		Normal tax on Column 1	Percentage on excess
Over (Column 1)	Not over (Note)		
0	C£ 6,000	—	—
C£ 6,000	9,000	—	20
9,000	12,000	C£ 600	30
12,000		1,500	40

Note:

Foreign employees of international business entities (i.e., entities exclusively owned by aliens and deriving their income from activities carried on exclusively outside Cyprus) are entitled to the following tax advantages.

1. An international business entity's foreign employees providing their services in Cyprus are liable to Cyprus income tax at reduced rates equal to one-half of the normal Cyprus tax rates.
2. An international business entity's foreign employees working outside Cyprus are liable to Cyprus income tax at reduced rates equal to one-tenth of the normal Cyprus tax rates. Such employees are, however, totally exempt from tax if they receive their salary in or through Cyprus.
3. An international business entity's foreign employees are fully exempt from social insurance and defense contributions.

INDIVIDUAL TAX CALCULATION

Calendar year 2002

Assumptions

Resident husband and wife; two children, both receiving full-time education in secondary schools in Cyprus; one spouse earns all the income.

Tax computation

Salary		C£ 42,000
Interest remitted to Cyprus on foreign investments		3,500
Bank deposit and public company debenture interest		900
Dividends from public companies		2,100
Interest on Cyprus Government securities and Government Savings Certificates		2,000
Capital gains		2,000
Total gross income		52,500
Less—Itemized deductions:		
Interest on foreign investments remitted to Cyprus	3,500	
Interest on bank deposits and public company debentures	600	
Dividends from public companies	1,200	
Interest on Cyprus government securities and Government Savings Certificates	2,000	
Capital gains	2,000	
30% of amount spent to acquire public company first-issue shares	800	
Professional tax	220	
Housing loan interest	500	
Other interest expense	100	
Charitable contributions	300	
Subscriptions	880	12,100
Net income		40,400
Less—Personal allowances:		
Deduction for children—C£500 x 2	1,000	
Deduction for spouse	500	
Social security contributions	1,350	2,850
Taxable income		C£ 37,550
Income tax thereon (see table above)		C£ 11,720
Add—5% tax on excess of interest on foreign investments remitted to Cyprus over 2,000, i.e., 5% on 1,500		75
Less—Foreign tax on foreign investment interest higher than 75; restricted to 75		(75)
Income tax liability		C£ 11,720

Notes:

1. The income tax liability as calculated is discharged partly by withholding at source and partly by direct tax payments.
2. Exchange rate of the Cyprus pound at December 31, 2001: US$1 = C£0.622.

Czech Republic

PwC contacts

For additional information on taxation in the Czech Republic, contact:

Monika Diekert, Partner in Charge, Tax and Legal Services
Zuzana Vaneckova, Tax Partner
Antoni Turczynowicz, Tax Partner
PricewaterhouseCoopers
Katerinska 40
120 00 Praha 2
Czech Republic
Telephone: (420) (2) 5115 1111
Fax: (420) (2) 5115 6111
e-mail: monika.svobodova-diekert@cz.pwcglobal.com
zuzana.vaneckova@cz.pwcglobal.com
antoni.turczynowicz@cz.pwcglobal.com

General note

Entirely new tax legislation was introduced in the Czech Republic on January 1, 1993. The legislation is subject to frequent amendments and changes in official interpretation as the market economy develops in the Czech Republic. These amendments frequently occur without prior notice and become effective immediately or even retroactively. Therefore, it is advisable to contact the experts listed above for up-to-date information.

Territoriality and residence

A resident of the Czech Republic is subject to tax on worldwide income, irrespective of whether the income is remitted to the Czech Republic.

An individual who spends at least 183 days in a calendar year or has a permanent place of abode in the Czech Republic is resident for tax purposes.

A nonresident is liable to tax on Czech-source income only, subject to double taxation treaties. Czech-source income includes income from work performed in the territory of the Czech Republic, even of just one day's duration, irrespective of the place of payment, if the employer is a Czech resident or has a permanent establishment in the Czech Republic. A nonresident is exempt from Czech tax on employment income resulting from work performed for a foreign employer resident abroad with no permanent establishment or deemed place of business in the Czech Republic as long as the time period related to the performance of the work does not exceed 183 days in a 12-month period.

Gross income

Employee gross income/The gross income of employees includes all wages, salaries and bonuses paid and any benefits in kind (subject to minor exceptions) received as a result of employment. Benefits in kind are valued in principle at open-market values, although a fixed rate of 12% per annum of the purchase price is applied to cars provided by the employer unless the employee makes no private use of the car. The reimbursement of travel expenses in excess of fairly low statutory limits is also a taxable benefit to the employee. Certain nonmonetary educational, sporting and health benefits are nontaxable. Accommodation provided by an employer as a nonmonetary benefit is not taxable if arrangements are properly structured. An accommodation allowance is taxable.

Nonresident directors' fees and fees payable to nonresident members of other statutory bodies of Czech companies are subject to a withholding tax of 25%. No further tax is payable on this income. When paid to tax residents, directors' fees and fees to members of other statutory bodies of Czech companies are taxed under the payroll administration, using the progressive tax rates.

Capital gains and investment income/Capital gains form part of total income and are therefore subject to income tax at the taxpayer's marginal rate. Exemptions are available for gains arising on the disposal of assets that have not been used for commercial purposes and that have been held for certain minimum periods, as follows.

1. Securities—Held for more than six months.
2. Cars and other movable assets—Held for more than 12 months.
3. Real estate—Held for more than five years.

A gain on the sale of an apartment or house that has been the taxpayer's residence for at least two years before the sale is, subject to certain conditions, also exempt, as is a gain on the sale of property by the first owner in restitution.

Interest earned on Czech savings deposits is subject to a final withholding tax of 15%. Dividends received from Czech companies are also subject to final withholding tax at the rate of 15%.

Interest, dividends, and other investment income received from foreign sources may be added to total taxable income and taxed at a progressive rate. Alternatively, the individual may choose to include this type of income in a separate tax base and have it taxed at a flat 15% rate. Foreigners who are not tax-resident in the Czech Republic are not liable to tax on investment income received from foreign sources.

Deductions

Business deductions/No deductions are available from income from employment. Sums received by way of reimbursement of expenses incurred in connection with employment are exempt from tax, provided they do not exceed the statutory limits. Private entrepreneurs may deduct ordinary business expenses.

Nonbusiness deductions/Necessary expenses incurred in the earning of income from sources other than trading sources can be deducted from the income earned. There are no standard deductions. For certain categories of income a fixed percentage of gross income can be claimed as a deduction instead of actual expenditures. Employees' mandatory social and health insurance contributions are deductible from employment income. Donations to Czech organizations for the purpose of financing science, education, culture, etc., are deductible up to a maximum of 10% of total taxable income, provided the total value of the donations exceeds 2% of the tax base or is at least CZK1,000.

Personal allowances/A basic allowance of CZK38,040 per annum is available to all individuals. A further CZK21,720 per annum is available to taxpayers supporting their spouse in a joint home, provided the spouse's income is less than CZK38,040 per annum. An allowance of CZK23,520 per dependent child is available. Further allowances are available for students and disabled people. The allowances are deducted from the tax base. The interest paid on a mortgage loan or a loan provided from a housing savings plan can be also deducted from the tax base in a maximum amount of CZK300,000 per annum. Spousal and child allowances are not available to individuals who are not tax-resident.

Tax credits

Based on Czech domestic tax legislation, when eliminating double taxation of income from abroad, the provisions of double taxation treaties concluded by the Czech Republic are to be followed. If no applicable treaty exists, the income from a dependent activity carried out abroad can be reduced by the tax paid on the income abroad.

Other taxes

Social security taxes/Individuals employed by a Czech entity must pay social and health insurance contributions totaling 12.5% of gross salary. Employers must pay corresponding contributions totaling 35% of gross salary. The employees' contributions are deductible from salary for income tax purposes. Neither foreign individuals nor their employers are required to make contributions if the employment arrangements are governed by foreign labor law. Under international treaties on mutual employment concluded by the Czech Republic, nationals of some countries must pay Czech social security taxes if they are employed by a Czech entity.

Private entrepreneurs must contribute at the rate of 43.1% on 35% of the annual insurance base, which is determined as gross income less expenses.

Local taxes on income/There are no local taxes on income.

Tax administration

Returns/A tax return must be filed by March 31 following the calendar year-end. The deadline is extended to June 30 if the return is prepared and filed by an authorized tax adviser under a power of attorney and the tax authorities have been so advised by March 31. Husbands and wives must file separate returns.

A tax return need not be filed if all income received has been subjected to tax at source in the Czech Republic. This applies if employment income paid by a Czech employer through local payroll is the only source of income. Furthermore, a tax return need not be filed if income other than employment income does not exceed CZK4,000.

Payment of tax/Income tax is withheld monthly at source from income from employment for employees of a Czech company or branch and for employees of a foreign company assigned to work in the Czech branch of that foreign company. The Czech law also contains a deemed employer rule whereby an employee of a foreign company who performs work for, and takes orders from, a Czech individual or company may be seen as an employee for payroll withholding purposes irrespective of the legal employment arrangements. Unless the relevant double taxation treaty provides otherwise, nonresident individuals working in the Czech Republic (e.g., consultants) who are not employees will be subject to 25% withholding by the Czech entity/person paying for the services.

For all sources of income that have not been liable to Czech tax at source, individuals are responsible for making payments of tax in advance on the basis of prior-year liability. This applies to the employment income of foreigners assigned to the Czech Republic by an employer, regardless of whether the employer has a permanent establishment in the Czech Republic.

Tax rates

The 2002 tax rates are as follows.

Taxable income Over (Column 1)	Not over	Tax on Column 1	Percentage on excess
0	CZK 109,200	—	15
CZK 109,200	218,400	CZK 16,380	20
218,400	331,200	38,220	25
331,200		66,420	32

INDIVIDUAL TAX CALCULATION

Calendar year ended December 31, 2002

Assumptions

The individual is a foreigner who is employed by a non–Czech-resident employer and who is assigned to work in the Czech Republic for a period of more than 183 days in a calendar year. The individual is married, supports a spouse and two children, and is considered to be a Czech tax resident. No social security contribution liability arises. Accommodation is provided directly by the employer.

Tax computation

Income from employment:		
Salary	2,245,000	
Company car (12% of purchase price of 800,000)	96,000	CZK 2,341,000
Less:		
Personal allowance	38,040	
Spouse allowance	21,720	
Child allowance (2 children)	47,040	106,800
Taxable income		CZK 2,234,200
Rounding		CZK 2,234,200
Tax due (2,234,200 – 331,200) x 32% + 66,420		CZK 675,380

Notes:

Exchange rate at December 31, 2001: US$1 = CZK36.259.

Denmark

PwC contact

For additional information on taxation in Denmark, contact:

Poul-Erik Skou Larsen
PricewaterhouseCoopers
Tuborg Boulevard 1
DK-2900 Hellerup, Denmark
Telephone: (45) (39) 45 39 45
Fax: (45) (39) 45 99 87
e-mail: psl@pwc.dk

Significant developments

There have been no significant tax or regulatory developments in the past year.

Territoriality and residence

Danish tax legislation distinguishes between full and limited tax liability. The main criteria are residence, length of stay, place of work, employer's residence, and type of income, as described below. Citizenship does not affect Danish tax liability.

Individuals are subject to full tax liability when they (1) take up residence or (2) stay in Denmark without taking up residence when the stay exceeds six consecutive months interrupted only by short stays abroad (and then as from the day of arrival). An individual subject to full tax liability in Denmark is taxed on worldwide income and gains received or accrued.

Individuals are subject to limited tax liability on Danish-situs services and other Danish-source income. Dividends are taxed separately.

Separate rules apply to contract labor and individuals participating in oil and gas exploration activities.

Gross income

Employee gross income/All remuneration from employment, whether in cash or in kind, is subject to tax when the employee has obtained a legal right to the remuneration, regardless of where payment is made and regardless of whether remitted. The liability extends to any living or housing allowance and any reimbursement of tax or other personal liability, whether paid directly to an employee or borne by the employer on the employee's behalf.

Payments to an employee for expenses of travel, entertainment or any other service to be performed on behalf of the employer are taxable only to the extent that they are not actually expended in the performance of the service. Special rules apply for free housing provided by the employer and some work-related benefits in kind of less than DKK4,600.

Capital gains and investment income/Taxable gains and investment income are added to taxable income. Certain allowances are available. Profit on the sale of a private house in which the owner has lived and that is situated on property having an area of less than, normally, 1,400 square meters is tax exempt. Gains on the sale of shares in a quoted company are exempt if the shares have been owned for at least three years and the shareholder's total shareholding of all quoted shares for at least three years has been worth less than DKK125,100 (DKK250,100 for a married couple).

The taxable income of an individual subject to full tax liability includes interest, cash dividends, profits from gains on sale of shares owned less than three years, rents, royalties, professional fees, pensions, annuities, and alimony from all sources, wherever located, subject to any limitation that may be imposed under a tax treaty.

Dividends received from both domestic and foreign companies by resident individuals are subject to income tax. Dividends from domestic companies and gains on sale of shares owned at least three years of up to DKK39,700 (DKK79,400 for a married couple) are taxed at 28%. Dividends and gains on the sale of shares in excess of this amount must be reported and are taxed at a rate of 43%.

Exit taxation applies on shareholders leaving Denmark. However, the tax applies only if the shareholder has been subject to full Danish taxation for at least five years within the last ten years before the cessation of tax liability. The rules apply to both Danish and foreign shares. To avoid the burden of paying tax on an unrealized profit, permission can be obtained to postpone payment until the taxpayer has actually disposed of the shares.

Deductions

Business deductions/An employee is entitled to deduct traveling expenses (in accordance with special rules), subscriptions to professional associations, necessary business literature, tools of trade, etc. (exceeding DKK4,600 per calendar year).

Expatriates taking up temporary residence in Denmark may be granted an annual allowance for extra costs of living equal to the lesser of (1) DKK8,000 plus 5% of gross earned income or (2) 25% of gross earned income. This allowance is granted for the first two years; it will be granted only if an expatriate intends to stay in Denmark for no more than three years. It is also a condition that the assignee continue to be paid by the foreign employer.

Special tax legislation covers foreigners who sign contracts for work in Denmark after June 1, 1991. According to this legislation, a tax of only 25% will be levied on their gross income, provided their stay in Denmark is more than 6 months but not longer than 36 months and their monthly income after ATP (ATP-bidrag) and labor market contribution exceeds DKK52,400 However, taking into account the 9% labor market (i.e., social) contribution (see below), the amount before ATP and this 9% tax is DKK57,657.

The tax rate of 25% applies for the first 36 months. The employee's stay in Denmark may be extended a further 48 months, but the income in this period is taxed at ordinary rates. If the employee stays for more than seven years, the total income for the period is taxed at ordinary tax rates (clawback).

Nonbusiness expenses/An individual subject to full tax liability can deduct all interest paid and contributions or premiums paid under certain pension schemes with a Danish pension fund or insurance company. Life insurance premiums paid to a foreign insurance company cannot be deducted, unless a tax treaty provides otherwise. Employee contributions to social security funds are withheld from salary payment and are not considered part of taxable income.

Special rules apply to counteract the avoidance of taxation by individuals leaving Denmark; e.g., persons with limited tax liability and nontaxable persons who cancel a Danish pension scheme pay a special tax of 60% of the insurance value.

For the year in which tax liability ceases and the previous four years, supplementary taxation is also imposed in respect of extraordinary increases in payments to a pension scheme.

Personal allowances/A personal allowance of DKK34,400 is granted that has the effect of reducing income tax payable. The allowance is granted to each individual, but where a spouse cannot utilize the whole personal allowance, the balance is transferred to the other spouse.

With regard to individuals who are subject to limited tax liability, the personal allowance is granted only for salaries and pensions. A special allowance of DKK34,400 is granted for salaries subject to limited tax liability if the spouse is not entitled to a personal allowance.

Tax credits

An individual is entitled to deduct foreign income taxes paid or accrued on foreign-source income from the Danish tax payable up to a maximum of Danish tax paid on that part of the taxable income that is foreign-source income. Relief according to the double taxation treaties can be claimed if their provisions are more favorable.

Personal allowances take the form of tax credits.

Other taxes

Social security taxes/Social security taxes consist of labor market contributions (AM-bidrag), special pension contributions (SP-bidrag) supplementary old-age pension contributions (ATP-bidrag) and work injury insurance.

The AM-*bidrag* to be paid by the employee is 9% of gross salary, and the ATP-*bidrag* to be paid by the employee is DKK895 per annum. The ATP-*bidrag* to be paid by the employer is DKK1,790 per annum. The work injury insurance is paid by the employer.

All social security contributions are tax deductible.

For banks and other financial institutions, a special social tax of 9.13% of gross salary must be paid.

Local taxes on income/County and municipal taxes are levied at flat rates. State and local taxes on income are not deductible for tax purposes.

Wealth tax/From 1997 the wealth tax has been abolished. However, individuals must still fill out asset explanations if requested by the tax authorities.

Tax administration

Returns/Husbands and wives file separate returns for the income year. Taxpayers receive a preprinted tax return in March, containing information that the tax authorities have already obtained from employers or financial institutions (for instance). If the tax return is not correct, it must be corrected, signed and filed no later than May 1.

Taxpayers with more complicated tax returns (most expatriates) must file tax returns no later than July 1.

The tax year for individuals is the calendar year.

When tax liability ceases as a result of leaving Denmark, an income tax return covering the period from the end of the last income year to the date tax liability ceases must be filed before the end of the calendar month following the month in which tax liability ceases. Postponements can normally be obtained upon application.

Payment of tax/There is income tax withholding from salaries (A-tax). For other types of income, an advance tax (B-tax) is paid in ten equal installments during the income year.

Tax rates

Tax rates in effect for calendar year 2002 are detailed below.

Personal income is taxed at a marginal rate up to 59%. Net capital income is taxed at a rate up to 59%, and negative net capital income and other allowances have a tax value of typically 32%, depending on local tax rates. People with independent businesses may choose a special tax system, whereby all business income is taxed at 30%, as long as the income is kept in the business.

Income and allowances are divided into the three categories shown below.

1. Personal income (salary less pension contributions).
2. Capital income (interest income less interest expenses, net taxable capital gain and tax value of notional rent).
3. Other allowances (also deductible in total taxable income).

Local income taxes are calculated on taxable income at flat rates ranging from 27% to 35%.

On income/State income tax is calculated as shown below.

1. Bottom tax—Total taxable income is taxed at 5.50%.

   Plus
2. Middle tax—The aggregate of personal income and positive net capital income in excess of DKK191,200 for a single taxpayer and DKK382,400 for a married couple is taxed at 6%.

   Plus
3. Top tax—The tax base for the top tax of 15% is the sum of all personal income and positive capital income. The tax is levied on the amount in excess of DKK285,200. Unutilized portions of this amount cannot be transferred to the taxpayer's spouse.

The combined top marginal income tax rate cannot exceed 59%.

Income and expenses are annualized if the tax return covers a period shorter than one calendar year.

The tax rates for nonresidents subject to limited tax liability are identical to the state tax rates for resident individuals, together with a local tax rate of 32%. This gives a tax rate of 38.25% for salary income up to DKK191,200, 44.25% from DKK191,200 to DKK285,200 and 59% above DKK285,200.

On wealth/Wealth tax is no longer imposed.

INDIVIDUAL TAX CALCULATION

Assumptions

A married couple with two children resident in Denmark in 2002. The husband, who earns all the income, is employed by a Danish employer. A composite local tax rate of 32.55% has been assumed. The employee is assumed to be covered by the Danish social security system. Total social security tax amounts to DKK895 per year plus the 9% social contribution withheld from the gross salary, all borne by the employee.

The tax consequences where the husband is temporarily employed by a Danish company are also indicated, assuming the employment conditions meet the requirements for the advantageous 25% taxation of gross income mentioned above.

Tax computation

Personal income

Salary and taxable benefits		DKK 1,000,000
Less:		
Social security taxes paid by employee	895	
Contribution to Danish pension scheme	24,000	
9% social contribution (on 975,105)	87,760	112,655
		DKK 887,345

Capital income (net)

Interest income	60,000	
Less—Interest expense	(30,000)	DKK 30,000

Other deductible expenses

Extra cost of commuting between home and place of work	DKK 10,000

Taxable income

Personal income	DKK 887,345
Capital income	30,000
Other deductible expenses	(10,000)
Taxable income	DKK 907,345

Taxes thereon

Taxable income (from above)		DKK 907,345
State income tax:		
Bottom tax—5.5% of taxable income	49,904	
Middle tax—6% of personal and capital income above 382,400)	32,097	
Top tax—(15% of personal income plus capital income exceeding 285,200	94,821	DKK 176,822
Less—Tax value of personal allowance for husband and wife—5.5% of 68,800		(3,784)
Less—Tax ceiling		(316)
Total state tax		DKK 172,722
Local tax—32.55% of taxable income		DKK 295,341
Less—Tax value of personal allowance for husband and wife—32.55% of 68,800		(22,394)
Total local tax		DKK 272,947
Total tax payable		DKK 445,669
Social security tax paid by employee:		
ATP	895	
9% tax on salary	87,760	88,655
Social security tax paid for by pension funds—(8% tax on ATP and pension contributions) (1)		1,992
Total tax expense (2)		DKK 536,316

Notes:

1. The 9% tax is calculated on gross income. However, if the taxpayer has a pension agreement with the employer, only 8% tax is withheld by the pension fund from the employee's pension contributions.
2. If the employee were covered by the 25% taxation of gross income, the total tax would be DKK221,836 plus social security charge of DKK895 plus 9% social contribution of DKK87,760.
3. Exchange rate of the krone at December 31, 2001: US$1 = DKK8.40.

Dominican Republic

PwC contacts

For additional information on taxation in the Dominican Republic, contact:

Freddy Perez
Ramón Ortega
Juan Jorge Pineda
PricewaterhouseCoopers
Lope de Vega esq. John F. Kennedy
Edificio Banco Nova Scotia, Third Floor
Santo Domingo, República Dominicana
Telephone: (809) 567 7741
Fax: (809) 541 1210
LN address: Freddy Perez@Americas-Carib
Ramon Ortega@Price Americas-Carib

General note

This entry is repeated from the 2001/2002 edition. For more up-to-date information, consult the contact listed above or Mark Friedlich at mark.friedlich@us.pwcglobal.com.

Significant developments

There have been no significant tax or regulatory developments in the past year.

Territoriality and residence

The Dominican Republic follows a territorial concept for the determination of taxable income. Dominican-source income is subject to tax, but foreign income is not. Residents and nonresidents are not taxed in the same manner.

Persons are resident in the Dominican Republic if they live in the country for more than 182 days during a calendar year.

Gross income

Employee gross income/Broadly, the entire remuneration for personal services rendered in the Dominican Republic is subject to income tax. However, with regard to compensation-in-kind, the employer is liable for paying tax (on a monthly basis) as set forth by the Tax Code. This additional compensation includes housing, living allowances, and automobiles.

Capital gains and investment income/Capital gains are taxed at a rate of 25%. Interest from time deposits, savings accounts, and other sources that is received from financial institutions in the Dominican Republic is tax exempt. Cash dividends to resident and nonresident individuals are subject to a withholding tax of 25%; the withholding represents a credit to be offset against future tax payable. Foreign investment and financial income of Dominican residents is subject to tax (according to the Tax Code).

Deductions

Business deductions/In general, all expenses incurred in the production of assessable income are deductible.

Nonbusiness expenses/Nonbusiness expenses are not deductible.

Personal allowances/Residents have a standard deduction of RD$8,150 per month (RD$97,800 annually). Christmas bonuses are tax exempt.

Other taxes

Social security taxes/Employers contribute 7% of salaries and withhold 2.5% from employees. Because employees with compensation exceeding RD$1,001 per week are excluded, foreigners are seldom required to be covered.

Technical education tax/A payroll-based contribution is imposed on employees and employers toward the financing of a program for the technical instruction and training of workers. The contribution of employers is 1% of total monthly payroll; for employees, it is 0.5% of bonuses received.

Other taxes on income/No other taxes are payable on income.

Tax administration

Returns/Spouses are required to file separate income tax returns covering their respective incomes. Income from property held in common is included in the return of the husband. Individuals are required to file a personal tax only when income from sources different from the salaries, wages, and bonuses (where the employer withholds tax) is received.

Payment of tax/Employers are required to withhold income tax on salaries, wages, and bonuses. Only a personal standard allowance of RD$97,800 yearly is allowed for withholding purposes.

Tax rates

Basic tax/Individuals pay tax on the excess of RD$97,800 received. Personal income is taxed at the following rates.

Taxable income		Tax on	Percentage
Over	Not over	Column 1	on excess
0	RD$ 97,800	—	0
RD$ 97,800	162,996	—	15
162,996	244,488	RD$ 9,779	20
244,488		26,078	25

INDIVIDUAL TAX CALCULATION

Calendar year 1999; Income year 1998

Assumptions

Resident alien, living in the Dominican Republic; husband and wife, two children; only one spouse is allowed to earn all the income.

Tax computation

Salary		RD$	900,000
Interest (other than nontaxable interest)			90,000
Christmas bonus			75,000
Total gross income			1,065,000
Less:			
Personal standard deduction	97,800		
Christmas bonus (maximum)	75,000		172,800
Taxable income		RD$	892,200
Income tax (1)		RD$	188,005

Notes:

1. Determined as follows.

Income	Amount subject to tax	Rate	Tax effect
	RD$	%	RD$
To 97,800	97,800	0	—
From 97,801 to 162,996	65,196	15	9,779
From 162,997 to 244,488	81,492	20	16,298
Over 244,488	654,792	25	161,928
	899,280		188,005

2. Official exchange rate of the peso at December 31, 2000: US$1 = RD$16.1216.

PwC contact

For additional information on taxation in Ecuador, contact:

Luciano Almeida C, Partner
PricewaterhouseCoopers del Ecuador Cia. Ltda.
Casilla 09-01-5820
Guayaquil, Ecuador
Telephone: (593) (4) 228 1555/228 8199
Fax: (593) (4) 228 6889
e-mail: luciano.almeida@ec.pwcglobal.com

Significant developments

On May 14, 2001 the tax law was once again amended, and new regulations to the Internal Tax Regime Law (ITRL) were issued and came into effect as of December 31, 2001. These new regulations moved the due date for filing of personal income tax returns from April to March.

A new Social Security Law came into effect as of November 30, 2001.

Territoriality and residence

Ecuador currently taxes its citizens and foreigners mostly on their Ecuador-source income. Ecuador-source income is defined as any income derived from activities executed in Ecuador, regardless of where the income is received. It also includes income obtained abroad by Ecuador-resident individuals and corporations, whether local or foreign.

Foreigners are subject to tax on their Ecuador-source income regardless of their domicile or place of residence. Foreigners residing in Ecuador for a short period of time (less than six months) are subject to a flat 25% income tax on income received from local sources, which is withheld at source. Payments made to foreigners occasionally working in Ecuador, when not charged to an Ecuadorian company or branch of a foreign entity, do not give rise to income tax. Foreigners with resident visas are subject to income tax on any earnings and are not entitled to exclusion of income for periods of temporary absence from Ecuador.

Gross income

For personal income tax purposes, it is necessary to differentiate between two main contractual relationships that may exist between a company and a person: labor and professional fee-based relationships.

A labor relationship exists where a person provides personal and legitimate services to a company under the provisions of the Labor Code. The employee is then under a labor contract and included in the company's payroll, thus receiving a fixed monthly remuneration.

A professional fee-based relationship exists when an individual provides professional services to a company on a free-lance basis or under a civil contract. This individual is not included in the company's payroll and is not subject to regulations established in the Labor Code.

Employee gross income/Residents (national or foreign) are taxed on their total labor compensation, net of social security contributions.

Total compensation includes any payments in cash, kind or services made by the employer exclusive of certain few statutory social benefits. Allowances such as cost of living, car, vacation travel, housing, and utilities are considered taxable.

In cases where the employer pays personal income taxes and social security contributions on account of an employee (net salaries), the income tax liability on the net salary is added only once to the total income to arrive at a taxable base and the social security deduction is not allowed.

Independent professional gross income/Residents (national or foreign) are taxed on the total fees invoiced. Under the new social security law professionals are required to pay social security contributions.

Capital gains and investment income/Occasional capital gains (defined as those obtained in the sale of real estate and stock transactions) are exempt from income tax. Other investment income forms part of an individual's taxable income. Dividends received from local corporations and interest received from savings accounts deposits are tax exempt.

Deductions

Business deductions/Expenses incurred in order to generate, maintain, or improve taxable Ecuadorian-source income are in principle deductible. For those under a fee-based relationship, only a few business deductions can be justified.

Nonbusiness expenses/Social security contributions are the only deductions allowed against income arising from employment. Independent professionals are also allowed such deduction.

Personal allowances/An annual personal allowance of $6,200 is built in the current progressive tax table which means that individuals pay income tax on income over and above $6,200.

Tax credits

Credit is available for income taxes paid to another country on income generated abroad, which however is considered taxable in Ecuador. The credit is limited to an amount equal to the Ecuadorian tax due on such income.

Other taxes

Social security contributions/The employee's personal contribution to the social security system is 9.35% of remuneration arising from employment (except certain statutory social benefits). Special rates apply to employees working on special sectors of the economy. Social security contributions are deductible, except when borne by the employer. Individuals under professional fee-based relationship are required to pay social security contributions at a rate of 20.15%.

Local taxes on income/There are no local (provincial, county or municipal) taxes on income.

Value-added tax (VAT)/No VAT applies on employment services on labor relationship. Personal services provided under a civil contract relationship are subject to VAT at 12%, which, when provided to companies, is subject to withholding by the company.

Tax administration

Returns/Annual tax returns need not be filed if the taxpayer's income does not exceed the taxable base (i.e., $6,200); the employer's annual withholding return is considered the employee's return in such cases. If taxable income is earned from other sources or from more than one employer, the employer must consolidate both incomes in a single annual return.

Individuals who end their economic activity prior to the end of the fiscal year are required to file their corresponding income tax return upon termination of activity. Once this return is filed, the individual must cancel the Taxpayer Identification Number (TIN) connected with the activity within 30 days of terminating same.

The fiscal year is the calendar year.

Husbands and wives must file separate returns on their separate employment income. Other joint income, if any, must be split with each spouse declaring half.

Payment of tax/In the case of employees, there is mandatory monthly withholding by the employer as long as the total annual net income exceeds the taxable base of $6,200. Independent professionals are required to make advance tax payments equivalent to 50% of the previous year's tax less withholdings for that year.

Tax rates

The tax table applicable in Ecuador as of January 1, 2002 is as follows.

Taxable income		Tax on base	Percentage on excess
Over	Not over		
(Base)			
0	$ 6,200.00	—	0
$ 6,200.00	12,400.00	—	5
12,400.00	24,800.00	$ 310.00	10
24,800.00	37,200.00	1,550.00	15
37,200.00	49,600.00	3,410.00	20
49,600.00		5,890.00	25

No other surtaxes or additional taxes apply.

INDIVIDUAL TAX CALCULATION

Calendar year 2002

Assumptions

Foreign person residing in Ecuador under labor relationship for an entire calendar year. Remuneration does not include Ecuadorian statutory social benefits. Taxpayer pays own social security contributions and income tax.

Tax computation

Remuneration		$ 30,000
Statutory social benefits		
Salary components ($24 per month)	288	
Christmas bonus (thirteenth salary)	2,500	
Educational bonus (fourteenth salary)	8	
Interest income in saving accounts (nontaxable)	1,000	
Capital gains, other than occasional	500	4,296
Total income		$ 34,296
Less:		
Exempt income	1,000	
Social security contributions (30,000 x 9.35%)	2,805	3,805
Taxable base (i.e., taxable work income)		$ 30,491
Income tax on first 24,800	1,550.00	
Income tax on excess at 15%	853.65	
Total income tax		$ 2,403.65
Less—Tax withheld by employer (estimate)		(2,328.65)
Tax due		$ 75.00

Reconciliation

Total income from all sources	$ 34,296.00
Total income tax	(2,403.65)
Total contributions to social security	(2,805.00)
Net income	$ 29,087.35

Notes:

1. At the moment that the company shares on its profits (statutory profit sharing) with its employee such profit sharing will become part of the person's taxable income.
2. The monetary unit is the U.S. dollar.

PwC contacts

For additional information on taxation in Egypt, contact:

Sherif Mansour, TLS Leader
Abdallah El Adly, Tax Partner
PricewaterhouseCoopers
22 El Nasr Street
New Maadi
Cairo, Egypt
Tel: (20) 2 516 8027/(20) 2 260 8500
Fax: (20) 2 516 8169/(20) 2 261 3204
e-mail: sherif.mansour@eg.pwcglobal.com
abdallah.eladly@eg.pwcglobal.com

Significant developments

There have been no significant tax or regulatory developments relating to individual taxation in the past year.

Territoriality and residence

Earnings of individuals working in Egypt are subject to taxes regardless of the place of payment, provided it is related to work performed in Egypt. Earnings paid by the overseas entity for purposes other than work done in Egypt are not taxable. An individual is considered to be a resident in Egypt if the period of work in Egypt exceeds 183 days in any calendar year, or the individual's principal residence is in Egypt.

Residents and nonresidents are treated equally, except that nonresident foreign experts are not entitled to any relief.

Gross income

Employee gross income/An alien is taxed on salary earned for work performed in Egypt regardless of where payment is made and regardless of whether it is remitted. The alien is not taxed to the extent compensation relates to services performed outside Egypt.

Reimbursement for expenses of spouse and dependents is taxable income. School tuition fees, long-term living expenses and overseas and hardship allowances are taxable.

Capital gains and investment income/An alien is taxed on real estate capital gains realized in Egypt. Capital gains on the sale of Egyptian securities are not taxable.

Interest income received from local banks is not taxable.

Deductions and exemptions

The items listed below are deductible for representation, (there is a maximum of £E4,000 for total representation, incentives and nature-of-work allowances).

1. Representation allowance up to £E2,500 per annum.
2. Family relief allowance of £E2,500 for married persons £E3,000 for married persons with children and £E2,000 for a single person.
3. 10% of gross pay less representation and nature-of-work allowances and special salary increase for all undocumented expenses and costs.

4. Special "Social increment" salary increase.
5. A nature-of-work allowance of up to £E480 per annum.
6. A £E2,000 tax exemption per annum.
7. Airfare for first arrival and final departure to/from Egypt.
8. Housing is exempt from salary if:
   a. It is provided in cash or kind to experts working for more than 183 days in any calendar year; or
   b. It is provided in a company guest house available for use by all employees.

Other taxes

Social security taxes/Expatriate employees working in Egypt are not subject to the social insurance scheme except in the following cases.

1. A treaty between Egypt and the expatriate's country is in force to exempt the citizens of the other country in Egypt and vice versa.
2. The expatriate's work agreement covers a period exceeding one year.

Additional taxes/Individuals making over £E18,000 (of taxable income) per annum are subject to an additional 2% tax (development duty) on the excess.

Tax administration

Returns/No tax year other than the calendar year is permitted.

Payment of tax/Employers must withhold taxes on a monthly basis and submit them to the Tax Department within the first 15 days of the following month.

Tax rates

The first £E50,000 of annual taxable salary is subject to tax at 20%; the excess is taxed at the rate of 32%.

Income such as real estate, professional, and commercial is taxed at rates starting from 20% to a maximum of 40% for income exceeding US$3,463 (approximately L£16,000).

Tax on revenue from movable capital applies to interest income from all sources, foreign and domestic, and foreign-source dividends at a rate of 32%. Certain exemptions are available for domestic-source interest.

INDIVIDUAL TAX CALCULATION—TAX ON SALARY ONLY

Calendar year 2002

Assumptions

An alien and wife, two children; one spouse earns all the income.

Tax computation

Gross income—(Includes representation allowance and nature-of-work allowance)		£E 176,000
Less—Deductions:		
Representation allowance (maximum)	2,500	
Nature-of-work allowance deductible (maximum)	480	
Social increment (if given)	0	
10% of (176,000 – 2,980) for undocumented expenses	17,302	
Tax-exempt amount	2,000	
Family relief allowance (maximum)	3,000	25,282
Taxable amount		£E 150,718
Tax thereon:		
First 50,000 at 20%	10,000	
100,718 at 32%	32,230	£E 42,230

Development duty

Taxable amount for unified tax purposes	£E 150,718
Less—Exempt amount	18,000
Applicable amount	£E 132,718
Duty at 2%	£E 2,655

Net salary

Gross income		£E 176,000
Less:		
Tax on salary	42,230	
Duty at 2%	2,655	£E 44,885
Net salary		£E 131,115

Note:

Exchange rate of the Egyptian pound at December 31, 2001: US$1 = £E4.62.

Estonia

PwC contacts

For additional information on taxation in Estonia, contact:

Aare Kurist
Tax Department
AS PricewaterhouseCoopers
Pärnu mnt 15
10141 Tallinn, Estonia
Telephone: (372) (6) 141 800
Fax: (372) (6) 141 900
e-mail: aare.kurist@ee.pwcglobal.com

Copies of all documents/inquiries to be sent to:

Cameron G. Greaves (TLS Baltic Leader)
PricewaterhouseCoopers UAB
T. Sevcenkos 21
LT-2009 Vilnius, Lithuania
Telephone: (370) 2 392 300
Fax: (370) 2 392 301
e-mail: cameron.greaves@lt.pwcglobal.com

Significant developments

Resident employees born after December, 31 1982 must contribute to the compulsory accumulative pension scheme from July 1, 2002.

Territoriality and residence

An individual who is a resident of Estonia is liable to tax on worldwide income, irrespective of the origin of the income. Nonresidents are taxed on their Estonian-source income. Individuals are considered residents of Estonia if they have a permanent place of residence, their stay during a calendar year is equal to or exceeds 183 days or they are Estonian public servants who are sent abroad on assignment.

Gross income

Employee gross income/Taxable income includes employment and private business income and income from other sources. Income from other sources not exempt from taxation includes nonstate pensions and scholarships, alimony received, interest, royalties, rental income, foreign dividends, certain insurance proceeds, and gains from the disposal of assets. Taxable income also includes income of a legal entity (CFC) located in a low-tax jurisdiction.

Certain nonstate scholarships, gains from the sale of a resident taxpayer's own residential dwelling and the first sale of land acquired in the process of property reform, and the winnings from certain lotteries, among other items, are excluded from gross income. Benefits in kind (e.g., residential housing, company car, etc.) are taxable to the employer and are not included in the taxable income of the individual.

There are no special taxation rules for expatriates.

Capital gains and investment income/Capital gains realized by resident individuals are generally taxed as ordinary income. However, the following gains are tax exempt for resident individuals.

1. Gains from the sale of a resident taxpayer's own immovable property, including dwellings, or movable apartment or house that was used as a permanent or primary place of residence by the taxpayer until its sale or that has been transferred to the taxpayer's ownership through restitution of illegally expropriated property.
2. Gains from the sale of a resident taxpayer's own immovable property, including dwellings, or movable apartment or house that has been transferred to the taxpayer's ownership through privatization with preemption (provided the immovable property is under two hectares).
3. Gains from the sale of a summer cottage or garden house, provided the taxpayer has owned it for more than two years and the immovable property is under 0.25 hectares.
4. Gains from the disposal of land granted as restitution to an individual in the course of property reform.

Gains derived by nonresidents from the disposal of property located in Estonia or registered in any Estonian register, as well as the disposal of rights in real estate, are generally liable to income tax of 26%. However, gains from the disposal of shares of Estonian corporate entities are subject to 26% Estonian tax only if the nonresident disposed of at least a 10% share in the company and 75% of its assets are represented by real estate or buildings.

Dividends are not taxed in the hands of the resident recipient if they have been received from a company registered in Estonia. Interest from resident credit institutions, Estonian branches of nonresident credit institutions and the Compensation Fund is exempt from income tax. However, interest derived by nonresidents from Estonian branches of nonresident credit institutions is subject to tax. Interest from other institutions is taxed at 26%.

Deductions

Business deductions/Only business-related expenses for individuals engaged in business and registered as such with the tax authorities are deductible. These individuals must follow the cash basis in accounting for their income and expenditure.

Nonbusiness deductions/Alimony paid during the tax period can be deducted from taxable income, provided the alimony is subject to tax under Estonian law. Interest on loans and/or capital rent for the purpose of acquiring a single-residence building or apartment are deductible if paid to resident credit and financing institutions or to Estonian branches of nonresident credit institutions during the taxation period.

Residents have the right to deduct from their taxable income interest on student loans and the costs of their own or their under 26 year-old dependents' (or instead, under 26 year-old permanent resident of Estonia) training in certified educational institutions.

Residents may deduct from taxable income documented gifts and charitable contributions made to nonprofit associations and foundations listed by the government and to public universities, as well as to cultural, sports, educational, health, or social security institutions belonging to state or local authorities. Also, entrance and membership fees to trade unions registered as nonprofit associations or foundations are deductible. The total deductions of such gifts, charitable contributions and entrance and membership fees may not exceed 5 percent of the individual's income for the tax period after the deduction of other allowable expenses.

The deduction of interest, education expenses, charitable contributions, and trade union membership fees cannot exceed the lesser of a) 50% of the taxable income for the tax year or b) a fixed amount of EEK100,000.

Premiums to certain annuity pension schemes and expenses incurred to buy the shares of approved resident pension funds may be deducted from taxable income. Such deduction is limited to 15% of income (after business deductions, if any) derived during the tax year.

Unemployment insurance contributions and contributions to compulsory accumulative pension schemes made during the tax year are deductible from the taxable income of a resident individual, without any limits.

General deduction/Annual income of up to EEK12,000 is not taxable. Resident parents with more than two children may take one additional general deduction (EEK12,000) for each additional child.

Tax credits

For Estonian residents, income taxes paid abroad as final tax on income during their period of residence are allowed as a credit against national tax payable in Estonia. The tax credit is limited to 26% of the foreign income.

Other taxes

Social security taxes/Employers must pay social security contributions for their employees at a rate of 33%. Individuals engaged in business must make personal social security contributions.

Unemployment insurance/From January 1, 2002 both employers and employees are obliged to pay unemployment insurance contributions on employment income at the rates of 0.5% and 1%, respectively.

Compulsory accumulative pension scheme/Resident employees born after December 31, 1982 are obliged to join the compulsory accumulative pension scheme and make contributions at 2% from gross salary from July 1, 2002. For resident employees born before 1983 joining the pension scheme is voluntary, but after joining, it becomes compulsory and employees may not subsequently leave the scheme. In addition to the 2% contribution made by the employee, 4 percentage points of the social security contribution payable by the employer (33% social security contributions) will be transferred to the employee's pension account. Both unemployment insurance contributions and contributions to compulsory accumulative pension scheme are withheld from employee's salary by the employer.

Local taxes on income/There are no local taxes on income.

Tax administration

Returns/A resident individual's annual tax return must be filed by March 31. Resident husbands and wives are treated as individual taxpayers, unless they apply to have their incomes combined.

A nonresident is obliged to file an income tax return generally by March 31 following the year of taxation on gains from the disposal of property and on certain types of income (wages, rent, royalties, interest, pensions, scholarships, awards and benefits) when these have been received other than under deduction of withholding tax. Gains from the disposal of real estate, buildings or apartments must be declared within one month of the transfer. Nonresidents are not required to submit tax returns for income that has been subject to final withholding tax.

Payment of tax/Income from employment is subject to withholding tax. It is the employer's responsibility to withhold taxes and to transfer them to the local tax authorities without delay. The calculation of tax withholding is based on the rates established for taxation of annual income. The amount withheld is credited against the employee's annual tax liability.

Final income tax due must be paid by resident individual to the tax authorities before July 1 following the year of taxation, except the income tax on gains from the disposal of property or business income, which is due by October 1 following the year of taxation.

The nonresident individual must pay final income tax due to the tax authorities by the due date of the income tax return.

Tax rates

Employee income is taxed at a flat rate of 26%.

As noted above, annual income of resident individual up to EEK12,000 is not taxable.

INDIVIDUAL TAX CALCULATION

Calendar year ending December 31, 2002

Assumptions

This calculation concerns a resident who has tax-exempt income of EEK12,000 per year (together, a married couple would have EEK24,000 of tax-exempt income).

Tax computation

Salary, premium and other payments	EEK 1,100,000
Other income	20,000
Gross income	1,120,000
Less—Tax-exempt income:	
Nontaxable minimum income	12,000
Unemployment insurance contribution paid by employee	11,000
Income subject to income tax	EEK 1,097,000
Income tax payable	EEK 285,220
Less—Income tax withheld	(280,020)
Additional income tax due	EEK 5,200

Note:

Exchange rate of the kroon at December 31, 2001: US$1 = EEK17.69.

PwC contact

For additional information on taxation in Faroe Islands, contact:

Ole Guldborg Nielsen
Rasmussen & Weihe
Statsautoriserað grannskoðarafelag, P/F
Á Gladsheyggi
P.O. Box 30
FO–110 Tórshavn
Faroe Islands
Telephone: (298) 31 10 17
Fax: (298) 31 10 18
e-mail: rasmussen@rasmussen.fo

Significant developments

There have been significant changes in the taxation of capital gains.

Territoriality and residence

Faroese tax legislation distinguishes between full and limited tax liability. The main criteria are residence, length of stay, place of work, employer's residence, and type of income, as described below. Citizenship does not affect Faroese tax liability.

Individuals are subject to full tax liability when they (1) take up residence or (2) stay in the Faroe Islands without taking up residence when the stay exceeds six consecutive months interrupted only by short stays abroad (and then as from the day of arrival). An individual subject to full tax liability in Faroe Islands is taxed on worldwide income and gains received or accrued. Individuals are subject to limited tax liability on Faroese-situs services and other Faroese-source income. Dividends are taxed separately.

Separate rules apply to contract labor.

With the introduction of a hydrocarbon tax bill in 1999, special rules apply for individuals participating in oil and gas exploration activities. Foreign subcontractors (self-employed) and foreign employees engaged in hydrocarbon activities in Faroese territory are subject to pay a final tax of 35.5% (combined 35% tax rate and 0.5% social contributions).

Gross income

The taxable income of an individual subject to full tax liability includes rents, royalties, professional fees, pensions, annuities, and alimony from all sources (wherever located), subject to any limitation that may be imposed under a tax treaty.

Employee gross income/All remuneration from employment, whether in cash or in kind, is subject to tax when the employee has obtained a legal right to the remuneration, regardless of where payment is made and regardless of whether remitted. The liability extends to any living or housing allowance and any reimbursement of tax or other personal liability, whether paid directly to an employee or borne by the employer on behalf of the employee.

Payments to an employee for expenses incurred for travel, entertainment or any other service to be performed on behalf of the employer are taxable only to the extent that they are not actually expended in the performance of the service. Special rules apply for free housing and other benefits in kind provided by the employer.

Capital gains and investment income/Capital gains and investment income are taxed separately and must be declared on a special self-assessment form. Gains on the sale of bonds and shares, options, debt, and dividends and on interest are not included in ordinary taxable income.

Profit on the sale of a private house owned for more than two years is normally tax exempt.

Capital gains, dividends, and interest are taxed at a fixed tax rate of 35%. Capital losses can only be deducted in the assessment of capital gain. Certain interim provisions apply for shares acquired before the new legislation was set in force.

For dividends from Faroese companies or interest from Faroese banks, the tax will be withheld by the company/bank.

Deductions

Business deductions/No business deductions are available to individuals. However, travel expenses will be (partly) reimbursed according to special rules. An application is necessary.

There are no special rules for expatriates taking up temporary residence in the Faroe Islands.

Nonbusiness expenses/An individual subject to full tax liability can deduct contributions or premium paid under certain pension schemes with a pension fund, a bank or an insurance company. Employee contributions under certain pension schemes are withheld from salary payment and are not considered part of taxable income.

Mortgage or other interest is not deductible. However, according to special rules, part of mortgage interest can be reimbursed, provided the mortgage is obtained for private housing purposes. For 2001 the rate of reimbursement is 44%, but it will gradually be reduced from 2002 (42%) until the reimbursement is 40% in 2003.

Personal allowances/Single individuals on old-age pension are eligible for an allowance of DKK16,200. For married people, the allowance is DKK10,500 each. There are also personal allowances for individuals with children under the age of 18. The child allowance ranges from DKK5,500 to DKK10,000 per child—the difference is due to the fact that the municipalities decide part of the child allowance. These allowances are deducted in figuring the computed tax.

Special provisions for fishermen/A special allowance is granted for fishermen. When computing the taxable income, 15% of income is deductible. However, this deduction may not exceed DKK75,000.

Tax credits

An individual is entitled to deduct foreign income taxes paid or accrued on foreign-source income from the Faroese tax payable up to a maximum of Faroese tax paid on that part of the taxable income that is foreign-source income. Relief according to double taxation treaties can be claimed if their provisions are more favorable.

Other taxes

Social security taxes/Social security taxes comprise contributions to a labor market unemployment fund (ALS), supplementary old-age pension contributions (AMEG), contributions to a maternity fund, and contributions to a security fund for wages.

The contributions paid by the employer are computed as a percentage of wages/salaries and amount to 1.25% to ALS, 0.5% to AMEG, 0.25% to a maternity fund, and 0.15% to the security fund. Employers are also required to hold work insurance. All social security contributions are tax deductible for the employer.

The employee contributes 1.25% to ALS, 0.25% to the maternity fund and 0.5% to AMEG. These employee contributions are nondeductible.

Banks and insurance companies must pay a special social tax of 5% of gross salary. Other VAT-exempt businesses are taxed at 2.5%. This tax is not deductible.

Local taxes on income/Municipal taxes are levied at flat rates and vary between 16% and 23%. State and local taxes are not deductible for tax purposes.

Tax administration

Returns/Husbands and wives file separate returns for the income year. Taxpayers receive a preprinted tax return in February or March containing information that the tax authorities have already obtained from employers or financial institutions. If the tax return is not correct, it must be corrected, signed and filed no later than March 15.

The tax year for individuals is the calendar year.

Postponements can normally be obtained upon application, but for no later than August 15.

Payment of tax/Any employer is obliged to pay out all wages and salaries through an authorized "payment office"—in reality, any bank, post office bank or savings bank in the Faroe Islands. At the time of payment the tax will be computed and withheld. For other types of income, an advance tax is paid in twelve equal installments during the income year.

Tax rates

Tax rates for calendar year 2001 are detailed below.

Residents/Income taxes are assessed on the basis of a single annual tax return. Both the state and the municipality collect income taxes. State taxes are progressive, with the highest rate at 37% for taxable income in excess of DKK150,000. Municipal taxes are set each year by the various municipal authorities. In 2001 they varied between 16% and 23%.

A special rule states that an individual can never pay more than 50% tax on his or her taxable income. Therefore, if an individual's tax is computed to be more than 50% of taxable income, the final tax will be lowered to 50% of taxable income.

Only 85% of income earned through fishing is taxable.

Nonresidents/Nonresidents are taxed at 42% of any wage/salary/fee arising in the Faroe Islands, with no deductions. In addition, 0.5% social security (AMEG) must be paid.

Employees liable to taxation according to the Hydrocarbon Tax Act are taxed at a rate of 35% on wages and salaries for work performed in the Faroes (including Faroe

Islands off-shore). The employee is also obliged to pay 0.5% to a pension fund, bringing the total tax up to 35.5%.

INDIVIDUAL TAX CALCULATION

Calendar year 2001

Assumptions

Individual receiving a salary of DKK1,000.000. Payment to a pension scheme of DKK41,400 (maximum). Two children under the age of 18. The individual is situated in the Municipality of Tórshavn (capital of the Faroe Islands).

Tax computation

Salary		DKK 1,000,000
Less—Contribution to pension scheme		41,400
		DKK 958,600
Municipality tax:		
Taxable income	958,600	
Less—Fixed deduction (no municipal tax is imposed for taxable income below DKK19,0000)	(19,000)	
	939,600	
Municipality tax of Tórshavn (18.75%)	176,175	
Deduction for two children	(7,000)	DKK 169,175
Church tax (0.3% of 939,600) – (voluntary)		2,819
State tax:		
Taxable income	958,600	
Tax on income up to 150,000	22,590	
Tax on income in excess of 150,000 (37.0%)	299,182	
Deduction for two children	(8,000)	313,772
Computed tax		DKK 485,766
Tax payable—The lower of:		
(1) 485,766 or (2) 958,600 x 50% = 479,300		DKK 479,300
Social security tax:		
Paid by the employer: 2.15% of 1,000,000		DKK 21,500
Paid by the employee: 1.50% of 1,000,000 and 0.50% of 958,600		DKK 19,793

Note:

Exchange rate of the Danish krone at December 31, 2001: US$1 = DKK8.40.

PwC contact

For additional information on taxation in Fiji, contact:

Jerome Kado
PricewaterhouseCoopers
Level 8, Civic Tower
262 Victoria Parade
(GPO Box 200)
Suva, Fiji
Telephone: (679) 313 955
Fax: (679) 300 981
e-mail: jerome.kado@fj.pwcglobal.com

Significant developments

The maximum tax rate has been reduced from 34% to 32% with effect from January 1, 2002.

A deduction up to $F1,000 is now allowable in respect to the discount on shares issued to employees under "qualifying employee share schemes" from January 1, 2001. See "Employee Share Scheme."

Resident dividend withholding tax of 5% has been removed. A deduction is available for dividends to the extent that they have been charged to tax. See "Dividends."

Territoriality and residence

Residents/Resident individuals are liable to tax on taxable income accruing in or derived from Fiji or elsewhere. Pursuant to the ruling in a recent case, foreign income sourced from a nontreaty country is subject to income tax in Fiji, with credits available for tax paid on such income.

Residents are those who have been in Fiji during more than half the year, unless the Commissioner is satisfied that their usual place of abode is outside Fiji and that they do not intend to take up residence in Fiji. Persons domiciled in Fiji are also considered resident, unless their permanent place of abode is outside Fiji.

Nonresidents/Nonresidents are liable to tax only on taxable income accruing in or derived from Fiji.

Foreign personnel/Income other than employment income is not subject to tax if one of the following applies.

1. It does not accrue in Fiji.
2. It is not derived from or received in Fiji by a person whose permanent place of abode is outside Fiji and who is in Fiji solely or mainly for the purpose of engaging in employment in Fiji under a contract of employment of not more than three years' duration.

Gross income

Employee gross income/A foreign person residing in Fiji solely or mainly for the purpose of engaging in employment is subject to tax on salary earned in Fiji regardless of where payment is made and regardless of whether it is remitted. Gross income includes wages, salaries, fees and other emoluments, living allowances, housing allowances, tax reimbursements, and other benefits received from any office or employment. These allowances and benefits are explained below.

1. Housing—Where furnished accommodation is provided by an employer, an employee is treated as receiving a taxable benefit amounting to one-eighth (one-ninth where it is unfurnished) of basic emoluments, with a maximum benefit of $F12,000 ($F10,667 if unfurnished), unless the actual rent paid by the employer exceeds $F20,000 per annum, in which case the greater of 50% of the actual rent paid or one-eighth (one-ninth if unfurnished) of basic emoluments is deemed to be the benefit. Twice the amount of a rent contribution made by the employee may be offset against this benefit.
2. Cars—A fixed sum of $F1,800, $F2,000 or $F2,4000 ($F1,350, $F1,500 or $F1,800 if the employee also owns a car), depending on engine capacity, is deemed to be the private benefit arising from the use of a company car. However, if the cost of the vehicle provided to the employee exceeds $F60,000, a sum of $F2,400 plus 10% of the cost in excess of $F60,000 is adopted, irrespective of the engine capacity (subject to reduction to 75% if the employee also owns a car).
3. Personal expenses of the employee borne by the employer. However, in the case of a foreigner recruited outside Fiji, passage costs borne by the employer or reimbursed to the employee for the employee and the employee's family for initial arrival and final departure, one return journey per annum for leave purposes and journeys made for urgent family reasons are not a taxable benefit to the employee. The exemption is limited to the cost of economy-class airfares using the most direct route between Fiji and the territory in which the employee was recruited. In all other cases, subsidized or free travel provided to employees is a taxable benefit.

Capital gains and investment income/There is no capital gains tax in Fiji. However, gains realized from the sale or other disposition of property acquired for purposes of resale or as part of a profit-making undertaking or scheme are taxable as ordinary income and are not treated as capital gains. The proposed capital gains tax, which was to be introduced from January 1, 1994, has now been deferred indefinitely.

A full exemption from tax is available on dividends received by residents of Fiji from shares held in companies listed on the Suva Stock Exchange. This measure is aimed at encouraging a wider spread of ownership of capital and the development of the Stock Exchange as a vehicle for widespread share ownership.

A foreign person's income from Fiji sources, including interest, dividends, rents, and royalties, is subject to income tax at graduated rates. However, there is a concession for dividend income from Fiji-incorporated companies.

Income from interest, dividends or royalties derived outside Fiji by a person resident in Fiji solely or mainly for the purpose of engaging in any employment under a contract of employment of not more than three years' duration is not subject to Fiji tax.

Deductions

Business deductions/In arriving at taxable income, deductions may be taken for expenses laid out wholly and exclusively for the purposes of deriving that income. Deductions are not available for personal or living expenses or for income taxes paid. However, reimbursements of relocation expenses and travel and automobile expenses for business purposes are not subject to tax.

Employee share scheme/From January 1, 2001, a maximum exemption of $F1,000 is now allowable on the assessable value of the discount on any shares issued to employees under a "qualifying employee share scheme" as defined under the Fiji Income Tax Act.

Nonbusiness expenses/Deductions for nonbusiness expenses are minimal and are unlikely to be available to a foreign employee.

Personal allowances/Resident individuals, including those in Fiji for employment purposes, may claim the allowances listed below.

1. Wife allowance of $F1,200 if wife's income is not separately assessed.
2. Child allowance of $F500 each for the first two children and $F300 each for three additional children (allowances cover a maximum of five children).
3. Life insurance premiums and approved retirement fund contributions up to $F1,500. From January 1, 2000 each spouse may claim $F1,500 for this allowance. Previously, this was limited to $F1,500 for a married couple.

The allowances are deducted for the purpose of determining taxable income.

Nonresidents may claim a portion of the allowance for a wife, the proportion being the same as that of their Fiji-source income divided by their worldwide income. Persons in Fiji for employment purposes for less than a full year may claim the allowances detailed above in proportion to either the period of their residence in Fiji or the period with respect to which they derive emoluments from their employment in Fiji, whichever is more favorable to the taxpayer.

Dividends/A deduction is available for dividends to the extent that they have been paid or credited from income that has been charged to tax. The deduction will not be allowed unless the taxpayer provides to the Commissioner a certificate issued by the company paying or crediting the dividends in accordance with the regulations. The regulations have yet to be issued by the Fiji tax office.

Tax credits

Tax credits apply to income derived from the countries with which Fiji has double taxation agreements—Australia, Japan, the Republic of Korea, Malaysia, New Zealand, Papua New Guinea, and the United Kingdom.

Other taxes

Resident interest withholding taxes/A withholding tax of 32% is deductible on payments or accrual of interest by banks and other financial institutions to resident depositors. However, this tax is not payable where the depositors provide the financial institutions with their tax identification numbers or where interest received does not exceed $120.

Social security taxes/No social security taxes are imposed.

Land sales tax/Certain profits arising from the sale of land that are not subject to income tax may be liable to land sales tax at rates varying from 6.5 to 30%, depending on the level of profits.

Local taxes on income/There are no local taxes on income.

Tax administration

Returns/Husbands and wives are required to file joint returns, since the income of a married woman is treated, for income tax purposes, as her husband's, with the exception of profits or earnings from a wife's "personal exertion" that arise from a source not connected with any trade or business associated with her husband or from a company in which her husband has an interest. Where a wife has such unconnected personal exertion income, she may, by election, be assessed to tax in her own name on that income.

The taxable year for the individual is the calendar year.

Payment of tax/There is income tax withholding from salaries. Generally, if taxpayers have sizable income not subject to withholding they will be required to make provisional payments of estimated tax in three installments.

Tax rates

Normal tax is assessed on taxable (chargeable) income, i.e., total income less personal allowances. From January 1, 2001, where the taxable income of a resident exceeds $F20,000, normal tax is $F3,025, plus 32% of the taxable income in excess of $F20,000. In the case of nonresidents with taxable income in excess of $F20,000, normal tax is $F5,175, plus 32% of the taxable income in excess of $F20,000.

INDIVIDUAL TAX CALCULATION

Year ending December 31, 2001

Assumptions

Resident foreign husband and wife, two children; one spouse earns all income. Capital gains, being currently exempt from tax, have been excluded from the computation. Ex-Fiji income being generally exempt, no tax credits are available against Fiji income tax liability.

Tax computation

Gross salary		$F 124, 900
Add—Taxable benefits:		
Furnished housing	12,000	
Use of company car (1800–1999 cc)	2,000	14,000
		138,900
Interest on bank savings account—Self and wife		1,000
Total income		139,900
Deduct—Allowances:		
Wife	1,200	
Children (two)	1,000	
Life insurance and contribution to superannuation funds (maximum)	1,500	3,700
Taxable income		$F 136,200
Normal tax payable		$F $40,209

Note:

Exchange rate (bank selling) of the Fiji dollar at January 15, 2002: US$1 = $F2.3343.

Finland

PwC contact

For additional information on taxation in Finland, contact:

Mr. Kai Wist
SVH PricewaterhouseCoopers Oy
P.O. Box 1015
FIN-00101 Helsinki, Finland
Telephone: (358) (9) 2280 1401
Fax: (358) (9) 2280 1240
e-mail: kai.wist@fi.pwcglobal.com

General note

This entry is repeated from the 2001/2002 edition. For more up-to-date information, consult the contact listed above or Mark Friedlich at mark.friedlich@us.pwcglobal.com.

Significant developments

The expatriate income regime, which expired on December 31, 1999, was restored at the beginning of 2001.

Territoriality and residence

Finland taxes residents on their worldwide income. Residents are taxed according to progressive tax rates for national tax purposes and flat rates for municipal (and church and social security) tax purposes.

A nonresident alien, for example, one occasionally working in Finland, is taxed on Finnish-source income only. Tax treaties may provide, however, that under certain conditions even this income may not be taxed in Finland. Nonresidents are taxed at flat rates in accordance with the Nonresidents' Tax Act. Nonresidents do not pay social security charges to Finland.

The expatriate regime is available again as from January 1, 2001. The regime provides for a flat tax rate of 35% for those foreign employees whose work requires special knowledge. Other conditions are that monthly cash salary is at least FIM35,000 and that the length of the assignment is 6 to 24 months. The expatriate regime applies for a maximum of 24 months from the start of the assignment; after that period, the expatriate is taxed according to the normal rules.

Individuals are deemed to be resident in Finland if they have their permanent home or habitual abode in Finland or if they are present in Finland for a continuous period of more than six months. A temporary absence from Finland does not prevent a stay from being deemed continuous. Finnish citizens are, however, considered resident in Finland for three full calendar years after they have left the country, unless they prove they had no essential connections therewith in the fiscal year in question. Residence may start or break off in the course of a year.

Gross income

Employee gross income/Taxable personal income of a resident employee includes, inter alia, wages and salaries in money and in kind, directors' bonuses, employee stock options, rental value of employee's free housing, pensions and annuities, living and housing allowances, car benefits, unemployment benefits, and capital gains (if taxable). The income is divided into earned income and capital income. Earned-income tax is imposed at progressive rates. Capital income is taxed at a flat rate of 29%. Dividends from stock other than that quoted on the Helsinki Stock Exchange are divided into capital income and earned income.

Finnish-source income of a nonresident alien is taxed definitively at source. Unless lower rates are provided for in a tax treaty, the rates are 35% on salaries and pensions and 29% on dividends, interest, and royalties. In principle, no deductions are allowed against the income. Finnish-source income other than that mentioned above is subject to income tax at flat rates of 35% or 29% (if it is in the nature of capital income) unless a tax treaty provides otherwise.

Capital gains and investment income/Capital gains are fully taxable at a flat rate of 29%.

A gain from the sale of a home is exempt from taxation if the house or apartment has been the taxpayer's home for at least two years continuously during the period of ownership.

Interest income from deposits in Finnish bank accounts and Finnish bonds is subject to tax at source at a flat rate of 29%. This tax is final.

Deductions

Business deductions/Expenses incurred in acquiring or maintaining taxable income are, in principle, deductible items. The maximum allowance for travel expenses to and from work is FIM23,000, with an own-risk share of FIM3,000. Generally, only travel expenses incurred though the least expensive means of transportation (public transportation: train, bus, streetcar, or ship) are deductible. Other deductions for earning income may include expenses for professional literature, own tools, etc., against original payment receipts. Moving, automobile, and entertainment expenses are generally not deductible.

A standard deduction of FIM2,700 from salary income is granted if actual business expenses are below that amount.

Nonbusiness expenses/The following deductions are available.

1. Pension premiums: Mandatory pension premiums are wholly tax deductible for both national and municipal tax purposes (see the calculation below). The deductibility of voluntary pension premiums is limited.
2. Unemployment insurance premiums: Mandatory unemployment insurance premiums are deductible for both national and municipal tax purposes (see the calculation).
3. Interest: Most interest expenses paid are deductible when calculating capital income.

Medical expenses are not deductible.

Tax credits

For their period of residence, Finnish residents can credit national taxes paid abroad as final tax on income against national tax payable in Finland on the same income.

Other taxes

Social security taxes/A sickness insurance premium of 1.5% is paid on income for municipal taxation.

Local taxes on income/Municipal tax is levied at flat rates on taxable income. This tax rate varies between 15% and 19.5%, depending on the municipality.

Church tax/Church tax is paid by members of the Evangelic Lutheran and Orthodox churches in Finland at flat rates on the taxable income as determined for municipal tax. Rates vary between 1% and 2.25%.

Wealth tax/If an individual owns assets with a net value of FIM1.1 million, wealth tax of FIM500 is applicable. A rate of 0.09% applies to the value in excess of FIM1.1 million.

Tax administration

Returns/Husbands and wives file separate returns; joint filing or income splitting is not possible. Salaried employees file returns on a calendar-year basis by the end of January each year. The tax year is the calendar year.

Nonresident aliens generally do not file any tax return because the final tax is withheld at source from their Finnish-source income. For income other than salary, pension, dividends, interest, or royalties (e.g., rental income), a tax return must be filed in accordance with the general procedures.

Payment of tax/There is preliminary income tax withholding from salaries and from most usual incomes, for example, pensions, remuneration, and dividends. Generally, if taxpayers have income not subject to withholding (e.g., salary paid from abroad), they will be required to make monthly payments of estimated tax.

Tax rates

Employment income/National taxation rates are as follows.

Taxable income		Tax on	Percentage
Over	Not over	Column 1	on excess
(Column 1)			
FIM 66,000	FIM 85,000	FIM 50	14
85,000	117,000	2,710	18
117,000	184,000	8,470	24
184,000	325,000	24,550	30
325,000		66,850	37

Capital income/The tax rate on capital income is a flat tax rate of 29%.

Other national and municipal taxation/In addition to the above-mentioned national tax, the taxpayer must pay municipal, church, and national pension and sickness insurance premiums (see "Other taxes" above). Church tax is included, since it applies to foreigners if they are members of the Evangelic Lutheran and Orthodox churches or the Finnish German church.

INDIVIDUAL TAX CALCULATIONS

Calendar year 2001

Computation I

Assumptions

Resident alien living in Helsinki, married, two children (ages 6 and 10). One spouse earns all the income.

Tax computation

Income from employment

	National tax	Municipal and other tax
Gross employment income, 2001	FIM 435,000	FIM 435,000
Less—Itemized deductions:		
Standard deduction	2,700	2,700
Compulsory pension premium (4.5%)	19,575	19,575
Compulsory unemployment insurance premium (0.7%)	3,045	3,045
Taxable income	FIM 409,680	FIM 409,680
National income tax:		
On first 325,000	FIM 66,850	—
37% on remaining 84,680	31,332	—
Municipal income tax—16.5% (Helsinki)	—	67,597
Church tax—1% (Helsinki)	—	4,097
Sickness insurance premium—1.5%	—	6,145
	FIM 98,182	FIM 77,839
Total tax on income from employment		FIM 176,021

Income from capital

Capital gain	FIM 50,000
Rental income	10,000
	60,000
Less—Interest paid	15,000
Total capital income	FIM 45,000
Capital income tax at 29%	FIM 13,060

Computation II

Calculation of estimated tax for the year 2001

Assumptions

Resident with Finnish social security.

Tax computation

Income from employment

Income:		
A. Cash salary		FIM 435,000
B. Fringe benefits		0
C. Total		FIM 435,000
Deductions:		
Standard deduction (maximum, 2,700)	2,700	
Travel costs between home and work (in excess of 3,000)	0	
Other business deductions (in excess of 2,100)	0	
Compulsory pension insurance (4.5%)	19,575	
Compulsory unemployment insurance (0.7%)	3,045	
Voluntary pension insurance contributions	0	25,320
		FIM 409,680

	Municipal	State
Taxable income:		
Earned income	FIM 409,680	FIM 409,680
Less—Earned-income deduction	0	—
Less—Basic deduction	0	—
Taxable income	FIM 409,680	FIM 409,680
Taxes:		
Municipal income tax—16.5% (Helsinki)		FIM 67,597
Church tax—1% (Helsinki)		4,097
Sickness insurance premium—1.5%		6,145
State tax (1)		98,182
		176,021
Deduction from taxes:		
Deficit compensation (28% of the amount of interest if it exceeds the amount of capital income) (2)		0
Total tax on income		FIM 176,021

Notes:

1. For the purposes of this calculation, state tax rates are the same as national tax rates.
2. Interest did not exceed capital income in 1998.
3. Exchange rate of the Finnish markka at December 31, 2000: US$1 = FIM6.38.

PwC contact

For additional information on taxation in France, contact:

Jean-Luc Pierre
Landwell & Associés
32, rue Guersant 75833 Paris Cedex 17
Telephone: (33) 1 56 57 83 92
Fax: (33) 1 56 57 21 35
e-mail: jean-luc.pierre@fr.landwellglobal.com

Significant developments

There have been no significant tax or regulatory developments as regards individual taxation in the past year.

Territoriality and residence

Individuals, whether French or foreign nationals, who have their tax domicile in France are generally subject to personal income tax on worldwide income unless excluded by a tax treaty. Individuals who are not domiciled in France (nonresidents) are subject to tax only on their income arising in France or, in certain instances, on imputed income.

Under domestic law, an individual is considered to be domiciled in France if at least one of the four criteria listed below is met.

1. The habitual abode of the person or family is in France.
2. France is the principal place of sojourn (more than 183 days in a calendar year).
3. Professional activities are carried out in France.
4. France is the center of economic interests.

Under bilateral tax treaties concluded with France, tax domicile is first determined under the law of the country that asserts the power to tax. If the individual is considered to be resident under the laws of two countries, the treaty provides "tie-breaker" provisions to determine the country of residence. These tie-breaker tests generally include as criteria, in order of importance, permanent residence, center of personal and economic relations, habitual abode, and, if none of the foregoing tests is determinative, the decision of the competent authorities.

Gross income

Employee gross income/Unless expressly excluded by tax treaty as subject to tax in another country or by domestic law, compensation earned in France and abroad by a resident is subject to French income tax, regardless of where payment is made and whether it is remitted.

Compensation includes both salary and cash allowances (e.g., cost-of-living, hardship, schooling, and home-leave allowances and income tax reimbursements) but excludes social security and pension contributions made to French and qualified foreign plans. Business expense reimbursements are not taxable. Since 1997, special concessions may be made to foreign nationals on short- or long-term assignments not exceeding six years. Exceptions may also be created either under tax treaties or pursuant to agreements negotiated with the French tax authorities for employees of headquarters operations located in France. Special relief also exists for one-time moving premiums.

Capital gains and investment income/Unless exempt under a tax treaty, capital gains arising from the sale of real property are taxable, but the tax base is reduced on the basis of the holding period. The sale of a principal residence is tax exempt.

Capital gains arising from the sale of quoted or unquoted securities, as well as of shares in SICAV and FCP, are subject to a 16% rate (plus 10% social surcharges) where the proceeds of such sales exceed €7,623 (2001 income).

If the taxpayer directly or indirectly holds 25% or more of the shares of an unquoted company and sells its shares, capital gains tax is assessed, regardless of the amount of total proceeds.

Taxable investment income consists of total income from dividends and interest actually or constructively received in a calendar year, adjusted for any related tax credits, less related investment expenses (e.g., brokers' and management fees).

For French-source dividends, individuals must add back to the cash dividend the tax credit recognized on the dividends paid by French companies, but they are entitled to deduct the tax credit from net tax payable on all income. For dividends received from tax treaty countries, the gross dividend (i.e., cash dividend received plus any withholding tax) is taxable, but a tax credit against total income is recognized. For dividends received from non–tax treaty countries, no tax credit is allowed, but only the net cash dividend is taxable. In addition income taxes dividend income is subject to social surcharges of 10% for 2001 income.

Net French-source interest income may be included in an individual tax return with other investment income; alternatively, for certain types of securities, the taxpayer may elect to have interest income taxed at flat tax rates that range from 15% to 60% (plus 10% social surcharges, depending on the nature of the underlying investment). Interest paid by a foreign company to persons having their tax domicile in France must be included in taxable income. Such interest is grossed up to include any tax credit granted pursuant to a tax treaty. All taxable interest income is also subject to 10% social surcharges.

For more details on the social surcharges and their applicability to capital gains and investment income, see below.

Deductions

Business deductions/Employees may elect either a standard 10% business expense deduction (limited to €12,229 on 2001 income) or itemized business expenses. Journalists benefit from an income tax exemption for the first €7,650 of their income.

Nonbusiness expenses/Residents may deduct their French social security, unemployment contributions, and pension contributions from gross income. Unless otherwise provided by treaty, optional contributions to foreign pension plans are not deductible.

Employees are entitled to a further 20% deduction, limited to €22,380 (2001 income).

Taxpayers may be entitled to one or more of the tax credits or general deductions shown below.

1. Limited tax credits are available for mortgage interest on principal residences (loans taken out before January 1, 1998), maintenance expenses and major repair

expenses on principal residences, insurance premiums, charitable contributions, domestic employees, students, and child care.

2. General deductions are available for support and alimony payments.

Tax credits

Unless specifically excluded by treaty, foreign-source income is taxable in France. Residents are entitled to tax credits for withholding tax paid on certain types of income from other tax treaty countries. Residents are also entitled to a tax credit (*avoir fiscal*) equal to 50% of the cash dividends paid by French companies. Foreign-source income exempt from French tax by virtue of a tax treaty is nevertheless added to income taxable in France, either to determine the French tax rate applicable to income taxable in France (exemption with progression) or to calculate gross French tax liability, from which tax paid abroad is deducted (tax credit system), depending on the applicable tax treaty.

Other taxes

Social security taxes/For 2002, the employee's share of social contributions represents approximately 18% to 23% of salary. (See also "Nonbusiness expenses.")

Wealth tax/Wealth tax is assessed on in individuals whose net wealth as at January 1, 1999, exceeds €720,000. Wealth tax rates range from 0.55% on net wealth between €720,000 and €1,160,000 to 1.8% on net wealth in excess of €15 million. French residents are subject to wealth tax on worldwide assets, while the tax base for nonresidents is limited to assets situated in France.

Wealth tax returns for calendar year 2001 must be filed by June 15, 2002. The tax is payable upon filing of the return.

Local taxes/Private occupiers of French real estate pay a local tax, known as habitation tax. Tax revenues go to some of the local government bodies (in descending order of geographical size, the departments, and communes). The tax is based on the assessed value of real estate. The assessment of the departmental portion of habitation tax is expected to be determined on prior-year income, as calculated for income tax purposes (subject to deductions from taxable income). However, it is not known at what date this modification will come into effect, because legislation concerning it has been temporarily suspended.

Tax administration

Returns/Husbands and wives must file joint returns. Separate filing status is not permitted, except under strictly limited circumstances. French residents' income tax returns are based on calendar-year income and must be filed by March 1 of the following year (however, by March 25, 2002, for 2000 calendar-year income). The total taxable income is divided into the number of shares ("parts") that reflects the taxpayer's marital status and number of dependents. Children under 18 years of age and disabled children of all ages can be claimed as dependents.

Children from the ages of 18 to 21, as well as children from the ages of 21 to 25 who are full-time students, can upon request be claimed as dependents. The tax benefit or dependent children is limited in most cases to a maximum of €2,017 (limit) for each of the first two children and €4,034 for each additional child.

Payment of tax/There is no income tax withholding from salaries, except for nonresidents deriving income from employment and professional activities in France. For nonresidents, tax at flat rates of 0%, 15%, and 25% is withheld at source. An annual income tax return is required if the income subject to withholding tax falls into the 25% withholding tax bracket.

Taxpayers must pay their current year's taxes in one of two ways: in two installments and a final payment, with each installment equal to one-third of the previous year's tax liability and the final payment equal to the excess of the actual tax liability over the two installment payments; or in monthly installments. Foreign nationals working in France for the first time normally pay their tax in September of the year following their arrival. Thereafter, they follow the standard system.

(In Euros)

			Income tax			
Total compensation	**Employee social contributions**	**Adjusted gross income**	**Single**	**Married**	**Married + 1 child (c)**	**Married + 2c**
38,112	8,025	31,192	4,132	1,910	1,208	756
41,924	8,780	34,355	5,002	2,388	1,687	985
45,735	9,535	37,518	5,936	2,867	2,165	1,463
49,546	10,289	40,682	6,870	3,421	2,643	1,942
53,357	11,806	43,845	7,804	4,127	3,121	2,420
57,168	11,799	47,009	8,738	4,833	3,600	2,898
60,980	12,554	50,172	9,672	5,539	4,125	3,377
64,791	13,309	53,336	10,653	6,246	4,831	3,855
68,602	14,065	56,499	11,718	6,951	5,537	4,333
72,413	14,819	59,663	12,783	7,658	6,243	4,828
76,225	15,627	62,826	13,847	8,364	6,949	5,534
80,036	16,328	65,990	14,983	9,202	7,655	6,240
83,847	17,083	69,153	16,184	10,136	8,361	6,946
87,658	17,838	72,317	17,385	11,070	9,067	7,653
91,470	18,593	75,480	18,587	12,004	9,987	8,359
95,281	19,348	78,644	19,789	12,983	10,921	9,065
99,092	20,102	81,807	20,990	13,871	11,854	9,837
102,903	20,857	84,970	22,191	14,805	12,788	10,771
106,714	21,582	88,164	23,404	15,748	13,731	11,714
110,526	22,199	91,466	24,658	16,722	14,705	12,688
114,337	22,816	94,837	25,938	17,717	15,700	13,683

Notes:

1. Social contribution rates are those average rates applicable to 2002 income. Income tax rates are those applicable to 2001 income.
2. The non deductible general social contribution (CSG) and contribution for reimbursement of the social debt (CRDS) surtaxes have been added to adjusted gross income.

Social surcharges/Social surcharges are applicable to various kinds of income. The total social surcharges on interest, dividends, and capital gains for 2001 are as shown below.

	%
General social contribution	7.5
Social tax	2.0
CRDS contribution	0.5
Total	10.0

The general social and CRDS contributions are discussed below.

General social contribution/A social contribution (contribution sociale généralisée) of 7.5% on employee compensation and investment income must be paid by all French-resident individuals. As a "universal" charge, it applies to all forms of gross income, including the following.

1. Employee compensation, including benefits in kind and stock option gains.
2. Pensions.
3. Income earned from independent services.
4. Investment income, including rental income, dividends, interest, and capital gains (as discussed under "Social surcharges").

The general social contribution is not deductible if assessed on income or capital gains taxed at a flat rate. 5.1% within the 7.5% overall rate is tax deductible if the general social contribution is assessed on income or capital gains taxed at graduated rates. The total 7.5% contribution is withheld directly by employers from salary. Special rules apply to foreign-source employee compensation. A separate tax bill is issued for CSG on investment income, based on the individual's annual tax return.

Contribution for reimbursement of the social debt/Since February 1, 1996, a social fax of 0.5% called the CRDS (contribution au remboursement de la dette sociale) has been levied on ail French residents on most categories of income (including foreign-paid compensation) and is also not deductible for fax purposes. This additional surtax is expected to remain in force for 18 years.

INDIVIDUAL TAX CALCULATION

2001

Assumptions

Resident employee, married with two children under age 18 (one in middle school (*college*) and one in high school (*lycée*)). The employee earned €121,960 net income in 2001, received €3,050 in U.K. dividend income, paid €1,525 of qualified life insurance premiums, and made support payments to his parents (in financial need) of €2,287, for which he has the receipts. He sold listed shares for €53,357 and realized an €2,134 net capital gain.

Tax computation

Net salary (after deduction of social security)		€ 121,960.0
Less—Standard deductions:		
Business expense deduction—10% (maximum 12,229)	12,196.0	
Standard deduction—20% (maximum 22,380)	21,953.0	34,149.0
Taxable salary		87,811.0
Add:		
U.K. dividends	3,050.0	
Less—Withholding tax: 15%	(457.5)	
Net amount	2,592.5	
Tax credit—17,000 x 18%	467.0	3,059.5
Total taxable income		90,870.5
Less—Support payments to parents		2,287.0
Taxable income after deductions		€ 88,583.5
Tax thereon:		
Income tax on 88,583.5 (3 shares) (1)		€ 22,750.0
Tax on capital gains (16% x 2,134)		341.5
Total income and capital gains tax		23,091.5
Less:		
Life insurance payments (total – 1,525; maximum allowed—910 (610 + 150 per child) x 25%)	227.5	
Student reduction (61 for middle school, 153 for high school)	214.0	(441.5)
Net tax due before tax credits:		22,650.0
Social tax on dividends and capital gains—2% x (3,059.5 + 2,134)		104.0
General social contribution—7.5% x (3,059.5 + 2,134) (2)		389.5
CRDS—0.5% x (3,059.5 x 2,134)		26.0
Less—Tax credits on dividends		(467.0)
Total net income tax		€ 22,702.5

Notes:

1. The method of calculating a household's income tax liability is first to calculate the tax for two shares and then to calculate the tax for the actual number of shares, including the children. If the difference between the two calculations exceeds €2,017 2001 income) for each of the first two children or €4,034 for each additional child, then maximum tax reduction per child is limited to €2,017 for each of the first two children and €4,034 for each additional child. If the amount per child is less than €2,017 for each of the first two children or €4,034 for each additional child, the actual amount is used in the calculation.
2. The general social contribution rate applicable to gross income is 7.5%. An additional CRDS tax of 0.5% is also payable on this amount, as well as on taxable income after deductions.
3. Exchange rate of the Euro at January 3, 2002: US$1 = €1.106.

PwC contact

For additional information on taxation in Gabon, contact:

Christophe Relongoue
Price Waterhouse/Fidafrica
B.P. 2164
Libreville, Gabon
Telephone: (241) 76 23 71
Fax: (241) 76 59.53
e-mail: christophe.relongoue@ga.pwcglobal.com

Significant developments

There have been no significant tax or regulatory developments regarding individual taxation in the past year.

Territoriality and residence

Gabon taxes its citizens and residents on their worldwide income from whatever source, subject to the application of international tax treaties. Individuals with no tax domicile in Gabon (nonresidents) are subject to tax only on income arising from Gabon.

Individuals are deemed to have their tax domicile in Gabon if they have either their place of abode or their principal place of residence in Gabon.

The basis of the personal income tax covers the taxpayer's total net income earned during a calendar year (January 1 to December 31).

Total net income is made up of the total of net incomes from the following categories:

- Property income.
- Handicraft, industrial and commercial profits.
- Noncommercial profits.
- Agricultural profits.
- Salaries and wages.
- Transferable securities income.

Tax is assessed on the head of the family for his own and his wife's income and for the income of his dependent children. It is strictly forbidden for companies to take in charge the personal tax of their employees.

Gross income

Employee gross income/Taxable income includes all cash remuneration, benefits in kind and bonuses. Benefits in kind, such as housing, electricity and water supply and domestic servants, are taxable according to a schedule of deemed values. Housing allowance is limited to 40% of monthly gross income, with a maximum of CFAF250,000 per month. Transportation allowance is nontaxable up to CFAF100,000 per month.

Capital gains and investment income/Gains on disposals of fixed assets are tax free. Dividends, interest from certificates of deposit and directors' fees are subject to a withholding tax. Residents must include the net amount received from dividends and directors' fees in taxable income (for nonresidents, withholding tax is a final tax). Withholding tax on CD interest is final for both residents and nonresidents.

Applicable rates are as follows.

	%
Dividends	20
Directors' fees	22
CD interest	15

Deductions

Business deductions/The deemed value of professional expenses (net taxable salary x 20%) is deductible in determining total taxable income (maximum, CFAF10 million). Alternatively, it is theoretically possible to deduct the exact and duly justified amount of professional expenses incurred (auto expenses essentially). However, this is never done in practice.

Nonbusiness expenses/Allowable deductions are shown below.

1. Social security (CNSS) contribution paid for housekeeper.
2. Retirement pension contribution—up to 10% of net taxable salary less professional expenses.
3. Life insurance premiums—up to 5% of net taxable salary less professional expenses.
4. Maintenance allowance.
5. Complementary tax on wages (TCS) (see below).
6. Loan interest for purchase/building of principal residence—up to CFAF6 million per year.

Personal allowances/The number of a taxpayer's dependents is taken into account in the income tax progressive schedule (taxpayer, 1 share; spouse, 1 share; each child, 0.5 share).

Tax credits

Unless specifically excluded by tax treaty, foreign-source income is taxable in Gabon. Taxes paid in the country of origin on this income are creditable for Gabon tax purposes if Gabon has a tax treaty with that country.

Other taxes

Social security taxes/Employers must pay 22.6% of gross salary to social security (up to a limit of monthly salary CFAF1,500,000), of which 20.1% is the employer contribution and 2.5% is withheld from salary.

Local taxes on income/No local taxes are levied on income.

Complementary tax/This tax affects employees who earn at least CFAF65,000 per month. For these taxpayers, all wages, fees, allowances, and public and private salaries are subject to the tax. Tax is imposed at the rates shown under "Tax rates"; it is deductible in determining taxable income.

Tax administration

Returns/Employers must file salary tax returns showing individual tax withheld. Adjusting declarations are filed by January 31 each year. Employees must file a personal tax return by February 28 of each year. Joint filing is required except in cases of pending divorce proceedings. The tax year is the calendar year.

Payment of tax/Withheld individual taxes are to be remitted by the 25th of each month for the preceding month. Personal returns are for information purposes; a later assessment is raised. Any tax not covered by salary withholding is paid upon receipt of a notice of assessment from the Tax Inspector.

Tax rates

Wages and salary tax/Tax is computed on taxable income as determined from a tax scale and is based on the "share" system. Tax rates range from 0 to 50%.

Complementary tax/Tax is calculated on net revenue, that is, salary plus benefits in kind less CNSS. Complementary tax is levied at the rates shown below.

	%
For the part of salary under or equal to 100,000 per month	1.0
For the part of salary over 100,000 per month	5.5

INDIVIDUAL TAX CALCULATION

2001 salary

Assumptions

Resident employee, married, two children (number of shares: 3).

Tax computation

Annual basic salary		CFAF 26,000,000
Benefits in kind (deemed value)		
(26,000,000 – 540,000) x 11%		2,800,600
		28,800,600
Less*:*		
Social security	450,000	
Complementary tax on wages	1,554,783	2,004,783
Professional expenses (deemed value)	5,359,163	5,359,163
Net taxable salary		21,436,654
Deductible charges:		
Loan interest (purchase of principal residence)	1,730,000	
Pension contribution	1,500,000	
Life insurance premiums	800,000	4,030,000
Net taxable income		CFAF 17,406,654
2001 income tax (3 shares) (1)		CFAF 2,809,996

Notes:

1. For a single taxpayer (1 share), income tax on net taxable income would be CFAF5,353,994 in 2001.
2. Exchange rate of the CFA franc at January 1, 2002: US$1 = CFAF775.00.

PwC contact

For additional information on taxation in Germany, contact:

Hans-Jürgen Heise
PricewaterhouseCoopers GmbH
Marie-Curie-Str. 24-28
D–60439 Frankfurt (Main), Germany
Telephone: (49) (69) 95856 432
Fax: (49) (69) 95856107 (Zentrale)
Fax (49) (69) 95856 307
e-mail: hans-juergen.heise@de.pwcglobal.com

Significant developments

Since January 1, 2002, only 50% of dividends paid to resident individuals has to be recognized as taxable income, albeit with no corporation tax imputation credit attached to the dividend.

As a result of the German tax reform, the top marginal tax rate was reduced to 48.5% for 2001 and 2002. Including the 5.5% solidarity surcharge, this leads to a combined top marginal rate of 51.17%. The top marginal tax will be further reduced to 47% for 2003 and 2004 and 42% for 2005 and thereafter. The 5.5% solidarity surcharge will most likely stay in place and must be considered accordingly.

For 2002, the employee monthly contribution to social security and unemployment taxes is limited to a maximum of €576 for an annual maximum of €6,912.

As of January 1, 2002, the employee monthly contribution to old-age medicare insurance is limited to a maximum of €29.

Territoriality and residence

All resident individuals are taxed on their worldwide income. Generally, individuals are deemed to be resident if they are physically present in Germany for more than six months in any one calendar year or for a consecutive period of six months over a year-end. Nonresident individuals are taxed (usually by withholding) on German-source income only.

Contrary provisions in double taxation treaties override German national law unless the latter is more favorable (from the German tax point of view only) to the taxpayer.

Nationality is not of itself a criterion for determining residence or tax liability, although it may serve as an indicator of residence in (unusual) cases of doubt.

Gross income

Employee gross income/Taxable compensation includes all remuneration, allowances and benefits-in-kind given to or provided for an employee. Benefits-in-kind are valued, in principle, at cost to the employer, although there are some cases of global allocations (mainly cars), mostly for administrative simplicity. Certain minor benefits-in-kind (such as annual employee outings) are not taxed. Reimbursement of an employee's relocation costs to Germany is not a taxable benefit, provided certain (basically adequate) limits are observed. There are no special concessions for foreigners.

Capital gains and investment income/Long-term capital gains are tax-exempt, while 50% of short-term gains totaling more than €511 are added to an individual's taxable income. The time limits for long-term gains are 10 years for land and buildings and 12 months for securities and other assets.

Special rules apply to the taxation of capital gains from the sale of a significant interest (1% or more) in a business.

Investment income is part of an individual's total income for tax purposes. It qualifies for an "investor's allowance" of €1,550 per taxpayer and a global deduction of €51 for related expenses, but otherwise does not lead to any special concessions. These amounts are doubled in the case of married taxpayers filing jointly.

If German-source interest and investment income exceeds the above-mentioned investor's allowance, interest and surcharge withholding tax of 26.375% is automatically withheld at source. The withholding tax is treated as a payment on account of the final income tax liability.

Short-term capital gains and investment income from abroad are taxed under normal German rules, subject to the provisions of the relevant double taxation treaty. If, under the treaty, they cannot be taxed in Germany, they are taken into account when determining the tax rate to be applied to taxable income.

Deductions

Business deductions/Various properly documented and necessarily incurred business expenses may be deducted by an individual unless they are reimbursed by the employer. This includes the cost of traveling to and from work, business literature, business subscriptions, and professional dues. There is a blanket employee allowance for business deductions of €1,044 per annum. To the extent actual employment-connected expenses exceed the lump sum of €1,044, they are deductible if they can be substantiated.

Nonbusiness expenses/Social security contributions and insurance premiums can be deducted up to specified limits. Mortgage interest is deductible but only against income from the property. Tax advisers' fees are fully deductible, as is church tax (see "Church tax"). Contributions to German charities and certain international charities are deductible up to 5% of adjusted gross income. For contributions for scientific purposes, the percentage is increased by another 5%. Contributions to political parties up to a total of €1,534 per annum are also deductible (€3,068 for married taxpayers filing jointly).

Personal allowances/The allowances shown below are deductible in computing gross income.

	Per annum €
Child allowance—Per child registered in Germany	3,648
Additional special allowance to dependent children under 16 years of age	2,160
Employee allowance	1,044

An educational allowance of €924 per child is allowed for dependent children registered in Germany but attending school away from home.

There are also a number of other specific allowances and reliefs, for example, for the elderly and the disabled.

Tax credits

Foreign withholding taxes on passive income from abroad are usually credited against the applicable German income tax unless the relevant tax treaty specifies otherwise. No credit is given for underlying income tax, and unused credit cannot, for passive income, be carried forward or applied to income from a third country.

Other taxes

Social security taxes/The employee's portion of German social tax contributions (social security and unemployment tax) is limited to €576 per month on amounts up to €4,500 per month) for a maximum annual contribution of €6,912. The employer must contribute an equal amount. Contributions covering sickness insurance are not compulsory for employees earning over €3,375 monthly.

An old-age medicare insurance contribution is payable by the employee and the employer in equal amounts. The employee contribution is limited to €29 per month (0.85% on amounts up to €3,375 per month).

Social security contributions and insurance premiums are deductible from adjusted gross income up to specified limits.

Church tax/Members of officially recognized churches pay church tax as a surcharge on their income tax. The rates are either 8% or 9%, depending on the state of Germany where the individual is resident.

Income tax surcharge/To improve the economic situation and infrastructure in the five new eastern states of Germany, the German government is levying a 5.5% income tax surcharge for an indefinite period. The surcharge is imposed as a percentage on all individual income taxes.

Local taxes on income/There are no local taxes applicable to employees.

Tax administration

Returns/Resident husbands and wives file joint returns unless they are legally separated or one spouse requests otherwise. The income is split for all purposes, including the calculation of allowances. The tax year is the calendar year.

Payment of tax/Payment of tax on salary and employment benefits is by withholding. The amounts withheld are treated as a payment on account of the final income tax liability. If taxpayers have other income, they will usually be asked to make quarterly payments on account, on the basis of final liability as determined by the most recent final assessment.

Tax rates

2002

Single taxpayer

Taxable income From	Taxable income To	Tax rate
0	€ 7,235	0
€ 7,236	9,251	19.9%
9,252	55,007	At geometrically progressive rates
55,008		48.5% less €9,872

Married taxpayer

Taxable income From	Taxable income To	Tax rate
0	€ 14,471	0
€ 14,472	18,502	19.9%
18,503	110,015	At geometrically progressive rates
110,016		48.5% less €19,744

2003/2004

Single taxpayer

Taxable income From	Taxable income To	Tax rate
0	€ 7,426	0
€ 7,427	12,755	19.9%
12,756	52,292	At geometrically progressive rates
52,293		47% less €9,232

Married taxpayer

Taxable income From	Taxable income To	Tax rate
0	€ 14,852	0
€ 14,853	25,510	19.9%
25,511	104,585	At geometrically progressive rates
104,586		47% less €18,464

INDIVIDUAL TAX CALCULATION

Calendar year 2002

Assumptions

Resident husband and wife, no religious affiliation, two children under 16 years of age.

Tax computation

Annual gross salary	100,000	
Less—Employment allowance or higher itemized business expenses	1,044	€ 98,956
Interest income (1,000)	1,000	
Dividend income (5,000, of which 50% is taxable)	2,500	
Less—Investor's allowance	(3,202)	298
Short-term capital gain	511	
Less—Exempt amount	(511)	0
		99,254
Less:		
Lump sum for social security and life insurance premiums	4,002	
Tax advisor's fee	1,500	5,502
Less—Child allowances (two)		11,616
Taxable income		€ 82,136
Income tax at joint return rates		€ 21,160
Less—Withholding tax on German investment income in excess of tax-free amounts		(75)
		21,085
Surcharge		1,160
Total tax payable		€ 22,245

Note:

Exchange rate of the Euro at January 3, 2002: US$1 = €1.106.

Ghana

PwC contact

For additional information on taxation in Ghana, contact:

Charles Egan
PricewaterhouseCoopers
PMB CT 42
Cantonments, Accra, Ghana
Telephone: (233) (21) 506217/8
Fax: (233) (21) 506216
e-mail: charles.a.egan@gh.pwcglobal.com

General note

This entry is repeated from the 2001/2002 edition. For more up-to-date information, consult the contact listed above or Mark Friedlich at mark.friedlich@us.pwcglobal.com.

Significant developments

There have been no significant tax or regulatory developments in the past year.

Territoriality and residence

Ghana taxes its resident individuals on any of the following income accruing in, derived from, brought into, or received in Ghana.

1. Gains or profits from trade, business, profession, or vocation.
2. Gains or profits from any employment, including any allowances or benefits paid in cash or given in kind to or on behalf of an employee other than in respect of medical or dental cost, or any passage from or to Ghana.
3. Dividends.
4. Any charge or annuity.
5. Royalties, premiums, and any other profits arising from property, including rents from immovable property, except with the first five years of completion of the property.
6. Receipts including royalties or periodic or deferred payments of any kind derived from any transaction wherever and whenever made, affecting directly or indirectly, and/or from any natural resources in Ghana, and notwithstanding whether the receipts are paid within or outside Ghana.

An individual is resident for tax purposes if that individual is one of the following.

1. A citizen of Ghana and present in Ghana for a period or periods equal in total to 183 days or more in any year beginning January 1.
2. An employee or official of the government of Ghana posted abroad during the year.
3. A Ghanaian who is temporarily absent from Ghana for a period not exceeding 365 continuous days, where that Ghanaian has a permanent home in Ghana.

Nonresidents are liable to Ghanaian income tax at the rate of 20% on any income derived in Ghana from any trade, business, profession, or vocation or which derives from an employment exercised in Ghana. This rate applies to income earned by a nonresident individual who has stayed in Ghana for a period or periods amounting to less than 183 days in a particular year.

Gross income

Employee gross income/Total emoluments paid to an employee or on the employee's behalf are included in the chargeable income of the employee for any year of assessment. All fixed cash allowances for housing and entertainment are taxable, but reimbursements for expenses actually incurred exclusively on behalf of and for the benefit of the employer are not taxable to the employee.

Chargeable income also includes any benefit derived from the use of a motor vehicle, furnishing, or accommodation provided by the employer. There are no concessions for foreigners.

Capital gains and investment income/A capital gains tax is payable by every person on any capital gains accruing or derived from the realization of any chargeable asset, including buildings of a permanent or temporary nature; business and business assets, including goodwill; land other than agricultural land; any right or interest in, to, or over any stocks and shares; and any assets declared as chargeable by a legislative instrument. The applicable rate is 10% on gains in excess of GHC500,000, regardless of the period for which the asset was held prior to disposal.

Withholding tax on interest income for individuals has been abolished.

Nonresidents are subject to a final withholding tax of 10% on any dividend income paid to them by a resident.

Deductions

Business deductions/Expenses of a private or domestic nature are generally not deductible. For all individuals other than employees, all outgoings and expenses incurred wholly, exclusively, and necessarily, in the production of the income that is subject to tax are deductible. These include the following.

1. Interest on money borrowed and employed in acquiring the income.
2. Rent payable on land or buildings occupied for the purpose of acquiring the income.
3. Repairs and maintenance expenses for premises, plant, machinery, etc., employed in acquiring the income.
4. Local rates and taxes on premises.
5. Bad debts.
6. Losses incurred.

No blanket or standard deductions are allowed.

Nonbusiness expenses/Apart from social security contributions, qualifying insurance premiums, and donations, no nonbusiness expenses are deductible, and no standard deductions are allowed.

Personal allowances/The tax-free threshold from January 1, 2001, is GHC1,200,000. In addition, there is an allowance of GHC300,000 for a married man, a married woman maintaining her husband and household, and an unmarried man or woman with two or more dependent children. Disabled persons (self-employed or employees) are allowed a tax-free deduction of 25% of the assessable income from any business or employment accruing to them. There is an old-age relief of GHC300,000, deductible from the total income of a self-employed individual or employee who is more than 60 years old. A children's education relief of GHC240,000 per child in a registered secondary school in Ghana is granted. This is restricted to three children and is claimable by one parent only. Persons who support aged relatives are granted a relief of GHC200,000 in respect of each, for a maximum of two such relatives. A relief of GHC500,000 is given in the case of professional, technical, or vocational training. All residents are entitled to these reliefs.

Tax credits

There are no tax credits available to short-term residents.

For both residents and nonresidents who have had tax withheld from any income received by them, there is a tax credit against their tax payable to the full amount of any such tax withheld.

Other taxes

Social security taxes/Social security contributions are 5% and 12.5% of basic salary for employees and employers, respectively. They are deductible for tax purposes.

Local taxes on income/There are no local income taxes.

Tax administration

Returns/There is no joint filing for husband and wife. A tax year other than the calendar year is not permitted.

Payment of tax/Every employer is required to make monthly deductions of tax from the total emoluments of each employee in accordance with regulations made under the law.

Tax rates

The following rates of tax are in effect from January 1, 2001.

Chargeable income		Tax on Column 1	Percentage on excess
Over (Column 1)	Not over		
0	GHC 1,200,000	—	0
GHC 1,200,000	2,400,000	—	5
2,400,000	5,400,000	GHC 60,000	10
5,400,000	24,000,000	360,000	15
24,000,000	48,000,000	3,150,000	20
48,000,000		7,950,000	30

The above rates are applicable only to residents.

INDIVIDUAL TAX CALCULATION

Year ending December 31, 2001

Assumptions

Resident husband and wife; two children in approved educational institution. (Neither the wife nor the children have any separate income.) Husband is provided with fully furnished accommodations and use of an official car with driver and fuel. Income includes salary of GHC131,200,000 (equivalent of approximately US$19,294 at GHC6,800 = US$1) and GHC500,000 gross interest.

Tax computation

Basic salary		GHC 131,200,000
Less—Employee's contribution to social security fund (5% of basic salary)		6,560,000
		124,640,000
Add:		
Rent element (15% of basic salary)	19,680,000	
Car element (15% of basic salary) (1)	3,600,000	23,280,000
		147,920,000
Less—Reliefs:		
Married	300,000	
Children's education	480,000	780,000
Chargeable income		GHC 147,140,000
Tax thereon:		
On first 48,000,000	7,950,000	
On remaining 99,140,000 at 30%	29,742,000	
Tax payable		GHC 37,692,000

Notes:

1. Restricted to GHC300,000 per month, that is, GHC3,600,000 per year.
2. Exchange rate of the cedi at December 31, 2000: US$1 = GHC6,800.00.

PwC contact

For additional information on taxation in Greece, contact:

Dimitris Varvaritis
PricewaterhouseCoopers Business Solutions SA
268 Kifisias Avenue
152 32 Halandri
Athens, Greece
Telephone: (30) (10) 6874 548
Fax: (30) (10) 6874 444
e-mail: diimitris.varvaritis@gr.pwcglobal.com

Significant developments

The final phase of European Monetary Union (EMU) commenced on January 1, 2002, when all the states of the Euro area replaced their national currency with the Euro as the standard currency. Therefore Greece, as a Euro zone country, replaced its national currency (drachma) with the Euro on January 1, 2002.

Effective January 1, 2002 the stamp tax of 1.2% (employee's share 0.6% and employer's share 0.6%) on gross salary was abolished.

Effective for income earned as from January 1, 2002 the brackets of taxable income of the personal tax scale changed. The first tax-free bracket increased to €7,400 (€13,206 for individuals who live permanently on islands with fewer than 3,100 inhabitants) and the (last) bracket (€50,033) was abolished after the elimination of the 42.5% (maximum) rate (see below). The last bracket is now up to €23,400.

The maximum rate of the personal tax scale decreased from 42.5% for income earned in the year 2001 to 40% for income earned in the year 2002 and thereafter.

Territoriality and residence

Subject to relevant tax treaty provisions, income tax is payable by all individuals earning income in Greece, regardless of citizenship or place of permanent residence. Permanent residents are taxed on their worldwide income. Individuals residing in Greece under certain circumstances indicating intent to remain permanently are considered permanent residents, but this intent must be apparent from objective evidence.

Gross income

Employee gross income/Nonresident aliens are taxed on salary earned for work performed in Greece, regardless of where payment is made and regardless of whether it is remitted. They are not taxed to the extent their compensation relates to services performed outside Greece.

All fringe benefits are normally considered taxable income to the employee. However, company-provided housing and furniture given to executives could be considered in the tax courts as nontaxable income. Similarly, tuition for children could also be considered nontaxable income.

Capital gains and investment income/Capital gains derived from sales of any rights connected with the operations of a business (sole trader), such as the right of leasing or subleasing, trademarks or patents and similar rights, are subject to income tax at 30% (25% on any lump-sum collected by the lessor from the lessee over and above the rentals of land and buildings). Realized goodwill, including gains on a business (sole trader) sold as a whole, is subject to income tax at a 20% rate.

Dividends paid to shareholders are not taxed in their names because the underlying profits have already been taxed in the name of the distributing corporation. Exemption is applicable to dividends from mutual funds and investment companies.

Interest on deposits of any kind with local banks is subject to a 15% income tax withheld at source. Interest on government treasury bills and bonds issued after December 31, 1997 is subject to a10% income tax withheld at source (7.5% for those issued within the period from January 1 through December 31, 1997). Effective January 1, 1999 interest earned from Greek government bonds by nonresidents is exempt from taxation (formerly 10%).

Gains earned by private individuals and sole traders (not keeping double-entry accounting records) on the sale of shares listed on the Athens Stock Exchange are not taxable. Effective January 1, 1999 and thereafter, gains from the sale of shares listed on a foreign stock exchange or other internationally recognized exchange are also exempt from capital gains tax. A 5% transfer tax is levied on the shares' real value when private individuals and sole traders, Greek or foreign, transfer shares not listed on the Athens Stock Exchange. Income earned from contracts or transactions on derivatives of financial products is subject to a withholding tax of 15%, provided that the beneficiary is a resident of Greece and is not an entrepreneur that keeps double-entry accounting records. This withholding tax (7.5%, 10%, 15%, or 20%) terminates the income tax liability for such income.

Deductions

Business deductions/As a general rule there are no business deductions allowable, because business-related expenses would be reimbursed by the employer.

Nonbusiness expenses/Deductible nonbusiness expenses must be supported by official invoices or receipts or by certificates.

The following are the main instances of nonbusiness expenses that can be deducted from the employee's gross income to arrive at taxable income.

1. Medical and hospitalization expenses under the following conditions:
    a. If the total amount of the family taxable income is up to €29,350, the total amount of medical and hospitalization expenses is deductible;
    b. For income up to €44,000, 50% of the expenses exceeding €29,350 is deductible. For income higher than €44,000 the deduction is limited to €36,675 (100% of expenses up to €29,350, plus 50% of expenses from €29,350 to €44,000). The amount of medical and hospitalization expenses of each spouse is deducted from his or her income. If the respective spouse's income is less than the deduction claimed and the total amount of the expenses is higher than the total family income and over €29,350, the deductible amount is divided between the spouses on the basis of the amount of their respective taxable income.
2. The amount of annual main residence rental. If this amount is up to €440, it is deductible in full; if it exceeds €440, 40% of it is deductible, but the deductible amount can neither be higher than €740 nor lower than €440. In addition, the amount of annual rental the taxpayer pays for children studying in recognized Greek or foreign schools operating in Greece is deductible; if this amount is up to €440, it is deductible in full; if it exceeds €440, 40% of it is deductible, but the

deductible amount can neither be higher than €740 nor lower than €440 per child.

3. Life and accident insurance premiums. If this amount is up to €440, it is deductible in full; if it exceeds €440, 40% of it is deductible, but the deductible amount can neither be higher than €740 nor lower than €440.
4. The annual amount paid for private lessons at home or tutorial schools. If this amount is up to €440, it is deductible in full; if it exceeds €440, 40% of it is deductible, but the deductible amount can neither be higher than €740 nor lower than €440 per person (taxpayer, children).
5. The amount paid for the purchase of computer hardware, its peripherals that constitute a single unit and training software as well as expenses for access to the Internet. If this amount is up to €440, it is deductible in full; if it exceeds €440, 40% of it is deductible, but the deductible amount can neither be higher than €740 nor lower than €440.
6. 25% of the amount paid for the purchase of parts of domestic mutual funds that have invested their assets in shares or in both shares and other securities. The deductible amount cannot exceed €3,650. This amount is deducted from the total declared income of the taxpayer in the third year after their purchase.
7. Accrued interest on mortgage housing loans from banks and certain other credit organizations for the purchase of a main residence. If the surface area of the main residence exceeds 120 square meters, the deductible amount is limited to the portion corresponding to 120 square meters (effective for loans concluded from January 1, 2000 and thereafter).
8. 30% of the total amount of annual family expenses for purchases of goods and services in general, excluding the following:
   a. Expenses for purchases of food and beverages and fuel in general;
   b. Expenses for water supply, sewage, transportation, electric power supply, insurance premiums, and circulation tax of private automobiles, as well as tuition fees to private schools; and
   c. Expenses that are deductible on the basis of other regulations. The deductible amount for both spouses cannot exceed €900. This amount is apportioned between the spouses on the basis of the income declared by each spouse. For each spouse the reduction of tax cannot be higher than 15% of the deductible amount (i.e., not higher than €135 in total for both spouses).
9. The following donations are deductible:
   a. Immovable property and amounts in cash to the state, municipalities and communities, and churches;
   b. Medical machinery and ambulances to hospitals;
   c. Cash to institutions aiming at the general public benefit, associations, etc.; and
   d. Sponsorships of an amount up to 10% of total taxable income to nonprofit legal entities aiming at cultural purposes.

If the total aggregate amount of donations and sponsorships to be deducted from the taxpayer's income exceeds €2,950 for any donee, the taxpayer (donor) must withhold income tax at the rate of 10% on the amount of the donation or sponsorship over €2,950. This withholding must be paid to the tax authorities by the due date for filing the annual income tax return, and the original receipt must be attached to the annual income tax return filed with the tax authorities.

Personal allowances/No allowances are available for individual taxation.

Tax credits

Income tax paid in a foreign country is deductible from Greek tax but only on reported income earned abroad and up to the applicable Greek income tax.

For those taxpayers who have dependent children, the amount of tax computed on the basis of the scale shown under "Tax rates" is reduced by the following tax credits.

1. One child: €90.
2. Two children: €105 for each child.
3. Three children: €205 for each child.
4. Four children: €240 for each child.

   This amount increases by €30 for each additional child after the fourth child (e.g., €270 for each child when there are five children; €300 for each child when there are six children; and so on).

For those taxpayers who perform employee services and live for at least nine months of the year in border areas, these amounts are increased by €30 for each dependent child.

Other taxes

Social security taxes/Employee contributions to social security are computed at the rate of 15.9% on monthly gross salary, currently up to a salary limit of €1,884.75 (effective January 1, 2002), 14 times annually. As from January 1, 1993 the ceiling does not apply to those employees who are insured for the first time with social security funds in Greece. However, the social security ceiling is valid for the following, inter alia, persons: Greek and foreign persons who have been insured up to December 31, 1992 in any member state of the EU; and those persons who have been insured before January 1, 1993 in countries with which Greece has signed a social security totalization treaty, or with which there is a treaty signed but not yet ratified, or with which a treaty has been initialed. Employee social security contributions are withheld by the employer.

Social security payments are deductible in determining net taxable income as shown in the tax calculation.

Stamp tax/There is a stamp tax of 0.6% on gross salary. This is withheld by the employer and is a deductible expense for the taxpayer. Effective January 1, 2002 the stamp tax of 1.2% (employee's share 0.6% and employer's share 0.6%) on gross salary was abolished.

Share transfer tax/A 5% transfer tax is levied when private individuals and sole traders (Greek or foreign) transfer shares not listed on the Athens Stock Exchange. The tax of 5% is calculated on the real value of the shares transferred as this is defined by a decision of the Minister of Finance.

A 0.3% tax (increased to 0.6% for sales made from October 8, 1999 and decreased again to 0.3% for sales of shares made from January 1, 2001 and thereafter) is imposed on sales of shares listed on the Athens Stock Exchange. This tax is calculated on the sales value of shares as shown in the table prepared by the brokerage company and is borne by the seller (individuals, regardless of citizenship or place of permanent residence) of the shares. This is effective for sales of shares on the Athens Stock Exchange as from February 19, 1998. Effective January 1, 1999 and thereafter, the

0.6% transaction tax (0.3% for sales of shares made from January 1, 2001 and thereafter) is also imposed on the sales of shares listed on a foreign stock exchange or other internationally recognized exchange made by Greek residents.

Mobile telephone subscribers' duty/Effective from February 1, 1998 a duty is imposed on all subscribers of mobile telephone companies. This duty is calculated monthly and ranges from €1.5 to €6 per month, depending on the value of the subscriber's account.

Local taxes on income/No local taxes are imposed.

Tax administration

Returns/Husband and wife are obligated to file a joint tax return, but the income of each spouse is taxed separately. However, the taxable income of one spouse from a business that is financially dependent on the other spouse is added to the taxable income of the other spouse. Taxable income of minor children is added, with certain exceptions, to the parent who declares the higher total income. If the parents declare equal amounts of total income, the income of minor children is added to the father's taxable income. If there is no father, the income is added to the mother's. No taxable years other than the calendar year are permitted.

Payment of tax/Income tax is withheld from salaries. Generally, if the taxpayer has income not subject to tax withholding, a tax prepayment of 55% on the current year's income tax is assessed by the tax authorities and is paid together with the balance, if any, of the previous year's income tax liability in three bimonthly installments, starting from the last working day of the month following the assessment. If the tax is assessed in August or September of the fiscal year, it is payable in two equal bimonthly installments, starting from the last working day of the month following the assessment. If the tax is assessed in October of the fiscal year and thereafter, the tax is payable in a lump sum by the last working day of the second month following the assessment. If the entire amount of tax due is paid in a lump sum within the time due for the first installment, a discount of 2.5% is given if the number of acceptable installments had been three. Furthermore when the income tax return is filed by electronic means through Internet an additional discount of 2.5% of the total amount due is given.

The withholding tax on salaries, pensions and wages is calculated on the amount of monthly salary after being reduced by the employee share of social security contributions and stamp tax, multiplied by 14 (12 monthly salaries, plus one monthly salary for Christmas bonus, one-half monthly salary for Easter bonus and one-half monthly salary for vacation bonus). This amount constitutes the employee's annual net salary before income tax. The annual withholding income tax is calculated on the basis of the personal income tax scale shown below (see "Tax rates").

The amount of tax computed is reduced by the amounts shown under "Tax credits", which depend on the family status of the employee/pensioner concerned.

The amount of tax that remains after these reductions (credits) constitutes the income tax levied on the annual salary of the employee. This amount is further reduced by 2.5%, and the balance constitutes the income tax that must be withheld on an annual basis. The employer must withhold 1/14 of this amount each month from the employee's salary. The same amount of tax must be withheld from the Christmas bonus, while 1/2 (i.e., 1/28 of the annual tax) is the amount of tax that must be withheld from both the Easter and the vacation bonus. Those paid through a daily wage who render services on the basis of a defined contract with a duration of less than one year are subject to a withholding tax rate of 3% for a daily wage over €24. Overtime pay, bonuses, allowances, and additional benefits of any kind, as well as retroactive income, are subject to withholding tax at the rate of 20%. As from January 1, 1998 the withholding tax is further reduced by 2.5% (i.e., 19.5% is the effective rate).

Tax withholding on salaries of civil aviation flying staff for services rendered on the aircraft is computed at the rate of 10% on remuneration earned in calendar year 1997, 12.5% on remuneration earned in calendar year 1998 and 15% on remuneration earned in calendar year 1999 and thereafter. In addition, a contribution in favor of the Farmers' Social Security Fund (OGA) is imposed, which is calculated at the rate of 10% on the amount of tax up to €177 and at the rate of 15% on the amount of tax over €177.

Withholding tax on salaries of merchant marine officers and lower staff is computed at the rates of 6% for officers and 3% for lower staff on remuneration earned in calendar year 2002 and thereafter. This is applicable irrespective of whether they are paid in foreign or local currency. Contribution in favor of the OGA has been abolished as of December 8, 1999.

Annual income tax withholding on salaries, wages and pensions is set off against the final income tax assessed on the basis of the individual income tax return. Any amounts withheld in excess of the annual income tax assessed are refunded.

Tax rates

Income tax on individual net income and on the corresponding nontaxable amount is calculated according to the table below.

Taxable income		Tax on	Percentage
Over	Not over	Column 1	on excess
(Column 1)			
0	€ 7,400	—	0
€ 7,400	8,400	—	5
8,400	13, 400	€ 50	15
13, 400	23,400	800	30
23,400		3,800	40

For taxpayers who earn income from salaries or pensions (or both), the amount of the first bracket increases by €1,000 with an equal decrease in the amount of the second bracket of the scale. This provision results in a reduction of €50 in the individual's income tax. The maximum rate decreased from 45% to 42.5% for income earned in the year 2001 and to 40% for income earned in the year 2002 and thereafter. For nonresident individuals (without a physical presence in Greece) who earn income from sources located in Greece, the tax computed on the basis of the above tax scale is increased by applying the 5% tax rate to the first €7,400 of income. EU residents who derive more than 90% of their total income from Greece are eligible for the tax-free bracket. In addition, for individuals who live permanently on islands with fewer than 3,100 inhabitants, tax rates are as follows.

Taxable income			Tax on Column 1	Percentage on excess
Over	Not over			
(Column 1)				
0	€13,206		—	0
€13,206	14,206		—	5
14,206	19,206		€ 50	15
19,206	29,206		800	30
29,206			3,800	40

For applicable tax credits, see "Tax credits" above.

INDIVIDUAL TAX CALCULATION

Calendar year 2002

Assumptions

Resident alien husband and wife, two children; wife without taxable income.

Tax computation

Gross income:		
Salary		€ 80,000
Interest on government bonds		600
Interest on bank deposits		600
Total gross income		81,200
Less—Interest on government bonds and bank deposits		1,200
Adjusted gross income		80,000
Less—Social security payments		4,195
Net income		75,805
Less—Deductions:		
Medical expenses	1,500	
Main residence rentals	740	
Life insurance premiums	740	
Amount for private lessons	1,480	4,460
Taxable income		€ 71,345
Corresponding tax		€ 22,978
Less:		
Tax credits for two children	210	
Tax credits for annual family expenses	135	(345)
Income tax liability		22,633
Plus—Withholding tax on interest from bank deposits		90
Plus—Withholding tax on interest on government bonds		60
Total income tax liability		€ 22,783

Note:

Exchange rate of the Euro at January 3, 2002: US$1 = €1.106.

PwC contacts

For additional information on taxation in Guatemala, contact:

Oscar Cordon
Juan Pablo Ortiz
PricewaterhouseCoopers
Edificio Tívoli Plaza
6a Calle 6-38, Zone 9
Guatemala City, Guatemala
Telephone: (502) (2) 345080
Fax: (502) (2) 312819
e-mail: oscar.cordon@gt.pwcglobal.com
juan.pablo.ortiz@gt.pwcglobal.com

General note

This entry is repeated from the 2001/2002 edition. For more up-to-date information, consult the contact listed above or Mark Friedlich at mark.friedlich@us.pwcglobal.com.

Significant developments

The information in this entry is current as of January 2001. There have been no significant tax or regulatory developments in the past year. For subsequent developments, consult the contacts listed above.

Territoriality and residence

Guatemala taxes its citizens and resident or nonresident individuals on their compensation attributable to services rendered in Guatemala and on other Guatemalan-source income.

Gross income

Employee gross income/Nonresident aliens are taxed on salary earned for work done in Guatemala, regardless of where payment is made and regardless of whether it is remitted. They are not taxed to the extent that their compensation relates to services performed outside Guatemala. Quantifiable fringe benefits, such as housing allowance, living allowance, house, tax reimbursement, etc., are considered taxable income.

Capital gains and investment income/Guatemalan-source capital gains are taxed at a flat rate of 10%. Capital gains and investment income from outside the country are not taxed by Guatemala. Capital losses can be netted only against capital gains.

A nonresident alien's income from a Guatemalan source is subject to income tax withholding at varying rates.

1. Interest: 10%, except when the related foreign-exchange proceeds are sold directly into the Guatemalan banking system.
2. Dividends: 10%, except when taxpayers have paid corporate income tax.
3. Salaries and professional fees: 10%.
4. Rents, royalties, and technical services: 25%.

Deductions

All individuals, including resident aliens, can deduct the following in determining taxable income.

1. Personal deduction: Q36,000.
2. Social security contributions (4.83% of salary).
3. Life insurance premiums.
4. Medical expenses (excluding medicine).

Tax credits

An income tax credit is granted for value added taxes paid on goods purchased and services contracted for one's exclusive personal use, up to the value-added tax (VAT) rate (10% of net income). This amount is to be reduced by 25% during the next year (i.e., July 2001 to June 2002) and an additional 25% during the following year.

Resident aliens cannot take income taxes paid to foreign countries or governmental units as a credit against their tax liability in Guatemala.

Other taxes

Social security taxes/The taxpayer's share of social security taxes is 4.83% of compensation, without a maximum limit.

Other taxes on income/Interest income earned by domiciled persons is subject to a flat 10% income withholding tax.

Tax administration

Returns/Husbands and wives cannot file joint returns. The tax year for individuals runs from July 1 to June 30.

Payment of tax/Income tax must be withheld from salaries; rentals; royalties; fees for technical, professional, or scientific activities; or any kind of individual services.

Tax rates

Taxable income		Tax on	Percentage
Over	Not over	Column 1	on excess
(Column 1)			
Q 0	Q 65,000	0	15
65,000	180,000	Q 9,750	20
180,000	295,000	32,750	25
295,000		61,500	31

INDIVIDUAL TAX CALCULATION

Assumptions

Resident alien husband and wife; two children; one spouse earns all the income. Individual tax amounts are in local currency.

Tax computation

Gross taxable income:		
Salary		Q 120,000
Incentive bonus		864
		120,864
Deductions:		
Personal deduction	36,000	
Insurance premiums	6,000	
Social security	5,800	47,800
Net taxable income		Q 73,064
Income tax assessment:		
Fixed tax on 65,000	9,750	
On excess (20% of 8,464)	1,613	Q 11,363
Less—Value-added tax credit (1)		(6,000)
Tax to be paid		Q 5,363

Notes:

1. The law permits a credit for VAT paid up to 10% of the total income; it is possible to use 100% of this credit. To claim it, the taxpayer must have supporting documents, such as invoices. In the example above, 50% of the taxpayer's total income was subject to VAT.
2. Exchange rate of the quetzal at December 31, 2001: US$1= Q7.7316.

Guyana

PwC contact

For additional information on taxation in Guyana, contact the following partner in the correspondent firm of Jack A. Alli Sons & Co.:

Ronald M. Alli
Jack A. Alli Sons & Co.
145 Crown Street
Queenstown, Georgetown, Guyana
Telephone: (592) (22) 62904, 66532, 37065-7
Fax: (592) (22) 53849
e-mail: ronald.alli@jaasco.com

Significant developments

There have been no significant tax or regulatory developments regarding individual taxation in the past year.

Territoriality and residence

Income is taxable when it accrues in or is derived from Guyana, whether or not the individual is resident in Guyana. Earned income derived from sources outside Guyana is taxable only if it is received in Guyana by a resident individual. Unearned income derived from sources outside Guyana is taxable, whether received in Guyana or not, on individuals who are ordinarily resident or domiciled in Guyana, but is taxable on a resident who is not ordinarily resident or domiciled in Guyana only if it is received in Guyana.

Individuals are resident in Guyana if they reside there permanently or, being in Guyana, intend to reside there permanently, except for such temporary absence as the Commissioner of Inland Revenue may deem reasonable and not inconsistent with the claim of such individuals to be resident in Guyana.

An individual who resides in Guyana for more than 183 days in a calendar year is considered as resident for tax purposes.

Gross income

Employee gross income/An employee is taxed on income received for services performed in Guyana whether or not the income is received in Guyana. Employment compensation includes all benefits and allowances derived from employment, except allowances for medical or dental expenses or for a passage to or from Guyana and allowances for subsistence, travel, company car, entertainment, security, or expense if explained to the satisfaction of the Commissioner.

Capital gains and investment income/Residents and nonresidents are subject to capital gains tax on net gains derived from Guyana, except for capital gains on the disposal of shares or stock in public companies, which are exempt from taxation for any person. Residents who are ordinarily resident or domiciled in Guyana are also subject to capital gains tax on gains arising outside of Guyana, while residents who are not ordinarily resident in Guyana or domiciled therein are subject to tax only to the extent the gain is received in Guyana.

Capital gains tax is chargeable at the rate of 20% on gains exceeding G$1,000 where disposal of the assets occurs within 1 to 25 years of their acquisition. Short-term gains (arising within 12 months) are subject to tax as ordinary income. Gains on disposal of assets occurring more than 25 years after acquisition are exempt from taxation. There are certain minimal exemptions on disposal of personal assets. The market value at January 1, 1991 of assets held prior to that date is taken into consideration when computing capital gains.

Investment income arising outside of Guyana to a nonresident is not taxable in Guyana. A resident who is not ordinarily resident or domiciled in Guyana is taxable only to the extent that such income is received in Guyana.

Tax at 15% is withheld from gross distributions and bank interest arising in Guyana to nonresidents and from bank interest in Guyana to residents. Such income, unless an election is made, is exempt from further taxation by residents. Certain categories of taxpayers are exempt from taxation on bank interest. Residents are exempt from income tax/withholding tax on dividends received from a resident company.

Tax at 15% is withheld from discounts earned on treasury bills.

Taxpayers who are working painters, sculptors, or authors are assessed over a two- or three-year period on income arising from the sale of work, depending on the period of production.

Deductions

Business deductions/Generally, all outgoings and expenses incurred wholly and exclusively in the production of income are deductible. However, for nonresidents, certain expenses are not allowable, for example, property rental expenses. In circumstances where expenses and consequently profits cannot be readily ascertained, the Commissioner (or a judge on appeal) may determine a fair and reasonable percentage of turnover of the business done by a nonresident person in arriving at taxable income.

Nonbusiness expenses/Expenses of a private, domestic, or capital nature are expressly excluded from deduction. Personal expenses, including home mortgage and improvement interest, life insurance and superannuation premiums, and charitable donations, are no longer deductible.

Personal allowances/A basic allowance of G$216,000 is deductible in determining taxable income. The allowance is apportioned according to the individual's earning period.

Tax credits

Credit is granted to residents for taxes paid in foreign countries in accordance with the relevant double taxation treaties. Where no treaties currently exist, there are provisions for the unilateral granting of relief from double taxation.

Other taxes

Social security taxes/There is a social security tax, referred to as "national insurance contributions," which is deducted at source and to which employees contribute 4.8% of their gross wages and employers contribute 7.2% of their employees' gross wages. There is a maximum total rate of G$9,622 per month for monthly incomes in excess of G$80,180.

Other taxes on income/There are no other taxes on income. Other taxes are levied in the form of local rates on property, customs and excise duties, and consumption tax on certain goods, as well as property tax on the net asset worth of taxpayers.

Tax administration

Returns/Tax returns must be filed in specified form by April 30 of the year following the calendar year-end or accounting year-end. Tax returns are filed for income earned in a calendar year (which coincides with the tax year), except in the case of a sole trader or a partnership where filing is done according to the accounting terminal date approved by the Inland Revenue.

Each individual is required to file a separate return.

Payment of tax/There is payroll withholding of income tax under the pay-as-you-earn (PAYE) system. Withholding tax is deducted at source on bank interest paid to residents and on gross distribution, bank interest and other specified payments made to nonresidents. Income tax on other income is paid in quarterly installments in the year in which the income arises.

Any shortfall of taxes deducted at source or paid in quarterly installments should be met by April 30 following the year of income.

Tax rates

Income tax on an individual's chargeable income is payable at the rate of 20% on the first G$134,000. Chargeable income over G$134,000 is taxed at the rate of 33 1/3%. There are special rates applicable to income arising from gold and diamond mining.

Withholding tax is payable at rates of 15% on gross distributions and interest payments and at 10% on other specified payments made to nonresidents and 15% on commercial bank interest and discounts earned on treasury bills paid to residents. Dividends received by a resident from a resident company are exempt from income tax/withholding tax.

INDIVIDUAL TAX CALCULATION

Year of income 2001/Fiscal year 2001

Income tax

Assumptions

1. Resident alien with employment income of G$7,980,800, maintaining a nonworking spouse and two children in Guyana and earning interest from a savings account with a local bank.
2. Resident alien pays mortgage interest for property acquired in country of origin. Interest is not an allowable deduction in Guyana.
3. Resident alien pays life insurance premiums for self in country of origin. Life insurance premiums are not allowable deductions in Guyana.

Tax computation

Salary		G$ 7,980,800
Bank interest	12,870	
Less—Withholding tax deducted at source	(1,930)	
Bank interest received	10,940	
Less—Amount exempt from further taxation	(10,940)	—
Short-term capital gains		2,000
		7,982,800
Less—Personal allowance		216,000
Taxable income		G$ 7,766,800
Income tax on taxable income of 7,766,800		G$ 2,571,067

Capital gains tax—Long-term gain

Assumptions

Individual alien considered a resident of Guyana disposes of land and building used as residence acquired in July 1984 at a cost of G$750,000 and sold in September 2001 for G$2,000,000, with a market value of G$1,500,000 at January 1, 1991. Legal expenses incurred on the sale of the property: G$1,200.

Tax computation

Cost of land and building	G$ 750,000
Proceeds of sale of land and building	G$ 2,000,000
Market value of land and building at January 1, 1991	1,500,000
Gain	500,000
Less—Legal expenses	1,200
Net gain	G$ 498,800
Capital gains tax on 498,800 at 20%	G$ 99,760

Note:

Exchange rate of the Guyanese dollar at December 31, 2001: US$1 = G$189.50.

Hong Kong

PwC contact

For additional information on taxation in Hong Kong, contact:

Rod Houng-Lee
PricewaterhouseCoopers
32/F Cheung Kong Center
Central Hong Kong
Telephone: (852) 2289 2472
Fax: (852) 2810 9888
e-mail: rod.houng-lee@hk.pwcglobal.com

Significant developments

There have been no significant tax or regulatory changes regarding individual taxation in the last year.

Territoriality and residence

Residence, domicile and citizenship are not relevant to tax liability, except for the purpose of the Mainland China double taxation arrangement (see "Tax credits" below), where the term "resident" is used. All individuals, resident or nonresident, are subject to tax on Hong Kong-source employment income, Hong Kong income from an office and Hong Kong pensions, as shown below.

1. Hong Kong employment income—Whether a person has a Hong Kong employment is usually determined by whether that person has entered into a contract of employment with a Hong Kong employer or Hong Kong-resident company. If the source of employment income is in Hong Kong, all the income is taxable, unless all of the services were rendered outside Hong Kong for a particular year of assessment. However, to provide unilateral relief for Hong Kong-source employment, income referable to services rendered outside Hong Kong will not be taxed in Hong Kong if the employee is liable to and has paid tax similar in nature to Hong Kong tax in the territory where the services are rendered.
2. Non–Hong Kong employment income—The Inland Revenue Department usually accepts that a person has a non-Hong Kong employment where three factors are present:
   a. The employer is resident outside Hong Kong;
   b. The contract of employment was negotiated and entered into, and is enforceable outside Hong Kong; and
   c. The employee's remuneration is paid outside Hong Kong.

   For a non–Hong Kong employment, only the income attributable to services rendered in Hong Kong is taxable. If all of the services for a year of assessment are rendered outside Hong Kong, salaries tax is not payable in Hong Kong. A person with a non-Hong Kong employment who only renders services in Hong Kong during visits not exceeding a total of 60 days in a tax year is treated as if no services were rendered in Hong Kong in that year. Income from an office and pensions do not qualify for the apportionment basis and exclusion of income under the "visits not exceeding 60 days" rule.
3. Income from an office (such as directors' fees)—The source of such fees is determined by reference to where the company is managed and controlled.

4. Pensions—Pensions are taxable if the funds out of which the payment is made are situated in Hong Kong.

Gross income

Employee gross income/Taxable income includes any wages, salary, leave pay, fees, commissions, bonuses, gratuities, perquisites, and allowances, subject to certain exemptions.

1. Benefits in kind. If the employer has sole and primary liability for payment of benefits, and no other person including the employee acts as surety in respect of the liability, the employee will generally not be taxed, except in two situations:
   a. If the benefit is capable of being converted into money by the employee; or
   b. If the employer pays any amount in connection with the education of a child of an employee.
2. Cash allowances for holiday warrants, insofar as used for travel and transportation of personal effects for such travel, are exempt.
3. Free housing or rental refunds are taxed only on the rental value computed as a percentage of total income, as follows:

	%
Hotel, one room	4
Hotel, not more than two rooms	8
Other accommodation	10

4. Any sum received by way of commutation of pension under a recognized occupational retirement scheme upon death, incapacity, retirement, or termination of service is exempt, with certain exceptions where there is a termination of service of less than ten years with an employer. Any sum received by way of commutation of pension under the Pensions Ordinance is exempt.
5. There are no special concessions for foreigners or short-term residents, except that an employee engaged in a non-Hong Kong employment will not be subject to salaries tax on income from services rendered in Hong Kong during visits not exceeding a total of 60 days in the basis period for a year of assessment.

Capital gains and investment income/All capital gains, dividends and interest on bank deposits are not taxable in Hong Kong.

Deductions

Business deductions/Expenses are allowable insofar as they are incurred wholly, exclusively and necessarily in the production of income subject to salaries tax. In practice, very few expenses meet these requirements. Some travel expenses (excluding private travel expenses, e.g., home to place of work) and entertainment expenses may qualify for deduction. There are no blanket or standard deductions. A deduction is allowed for self-education expenses paid up to a maximum of $40,000.

Nonbusiness expenses/"Concessionary deductions" are available in respect of approved charitable donations, home loan interest, elderly residential care expenses, and contributions to recognized retirement schemes.

1. Charitable donations made in cash to approved charities are allowable when the aggregate is not less than HK$100. The allowance for donations is restricted to 10% of the income of the tax year.

2. From 1998/1999 onward, home loan interest paid is deductible for five years of assessment. The place of residence must be situated in Hong Kong. For 1998/1999 to 2000/2001, the maximum deductible is HK$100,000. For 2001/2002 and 2002/2003, the maximum deductible is HK$150,000.
3. Elderly residential care expenses paid to a residential care home in respect of a parent or grandparent of a taxpayer or spouse are deductible up to a maximum of HK$60,000 per year for each parent or grandparent.
4. Contributions to recognized retirement schemes, including the Mandatory Provident Fund, are deductible up to a maximum of HK$12,000 per year.

Personal allowances/Allowances are granted as listed below for the taxpayer, spouse (provided the individual was married at any time during the tax year and, in the case of a wife living apart from her husband, provided he was maintaining or supporting the wife), unmarried children under the age of 25 years (provided children aged 18 to 24 are receiving full-time education), children over the age of 18 physically or mentally incapacitated for work, disabled dependents eligible to claim a disability allowance from the Hong Kong government, and the taxpayer's or spouse's parents or grandparents maintained by the taxpayer if the parents or grandparents are ordinarily resident in Hong Kong and are aged 60 or more or eligible to claim a disability allowance from the Hong Kong government.

Amounts for 2000/2001 and 2001/2002 are show below:

	HK$
For a single person (Note)	108,000
For a married couple (Note)	216,000
Child allowances:	
First	30,000
Second	30,000
Third and additional (each)	15,000
Maximum child allowances are restricted to	165,000
Dependent parent or grandparent allowance (each)	30,000
Dependent parent or grandparent living together with taxpayer (each)	60,000
Dependent brother or sister allowance	30,000
Single parent allowance (for single parent with sole or predominant care of a child)	108,000
Disabled dependent allowance	60,000

Note:

If a married couple both have income liable to salaries tax, they are taxed as two single persons. The married allowance is given only if one spouse has no income liable to salaries tax, where the married couple have elected for joint assessment to salaries tax or where an election has been made for personal assessment. A couple must state which spouse will claim the child allowance.

Mandatory Provident Fund

Hong Kong's Mandatory Provident Fund (MPF) system came into operation on December 1, 2000. The MPF is designed to provide a formal, compulsory system of retirement protection by way of a privately managed contribution scheme. All benefits derived from mandatory contributions must generally be preserved until the contributor reaches the prescribed retirement age of 65.

An employee is required to contribute 5% of his/her monthly income and the employer has to match this amount. The maximum level of income for contribution purposes is HK$20,000 (approximately US$2,564) per month, so the maximum mandatory contribution for each of the employee and employer is HK$1,000 (US$128) per month.

Employees' mandatory contributions are tax deductible, up to a limit of HK$12,000 (US$1,538) per annum. Employers' MPF contributions are tax deductible to the extent that they do not exceed 15% of each employee's yearly emoluments.

Exemption from the MPF system is provided for some very limited categories of employees, including a person from overseas who enters Hong Kong for employment for less than one year or who is a member of a provident, pension, retirement or superannuation scheme (however described) of a place outside Hong Kong.

Tax credits

In practice, few foreign tax credits apply. However, an arrangement has been entered into between Mainland China and the Hong Kong Special Administrative Region for the avoidance of double taxation of income. The arrangement applies in Hong Kong in respect of income derived in any year of assessment commencing on or after April 1, 1998. Where a resident of Hong Kong derives income from Mainland China, the amount of tax paid in Mainland China in respect of that income is allowed as a credit against any Hong Kong tax imposed on that resident in respect of the same income. However, the amount of credit is not to exceed the amount of Hong Kong tax computed in respect of that income.

Other taxes

Hong Kong has no social security taxes or other taxes on income and no wealth tax, gift tax or inheritance tax. Estates of deceased persons are subject to estate tax, but not on property situated outside Hong Kong. There are no local taxes.

Tax administration

Tax returns/Returns are filed in specified forms on the basis of a tax year ending March 31. Although husbands and wives who each have taxable earnings are required to file separate salaries tax returns, they may elect for joint assessment if such an election would result in reduced total salaries tax liability.

Payment of tax/There is no withholding on wages and salaries, with the exception that an employer is under an obligation to withhold any payment to an employee who is about to leave Hong Kong other than on a normal business trip.

Provisional salaries tax is a prepayment during the current year of the salaries tax payable in respect of income being earned during that year. It is based on the salaries tax payable for the previous year. It is credited against the salaries tax finally assessed for the current year. This assessment will also include a charge of provisional salaries tax for the following year.

Tax rates

Net taxable income		Tax on	Percentage
Over	Not over	Column 1	on excess
(Column 1)			
0	HK$ 35,000	—	2
HK$ 35,000	70,000	HK$ 700	7
70,000	105,000	3,150	12
105,000		7,350	17

The maximum tax, however, is limited to tax at the standard rate (15%) on the net assessable income (after any business deductions) less concessionary deductions but without the deduction of personal allowances.

INDIVIDUAL TAX CALCULATION

Assumptions

1. The individual is employed by a non-Hong Kong employer under an overseas employment contract and is required to travel extensively to other areas. The remuneration has been paid outside Hong Kong.
2. The individual is married and has two children. Wife does not work.
3. Salary calculation—year of assessment 2001/2002. Income based on the year April 1, 2001 to March 31, 2002. Provisional tax payable for the year of assessment 2002/2003.
4. Accommodation provided by employer is rent-free.
5. Days spent out of Hong Kong on business—120.
6. Children's education expenses paid by employer: HK$80,000.
7. Perquisites capable of being converted into money, e.g., a gift of a car: HK$100,000.
8. Perquisites not capable of being converted into money (not taxable): HK$8,000.
9. Interest income (not taxable): HK$10,000.
10. Long-term capital gain (not taxable): HK$60,000.
11. Approved charitable donations: HK$2,000.
12. The individual is a member of an overseas retirement scheme and is not required to join Hong Kong's MPF scheme.

Salaries tax computation

Base salary		HK$ 620,000
Add:		
Perquisites—Education expenses	80,000	
Other taxable perquisites	100,000	180,000
		HK$ 800,000
Portion of income attributable to time spent in Hong Kong		
800,000 x (245 ÷ 365) (1)		HK$ 536,986
Rental value of residence:		
(10% of 800,000 = 80,000 x (245 ÷ 365))		53,698
Assessable income		590,684
Less—Concessionary deductions:		
Approved charitable donations		2,000
Net assessable income after concessionary deductions		588,684
Less—Personal allowances (2):		
Married allowance	216,000	
Children (two)	60,000	276,000
Net chargeable income		HK$ 312,684
Salaries tax liability for year of assessment 2001/2002 (3):		
35,000 at 2%	700	
35,000 at 7%	2,450	
35,000 at 12%	4,200	
207,684 at 17%	35,306	HK$ 42,656
Less—Provisional tax previously paid, say		(37,868)
Additional tax due 2001/2002		4,788
Provisional tax payable for year of assessment 2002/2003		42,656
Total tax due		HK$ 47,444

Notes:

1. If the individual in this case had signed a contract of employment with a Hong Kong company and thus had a Hong Kong employment, his/her gross income of HK$800,000 would be fully taxable and not be apportioned.
2. Personal allowances are not apportioned.
3. If the individual's net assessable income after concessionary deductions had been HK$2,871,000 or above, it would be taxed at the standard rate of 15%.
4. Exchange rate of the Hong Kong dollar at January 1, 2002: US$1 = HK$7.80.

Hungary

PwC contact

For additional information on taxation in Hungary, contact:

Paul Grocott
PricewaterhouseCoopers Kft
Wesselényi u. 16.
H–1077 Budapest, Hungary
Telephone: (36) (1) 461 9260
Fax: (36) (1) 461 9110
e-mail: paul.grocott@hu.pwcglobal.com

Significant developments

- As from January 1, 2001 gross income received from a foreign employer can no longer be classified as "independent income," which means that 100% of this income will be included in the taxable base and the 10% flat deduction or an actual cost deduction can no longer be applied to such income.
- As from January 1, 2001 quarterly tax advance payments are due on "other income."
- As from January 1, 2002 certain types of income that are taxed separately are classified as "other income" where this income originates in a country with which Hungary has not concluded an agreement for the avoidance of double taxation.

Territoriality and residence

Hungarian personal income tax is assessed on the following.

1. Domestic-source income.
2. Foreign-source income, provided the individual is resident in Hungary.

Income derived in relation to any activity performed in Hungary is considered domestic-source income, even if it is paid from abroad. In the case of income paid from abroad, income tax will be due whether or not this income has been transferred or brought into the country.

Individuals are resident in Hungary if they have their "regular place of stay" in Hungary (they stay in the country at least 183 days during a given calendar year) or have their permanent home in Hungary.

Gross income

Employee gross income/The gross income of employees includes all cash remuneration and most personal expenses (overseas allowances, insurance, pension, tax reimbursement, tax equalization payments, etc.) paid by the employer. Housing can still be provided tax free by either the foreign or the Hungarian company, provided certain conditions are met.

Fringe benefits (e.g., home leave, school fees) are taxable to the employer at a flat rate of 44%. Where the fringe benefits tax cannot be levied by the Hungarian tax authorities (e.g., where the company providing or paying for the benefit is an overseas company), the benefit will be treated as compensation taxable in the individual.

Capital gains and investment income/Capital gains on the sale of real estate, investments, and certain high-value items are taxed at a flat 20% rate. Interest income is effectively zero-rated in most cases. Dividend income from Hungarian companies is taxed at flat rates of 20% or 35%, depending on the ratio of the dividend distribution to the shareholders' equity in the company. For dividend income from abroad, the flat rate is 20%. This can be reduced by credit for any foreign withholding taxes. However, there is a minimum Hungarian tax of 5% on dividends from nontreaty countries.

In most cases taxes on capital gains are paid by withholding. In all cases they are the final tax burden.

Deductions

Business deductions/Fees for membership in professional associations and trade unions are deductible from employment income.

Nonbusiness expenses/None.

Personal allowances/A few personal reliefs are available in the form of tax rebates. These are generally of little relevance to expatriates on medium-term assignments, partly because of lower limits in most cases and partly because of direct links to Hungarian institutions. Examples include life insurance, building society savings schemes, university (but not school) fees for dependents, a new child allowance and charitable donations.

There is also a tax deferral scheme for the encouragement of portfolio investments in Hungarian shares, and an individual may determine that up to 1% of net tax payable be paid to a listed Hungarian charity and another 1% to a registered Hungarian church rather than to the tax office.

Tax credits

If a double taxation treaty does not apply, Hungarian residents are taxed at marginal rates on foreign-source income, but credit is given for foreign taxes paid. The credit may exceed neither 90% of the foreign tax paid abroad, nor the Hungarian personal income tax calculated applying an average tax rate (which is determined by dividing the calculated tax by the consolidated tax base). Most treaties provide for an exemption with progression rather than a credit for active income (e.g., from second employment).

Other taxes

Social security taxes/The individual's share of social security contributions is a flat 11% of gross salary (health care contribution: 3% (no cap), pension contribution: 8% (capped at income of HUF2,368,850/year)). An additional 1.5% of gross salary must be contributed as employees' unemployment contribution (no cap). Foreign individuals are exempt from mandatory social security contributions but not from the 1.5% employees' unemployment contribution. 25% of the pension contribution paid is deductible from the calculated tax.

Social security contribution at the rate of 29% and employers' unemployment contribution at a rate of 3% of gross salary (no cap) are payable by Hungarian employers. Fringe benefits are subject to either the 29% employers' social security contribution or an 11% health tax where there is no insurance (e.g., employment) relationship. In the absence of a mandatory insurance relationship, neither 29% employers' social security contribution nor 11% health tax contribution should be paid in respect of any remuneration paid by a foreign company or a partially or wholly foreign-owned entity to a foreign individual.

Other contributions (training fund) are 1.5% of the total salary paid to all employees, including foreign individuals.

There are social security agreements in force between Hungary and Austria, Bulgaria, Croatia, the Czech Republic, Germany, Poland, Romania, Russia and the other members of the Commonwealth of Independent States, the Slovak Republic, Slovenia, Switzerland, and Yugoslavia.

Withholding taxes/For resident individuals, withholding tax rates are as follows.

1. Dividends—20%, or 35% on dividends of more than twice the prime rate quoted by the National Bank of Hungary (currently 2 x 9%) multiplied by the shareholders' equity.
2. Interest—Generally nil.
3. Royalties—Royalties are taxed at normal rates, although in most instances only a portion of the income is subject to tax.

Local taxes on income/Local authorities have the right to levy certain minor taxes.

Tax administration

Returns/Returns must be filed for each tax year (i.e., the calendar year) by March 20 of the following year.

Returns need not be filed where the individual does not have taxable income or where the individual's only taxable income is from a sole Hungarian employer. At the taxpayer's option, this can be extended to successive employments, provided appropriate details are given to the employer by January 15 of the following year. In this case the employer may file on behalf of the employee.

Individuals must file separate returns; there is no joint filing for husband and wife.

Payment of tax/Income tax is withheld from salaries and most investment income. For other income, individuals must pay income tax themselves. Taxpayers with income not subject to withholding generally must make quarterly payments. Employers are required to notify the tax office of total pay, benefits and expenses paid or reimbursed (employment income).

Tax rates

With effect from January 1, 2002, the tax rates are as follows.

Taxable income		Tax on Column 1	Percentage on excess
Over (Column 1)	Not over		
0	HUF 600,000	—	20
HUF 600,000	1,200,000	HUF 120,000	30
1,200,000		300,000	40

INDIVIDUAL TAX CALCULATION

Calendar year 2002

Assumptions

Expatriate employee with salary from foreign employer and benefits as shown, and with foreign investment (dividend) income.

Tax computation

Income tax

Gross salary	HUF	21,955,200
Add—Other cash allowances paid by the Hungarian disburser directly to the foreign individual		3,600,000
Less—Housing invoiced to and paid directly by the foreign individual, limited to the amount received in respect of the housing		2,500,000
		23,055,200
Add—Insurance premiums paid by employer (e.g., life insurance, savings type)	HUF	500,000
Total income taxable at scale rates	HUF	23,555,200
Tax due:		
On the first 1,200,000	HUF	300,000
On the remaining 22,355,200 at 40%		8,942,080
Total Hungarian income tax borne on aggregated income	HUF	9,242,080

Fringe benefit tax

School fees	HUF	1,000,000
Total fringe benefits provided by employer	HUF	1,000,000
Fringe benefit tax payable by employer (44%)	HUF	440,000

Tax on dividends

Foreign dividend	HUF	500,000
Tax liability on dividend (20%)	HUF	100,000

Note:

Exchange rate of the forint at December 31, 2001: US$1 = HUF274.44.

India

PwC contact

For additional information on taxation in India, contact:

Rathin Datta
Price Waterhouse
20A Park Street
3rd Floor
Calcutta 700016, India
Telephone: (91) (33) 2494680, 2263275, 2495380, 2295789
Fax: (91) (33) 2490759
e-mail: rathin.datta@in.pwcglobal.com

Significant developments

There have been no significant tax or regulatory developments as regards individual taxation in 2001.

Territoriality and residence

Residents are taxed on their worldwide income. Nonresidents are taxed only on income that is received in India or that accrues or is deemed to accrue in India. A person not ordinarily resident is taxed like a nonresident but is also liable to tax on income accruing abroad if it is from a business controlled in or a profession set up in India.

A person is resident if present in India (1) for 182 days in a year or (2) for 60 days in a year and 365 days during the preceding four years. Individuals fulfilling neither of these conditions are nonresidents. A resident who was away from India for 730 days during the preceding seven years or who was nonresident for nine out of ten preceding years is not ordinarily resident. In effect, a newcomer to India remains not ordinarily resident for the first nine years of stay in India. (The rules are slightly more liberal for persons of Indian origin residing abroad and visiting India or for Indian citizens leaving India for employment abroad.)

Gross income

Employee gross income/An individual's entire remuneration (including benefits in kind valued as per the tax rules) received from an employer is taxable. Concessional treatment is accorded to leave passage, reimbursement of medical expenses and certain retirement benefits.

A foreign employee of a foreign enterprise who is not present in India for more than 90 days in a year is not taxed on remuneration received from the foreign employer for services performed in India, provided the foreign enterprise is not engaged in any trade or business in India and provided the remuneration is not deductible in computing the employer's taxable income in India. In a treaty situation, the 183-day rule applies. A foreign technician or a nonresident Indian technician fulfilling certain conditions will have no further tax liability during the first 48 months if the tax on the technician's remuneration is paid by the employer. Concessions are also available under tax treaties.

Specified income of a foreign citizen and a person not ordinarily resident is exempt from tax if he or she is engaged with the approval of the prescribed authority to render technical services under an agreement entered into by an international organization with the government of India and funded by the government of a foreign state.

Capital gains and investment income/Residents are taxed on capital gains and investment income irrespective of place of accrual. Nonresidents and persons not ordinarily resident pay tax only on capital gains and investment income accruing in India or received in India. Capital gains on assets held for over three years (one year in the case of shares) are determined after adjusting costs by prescribed inflation factors and are taxed at 20.4%. Other capital gains are aggregated with taxable income, which is taxed at the applicable rates. Capital losses can be offset only against capital gains. In the case of nonresident Indians the rate is 10% on long-term capital gains arising on sale of specified assets purchased in foreign currency.

In respect of long-term capital gains arising on sale of securities listed in India, taxpayers can either choose the above methodology of indexation and pay tax at 20.4% or pay 10.2% on the gain amount computed without inflation adjustment. Income from specified investments is exempt, up to certain limits.

Deductions

Business deductions/In computing the taxable income from salaries, a standard deduction equal to the lesser of 33.33% of salary or Rs30,000 is allowed to all employees drawing salary of Rs150,000 or less. For employees drawing salary of more than Rs150,000 but not more than Rs300,000, the deduction is Rs25,000 while for employees drawing salary of more than Rs300,000 but not more than Rs500,000, the deduction is Rs20,000. Employees drawing a salary of more than Rs500,000 are not eligible for the deduction. No other deduction is available for business-connected expenses, unless a special allowance is specifically granted to meet certain specified employment-related expenses (conveyance in performance of duties, cost of travel on tour or transfer, etc.), in which case, in addition to the standard deduction, the expenses within the amount of the allowance are deductible.

Nonbusiness expenses/No deductions are available from salaries for interest or taxes. Deductions up to certain limits are allowed for approved charitable contributions, medical insurance premiums and, to a very limited extent, children's education/hostel allowance received from the employer.

Personal allowances/There are no personal allowances apart from the standard deduction mentioned above, professional tax (see below) and a limited deduction for certain allowances in connection with a posting in specified hilly, border, remote, or tribal areas.

Tax credits

Tax rebate/A rebate equal to 20% (30% for individuals having total income not exceeding Rs100,000) of the amount invested in life insurance premiums, specified schemes, long-term investments, amounts spent on construction/purchase of a residential house or repayment of certain loans, subscription to specified infrastructure bonds, etc., taken for that purpose is allowed from the gross tax up to a maximum of Rs16,000, out of which the amount in excess of Rs12,000 must be investment in infrastructure bonds A rebate of 100% of the gross tax, subject to a maximum of Rs5,000 for resident women below sixty-five years of age and Rs15,000, to resident individuals aged 65 years or more are allowed. Tax rebates cannot exceed the gross tax payable.

Foreign taxes paid/Only residents are allowed credit against their Indian tax liability for income tax paid abroad on income arising abroad (limited to the Indian tax on the doubly taxed income).

Other taxes

Social security taxes/There are no social security taxes.

Local taxes on income/Professional taxes imposed by certain states are minimal and are deductible in computing taxable income.

Tax administration

Returns/Husbands and wives file returns separately. Joint filing is not permitted. For tax purposes, the year ends on March 31.

Payment of tax/Income tax is withheld from salaries. If the taxpayer has other taxable income, then the taxpayer must pay advance tax on the basis of estimated income.

Tax rates

Income tax is calculated at graduated rates. On income of Rs150,000, the tax is Rs19,000, and income in excess of Rs150,000 is taxed at 30%. Long-term capital gains are taxed at 20%.

For residents whose taxable income exceeds Rs60,000, the tax amount calculated in the manner prescribed above is increased by a surcharge of 2% of the tax liability.

INDIVIDUAL TAX CALCULATION

Assumption

The taxpayer is a not ordinarily resident alien (1).

Tax computation

Salary		Rs 3,500,000
Add:		
Value of accommodation provided (10% of 3,500,000)	350,000	
Value of car/chauffeur provided (1,600/600 per month)	26,400	376,400
		3,876,600
Less—Standard deduction		Nil
		3,876,600
Add:		
Interest accruing in India (to the extent taxable)	20,000	
Short-term capital gain accruing in India	24,000	
Long-term capital gain accruing in India (2, 3)	35,000	79,000
		3,955,600
Less—Contribution to approved charities (10,000 at 50%)		5,000
Taxable income		Rs 3,950,600
Gross tax (excluding tax on long-term capital gains)		Rs 1,159,180
Less—Tax rebates:		
Contribution to provident fund	350,000	
Infrastructure bonds purchased	20,000	
	370,000	
Rebate allowable: 20% of 370,000, up to maximum of 16,000		(16,000)
Tax payable		1,143,180
Add—Tax on long-term capital gains (10.2%) (3)		3,570
		1,146,750
Add—Surcharge (2% of 1,146,750)		22,935
Total tax payable		Rs 1,169,685

Notes:

1. In the case of a foreign technician or a nonresident Indian technician, if the employer pays the tax the technician has no further tax liability for the first 48 months.
2. 500 shares of Company X (assumed to be listed) sold in financial year 2000/2001 (purchased in financial year 1991/1992 at Rs10 per share) at Rs.80 per share. Cost inflation index: 1991/1992—199; 2000/2001—406.
3. Capital gains arising on sale of long-term listed securities can be taxed at a reduced rate of 10.2%, but availing indexation benefits, at the option of the taxpayer.
4. Exchange rate of the rupee at December 31, 2001: US$1 = Rs48.01.

PwC contact

For additional information on taxation in Indonesia, contact:

Firdaus Asikin
Tax Partner to Kantor Akuntan Publik
Drs Hadi Sutanto & Rekan
Gedung PricewaterhouseCoopers
Jalan HR Rasuna Said Kav. C-3
Kuningan
Jakarta 12940, Indonesia
Telephone: (62) (21) 521 2901–6
Fax: (62) (21) 521 2911–2
e-mail: firdaus.asikin@id.pwcglobal.com

Significant developments

Indonesia is slowly recovering from the severe economic crisis that began in 1997 and subsequent political turmoil. A new government was democratically elected in 1999 followed by a couple of cabinet reshuffles up to the end of 2000. Heavy reliance on support from the International Monetary Fund, the World Bank and other international financial institutions for the survival of its economy still continues in 2002.

Territoriality and residence

Resident individuals are, by law, taxed on worldwide income, whether or not remitted to Indonesia. A resident taxpayer is an individual who is present in Indonesia for more than 183 days during any 12-month period or has the intention to reside in Indonesia.

A nonresident is taxed on compensation received for work performed or utilized in Indonesia, regardless of where payment is made, at a rate of 20% (constituting a final tax). However, if the cost of this compensation is not borne by an Indonesian entity, this compensation is, in practice, not taxable in Indonesia. In addition, residents of tax treaty countries on short-term assignment in Indonesia may be protected from Indonesian tax where certain conditions are satisfied.

Gross income

Employee gross income/"Income" is widely defined to include almost any increase in economic prosperity. Resident taxpayers are not normally taxed on compensation received in kind (e.g., housing, cars) for work or services performed. Cash allowances for home-leave travel, education and similar costs are taxable in full to the individual taxpayer. Benefits in kind paid by certain tax-exempt, deemed-profit-basis or nontaxpayer entities are taxable.

Capital gains and investment income/Capital gains, excluding gains from sales of land and/or buildings and from sales of certain shares, form part of an individual's taxable income. Capital gains are taxable as income at the individual income tax rates.

Individuals who sell land and/or buildings valued at more than Rp. 60,000,000, or less than Rp. 60,000,000 but have an income of more than the PTKP (nontaxable income) threshold, should pay income tax (a final tax) on the gross amount of the sales transaction. The tax rate is 5%.

Sales of shares listed on an Indonesian stock exchange are subject to final withholding tax of 0.1% of the gross sales consideration. An additional final tax of 0.5% applies to the share value of founder shares at the time an initial public offering takes place, irrespective of whether the shares are held or sold. Shareholders can elect not to pay this tax; in this case, the actual gain will be subject to normal tax at the time the shares are sold.

Investment income, excluding interest on savings schemes, is also included as part of an individual's taxable income. Interest income on time deposits with Indonesian banks or their overseas branches as well as interest income on time deposits placed through Indonesian branches of foreign banks (in any currency) are currently taxed at a final flat preferential rate of 20%. Interest on bonds listed on Indonesian stock exchanges continues to be subject to final withholding tax at 15%.

Deductions

Business deductions/A specific tax exemption or concessional deduction covering approved business and occupational expenses is granted, amounting to 5% of the gross income up to a maximum of Rp1,296,000 per annum.

Nonbusiness expenses/Contributions to a pension fund approved by the Minister of Finance are recognized as allowable deductions. Other nonbusiness expenses, such as income taxes, mortgage interest and charitable contributions, are not tax deductible.

Personal allowances/The annual personal allowances shown below are available. These allowance amounts came into effect in 1999 and are valid for the 2002 tax year.

	Rp
Taxpayer	2,880,000
Wife	1,440,000
Dependents (maximum three), each	1,440,000
Occupational expenses 5% of gross income, max	1,296,000

These personal allowances take the form of deductions; they are not available to nonresident taxpayers.

Tax credits

A credit is granted for tax paid or due abroad in connection with income received or accrued abroad. The tax credit is calculated at the rate this income would have been taxed had it been earned and taxed in Indonesia, unless the amount of tax paid or due abroad is lower.

Other taxes

Social security taxes/Indonesia does not have a comprehensive social security system. However, the Worker's Social Security Act (Jamsostek) encompasses occupational accident security, death security, old-age security, and health maintenance security, and operates as follows.

Employers are responsible for full contributions to occupational accident security, death security and health maintenance security funds. The contribution for old-age security is borne jointly by the employer and the employee; at 3.7% and 2% of monthly pay, respectively. Employee contributions to Jamsostek are collected by the employer through payroll deductions.

There are five major classifications under the occupational accident security component, with rates ranging from 0.24% to 1.74% of monthly pay, depending on the employer's type of business.

Death security contributions are made at 0.30% of monthly pay.

Health maintenance security is payable by the employer under Jamsostek if the company does not have in place an existing health scheme for employees that meets the government's minimum standard. The contribution amounts are 6% of monthly pay for married employees and 3% of monthly pay for single employees, subject to a maximum of Rp60,000 per month for married employees and Rp30,000 per month for single employees.

Expatriates are not required to participate in Jamsostek.

Fiscal exit taxes/This tax (Rp1 million per exit from Indonesia by plane, Rp500,000 by ship or Rp200,000 by land) is payable by most residents and, by law, represents a prepayment of the personal income tax liability. Where the tax is borne by a company for its employees' business trips, the tax is considered a prepayment of the company's income tax liability. In most other circumstances, this tax becomes a cost unless the individual files personal income tax returns (see "Tax administration"). There are a number of exemptions to the payment of fiscal exit tax, including children below the age of 12.

Other taxes on income/There are no other taxes on income.

Tax administration

Individual taxpayers with income of more than the nontaxable threshold are required to register with the Indonesian Tax Authorities to obtain a personal tax identification number (NPWP) and to file annual individual tax returns (there are some exceptions) within three months of the end of the tax year (which is the calendar year).

In mid-2000, the Indonesian tax authorities issued a new ruling regarding individual taxation, under which expatriate tax residents are required to register and file tax returns on their worldwide income.

Effective from January 1, 2001, the requirement also applies to national Indonesian tax residents.

Payment of tax/An employer is responsible for the deduction of taxes from its employees' earnings and for the remittance of those taxes to the tax authorities. In addition, at the end of the calendar year, the employer is obliged to recalculate the income taxes of its employees. If it appears that the total amount of taxes paid monthly during the year is less than the total tax payable, the balance must be paid by the following March 25 at the latest.

Individual taxpayers are also required to pay monthly tax installments on income that has not been subject to withholding tax. However, the income tax withheld from their employment income will constitute a tax credit against the overall income tax liability declared in their individual tax returns.

Tax rates

The rates applied to taxable income, effective as of January 1, 2001 and are still applicable for 2002, are shown below.

Individual tax rates/For resident individuals (general), the following tax rates apply.

Taxable income	Rate	Tax
	%	Rp
On the first Rp25,000,000	5	1,250,000
On the next Rp25,000,000	10	2,500,000
On the next Rp50,000,000	15	7,500,000
On the next Rp100,000,000	25	25,000,000
Over Rp200,000,000	35	

Tax on severance payments/Severance payments are taxed separately at the following rates:

Taxable income	Rate	Tax
	%	Rp
On the first Rp25,000,000	—	Nil
On the next Rp25,000,000	5	1,250,000
On the next Rp50,000,000	10	5,000,000
On the next Rp100,000,000	15	15,000,000
Over Rp200,000,000	25	

INDIVIDUAL TAX CALCULATION

Calendar year 2001

Assumptions

Resident taxpayer and wife with two children; salary is paid on a gross basis (1).

Tax computation

Gross wages paid in 2001		Rp 600,000,000
Employer's contribution for Jamsostek (0.54%)		3,240,000
Capital gains (domestic) on sales of assets other than land, buildings or shares		30,000,000
		633,240,000
Less—Allowable deductions:		
Taxpayer	2,880,000	
Wife	1,440,000	
Children (two)	2,880,000	
Business expenses	1,296,000	
Employee contribution to Jamsostek (2%) (2)	12,000,000	20,496,000
Net paid taxable income		Rp 612,744,000
Income tax thereon:		
On first 25,000,000	1,250,000	
On the next 25,000,000	2,500,000	
On the next 50,000,000	7,500,000	
On the next 100,000,000	25,000,000	
On remainder (412,744,000)	144,460,400	Rp 180,710,400
Payable thus:		
Income tax withheld on wages received		Rp 171,250,000
Balance payable		9,460,400
		Rp 180,710,400

Notes:

1. To apply the above calculations to an expatriate living in Indonesia, omit the employer and employee contributions to Jamsostek.
2. The employer's contribution to Jamsostek consists of the occupational accident security contribution of 0.24% and the death security contribution of 0.3%.
3. Exchange rate of the Indonesian rupiah at December 29, 2001: US$1 = Rp10,400 The exchange rate has varied significantly in recent years. The official rates published weekly by the Tax Office are used in computing taxable income.

PwC contact

For additional information on taxation in Iran, contact:

Abbas Hoshi
Hoshiyar/Behmand & Co.*
130, Ghaemmagham Farahani Avenue
(P.O. Box 15815-1619)
Tehran, Iran
Telephone: (98) (21) 8305391–4, 8844684, 8843704–5
Fax: (98) (21) 8844685
e-mail: hb-ir-pwc@dpi.net.ir (Fax is also recommended.)

*A cooperative firm of PricewaterhouseCoopers in Iran.

Significant developments

A new tax law was approved in February 2002, based on which the salary tax rate has been decreased. This new tax rate is applicable on the salary earned from February 17, 2002.

Territoriality and residence

All Iranians residing in Iran are subject to tax on their worldwide income. Iranians resident abroad and foreigners resident in Iran are subject to national taxes on income earned in Iran. Iranian nationals are considered resident in Iran if they have a place of residence in Iran or have resided for a total of more than six months in Iran during any one year.

In computing worldwide income, an Iranian resident in Iran must include the net amount of income received abroad or remitted from abroad. This implies that relief for tax paid in other countries is given by deducting this tax from gross income.

A foreign national resident in Iran will be subject to tax only on income earned in Iran, and not on worldwide income.

In the case of income earned from sources in Germany, France, South Africa, and a few of the new republics in Central Asia with which there are double taxation treaties, either such income is excluded from income tax or the gross amount will be taken as income and tax paid at source will be taken as an advance payment. General rules of 183-day residence and the taxpayer's not being subject to the other country's tax apply in Iran.

Foreign nationals who work in Iran and have obtained a work permit are treated as resident. The resident permit is issued accordingly.

Foreign currency transfer/An expatriate working in Iran as an employee of a registered company or branch is allowed to transfer net salary abroad in foreign currency purchased from official money dealers, owners of funds resulting from export activities or transferred from foreign-source funds (such funds should be kept in an Iranian bank account) and even from Iranian commercial banks (since July 2001).

Gross income

Employee gross income/Taxable income is deemed to include, for both foreigners and Iranians, all of their income (as limited above), together with free housing (as explained below), cost-of-living allowances or other cash payments, tax payments made by the employer on behalf of the employee, bonuses (less Rls1,300,000 per month or Rls1,500,000 per month from March 21, 2002, the first day of the new Iranian year), and a free car (as explained below).

Nonpecuniary benefits liable to salary tax are assessed and computed as noted below.

1. Free housing:
   a. Furnished—Equal to 25% of salary;
   b. Unfurnished—Equal to 20% of salary and taxable recurring compensation after the relevant deduction, if any.
2. Allocated car with driver—Equal to 10% (without driver, equal to 5%) of salary and taxable recurring compensation after the relevant deduction, if any.
3. Such other no pecuniary income as may, at the proposal of the Ministry of Finance and with the approval of the Council of Ministers, be considered as benefits received—An amount equal to the cost price incurred by the payer.

There are no concessions to foreigners working in Iran on a short-term or a long-term basis.

Note: In practice, since the expatriate's salary agreement is not sent to the Tax Office, taxable salary is assessed on a deemed-salary rather than on a reported-salary basis. The employers' reason for this decision is mostly because of the fact that the actual salary package is more than the deemed salary (as stated in the table). The arbitrary amount of the salary subject to income tax is determined by the Tax Office for each year, on the basis of the expatriate's nationality and the nature of the assigned job (which is specified in the work permit). The employer of an expatriate employee is required to provide the Tax Office with the employee's salary agreement, the amount of which should not be less than the deemed taxable salary of US$1,000 to US$7,000 per month (depending on the job description and nationality of the employee).

Capital gains and investment income/Capital gains and income from investments are taxable and the related tax is withheld at source. For a short-term resident, this income is subject to income tax in Iran, provided the capital asset or investment has been acquired/made and reported during the stay in Iran and provided the income is realized during this period.

Deductions

An annual basic deduction of Rls15,600,000 (Rls1,300,000 per month) is allowed between February 17, 2002, to March 20, 2002. From the next new Iranian year (starting March 21, 2002) the basic annual deduction will be increased to Rls17,400,000 (Rls1,450,000 monthly).

Business deductions/There are no specific business deductions except for family medical expenses of employees working in underdeveloped areas (the list of which is announced by the Planning and Management Organization), which are subject to a 50% discount on the tax amount applicable to the salary income.

Personal allowance/Personal, spouse, or dependent allowances are not available.

Tax credit

Since the withholding tax on salary is calculated on an annual income basis, and the requirement of filing annual personal tax return is no longer a tax requirement, withheld tax constitutes a final tax.

Other taxes

Social security taxes/The social security organization provides coverage in the following cases for laborers and employees falling within the regulations.

1. Accidents at work and occupational diseases and their consequences.
2. Ordinary accidents and illnesses, pregnancy, and childbirth.
3. Disability.
4. Retirement.
5. Death.

An insured person has the right to benefit from family assistance. Members of the insured person's immediate family can benefit from this law in respect of illness.

All employers are required to arrange for the insurance of their workers, irrespective of the type of employment or contract or the method of payment of wages or salary (cash or otherwise). The social security organization may insure the self-employed or employees and owners of enterprises in accordance with special regulations for all or certain of the cases enumerated in this law, but any insurance of domestic servants and occasional workers is dependent on mutual agreement between the employer and the employee.

Insurance contributions are to be made at a rate of 27% of salary and other regular compensation—7% payable by the employee (usually withheld from the monthly salary) and the balance of 20% at the employer's expense. The ceiling of the salary and wages subject to this contribution is determined by the government and is based on the annual basic salary. For the year ending March 20, 2002 basic salary is Rls67,900 per day (Rls2,037,000 per month). From March 21, 2002, the new Iranian year, the ceiling is Rls83,580 per day (Rls2,507,400 per month).

Expatriates working in Iran are subject to the above-mentioned regulation, except in the cases described below.

1. If there is a contract or agreement between the Iranian government and the government of the concerned country, the terms of this contract should be observed.
2. If the employee provides the Iranian social security organization with a legal certificate that confirms that the employee is insured with the social security organization of the home country or any other country for the period that the employee is working in Iran, the employee is exempt from payment of a social security premium for that period.

Unemployment insurance charges/An unemployment charge equal to 3% of salary, subject to a social security premium, is levied. The charges are payable directly by the employer. The Social Security Organization is in charge of collecting this amount through the monthly payroll submitted by the employer.

Ministry of Labor charges/All expatriates' salaries (except in a few cases) are subject to a fixed charge equal to 30% (according to the Annual Budget Law) of salary (to be determined on a deemed basis) plus 3% on employment charges (which is calculated on the maximum salary subject to the social security deduction). This is payable to the Ministry of Labor by the employer. Salary is determined on an arbitrary basis and is equivalent to US$1,000 to US$7,000, depending on the expatriate's nationality and job title. By taking the new tax procedure (deemed-salary tax table) into consideration, this base may be changed.

Local taxes on income/There is no local income tax.

Property tax/According to the new tax law property tax is no longer assessed on the assets of an individual.

Tax administration

Returns/In Iran, there is no aggregation of the incomes of a husband and wife for determining total taxable income. Tax is payable by each individual on the basis of that individual's income. The taxable year is the year ended March 20.

Payment of tax/According to the new tax law, tax is withheld at source and individuals are no longer required to file annual tax return. An individual who has a business practice is required to keep financial records and also file an annual tax return. Such individual's income is subject to tax rate as stated in Article 131 (15% to 35%).

Foreigners' tax procedure/Expatriates are allowed to work in Iran under the conditions established by the Ministry of Labor. A work permit and a residence permit are issued on the basis of the request of either the Iranian company or the government offices that have contracted with the foreign company. If the work visa is issued, the employee should obtain the work permit, which is valid for one to twelve months. The company (or branch) in Iran is responsible for payment of the related salary tax, and the expatriate employee will be able to obtain an exit visa upon providing the authorities with the salary tax clearance (in the form of clearance against payment of taxes or issuance of a guarantee letter by the employer accepting the responsibility of payment of taxes). If the expatriate is also a branch manager or the managing director of a company, an additional branch or company corporate tax clearance is also necessary.

In the case of expatriate employees employed by a government office, a guaranteed letter (accepting the tax responsibility) issued by the employer is sufficient to issue the clearance letter (which is necessary to get exit visa).

Individuals who stay in Iran for less than one year (as defined for Iranian tax purposes) and pay income tax for a period of assignment in Iran of more than the income tax due for their part-year stay are allowed to claim a credit for the extra taxes (according to the new tax law), but the tax procedure has not yet been announced.

Tax rates

The tax rates shown below are according to Article 131.

Income tax/Individuals are taxed at rates varying between 15% to 35% as shown below.

Taxable income Over (Column 1)	Not over		Tax on Column 1	Percentage on excess
0	Rls 30,000,000	....	—	15
Rls 30,000,000	100,000,000	....	Rls 4,500,000	20
100,000,000	250,000,000	....	18,500,000	25
250,000,000	1,000,000,000	....	56,000,000	30
1,000,000,001		....	281,000,000	35

Salary withholding tax/Tax is withheld from wages and salaries at progressive rates; the first annual salary of Rls15,600,000 is exempt, and the extra amount up to Rls42,000,000 is subject to a 10% tax. The excess of this amount is subject to tax rates according to Article 131, as follows.

Taxable income Over (Column 1)	Not over		Tax on Column 1	Percentage on excess
0	Rls 15,600,000	....	—	—
Rls 15,600,000	57,600,000	....	—*	10
57,600,000	115,600,000	....	Rls 4,200,000	20
115,600,000	265,600,000	....	15,800,000	25
265,600,000	1,015,600,000	....	53,300,000	30
1,015,600,001		....	278,300,000	35

*Exempt.

For the year commencing from March 21, 2002, rates are as follows.

Taxable income Over (Column 1)	Not over		Tax on Column 1	Percentage on excess
0	Rls 18,000,000	....	—	—
Rls 18,000,000	42,000,000	....	—*	10
60,000,000	118,000,000	....	Rls 4,200,000	20
118,000,000	268,000,000	....	15,800,000	25
268,000,000	1,018,000,000	....	53,300,000	30
1,018,000,001		....	278,300,000	35

*Exempt.

Exchange rate

At present there are two exchange rates in use: (1) the official floating rate for government use only, and (2) the market exchange rate. The exchange rate at December 31, 2001 was:

	US$1 =	
	Buy	**Sell**
Floating exchange rate	Rls 1,750	Rls 1,770
Market exchange rate	Rls 8,000	Rls 8,020

Note:

From March 21, 2002, one unique exchange rate, the market rate, will be in use, and the floating rate will be removed from existing system. The exchange rate is expected to be US$1 = Rls7,700 to Rls7,900.

PwC contact

For additional information on taxation in Ireland, contact:

Enda Faughnan
PricewaterhouseCoopers
Wilton Place
Dublin 2, Ireland
Telephone: (353) (1) 6789999
Fax: (353) (1) 6626616
e-mail: enda.faughnan@ie.pwcglobal.com

Significant developments

The information in this entry is current as of January 2002. For subsequent developments consult the contact listed above.

Territoriality and residence

Irish income tax is imposed on the following.

1. The worldwide income of an individual resident and domiciled in Ireland.
2. Income arising in Ireland and the United Kingdom and foreign income remitted to Ireland of an individual resident but not domiciled in Ireland.
3. Income arising in Ireland of an individual not resident in Ireland.

The following two rules determine the tax residence position of an individual for 2002.

1. An individual who spends 183 days in Ireland during a tax year is resident for that year.
2. An individual who spends 244 days in aggregate in Ireland between that year and the preceding year will be resident in that year, provided more than 30 days are spent in Ireland in that year.

Additional rules apply in relation to ordinary residence, which may impact on the scope of income within the charge to Irish tax.

Gross income

Employee gross income/Expatriate employees regarded as resident but not domiciled in Ireland, will be liable to Irish tax on that portion of their foreign salary that they remit to Ireland, together with any benefits-in-kind (such as a house or car) or allowances that are provided to them by their foreign employer. The remittance basis does not apply to income from the United Kingdom. If, in addition, the individuals are in receipt of salary, benefits or allowances from an Irish-affiliated company, these items are fully taxable.

Capital gains and investment income/A single rate of 20% applies to most capital gains, (excluding certain interests in funds and life insurance policies where the rate of 23% applies). In computing capital gains, the base cost is indexed by reference to the level of Irish inflation during the period of ownership. Annual gains of up to €1,270 for an individual are exempt from capital gains tax. This exemption is not transferable between spouses.

A nondomiciled Irish resident individual is liable to Irish capital gains tax on the full amount of gains arising in Ireland or the United Kingdom and on that portion of foreign gains that is remitted to Ireland.

Income tax on interest paid on normal deposit accounts held by Irish resident individuals in banks and other financial institutions is confined to the standard rate of tax (20% from January 1, 2002) and is deducted at source. Individuals who are both nonresident and non–ordinarily resident and who make a relevant declaration can receive deposit interest gross.

Furthermore, certain tax-efficient investment accounts are available to individuals. A new monthly savings scheme is available to individuals over 18 years of age who are resident in Ireland at the time of opening the account. The individual must remain resident and/or ordinarily resident for the period of five years during which the account must be held. The scheme commenced on May 1, 2001 and accounts must be opened before April 30, 2002. The state will match the monthly savings (minimum €13, maximum €256) for a five-year period with a contribution of 25% of the savings. Income or gains on the account will be taxed at 23% at the end of the five-year period. If the funds are withdrawn or the individual ceases to satisfy the residence criteria before the end of the five years, the full amount (savings plus investment return) will be liable to tax at 23%.

Interest on special-term accounts of up to €476 per year (three-year term) or €635 per year (five-year term) may be paid tax-free. Any excess interest is subject to standard rate tax. Individuals are limited to one special-term account.

Investment income of a nondomiciled person arising outside Ireland and the United Kingdom is taxed only to the extent that it is remitted to Ireland.

Deductions

Business deductions/Individuals may claim a deduction for expenses incurred wholly, exclusively and necessarily in the course of their employment. These expenses would include travel costs when the employment requires absence from home, as well as reasonable maintenance expenses for such absences. Expenses incurred travelling to and from work are not deductible. There are no standard deductions.

An Irish resident individual may, in certain circumstances, obtain a deduction from taxable employment income for periods spent working outside Ireland and the United Kingdom. In order to claim the relief, an employee must spend at least 90 "qualifying days" in aggregate working outside Ireland and the United Kingdom in a 12-month period. Only periods of at least 11 consecutive days, throughout the whole of which the individual is absent from the state count as qualifying days.

Following the introduction of various restrictions, the deduction is now limited to cash earnings and subject to a ceiling of €31,744.

Nonbusiness expenses/The principal nonbusiness expenses that may be deducted are interest on loans for investments in certain private trading or rental companies. Other expenses that may be deducted are retirement annuity premiums for self-employed individuals and employees in nonpensionable employment. Contributions to revenue-approved pension schemes are allowable deductions for employees.

There are no standard deductions.

Tax relief has been introduced with effect from April 6, 2001 for donations by individuals to certain approved bodies (charities/educational establishments).

With effect from January 1, 2002 tax relief at source will be introduced for mortgage interest the effect of which will mean the tax relief will be granted by the mortgager prior to the payment of the interest. The relief is given at source at the standard rate of 20%.

Personal tax credits/Tax credits are available at the standard rate of tax. For 2002 the main personal tax credits are €1,520 single, €3,040 married and €1,820 widowed. A home carer credit of €770 is available to married couples where one spouse works in the home caring for a dependent person. Certain income restrictions apply.

No child credit is available except for incapacitated children, for whom the credit is €500. Individuals are entitled to a pay-as-you-earn (PAYE) credit of €660 if they have employment income from which income tax is deducted at source.

Additional credits may be available (e.g., for rent paid, medical expenses incurred, etc.).

Tax credits on dividends

Dividend withholding tax was introduced on April 6, 1999 and applies to dividends and other distributions made by Irish resident companies. The standard rate of income tax is withheld on these dividends. Exemptions apply in the case of certain categories of individuals who are neither resident nor ordinarily resident.

Other taxes

Social security taxes/The individual's share of social security contributions is 6% (4% plus 2% health levy) on the first €38,740 of income and 2% on earnings in excess of €38,740. The first €127 per week of earnings is exempt from PRSI contributions. The PRSI contribution rate for employers will be reduced by 1.25% from 12% to 10.75% with effect from March 1, 2002. For self-employed persons and certain directors a rate of 5% applies to all income.

Local taxes on income/There are no local taxes on income in Ireland.

Tax administration

Tax year/With effect from January 1, 2002 the Irish tax year is aligned with the calendar year.

Returns/In the absence of an election to the contrary, the incomes of a husband and wife are aggregated, and the income tax is assessed on and paid by the higher earner. Either spouse may elect to be taxed as a single person. Income of children is not generally aggregated with that of the parents, although there are provisions for this in certain cases. Tax returns are made for the tax year and must be filed by October 31, following the year end.

Payment of tax/Income tax is withheld from all salaries paid from Irish pay points. For other income, a system of self-assessment applies, and payment is made in two installments. The revenue authorities retain the power to raise assessments as necessary; and payment is made in one installment. The revenue authorities now have a power of attachment whereby they can seize assets of defaulters.

Tax rates—Full tax year

Single or widowed person—No dependent children

Taxable income Over (Column 1)	Not over	Tax on Column 1	Percentage on excess
0	€ 28,000	—	20
€ 28,000		€ 5,600	42

Single or widowed person—Dependent children

Taxable income Over (Column 1)	Not over	Tax on Column 1	Percentage on excess
0	€ 32,000	—	20
€ 32,000		€ 6,400	42

Married couple—One income

Taxable income Over (Column 1)	Not over	Tax on Column 1	Percentage on excess
0	€ 37,000	—	20
€ 37,000		€ 7,400	42

Married couple—Two incomes

Taxable income Over (Column 1)	Not over	Tax on Column 1	Percentage on excess
0	€ 56,000	—	20
€ 56,000		€ 11,200	42

INDIVIDUAL TAX CALCULATION

Tax year 2002 (January 1, 2002 to December 31, 2002)

Assumptions

Irish-resident, non–Irish-domiciled husband and wife, two children; one spouse who is employed by an Irish company earns all the income.

Tax computation

Salary		€ 61,000
Dividend from Irish company—Gross		€ 2,500
Total gross income		€ 63,500
Capital gain (after relief for inflation and exemption)		€ 5,000
Taxable income		€ 63,500
Taxed as follows:		
37,000 @ 20%	7,400	
26,500 @ 42%	11,130	
Income tax (see table above)		€ 18,530
Less—Tax credits:		
Personal credit	3,040	
PAYE credit	660	
Home carer credit	770	
Dividend withholding tax (2,500 at 20%)	500	(4,970)
Net income tax liability		€ 13,560
Capital gains tax (5,000 at 20%)		€ 1,000

Notes:

1. Other payments:

	€
Pay-related social insurance (rate 4%)	1,314
Levies (rate 2%)	1,270
Total	2,534

2. Exchange rate of the Euro at January 3, 2002: US$1 = €1.106.

Isle of Man

PwC contact

For additional information on taxation in the Isle of Man, contact:

David Churcher
PricewaterhouseCoopers
Sixty Circular Road
Douglas, Isle of Man
Telephone: (44) (1624) 689689
Fax: (44) (1624) 689600
e-mail: churcher.david@iom.pwcglobal.com

Significant developments

There have been no significant tax or regulatory developments in the past year.

Territoriality and residence

Residents/Individuals who are resident in the Isle of Man are liable to tax on their worldwide income from all sources. Generally, a person present on the Island for six months or more in the tax year is regarded as resident. However, individuals may be judged to be resident with less than six months' presence in one year, depending on such factors as the maintenance of a home available for their use on the Island and the purpose of their visits to the Island and abroad.

By concession, an individual who has accommodation available for use in the Island is not treated as resident if visits to the Island in any two consecutive years of assessment do not exceed four months in aggregate.

Nonresidents/A nonresident is liable to tax on income arising or accruing from any source whatsoever in the Island, with the exception of bank interest, building society interest, and dividends paid by certain companies included in a list held by the Treasury for this purpose.

International limited partnerships/A limited partner in an international limited partnership is not liable to income tax on income received from that partnership as long as the partnership has been granted a "certificate of status" as an international limited partnership.

Gross income

Employee gross income/A resident is assessable on income from employment (including most benefits), wherever carried out. There is no remittance basis of assessment. A nonresident is assessed on income from employment carried on in the Isle of Man.

Capital gains and investment income/There is no capital gains tax in the Isle of Man. Similarly, there are no death or estate duties or capital transfer, gift or wealth taxes.

Investment income is charged to tax as follows.

1. For a resident, on income from any source inside or outside the Island.
2. For a nonresident, on income arising in the Island, at the prevailing higher rate of income tax (see "Tax rates" below). However, by extrastatutory concession, the Treasury will take no action to pursue the liability to income tax on bank interest, building society interest and dividends paid by certain companies to nonresidents.

Deductions

Business deductions/Business deductions are applicable to individuals only for disbursements or expenses incurred wholly and exclusively in acquiring the income on which income tax is payable. They would include travel expenses, professional expenses and a proportion of household expenses. The expense of traveling to and from work is not deductible. There are no standard deductions.

Nonbusiness expenses/Deductible nonbusiness expenses are as follows.

1. Interest paid by a resident on any mortgage or loan, provided, in most cases, that the lending institution is based in the Isle of Man. If interest is paid at more than a reasonable commercial rate, the excess is not deductible.
2. Pension contributions paid to approved superannuation funds.
3. Within certain limits, 50% of the annual amount of life insurance premiums.
4. Charitable covenants to charities, whether based in the Isle of Man or the United Kingdom, and certain covenanted educational payments.

Personal allowances/Nonresidents are not generally entitled to personal allowances, and all of their taxable income is taxed at the prevailing higher rate. However, a nonresident subject to deduction of tax under the ITIP (Income Tax Installment Payments) scheme would be granted a portion of the single person's allowance.

Allowances for 2001/2002 are as follows.

	£
Single person	7,700
Married couple (Combined allowance—totally transferable)	15,400
Single parent (entitled to single parent benefit)	5,270*
Blind person/Disabled person	2,120*

*Paid in addition to a single person allowance.

Tax credits

Foreign tax credits are available under the U.K./Isle of Man treaty. The treaty does not cover dividends or debenture interest. U.K. personal allowances may be given under U.K. legislation to Isle of Man residents, provided a claim is made to the U.K. authorities. The Island does not have a treaty with any other country. Where no bilateral agreement exists, Isle of Man residents paying or liable to pay foreign tax (other than U.K. tax covered by the treaty) as well as Isle of Man tax on income arising outside the Island are entitled to relief from Isle of Man tax on the lesser of the marginal amount or the amount of foreign tax on which the deduction is claimed. The marginal amount is calculated as the difference between (1) the tax on the total amount including foreign taxed income and (2) the tax on total income excluding the foreign income in respect of which the relief is to be allowed. This is known as unilateral relief.

Other taxes

Social security taxes/No national insurance contributions are payable where earnings are less than £87 per week. Above this limit, 10% is paid by employees on earnings up to a limit of £575 per week, giving a maximum contribution of £2,538 per annum (on a salary of more than £29,900 per annum). National insurance contributions are not payable on the benefit of cars and car fuel provided by employers.

Self-employed persons earning £3,995 or more per annum pay a flat-rate contribution of £2.00 per week. In addition, there is a contribution of 7% of profits between £4,535 and £29,900 per annum. Therefore, the maximum additional contribution is £1,775 (on earnings of more than £29,900 per annum). This additional contribution is allowable in full for tax purposes.

Other taxes on income/There are no other taxes on income. Other taxes are raised in the form of customs and excise duties on certain goods and through value-added tax on the purchase of most goods and services.

Tax administration

Returns/The tax year runs from April 6 to April 5. Tax returns must be filed before June 30 for total income of the preceding tax year.

A wife's separate income is deemed to be her husband's for income tax purposes, and such income must be recorded on the husband's tax return. Husband and wife can elect to be taxed separately.

Payment of tax/An employee's tax and national insurance contribution are deducted by the employer under the ITIP system, and the employer is accountable to the Assessor each month for the amounts due. Income tax (other than that paid under the ITIP system) is payable on or before January 1 for the year ending on the preceding April 5 (i.e., on income from the previous tax year).

Tax rates

A standard rate of 12% is charged on taxable income of resident individuals up to £10,000 for single persons and £20,000 for married couples. A higher rate of 18% is charged on taxable income exceeding the standard rate limits. The nonresident tax rate is 18% on total taxable income.

INDIVIDUAL TAX CALCULATION

Tax year 2001/02

Assumptions

Resident husband and wife, two children; one spouse earns all the income.

Tax computation

Salary		£ 50,000
Interest (1)		10,000
Capital gains—Not assessable		—
		60,000
Less:		
Mortgage interest	5,000	
Life insurance premiums (50% of 1,500)	750	
Charitable covenants	1,000	6,750
		53,250
Less—Personal allowance		15,400
Taxable income		£ 37,850
Tax thereon:		
First 20,000 at 12%	2,400	
Balance of 17,850 at 18%	3,213	
Total tax due (2)		£ 5,613

Notes:

1. Interest and dividends paid by Isle of Man companies are paid gross to residents.
2. Manx effective rate (5,613 ÷ 60,000) x 100 = 9.355%.
3. Exchange rate of the pound sterling at December 31, 2001: US$1 = £0.6905.

Israel

PwC contacts

For additional information on taxation in Israel, contact:

Gerry Seligman
Shlomi Zehavi
Kesselman & Kesselman
Trade Tower, 25 Hamered Street
P.O. Box 452
Tel-Aviv 61003
Telephone: (972) (3) 795 4555
Fax: (972) (3) 795 4506
e-mail: gerry.seligman@il.pwcglobal.com
shlomi.zehavi@il.pwcglobal.com

Significant developments

A special taxation levy of 0.5% will be applicable to income earned in the year 2002. The tax will be imposed on individuals whose taxable income in excess of NIS500,000 or upon employment and business income is excess of NIS360,000 (certain reductions are available).

A real estate reform has been enacted into law on March 2002. The tax rate on gains accumulated after November 7, 2001 from the sale of or disposition of real estate has been reduced to 25% (instead of up to 50%). Sales tax has been annulled regarding assets that were purchased after November 11, 2001. Acquisition tax on residential dwellings has also been temporarily reduced from 5% to 4.5% and 4.75%.

Territoriality and residence

Israeli-resident individuals are subject to taxation on Israeli-source income (i.e., income accrued in, derived from or received in Israel). The individual taxpayer is given relief for foreign taxes paid either in accordance with the relevant double taxation treaty or unilaterally. In addition, certain income, although from foreign sources, is deemed to be Israeli-source income in the hands of a resident, namely the following.

1. Income from a profession or vocation that an Israeli resident generally conducts in Israel. For these purposes, a change in the character of the income (e.g., business income vs. employment income or vice versa) generated from the same vocation would not be considered a change in the vocation itself.
2. Income of an Israeli-resident employee from work performed outside of Israel for an Israeli resident employer within four years from the employee's departure from Israel. If the work is of the same nature as that in which the employee was engaged in Israel, the income is taxable even if the four years have elapsed. The four-year limit also does not apply if the employer is the state of Israel or a specified quasi-government body.
3. Profits from a business controlled and managed in Israel.
4. Capital gains that accrue to an Israeli resident outside of Israel (in respect of assets held outside Israel), even if the proceeds are not remitted to Israel.

Nonresident individuals are subject to income tax on Israeli-source income and to capital gains tax on capital gains from assets situated in Israel or a right to an asset in Israel, as well as the profits of a business controlled and managed in Israel. They are also subject to tax on income arising abroad and received in Israel, unless the income is received by a person who is in Israel for some temporary purpose only, without any intention of establishing a permanent residence in Israel and who, during the tax year, has not actually resided there, whether continuously or with interruptions, for a total of more than six months. A nonresident can be assessable and chargeable to tax in the name of a trustee, guardian, committee, attorney, factor, agent, receiver, branch, or manager, irrespective of whether such appointee is in receipt of the relevant income.

The Israel Income Tax Ordinance defines a "resident" as "an individual who resides in Israel except for such temporary absences which to the assessing officer may seem reasonable and not inconsistent with the claim of such individual to be resident in Israel." In practice, all circumstances relating to the question of residence of the taxpayer should be examined, including such factors as birthplace, ownership of property in Israel, close family residing in Israel, the type of visa used for entry into Israel, the taxpayer's own representations, military service, the nature of the taxpayer's living quarters in Israel, and, above all, the length of time spent in Israel. If these and any other relevant factors show that a home has been established in Israel, then the taxpayer will be considered resident for tax purposes.

Should an individual be deemed an Israeli resident while at the same time resident of another country, the tie-breaker tests set out in the applicable treaty will determine in which country the employee will be viewed as resident. Generally, the treaties focus on factors relating to where the person's permanent home is maintained, in which country the person's personal and economic relations are closest ("center of vital interests" test) and in which country the person is a national.

The Israel Income Tax Ordinance defines a nonresident taxpayer as being anyone other than a person resident in Israel. It elaborates on this definition by including, inter alia, any person who is in Israel for some temporary purpose only, as described above.

Gross income

Employee gross income/All remuneration derived from employment, including allowances paid to an employee for cars, clothes, transport, professional literature, and the like, are taxed as ordinary income. If the interest rate charged on loans to employees is less than the rate of increase in the consumer price index (CPI) (with an addition of 4% annual interest), the resulting benefit for each month in which these loans are outstanding (i.e., the difference between actual interest charged and the increase in the CPI plus interest) is also taxed as ordinary employment income. The prescribed value of the regular use of a company car is considered to be income of the employee. Any benefit arising from exercising a right or option at a price below its market value is considered to be income of the employee. The only benefits that are exempt from tax are employers' contributions to further education and training schemes and their contributions to approved pension and benefit schemes (subject to certain requirements and maximum levels of contribution).

Nonresidents that have qualified as "foreign experts" are entitled to certain deductions as follows. A nonresident employee who satisfied the following criteria would be regarded as a foreign expert.

1. Was invited by a resident employer to perform duties in his or her area of expertise, which is not a manpower company or temporary agency;
2. Is legally employed in Israel (i.e., with work permits issued by the Ministry of the Interior);
3. Earns more than NIS10,000 per month; tax is withheld from salary on a monthly basis.

Such foreign experts can deduct from their remuneration earned in Israel accommodation expenses and a daily allowance for meals for a period not exceeding 12 months. The daily meal deduction is restricted to the lower of (1) a prescribed amount, currently NIS250 per day or (2) 50% of gross employment income (according to the tax authorities guidelines). Otherwise, all earnings from employment performed in Israel are generally taxable as for other residents. Certain personal tax credit points are also allowed to foreign residents.

"Approved specialists" (nonresidents approved by the director of the Investment Center at the Ministry of Industry and Trade), provided they are experts who possess skills not readily available locally, are taxed at a maximum rate of 25% on their earnings for a period of three years, with a possible extension of up to a further five years. They are also entitled to the benefits available to foreign experts in the first 12 months. Approval is normally given on income up to US$75,000 per annum.

Capital gains and investment income/Capital gains tax is payable on capital gains (with some exceptions) by residents of Israel on the sale of assets (irrespective of the location of the assets) and by nonresidents on the sale of assets located in Israel or of the direct or indirect right to an asset located in Israel.

For the purposes of assessing tax, the capital gain is generally calculated in local currency terms, and provisions exist for segregating the taxable gain into its real and inflationary components. The inflationary amount is the total of two components: (i) net cost indexation difference and (ii) share of retained profits (in the event of a disposal of shares).

The net cost indexation difference is equal to the original cost of the asset less depreciation (where applicable) multiplied by the percentage increase in the Israeli consumer price index from the date of acquisition of the asset to the date of its sale. This component of the inflationary amount is exempt to the extent it accrued after January 1, 1994 and is generally subject to tax at the rate of 10% if it accrued before then.

A nonresident who invests in taxable assets with foreign currency may elect to calculate the inflationary amount in terms of the foreign currency originally invested. Under this option, in the event of sale of shares in an Israeli resident company, the inflationary amount attributable to exchange differences on the investment is exempt from Israeli tax.

In the case of a disposal of shares, the share of retained profits is the amount of gain equal to the proportional part of the retained profits of the company that the seller of the shares would have rights to by virtue of those shares. Profits for this purpose are generally defined as financial statement profits available for distribution which accumulated over the period from the end of the tax year prior to the year of acquisition of the shares to the end of the tax year prior to the year of sale, but no more than seven years prior to the year of sale. The amount of the profits is not to exceed the amount of income taxed in the above-mentioned period, less the taxes thereon and any dividend distributed therefrom, with the addition of tax-exempt income. A nonresident is not exempt from tax on this type of inflationary amount.

The remaining "real gain," if any, is generally taxable at the regular tax rates (30% to 50%).

Special tax rates apply to assets purchased prior to April 1, 1961.

Profits on the sale of securities traded on the Tel Aviv Stock Exchange and certain Israeli securities traded overseas are exempt from tax, unless the profits are determined to be from trading in securities. Special provisions of the law apply to the sale of securities that were acquired prior to their listing on such an exchange.

Israeli resident individuals who dispose of foreign securities that are listed for trading on overseas exchanges are generally liable to Israeli tax of 35% of the capital gain arising thereon, calculated in terms of the foreign currency invested.

Capital gains realized by a nonresident from the sale of assets that are not attributable to an Israeli permanent establishment or are not real estate rights may qualify for treaty exemption, depending upon the particular circumstances.

Dividends from resident companies are generally subject to 25% withholding tax (15% for dividends distributed from approved enterprises), which represents the final tax to the individual. Dividends received from foreign companies are liable to a maximum tax of 25% (35% in the case of traded securities) on receipt in Israel. Nonresidents who are in Israel for some temporary purpose for less than six months in the tax year will not be liable to tax in Israel on such dividends received from foreign companies.

Deductions

Business deductions/Business expenses deductible from business-source income must be incurred wholly and exclusively during the tax year for the purposes of producing this income. Employees are entitled to relatively few deductions. However, subsistence expenses if required to travel out of town and subsistence expenses abroad may be deducted.

Self-employed individuals are subject to special rules for determining the deductibility of expenditure on the maintenance of private and small commercial vehicles, as well as other expenditures such as telephone costs when the business is conducted from the taxpayer's house.

Nonbusiness expenses/Contributions to an approved provident fund and a training fund are deductible up to predetermined limits for the self-employed and certain employees. Mortgage interest and medical expenses are not deductible. Charitable contributions are not deductible, but a tax credit may be allowed (see below).

Personal allowances/Residents are entitled to personal tax credits against their tax liabilities according to their status. At January 2002 each point is worth NIS170 per month, resident individuals being entitled to a minimum of 2.25 points. Additional points are granted for, among other items, dependent children, new immigrants and single-parent families.

Tax credits and deductions are granted for certain payments for life insurance premiums and payments to provident and pension funds.

Tax credits

Foreign residents are not entitled to personal tax credits or unilateral tax relief on foreign income. However, in circumstances where it can be shown that the amount of tax payable in Israel exceeds the amount of tax credit available in the home country on specific Israeli-source income, the Minister of Finance is permitted to order a total or partial tax refund.

Donations to recognized public institutions entitle the taxpayer to a tax credit of 35% from donations that in aggregate are not less than NIS340, provided the donations do not exceed 30% of annual taxable income or NIS480,000, whichever is less.

Personal tax credits are available; see "Personal allowances."

Other taxes

Social security taxes/Employees' National Insurance contributions are 2.66% on the first NIS3,525 of income per month and 4.9% on additional income up to a maximum of five times the average national wage (currently, NIS35,250 per month). Employers' contribution is 4.93% up to maximum of four times the average national wage (currently, NIS28,200). Contributions for nonresidents are funded by the employee at 0.33% and 0.6% in accordance with the above limits and by the employer at a single rate of 0.7% up to maximum of NIS28,200. Special detailed rules and rates apply to the self-employed and to other sources of income generated by an Israeli resident (i.e., rent, interest, dividends, pension, etc.). Capital gains are not subject to National Insurance contributions.

National Health Insurance premiums/Health Insurance premiums are levied at 3.10% on the first NIS3,525 of income per month and 4.8% on additional income up to a maximum income of five times the average national wage (currently NIS35,250 per month). Nonresidents are not subject to National Health Tax.

Local taxes on income/There are no local taxes on income.

Land appreciation tax/Capital gains on real estate are assessed to land appreciation tax. The law relates to any real estate in Israel, including houses, buildings and anything permanently fixed to land; real estate rights and leases for 25 years or more. Tax calculations closely follow the calculation of tax on capital gains (see below). The tax rate on the real gain has been reduced from up to 50% to 25% on assets that were purchased after November 7, 2001. Regarding assets purchased prior to November 7, 2001, the reduced tax rate will be applicable only to the gain accumulated after November 7, 2001. The gain will be attributed to the period commencing on November 7, 2001 in accordance with the ratio of the holding period after this date to the entire holding period. Other beneficial provisions apply to the sale of real estate between November 11, 2001 and December 31, 2002.

The purchaser of real estate is subject to acquisition tax at the rates of 0.5% to 5%. A temporary reduction in acquisition tax has been granted as follows.

1. The 5% will be reduced to 4.5% on apartments (residential dwellings) purchased between November 7, 2001 and December 31, 2002.
2. Acquisition tax at a rate of 4.75% (instead of 5%) will apply to apartments (residential dwellings) purchased between January 1, 2003 and December 31, 2003.

Sales tax/Sales tax at the rate of 2.5% is applicable to the sale of most real estate rights. The sales tax does not apply to certain types of apartments (residential dwellings) that are classified as inventory (the 0.8% rate that had been imposed on this type of transaction was annulled as of November 7, 2001). Sales tax will not apply to sales of real estate purchased after November 7, 2001. Certain other exemptions will be available.

Tax administration

Returns/A taxpayer whose income consists of earnings from employment in Israel and who is taxed by deductions at source from wage, salary, pension, or severance pay ("employment income") not exceeding NIS490,000, plus certain additional income not exceeding NIS260,000 or 50% of employment income (and on condition that income from the sale of securities does not exceed NIS51,000), whichever is the lower, from which tax was deducted at source at prescribed rates (2001 tax return figures), is not required to file a tax return unless one is specifically demanded. Foreign residents are also exempt from filing tax returns if their income relates to (1) a business or profession where the activities were conducted during a cumulative period not exceeding 180 days in the tax year or (2) salary, interest, dividends, royalties, and other instances where tax was deducted at source.

Married couples are permitted to file separate or joint returns. In the latter case, a separate calculation may still be obtained for tax on income from personal exertion in any business or vocation or from employment, provided the income is from independent sources.

Tax returns are filed on a calendar-year basis.

Payment of tax/Payroll withholding of income tax is statutory, irrespective of the residence of the employer or employee. In general, withholding taxes in respect of salary payments effected from the 14th day of one month to the 13th day of the following month are payable on the 15th day that following month.

Self-employed individuals are generally required to make monthly or bimonthly advance tax payments, usually based on a percentage of turnover.

Tax rates

Income tax is calculated at graduated rates, as follows (2002 estimate, subject to possible adjustment for inflation in the course of the year).

Taxable income		Accumulated tax on Column 1	Percentage on excess
Over (Column 1)	Not over		
0	NIS 28,410	—	10
NIS 28,410	42,630	NIS 2,841	20
42,630	124,800	5,685	30
124,800	226,080	30,336	45
226,080		75,912	50

A minimum tax rate of 30% generally applies to passive income not derived from business or employment and to real capital gains.

Various special tax rates and benefits are prescribed in certain instances.

A special taxation levy of 0.5% is applicable to income earned in the year 2002. The tax will be imposed on individuals whose taxable income in excess of NIS500,000 or on employment and business income in excess of NIS360,000 (certain reductions are available).

INDIVIDUAL TAX CALCULATION

Tax year 2002 (estimate)

Assumptions

Resident husband and wife, two children; wife has no taxable income.

Tax computation

Salary		NIS 300,000
Interest on government bonds		40,000
Bank interest on foreign-currency-linked deposit		40,000
Profit on sale of Tel Aviv Stock Exchange-quoted securities		20,000
		400,000
Less:		
Interest on bonds and bank deposits (taxed at a Reduced tax rate)	80,000	
Profit on quoted securities (exempt)	20,000	100,000
		300,000
Less—Personal contribution to provident fund		5,580
Net income		NIS 294,420
Tax according to tax tables		NIS 110,082
Add:		
Interest on government bonds at 35%	14,000	
Bank interest at 35%	14,000	28,000
		138,082
Less:		
Personal tax credits (2.25 points as resident, 1 point for wife not working)—3.25 x 170 x 12	6,630	
Donations—5,000 x 35%	1,750	
Provident fund contribution	1,395	(9,775)
Total income tax liability		NIS 128,307

Note:

Average exchange rate of the new shekel in 2001: US$1 = NIS4.2056.

PwC contact

For additional information on taxation in Italy, contact:

Luca Barbera
International Assignment Solutions
Pirola Pennuto Zei & Associati
Via Vittor Pisani, 19
20124 Milan, Italy
Telephone: (39) (02) 66995481
Fax: (39) (02) 66995460
e-mail: luca.barbera@studiopirola.com

Significant developments

New rules are in force on inheritance and gift taxes, and apply to inheritances and gifts transferred after October 25, 2001. Tax on inheritance no longer applies, regardless of the relationship with the heirs. The only taxes applied are mortgage and cadastral taxes. Tax on gifts is levied only in the case of gifts made to relatives beyond the fourth degree (therefore, it does not apply in the case of gifts made to spouse, parents, children, grandparents, grandchildren, uncles, aunts, and cousins) when the estate or gift value exceeds €180.759,91 (€516,456.90 if the beneficiary is a minor or handicapped person). The only taxes applied are mortgage and cadastral taxes plus the "registry tax." Where the donor makes several donations during his or her life, these must be taken into account in calculating the tax rate to be applied. Donations of state bonds are also subject to gift tax (not to inheritance tax).

Territoriality and residence

An individual is considered to be resident in Italy if, for the greater part of the fiscal year (i.e., for more than 183 days), he/she is registered with the Registry of the Resident Population (*Anagrafe*); or has his/her residence or his/her domicile (principal place of business and interests) in the territory of the state.

The exemption from tax on income deriving from employment activities performed abroad has been abrogated as of January 1, 2001. Double taxation may be mitigated through the application of a tax credit.

The taxation of employment income deriving from an activity performed abroad is now applicable as follows.

1. Italian tax residents working abroad are taxed on income, wherever produced, on the basis of the "world wide taxation" principle.
2. In respect of Italian resident employees working abroad for more than 183 days in a 12-month period, in a permanent and coordinated way and having the working activity performed abroad as the only object of the work relationship, the taxable basis is now determined on the basis of "figurative salaries" (*retribuzioni convenzionali*), based the employees' level and sector of activity. Figurative salaries are capped, despite the actual income received by the employee.

Figurative salaries do not apply for social security purposes if there is a social security agreement in force with the other country.

An anti-abuse rule provides that Italian citizens who move to countries considered as "tax havens" (these are determined through a decree of the Ministry of Finance), are deemed to be resident in Italy even if they cancel from the Registry of the Resident Population, unless otherwise proven by the individuals.

The main income tax levied on individuals is the personal income tax (IRPEF).

Gross income

Employee gross income/Taxable salary includes all compensation (money or benefits in kind) and emoluments received in relation to employment, including any received as a share of profits or through subsidy or an act of generosity.

Out-of-town travel indemnities exceeding €46.48 per day in Italy or €77.47 per day abroad are included in taxable income if no meal and accommodation costs are reimbursed.

Some fringe benefits are taxable on a lump-sum basis, such as housing, loans, company car.

Transfer indemnities are taxed for the 50% of their amount, for a sum that can not exceed €1,549.37 for transfers inside the national territory, and €4,648.11 for transfers outside the national territory.

Please note that this kind of taxation is valid only for the first year.

There are no special concessions to foreigners on calculating taxable income.

Capital gains and investment income/For individuals, capital gains are normally taxable, even if not arising from speculative intent or by way of a business.

There are no taxes on capital gains deriving from the following.

1. The sale of a real estate used as principal residence if owned for more than five years.
2. The sale of a real estate, even if owned for less than five years, if it has been used as principal residence for most of the period of ownership.

Capital gains tax on securities is levied at the flat rate of 12.50% where the shares sold or transferred do not exceed 2% of voting rights or 5% of capital in the case of quoted shares or 20% of voting rights or 25% of capital in case of other participation; and 27% where the shares sold or transferred exceed the above limits.

Investment income, such as interest on bonds, is taxable at the flat rate of 12.5% or 27%, depending on the source. Dividends granted by Italian companies may be subject to final withholding tax at 12.5% if received by resident individuals and 27% if received by nonresident individuals, unless any tax treaty provision applies. Italian resident individuals may opt to have no final tax withheld on said dividends. In this case, the individual must include dividend income in the Italian tax return (where it is taxed at the progressive rate) and is entitled to claim a tax credit equal to 56.25% for dividends distributions decided in the tax year following the one in course on January 1, 2001. This tax credit may be full or limited (refer to *Corporate Taxes—Worldwide Summaries*).

If the stocks are included in a so-called "managed saving" (*risparmio gestito*), dividend income is not subject to withholding tax. Such dividends are included in the profit (or loss) of said *risparmio gestito,* which is taxable at a 12.5% rate. No tax credit is available.

Dividends distributed by a foreign entity and paid through a resident broker are subject to a withholding tax at the rate of 12.50%. In addition, they must be reported in the tax return and are taxed at the marginal rate. When a nonresident broker is used, these dividends are included in the Italian tax return and taxed at the marginal rate. In both cases, any foreign tax paid may be deducted from the tax due on the dividends.

Deductions and tax credits

Business deductions/There are no special deductions for business related expenses. Starting from January 1, 2001, self-employment income arising from the activities of managing directors, auditors, contractors, directors, and accountants is treated as employment income and therefore benefits from the same tax credits as employment income. Income from patents, trademarks, and so on, gives the right to a 25% deduction.

Some business-related expenses are not included in taxable income.

Nonbusiness expenses/Allowable deductions from taxable income include medical expenses related to handicaps, social security contributions and charitable contributions to the Roman Catholic Church; the principal residence income (i.e., figurative income) is totally deductible from the taxpayer's aggregate income.

For mortgage interest (up to €3,615.20), medical expenses (over €129.11) and insurance premiums (for the part of the premium related to the risk of death, disability or non–self-sufficiency, up to €1,291.14), a tax credit is allowed equal to 19% of the total amount of the expenses for fiscal year 2001. Starting from January 1, 2001, it is possible to deduct the contributions paid to certain kinds of pension funds; such a deduction is allowed up to 12% of gross income (gross of tax credits), limited to €5,164.57.

Employment income tax credit/For fiscal year 2002, an employee is entitled to the following tax credit, equal to the tax credit foreseen for fiscal year 2001 (prorated for a calendar year).

Taxable income		2002
Over	Not over	Tax credit
0	€ 6,197.48	€ 1,146.53
€ 6,197.48	6,352.42	1,084.56
6,352.42	6,507.36	1,032.91
6,507.36	7,746.85	981.27
7,746.85	7,901.79	903.80
7,901.79	8,056.73	826.33
8,056.73	8,211.66	748.86
8,211.66	8,263.31	686.89
8,263.31	8,779.77	650.74
8,779.77	9,296.22	614.58
9,296.22	9,812.68	578.43
9,812.68	15,493.71	542.28
15,493.71	20,658.28	490.63
20,658.28	25,822.84	438.99
25,822.84	30,987.41	387.34
30,987.41	31,142.35	335.70
31,142.35	36,151.98	284.05
36,151.98	41,316.55	232.41
41,316.55	46,481.12	180.76
46,481.12	46,687.70	129.11
46,687.70	51,645.69	77.47
51,645.69		51.65

Independent work and self-employed income tax credit/Tax credits (prorated for a calendar year) for independent workers and self-employed taxpayers in year 2002 are the same as for 2001, as follows.

Earnings		2002
Over	Not over	Tax credit
0	€ 4,699.76	€ 573.27
€ 4,699.76	4,803.05	516.46
4,803.05	4,957.99	464.81
4,957.99	5,112.92	413.17
5,112.92	7,746.85	361.52
7,746.85	7,901.79	309.87
7,901.79	8,263.31	247.90
8,263.31	8,779.77	211.75
8,779.77	9,296.22	175.60
9,296.22	9,812.68	139.44
9,812.68	15,493.71	103.29
15,493.71	30,987.41	51.65

Personal allowances/Personal allowances are granted in the form of tax credits.

1. The tax credit for dependent spouse who earns less than €2,840.51 per annum is as follows:

Taxable income		2002
Over	Not over	Tax credit
0	€ 15,493.71	€ 546.18
€ 15,493.71	30,987.41	496.60
30,987.41	51,645.69	459.42
51,645.69		422.23

2. Dependent children—€285.08 for the tax year 2001, to be allocated between the parents. This deduction works as follows: if the income is under €51,645.69, the deduction is of €285.08 for the first child, and of €318.14 for each one of the others, if the income is over €51,645.69, the deduction is of €266.49 for each child.
3. Dependent children in the absence of a spouse—equal to dependent-spouse deduction.
4. Any other dependent with an income lower than €2,840.51—same as for dependent children.
5. Dependent children less than three years old: add €123.95 each to the normal deduction, with effect from January 1, 2001.
6. Amount of dependent children deduction for 2002 tax year (applicable starting from 2003 tax return):
   a. €516.46 where:
      i. Income is less than €36,151.98 and with one dependent child;
      ii. Income is less than €41,316.55 and with two dependent children;
      iii. Income is less than €46,481.12 and with three dependent children;
      iv. Four dependent children.
   b. €303.68 if income is less than €51,645.69, for the first child;
   c. €336,73 where Income is less than €51,645.69, for second and subsequent children.

The deduction for children younger than three years old not applicable if the €516.46 deduction applies.

Tax credits

Taxes paid abroad as a tax on income included in the Italian taxable base are allowed as a credit against personal income tax. Taxes withheld at source are deductible from total taxes due. Taxpayers are entitled to a refund should the taxes withheld exceed the final tax due.

Other taxes

Social security contributions/Participation in the Italian social security scheme is compulsory for virtually all salaried employees and wage earners. An Italian employer must therefore register with the Italian Social Security Administration (INPS).

Social security contributions are due from both the employee and the employer. Only the workers' charges are considered in the following discussion.

INPS contributions to be paid by employees (white-collar workers and cadres) are about 10% of their gross annual compensation.

For fiscal year 2002 social security contributions due from managers and executives (i.e., "*dirigenti*") are as described below.

Commercial agreement..........	8.89% (INPS) on total gross income, *plus* 1% (Fondo Mario Negri, a pension fund) on a notional remuneration of €53,718.39 per annum of gross income, and €129.11 per annum as professional training charges, *plus* 1.95% (FASDAC, a separate supplementary medical care plan) on a notional remuneration of €44,194.25 per annum of gross income, *plus* €929.62 (PREVIR, entity consisting of a combination of insurance and investment). Not compulsory.
Industrial agreement	8.89% (INPDAI) on income up to a ceiling of €36,093 of income and 9.89% on income ranging from €36,093 to €78,507 or €143,105, depending on how long the manager has contributed to the mandatory social security scheme, *plus* A flat contribution of €610.45 (FASI), plus €206.58 for the first inscription, *plus* PREVINDAI (an additional pension fund) as follows: • *"Dirigenti"* enrolled before April 28, 1993: 3% up to a maximum annual earning of €100,709.10, 4% starting from a maximum annual earning over €100,709.10 up to €139,443.36, • "Dirigenti" enrolled after April 28, 1993: 2.5% up to an annual earning of €77,468.53

Self-employed individual not covered by a mandatory pension fund must register with a special "pension fund." The contribution is equal to 14% of the fees (contribution ceiling, annually revised, of Lit148,014,000 for 2001 and of €78,507 for 2002). Two-thirds of the total amount is the contractor's share, and one-third is the self-employed individual's share.

Also see "Nonbusiness expenses."

IRAP/This tax is applicable on productive activity exercised in any of the 20 Italian regions. IRAP has replaced, inter alia, local tax on income (ILOR).

Taxpayers for IRAP purposes are, among others, self-employed individuals, nonresident taxpayers who exercise business activities in Italy through a permanent establishment, and partnerships.

Briefly, the IRAP taxable base is the difference between compensation received and directly related business expenses (depreciation of tangible and intangible assets included). Personnel and interest costs are nondeductible.

The IRAP tax rate is fixed at 4.25%.

Additional income taxes/There are two additional income taxes in force: a "regional additional tax" (ranging from 0.9% to 14%), and a municipal additional tax (up to 0.5%). Both these additional taxes are regulated under IRPEF rules.

Note that, even if the regional additional tax ranges from 0.9% to 1.4%, regions can decide to adopt a higher rate or to fix special criteria to determine the rate applicable.

Below is the list of the regions that have significantly different 2002 regional tax rates:

1. Lombardia:
   a. 1.2% on income up to €15,493.71;
   b. 1.3% on income from €15,493.71 up to €30,987.41;
   c. 1.4% on income exceeding €30,987.41.

   The rate remains equal to 0.9% for income deriving only from pension and main residence.
2. Marche:
   a. 0.9% on income up to €15,493.71;
   b. 1.91% on income from €15,493.71 up to €30,987.41;
   c. 3.60% on income from €30,987.41 up to €69,721.68;
   d. 4% on income exceeding €69,721.68.
3. Piemonte:
   a. 0.9% on income up to €10,329.14;
   b. 1.4% on income exceeding €10,329.14.
4. Umbria:
   a. 0,.9% on income up to €10,329.14;
   b. 1.1% on income exceeding €10,329.14.
5. Veneto:
   a. 1.2% on income up to €10,329.14;
   b. 1.3% on income from €10,329.14 up to €15,493.71;
   c. 1.4% on income from €15,493.71 and €69,721.68;
   d. 1.9% on income exceeding €69,721.68.

   The tax rate is equal to 0.9% for families with an income not exceeding €30,987.41 and a disabled family member.

Tax administration

Returns/2001 returns must be filed by May 31, 2002. The definitive instructions are still to be approved, and the deadline will likely be postponed to July 31. The tax year for individuals is the calendar year.

Payment of tax/An income withholding tax is imposed on salaries on the basis of the tax rates applicable to the annual employment income. For tax year 2000 the estimated payment due is 95%.The on-account payment is payable in two installments: 40% of 95% in May/June 2001 and 60% of 95% in November 2001. For tax year 2001 the estimated payment due is 98%.The on-account payment is payable in two installments: 40% of 98% in May/June 2002 and 60% of 98% in November 2002. The balance is due when the annual tax settlement is submitted.

Tax rates

Tax rates for 2002 (equal to those for 2001) for the normal computation of IRPEF are determined on a graduated scale, as shown below.

Taxable income			Tax on Column 1	Percentage on excess
Over (Column 1)	Not over			
0	€ 10,329.14		—	18
€ 10,329.14	15,493.71		€ 1,859.25	24
15,493.71	30,987.41		3,098.75	32
30,987.41	69,721.68		8,056.73	39
69,721.68			23,163.10	45

The tax rates above do not include regional tax (ranging from 0.9% to 1.4%) or municipal tax (up to 0.5%).

INDIVIDUAL TAX CALCULATION

Income 2001 year (2002 tax return)

Assumptions

Husband (employee), dependent wife and two children. Employment income of US$80,000, mortgage interest for main residence of €3,600, net income of owner's home of €0.

Tax computation

Gross employment income		€ 89,322.60
Less—Social security contributions (10%)		8,932.26
Taxable income		€ 80,390.34
Gross income tax		€ 27,963.89
Less—Personal allowances/Tax credits:		
Dependent spouse	422.23	
Dependent children (two)	532.98	
Employment tax credit	51.65	
Mortgage interest (19% of €3,600)	684.00	(1,690.86)
Net income tax		26,273.03
Additional regional income tax (up to 1.4% of taxable income) (1)		1,125.46
Additional municipal income tax (up to 0.5% of taxable income) (2)		401.95
Total income taxes due		€ 27,800.44

Note:

1. The regional tax ranges from 0.9 up to 1.4% of taxable income, therefore the amount of this tax depends on the place where the individual is located or performs work.
2. Municipal tax ranges from 0 to 0.5% of taxable income; therefore the presence and the amount of this tax depends on the place where the individual is located or performs work.
3. Exchange rate of the Euro at January 3, 2002: US$1 = €1.106.

PwC contact

For additional information on taxation in the Ivory Coast, contact:

Alioune Touré
PricewaterhouseCoopers
Alpha 2000, 23rd Floor
(01 B.P. 2921)
Abidjan 01, Côte d'Ivoire
Telephone: (225) 21 22 88, 21 22 76
Fax: (225) 21 08 85
e-mail: alioune.toure@ci.pwcglobal.com

General note

This entry is repeated from the 2001/2002 edition. For more up-to-date information, consult the contact listed above or Mark Friedlich at mark.friedlich@us.pwcglobal.com.

Significant developments

There have been no significant tax or regulatory developments in the past year.

Territoriality and residence

The Ivory Coast taxes residents on their worldwide income.

Individuals resident in the Ivory Coast are subject to specific direct income tax, depending on the kind of revenue earned, and to general revenue tax (IGR).

Gross income

Employee gross income/Four taxes presented below are withheld from taxable gross income (strikethrough: as defined below). Taxable gross income is also the basis for calculation of taxes paid by the employer (tax on salaries and a social security contribution).

Taxable income includes all cash remuneration, including living allowances, housing allowances, bonuses, and social contributions paid by the employer. However, social contributions are not taxable if they do not exceed both 10% of total gross income and CFAF3,600,000 a year.

In-kind benefits, such as housing, electricity, water, and air conditioning, are taxed according to a schedule of deemed values. Reimbursements of business expenses are not taxed up to an amount that equals 10% of taxable cash income plus reimbursements.

There are no allowances for short-term residents.

Expatriate tax concessions/Holiday fare of an expatriate and expatriate's family paid by the employer is not taxable.

Reimbursements paid after leaving the country are not reported, to the extent that these reimbursements are not paid by the local employer.

Capital gains and investment income/Capital gains are not taxable, except for certain gains arising from the sale of shares.

Deductions

Business deductions/Individuals may take a standard 15% IGR deduction on their gross income for business-related expenses, such as travel fees, representation costs, and business materials. The deduction is applied to the adjusted gross income, derived by first calculating the 20% general deduction, described below, and deducting IS (salary tax) and CN (national contribution) taxes.

Nonbusiness expenses/A general or standard deduction of 20% is applied to gross taxable income and is the highly recommended tax choice for resident aliens. See "Tax rates" below for the formula used to apply this deduction.

Although the deduction of specific nonbusiness expenses is permitted under tax law, the practice rarely is used, since the results usually are less favorable than the result from taking the standard deduction.

Specific nonbusiness deductions include the following.

1. Interest on loans and debts.
2. Mandatory payment of freely paid arrears on rents.
3. Maintenance or alimony payments.
4. Life insurance premiums paid to an insurance company, up to 6% of the taxable income before deduction of the premiums.
5. Voluntary payments to a retirement account with concurrent life insurance, up to 6% of the net income with a ceiling of CFAF200,000, increased by CFAF40,000 for each dependent child.
6. Direct and equivalent taxes, including the general revenue tax (the effective IGR rate adjusted accordingly).
7. 50% of monetary gifts made to recognized athletic associations, up to 5% of the declared gross income.

Personal allowances/The number of a taxpayer's dependents does not affect IS (salary tax), CN (national contribution), CNS (solidarity contribution), or CNPS (social security) but is reflected in the progressive IGR schedule.

IGR allowances are based on deductions ratios called "parts" that relate to the taxpayer's family status. Unmarried taxpayers may deduct one part, married taxpayers may deduct two parts, and taxpayers may add one-half part for each dependent child, up to a maximum per family of five parts. See also "Individual tax calculation" below.

Tax credits

No tax credits are granted. However, the tax obligations of nonresidents may be affected by a tax treaty in effect between the Ivory Coast and the country where the taxpayer is resident. The Ivory Coast has such treaties with Belgium, Canada, France, Germany, Italy, Norway, Switzerland, and the United Kingdom. Tax credits and requirements are specified by the treaty.

Social taxes paid to the home country by expatriates are not creditable against Ivory Coast taxes.

Other taxes

Social taxes/Employers must contribute to the social security system (CNPS). The employer also pays 8% of the taxable salary to the CNPS Retirement Fund, of which

4.8% is the employer's contribution and 3.2% is withheld from the employee's salary up to a monthly ceiling of CFAF1,647,315.

Other taxes/None.

Tax administration

Returns/Employers must calculate and withhold taxes due by employees, and they must file monthly salary tax returns for both employee tax and the employer's payroll tax. Adjustment declarations are filed annually by January 31. Employees are not required to file individual tax returns unless they work for more than one employer or they work for an employer that is not established in the Ivory Coast. Returns must be filed on a calendar-year basis.

A husband and wife are taxed separately. The husband's salary is taxed under the head-of-household category, with the relevant deductions for dependents. The wife's salary is taxed as an unmarried taxpayer without dependents. Husband and wife, however, may also file jointly.

Payment of tax/Taxes, including withholding taxes, are remitted by the 15th of each month for the preceding month.

Tax rates

1. Salary tax (IS):

   1.5% of 80% of gross income (GI).

2. National contribution (CN):

   80% of gross income taxed at progressive rates from 1.5 to 10%, based on varying tax brackets as shown below.

   Formula: CN = 80% x GI x (Rate) – (Variable)

Taxable base		Rate	
Over	**Not over**	**of tax**	**Variable**
0	CFAF 600,000	Nil	CFAF Nil
CFAF 600,000	1,560,000	1.5%	9,000
1,560,000	2,400,000	5%	63,600
2,400,000		10%	183,600

3. General income tax (IGR)

   Taxable base:

   The taxable base (T) is derived as shown below, and includes a 15% deduction.

   Formula: IGR = (T/N x (rate) – V) x N, where:

   T = [GI x 80% – (IS + CN)] x 85%

   GI = Gross income

   IS = Tax on salary

   CN = National contribution

   V = Predetermined variable

   N = Number of parts

Taxable base	Net tax	–	Tax thereon Variable	x	Number of parts
From 0 to 300,000		Nil			
300,001 to 547,000	(R x 10/110	–	27,273)	x	N
547,001 to 979,000	(R x 15/115	–	48,913)	x	N
979,001 to 1,519,000	(R x 20/120	–	84,375)	x	N
1,519,001 to 2,644,000	(R x 25/125	–	135,000)	x	N
2,644,001 to 4,669,000	(R x 35/135	–	291,667)	x	N
4,669,001 to 10,106,000	(R x 45/145	–	530,172)	x	N
Over 10,106,000	(R x 60/160	–	1,183,594)	x	N

4. Solidarity contribution (CNS):

   1% of gross income.

5. Social security contribution (CNPS):

   3.2% of gross income, without any deduction, up to a monthly ceiling of CFAF1,647,315.

INDIVIDUAL TAX CALCULATION

Assumptions

Resident alien, married, two children; employer classified in highest-risk category for CNPS Workmen's Compensation Fund.

Tax computation

Annual base salary		CFAF 40,000,000
Taxes withheld from salary:		
Salary tax (IS) (40,000,000 x 80% x 1.5%)	480,000	
National contribution (CN) (40,000,000 x 80% x 10%) – 183,600	3,016,400	
General income tax (IGR)—Taxable base [(40,000,000 x 80%) – (480,000 + 3,016,400) x 85%] = 24,228,060		
24,228,060 ÷ 3 = 8,076,020		
IGR—Tax [(8,076,020 x 31%) – 530,172] x 3	5,920,183	
Solidarity contribution: (40,000,000 x 1%)	400,000	
CNPS Retirement Fund	632,569	
Total tax and social security		CFAF 10,449,152
Net income		CFAF 29,550,848
Employers contributions:		
Local payroll tax	4,800,000	
Family Allowance Fund	48,300	
Workmen's compensation	42,000	
Retirement Fund	948,853	
Total employer contributions		CFAF 5,839,153

Note:

Exchange rate at January 1, 2001: US$1 = CFAF699.260.

Parity remains fixed between the CFA franc, used in 14 French-speaking African countries, and the French franc. The rate is CFAF100 = FF1. The convertibility of the CFA franc continues to be assured, as long as transfers are made through banking channels.

PwC contact

For additional information on taxation in Jamaica, contact:

Eric A. Crawford
PricewaterhouseCoopers
Scotiabank Centre
Duke Street
Kingston, Jamaica
Telephone: (1) (876) 922 6230
Fax: (1) (876) 967 1949
e-mail: eric.crawford.jm@pwcglobal.com

Significant developments

There have been no significant tax or regulatory developments in the past year.

Territoriality and residence

In general, Jamaica taxes its citizens and residents on their worldwide income. An individual working in Jamaica is taxed on the compensation attributable to the Jamaican services and other Jamaican-source income.

Individuals are treated as being resident in Jamaica for a tax year if they satisfy any one of several conditions.

1. They spend at least six months in Jamaica in the tax year or visit Jamaica with the intention of remaining there permanently and have actually been in the island for six months in the tax year.
2. They (or their spouses) have a place of abode available for their use in Jamaica, and they visit the island at any time during the tax year, no matter how short the stay.
3. They habitually visit Jamaica for substantial periods. The Commissioner of Income Tax would probably regard periods totaling three months as substantial and visits occurring in four consecutive years as habitual.

An individual not domiciled in Jamaica is taxable in Jamaica on any Jamaican-source income and, where resident, on remittances of foreign income to the island.

Gross income

Employee gross income/An individual resident but not domiciled in Jamaica is taxed on the emoluments (salary, living allowances, benefits-in-kind, cars, etc.) paid for work done for or on behalf of Jamaica, regardless of where payment is made and regardless of whether the emoluments are remitted to Jamaica. Income for services rendered outside Jamaica is not taxed if the services are not related to Jamaica.

Benefits, whether in cash or kind, payable for services rendered are taxable. Accommodation is ascribed a maximum taxable value of 15% of total taxable emoluments/other than the value of the accommodation. If the cost or market value of the accommodation exceeds other emoluments, the value is 15% of the average of other emoluments including those paid by connected parties and annual cost/market value of the accommodation.

The taxable benefit arising from the private use of a company car ranges from J$30,000 to J$140,000 and is determined by reference to the cost, the age and the relative percentage of private and business use.

Persons to whom allowances for laundry and uniforms (up to a specified limit) can be paid tax-free must be designated by the Commissioner of Income Tax.

Tax reimbursement is exempt from tax, provided it does not exceed the excess of Jamaican taxes paid over the tax liability on the same amount of income in the recipient's home country.

Capital gains and investment income/No tax is levied on capital gains. There is, however, a tax of 7.5% of the consideration paid on the transfer of certain assets, e.g., land and company securities (including stock). The tax is limited to 37.5% of the capital gain. Resident individual recipients of unfranked dividends and interest are subject to 25% withholding tax at source (corporate recipients, 33 1/3%). Franked income is distributions received by a corporate body subject to income tax that is resident in the island and from which distribution tax has been deducted at source.

An individual resident but not domiciled in Jamaica is taxed in Jamaica on investment income arising outside Jamaica to the extent that the income is remitted to Jamaica.

Dividends from listed companies/Between the period June 1, 2000 and April 1, 2001, dividends paid by a Jamaican corporation whose shares are quoted on the Jamaican Stock exchange were taxed at the rate of 20%. Since April 1, 2001, similar dividends have been taxed at the reduced rate of 10% and will eventually be taxed at the rate of 0% from April 1, 2002.

The rate of tax on dividends from unlisted companies remains at 25%.

Long-term savings accounts (LSAs)/Certain categories of interest income earned on long-term savings accounts (LSAs) were made tax exempt. These are the following.

1. Interest paid or credited in respect of investments or deposits made by individuals with prescribed persons if:
   a. The deposit remains for a minimum of five years without any withdrawal from the principal sum invested;
   b. The deposit or investment (other than interest accrued or credited) does not exceed one million dollars in any year;
   c. The account is not transferable, except on the death or bankruptcy of the depositor or investor;
   d. Not more than 85% (75% after July 2001) of the interest accrued in any year is withdrawn during that year.
2. Benefits derived from investments in certain life insurance policies may also be exempt from income tax if specified criteria are satisfied.

Deductions

Business deductions/To the extent not reimbursed, individuals (resident or nonresident) can deduct all expenses that are incurred wholly and exclusively by them in earning their income, e.g., business-related travel, automobile and entertainment expenses. Expenses for travel to and from work are not deductible. There are no standard deductions or deductions for expenses that are wholly personal.

Nonbusiness expenses/Social security and superannuation contributions to approved pension schemes are deductible in determining taxable income, as is interest paid in acquiring income. Approved charitable contributions, restricted to 5% of taxable income, are also deductible.

There are no standard deductions.

Relief is not available for medical expenses, insurance premiums and mortgage interest paid on a local dwelling.

Personal allowances/There are no personal allowances.

Tax credits

Foreign tax paid on income that is not taxed in Jamaica is not available as a credit against the individual's Jamaican tax liability on other income.

Other taxes

Withholding tax/Prescribed persons are required to withhold tax at source at a rate of 25% on interest income earned on investment instruments (subject to any lower rate as prescribed in a double taxation treaty). "Prescribed persons" are entities defined as such and include: the Accountant General, any bank operating under the Banking Act or the Bank of Jamaica Act; any institution operating under the Financial Institutions Act; any building society; any society registered under the Cooperative Societies Act, licensed securities dealers; societies registered under the Industrial and Provident Societies Act (unless certain conditions are met); the Ministry of Finance; life insurance companies; companies registered under the Companies Act in which the government, or an agency of the government holds more than 50% of the ordinary shares and which issues interest bearing securities; issuers of commercial paper; unit trust management companies; and any person connected with any of the persons mentioned above.

Social security taxes/Effective February 1996 there was an increase in the insurable wage ceiling under the National Insurance Act, resulting in a new maximum of J$120.25 per week or J$6,250 per annum.

Other taxes on income/The National Housing Trust Contributions and Education Tax, which are payroll taxes, are each payable by employees at the rate of 2% on taxable compensation for employment in the island. They are not deductible for income tax purposes. Expatriate employees are entitled to claim a refund of their National Housing Trust contributions when leaving the island permanently.

Concessionary loans/There is a taxable benefit on loans made to employees, as well as directors, of specified financial institutions where the interest on those loans is at less than market value. Market value is prescribed by the Minister of Finance and is currently 18%. The taxable benefit is treated as an emolument for the purposes of income tax and is subject to pay-as-you-earn (PAYE) regulations. Tax is not payable in respect of the benefit derived from certain types of loans where the aggregate amount loaned for the purposes specified does not exceed J$1.5 million.

Tax administration

There are six taxation departments.

1. Tax Administration Services Department (TASD)—deals with administrative issues.

2. Taxpayer Audit and Assessment Department (TAAD)—deals with the audit and assessment functions of Income Tax, General Consumption Tax (GCT/VAT), Stamp Duty and Transfer Tax.
3. Taxpayer Appeals Department (TAD)—processes appeals to decisions made by tax Commissioners.
4. Revenue Protection Department (RPD)—investigates customs breaches and fraudulent acts in respect of the various tax Acts.
5. Inland Revenue Department—deals with all compliance and tax collection functions.
6. The Customs Department.

Returns/Husbands and wives generally file separately and must elect in writing to be jointly assessed. Such a choice is unlikely to be beneficial.

The income tax year runs from January 1 to December 31. Taxpayers normally file their returns on a calendar-year basis, but a fiscal-year basis may be approved by the Commissioner of Income Tax.

Payment of tax/There is withholding of income tax from salaries. If withholding is not possible, for example, because the employer is not resident in Jamaica, the taxpayer will be required to make payment of estimated tax in quarterly installments.

Tax rates

The rates shown below are applied to taxable income for 2001.

Taxable income	%
On first J$120,432	Nil
On excess over J$120,432	25

INDIVIDUAL TAX CALCULATION

Calendar year 2001

Assumptions

Resident, non–Jamaican-domiciled married man.

Tax computation

Salary		J$ 3,200,000
Car benefit (scale rate) (1)		40,000
Housing accommodation—15% of $3,240,000 (2)		486,000
		3,726,000
Less:		
National insurance contributions (social security)	6,250	
Superannuation contributions	320,000	326,250
		3,399,750
Add:		
Bank deposit interest (net 24,000 + 8,000 tax withheld)	32,000	
Dividends received from listed companies	10,000	
Capital gains (exempt)	0	42,000
		3,441,750
Less—Approved charitable donations (3)		91,286
Taxable income		J$ 3,350,464
Tax payable:		
On first 120,432	0	
On dividends from listed company 10,000 at 10%	1,000	
On remaining 3,220,032 at 25%	805,008	J$ 806,008
Less—Credit for tax deducted from local bank interest and dividends		(9,000)
Net tax payable		J$ 797,008

Notes:

1. Assume car purchased in 1994 costing J$500,000, having under 50% private use. If the annual value of accommodation is greater than other emoluments, then the benefit assessed is 15% of ($3,240,000 + annual value) ÷ 2.
2. Annual value is less than other emoluments in this instance.
3. Limited to 5% of statutory income.
4. Exchange rate of the Jamaican dollar at December 31, 2001: US$1 = J$47.29.

PwC contact

For additional information on taxation in Japan, contact:

Hiroyuki Suzuki
PricewaterhouseCoopers—Tax
Kasumigaseki Bldg. 15F
2-5, Kasumigaseki 3-chome
Chiyoda-ku
Tokyo 100-6015, Japan
Telephone: (81)(3) 5251 2400
Fax: (81)(3) 5251 2424
e-mail: hiroyuki.suzuki@jp.pwcglobal.com

Significant developments

There is no significant change to individual income tax during 2001, except for taxation on capital gains arising from sales of shares, as discussed below. The new rules were introduced to stimulate the Japanese stock market.

Territoriality and residence

Nonresident taxpayers are taxed only on their Japan-source income. Nonpermanent resident taxpayers are taxed on Japan-source income plus that part of non–Japan-source income that is paid in or remitted to Japan. Permanent resident taxpayers are taxed on their worldwide income. Expatriate taxpayers are generally classified as nonpermanent resident taxpayers for the initial 60 months of residency, unless their Japan assignment period is limited to less than 12 months (if limited to less than 12 months, they are classified as nonresident). After the first 60-month period, the expatriate becomes a permanent resident taxpayer.

Gross income

Employee gross income/Salary, foreign-service premiums, cost-of-living allowances, tax reimbursements, and other benefits-in-kind (except for certain tax-exempt items) are classified as taxable remuneration (employment income). Japan-source employment income is remuneration earned for services rendered in Japan, regardless of when or where the remuneration is paid.

Reasonable relocation expenses, including expenses for a spouse and children, that are borne by the employer do not constitute taxable income. A reasonable amount of airfare for home leave, including airfare for family members, is not taxable. Where an employer provides housing, the amount of the taxable benefit is determined on a formula basis and, provided the housing arrangements are structured properly, generally is less than actual rent. In the case of housing provided for a director (a board member) of a domestic or foreign company, the taxable value would generally be 50% (35% if it can be substantiated that the house is also used for business purposes by the employer) of the actual rent. However, if the housing provided by the company is considered too luxurious, the market rent is taxable.

For directors and employees, income arising from the exercise of stock options is generally treated as employment income and taxed when exercised. However, income arising from certain qualified stock options is not taxable when exercised but taxed as capital gains when the stocks given by exercising the options are transferred if certain conditions are met.

Capital gains and investment income/Capital gains are, in principle, aggregated with other income after deductions for necessary expenses and after a statutory deduction of a maximum of ¥500,000. If the transferred assets were owned for more than five years, the gain is regarded as a long-term capital gain, and the taxable basis is reduced to 50% of the net capital gain.

Special taxation measures may be applicable to the taxation of capital gains derived from a transfer of real property (land, building and structures).

Capital gains arising from sales of certain designated securities (including shares in corporations, convertible debentures, etc., but excluding bonds and/or ordinary corporate debentures, etc.) are taxed at a flat tax rate of 26% (combination of national tax of 20% and local inhabitants tax of 6%) separately from other sources of income. This tax rate will be reduced to 20% (combined 15% national tax and 5% local inhabitants tax) for gains realized on or after January 1, 2003. Also, capital gains arising from a transfer of listed shares during the period from January 1, 2003 to December 31, 2005 are subject to a tax rate of 10% (combined 7% national tax and 3% local inhabitants tax), provided the shareholding period exceeds 12 months.

A taxpayer may opt to be taxed on the gains at a flat rate of 1.05% on gross sale proceeds through withholding of the tax, provided the designated securities are sold to or through securities companies operating in Japan. However, this optional tax scheme will be abolished as of December 31, 2002.

Capital losses arising from a transfer of listed shares on or after January 1, 2003 can be carried forward for three years.

During the period from October 1, 2001 to March 31, 2005, the capital gains arising from sales of listed securities can be reduced by ¥1 million, provided the holding period exceeds one year. This treatment has been applied to transactions made on or after October 1, 2001.

Under the following conditions, capital gains from the transfer of listed shares may be exempt from income tax.

1. The shares must be acquired during the period from November 30, 2001 to December 31, 2002;
2. The shares must be transferred during the period from January 1, 2005 to December 31, 2007; and
3. The total acquisition cost must not exceed ¥10 million.

Interest on bank deposits and/or certain designated financial instruments is taxed separately from other income and is subject to 20% withholding tax (a combination of national tax of 15% and local inhabitants tax of 5%).

Dividends are generally subject to 20% withholding tax and are taxed after being aggregated with other income. However, at the taxpayer's option, certain dividends are subject to 35% withholding tax and are taxed separately from other income.

A nonresident's income from Japan-source interest, dividends, rents, and royalties is subject to tax at a 20% rate (15% in the case of interest on bank deposits and/or certain designated financial instruments) or lower treaty rates through a withholding tax at source.

Deductions

Business deductions/Business expenses are generally not tax deductible against employment income. An employer's reimbursements of business expenses, such as moving, travel and entertainment expenses, do not constitute taxable income to the employee, provided the expenses are required for the employer's business.

Instead of a tax deduction for (unreimbursed) business expenses, a permanent and/or nonpermanent resident employee can deduct an earned income relief, computed by applying an appropriate rate to gross employment income as follows. (The minimum standard deduction is ¥650,000 or gross employment income, whichever is lower).

Gross employment income				
Over	Not over		Standard deduction	Percentage on excess
(Column 1)			(On Column 1)	
¥ 1,625,000	¥ 1,800,000	....	¥ 650,000	40
1,800,000	3,600,000	....	720,000	30
3,600,000	6,600,000	....	1,260,000	20
6,600,000	10,000,000	....	1,860,000	10
10,000,000	....	....	2,200,000	5

A self-employed taxpayer is allowed to claim a tax deduction for business expenses, provided it can be substantiated that the expenses are necessary.

Nonbusiness expenses/Interest, including mortgage interest, is not tax deductible. Japanese social security contributions are fully deductible. Medical expenses (irrespective of where they were paid), charitable contributions designated by the Ministry of Finance in Japan and insurance premiums paid in Japan are tax deductible, with certain limitations.

Personal allowances/Permanent and nonpermanent resident taxpayers are entitled to a personal allowance (¥380,000 for national income tax purposes, ¥330,000 for local inhabitants tax purposes) for themselves, for their dependent spouses and for each of their dependents. An additional special allowance for a spouse (maximum ¥380,000 and ¥330,000 for national income tax purposes and local inhabitants tax purposes, respectively, depending on the spouse's income) is deductible for taxpayers whose income amount does not exceed ¥10,000,000. Also, an additional special allowance (¥250,000 and ¥120,000 for national income tax purposes and local inhabitants tax purposes, respectively) may be claimed for a dependent aged 16 to 22.

In general, a nonresident is not permitted any of these deductions.

Tax credits

Resident taxpayers can credit foreign income taxes against their Japanese national tax and local inhabitants tax liabilities (with certain limitations) for non-Japan-source income taxed in Japan. A nonresident is not entitled to a foreign tax credit.

Withholding tax on Japan-source dividends is generally creditable against a resident's annual tax liability. A special deemed tax credit is available in addition to the tax withheld on dividends received from domestic companies for both national tax and local inhabitants tax purposes.

Fixed-percentage reduction

1. National tax—As a permanent measure for tax reduction effective for the year 1999 and thereafter, the Japanese government has granted each taxpayer a fixed-percentage reduction. For national income tax purposes, the tax due has been reduced by 20% (the maximum reduction is ¥250,000 per year).
2. Inhabitants tax—Local inhabitants tax due was reduced by 15% (maximum reduction is ¥40,000 per year). The new reduction applies for the calendar year 1999, which is due on 1998 taxable income, and thereafter.

Other taxes

Social security taxes/An employee whose salary is paid in Japan by a local employer, including a Japanese branch of a foreign corporation, is generally liable to pay a share of social security premiums. The employee's share consists of the following contributions.

	Premiums on monthly salary	Premiums on bonuses
Health insurance	4.25% (Maximum ¥41,650 per month)	0.3%
Long-term care insurance	0.545% (Maximum ¥5,341per month)	—
Welfare pension	8.675% (Maximum ¥53,785 per month)	0.5%
Unemployment insurance	0.6%	0.6%
Total	14.07%	1.4%

In the case of an expatriate, the above total rate will be reduced to 13.47%, since enrollment in an unemployment insurance program generally is not required. This is because an expatriate will not be unemployed in Japan, since the company guaranteed to employ the expatriate as a condition for obtaining a working visa. And the expatriate will return to the home country upon termination of the assignment in Japan. In this case, the employee's maximum share of monthly premiums is limited to ¥100,776. As noted above, social security contributions are deductible.

Totalization agreements/Designed to avoid overlaps in social security enrollment, the social security agreement between Japan and Germany became effective as of February 1, 2000, and that between Japan and the United Kingdom became effective as of February 1, 2001. The agreements between Japan and the United States and between Japan and France are now under negotiation. However, the agreement between Japan and the United States may become effective first.

Local taxes on income/Japanese local governments (prefectural and municipal governments) levy local inhabitants tax on taxpayers' previous year's income if they are residents of Japan as of January 1 of the current year. For inhabitants tax purposes, an equalization "per capita" tax is also assessed, at a minimum rate of

¥3,000 and a maximum rate of ¥4,000 per annum, depending on the locality in which the taxpayer resides. Local inhabitants tax is not deductible.

If taxpayers engage in their own business, a business enterprise tax will be levied on their business income by the local prefectural government. Business enterprise tax is deductible for calculation of business income.

Tax administration

Returns/Joint tax returns are not permitted in Japan. The tax year is the calendar year for all resident-status individuals, and a taxpayer is required to file a national tax return by March 15 of the following year.

If a taxpayer's income consists only of employment income from one employer that does not exceed ¥20,000,000 in a year, the payer of the income makes a so-called "year-end adjustment" on the employment income, and if total income other than employment income is ¥200,000 or less, the employee is not required to file an income tax return.

Payment of tax/If salary is paid in Japan by a local employer, including a Japan branch of a foreign corporation, monthly withholding of both national and local income taxes is required. The tax due on overseas payments of salary is payable when the tax return is filed, rather than through payroll withholding. Provisional payments of national tax are required in July and November if the previous year's final tax liability with adjustments based on the current tax rates (after the deduction of withholding tax) is ¥150,000 or more.

Tax rates

National tax

Taxable income		Tax on	Percentage
Over (Column 1)	Not over	Column 1	on excess
0	¥ 3,300,000	—	10
¥ 3,300,000	9,000,000	¥ 330,000	20
9,000,000	18,000,000	1,470,000	30
18,000,000		4,170,000	37

Local inhabitants tax/Combined prefectural and municipal taxes are applied at the rates shown below.

Taxable income		Tax on	Percentage
Over (Column 1)	Not over	Column 1	on excess
0	¥ 2,000,000	—	5
¥ 2,000,000	7,000,000	¥ 100,000	10
7,000,000		600,000	13

Nonresidents/A nonresident's Japan-source compensation (employment income) is subject to a 20% national income tax on gross compensation.

INDIVIDUAL TAX CALCULATION

Calendar year 2001

Assumptions

1. Nonpermanent resident taxpayer with a wife (no income) and two children who are younger than 15 years old.
2. Remuneration is fully paid in Japan or, if partly paid outside of Japan, no business days were spent outside of Japan during the taxable year.
3. Interest on bank deposit in Japan: ¥100,000 (1).
4. Capital gain on sale of shares in foreign company: ¥500,000 (2).
5. There is no remittance of money from abroad to Japan during the taxable year.

Tax computation

Gross remuneration		¥ 10,000,000
Less—Earned income relief:		
Up to 6,600,000	1,860,000	
10% of excess	340,000	2,200,000
Taxable income		¥ 7,800,000

	National tax	Inhabitants tax
Income as above	¥ 7,800,000	¥ 7,800,000
Deductions:		
Basic exemption	380,000	330,000
Dependent spouse (including special allowance)	760,000	660,000
Other dependents (two)	760,000	660,000
Social insurance premium paid	1,068,720	1,068,720
Taxable basis (rounded)	¥ 4,831,000	¥ 5,081,000
Income taxes:		
330,000 plus 20% on excess over 3,300,000	¥ 636,200	—
20% on interest income of 100,000 (1)	15,000	¥ 5,000
100,000 plus 10% on excess over 2,000,000	—	408,000
Equalization per capita tax (maximum)	—	4,000
Special tax reduction (3, 4)	(127,240)	(40,000)
Total taxes	¥ 523,960	¥ 377,000

Notes:

1. Taxation of interest on bank deposits is fully settled by the withholding of tax at the source of payment at a rate of 20% (combined national tax at 15% and local tax at 5%).
2. Foreign-source capital gain derived by a nonpermanent resident taxpayer is not taxable unless it is remitted to Japan.
3. For national tax purposes—20% of ¥636,200 or ¥250,000, whichever lower.
4. For inhabitants tax purposes—15% of ¥408,000 or ¥40,000, whichever lower.
5. Exchange rate of the yen at December 28, 2001: US$1 = ¥131.95 (TTM).

PwC contacts

For additional information on taxation in Kazakhstan, contact:

Rusty Lambert, Partner
Zaid Sethi, Tax Director
Krzysztof Lipka, Tax Director
Natalya Revenko, Senior Tax Manager
PricewaterhouseCoopers
29/6 Satpaev Avenue, 3rd Floor
Almaty 480070, Kazakhstan
Telephone: (7) (3272) 980448
Fax: (7) (3272) 980252
e-mail: russell.w.lambert@kz.pwcglobal.com
zaid.s.sethi@kz.pwcglobal.com
krzysztof.lipka@kz.pwcglobal.com
natalya.revenko@kz.pwcglobal.com

General note

This entry is repeated from the 2001/2002 edition. For more up-to-date information, consult the contact listed above or Mark Friedlich at mark.friedlich@us.pwcglobal.com.

Significant developments

The bands for personal income tax have been narrowed so that the top personal income tax rate of 30% now applies on taxable income of more than approximately US$4,000. With effect from January 30, 2001, an employer is liable to pay social tax at a rate of 26% of gross remuneration of employees (including foreign citizens and individuals without citizenship).

Territoriality and residence

Individuals are classified as nonresidents and are subject to taxation on their Kazakhstan-source income if they have been present in Kazakhstan for less than 183 days in any continuous 12-month period. They are classified as residents and subject to taxation on their worldwide income if they remain in Kazakhstan for 183 days or more in any continuous 12-month period, subject to double taxation treaty protection.

Gross income

Employee gross income/All types of direct and indirect income are included in taxable compensation. There are no concessions to short-term residents.

Capital gains and investment income/Capital gains are generally taxed as regular income. Capital gains from selling a share participation in a resident legal entity are taxed to individuals at a reduced rate of 15%, which is withheld at the source of payment.

Deductions

Business deductions/There are no business deductions allowed for employees. An individual may claim business deductions if registered as an entrepreneur.

Nonbusiness expenses/There are no deductions for nonbusiness expenses.

Personal allowances/These allowances take the form of deductions (currently approximately US$64) per dependent per year.

Tax credits/Taxpayers are allowed a tax credit for foreign taxes paid, limited to Kazakhstan taxes due on that income.

Other taxes

Social security taxes/Effective as of January 1, 1999, social security contributions have been restructured and now take the form of payments to the State Budget. These payments are social tax and obligatory pension contributions. Social tax is payable at the expense of an employer at a rate of 26% of gross income of employees. Obligatory pension contributions are payable by Kazakhstani citizens and permanently resident foreign citizens at their expense at a rate of 10% of their gross income.

Social tax/With effect from January 30, 2001, social tax on the foreign labor is payable at a rate of 26% of gross remuneration.

Additional local taxes on income/There are no additional local taxes on income.

Tax administration

Returns/Taxable years other than the calendar year are not permitted. Kazakhstan applies a self-assessment system whereby all taxpayers who have taxable income are required to submit a tax declaration detailing both taxable income and outstanding tax payable.

Tax returns are due on or before March 31 of each year following the tax year for which tax is due. Any additional tax amounts required to be paid should be transferred within 10 days of filing the return, but not later than April 10.

If an individual leaves Kazakhstan permanently during a tax year, his or her tax return is due on departure.

Payment of tax/Depending on the circumstances of employment, either taxes should be withheld by the employer or advance payments of estimated tax should be made quarterly by the individual.

Tax rates

The 2000 and 2001 individual tax rates are graduated, with indexed brackets taxed at rates ranging from 5 to 30%.

INDIVIDUAL TAX CALCULATION

Year 2000

Assumptions

1. Nonresident.
2. Annual salary—US$80,000.
3. Bonuses—US$2,000 (assumes Kazakhstan-source income).
4. Living allowance—US$1,000 (assumes Kazakhstan-source income).
5. Personal exemptions—Three dependents.
6. No tax credits or nonbusiness expenses.
7. Tax is paid by the individual.

Tax computation

		Total for the year
Salary	US$	80,000
Bonuses		2,000
Living allowance		1,000
Total income	US$	83,000
Exchange rate—US$1 to KZT		144.50
Total amount of income	KZT	11,993,500
Less—Allowable deduction (1)		34,800
Taxable income	KZT	11,958,700
Tax thereon	KZT	3,498,435
Less—Tax paid		(3,145,200)
Tax due	KZT	353,235

Notes:

1. The annual allowable deduction per person for the year 2000 was KZT8,700.
2. Exchange rate of the tenge at December 31, 2000: US$1 = KZT144.50.

Kenya

PwC contacts

For additional information on taxation in Kenya, contact:

Shaira Adamali
Gavin McEwan
PricewaterhouseCoopers
The Rahimtulla Tower
Upper Hill Road
Nairobi, Kenya
Telephone: (254) (2) 711195, 711196
Fax: (254) (2) 711184
e-mail: shaira.adamali@ke.pwcglobal.com
gavin.mcewan@ke.pwcglobal.com

General note

This entry is repeated from the 2001/2002 edition. For more up-to-date information, consult the contact listed above or Mark Friedlich at mark.friedlich@us.pwcglobal.com.

Significant developments

There has been a marginal reduction on the tax on personal income brought about by the widening of the tax bands and an increase in personal tax reliefs.

Presumptive income tax on certain agricultural produce has now been abolished with effect from June 15, 2000. As a result, individuals in the specified farming businesses are now required to file self-assessment tax returns.

Territoriality and residence

Kenyan residents and citizens are subject to Kenyan income tax on their worldwide earned income. Residence is defined as either having a permanent home in Kenya or spending more than 182 days in Kenya in any one tax year or an average of more than 122 days over three consecutive tax years.

Gross income

Employee gross income*/*Nonresident employees are taxable only on their income earned from within Kenya or derived from Kenya. Residents are taxed on worldwide earned income, regardless of source. Income of an individual for tax purposes includes all payments made by an employer on behalf of an employee. This will include salaries, wages, bonuses, and fringe benefits received or enjoyed by virtue of employment.

Fringe benefits usually give rise to taxable income at cost to the employer, although some benefits are taxed at standard amounts.

For employees other than directors with gross emoluments of less than KShs50,000 per month, the taxable housing benefit is computed at 15% of gross salary plus benefits (10% for agricultural employees residing on a plantation or farm). For employees earning above KShs50,000 per month and directors, the housing benefit is the actual rent paid or, where the premises are owned by the employer, the fair rental market value of the premises.

Motor vehicles supplied by the employer are assessed at the higher of 2% of the cost of the vehicle or prescribed standard rates.

Interest-free or low-interest loans granted to employees prior to June 11, 1998, are taxed on an imputed interest benefit of the lower of 15% or rates prescribed by the Commissioner. For loans granted after June 11, 1998, the tax burden has been shifted to the employer.

Education fees borne by the employer are not taxed on the employee, except where the employer has tax-exempt status. However, the fees are not an allowable expense for the employer.

Where a contract of employment states that remuneration should be paid free of all taxes, the amount received by the employee is deemed to be net income, and the figure is grossed up to determine the tax liability.

All benefits should be taxed under the pay-as-you-earn (PAYE) system.

Capital gains and investment income/Capital gains tax is not currently imposed.

Income from dividends within Kenya is subject to withholding tax of 5% for residents, and this is a final tax. Interest income within Kenya is subject to a general withholding tax of 15% for residents. However, different withholding rates apply as follows, depending upon the kind of financial instruments.

	%
Housing bonds	10
Bearer instruments (other than government bearer bonds and treasury bills)	25
Any other interest	15

On housing bonds, interest up to KShs300,000 per annum is subject to 10% withholding tax, which is a final tax. Income in excess thereof is subject to 15% tax, which is a final withholding tax. Withholding tax on interest income is the final tax.

The nonresident withholding tax rates on interest and dividends are 15% and 10%, respectively, and this amounts to the total tax liability. The tax withheld on payments to unit trusts is 15% for interest and 5% for dividends, and this represents the final tax.

Exempt income includes interest on tax reserve certificates and from savings accounts with the Kenya Post Office Savings Bank.

Deductions

Business deductions/An individual may claim a deduction for any expense incurred wholly and exclusively in the production of employment income. Reimbursements of business expenses such as entertainment, travel, and car expenses are not part of taxable income. Airfares and moving expenses paid to expatriate employees recruited outside Kenya and there solely to perform their duties are not taxable. Leave passages for such employees are also not taxable.

Nonbusiness expenses/Reimbursed medical insurance or medical expenses are not normally taxable.

Relief of up to KShs17,500 per month is given for contributions to registered pension funds or provident funds. The employee is entitled to claim this deduction in preference to the employer.

Interest payments on loans borrowed for the purposes of improvement or construction of residential premises are deductible, subject to a limit of KShs100,000 per annum.

Special deduction/Under certain circumstances, expatriates may claim a one-third deduction from taxable income if they are employed by a regional office that carries on no business in Kenya and if they are absent on business for at least 120 days in any tax year.

First-time buyers of houses can obtain a special KShs480,000 deduction, provided the following conditions are met.

1. The deduction is limited to KShs48,000 per year for each of 10 consecutive years.
2. The amount must be deposited with prescribed financial institutions.
3. The funds must be withdrawn at the end of the 10th year and, within one year of withdrawal, applied only toward the purchase of a house.

Any income earned on the funds in this 10-year period is also tax free, subject to all conditions being met.

Personal allowances/Allowances are minimal, amounting to KShs11,520 per annum for all individual taxpayers, and applied as credits against the tax liability.

Tax credits

Relief is given for double taxation only where a treaty exists. Available personal allowances are in the form of tax credits.

Other taxes

Social security taxes/Every employee must contribute to the National Social Security Fund. The contribution is 5% of salary subject to a maximum of KShs80 (K£4) per month. The employer makes a corresponding contribution. Overseas personnel who are expected to be employed for less than three years can sometimes claim exemption if they can show that they contribute to a similar scheme in their home country.

Hospital insurance/Employees earning over KShs1,000 per month must contribute approximately 2% of their salaries to the National Hospital Insurance Fund, subject to a maximum of KShs320. This entitles the payers and their families to a maximum refund of KShs450 per day should they be admitted to a hospital.

Local authority service charge/The local authority service charge has been abolished.

Tax administration

Returns/Wives with income from employment, self-employment, or certain professions can now opt to file separate self-assessment returns from their husbands. A wife's income from employment (or self-employment in certain professions) is taxed at special rates equal to the normal basic rates of tax. This has the effect of separating the income of husband and wife so that lower rates apply to both.

Self-assessment returns must be filed by June 30 in the year following the year of income. The year of income is a calendar year. Any balance of tax due must be paid by April 30.

Payment of tax/The majority of tax on employees is paid by withholding from salaries and benefits in the form of PAYE. Any further tax liability is based on self-assessment, and it must be paid by April 30 following the year of income to which the liability relates. An individual (other than one whose total taxable income has been subjected to tax at source) whose tax liability exceeds KShs40,000 per annum is required to pay four installment taxes by April 30, June 20, September 20, and December 20.

The installment tax payable on each due date is 25% of the lower of 110% of tax assessed in the prior year or the taxpayer's estimate of the current year's tax liability.

The airport tax paid by air passengers is collected at the time of ticket purchase.

Tax rates

The rates applied to taxable income from January 1, 2001, are shown below.

Taxable income		Tax on	Percentage
Over (Column 1)	Not over	Column 1	on excess
0	KShs 109,440	0	10
KShs 109,440	218,880	KShs 10,944	15
218,880	328,320	27,360	20
328,320	437,760	49,248	25
437,760		76,608	30

The above rates also apply to a wife's employment income and self-employment income from certain professions.

As shown above, the maximum rate of 30% is charged on income in excess of KShs437,760 (approximately US$5,612).

INDIVIDUAL TAX CALCULATIONS

Year 2001

I—Resident Kenya citizen

Assumptions

Resident Kenya citizen, married with two children. Gross income of husband is KShs5,840,000; of wife, KShs800,000. Benefits provided to the husband by his employer include an 1,800 cc motor vehicle (cost, KShs1,000,000) and a telephone; wife receives no benefits. Received bank deposit interest of KShs70,000 and dividend income of KShs40,000 and paid mortgage interest of KShs120,000 on owner-occupied property. Made capital gains of KShs500,000 on sale of residential property.

Tax computation

Husband

Gross income		KShs 5,840,000
Add—Benefits at standard rates:		
1,800 cc motor vehicle (1)	240,000	
Telephone	3,600	243,600
Total		6,083,600
Add—Bank deposit interest (2)		Nil
		6,083,600
Less—Mortgage interest (maximum deduction)		100,000
Taxable income		KShs 5,983,600
Tax thereon:		
On first 437,760 of taxable income	76,608	
On remaining 5,545,840 at 30%	1,663,752	1,740,360
Less—Personal relief		(11,520)
Tax payable		KShs 1,728,840
Dividend income—Gross		KShs 40,000
Tax on dividend income—Deducted at source (final tax)		KShs 2,000
Interest income—Gross		KShs 70,000
Tax on interest income—Deducted at source (final tax)		KShs 10,500
Capital gain on sale of property		KShs 500,000
Tax on gain		KShs Nil

Wife

Gross income		KShs 800,000
Tax thereon:		
On first 437,760	76,608	
On remaining 362,240 at 30%	108,672	185,280
Less—Personal relief		(11,520)
		173,760

Total liability to taxation

Total tax liability:	
Husband	KShs 1,728,840
Wife	173,760
	KShs 1,902,600

Notes:

1. Benefit is the higher of KShs86,400 or 24% per annum of capital cost.
2. Withholding tax borne at source represents final tax.
3. Credit for tax deducted under the PAYE system to be given against total liability, as above.

II—Expatriate employed by a regional office

Assumptions

Expatriate employed by a regional office; married with two children; gross income KShs3,600,000. Business travel, excluding leave, totals 140 days. Benefits provided by employer include an 1,800 cc motor vehicle (cost, KShs1,500,000), a telephone, housing, and furniture. Housing cost to the employer is KShs1,000,000 per year. This calculation only applies where certain conditions have been met.

Tax computation

Gross income		KShs 3,600,000
Add—Benefits at standard rates:		
1,800 cc motor vehicle (1)	360,000	
Telephone	3,600	
Furniture	4,800	
Housing at cost	1,000,000	1,368,400
		4,968,400
Less—Regional deduction (4,968,400 x 33.333%)		(1,656,117)
Taxable income		3,312,267
Tax thereon:		
On first 437,760	76,608	
On remaining 2,874,507 at 30%	862,352	KShs 938,960
Less—Personal relief		(11,520)
Tax payable		KShs 927,440

Notes:

1. Benefit is the higher of KShs86,400 or 24% of capital costs.
2. Credit for tax deducted under the PAYE system to be given against total liability, as above.
3. Exchange rate of the Kenya shilling at January 1, 2000: US$1 = KShs78.00.

PwC contact

For additional information on taxation in Korea, contact:

Ando Yun
Samil Accounting Corporation
Hanil Group Building, 21F
#191, 2-ka
Han-Kang-Ro, Yong-San-ku
Seoul 140-702, Korea
Telephone: (82) (2) 709-0551
Fax: (82) (2) 796-7027, 790-1507
e-mail: ando.yun@kr.pwcglobal.com

Significant developments

There have been no significant tax or regulatory developments regarding individual taxation in the past year. The information below is current as of January 2002. For subsequent developments consult the contact listed above.

Territoriality and residence

All individuals in Korea are classified for income tax purposes, as listed below.

1. Citizen—Korean national.
2. Resident—Non-Koreans having a domicile or residence within Korea for one year or more, individuals having an occupation that would generally require them to reside in Korea for one year or more, or individuals whose families accompany them to Korea and who retain substantial assets in Korea. Generally, residency is determined on a "facts and circumstances" test, evaluated on an individual basis.
3. Nonresident—An individual who is not deemed to be a resident.

Korean citizens and individuals considered as residents for tax purposes are subject to Korean income tax on worldwide income. An expatriate who is deemed to be a nonresident is taxed only on Korean-source income. A nonresident is not allowed all the personal deductions granted to residents, except for a basic deduction of W1,000,000 and additional personal deduction of W1,000,000.

Gross income

Employee gross income/Individual income can be categorized as taxable, nontaxable or tax exempt. Taxable income includes global income, capital gains and severance pay, each of which is subject to tax on a unique tax rate structure. There are certain elements of income on which the government has waived its taxing rights, whether or not an application for exemption is filed by an individual. There are other items of income for which a taxpayer can submit an application for tax.

Global income is subject to global taxation and includes earned income (salaries, wages, bonuses, and other amounts received for personal services rendered), interest income, dividend income, rental income, personal business income, and other income (prize winnings, royalties, rewards, etc.).

Korean tax law segregates earned income into Class A or Class B income, depending on the income source.

1. Class A earned income—Employment income received from a domestic (Korean) corporation or a Korean branch office of a foreign corporation for

services rendered in Korea. Such income is subject to payroll withholding taxes by the employer on a monthly basis.

2. Class B earned income—Employment income received in foreign currency from a foreign corporation outside Korea. However, even if foreigners who work in Korea are paid their wages overseas, the wages are considered Class A earned income rather than Class B earned income where the wage is deducted as an expense in calculating the taxable income of a permanent establishment of the foreign corporation in Korea.

   The employer is not required to withhold Korean taxes at the time of payment of Class B income; however, the individual is required to declare this income annually and pay income taxes thereon on a voluntary basis. Alternatively, the individual may elect to pay Class B income taxes through a licensed taxpayers' association, which collects and remits such taxes on a monthly basis. Taxpayers who join such an association are eligible to receive a 10% reduction in the amount of income tax payable.

Capital gains and investment income/Gains arising from the disposal of capital assets are included in an individual's taxable income but are taxed separately from global income. Certain capital gains are specifically exempt from tax. These include gains from certain transfers of farmland and other real estate; gains from the transfer of one house, including land, per household; and gains from the transfer of listed stock (corporate equity share certificates). However, exceptionally, when the total stake of a shareholder together with any related parties in a listed company exceeds 3% and total market value is W10 billion or more, the capital gains are taxed at the rate of 22% (if the holding period is less than one year, 33% would be applied). If the stake is in a small- and medium-sized company, the gains are subject to tax at 11%.

Gains from the disposal of foreign assets are taxable where the transfer is made after January 1, 1999 and the transferor has been a Korean resident for five years or more at the time of sale.

Capital losses are deductible only against capital gains. Unused losses may not be carried forward.

Interest income earned on other than National Savings Association deposits and dividend income received from both domestic and foreign corporations are taxable. Most interest and dividend income earned from Korean sources is subject to 16.5% tax withholding at source. Resident taxpayers are required to include any interest and dividends received from non-Korean sources in global income and to pay taxes thereon at basic global tax rates (discussed below).

Nontaxable income/The following elements of employee income are nontaxable.

1. Housing and related costs paid by an employer directly to a landlord on behalf of an expatriate employee. However, utility costs paid by an employer are taxable to the employee.
2. Reimbursement of business expenses, including social membership costs and entertainment expenses incurred by an employee for business purposes.
3. Cost of an automobile and driver and related maintenance and insurance expenses provided by an employer, provided the automobile is registered in the name of the employer and the driver is on the employer's payroll register.
4. Reimbursement of operating costs for a personal automobile used for business purposes, up to W200,000 per month.

5. Relocation and moving expense reimbursements.
6. Reasonable amounts of employer-reimbursed home-leave travel expenses for expatriate employees.

Special exclusion for overseas expatriate allowances/Overseas service allowances received by expatriates employed in Korea in excess of the regular salary they would be paid while working in their home country, such as cost-of-living allowances, hardship provisions, housing, transportation, education, utilities, domestic help, and security services, can be excluded from taxable income. The total amount of such allowances considered to be nontaxable is limited to 20% of an expatriate's monthly base salary or one-sixth of the total monthly compensation, including taxable allowances, whichever is greater.

Tax-exempt income/Individuals can request tax-exempt treatment for certain types of income (specified below) by submitting through their employer an application to the appropriate tax authorities.

1. Wages and various allowances received by a foreigner providing services under a high-technology inducement contract prescribed under the Foreign Investment Promotion Law, for a period of five years from the acceptance date of the technical service agreement.
2. Wages received by a qualified foreign technician/engineer providing services in Korea to a domestic entity under a engineering technology inducement agreement under the Engineering Technology Promotion Law (of which consideration amounts to US$300,000 or more) for five years from the date the expatriate commences rendering services in Korea.
3. Wages received by a foreign technician with five or more years' working experience at mining, construction, manufacturing, or certain technology-intensive industries or having a bachelor's degree and three or more years' working experience at these industries.
4. Wages and salaries received by a foreign researcher working in a qualified research center.

Deductions

Business deductions/All business-related expenses, such as moving expenses, travel expenses, automobile expenses, and certain amounts of entertainment expenses, are tax deductible. Alternatively, reimbursements for such expenses can be claimed by the business as deductible expenses and need not be included in the individual's taxable income.

Nonbusiness expenses/Certain other allowable deductions are outlined below.

1. An earned income deduction is allowed for salary or wage earners as follows:
   a. Entire income up to W5 million;
   b. 45% of the income from W5 million up to W15 million;
   c. 15% of the income from W15 million up to W30 million;
   d. 10% of the income from W30 million up to W45 million;
   e. 5% of the income in excess of W45 million.
2. A deduction for certain insurance premiums paid by an individual and other dependents, up to a maximum of W700,000.
3. A deduction for deposits in a qualified personal pension program (enrolled before December 31, 2000), up to a maximum of W720,000.

4. A deduction for medical expenses incurred by a taxpayer, up to a maximum of W3 million, to the extent that the expenses exceed 3% of total earned income. However, medical expenses paid for parents aged 65 or over and living together with the taxpayer and for the handicapped are not subject to the above W3 million limit.
5. A deduction for all of an employed taxpayer's own education expenses (including graduate school fees). Other education expenses within certain limits incurred by a taxpayer's dependents are deductible (W3 million for each dependent attending university, W1.5 million for each dependent attending elementary school, middle school or high school, W1 million for each dependent attending preschool).
6. A deduction for certain types of charitable contributions, generally up to a maximum of 10% of gross global income after the earned income deduction described above.
7. A deduction of W3 million (maximum) for wage earners who do not own a home or who are owners of a house of a certain size and who subscribed to a particular savings program for home ownership.
8. In lieu of one of the deductions listed above (except for the earned income deduction), a standard special deduction of W600,000 is available.
9. A deduction for expenditure paid by credit cards, up to 20% of the amount in excess of 10% of earned income. This deduction is limited to a maximum of W5 million.

Personal exemptions/Korean tax law provides all resident taxpayers with the following standard personal exemptions from individual taxable income.

1. A basic exemption of W1 million per year.
2. An exemption of W1 million for a spouse who lives with the taxpayer and who has income (other than interest, dividends and rental income) of less than the W1 million.
3. An exemption of W1 million for each eligible dependent who lives with the taxpayer and has income of less than the W1 million.
4. An exemption of W1 million for each handicapped person in the taxpayer's household. The handicapped person may be the taxpayer, spouse or other dependent. To qualify for the exemption, the spouse and or dependent are not permitted to have income in excess of W1 million.
5. An additional exemption of W1 million for each taxpayer, spouse or dependent aged 65 or over in the taxpayer's household. To qualify for this additional exemption, the spouse or other dependent should not have income in excess of W1 million.
6. An additional exemption of W500,000 for a woman householder with dependents.
7. An additional deduction of W500,000 for a woman salary earner in the case of a two-earner married couple.
8. An additional deduction of W500,000 per child for a working woman who has children under the age of six.
9. In cases where there is only one family member (including the taxpayer) qualified for personal exemption, a special deduction of W1 million and W500,000 for two family members (including taxpayer) who qualify for personal deduction is available in addition to the deductions listed above.

Nonresidents of Korea are only allowed to claim the personal exemption noted in 1 and 9.

Tax credits

Certain tax credits against the global income tax are available to resident taxpayers. These include the items shown below.

1. A tax credit for Class A and Class B wages (up to a maximum of W400,000 per year):
   a. Where the calculated tax amount is W500,000 or less, the credit is the amount of the calculated amount multiplied by 45%, that is, W225,000.
   b. Where the calculated tax amount is more than W500,000, the credit is W225,000 plus 30% of the calculated tax amount in excess of W500,000.
2. A tax credit of 10% of the income tax for Class B wage earners who voluntarily report their monthly earnings and pay monthly income taxes through a licensed taxpayers' association.
3. A tax credit of 19% of certain dividends received by each shareholder against the individual income tax calculated on the global income increased by 19% of dividends received.
4. A tax credit for foreign income taxes paid abroad by Korean residents, up to a limit of the amount of Korean income taxes before the foreign tax credit times the ratio of foreign-source income to worldwide total taxable income. Any excess over the maximum allowable credit may be carried forward for five years. Alternatively, foreign tax paid can be deducted from taxable income.

Other taxes

Minimum tax/A minimum tax, with exceptions, will be calculated at the greater of 40% of income tax liability before exemptions or actual tax after exemptions.

The minimum tax is applied to business income of a resident individual and Korean-source business income of a nonresident individual, but it is not applied to employment (earned) income.

Social security taxes/Under the national pension program, companies are required to contribute an amount equal to 4.5% of employee salaries to the national pension fund. Employees are also required to contribute an amount equal to 4.5% of their salaries. The employee contributions to the national pension program are tax deductible. This national pension contribution is capped at a monthly salary of W3,600,000. Thus, the maximum monthly pension contribution to be paid by an employee is W162,000.

There is also a severance pay system that requires no employee contribution. Severance pay, or retirement income, is taxed separately from global income.

Local taxes on income/Besides the basic income tax (which is paid to the national tax office), there is also a local residence tax surcharge, which is paid to the city or province that is the domicile of the taxpayer. The residence tax is calculated as 10% of the basic income tax liability.

Tax administration

Returns/A tax return must be filed by taxpayers who have both of Class A and Class B income or Class B income if not declared through a licensed taxpayer's association. Taxpayers must file returns for the calendar year during May (before May 31) of the following year or prior to leaving Korea permanently. There is generally no provision for filing joint tax returns under Korean tax law.

Payment of tax/A taxpayer who receives only Class A and/or retirement income is generally not required to file an annual tax return. The employer is required to withhold income taxes at source on a monthly basis and to finalize the employee's tax liability and issue a final tax settlement certificate at the end of February of the following tax year.

The employer is not required to withhold Korean taxes at the time of payment of Class B income; however, the individual is required to declare this income annually and pay income taxes thereon on a voluntary basis. Alternatively, the individual may elect to pay Class B income taxes through a licensed taxpayers' association, which collects and remits such taxes on a monthly basis. Taxpayers who join such an association are eligible to receive a 10% reduction in the amount of income tax payable. A member firm of PricewaterhouseCoopers in Seoul, the Samil Accounting Corporation, operates such an association (Samil Taxpayers' Association).

Tax rates

Effective from January 1, 2002, individual income tax rates on global income range from 9% to 36%. The top marginal tax rate, including the residence surcharge (see below), is 39.6% on taxable income in excess of W80 million.

Basic global income tax/The following tax table summarizes the basic global tax rates applicable for the income received from January 1, 2002 and thereafter.

(In Won thousands)

Annual taxable income			
Over	**Not over**	**Tax on Column 1**	**Percentage on excess**
(Column 1)			
0	W 10,000	—	9
W 10,000	40,000	W 900	18
40,000	80,000	6,300	27
80,000		17,100	36

Residence tax surcharge/A residence tax surcharge is assessed at a rate of 10% of the income tax liability.

INDIVIDUAL TAX CALCULATION

Calendar year 2002

Assumptions

Resident alien husband and wife, two children under the age of 20; one spouse earns all the income; salary is paid in either Korean or non-Korean currency.

Tax computation

Salary		W 40,000,000
Overseas allowances		26,000,000
Gross income		66,000,000
Less—Exclusion for overseas allowances (1)		11,000,000
Adjusted gross income		55,000,000
Less:		
Earned income deduction	13,750,000	
Standard deduction	600,000	
Basic allowance	1,000,000	
Spouse allowance	1,000,000	
Dependent allowance (1,000,000 x 2)	2,000,000	18,350,000
Taxable income		W 36,650,000
Income tax		W 5,697,000
Income tax credit (2)		(400,000)
		5,297,000
Residence tax (10% of income tax)		529,700
		5,826,700
Less—Tax payable through payroll tax withholding or with return		(3,480,000)
Total tax payable		W 2,346,700

Notes:

1. Computed as one-sixth of gross income.
2. A 10% tax credit (limited to W400,000) is available if an expatriate who is paid in non-Korean currency joins a licensed taxpayers' association and pays taxes voluntarily on a monthly basis. (Samil Accounting Corporation operates such an association.)

   A tax credit of up to a maximum of W400,000 per year is also available related to income tax.
3. Exchange rate (base rate) of the won at January 1, 2001: US$1 = W1,326.1.

PwC contact

For additional information on Kuwait, contact:

Thomas A. George
Pricewaterhouse Coopers
KIC Building, 4th floor
Opposite Al Ahli Bank
(P.O. Box 20174, Safat 13062)
Kuwait
Telephone: (965) 2408844
Fax: (965) 2408855
e-mail: t.george@kw.pwcglobal.com

Note

The following information on taxation in Kuwait is accurate as of January 1, 2001. For subsequent developments, refer to the contact above.

Absence of taxation

Income tax is not imposed on individuals in Kuwait.

Note

Exchange rate of the dinar at January 1, 2002: US$1 = KD0.308.

PwC contacts

For more information on taxation in Laos, contact:

Richard Irwin
Dean Wheeldon
PricewaterhouseCoopers (Vietnam) Ltd.
Unit # 01, 4th Floor, International Center
17 Ngo Quyen Street
Hanoi, Vietnam
Telephone: 844 8251 215
Fax: 844 8251 737
e-mail: r.irwin@vn.pwcglobal.com
dean.wheeldon@vn.pwcglobal.com

Ms. Xaynari Chanthala
PricewaterhouseCoopers (Laos) Ltd.
Vientiane Commercial Building
Unit 1-3, 4th Floor
33 Lane Xang Avenue
Vientiane, Laos
Telephone: 856 21 222 718
Fax: 856 21 222 723
e-mail: pwclaos@loxinfo.co.th

General note

This entry is repeated from the 2001/2002 edition. For more up-to-date information, consult the contact listed above or Mark Friedlich at mark.friedlich@us.pwcglobal.com.

Significant developments

There have been some changes to the rates of tax applying to individuals who earn income from rental of immovable property.

The Ministry of Labour and Social Welfare has issued a Decree, effective from July 1, 2000, which implements a social security system for employees. The Board of Directors of the Lao Social Security Organization has determined a total contribution rate of 9.5% to the social security fund, of which employers contribute 5% and employees contribute 4.5%.

Territoriality and residence

Foreign persons who work in the Lao PDR and receive salary payments abroad are subject to personal income tax in the Lao PDR if they reside in the Lao PDR for more than 180 days in a calendar year. Foreign persons who receive salary payments in the Lao PDR are subject to personal income tax in the Lao PDR, regardless of the number of days spent in Laos.

Gross income

Employee's gross income includes all remuneration, such as salary and wages, bonuses, overtime, allowances, and director's position fees. The Tax Law and Decree impose tax on most ancillary and in-kind remuneration. In addition, the Decree specifies material benefits, such as provision of housing, motor vehicles, and food, as taxable.

Where an amount is paid as a one-time payment, it is generally not treated as taxable. Such payments could include redundancy/retirement payments or moving allowances.

Exempt income includes family and medical allowances.

Capital gains and investment income/Income from dividends, interest on loans, and security fees are subject to 10% tax.

Deductions

There are no deductions or family-type allowances in respect of personal income tax.

Tax credits

Individuals are not taxable on foreign work; accordingly, foreign tax credits are not applicable. Currently, Laos has double taxation agreements only with Russia, Thailand, and Vietnam. The Lao PDR government has negotiated double taxation agreements with North Korea, Brunei, and Myanmar, but these have not been signed.

Other taxes

Social security taxes/A Decree on social security has been passed, effective from July 1, 2000; however, regulations have not been issued outlining the rate of social security taxes that will apply or whether this will be funded by employers, employees, or the government. The Board of Directors of the Lao Social Security Organization has determined a total contribution rate of 9.5% to the social security fund, of which employers contribute 5% and employees contribute 4.5%.

However, the structures to operate the social security system are not yet in place, and, accordingly, contributions are not being made at present. Whether this delay in implementation will require retrospective contributions is unknown at present.

Local taxes on income/There are no such taxes at this time.

Tax administration

Returns/Employers must submit to the tax authorities, together with the payment of tax withheld, a monthly tax declaration for the withholding tax on salary within 10 days of the day of making payment. There is no employee annual return.

Payment of tax/All enterprises are required to withhold applicable personal income taxes upon payment and remit the tax withheld to the Tax Department monthly.

Taxes on income from dividends, interest on loans, security fees, and intellectual property rights must be withheld at source. The owner of immovable property must pay taxes on income from the rent of land, real estate, and other property within 10 days of the day the income is received.

Tax rate

The salaries of foreign employees working for a business having a foreign investment license are taxed at a flat rate of 10%. Lao nationals and expatriate employees working for domestic investors are taxed on a progressive scale, after an LAK36,000 monthly deduction. Rates on this scale range between 5% and 40%.

Monthly progressive scale for Lao employees/For Lao workers, tax is levied on an escalating scale based on income, as shown below.

Monthly taxable salary			Tax on	Percentage
Over	Not over		Column 1	on excess
(Column 1)				
0	LAK 30,000	....	—	—
LAK 30,000	125,000	....	—	5
125,000	250,000	....	LAK 4,750	10
250,000	500,000	....	17,250	15
500,000	1,000,000	....	54,750	20
1,000,000	2,000,000	....	154,750	25
2,000,000	3,000,000	....	404,750	30
3,000,000	5,000,000	....	704,750	35
5,000,000		....	1,404,750	40

The following tax rates are applied under the Profit Tax and Personal Income Tax headings of the Tax Law.

1. Income from intellectual property rights is subject to 5% tax.
2. Income from real estate is subject to a tax of 30%, 25%, or a rate per square meter (e.g., US$2 per square meter per month), depending on the type of house and whether it is rented to a foreigner or a Lao national. Income from the rent of land and other property is subject to a flat tax of 25%.
3. For foreign workers, the tax is 10% of income.

Official exchange rates are provided for translation of foreign currencies into kip.

INDIVIDUAL TAX CALCULATION

Assumptions

A foreign employee of a foreign-invested enterprise and a spouse who resides in Laos with two school-aged children; one spouse earns all the income. Annual gross salary of US$80,000; employer pays US$3,000 per month for accommodation. Calculations are given in local currency.

Tax computation

Gross monthly salary:	
Salary	LAK 50,666,667
Accommodation	22,800,000
Net monthly taxable income	LAK 73,466,667
Income tax assessment:	
Monthly salary tax payable (tax at 10% flat rate)	LAK 7,346,667

Note:

Exchange rate of the kip at January 1, 2001: US$1 = LAK7,600.76.

Latvia

PwC contacts

For additional information on taxation in Latvia, contact:

Helen Barker/Gunita Puzule
PricewaterhouseCoopers SIA
Kr. Valdemara 19
LV–1010 Riga, Latvia
Telephone: (371) 709 44 00
Fax: (371) 783 00 55
e-mail: helen barker@lv.pwcglobal.com
gunita.puzule@lv.pwcglobal.com

Copies of all documents/inquiries to be sent to:

Cameron G. Greaves (TLS Baltic Leader)
AS PricewaterhouseCoopers
T. Sevcenkos 21
LT–2009 Vilnius, Lithuania
Telephone: (3702) (26) 392 300
Fax: (3702) (26) 392 301
e-mail: cameron.greaves@lt.pwcglobal.com

Significant developments

The most essential changes include taxability of gains. From January 1, 2002, only gains arising on disposal of immovable property held for less than 12 months will be taxable.

From January 1, 2002, foreign nationals assigned to work in Latvia for a period not exceeding 12 months will be exempt from paying National Social Insurance (NSI), provided they file an approved document from their home tax authorities as evidence that they pay NSI or an equivalent insurance in their home country. The Cabinet of Ministers accepted amendments to regulations on the maximum amount of income subject to yearly NSI contributions in 2002, which have been increased from LVL16,000 to LVL17,300. Slight rate alterations have affected all categories of social insurance contributors.

As regards the calculation of wages and salaries, as well as other statutory compensation, it is useful to remember that from July 1, 2001 the minimum monthly wage is fixed at LVL60.

Territoriality and residence

Latvian residents are liable to Latvian income tax on their worldwide income. Nonresidents are liable to income tax on Latvian-source income.

Persons satisfying one of the following conditions are considered to be resident in Latvia.

1. Individuals who have their permanent place of residence in Latvia;
2. Individuals present in Latvia for 183 days or more during any 12-month period; or
3. Latvian citizens employed abroad by the Republic of Latvia.

Gross income

Employee gross income/Gross income includes salary, bonuses, gifts from employer, benefits-in-kind, and so on. Benefits include accommodation allowances, private use of company cars, relocation allowances, and so on. Reimbursement of relocations costs related to an assignment to Latvia and contributions toward approved pension schemes are not taxable.

Capital gains and investment income/For Latvian residents, dividends received from Latvian companies (out of taxed income) are tax exempt, as is interest received from Latvian banks and credit institutions. Foreign investment income is fully taxable, and foreign tax suffered may be credited against the Latvian tax liability.

Generally, there is no tax on income from the sale of personal property, with the exception of immovable property held for less than 12 months before sale. Also, if an individual buys and sells enough personal property to be viewed as engaging in a trade or business, the gains will be taxed. Securities are considered personal property.

Deductions

Business deductions/If the person has been registered as a sole trader, expenses directly relating to obtaining income earned during the ordinary course of business or during the lease of property are deductible, provided they can be supported by documentation.

Nonbusiness expenses/Residents may deduct the following nonbusiness expenses.

1. Compulsory National Social Insurance contributions.
2. Expenditures of up to LVL150 per taxpayer and each family member for certain qualifying education expenditure and medical costs (can be carried forward for five consecutive years).
3. Charitable contributions.
4. Employer's pension contributions to private pension funds registered in Latvia and life insurance premiums up to the limit of 10% of gross salary.

Personal allowances/Residents may be entitles to the following types of personal allowances.

1. Nontaxable minimum of LVL21 per month.
2. Allowance for a qualifying dependent of LVL10.50 per month (children up to the age of 18, unemployed spouse).

Tax credits

Residents are entitled to relief from double taxation under tax treaties.

Tax paid abroad on income included in the taxable base is allowed as a credit against personal income tax. However, the credit may not exceed the Latvian tax attributable to the income taxed abroad.

Other taxes

National social insurance/The contribution rates are summarized in the following table.

Employment	2001 %	2002 %
Employment with company registered in Latvia:		
Employer	26.09	26.09
Employee	9.00	9.00
Employment with company registered in Latvia (employee eligible for retirement):		
Employer	21.02	21.24
Employee	7.24	7.32
Foreign employee employed by foreign nonresident employer:		
Employer	—	—
Employee	8.43	8.52
Self-employed	32.10	32.27
Self-employed (eligible for retirement)	28.17	28.47

Beginning January 1, 2002 contributions are due only on the first LVL17,300 earned in a calendar year.

Local taxes/There are no local taxes, such as municipal taxes.

Real estate tax/Real estate tax is applied annually at the rate of 1.5%, calculated on the registered value of the land owned by individuals. Some municipalities offer certain reliefs to landowners using land for residential purposes only.

Tax administration

Returns/Income tax returns are filed individually on a calendar-year basis and must be submitted by April 1 of the year following the income year. Husbands and wives may not file joint returns. National insurance contributions made should be reported quarterly.

Payment of tax/Latvian employers are obliged to withhold income tax on salaries paid to employees and remit the taxes to tax authorities. If necessary, the taxpayer is obliged to make an additional tax payment in order to cover the remaining tax liability, no later than 15 days after the tax return was submitted to the tax authorities. If the additional tax exceeds LVL100, the taxpayer may transfer the amount in three equal installments within three months.

Residents employed by foreign employers are required to calculate and pay income tax once a month. Social insurance contributions are to be calculated and paid on quarterly basis.

Tax rates

Individual income tax is levied at the flat rate of 25%.

INDIVIDUAL TAX CALCULATION

Calendar year ending December 31, 2002 (income year 2002)

Assumptions

Resident, employed in a Latvian-resident company, who earns all the income; with spouse and two children.

Tax computation

Gross salary		LVL 45,520
Less—Nonbusiness expenses:		
National Social Insurance contribution (9%) (1)	1,557	
Personal allowance (21 per month)	252	
Allowance for unemployed spouse (10.50 per month)	126	
Allowance for 2 children (10.50 per month per child)	252	
Medical costs	150	2,337
Annual taxable income		LVL 43,183
Personal income tax liability—25%		LVL 10,796

Notes:

1. National Social Insurance contribution paid by employer—26.09% of 17,300 (2002 limit) = 4,514.
2. Exchange rate of the lat at December 31, 2001: US$1 = LVL0.638.

Liechtenstein

PwC contacts

For additional information on taxation in Liechtenstein, contact:

Werner Schmid, Tax Partner
Victor Meyer, Tax Partner
PricewaterhouseCoopers AG
Stampfenbachstrasse 73
8022 Zurich, Switzerland
Telephone: (41) (1) 630 11 11
Fax: (41) (1) 630 41 15
e-mail: werner schmid@ch.pwcglobal.com
victor.meyer@ch.pwcglobal.com

Significant developments

There have been no significant tax or regulatory developments in the past year.

Territoriality and residence

Individuals are regarded as resident in Liechtenstein if they are residing within Liechtenstein with the intention of staying there permanently. In addition, individuals are deemed to be resident for tax purposes if they are residing in the country and performing a gainful activity (employed or self-employed).

In principle, tax is levied on the resident taxpayer's worldwide earned income and net wealth. There are important income items that are exempt from income tax, as described below.

Gross income

Employee gross income/An employee resident in Liechtenstein for tax purposes is taxed on any salary and any other monetary benefits (including reimbursements of living expenses) received from the employer, regardless of where the work has been performed, where payment is made or whether it is remitted.

Capital gains and investment income/Any capital gains are included in the determination of gross income, except for those realized on the sale of real estate that are subject to the Liechtenstein real estate profits tax or to a foreign tax if located abroad.

Income from investments (mainly dividends, interest, rental income) is exempt from income tax, provided net wealth tax has been paid on the underlying assets.

Deductions

Business deductions/Individuals with income from employment are entitled to a deduction, generally CHF1,500, as compensation for outlays relating to employment, such as travel to and from work and extra costs for outside meals.

Nonbusiness expenses/Deductible expenses include premiums for life, sickness and accident insurance up to a maximum of CHF5,000 per married couple, CHF2,500 per single taxpayer and CHF1,500 per child; contributions to pension funds up to 12% of taxable income and all social security contributions required by law; the cost for higher education for children up to CHF12,000 per child; and medical expenses, as well as expenses for dentistry borne by the taxpayer up to CHF6,000 per person.

Personal allowances/Personal allowances, deductible in determining taxable income, are granted as follows. See also "Tax credits" below.

	CHF
Taxpayers without own household	2,400
Taxpayers with own household but without children	4,800
Taxpayers with own household and with dependent children	6,000
Allowance per child	6,000
Allowance per person for private capital gains	5,000
Allowance in the amount of the effective contribution per person whom the taxpayer is legally required to support, other than children	No limit

Tax credits

Apart from those deriving from the double taxation treaty with Austria, there are no foreign tax credits available. For couples, total income and wealth tax is reduced by one-third for a tax amount of up to CHF2,897, by 30% for a tax amount of more than CHF2,897, and by 28% for a tax amount of more than CHF3,549, with a minimum of CHF550 and a maximum of CHF5,500. Single mothers and fathers can deduct one-half of the above-mentioned reduction.

Other taxes

Social security taxes/For 2001 the taxpayer's share of social security contributions (old-age and dependent pension schemes, disability insurance) is 4.4% with no upper limit (maximum 11.336% for self-employment income) and 0.25% for unemployment insurance on the first CHF97,200 of compensation (see also "Nonbusiness expenses").

Other taxes on income/There are no other taxes on income.

Wealth tax/Wealth tax is levied on the net assets of the taxpayer. All assets of the taxpayer, including domestic real estate, investments in securities, cash, time deposits, precious metals, and all other personal property, are included in the determination of net assets. Related liabilities, such as mortgages and other borrowings, may be deducted. Assets are, in general, assessed at their approximate fair market value. (The related unrealized gains or losses are not included in taxable income.) Additionally, the first CHF70,000 for a single taxpayer (CHF140,000 for a married taxpayer) of the taxpayer's net assets is not subject to taxation.

Tax administration

Returns/The income and wealth of both spouses are always taxed jointly. Returns must be filed annually, normally by late April. Employees must enclose a certificate of remuneration issued by their employers. Taxpayers must always file their returns on a calendar-year basis.

Payment of tax/There is income tax withholding from salaries, provided the employer is resident in Liechtenstein. In computing the tax payable by an individual, the tax liability is reduced by the payments of tax already made by wage tax withholding. The balance is payable within 30 days after receipt of the assessment. For employees whose employer is a nonresident, there is no wage tax withholding; the payment of tax is based on the tax bills received and must be made within 30 days after receipt.

Tax rates

Individual income tax rates are determined not only by taxable income but also by taxable wealth (see "Individual tax calculation").

Basic tax rates/The basic tax rates are specified below.

	Tax rate
	%
On income	1.080
On wealth	0.054

Communal tax/The communes levy a communal tax of 200% of the national tax (Schaan, 170%, Vaduz 180%); the top income tax rate is thus 17.01% (excluding Vaduz and Schaan), 15.88% in Vaduz and 15.31% in Schaan, and the top wealth tax is 0.8505%.

Surcharge/The following surcharges on the basic tax on income and wealth are levied and result, in total, in the national tax due.

From	To	Surcharge
CHF	CHF	%
397	417	5
417	438	10
438	460	15
460	483	20
483	507	25
507	532	30
532	556	35
556	581	40
581	607	45
607	634	50
634	663	55
663	693	60
693	724	65
724	757	70
757	791	75
791	827	80
827	860	85
860	894	90
894	930	95
930	967	100
967	1,006	105
1,006	1,046	110
1,046	1,088	115
1,088	1,132	120
1,132	1,177	125
1,177	1,224	130
1,224	1,267	135
1,267	1,311	140
1,311	1,357	145
1,357	1,404	150
1,404	1,453	155
1,453	1,504	160
1,504	1,557	165
1,557	1,611	170
1,611	1,667	175
1,667	1,725	180
1,725	1,777	185
1,777	1,830	190
1,830	1,885	195
1,885	1,942	200
1,924	2,000	205
2,000	2,060	210
2,060	2,122	215
2,122	2,186	220
2,186	2,252	225
2,252	2,320	230
2,320	2,378	235
2,378	2,437	240
2,437	2,498	245
2,498	2,560	250
2,560	2,624	255
2,624	2,690	260
2,690	2,757	265
2,757	2,826	270
2,826	2,897	275
2,897	2,969	280
2,969	3,028	285
3,028	3,089	290
3,089	3,151	295
3,151	3,214	300
3,214	3,278	305
3,278	3,344	310
3,344	3,411	315
3,411	3,479	320
3,479	3,549	325
3,549	3,620	330
3,620	3,656	335
3,656	3,693	340
3,693	3,730	345
3,730	3,767	350
3,767	3,805	355
3,805	3,843	360
3,843	3,881	365
3,881	3,920	370
3,920	4,270	375
4,270	4,620	380
4,620	4,920	385
4,920	5,320	390
5,320	5,520	395
5,520	5,720	400
5,720	5,920	405
5,920	6,120	410
6,120	6,320	415
6,320	6,520	420
6,520		425

INDIVIDUAL TAX CALCULATION

National and communal tax for tax year 2001

Assumptions

1. Married man with two children, resident in Vaduz.
2. Employment income of CHF175,400 net of social security contributions.
3. Compensation as director of CHF2,500.
4. Securities and savings accounts total of CHF140,000; income thereon of CHF7,000.
5. Capital gains on security transactions of CHF20,000.
6. Insurance premiums for life insurance of CHF2,500; surrender value of CHF15,000.
7. Motorcar with market value of CHF25,000.
8. Living in own apartment; assessed value of CHF180,000, mortgage of CHF100,000, mortgage interest of CHF6,000.

Determination of taxable income

Gross income:		
Income from employment		CHF 175,400
Compensation as director		2,500
Income from securities and savings accounts		7,000
Capital gains on security transactions		20,000
		CHF 204,900
Less—Tax-exempt income—Income from securities and savings accounts		7,000
Total gross income		197,900
Less—Deductions:		
Income-connected expenses	1,500	
Insurance premiums, say	2,500	
Cost for children's higher education (maximum, 2 x 12,000)	24,000	
Medical and dental expenses, say	3,650	
Mortgage interest (not allowed as deduction)	—	31,650
Net income		166,250
Less—Personal allowances:		
For taxpayer having own household	6,000	
Allowance for children (2 x 6000)	12,000	
Allowance for capital gain (4 x 5,000)	20,000	38,000
Taxable income		CHF 128,250

Determination of taxable wealth

Year ended December 31, 2001

Assets:		
Apartment		CHF 180,000
Securities and savings accounts		140,000
Surrender value of life insurance		15,000
Household effects (33% of insurance value), say		50,000
Car		25,000
Total assets		CHF 410,000
Less—Liabilities:		
Mortgage		100,000
Net assets		310,000
Less—Allowances:		
Increase in wealth during the year (capital gain)	20,000	
Tax exemption	140,000	160,000
Taxable wealth		CHF 150,000

Tax computation

National tax:		
1.08% on taxable income of 128,250	1,385	
0.054% on taxable wealth of 150,000	81	CHF 1,466
Progression surcharge according to table—160%		2,346
		3,812
Less—Allowance for couples (33.33% of 1,385)		(462)
Total national tax		3,350
Communal tax—180% of national tax		6,030
Total income and wealth tax		CHF 9,380

Notes:

1. The unit of local currency is the Swiss franc.
2. Exchange rate of the Swiss franc at December 31, 2001: US$1 = CHF1.63.

Lithuania

PwC contacts

For additional information on taxation in Lithuania, contact:

Algirdas Vaitiekunas
PricewaterhouseCoopers UAB
T. Sevcenkos 21
LT-2009 Vilnius
Telephone: (370) 2 39 23 00
Fax: (370) 39 23 01
e-mail: algis.vaitiekunas@lt.pwcglobal.com

Copies of all documents/inquiries to be sent to:

Cameron G. Greaves (TLS Baltic Leader)
PricewaterhouseCoopers UAB
T. Sevcenkos 21
LT-2009 Vilnius
Telephone: (370) (2) 39 23 00
Fax: (370) (2) 39 23 01
e-mail: cameron.greaves@lt.pwcglobal.com

Significant developments

The Lithuanian currency, the Litas, was unpegged from the U.S. dollar and pegged to the Euro on February 2, 2002 at a rate of LTL3.4528 = €1.

From April 1, 2002 the monthly tax-exempt minimum will be increased from LTL214 to LTL250.

Territoriality and residence

Income tax on natural persons is paid by the following.

1. Lithuanian citizens, foreigners and noncitizens deriving income through their labor in Lithuanian enterprises, institutions and organizations, including permanent establishments of foreign corporations in Lithuania, Lithuanian representative offices of foreign corporations, and Lithuanian enterprises, institutions and organizations registered abroad.
2. Lithuanian residents deriving income through their labor in foreign enterprises, institutions and organizations.
3. Foreigners and noncitizens deriving income through their labor in Lithuania in foreign enterprises, institutions and organizations.
4. Lithuanian citizens, foreigners and noncitizens deriving nonsalary income from Lithuanian residents, enterprises, institutions, and organizations, including permanent establishments of foreign corporations in Lithuania, Lithuanian representative offices of foreign corporations, and Lithuanian enterprises, institutions and organizations registered abroad.
5. Lithuanian residents deriving nonsalary income from foreign residents, enterprises, institutions, and organizations.

The following persons are considered residents of the Republic of Lithuania.

1. Any individual whose main place of residence is within Lithuania. The main place of residence is considered to be the place where the person lives

permanently or most of the time, or the place of the person's personal, social or economic interests.

2. Any individual who has stayed within Lithuania continuously or with breaks for 183 days or more within the 12-month period for which taxes are charged.
3. Lithuanian citizens employed in diplomatic representations and consular offices or other institutions of Lithuania abroad.

Gross income

Employee gross income/Taxable monthly earnings in cash and kind received from the principal workplace include wages; various additional payments such as sickness and maternity benefits paid from social insurance; bonuses, incentive payments, taxable allowances, and other such payments; and compensation upon discharge from work, such as compensation for remaining vacation, gratuities and compensation for unlawful dismissal from work.

Capital gains and investment income/Individuals are not subject to capital gains tax.

Deductions and exemptions

Exemptions/The following income derived from employment in a Lithuanian legal entity is exempt from personal income tax.

1. Social security and social assistance benefits paid from state and social insurance funds, excluding sickness and maternity (paternity) allowances.
2. Benefits paid by an employer upon the death of a spouse or certain other heirs of an employee, as well as in cases of natural calamity or fire.
3. Compensation for moral and material damage adjudged by the courts.
4. Insurance premiums in accordance with the provisions of the Law on Insurance.
5. Business trip expenses in the amounts established by the legislation, reimbursement of other expenses related to employment, and fines imposed for delay in payment if in connection with labor.
6. Prizes received during personal celebrations or competitions or on any other occasion, provided that the value of these gifts and prizes during the calendar year does not exceed the tax-exempt earnings limit.

Nonbusiness deductions/Taxable income is reduced by the following.

1. The amount expended on charity and sponsorship according to the procedure established by the Law on Charity and Sponsorship, but not exceeding 15% of a person's annual income.
2. Pension payments made to pension program participants' personal accounts, up to a limit of 25% of annual employment income.

Other taxes

Social security taxes/The current mandatory social insurance contribution rates are as follows.

Employers	28%
Employees	3%
Farmers	20% of the amount of basic pension
Self-employed	50% of the amount of basic pension

State social insurance is mandatory for the following persons.

1. Persons receiving remuneration for working under employment agreements, as well as those who are employed on the basis of membership in elective institutions, in partnerships, agricultural companies or cooperative organizations, as well as candidates to notary and employees of public administration.
2. Sole proprietors, self-employed persons and partners in partnerships.
3. Farmers and other adults working on their farms.
4. Individuals who acquire a patent to carry out certain business activities.

The following persons are compulsorily insured by state social pension insurance.

1. Persons employed under employment or diplomatic service agreements, as well as those who are employed in elective institutions on the basis of membership or working in partnerships, agricultural companies or cooperative organizations for remuneration.
2. Officers of the Ministry of Internal Affairs, police and other persons serving in the Ministry, noncommissioned reenlistees and soldiers, and Prosecution Office officials.
3. Professional military service personnel.
4. Officers of state security.
5. Unemployed diplomats' spouses during the Lithuanian diplomats' service and residence abroad.
6. Sole proprietors, self-employed persons and partners in partnerships.
7. Farmers and other adults working on their farms.
8. Individuals who acquire a patent to carry out certain business activities.
9. Compulsory military service and alternative national defense personnel.
10. Mothers (or fathers) during maternity (paternity) leave.
11. Mothers (or fathers) not on maternity (paternity) leave but raising a child up to three years of age.
12. Clergymen of traditional religious communities and monks with sole employment in monasteries.
13. One of the parents of a fully disabled person, engaged in home care.

In addition, for certain categories of individuals, voluntary social insurance is available, providing payment of social insurance benefits in case of illness, pregnancy and maternity (paternity).

Only pension insurance is mandatory for self-employed persons. They may contribute voluntarily to health insurance. Rates of contribution of health insurance are as follows.

Rates of obligatory health insurance:	
Enterprises	3% of the salary of an employee, a person rendering management services in accordance with management services agreement, a person working on the basis of membership
Enterprises situated in Lithuania and Lithuanian enterprises situated abroad	30% of the amount of income tax calculated on the salary of an employee

Rates of voluntary health insurance:	
Partnerships and private enterprises pay for owners and partners	Not less than 30% of the amount of income tax or patent tax, but no less than 10% of the minimum monthly salary
Persons having patents obtained to engage in certain commercial activity	30% of the amount of the patent tax, but no less than 5% of the minimum monthly salary
Farmers and other land users (except those insured by state funds), pay for themselves and other adults working on the farm:	
If the land plot exceeds 3 hectares	3.5% of the minimum monthly salary
If the land plot is less than 3 hectares	1.5% of the minimum monthly salary
Other persons	10% of the official average monthly salary

Local taxes on income/There are no local taxes on income.

Gift and inheritance tax/Property for the purpose of taxation is considered to be real estate and movable property for which statutory registration is required. Shares, obligations, paper credit, other securities, precious metals, gemstones, and money are also considered to be property for tax purposes.

Tax is also applied on property that is the object of a donation contract confirmed in the Notaries Bureau, as well as on inherited property. The tax is paid into the local budget by natural persons who have inherited property or acquired it under a donation agreement in Lithuania. Foreigners pay this tax in the same manner as citizens of Lithuania.

The tax rates are as follows.

1. Inherited property:
   a. Taxable value up to LTL0.5 million—5%;
   b. Taxable value of LTL0.5 million and above—10%.
2. Gifted property—10%.

The tax is not applicable in the following situations.

1. If the recipients are the donor's children (including adopted children) or parents (including stepparents) in accordance with an agreement on gifts.
2. If the property is donated by a spouse, or inherited after a spouse's death.
3. If the property is inherited by children (or adopted children), parents (or step-parents), guardians, wards, grandparents, grandchildren, brothers, or sisters.

The Municipal Council may postpone the obligation to pay tax for one year after legal registration of property, issue of heritage documents or conclusion of an agreement on gifts.

Wealth tax/There are no taxes on wealth.

Real estate tax/There is no real estate tax for individuals.

Tax administration

Returns of individuals and tax payment/Natural persons deriving miscellaneous receipts from other natural persons, and persons working in Lithuania while employed in foreign companies must file tax returns.

The law requires that the tax returns of individuals must be filed with the territorial State Tax Inspectorate, situated in the place of their permanent residence. Foreign nationals and stateless persons (without a Lithuanian registration of their place of residence) must file their tax returns with the State Tax Inspectorate, within the catchment area of their place of residence or work. The tax return is filed in the following cases and by the following deadlines.

1. The tax return for expected permanent income of the current year is filed by February 1 of the current year.
2. The tax return for income received in the current year is filed within five days upon expiration of one month following the date of receipt of income.
3. The adjusted annual tax return (to be filed by February 1) need not be filed when extraordinary income received in the current year is reported, except for capital gains on disposal of securities.
4. In respect of income earned abroad, the tax return must be filed within five days after expiration of one month following the date of return to Lithuania, or after the foreign-source income ceases to be derived. This income must be reported irrespective of whether taxes have been paid abroad.
5. Upon any substantial change (increase or decrease) in the amount of income received in the current year, individuals, who previously reported their expected income and who paid advance amounts of tax, may file a new tax return, on the basis of which the amount of assessed income tax is adjusted.
6. Upon expiration of a source of income in the current year, an adjusted tax return for income actually received may be filed. The actual difference between the amount of assessed income tax and that demanded for payment is recovered or refunded.
7. The tax return may be filed on the basis of data collected in the course of inspections carried out by the State Tax Inspectorate or on other available information regarding the taxpayer's income.

Income tax on expected permanent income as well as on income actually received at any time of the year is assessed and paid in equal parts on a quarterly basis by the 15th day of the second month of each quarter. Tax on income received at any time of the year must be paid by the end of the year in compliance with the remaining deadlines.

If a tax return is filed after November 15 (beyond the last deadline), income tax must be paid within one month after the date of the tax return.

Tax rates

Employment income tax/The income tax rate for employment income is 33% of the amount exceeding the TEM. The monthly TEM from February 1, 1998 is LTL214. From April 1, 2002 the tax-exempt minimum will be increased from LTL214 to LTL250. It is greater for certain groups, as follows.

	LTL
Disabled:	
Group 1	368
Group 2	324
Group 3	242
Persons with three or more children under 18 years of age	368
Mother or father in a single-parent family with one child under 18	287
Employers of enterprises producing agricultural products whose monthly income generated from activities not Connected with production or processing of these products does not exceed 20% of gross monthly income	278

Note:

For a mother or father with two or more children under age 18, the TEM is increased by LTL45 for the second and each successive child.

In addition, for visually handicapped persons of Groups 1 and 2, for parents with at least one handicapped child and for the fourth and each successive child of parents with four and more children the calculated tax is reduced by LTL10.

The rates of tax on monthly wages from extra work are as follows.

	%
0 to 0.5 TEM	10
0.5 to 1.0 TEM	20
Over 1.0 TEM	35

Employment income generated from foreign entities is taxed at the flat rate of 20%, unless a double taxation treaty provides otherwise.

INDIVIDUAL TAX CALCULATION

Gross monthly salary	LTL	1,000.00
Less—TEM		214.00
Taxable income		786.00
Tax at 33%	LTL	259.38
Net monthly salary calculation:		
Gross salary	LTL	1,000.00
Less—Income tax		259.38
		740.62
Less—Social security charges (3% of 1,000)		30.00
Net monthly salary	LTL	710.62

Notes:

1. The TEM from February 1, 1998 (LTL214) is used in the calculation.
2. Exchange rate of the litas on February 2, 2002: €1 = LTL3.4528; US$1 = LTL4.0127.

Luxembourg

PwC contact

For additional information on taxation in Luxembourg, contact:

Michiel Roumieux
PricewaterhouseCoopers
400, route d'Esch
B.P. 1443
L–1014 Luxembourg
Telephone: (352) 49 48 48 1
Fax: (352) 49 48 48 2900
e-mail: Michiel.Roumieux@lu.pwcglobal.com

Significant developments

The Luxembourg government enacted a tax reform applicable as from January 1, 2002. This reform includes a reduction of progressive income tax rates.

The currency unit in Luxembourg is now the Euro.

Territoriality and residence

Individual income tax is levied on the worldwide income of individuals residing in Luxembourg, as well as on Luxembourg-source income of nonresidents. Generally, an effectively used abode in Luxembourg or a stay in Luxembourg in excess of six consecutive months entails residence, even if the period overlaps two fiscal years or is interrupted by short absences.

Gross income

Employee gross income/Income from employment includes all benefits in cash and in kind received by an individual. If an employer provides a house or apartment to an employee, the monthly benefit in kind is valued at 25% of its unitary value, with a minimum of three-quarters of the rent effectively paid by the employer. Furniture put at the disposition of the employee gives rise to an additional 10%. If the employer pays electricity and other charges, these must be added to the benefit at their nominal value. If the employee rents a house or an apartment and pays the rent, reimbursement of the rent by the employer is taxed entirely as a benefit. The monthly benefit in kind arising from the private use of a company car corresponds to private mileage multiplied by the car's kilometer cost. This evaluation can be replaced by a lump-sum evaluation method, according to which monthly taxable fringe benefit corresponds to 1.5% of the full purchase price (including VAT) of the new car. A number of items are exempt from tax, such as debtor-interest savings on a reduced- or nil-interest loan granted by the employer (within certain limits) and overtime payments, up to a certain limit.

Under specific conditions, moving expense reimbursements are tax exempt. Nonresidents are taxed on salaried income if their occupation is exercised in Luxembourg or if their salary is paid from Luxembourg. Tax treaties generally grant exemption if the nonresident stays for less than 183 days in the calendar year and if the remuneration is paid and borne by a party in the other country.

Capital gains and investment income/Short-term capital gains (see comments on speculation profits below) are included in normal taxable income. However, long-term capital gains on buildings and land (owned longer than two years) and capital gains derived from the disposal of a participation of more than 10% in a company (owned longer than six months) are taxed as extraordinary income at half the average global tax rate (maximum 19.475%). Inflation is taken into account by multiplying the acquisition cost by a coefficient. The first €50,000 of cumulative capital gains realized over a 10-year period is tax exempt. The 10-year allowance is increased to €100,000 in the case of collectively taxed spouses. In the case of a capital gain on a building acquired through direct inheritance, an allowance of up to €75,000 may be granted. Capital gains on the sale of a main residence are exempt from taxation. Long-term capital gains realized on investments other than in land, buildings, and on minor participations (less than 10%) are also exempt from taxation.

So-called speculation profits over €500 on buildings, land and investments are treated as ordinary income. Speculation arises when purchase and sale occur within two years for real estate and within six months for other property.

Capital losses can be offset only against capital gains in the same year.

Gross income from capital and investments is included in taxable income. An exemption of €1,500 is granted on portfolio income. It is doubled in the case of collectively taxed spouses. Half of the dividend income received is tax exempt if paid by a qualifying company.

Deductions

Business deductions/Income-related expenses are normally deductible.

Employees benefit from minimum standard deductions of €540 for job-related expenses. These deductions are doubled if the spouse is also employed. If expenses for tools, specific work clothes, and so on, exceed the minimum, the actual expenses may be deducted. Commuting expenses are tax deductible, with a minimum yearly amount of €396 and a maximum of €2,970 per year.

A minimum lump-sum allowance of €25 is deductible from income from capital and investments. The minimum lump-sum allowance is doubled in the case of collectively taxed spouses if both earn income from capital and investments. Actual expenses exceeding this lump-sum allowance can be deducted. Nonresidents can deduct only expenses related to income subject to Luxembourg taxation.

Nonbusiness expenses/For residents, certain premiums paid for life, sickness, accident, disability and third-party liability insurance are deductible, up to €672 per family member. This allowance is increased for a one-time premium for temporary death insurance subscribed to assure the reimbursement of a loan taken up for the purchase of a house. The related tax deduction varies with the age of the taxpayer.

Insurance premiums paid within the context of a private pension scheme qualifying under Luxembourg tax law are also tax deductible. Based on the taxpayer's age, the maximum tax deduction varies from €1,500 to €3,200. If each spouse subscribes to a qualifying private pension insurance contract, the ceiling is doubled.

Certain contributions to savings and home-loan associations are deductible up to €672 per family member. Interest arising on a loan contracted to purchase a car, furniture, and so forth, is deductible up to €672 per family member. A minimum standard deduction of €480 is granted for the above expenses; it is doubled if the spouse is also employed.

Compulsory Luxembourg and foreign legal social contributions covered by a social security treaty, as well as donations under certain conditions, are also deductible.

Nonresident employees may deduct compulsory social security contributions and donations to qualifying institutions, as well as the flat allowance of €480.

Personal allowances/Residents may deduct extraordinary charges for sickness, accidents, living costs of parents, and so on, up to a certain limit.

A specific deduction is also available for kindergarten costs.

A salaried-income-related allowance of €600 is granted to residents, as well as to nonresidents. This deduction is doubled if the spouse also is employed.

Spouses who both exercise a professional activity taxable in Luxembourg benefit from a lump-sum allowance of €4,500.

Within specific conditions, residents who acquire shares in Luxembourg based companies can deduct the underlying acquisition up to €1,500. To qualify for the underlying deduction, the individual must notably hold the shares for at least the subsequent four fiscal years (calendar years) following the year of acquisition.

Nonresident taxpayers/If at least 90% of the professional income of a nonresident is taxable in Luxembourg, the taxpayer may opt to be treated as a resident for tax purposes, thus benefiting from the same deductions and allowances as a resident. The tax rate applied to Luxembourg-source income is then determined on the basis of the taxpayer's household total worldwide professional income.

Tax credits

Foreign income received by residents that is subject to a tax equivalent to Luxembourg income tax and is not exempted by a double taxation agreement is granted a tax credit; any nonimputable tax in excess is deductible as a tax-deductible expense.

Other taxes

Social security taxes/Compulsory social security contributions for employees are listed below.

1. For sickness: 2.65% of gross periodic remuneration, limited to an annual ceiling of €78,541.9.
2. For pension: 8% of gross remuneration, limited to an annual ceiling of €78,541.9.

Certain multilateral and bilateral social security agreements protect the interests of temporarily resident employees.

See also "Nonbusiness expenses" above.

Employees subject to Luxembourg social security contributions are subject to the so-called dependency contribution on their gross professional income, less €3,927.09 for 2002. Net portfolio income and taxable capital gains of Luxembourg-resident taxpayers are also subject to the dependency contribution. The dependency contribution rate amounts to 1% (flat rate).

Wealth taxes/Wealth taxes are assessed on resident taxpayers' worldwide taxable wealth and on nonresident taxpayers' Luxembourg taxable wealth. Taxable wealth corresponds to gross value of the elements comprising wealth, less qualifying deductions. Wealth taxes are assessed at a flat rate of 0.5% of the global taxable wealth value.

Tax administration

Income tax returns/The total income of husband and wife and the nonsalary income of minor children forming part of the household are aggregated for purposes of the annual tax computation. Combined assessments are due in principle if the spouses are not separated on the basis of a legal or judicial dispensation. The fiscal year corresponds to the calendar year.

Payment of income tax/Payroll income taxes are withheld by the employer on a monthly basis. At year-end, the salary income tax payments are, in principle, regularized by the employer or the tax administration, as appropriate.

Wealth tax returns/An individual's wealth tax is determined on the basis of a specific tax return. An assessment of the taxpayer's taxable wealth takes place, in principle, every three years at a predetermined valuation date. Where the taxpayer's taxable wealth changes significantly between two valuation dates, a new evaluation is made for the next predetermined valuation date.

Payment of wealth tax/Wealth taxes are paid quarterly.

Income tax rates

Tax is calculated in accordance with a graduated table, ranging from 8% on taxable income in excess of €9,750 to 38% on income in excess of €34,500 for 2002. A solidarity tax of 2.5% of taxes is added. Married nonresident taxpayers who are not separated are put into Tax Class 2 (generally the tax class for resident unseparated spouses) if they are taxable in Luxembourg for more than 50% of the professional income of their household. If both spouses derive professional income taxable in Luxembourg, the application of Tax Class 2 leads to a combined assessment. Unseparated married nonresident taxpayers who do not comply with the above condition are put into the higher intermediary Tax Class 1a.

The following tables show taxes for taxable salaried income between €20,000 and €155,000. (Taxable salary income equals gross salary income minus all qualifying deductions under Luxembourg income tax law.)

Single taxpayer (class 1)
Single taxpayer with dependent children (class 1a.x)

(In Euros)

Taxable salaried income	Income tax				
	Single (S) (Class 1)	Single: special rate (Class 1a)	S + 1 Child (C) (Class 1a.1)	S + 2 C (Class 1a.2)	S + 3 C (Class 1a.3)
20,000	1,390	61	—	—	—
38,700	7,217	6,057	5,135	4,212	3,290
58,000	14,734	13,575	12,652	11,730	10,807
77,400	22,290	21,131	20,208	19,286	18,363
96,700	29,808	28,648	27,726	26,803	25,881
116,000	37,325	36,166	35,243	34,321	33,398
135,500	44,920	43,761	42,838	41,916	40,993
155,000	52,515	51,356	50,434	49,511	48,589

Married taxpayer (class 2)
Married taxpayer with dependent children (class 2.x)

(In Euros)

Taxable salaried income	Income tax			
	Married (M) (Class 2)	M + 1 Child (C) (Class 2.1)	M + 2 C (Class 2.2)	M + 3 C (Class 2.3)
20,000	41	—	—	—
38,700	2,527	1,605	682	—
58,000	7,373	6,451	5,528	4,606
77,400	14,434	13,511	12,589	11,666
96,700	21,951	21,028	20,106	19,183
116,000	29,468	28,546	27,623	26,701
135,500	37,064	36,141	35,219	34,296
155,000	44,659	43,736	42,814	41,891

INDIVIDUAL TAX CALCULATION

Assumptions

Collectively taxed spouses with two children who reside in Luxembourg during the entire year 2002. They have the following income.

1. One spouse receives a salary.
2. Both spouses earn dividend and interest income from Luxembourg.

The standard deductions are exceeded because of the following.

1. They live in the countryside at a distance of some 20 kilometers from the workplace of the salaried spouse.
2. They pay debtor interest on a loan taken up for the purchase of a car and computer equipment, as well as life, sickness, and personal liability insurance premiums.
3. They make donations to qualifying institutions.
4. They invest in shares in qualifying companies.

Tax computation

Determination of taxable income

Salary		€ 90,000
Less:		
Standard deduction	540	
Deduction for travel between home and work	1,980	2,520
		87,480
Income from securities:		
Dividends	2,000	
Interest	2,000	
Less:		
Exemption on income from securities	(3,000)	
Exemption of half of dividends	(1,000)	0
Net income		87,480
Less:		
Maximum deduction for debtor interest on a consumer loan	2,688	
Maximum deduction for insurance premiums	2,688	
Compulsory social security on salary (dependency contribution not included)	8,364	
Donations	250	13,990
Taxable income		73,490
Less:		
Qualifying shares acquisition	3,000	
Standard salaried income allowance	600	3,600
Adjusted taxable income		€ 69,890

Determination of tax

Adjusted taxable income rounded		€ 69,850
Tax on ordinary income 1		€ 9,413
Solidarity tax (9,413 x 2.5%)		235
Total income tax		9,648
Less:		
20% withholding taxes on dividends from Luxembourg	400	
Tax withheld on salary	12,385	(12,785)
Tax to be reimbursed by the tax authorities		€ 3,137

Summary of income tax and social security charges

Social security contributions (employee's part)	€ 8,364
Dependency contribution	€ 860
Income taxes	€ 9,648

Note:

Exchange rate of the Euro at January 3, 2002: US$1 = €1.106.

PwC contact

KK So, Tax Partner
PricewaterhouseCoopers Ltd
33/F Cheung Kong Center
2 Queen's Road Central
Hong Kong
Telephone: (852) 2289 3789
Fax: (852) 2882 5087
e-mail: kk.so@hk.pwcglobal.com

Significant developments

A one-off 25% reduction applies to the professional tax payable in 2002.

Territoriality and residence

Residence and/or domicile is irrelevant for Macau individual tax purposes. Individual tax is levied and payable only where Macau-source income is earned. The income of all entities (i.e., companies, partnerships, sole proprietors, etc.), including individuals who receive income for work done in the territory, is subject to complementary tax. Earnings of salaried employees and self-employed persons are also taxed under the professional tax regulations.

Certain overseas specialized technicians or managers who are seconded to an approved offshore institution established in Macao may enjoy an exemption from professional tax for the first three calendar years of their employment.

Unless otherwise stated, the information below relates to the regulations applicable to professional tax.

Professional tax is payable by anyone receiving income from work done in Macau irrespective of (a) where the income was received, (b) whether the recipient is a resident or not, and (c) whether the recipient is paid in money or in kind. Where income other than cash is received, the Inland Revenue Department may assess the value so received.

Gross income

Employee gross income/Employee gross income comprises the items shown below.

1. Salary, overtime, commissions, and bonuses, but not lump-sum payments on retirement.
2. Rental accommodation paid for by the employer. This is valued for tax purposes as follows:
   a. MOP2,000 per month for a company-owned residence;
   b. Rent actually paid as per lease agreement and receipt if lower than MOP2,000; or
   c. MOP2,000 per month, where the rent actually paid exceeds this amount or 15% of the remuneration received in cash, whichever is greater.
3. Passages for holidays.
4. Other benefits, i.e., car (valued at MOP12,000 per annum if chauffeur-driven and at MOP6,000 per annum if self-driven); domestic help (MOP18,000 per annum); telephone (MOP720 per annum); and electricity (MOP6,000 per annum).

5. Other allowances paid by the employer (other than reimbursements of expenses incurred on behalf of the employer) are also subject to professional tax.

Capital gains and investment income/Gains and investment income are tax exempt (i.e., not subject to either professional or complementary tax) with the exception of dividends received from local corporations, which are subject to complementary tax.

Deductions

Business deductions/Business deductions are only applicable to self-employed individuals (i.e., business or professional income), whose income is taxed under the professional tax regulations.

For salaried employees, there are no provisions in the tax regulations to claim business deductions.

Nonbusiness expenses/None.

Personal allowances/The allowances shown below are deductible in determining taxable income for professional tax purposes.

1. Personal allowance of MOP85,000 per annum or MOP7,084 per month.
2. Sickness and hospitalization allowances up to the actual amount paid if properly documented.
3. Family allowance for married individuals:
   a. Family subsidy—MOP2,040 per annum; and
   b. Child subsidy—MOP2,640 per child per annum.

The allowances listed below are deductible in determining taxable income for complementary tax purposes.

1. Basic allowance—MOP12,000.
2. Employment income allowance—20% of income from employment.
3. Business registration tax paid.
4. Spouse allowance—MOP6,000.
5. Child allowance:
   a. Each child up to 7 years old—MOP1,500;
   b. Each child between 7 and 11 years old—MOP2,000;
   c. Each child between 11 and 16 years old—MOP2,500;
   d. Each child between 16 and 21 years old—MOP3,000;
   e. Each child younger than 26 years old and studying overseas without receiving any scholarship—MOP6,000.
6. Personal allowance is MOP120,000 for employees over 65 years old and for those disabled with proven incapacity above 60 percent.

Tax credits

A credit is available for professional tax (less surcharges) for purposes of determining complementary tax payable.

Other taxes

Apart from professional and complementary taxes and their respective surcharges (stamp duty), there is also the monthly social security fund's contribution in the amount of MOP15 imposed on resident employees.

Tax administration

Returns/Husbands and wives are taxed separately in Macau on a calendar-year basis.

Payment of tax/For salaried individuals only, the employer is obliged to collect the amount of professional tax payable from its employees each month and make such payments to the Inland Revenue Department before the 15th of the month following the quarter-end. This is similar to the pay-as-you-earn (PAYE) system used in other countries.

Tax rates

Professional tax/The professional tax rates are progressive and cumulative up to a maximum rate of 15%.

Assessable income		Tax on Column 1	Percentage on excess
Over	Not over		
(Column 1)			
0	MOP 85,000	—	—
MOP 85,000	100,000	—	10
100,000	115,000	MOP 1,500	11
115,000	145,000	3,150	12
145,000	205,000	6,750	13
205,000	295,000	14,550	14
295,000		27,150	15

A surcharge (stamp duty) of 5% on the professional tax payable is also levied.

Complementary tax/Complementary tax rates range form 2% to 15% if income is below MOP300,000. If income exceeds MOP300,000, the tax is 15%. (Tax rates from 2% to 15% are applied with complicated adjustments.)

Professional tax paid (including surcharges) is deductible in determining taxable income for complementary tax purposes.

A surcharge (stamp duty) of 5% on the complementary tax payable is also levied.

INDIVIDUAL TAX CALCULATION

Assumptions

Taxpayer, married with two children, both less than seven years old.

Tax computation

Calculation of professional tax payable

Salary, overtime, commissions and bonuses		MOP 640,000
Less:		
Personal allowance	85,000	
Family subsidy, including allowances for children	7,320	92,320
		547,680
Add—Other benefits:		
Rental accommodation	96,000	
Holiday passage for family	60,000	
Car	6,000	
Domestic help	18,000	
Telephone	720	
Electricity	6,000	186,720
		MOP 734,400
Professional tax (1):		
Tax on next 210,000		MOP 27,150
On remainder—524,400 at 15%		78,660
		105,810
Surcharge—5% of 105,810		5,290
		MOP 111,100

Calculation of complementary tax payable

Salary, overtime, commissions, and bonuses		MOP 640,000
Income from a commercial activity		300,000
Total income		940,000
Deductions:		
Basic allowance	12,000	
Employment income relief (20% of income from employment	168,000	
Spouse allowance	6,000	
Child allowance (two)	3,000	
Business registration tax paid	300	189,300
Taxable income		MOP 750,700
Tax thereon—750,700 at 15%		MOP 112,605
Less—Professional tax paid		(111,100)
Complementary tax payable		1,505
Surcharge—1,505 at 5%		75
		MOP 1,580

Amount of tax payable

Professional tax and surcharge	MOP 111,100
Complementary tax and surcharge	1,580
	MOP 112,680

Notes:

1. A one-off 25% reduction applies to the tax payable in 2002, reducing the amount payable to MOP83,325.
2. Exchange rate of the pataca at December 31, 2001: US$1 = MOP8.37090.

Malaysia

PwC contacts

For additional information on taxation in Malaysia, contact:

Chuan Keat Khoo, TLS Director
Peter K. S. Chow, TLS Director
PricewaterhouseCoopers
Wisma Sime Darby, 11th Floor
Jalan Raja Laut
50350 Kuala Lumpur, Malaysia
Telephone: (60) (3) 2693 1077
Fax: (60) (3) 2693 0997
e-mail: chuan.keat.khoo@my.pwcglobal.com
peter.chow@my.pwcglobal.com

Significant developments

Changes to tax rates for resident individuals were introduced with effect from year of assessment 2002. The maximum rate was reduced from 29% to 28%, with the intervening bands broadened (see "Tax Rates"). The tax rates for nonresident individuals were also reduced from 29% to 28%.

The exit levy that was imposed on the repatriation of profits from portfolio investments was abolished as from May 2, 2001.

Territoriality and residence

An individual resident in Malaysia is taxed on any income accruing in or derived from Malaysia or received in Malaysia from outside Malaysia. A nonresident is taxed only on income accruing in or derived from Malaysia.

The status of individuals as residents or nonresidents determines whether or not they can claim personal allowances and the benefit of graduated tax rates. Resident status is determined by reference to the number of days an individual is present in Malaysia. Generally, an individual who is in Malaysia for a period or periods amounting to 182 days or more in a calendar year will be regarded as a tax resident.

Basis of assessment/As from year of assessment 2000, assessment of income is on a current-year basis. An individual is taxed on income from nonbusiness sources for a year of assessment on a calendar-year basis. Business sources of income are assessed for a year of assessment on the basis of the financial/accounting year ending on a day in that particular year of assessment.

Gross income

Employee gross income/An employee is taxed on employment income earned for work performed in Malaysia, regardless of where payment is made. Employment income includes salary, allowances, perquisites, benefits-in-kind, tax reimbursements, and rent-free accommodation provided by the employer.

Medical benefits, as well as childcare benefits provided by the employer, are not taxable. Leave passages, restricted to one overseas trip, up to a maximum amount of RM3,000 and three local trips per year, are also tax exempt in the hands of the employee. Cars or other household items provided for private use are valued at prescribed rates that are lower than the actual cost incurred by the employer. Rent-free accommodation provided by the employer is valued at the lower of 30% of the employee's total cash remuneration or the actual rental value. Gifts of new computers by employers are not deemed benefits in kind and hence not taxable.

Short-term visiting nonresident employees are not subject to tax on income from employment exercised in Malaysia if the period of employment does not exceed 60 days in a calendar year. If the period of employment straddles two calendar years, they are exempt if the total period of their employment over the two years does not exceed 60 days.

Area representatives of nonresident companies using Malaysia as a base for activities extending to other countries in the Far East are taxed on the remuneration relating to the time actually spent in Malaysia.

Capital gains and investment income/Capital gains on the disposal of real property (including shares in a real property company—"RPC") situated in Malaysia, are subject to real property gains tax. The tax is levied at rates ranging from a maximum rate of 30% (for assets held for less than two years) to 0% (for assets held for more than five years). Capital losses on the sale of real property (other than losses on the disposal of RPC shares) are allowed as offset against gains arising on the sale of real property. (A real property company is a controlled company that owns real property or RPC shares with a defined value of not less than 75% of its total tangible assets.) Other capital gains are not subject to tax.

An individual who is not a citizen or a permanent resident in Malaysia is subject to real property gains tax on gains arising from the disposal of real property or RPC shares on or after October 17, 1997 at a rate of 30% on disposals within five years and at 5% on disposals after five years.

A resident is generally subject to income tax on all investment income accruing in or derived from Malaysia or received in Malaysia from outside Malaysia. A nonresident is not taxed on income derived outside Malaysia.

Interest received by a resident individual is subject to income tax at a flat rate of 5%. Interest received on deposits for a period of 12 months or more is tax exempt. Interest received from certain types of bonds or securities is also exempt from tax.

Interest paid to a nonresident individual by commercial or merchant banks or finance companies operating in Malaysia is exempt from tax.

Deductions

Business deductions/Employees are allowed a deduction for any expenditure incurred wholly and exclusively in the performance of their duties, but no allowance is given for tax depreciation. Expenses of a private or domestic nature are expressly excluded from deduction; for example, the cost of traveling to and from a place of employment is not deductible.

Nonbusiness expenses/Nonbusiness expenses, for example, domestic or household expenses and taxes, are not deductible. Mortgage interest incurred to finance the purchase of a house is deductible only if income is derived from the house. Donations to approved funds and subscriptions to associations related to the individual's profession are deductible.

Personal allowances/A resident individual receives a personal deduction of RM8,000, an allowance of RM3,000 for the spouse (except in a case where a husband and wife have ceased to live together during the year) and child allowances of RM800 for each child. A child allowance of up to two or four times the normal deduction is given where certain conditions are satisfied. Instead of the normal child relief, an allowance of RM5,000 is granted for each physically or mentally handicapped child. Child relief can be claimed by a wife filing a tax return separately. Additional deductions of RM5,000 (personal relief) or RM2,500 (spouse) will be granted if the individual or spouse is disabled.

Medical expenses incurred for the individual's parents qualify for deduction, but this deduction is limited to a maximum of RM5,000. An additional amount of up to RM5,000 is given for medical expenses for self, spouse or child on treatment of a serious disease (e.g., AIDS, leukemia). This amount includes medical examination fees of up to RM500 incurred for self, spouse or child. A wife filing a return separately is also eligible for these deductions.

Expenses of up to RM5,000 incurred for the purchase of disability-supporting equipment for the individual's own use if the individual is a disabled person, or for the use of a spouse, child, or parent who is disabled, would be allowed as a deduction.

Contributions to approved pension/provident funds and annual premiums for insurance policies taken out by a resident employee on that employee's own life, a spouse's life or jointly are allowed, subject to a limit of RM5,000. An additional amount of up to RM3,000 is given for premiums for insurance on education or for medical benefits incurred for the individual, spouse or child. Similar relief subject to limits of RM5,000 and RM3,000 is also given for contributions/premiums incurred by a spouse, where the spouse's income is separately taxed. An additional amount of up to RM1,000 is also given for premiums on an insurance for annuity benefits.

A deduction limited to a maximum of RM5,000 is allowed for fees paid for a course of study in Malaysia undertaken to acquire technical, vocational or industrial, scientific, technological skills up to tertiary level. A deduction of up to RM500 is given for purchase of books, journals, magazines and other similar publications for purpose of enchancing knowledge.

Personal allowances are deducted in arriving at chargeable income of the resident individual.

Tax credits

A tax resident is entitled to claim foreign tax credits against Malaysian tax. Where a treaty exists, the credit available is the whole of the foreign tax paid or the Malaysian tax levied on the foreign-source income, whichever is lower. In the absence of a tax treaty, the credit due is restricted to one-half of the foreign tax paid.

Other taxes

There are no social security taxes or local taxes on income.

Real property gains tax/Real property gains tax is imposed at rates from 0% to 30% on gains arising from the disposal of real property (which includes the disposal of shares in a real property company) situated in Malaysia (see "Capital gains and investment income").

Exit levy/With effect from May 2, 2001, the exit levy that had been imposed on repatriation of profits from portfolio investments was abolished altogether.

Tax administration

Returns/Returns are filed jointly by the taxpayer and the taxpayer's wife. The income of a wife living with her husband is taxed separately from that of the husband. However, a wife who is a resident or a Malaysian citizen can elect to be taxed jointly with her husband.

From year of assessment 2001, a husband who has no income may also elect to be assessed jointly with his wife under the wife's name. Where husband and wife are jointly assessed in the wife's name, she is entitled to claim "husband relief" of RM3,000. Up to year of assessment 2000, only a husband can claim "wife relief" of the same amount.

Returns are required by law to be filed within 30 days from the date of the issue of the tax return form.

Payment of tax/Tax is payable 30 days from the issue of an assessment notice. However, tax payments by employees are collected through compulsory deductions from salary. From the year 2000, all deductions are made on a PAYE basis.

Tax rates

The following are the rates which are applicable to resident individual taxpayers from the year of assessment 2002.

Taxable income		Tax on Column 1	Percentage on excess
Over (Column 1)	Not over		
RM 50,000	RM 70,000	RM 3,475	19
70,000	100,000	7,275	24
100,000	150,000	14,475	27
150,000	250,000	27,975	27
250,000		54,975	28

A nonresident individual is taxed at a flat rate of 28% on total taxable income.

INDIVIDUAL TAX CALCULATION

Year of assessment 2002

Assumptions

Resident employee and wife, two children; one spouse earns all the income.

Tax computation

Gross income:		
Salary		RM 200,000
Interest (18,640) (1)		—
Total gross income		200,000
Less—Approved donations		1,000
		199,000
Less—Personal exemptions:		
Self and wife	11,000	
First child (over 18 and attending university)	3,200	
Second child (under 18)	800	
Medical expenses for parents (maximum)	5,000	
Life insurance premiums and provident fund contributions (maximum)	5,000	
Premiums on education/medical insurance (maximum)	3,000	
Purchase of books for enhancing knowledge (maximum)	500	28,500
Taxable income		RM 170,500
Income tax at joint return rates (see table above)		RM 33,510

Notes:

1. Nonexempt interest received from banks and finance companies is subject to a withholding tax of 5%, which is a final tax. No further tax is payable thereon.
2. From September 1, 1998 the exchange rate of the ringgit is fixed at: US$1 = RM3.80.

PwC contacts

For additional information on taxation in Malta, contact:

Dr. Antoine Fiott
Dr. Neville Gatt
PricewaterhouseCoopers
167 Merchants Street
Valletta VLT03
Malta
Telephone: (356) 247000
Fax: (356) 244768
e-mail: antoine.fiott@mt.pwcglobal.com
neville.gatt@mt.pwcglobal.com

Significant developments

1. The income tax rates for married individuals have been reduced.
2. An investment registration scheme has been introduced so as to provide a one-time opportunity for Maltese persons having undeclared investments outside Malta to regularize their position.
3. It was announced in the government's budget for 2002 that simplification measures for small businesses will be introduced in order to inter alia alleviate compliance requirements.
4. Consistent with previous years, a further liberalization of exchange controls has been effected.

Territoriality and residence

Malta taxes individuals who are both domiciled and ordinarily resident in Malta on their worldwide income. Any person who is not ordinarily resident or domiciled in Malta is taxable only on income arising in Malta and on any foreign income remitted to Malta. A nonresident individual is taxed only on income arising in Malta. There are few specific rules relating to residence, ordinary residence, domicile, locality of income, or the remittance of income to Malta. Persons are usually held to be domiciled in a country where they actually have their permanent home. The locality where income arises is determined in accordance with the category of income concerned; different criteria may apply to different sources of income. Persons are considered to be ordinarily resident in Malta when they are so resident in the ordinary or regular course of their lives. The remittance of income to Malta is a question of fact.

Gross income

Employee gross income/Gains or profits from employment with a Maltese employer are usually fully taxable, including the value of "any benefit provided by reason of any employment or office." Remuneration received for services rendered outside Malta by persons not domiciled or not ordinarily resident in Malta should not be liable to tax in Malta. Apportionment is resorted to where necessary. All rewards for services rendered, including fringe benefits and benefits in kind, are taxable, although some exemptions are provided, some of which may be of general application while others are intended for expatriates rendering services to or employed with certain Maltese-licensed investment services companies or Maltese-licensed insurance companies.

Taxable benefits include living allowances, housing allowances, tax reimbursements (grossed up), use of car, paid vacation trips, and stock options.

Fringe benefits/Regulations outlining the valuation criteria for fringe benefits and the instances where a fringe benefit is deemed not to arise have been issued. The provisions on fringe benefits apply for benefits provided with effect from January 1, 2001.

Three main categories of fringe benefits are being identified by the regulations.

1. Category 1—Use of motor vehicles:

   The valuation of a fringe benefit arising on the use of a car would be calculated on the basis of three elements, i.e., the car use value, the maintenance value and the fuel value. The car use value is equivalent to 17% of the car value or to 10% of the car value if the car is more than six years old. In respect of both the maintenance and fuel value, the basis of valuation is in each case 3% of the car value if the latter does not exceed Lm12,000 and 5% of the car value in any other case. The fringe benefit is equal to the aggregate of these three elements multiplied by a percentage signifying the private use of the car. The private use percentage varies depending on the respective car value and may go up to 60%.

   The private use element (i.e., the taxable element) of a car cash allowance is 50% of the allowance if the allowance is Lm1,000 or less, or the cash allowance less Lm500 if the allowance exceeds Lm1,000.

2. Category 2—Use of other assets, including accommodation:

   Use of property/accommodation involves a chargeable fringe benefit of 5% of the higher of the market value and the original cost of the property. No fringe benefit is deemed to arise in certain situations, e.g., use of an official residence by the holder of public office, temporary accommodation for security purposes, etc. The cost of making the property available for use by the employee (such as water, electricity, ground rent, redecoration, repairs and maintenance and professional fees) is also a fringe benefit.

3. Category 3—Other benefits:

   The fringe benefit on the use of other assets (other than property and motor vehicles) stands at 12% of the higher of the market value and the original cost of the asset. The original cost is reduced by 40% in the case of assets that are owned for more than six years. Use of computers, related equipment and internet connection service is not considered a fringe benefit.

   In this case the fringe benefit is the actual cost to the employer of providing the relative fringe benefit or the market value thereof. This category of fringe benefits includes, among other items, beneficial loan arrangements, share option schemes, reimbursement of private expenses, discounted goods and services, free or subsidized meals, and gifts. Valuation criteria differ according to the type of benefit with the possibility of a partial or a full exemption in certain cases.

The provision of telephony services, computer equipment, recreational, and child-minding facilities, certain awards and certain training courses, among other items, are not considered to be fringe benefits.

Capital gains and investment income/Tax on capital gains is imposed on any gain realized on the transfer of immovable property (real estate), shares and other securities (excluding certain securities listed on the Malta Stock Exchange and investments that yield a fixed rate of return), business goodwill, copyright, patents, trade names, and trademarks. Gains from the transfer of other assets fall outside the scope of the tax. The rate of tax is the marginal rate of tax applicable to the particular taxpayer. Gains arising outside Malta and derived by a person who is either not domiciled or not ordinarily resident in Malta or is a returned migrant who qualifies for a reduced rate of income tax are not subject to tax even if remitted to Malta.

Subject to the applicable statutory requirements, nonresidents and expatriates working in investment services or insurance are exempt from tax on any interest, royalties and capital gains from specified sources, e.g., disposal of units in collective investment schemes and of shares or securities in companies satisfying certain conditions.

A final withholding tax system operates for certain types of investment income (see "Tax administration, Payment of tax"), paid by certain payers to specified categories of (Maltese-resident) recipients. The investment income provisions charge to tax investment income received by certain resident collective investment schemes and tax resident investors on gains realized on disposal of units in funds investing a certain level of their assets outside Malta.

Deductions

Business deductions/Certain allowances are available for business-related expenses in the case of persons exercising a trade, business, profession, or vocation. These include, inter alia, scientific research, bad debts and losses carried forward. To be deductible, expenses of an employee must be incurred wholly and exclusively in the production of the income and must be necessarily incurred. Where the employer reimburses employees for expenses incurred on the employer's behalf, no tax liability should arise in the hands of the recipients unless a gain or profit accrues to them from the arrangement.

Nonbusiness expenses/Alimony payments paid by a taxpayer to an estranged spouse are allowed as a deduction. A new deduction is also allowable in respect of private school fees (capped to a maximum amount). No other nonbusiness expenses are allowed.

Personal allowances/No personal allowances by way of credits or deductions are granted.

Tax credits

There are no special credits for short-term residents. Income taxes paid abroad on income that becomes taxable in the hands of a Maltese resident may qualify for a credit if a double taxation treaty has been concluded with the relevant country or under the unilateral relief provisions of Maltese law.

Other taxes

Social security taxes/For employees who do not earn more than Lm6,618 per annum, the employer and the employee each pay social security tax of 10% of salary. Employees earning in excess of Lm6,618 contribute Lm12.73 per week (the same amount is contributed by the employer). Self-employed persons who earn less than Lm6,618 pay a flat contribution percentage of 15% on net income. Those earning in excess of Lm6,618 contribute Lm19.09 per week.

Local taxes on income/There are no local or municipal taxes in Malta.

Other taxes/Other taxes imposed include customs and excise duties on certain goods; a tax on air travel; value-added tax on the importation and purchase of most goods and services; and stamp duty on certain documents and transfers, including transfers of immovable property and marketable securities; and issues and renewals of insurance policies. Stamp duty is also imposed on transmissions by death of immovable property and shares in Maltese companies.

Tax administration

Returns/Returns are filed on a calendar-year basis. Husband and wife are jointly responsible for filing tax returns and spouses must choose which of them is to be registered as the taxpayer. The election of a "responsible spouse" remains effective for five years. The responsible spouse may elect to have the tax on the other spouse's earned income computed separately. If a separate computation is chosen, husband and wife are assessed separately at single taxpayers' rates. Unearned income is assessable in the hands of the spouse earning the higher level of income.

The tax return, together with a self-assessment, must be submitted by the end of June of the year following the basis tax year. Under certain conditions, a taxpayer may file a declaration instead of a full tax return, in which case this should be filed by the end of April of the year following the basis year. Penalties are incurred on late filing of returns. The self-assessment is deemed to represent the correct tax position, and unless the Commissioner of Inland Revenue disagrees with the self-assessment, an assessment will not be raised.

Payment of tax/Income tax is withheld from salaries (including taxable fringe benefits) under the Final Settlement System (FSS), which in most cases equals the individual's total tax liability. Where income is not subject to the FSS (e.g., self-employed persons), the taxpayer is required to make three payments in the basis tax year under the provisional tax (PT) system. The provisional tax payments based on the last self-assessment filed by the individual and payments are divided into three installments of 20%, 30%, and 50%, respectively. The tax liability that is still due at the tax return date after deducting all tax credits must be settled immediately with the submission of the return. Interest at 1% per month is charged on any unpaid tax.

Provisional tax is also payable at 7% on the selling price of certain assets disposed of on account of tax imposed on capital gains. A final withholding tax of 15% is imposed on specified types of investment income (e.g., banking interest paid to Maltese residents), and on income from most part-time work. Taxpayers may opt out of this scheme, in which case tax on investment income will be charged at normal rates.

Tax rates

Income is taxable at graduated rates. For year of assessment 2003 (year of income 2002), in the case of single individuals (including married individuals opting for separate computation) there is a tax liability of Lm650 on the first Lm6,000 of income. Married individuals will be liable to Lm895 tax on the first Lm8,400 of income. For amounts exceeding these thresholds, the tax rate is 35% for both single and married individuals. The single rates apply also to married couples opting for a separate computation. The married rates apply also to single parents, widows/widowers and separated parents.

Tax rates for basis tax year 2002 are as follows.

Married resident taxpayers

Taxable income Over (Column 1)	Not over	Tax on Column 1	Percentage on excess
0	Lm 4,100	—	0
Lm 4,100	5,900	—	15
5,900	8,400	Lm 270	25
8,400		895	35

Single resident taxpayers

Taxable income Over (Column 1)	Not over	Tax on Column 1	Percentage on excess
0	Lm 3,000	—	0
Lm 3,000	4,000	—	15
4,000	6,000	Lm 150	25
6,000		650	35

Nonresident individuals (married or single)

Taxable income Over (Column 1)	Not over	Tax on Column 1	Percentage on excess
0	Lm 300	—	0
Lm 300	1,300	—	20
1,300	3,300	Lm 200	30
3,300		800	35

Residence permit holders and returned migrants are taxed at 15% on income over Lm2,500 for married taxpayers, and 15% on income over Lm1,800 for single taxpayers, subject to a minimum tax liability of Lm1,000 per annum.

INDIVIDUAL TAX CALCULATION

Year of assessment 2003 (year of income 2002)

Assumptions

Resident married expatriate employed by a Maltese company.

Tax computation

Gross income:		
Salary		Lm 29,500
Foreign bank interest remitted		2,000
Capital gains arising in Malta		2,500
Total gross income		34,000
Less—Expenditure necessarily incurred in producing the income		3,500
Total taxable income		Lm 30,500
Tax thereon:		
On the first 8,400	895	
On balance at 35%	7,735	
Total tax liability		Lm 8,630
Less:		
Tax withheld by deduction from salary	7,500	
Provisional capital gains tax	700	(8,200)
Net tax payable		Lm 430

Note:

Exchange rate of the lira at December 31, 2001: US$1 = Lm0.4492.

PwC contact

For additional information on taxation in Mauritius, contact:

N. M. Robert Bigaignon
PricewaterhouseCoopers
Cerné House, 6th Floor
Chaussée
Port Louis, Mauritius
Telephone: (230) 212 5011, 208 8036, 208 8038
Fax: (230) 208 8037
e-mail: robert.bigaignon@mu.pwcglobal.com

Significant developments

There have been no significant tax or regulatory developments in the past year.

Territoriality and residence

Individuals, irrespective of nationality, deriving income from sources within Mauritius are subject to Mauritian income tax on all such income, whether or not they are resident.

Resident individuals are subject to Mauritian income tax on their worldwide income from all sources. However, earned income derived from outside Mauritius is taxable only to the extent that it is received in Mauritius. Credits are available for foreign taxes paid on income derived from foreign sources. Income from employment duties performed in Mauritius is deemed to have been derived from Mauritius, even if the related remuneration is received outside Mauritius.

An individual is resident in Mauritius in an income year in the following cases.

1. The individual's domicile is in Mauritius, unless his or her permanent place of abode is outside Mauritius;
2. Presence in Mauritius in that income year and the two preceding income years is for an aggregate period of 270 days or more;

   or
3. Presence in Mauritius is for a period of or periods amounting in the aggregate to at least 183 days in that income year.

Gross income

Employee gross income/All income derived from employment exercised in Mauritius is liable to tax in Mauritius, regardless of where payment is made or who the employer is. Employment income includes salary, wages, leave pay, overtime pay, perquisites, allowances, bonuses, gratuities, commissions, compensation for loss of office, tax borne by employer, pensions, retiring allowances, annuities, all benefits in kind, and reward or remuneration in relation to employment. Passages by sea, air or land between Mauritius and another country provided under a contract of employment are not considered as income from employment.

Benefits in kind include the annual value of residential accommodation, use of cars, free meals, and full board provided for employees, as well as pecuniary liabilities of employees that are borne or reimbursed by the employer. Most benefits in kind are valued at standard scale rates that are usually less than the actual cost to the employer. For example, the benefit of rent-free unfurnished accommodation does not normally exceed 10% of assessable emoluments. For furnished accommodation, the corresponding percentage is 12.5%. For cars, the yearly benefit is a fixed sum of Rs12,000, but it may be higher for expensive cars. These rates, which date back to 1979, are expected to be revised soon.

Expatriate employees and qualifying Mauritian employees of a global bank, global business company (formerly offshore bank or offshore company), offshore trust, or company operating in the freeport zone or holding a pioneer financial services certificate are entitled to a deduction from their tax bill of 50% of the income tax payable by them on emoluments derived from such entities. A similar deduction of 50% is allowable to expatriate employees and qualifying Mauritian employees of a pioneer-status enterprise, an export enterprise, any company engaged in electronics and high-technology activities, or a company engaged wholly in the management of a venture capital fund, provided the number of employees entitled to the deduction does not exceed two for each company. In neither case may the period of exemption exceed in aggregate four income years for each enterprise or company.

Income derived by a nonresident expatriate from consultancy services or training provided in Mauritius, other than under a contract of employment, is free of income tax, provided the period during which the services are rendered does not exceed 183 days in a fiscal year. The income of nonresident expatriates who are engineering and support service personnel required by a pioneer-status enterprise or a company engaged in electronics and high-technology activities for the installation and maintenance of equipment and training of local staff is also exempt from income tax. Director's fees payable to a nonresident director of a resident company are free of tax.

Capital gains and investment income/There is no capital gains tax in Mauritius. Where individuals enter into a series of purchases and resales of property, the tax authorities may take the view that they are carrying on a trade and assess them to tax accordingly. Income derived from dealings in units and securities is, however, exempt from tax. Capital gains received by a resident or nonresident from outside Mauritius are not taxable.

Investment income derived from outside Mauritius is taxable in a resident recipient's hands whether or not it is received in Mauritius. However, a tax credit in respect of foreign tax paid on such income is allowable against Mauritius tax computed with reference to that income. This normally nullifies any tax incidence in Mauritius on foreign income.

Deductions

Business deductions/Where an individual derives income from a trade, business, profession, or vocation, deductions are allowed for all outgoings incurred wholly and exclusively in the production of the assessable income, including capital allowances on qualifying assets. Land and nonindustrial buildings do not qualify for capital allowances, with the exception of school buildings and consulting rooms of medical practitioners. An individual may also claim a deduction for any fees or expenses payable to a recognized institution for education or training, subject to a maximum of Rs25,000. Unauthorized deductions include all expenditure of a capital, domestic or private nature; expenditure relating to exempt income; all taxes; any reserve or provision (e.g., reserve for doubtful debts); gifts and donations; and entertainment expenses.

Employees are allowed a deduction for expenses necessarily incurred in the performance of their duties. A very restrictive interpretation of the term "necessarily incurred in performing the duties" is adopted by the tax authorities, and in practice few claims are admitted. Moving expenses are not allowable. Expenses incurred by members of professional bodies in respect of continuing professional education are allowable, subject to a limit of Rs20,000.

Nonbusiness expenses/Deductions may be claimed for mortgage interest or interest on loans raised on the security of a life insurance policy or of a standing crop or on the pledge of shares or debentures, provided the loan is taken for the acquisition of property for residential purposes or for financing the tertiary education of the taxpayer's children. Interest paid to a nonresident that is not assessable to Mauritian tax on the interest received is normally not allowable. The deduction in respect of interest incurred is limited to Rs200,000 (Rs100,000 per working spouse).

Medical expenses, contributions to medical schemes and contributions to the National Pension Fund are allowable, with certain restrictions, as personal reliefs and deductions in determining chargeable income.

Relief by way of a deduction is given for life insurance premiums and certain investments, such as the acquisition of units or shares issued by tax incentive companies or companies listed on the stock exchange. With regard to the investments, the deduction is limited to 40% of the amount invested or Rs50,000, whichever is less. Any amount in excess of Rs50,000 is deductible in the two succeeding income years, subject to a maximum of Rs50,000 in any income year.

Taxes are not allowable as a deduction, and there are no standard deductions other than the personal reliefs and deductions enumerated below.

Personal allowances/Resident individuals may claim the following reliefs and allowances that are deductible from their total net income to arrive at the income chargeable to tax.

	Rs
Basic personal deduction	70,000
Deduction for dependent spouse, i.e., a spouse who has no income or whose income for the income year does not exceed Rs55,000	55,000
Additional allowance if individual, spouse or any dependent child is permanently disabled	50,000
Dependent unmarried children (limited to three in number):	
Under 18 or, if 18 or over, receiving full-time instruction at an educational institution or being unemployed	23,000
Receiving full-time instruction at the University of Mauritius, attending a course at a polytechnic or at an appointed educational institution providing tertiary education in Mauritius or serving under articles of indenture overseas	50,000
Receiving full-time instruction at a university outside Mauritius or attending a course at a polytechnic outside Mauritius	100,000
If child is attending a course at the Industrial and Vocational Training Board or at a state-owned or -approved technical school	30,000
If child is over 18 and handicapped	50,000
Retirement pension relief—100% of pension, subject to a maximum of	65,000
Alimony and maintenance paid to a spouse in accordance with a court order	Amount paid

Emoluments relief—15% of emoluments, subject to a maximum of	100,000
Agricultural income relief—15% of agricultural income, subject to a maximum of	100,000
Contributions to prescribed funds or schemes such as superannuation funds or schemes, civil service Family Protection Scheme and the National Pensions Fund	Amount paid
Premiums on life insurance policy	(Note)
Premiums on retirement annuities allowable to self-employed persons or persons who derive income from nonpensionable offices	(Note)
Premiums on personal pension schemes	(Note)
Contributions to approved medical schemes	(Note)
Medical expenses incurred in a health institution or hospital for self, spouse or dependent children—50% of difference between expenses incurred and amounts reimbursed, subject to a maximum of:	
Treatment in Mauritius	20,000
Treatment outside Mauritius	30,000
Contributions to retirement savings schemes, subject to a maximum of	50,000

Note:

Deductions for contributions to medical schemes, premiums on personal pension schemes or retirement annuities are limited in the aggregate to 20% of net income. Life insurance premiums are deductible, subject to a maximum of Rs80,000 per year.

A nonresident individual is not entitled to any personal allowances or deductions other than emoluments relief, agricultural income relief and pension relief. A nonresident citizen of Mauritius may, however, claim the basic personal deduction.

Tax credits

The following reliefs are allowable by way of deduction from tax payable.

On income tax payable by an expatriate or qualifying Mauritian employee of a global business company or global bank (formerly an offshore company or offshore bank), offshore trust, or a company operating in the freeport zone or holding a pioneer financial services certificate on emoluments derived from such entities.	50% of tax otherwise payable
On income tax payable by an expatriate or qualifying Mauritian employee of a pioneer-status enterprise, an export enterprise, a company engaged in electronics and high-technology activities, or a company engaged wholly in the management of a venture capital fund, provided the number of employees entitled to the deduction does not exceed two for each company.	50% of tax otherwise payable

Unilateral foreign tax credit is allowed for foreign taxes paid, limited to Mauritius tax referable to the relevant foreign income subject to tax. Foreign tax credit available under a tax treaty will be allowed if it is more favorable.

Other taxes

Social security taxes/Contributions to the National Pensions Fund are payable by the employer at 6% and by the employee at 3% of cash remuneration up to a maximum remuneration of Rs6,000 monthly. Monthly contributions for remuneration exceeding Rs6,000 are made at the standard flat rates of Rs359.50 for the employer and Rs179.50 for the employee. In addition, employers are required to contribute 2.5% of remuneration, subject to a maximum of Rs149.50 per month per employee and to pay a monthly levy of 1% of basic salaries and wages of every employee.

Local taxes on income/There are no local taxes on income in Mauritius.

Tax administration

Returns/Income tax returns are filed on prescribed forms for a year of assessment ending June 30 on the basis of the income earned during the preceding income year ended June 30. With the approval of the Commissioner of Income Tax, a self-employed taxpayer may file a tax return relating to a 12-month period ending on a date other than June 30 in the preceding year.

Every individual taxpayer is required to file on or before September 30 following the end of the income year an annual return on a prescribed form, disclosing income from all sources as well as full particulars of deductions, allowances and tax credit reliefs claimed.

A married woman is assessed separately from her husband with regard to all income derived by her. She is entitled to claim all personal reliefs and deductions available to an individual taxpayer, including deductions for children. However, the number of children for whom deductions may be claimed is limited to three per married couple.

Payment of tax/Under the pay-as-you-earn (PAYE) system, income tax is withheld from wages and salaries on a noncumulative basis, and a final adjustment is made at the end of the income year when the taxpayer files the annual return of income. If tax is underpaid under the PAYE system, the unpaid balance becomes payable on or before September 30 following the end of the income year. If tax is overpaid, a refund of the excess tax is made to the taxpayer, normally within three months from the date of filing of the annual return of income. Tax withheld under PAYE from the emoluments of expatriate pilots and flight engineers approved by the Minister of Finance is deemed to be a final tax.

Under the current payment system (CPS), self-employed individuals must pay tax on their business income semiannually. The first payment is due on March 31 in the income year and is based on income for the preceding period from July 1 to December 31. The second and final payment and the annual tax return are due on September 30 following the income year.

Tax rates

Income tax is calculated at graduated rates as shown below.

Chargeable income		Tax on	Percentage
Over (Column 1)	Not over	Column 1	on excess
0	Rs 25,000	—	15
Rs 25,000		Rs 3,750	25

INDIVIDUAL TAX CALCULATION

Year of assessment 2002/2003 (income for the year ending June 30, 2002)

Assumptions

The employee is resident in Mauritius but domiciled in Australia, is married and has two unmarried children, ages 16 and 19. The latter is receiving full-time instruction at a university in Australia. A furnished house is provided by the employers, who pay an annual rent of Rs120,000 plus all electricity, telephone and gas bills. The employers also provide a new automobile of 1,800 cc that they purchased for Rs900,000. The employee has not derived any income from Australia.

Tax computation

Salary		Rs 1,080,000
Yearly December gratuity		90,000
Electricity, telephone and gas bills		48,000
Car benefit		12,000
Housing accommodation		120,000
Total income from employment		1,350,000
Add:		
Interest on bank savings account	12,000	
Less—Exemption	(75,000)	—
Total gross income		1,350,000
Less—Emoluments relief		100,000
		1,250,000
Less—Personal reliefs and deductions:		
Basic personal deduction	70,000	
Wife	55,000	
One child aged 16	23,000	
One child aged 19 attending university overseas	100,000	
Contribution to National Pensions Fund	2,154	
Contribution to approved medical scheme	5,000	
Life insurance premiums paid	15,000	270,154
Chargeable income		Rs 979,846
Tax payable:		
On first 25,000	3,750	
On remaining 954,846 at 25%	238,711	
Tax payable		Rs 242,461

Notes:

1. Tax is withheld from the salary of the employee under the PAYE system. Any tax underpaid will become payable on or before September 30, 2002; any tax overpaid will be refunded by the tax authorities within three months from the date the annual return of income is filed.
2. Exchange rate of the rupee at December 31, 2001: US$1 = Rs30.20.

PwC contacts

For additional information on taxation in Mexico, contact:

Carlos Montemayor
Jeff Tollers
PricewaterhouseCoopers
Mariano Escobedo No. 573
Col. Rincón del Bosque
11580 México, D.F.
Telephone: (52) 5 2 63 60 66 (Montemayor)
(52) 5 2 63 57 70 (Tollers)
IAS fax: (52) 5 2 63 86 76
e-mail: carlos.montemayor@mx.pwcglobal.com
jeff.tollers@mx.pwcglobal.com

General note

This entry is repeated from the 2001/2002 edition. For more up-to-date information, consult the contact listed above or Mark Friedlich at mark.friedlich@us.pwcglobal.com.

Significant developments

Limited tax amnesty/In an effort to increase individual tax compliance, a transitory resolution was passed that limits audits of certain taxpayers. If a taxpayer files an accurate 2000 tax return, the tax authorities will not be able to audit the previous five years. However, to maintain this protection from audit, all subsequent-year returns must be accurate as well.

However, even this limited protection is not applicable to income received from abroad. Therefore, for most international assignees, only salary reported on a Mexican payroll will be protected.

Territoriality and residence

Resident individuals are subject to Mexican income tax on their worldwide income, regardless of their nationality. Nonresidents, including Mexican citizens who can prove residence for tax purposes in a foreign country, are taxed only on their Mexican-source income.

The Federal Tax Code provides that foreign individuals will be considered as residents of Mexico for tax purposes when they have established their home in Mexico, unless they are present in another country for more than 183 days, consecutive or not, in a calendar year and are able to prove residence for tax purposes in that other country.

Gross income

Employee gross income/Income from personal services (earned income) includes salaries, commissions, and allowances of all types, including those for housing, living expenses, education, foreign service, tax reimbursements, and employer profit-sharing distributions. Benefits in service may be free of tax, except for low-interest or interest-free loans to employees, which are considered to produce taxable income to the employees in the form of imputed interest. This statute was overturned by the Mexican Supreme Court on constitutional grounds in August 1999. For years 2000 and 2001, the minimum interest rate that needs to be used to avoid income imputation is fixed at 15% per year. The use of a fixed interest rate is intended to remedy the constitutional defect of the prior statute.

Fringe benefits such as "social welfare benefits" may be considered as totally or partially exempt income if the employer satisfies certain eligibility requirements (e.g., nondiscrimination). However, the exempt amount of social welfare benefits is limited to the equivalent of one annual minimum wage (currently, Ps14,727.75) once the employee's salary (together with these benefits) exceeds the equivalent of seven times the minimum wage.

The personal use of an employer-provided automobile is usually not considered to represent additional taxable income to the employee. However, the employer's deductibility of automobile costs and expenses is subject to certain limitations, concerning mainly the maximum value of the vehicle and restrictions on the use of the vehicle outside of normal office hours. A per diem rate for business travel is treated as a taxable allowance unless supported by third-party receipts for travel expenses that are limited to lodging, meals, and transportation. Travel expenses are subject to certain maximum limits for domestic and foreign travel and are deductible (and thus not imputed as income to the employee) only when incurred outside a 50-kilometer radius from the employer's base.

Living expense reimbursements, including housing and rental allowances, are generally taxable to the employee, even if paid directly to third parties.

Reimbursements of expenses of a spouse or dependents usually represent taxable income to the employee.

Nonresidents' wages, salaries, and other remuneration for personal dependent services rendered in Mexico are taxed on the basis of income received in a 12-month fiscal year, as follows.

Cumulative income		
Over	**Not over**	**%**
0	Ps 27,829	Exempt
Ps 127,829	1,029,726	15
1,029,726		30

The rates are applied to the cumulative income as it is earned over a 12-month period, whether or not the period coincides with a calendar year.

The tax rate applicable to independent personal services performed by a nonresident in Mexico is a flat 21%. Fees paid to nonresident members of boards of directors or advisory boards (regardless of where the services are performed) are taxed at a flat 30%.

However, no tax is imposed when the compensation (other than board fees) is paid by a nonresident of Mexico (even if not subject to tax) who does not have in Mexico any kind of establishment to which the services relate, provided always that the individual is physically present in Mexico less than 183 days (consecutive or not) in any 12-month period. A nonresident who has become subject to the nonresident tax on service income continues to be subject to tax until it is shown that the nonresident has been out of Mexico for at least 183 consecutive days. Under some circumstances, tax treaties exempt Mexican-source income paid by a nonresident of Mexico to a resident of a treaty country.

The tax, when applicable, is withheld if the income is paid by a resident (or a nonresident with a permanent establishment in Mexico). Otherwise, the tax is payable on a monthly basis by the individual earning the Mexican-source income, generally by the 17th day of the following month.

Capital gains and investment income/Gains on the disposition of real property or shares of capital stock receive favorable income tax treatment in that historical costs may be adjusted (increased) for inflation (on the basis of the number of months the asset had been held). In the case of shares of capital stock of a Mexican corporation, the adjustment also includes amounts intended to partially cover net retained earnings, whether capitalized or not. The resulting net gain for tax purposes is taxed under a formula favorable to the taxpayer, depending on the number of years the asset was held before sale. Gains on sales of securities through the Mexican Stock Exchange, provided the securities are classified as available to the general public, are exempt from tax. Shares of Mexican companies traded abroad in authorized exchanges (e.g., ADRs) are also exempt when determined by the Mexican Ministry of Finance to be placed among the general investing public.

Gains from the sale of the taxpayer's principal residence are exempt, provided the taxpayer occupied it as such during the two years before the sale.

Persons considered as residents of Mexico are taxed on their worldwide capital gains, whereas nonresidents are subject to Mexican tax only on gains arising from sales of real property located in Mexico (including shares of foreign companies holding a significant amount of Mexican real property) or nonexempt sales of shares of Mexican companies, regardless of where the sale takes place.

Residents are required to include investment income received during the year in their annual returns, except for (1) the previously mentioned exempt capital gains; (2) interest from the Mexican banking system and government obligations, which either is subject to a definitive withholding tax or is exempt; and (3) dividend income from Mexican corporations or investment funds, which is subject to an additional 5% withholding after 1998.

However, resident individuals may elect to include dividends received from Mexican corporations (grossed up for the corporate income tax paid by the corporation) in their individual income tax returns and claim the underlying corporate income tax paid as a credit against their tax liability, as well as the 5% tax withheld on the payment of the dividend. This "deemed paid" credit system allows individual taxpayers to compute their tax on dividends at their own personal tax rate, which may be lower than the combined corporate rate of 35% plus the 5% tax withheld.

Taxable investment income includes income earned (even if not distributed) by investments of any kind located in countries considered to be tax havens in proportion to the ownership percentage of the resident taxpayers. If the taxpayer does not have effective control of the administration of the tax haven investment or the total amount of the investments are maintained at less than Ps160,000, the income need not be recognized until it is received.

Nonresidents are subject to withholding taxes on Mexican-source interest income at rates varying from 0% to 40%, depending on several factors. Other types of Mexican-source income (including rents and royalties) are also subject to withholding taxes when paid to a nonresident. In the case of dividends and other corporate distributions, there is a 5% tax withheld on the dividend (grossed up for the corporate income tax paid by the corporation), and no further tax is imposed on the nonresident investor/shareholder.

Residents are also required to file a separate report with the tax authorities by February 28 of each year regarding their direct and indirect investments during the previous calendar year in countries considered to be tax havens. Failure to file the information report may subject the resident individual to severe penalties, including a prison sentence. If the total tax-haven investments are maintained at less than Ps160,000, the report is not required.

Tax treaties may reduce or eliminate tax withholding to nonresidents, and the treaty provisions should be analyzed accordingly, depending on the country of residence of the individual receiving Mexican-source income. See the PricewaterhouseCoopers publication *Corporate Taxes—A Worldwide Summary* 2002–2003 for details on treaty countries and rates.

Deductions

Employees are allowed to exclude an amount equal to 30 days' minimum wages if they receive a year-end bonus, 15 days' minimum wage each if they receive a vacation bonus or employees' participation in profits, and up to five times the daily minimum wage per week of overtime, with certain limitations. These exclusions are taken into account by the employer when calculating the income tax withholding.

Business deductions/Employees are allowed no business-related deductions, but employer reimbursements of properly supported business-related moving and traveling expenses are not taxable to the employee.

Nonbusiness expenses/Resident taxpayers are allowed to deduct unreimbursed medical, dental, or funeral expenses for themselves and their dependents, as well as certain charitable contributions, deposits in special interest-bearing savings accounts (investment retirement accounts) or retirement insurance premiums in lieu thereof, and investments with a five-year minimum duration in special investment funds placed with the general investing public. The maximum deductible deposit or investment in the special interest-bearing accounts is Ps151,605 per year. Withdrawals from these savings accounts become taxable income. There are no standard deductions (except that an individual may deduct an amount equal to 50% of gross rental income—35% if the property rented is nonresidential—instead of actual expenses and depreciation of the property).

Tax credits

Residents may credit against their Mexican tax liability, subject to limitations, foreign income tax paid on foreign-source taxable income.

A credit on salary also reduces the tax liability by up to Ps1,820. Higher benefits are provided to employees with an income of under four minimum wages per year.

A nonrefundable low-income tax credit designed to reduce the tax burden of taxpayers with lower incomes is also granted. This credit, which can be as high as Ps44,733, is phased out if the taxpayer's employer provides tax-exempt benefits to its employees.

Other taxes

Social security taxes/Employee contributions to the Mexican Social Security Institute are withheld at source. The employer also makes contributions. Both contributions are calculated at varying rates and subject to various limits based on multiples of the minimum wage.

The maximum annual contribution for employees is about US$1,250. The employer's maximum annual contribution is about US$6,425, excluding occupational risk premiums, which vary, depending on the activity of the employer. These maximum contributions apply to employees earning more than approximately US$37,000 per year or US$3,080 per month.

Local taxes on income/Most Mexican states levy a relatively low rate of tax on salaries (but not on income in general), which in most cases is payable by the employer. The Federal District imposes a 2% payroll tax, but it is payable by the employer and constitutes a tax-deductible expense.

Tax administration

Returns/All residents receiving income during the calendar year are required to file an annual tax return no later than April 30 of the succeeding year, except in certain cases, such as when an individual earns Mexican bank interest only—regardless of the amount thereof—or when the taxpayer's only income consists of salaries paid by a single Mexican employer. In this latter case, if the taxpayer was employed through December 31, the employer computes the final tax liability and makes an adjustment in the employee's withholding; no return is required (unless requested otherwise by the employee, to claim personal deductions or other credits, in which case the employee is personally responsible for filing the annual tax return). Joint returns are not allowed, and personal service income should be declared by the spouse earning it, because income splitting is not allowed. In addition, see "Capital gains and investment income" above regarding the obligation to file an annual tax-haven investment information report by February 28, irrespective of the need to file an annual tax return. However, residents receiving only compensation income will be required to file an annual income tax return if total compensation is more than Ps$2,182,969.87, compensation was paid by more than one employer, or compensation was paid by a foreign employer.

Payment of tax/Tax is payable upon filing the return. The full tax on salary income and certain interest and dividend income is withheld at source. However, in the case of salaries received by resident individuals from nonresident employers (and nonresident employees subject to the nonresident tax discussed above), Mexican law requires the filing of monthly estimated tax returns to pay an amount equal to the tax withholdings applicable to these wages. The monthly returns are generally due by the 17th day of the following month.

Tax rates

Effective calendar year 2001

Taxable income		Basic tax	
Over	Not over	Tax on Column 1	Percentage on excess
(Column 1)			
Ps 0.01	Ps 5,077.91	0.00	3.00
5,077.92	43,099.31	Ps 152.28	10.00
43,099.32	75,743.15	3,954.36	17.00
75,743.16	88,048.07	9,504.00	25.00
88,048.08	105,417.47	12,580.20	32.00
105,417.48	212,611.91	18,138.36	33.00
212,611.92	619,825.79	53,512.56	34.00
619,825.80	1,859,477.03	191,965.08	35.00
1,859,477.03	2,479,302.95	625,843.20	37.50
2,479,302.96		858,277.80	40.00

Notes:

1. The above brackets are effective as of January 2001 and will be adjusted semiannually to reflect the effects of inflation as measured by the increase in the National Consumer Price Index (NCPI) for the particular year.
2. As mentioned earlier, in addition to the low-income credit discussed below, an additional credit on salary is allowed.

Low-income credit on annual return/A nonrefundable credit of up to 50% of the tax on lower incomes based on the tax rate schedule, designed to reduce the tax burden of taxpayers earning lower incomes, is granted. The credit is reduced proportionately for higher levels of income and phased out if taxpayers receive tax-exempt fringe benefits from their employer. At year-end, the employer computes the amount of the credit, and the employees claim it in their personal returns.

The following table is used to compute the preliminary amount of credit. The portion of the credit that is nonallowable because of nontaxable fringe benefits is equal to twice the percentage that nontaxable income is of total remuneration. Thus, when the nontaxable portion reaches 50% of total remuneration, no credit is allowed. This ratio is computed by the employer on a global companywide basis.

The following table shows the rates for computing the preliminary annual low-income tax credit.

Lower limit	Upper limit	Credit on tax on lower limit	% of credit on marginal tax
Ps 0.01	Ps 5,077.91	Ps 0.00	50
5,077.92	43,099.31	76.08	50
43,099.32	75,743.15	1,977.24	50
75,743.16	88,048.07	4,751.64	50
88,048.08	105,417.47	6,290.04	50
105,417.48	212,611.91	9,069.00	40
212,611.92	335,105.51	23,218.92	30
335,105.52	425,223.47	35,713.20	20
425,223.48	510,267.35	41,841.36	10
510,267.36		44,732.52	0

In addition to the low-income credit, there is a refundable credit that is capped at Ps1,820 for salaries above four minimum wages.

INDIVIDUAL TAX CALCULATION

Assumptions

1. Resident alien who earns a salary, with wife and two children.
2. Wife and children have no income.
3. Husband's income is as follows.

	Ps
Salary, allowances, and bonus	1,000,000
Nontaxable fringe benefits	100,000
Investment income from abroad, on which a foreign tax of 30% (Ps16,500) was paid to the foreign country on a nonresident basis	55,000
Long-term capital gains on sales of shares in Mexican stock market (exempt)	30,000

4. Allowable deductions include the following.

	Ps
Medical expenses	54,000
Charitable contributions	30,000
	84,000

5. Companywide nontaxable benefits are equal to 10% of total remuneration. The nonallowable portion of the low-income credit is therefore 20%.

Tax computation

Income:		
Salary, allowances, bonus, and fringe benefits		Ps 1,100,000
Less—Earned-income exclusions:		
Nontaxable fringe benefits	100,000	
Excludable portion of Christmas bonus	1,211	
Excludable portion of vacation premium	605	101,816
Taxable earned income		998,184
Add—Foreign-source investment income		55,000
		1,053,184
Deduct:		
Medical expenses	54,000	
Charitable contributions	30,000	84,000
Taxable income		Ps 969,184
Tax thereon		Ps 314,240
Less—Tax credits:		
Low-income credit (80% of 44,732.52)	35,786	
Annual credit on salary	1,820	(37,606)
		276,634
Less—Foreign tax credit (1)		(15,697)
Net tax liability		Ps 260,937

Notes:

1. The foreign tax credit allowed is the lesser of the foreign tax paid on the foreign-source income (limited to the equivalent of the foreign taxes paid on a nonresident basis) or the foreign tax credit limitation (as in this example), which (under current regulations) is computed by applying the effective tax rate to the foreign income, as follows.

   Effective tax rate: Ps276,634 ÷ Ps969,184 = 28.54%

   Limitation: 28.54% of 55,000 = Ps15,697

   Foreign tax paid: Ps16,500
2. Exchange rate of the peso at December 31, 2000: US$1 = Ps9.5997.

PwC contact

For additional information on taxation in Monaco, contact:

Christophe Goudou
Roland Melan (associated firm)
14 Boulevard des Moulins
Monte Carlo MC 98000, Monaco
Telephone: (377) 92 16 5400
Fax: (377) 92 16 5420
e-mail: christophe.goudou@fr.pwcglobal.com

General note

This entry is repeated from the 2001/2002 edition. For more up-to-date information, consult the contact listed above or Mark Friedlich at mark.friedlich@us.pwcglobal.com.

Absence of individual taxation

With the exception of French nationals, persons resident in Monaco are exempt from any form of Monegasque taxation on their income or wealth, as well as from any local taxes. The absence of any kind of taxation on individuals means that there is no legal definition of the concept of tax residence.

Monegasque citizens are defined as those persons who meet the conditions laid down in Monegasque Law No. 1155, dated December 18, 1992 (*Journal Officiel de Monaco*/Monaco Gazette, dated December 25, 1992), and individuals with French and Monegasque dual nationality.

Nationals other than Monegasque or French nationals are not subject to any taxation of their income or wealth in Monaco. These persons may, however, be subject to taxation on their income or their wealth according to specific provisions of the tax legislation of the country of which they are citizens and/or residents or of any income placed at their disposal.

French nationals residing in Monaco are deemed to have their tax residency in France, with the exception of those who had their domicile in Monaco for more than five years as from October 13, 1962, and of some individuals of dual nationality who have transferred their domicile outside France.

Note

Exchange rate of the French franc at December 31, 2000: US$1 = FF6.9664.

Morocco

PwC contacts

For additional information on taxation in Morocco, contact:

Aziz Bidah or Abdelwaret Kabbaj
PricewaterhouseCoopers
101 Bd Massira Al Khadra
20100 Casablanca, Morocco
Telephone: (212) (22) 77 90 00/98 40 40
Fax: (212) (22) 77 90 90
e-mail: aziz.bidah@ma.pwcglobal.com
abdelwaret.kabbaj@ma.pwcglobal.com

Significant developments

The financial law for the year 2002 has introduced an exemption of IGR for gains on certain share transfers through 2005.

The information in this entry is current as of January 2002. For subsequent developments consult the contact listed above.

Note

Individuals are subject to *Impôt Général sur le Revenu* (IGR), which applies to earnings, business and agricultural profits, land and real estate gains, rental income, and capital gains and investment income (e.g., dividends, interest).

Territoriality and residence

Residents are subject to taxation on their worldwide income. Nonresidents are taxed only on income from Moroccan sources.

In the absence of a ratified tax treaty, an alien is considered as resident when at least one of the following conditions is fulfilled.

1. The individual maintains a permanent home in Morocco;
2. The individual's economic interests are in Morocco;

   or
3. The individual is present in Morocco for a period or periods aggregating more than 183 days within any period of 365 days.

Gross income

Employee gross income/IGR is levied on all earnings (salaries, wages, premiums, living allowances, reimbursement of taxes and other personal expenses, benefits in kind, etc.). Business expenses are not included in taxable income.

Capital gains and investment income/Capital gains on investments are subject to IGR. net profits of individuals resident in Morocco is imposed on transfers of shares, issued by companies other than real estate companies. The rates of this tax are 10%, 15%, or 20%, depending on nature of the security. Profits attached to transfers made within a calendar year and amounting to less than DH20,000 are tax exempt.

However, the financial law for the year 2002 has introduced an exemption of IGR for capital gains on the transfer of the following.

1. Shares of companies listed in the Stock Exchange of Morocco.

2. Shares of OPCVM (organisme de placements collectifs en valeurs mobilières) whose assets are vested permanently at least 85% in listed shares.

This exemption of the IGR applies to the nets profits realized within the period from January 1, 2002 to December 31, 2005.

Beneficiaries of dividends from a Moroccan source may have the IGR withheld at source at the rate of 10%. The assessment for IGR is calculated without taking this income into account.

Interest is liable to tax at a rate of 30% for physical persons that are not subject in terms of their professional revenues to the "bénéfice net reel" or "bénéfice net simplifiée" systems. For professional revenues of physical and legal persons that are subject to these systems, the tax rate is 20%. Tax payable at the rate of 20% is deductible from IGR. If the 30% rate is applicable, the assessment for IGR is calculated without taking this income into account.

Rental income is subject to IGR. Net rental income is determined by applying to gross income a standard deduction of 40%. The rental income related to anew building is exempt from IGR for the three years following the year of the completion of construction.

Gains on the sale of land and real estate are subject to IGR at the discharging rate of 20%. The amount of tax can not be less than 3% of the proceeds attached to disposals from the real estate. However, some transfers are tax exempt:

1. Profits from the sale of a primary residence:
   a. The whole profit where the disposal is of a primary residence occupied for a period not less than 10 years;
   b. The whole profit corresponding to proceeds up to DH1 million if the said period is more than 5 years but less than or equal to 10 years. The tax on profit exceeding DH1 million is reduced by 50%.
2. The whole profit if the gross proceeds from disposals of real estate within a calendar year do not exceed DH60,000.
3. Where transfers are made free of charge between spouses, brothers and sisters.

Business income and professional and consultancy fees/These types of income are subject to IGR.

Deductions

Business and nonbusiness deductions/An initial 17% standard deduction from salary revenue (professional expenses) is available. The maximum amount deductible is DH24,000 per annum. Employee retirement contributions are deductible, as are employee contributions for social security and medical insurance.

The financial law of 1999/2000 provides for a tax exemption in terms of the amount that employers grant to their employees to cover food expenditures within the limit of DH10 per employee per working day, up to 20% of gross salary.

The financial law for year 2001 introduced a tax system applicable to stock options granted by Moroccan companies to their employees. The framework provides that the discount (difference between the value of shares at grant and the price paid by the employee for the shares) afforded by the company granting the shares is exempt from tax provided the following conditions are satisfied.

1. The discount does not exceed 10% of the share's value at grant; and
2. The sale of shares purchased by the employees does not occur before a five-year vesting period that starts at the grant date. In addition, the time span between the exercise and the sale dates should not be less than three years.

Interest charges on loans granted by Moroccan banks for the construction or purchase of primary housing are deductible up to 10% of net taxable income.

Personal allowances/Deductions from tax payable that are equivalent to DH180 per annum for a spouse and for each dependent child are allowed. The maximum amount deductible is DH1,080 per annum.

Tax credits

Tax that is paid in the country of origin on foreign income that is included in an IGR return can be deducted within the limit of IGR payable on this foreign-source income.

Other taxes

Social security taxes/The maximum amount of an employee's social security contribution is DH1,956 per annum. This amount is deductible from IGR in determining taxable income.

Cotisation minimale/Professional income, whether determined on the accrual basis or the cash basis, is subject to cotisation minimale (CM), even in the absence of profits. The CM can be set off against tax due. The CM is calculated by applying the following rates to turnover plus any other income.

	%
Liberal professions	6.0
Others	0.5

Tax administration

Payment of tax/Each resident employer is required to withhold the applicable IGR from each employee's monthly salary. The tax should be paid by the employer to the tax authorities within the month following that in which the taxes were withheld.

For individuals who receive income other than earnings from a Moroccan source, the amount assessed must be paid before the end of the second month following the month of the assessment.

Returns/There is no joint filing for husband and wife. Individuals resident in Morocco who receive earnings paid from a foreign source and those who receive unearned income (e.g., interest, dividends and rental income) must submit, by the end of March, an annual return based on their total income for the previous calendar year. The return is reviewed by the tax authorities, who calculate the tax liability and send an assessment.

Among the provisions adopted to improve transparency in tax matters, from January 1, 1993 the tax authorities have the possibility of verifying the taxpayer's declarations, using expenses incurred by taxpayers during the year.

Tax rates

IGR tax rates range from 13% to 44%. The tax on income of DH60,000 is DH11,440. A rate of 44% applies to income over that amount.

The rate of tax payable on remuneration or indemnities paid to temporary workers is 30%. For temporary teachers, the applicable rate is 17%. Such income is not included in taxable income for purposes of IGR. There is no obligation to make an annual declaration for such revenue.

INDIVIDUAL TAX CALCULATION

Calendar year 2001

Assumptions

1. The taxpayer is resident for the entire calendar year 2001.
2. The taxpayer is married, with two dependent children.
3. Income:

	DH
Salary	640,000
Interest (1)	60,000
Capital gains on investments (2)	40,000
Employee retirement contribution	40,000
Social security contribution	1,956

Tax computation

Salary		DH 640,000
Less:		
17% standard deduction (maximum 24,000)	24,000	
Retirement contribution	40,000	
Social security contribution	1,956	65,956
Net salary income		574,044
Investment income—Interest		—
Taxable income		DH 574,044
Tax payable:		
On first 60,000	11,440	
On remaining 514 ,044 at 44%	226,179	DH 237,619
Less—Personal deductions (180 x 3)		(540)
Net tax payable		DH 237,079

Notes:

1. Interest revenue is subject to IGR at 30%; this discharges all tax obligations.
2. Capital gain revenue is subject to IGR at 10%; this discharges all tax obligations.
3. Exchange rate of the dirham at December 31, 2001: US$1 = DH11.444.

Mozambique

PwC contact

For additional information on taxation in Mozambique, contact:

Fernando Barros
PricewaterhouseCoopers
Rovuma Carlton Hotel
Centro de Escritórios, 3º andar, 1
Maputo, Mozambique
Telephone: (258) (1) 307620
Fax: (258) (1) 307621
e-mail: barros.fernando@mz.pwcglobal.com

Significant developments

There were no significant tax or regulatory changes in Mozambique during last year.

Territoriality and residence

Residence and/or domicile are irrelevant for Mozambique individual tax purposes. Individual tax is levied and payable only where Mozambique-source income is earned.

Income tax on individuals is applicable both for Mozambican and foreign workers earning profits/remuneration received from employment in Mozambique and for those providing services on an independent or freelance basis.

Income tax is also applicable to outside resident individuals providing permanent services to entities based in Mozambique.

A complementary tax is levied on the global earnings of individuals not taxed under earned income tax.

A resident is defined as a person who fulfills one of the following criteria.

1. Resides permanently in Mozambique;
2. Has resided in Mozambique for more than 180 days in a fiscal year;

   or
3. Has resided in Mozambique for 180 days or less, but on December 31, the last day of the fiscal year:
   a. Occupies a residence under circumstances indicating intent to continue occupancy on a regular basis;
   b. Is a member of the crew of a vessel that has its port of registry in Mozambique; or
   c. Is a member of the crew of an airplane registered in Mozambique.

Gross income

Employee gross income/Income tax is levied on income from all sources, including: salaries and other benefits in money or in kind, owed to national or foreign workers in Mozambique, income earned by independent professionals, income from freelance work, income from business activities, and other sources.

In addition to the activities referred above, the following are also considered as taxable earnings.

1. Salaries received by members of company's corporate bodies (e.g., for the members of the board of directors).

2. Income received as salary by the owners of individual ventures.
3. Travel and entertainment payments.
4. Tax expenses of the employee assumed by the employer.

According the earned income tax regulations, there are no concessions to short-term residents.

Capital gains and investment income/As mentioned above, complementary tax is levied on capital gains from the disposal of shares, including amortization, at a flat withholding tax of 18%, except in cases where the profits from debtor bonds, dividends from stock shares and the value added resulting from the alienation or acquisition of shares on the stock exchange are exempt from complementary tax.

Deductions

Business deductions/No deductions are allowed in calculating earned income tax rate.

Nonbusiness expenses/In computing the net aggregated income for calculation of the complementary tax, individuals are allowed to deduct the following.

1. Corporate tax;
2. Contributions to social security entities, to public health, charity, education, scientific, artistic and other related entities (up to 15% of the previous year's income);
   and
3. Contributions to state entities and foreign taxes paid.

Personal allowances/None.

Tax credits/None.

Other taxes

Social security taxes/Social security contributions are payable monthly on all salaries, wages, regular bonuses, or other regular income, excluding meal subsidies. The employer contributes an amount equal to 4% of monthly salary and the employee contributes 3% of monthly salary. The employer withholds employees' contributions.

Local taxes on income/None.

Tax administration

Returns/The tax year is the calendar year.

Husbands and wives are taxed separately for earned income tax purposes.

Employers withhold earned income tax on a monthly basis for work carried out in Mozambique. In January, taxpayers must file returns for earned income tax covering income from the previous year. The balance of tax due is payable by July.

In July, taxpayers must file declarations of the previous year's income subject to complementary tax. The balance of tax due is payable by November.

Payment of tax/As stated above, an employer is obliged to collect the amount of earned income tax payable from its employees each month and make payments to the Finance Department within the following month.

Tax rates

Earned income tax/The following are the general rules on salaries and incidental monthly remuneration.

Monthly net income			
Over	Not over	Rate	Deduction*
		%	
0	MZM 700,000	0	—
MZM 700,000	2,800,000	10	MZM 70,000
2,800,000	11,200,000	15	210,000
11,200,000		20	770,000

*Amount deductible after applying rate to whole amount.

Specific rules and taxes apply to income received by owners of individual ventures or by shareholders working as directors of a company; and income arising from independent work (e.g., lawyers, doctors, etc.), as well as for occasional remuneration, fees, gratification, commissions, and so on. Regarding these earnings, the following taxation rates apply.

Net income	%
Up to MZM 9,000,000	15
Over MZM 9,000,000	20

Non-Mozambican residents are subject to the earned income tax, which is withheld and remitted by the employer or other payer at a flat rate of 20%.

Complementary tax rates/Applied as follows.

1. Capital gains, dividends, profits on shares transfers, etc.—Flat withholding tax of 18%.
2. Individual earnings—Progressive rates from 8% to 40%, as follows:

Net aggregated income			
Over	Not over	Rate	Deduction*
		%	
0	MZM 10,000,000	8	—
MZM 10,000,000	40,000,000	15	MZM 700,000
40,000,000	80,000,000	27	5,500,000
80,000,000		40	15,900,000

*Amount deductible after applying rate to whole amount.

INDIVIDUAL TAX CALCULATION

Year ended December 31, 2001 (calendar-year basis)

Employee income		
Salary, overtime, commissions and bonuses		MZM 10,000,000
Calculation of professional tax		
Net income		MZM 10,000,000
Tax at 15%		MZM 1,500,000
Less—Deduction		210,000
Total tax		MZM 1,290,000
Calculation of complementary tax payable		
Income from a commercial activity (1)		MZM 18,800,000
Dividends (2)		200,000
Total income		19,000,000
Less—Deductions:		
Corporate tax	320,000	
Social security contributions	564,000	
Charity contributions	2,000,000	2,884,000
Taxable income		MZM 16,116,000
Tax thereon:		
Complementary tax at 15%		MZM 2,417,400
Less—Deduction		(700,000)
		MZM 1,717,400

Notes:

1. The corporate tax corresponds to MZM320,000.
2. Complementary tax is levied on dividends at a flat withholding tax of 18%.
3. Exchange rate of the metical at December 31, 2001: US$1 = MZM23,358.

Namibia, Republic of

PwC contact

For additional information on taxation in Namibia, contact:

Albè Botha
PricewaterhouseCoopers
P.O. Box 1571
Windhoek, Namibia
Telephone: (264) (61) 2841000
Fax: (264) (61) 2841003
e-mail: albe.botha@na.pwcglobal.com

Significant developments

Namibia now has a system of self-assessment.

The following information on taxation in Namibia is accurate as of January 1, 2002. The 2001/2002 budget amendments are not included. For subsequent developments, refer to the contact above.

Territoriality and residence

The general rule is that tax is payable only on income derived or deemed to be derived from sources within Namibia.

The most important "deemed Namibian sources" relate to the following.

1. Interest (taxable in the hands of residents on a worldwide basis).
2. Income derived outside Namibia in the course of a trade conducted in Namibia.
3. Royalty and similar payments in respect of the use of intellectual property in Namibia.

Otherwise, residence, domicile and citizenship are not normally relevant, and there are no special concessions for nonresidents unless a tax treaty applies. Namibia has treaties with France, Germany, India, Mauritius, Romania, Russia, South Africa, Sweden, and the United Kingdom.

Gross income

Employee gross income/Gross income includes all receipts in respect of services rendered, in cash or in kind, in particular the following.

1. Salaries and fees.
2. Deemed value of accommodation provided by employer.
3. Deemed value of the use of a company motor vehicle.
4. All cash allowances and subsidies, subject to deductions for business expenses.

The principal exemptions are as follows.

1. Under certain conditions, the remuneration of heads of foreign governments and U.N. employees stationed in Namibia is exempt from taxation.
2. Relocation expenses paid by the employer are not taxed as fringe benefits in the employee's hands.
3. Where an approved scheme by the Receiver of Revenue is established for the provision of employee housing, the taxable fringe benefit arising from provision of accommodation, housing allowances or mortgage interest subsidies is reduced by at least one-third, provided the annual remuneration of the employee exceeds

N$30 000. If not, a formula is used if the remuneration of the employee exceeds N$15 000 but not N$30 000.

4. Employer contributions to approved retirement funds and medical aid schemes (private health insurance) are not taxable in the hands of employees.

Capital gains and investment income/The general rule is that capital gains are not taxable and capital losses are not deductible in the calculation of taxable income. Capital receipts are not defined by statute. Profits on the realization of assets are likely to be treated as exempt if the assets are income-producing. Profits on assets acquired with the intention of resale at a profit are generally taxable as income. Duration of ownership and the intentions of the taxpayer at the time of acquisition are also relevant, but there is no prescribed holding period.

Dividends are exempt from taxation (with the exception of local building society dividends). Interest is normally taxable on a worldwide basis; broadly speaking, however, a temporary resident is taxed only on locally sourced interest, i.e., interest earned overseas on foreign capital is exempt. The first N$500 of interest from Namibian financial institutions, in respect of a natural person, is exempt. As a result of the source rules and the exempt status of dividends, few items subject to foreign tax are liable to Namibian taxation. There is no general unilateral provision for relief from double taxation, although a specific provision prevents double taxation of royalties.

Deductions

Business deductions/There are no standard deductions for employees for business expenses. Travel, entertainment and motor vehicle expenses are potentially deductible, but the onus is on the employee to prove they were incurred in the production of taxable income. Where allowances are provided by the employer, this onus is more readily discharged, but the deduction cannot normally exceed the allowance.

Nonbusiness expenses/An employee may deduct contributions of up to N$30,000 per annum to an approved pension, retirement annuity, provident, or educational policy fund registered in Namibia.

Domestic mortgage interest is not deductible. There are minor deductions for donations to educational institutions.

Personal allowances/There are no personal allowances.

Other taxes

Namibia has no local income taxes, estate duty or capital transfer tax.

Social security/Namibia has a limited social security system. The Maternity Leave, Sick Leave and Death Benefit Fund became operational in 1996, and membership is compulsory for all employees. It is funded by employer and employee contributions of 0.9% of salary, with a maximum contribution of N$27 per month each.

Enabling legislation provides for the following three additional funds, which are not yet operational.

1. National Medical Benefit Fund.
2. National Pension Fund.
3. Development Fund.

Membership in the Medical Benefit and Pension Funds will not be required if employees are members of approved schemes provided by employers. The

Development Fund (to provide training and employment schemes, student funding, etc.) is not expected to be funded by dedicated contributions.

Workmen's compensation/Under the Workmen's Compensation Act, employers are required to contribute to a fund that provides cash benefits for industrial injury, disability and death. Contribution rates vary according to inherent occupational risk, from less than 1% in most low-risk commercial/administrative occupations to 8% for high-risk sectors (drilling, tunneling and rock-blasting). Employees whose annual remuneration exceeds N$36,000 are normally excluded from coverage.

Tax administration

Returns/The tax year runs from March 1 to February 28/29 of the following year. Tax returns must normally be filed within four months from the end of the financial year.

Namibia has a system of self-assessment, which must include a computation of the taxpayer's taxable income and tax payable, and the payment of tax due on the income so computed.

The payment of tax must be made within four months of financial year-end. Interest at 20% per annum is levied on any late payments.

Husbands and wives submit separate tax returns and are taxed separately.

Payment of tax/Pay-as-you-earn (PAYE) tax is withheld from an employee's salary by the employer and must be remitted to the revenue authorities monthly. Any individual who earns income in excess of N$5,000 (e.g., interest or profit from trade) that is not subject to PAYE is required to register as a provisional taxpayer.

Provisional taxpayers are required to submit half-yearly estimates of their income at end-August and end-February each year and pay the applicable taxes thereon. Where the taxpayer is unable to forecast such income accurately, the return may be based on the last year assessed.

Tax rates

Personal income tax rates for the year ended February 28, 2002 are as follows.

Taxable income: Over (Column 1)	Taxable income: Not over	Tax on Column 1	Percentage on excess
0	N$ 20,000	—	0
N$ 20,000	40,000	—	18
40,000	80,000	N$ 3,600	30
80,000	200,000	15,600	35
200,000		57,600	36

INDIVIDUAL TAX CALCULATION

Year ending February 28, 2002

Tax computation

Salary		N$ 280,000
Add—Fringe benefits:		
Use of company motor vehicle costing 100,000 (1)	18,000	
House provided by employer, in Windhoek (2)	21,600	
Entertainment allowance	12,000	51,600
		331,600
Deduct:		
Pension contribution (Namibian-registered fund)	14,000	
Entertainment expenses	11,600	25,600
		306,000
Add:		
Interest from Namibian bank	4,500	
Less—Standard exemption	(500)	4,000
Taxable income		N$ 310,000
Income tax:		
On 200,000		N$ 57,600
On 110,000 at 36%		39,600
Total income tax payable		N$ 97,200

Notes:

1. Car benefit calculated at 1.5% per month of cost of vehicle to employer.
2. Assuming three bedrooms and two reception rooms. Rates vary according to location and number of rooms.
3. Exchange rate of the Namibian dollar at January 31, 2002: US$1 = N$11.60. The Namibian dollar trades at par with the South African rand.

Netherlands

PwC contact

For additional information on taxation in the Netherlands, contact:

Louis de Vries
PricewaterhouseCoopers
De Entree 201
1101 HG Amsterdam Z-O
The Netherlands
Telephone: (31) (20) 568 6666
Fax: (31) (20) 568 6888
e-mail: louis.de.vries@nl.pwcglobal.com

Manon Ultee, Knowledge Manager
PricewaterhouseCoopers
Marten Meesweg 25
3068 AV Rotterdam
The Netherlands
Telephone: (31) (10) 407 5500
Fax: (31) (10) 407 5720
e-mail: manon.ultee@nl.pwcglobal.com

Significant developments

There have been no significant tax or regulatory developments in the past year.

Territoriality and residence

The Netherlands taxes its residents on their worldwide income; nonresidents are subject to tax only on income derived from specific sources in the Netherlands (mainly income from employment, director's fees, business income, and income from Dutch immovable property).

Article 4 of the General Taxation Act prescribes that the facts and circumstances determine an individual's residence. In case of a dispute the Dutch tax courts will examine the durable ties of a personal nature with the Netherlands.

Gross income

Box 1—Employee gross income and primary residence/Income from current or past employment, self-employment and the deemed rental income from the taxpayer's primary residence is assessed in box 1. Mortgage interest payments in relation to the financing, renovation or maintenance of the primary residence may be deducted from box 1 income.

All benefits in kind are, in principle, considered as taxable income. Such benefits include accommodation allowances, private use of company, home-leave allowances and pre- and postassignment bonuses. Reimbursement of relocation costs relating to the acceptance of a new employment and employer contributions toward approved pension schemes are not taxable.

Costs relating to the assignment to the Netherlands incurred by a foreign employee may be reimbursed tax-free. These so-called "extraterritorial" costs include all costs that the employee would not have incurred, had he or she not been assigned to the Netherlands. Double housing costs, cost-of-living allowances, language courses, etc., qualify as extraterritorial costs.

If certain conditions are met (see "30% ruling"), a foreign employee working in the Netherlands may be granted a tax-free allowance amounting to 30% of the income from current employment (the so-called "30% ruling"). The tax-free 30% allowance is intended to cover all extraterritorial costs. If the foreign employee benefits from the 30% ruling, extraterritorial costs may not be reimbursed tax-free in addition to the 30% tax-free allowance.

Nonresident employees are taxed on salary earned for employment activities performed inside the Netherlands. If the employment is exercised for a Dutch employer the work is deemed to be performed in the Netherlands, unless the employment is fully exercised outside the Netherlands or unless the salary earned in connection with foreign duties is taxed abroad. As a general rule a statutory director of a Dutch company is subject to Dutch taxation irrespective of the country where the duties relating to the directorship are actually performed. An exception is made only if a double taxation treaty stipulates otherwise. The box 1 income is taxed at progressive rates up to a maximum of 52%.

Box 2—Income from substantial interest/A Dutch resident who, alone or together with a spouse or other close relatives holds at least 5% of the shares of a company or who holds rights to acquire a 5% interest in a company, has a so-called substantial interest. The benefits derived from this substantial interest are taxable in box 2. These benefits include dividends and the gain on the sale of one or more of the shares or rights. Taxation in box 2 will apply only to a nonresident who holds a substantial interest in a Dutch-based company. All box 2 income is taxed at a flat rate of 25%.

Box 3—Income from savings and investments/Income from investments (e.g., dividends and interest) is as such not taxable. However, the net assets (assets minus debts) of an individual are deemed to generate a fixed return on investment of 4% per year. This fixed return is taxed in box 3. All net assets that are not intended for daily use and that are not taxed in box 1 or box 2 belong to the box 3 taxable base. For Dutch residents, part of the taxable base is exempt and several specific deductions apply.

Nonresidents are subject to taxation only on the net value of a limited number of Dutch assets, including the following.

1. Dutch real estate not used as the primary residence.
2. Profits rights unrelated to shares or an employment.

Capital gains and investment income/For residents and nonresidents, capital gains and investment income as such are not taxable, except as detailed for box 2 and box 3 above.

Deductions

Box 1—Business deductions/The following deductions may be claimed relating to employment income when filing a Dutch tax return.

1. A fixed annual amount for commuting by public transport.
2. A fixed annual amount for commuting by bicycle.
3. A fixed daily deduction for sailors.

30% ruling/As stated above, foreign employees qualifying for the 30% ruling may receive a tax-free allowance amounting to 30% of their income from current employment. To qualify for the 30% ruling, the foreign employee should have specific expertise that is not or scarcely available on the Dutch labor market, and should have at least 2.5 years of relevant (international) working experience.

The 30% ruling may apply for a maximum period of 120 months. Under the provisions of the 30% ruling, employees who are, based on facts and circumstances, considered as resident taxpayers may opt to be treated as partial nonresidents. Partial in this respect implies that they are treated as residents for box 1 and as nonresidents for box 2 and 3 purposes. The 30% ruling must be applied for within four months of starting the Dutch employment. If not applied for within this time, the ruling, if granted, will not apply retroactively as of the beginning of the Dutch employment, but only as of the month following the month in which the application was filed.

Nonbusiness deductions/Under certain conditions, residents and nonresidents may deduct premiums for life annuities and child day-care expenses (above a certain threshold).

In addition, residents (and partial nonresidents) are also entitled to claim deductions mainly relating to their personal or family circumstances: maintenance payments to a former spouse, expenses arising from sickness or disability, educational expenses, support payments to children, weekend expenses of disabled children, charitable donations, and losses of specified venture capital investments (deductions for certain expenses are capped or subject to thresholds).

Levy rebates/Resident and partial nonresident taxpayers are entitled to so-called "levy rebates." Except for the general levy rebate, several levy rebates, depending on the personal situation of the taxpayer can be claimed (children levy rebate, single parent levy rebate, etc.). The levy rebates cannot be transferred to the taxpayer's partner. The rebates reduce the amount of tax due and can therefore be considered as tax credits. There are several tax levy rebates varying from as less as €40 to €1,647.

Election to be treated as a resident taxpayer/The taxation of nonresidents is limited to specific sources of Dutch income, but few deductions may be claimed. Nonresidents may therefore opt to be treated as resident taxpayers, which enables them to claim levy rebates and other deductions that are available only to residents and partial nonresidents.

If a taxpayer elects to be treated as a resident taxpayer, the worldwide income of the nonresident is taken into account, and a relief for double taxation, mostly based on the exemption-with-progression method, will be granted for all items of income that are, based on the tax treaties, not allocated to the Netherlands. Opting to be treated as a resident is a possibility only for residents of most of the countries that have concluded tax treaties with the Netherlands.

Tax credits

Only residents are entitled to relief from double taxation under unilateral relief provisions or tax treaties.

Other taxes

Social security/Employee insurance contributions and national insurance tax are levied on residents and nonresidents under a number of different regulations.

Under the national insurance tax regulations, tax is levied on income up to a maximum of €27,847. At present, the tax is capped at €8,187 per annum. From this amount several levy rebates may be deducted varying from €36 to €1,497.

Under the employee insurance regulations, contributions are levied on income up to a maximum of €41,499. The contribution rate depends on the line of industry the employee belongs to, but on average the contributions are capped at €1,343 for the employee and €4,595 for the employer.

In addition, employees earning less than €28,188 a year are mandatorily covered by the state medical plan. In this case fixed health insurance premiums are due by the employee amounting to at maximum €479 per annum as well as additional variable premiums. The employer contributions amount to a maximum of €1,761.

Local taxes on income/There are no local taxes on income.

Tax administration

Returns/If both husband and wife are resident taxpayers, they are taxed separately for their business income, employment income, pension income, and other periodic payments less premiums for life annuities and for certain other periodic payments. Spouses and persons living as a joint household for at least six months in a calendar year can choose to whom of both they want to allocate the following income or deductions for Dutch income tax purposes: the taxable income from the primary residence, childcare expenses, the taxable income from a substantial interest (box 2), the fixed return of box 3, and the nonbusiness deductions relating to the taxpayers' personal circumstances.

Tax returns must be filed after each calendar year, in principle, before April 1, 2002.

Payment of tax/There is wage tax withholding from salaries if an employee is on a Dutch payroll. Generally speaking, if taxpayers have sizeable income that is not subject to wage tax withholding, they may be required to make advance payments of estimated additional tax.

Tax rates

Calendar year 2002

Box 1 income

Taxable income		Tax on	Percentage
Over	Not over	Column 1	on excess
(Column 1)			
0	€ 15,331*	—	2.95
€ 15,331	27,847*	€ 452	8.45
27,847	47,745	1,509	42.00
47,745		9,866	52.00

*In the first and second bracket of box 1, national insurance tax is levied at a rate of 29.40%.

Box 2 income/Box 2 income is taxed at 25%.

Box 3 income/Box 3 income is taxed at 30%.

INDIVIDUAL TAX CALCULATION

Calendar year 2002

Assumptions

The taxpayer is a foreign national residing in the Netherlands and benefiting from the 30% ruling; spouse and two dependent children under 12 years of age. The husband is the sole earner. Salary is paid from a Dutch payroll. The taxpayer owns a mortgaged home in the Netherlands and has requested that the Dutch Revenue consider him a partial nonresident taxpayer.

Tax computations

Box 1

Worldwide gross income:		
Gross Dutch salary	52,500	
30% tax free allowance	22,500	
Total gross income		€ 75,000
Taxable salary		€ 52,500
Less—Employee insurance contributions		1,343
		51,157
Less—Mortgage interest paid for house in the Netherlands		12,500
Taxable income		€ 38,657
Calculated tax	6,049	
Less—Levy rebates	258	€ 5,791
Calculated national insurance tax	8,187	
Less—Levy rebates	2,568	5,619
Amounts due/paid:		
Income tax	5,791	
National insurance tax	5,619	
Employee insurance contributions	1,343	
Total withholdings		€ 12,753
Net income		€ 62,247

Box 2*

Capital gain on sale of 10% of shares in a foreign company	€ 50,000
Dividends from Dutch company	2,000
Calculated tax for resident	13,000
Calculated tax for partial nonresident	500

*Partial nonresidents (a provision under the 30% ruling) are taxable only on Dutch-source income.

Box 3*

Summer house abroad	€ 300,000
Balance savings account abroad	20,000
Taxable income	9,697
Calculated tax for resident	2,909
Calculated tax for partial nonresident	0

*Partial nonresidents (a provision under the 30% ruling) are taxable only on Dutch-source income.

Note:

Exchange rate of the Euro at January 3, 2002: US$1 = €1.106.

Netherlands Antilles

PwC contacts

For additional information on taxation in the Netherlands Antilles, contact:

Peter Bolwerk/Steve Vanenburg
PricewaterhouseCoopers N.A.
Julianaplein 38
Curaçao, Netherlands Antilles
Telephone: (599) (9) 4300000
Fax: (599) (9) 4611119
e-mail: peter.j.bolwerk@an.pwcglobal.com
steve.r.vanenburg@an.pwcglobal.com

Significant developments

New Fiscal Framework/On December 29, 1999 the Parliament of the Netherlands Antilles approved three tax bills, which together are known as the New Fiscal Framework (NFF), published under P.B. 244, 245 and 246. The government's objectives of parting from its tax-haven image and revitalizing its financial services industry are the principal reasons for the NFF's enactment.

The main elements of the NFF with regard to individuals include the following.

1. Income Tax Ordinance:
   a. Introduction of deemed-income provisions;
   b. Amendment of the substantial interest provisions.
2. Introduction of a dividend withholding tax of 10%. This tax will take effect only on a date to be announced in a separate Ordinance, but this is not expected to happen in the near future.

Turnover tax/In Curaçao and Bonaire, turnover tax is levied on the provision of services and deliveries by entrepreneurs and companies. A limited number of services and deliveries are exempt. "Services" does not include advisory and management services provided to or by offshore companies and offshore banks.

An entrepreneur liable to the turnover tax must file a declaration with the Tax Inspectorate before the 16th day of the following month at the Tax Collector's office. The rate amounts to 5%.

Territoriality and residence

An individual's specific circumstances determine residence for tax purposes. These circumstances include permanent home, habitual stay, and center of economic and social interest. Residents are taxed on worldwide income, while nonresidents are taxed only on certain specified income generated within the Netherlands Antilles. Individuals are taxed from their date of arrival. Accordingly, there is no significance as to the timing of arrival.

Gross income

Residents/Gross income of residents includes gains, profits and income derived from the sources below.

1. A business or profession.
2. Employment.

3. Proceeds from immovable property.
4. Net income from capital.
5. Certain periodic receipts.
6. Net income from capital.

Deemed income

For individual income tax purposes, a resident taxpayer can be taxed on deemed annual income from capital if he or she owns shares in a Netherlands Antilles Exempt Company, or shares, membership rights or an interest in a nonresident company ("foreign investment company"), the activities of which, on a consolidated basis, consist mainly of lending, portfolio investments and similar activities.

Resident taxpayers are obliged to include the fair market value of such Exempt Company or foreign investment company in their annual taxable income. An amount equal to 4% of the fair market value of the shares, membership rights or interest at the beginning of the year will be considered as taxable income each year.

Where the actual income received exceeds the deemed amount, the income actually received does not have to be included in the taxable income rather than the amount of the deemed income.

The deemed income provision will also apply to the value of receivables on, profit sharing certificates in and rights in an Exempt Company or in a foreign investment company.

Substantial Interest

A substantial interest exists if a resident taxpayer owns at least 5% of the shares in a resident or nonresident company, the capital of which is divided into shares, or if a qualifying nonresident tax payer owns at least 5% of the shares in such a domestic company. The gain realized on the alienation of the shares is subject to income tax. The gain is defined as the difference between the sales price and the historic acquisition price of the shares.

Termination of residence

The termination of the residency of a taxpayer other than by death will also be considered as an alienation of shares. Upon the emigration the tax administration will impose a preserving assessment for the accrued capital gain (although not yet realized). If certain conditions are fulfilled, deferral of payment of this tax can be obtained. The tax due becomes payable if the shares are sold within a period of 10 years after the emigration. If the shares are not sold within this 10-year period the debt will be forgiven.

Retirees

Legislation regarding the so-called "pensionado" arrangement has been enacted whereby (retired) individuals who meet certain requirements may opt to be taxed at low rates. To qualify. the individual should not have been a N.A. resident in the five years before taking up residence in the Netherlands Antilles and applying for this tax incentive. Furthermore, the qualifying pensioner/retiree must be a minimum of 50 years of age, and must own and use a house in the Netherlands Antilles with a value of at least NAf450,000.

There are at present two retiree incentives: one that qualifies for applicability of the TAK (Tax Agreement for the Kingdom of the Netherlands—see "Tax treaties"), and one that does not. The pensioner/retiree may opt to pay one of the following.

1. A flat 10% tax rate on foreign income (minus allowable deductions) (TAK remains applicable);

   or

2. A fixed annual tax of approximately NAf269,600 (TAK is not applicable).

Nonresidents/Individuals living in the Netherlands Antilles for more than one year are generally considered residents. Residents are taxed on their worldwide income. Individuals not residing in the Netherlands Antilles are subject to individual income tax on their net income from certain specified sources in the Netherlands Antilles. The following are the more important sources of such income.

1. A business or profession carried out within the Netherlands Antilles personally or through a permanent representative or proxy holder. An exemption can be granted if the practice is of a temporary nature or lasts less than three consecutive months.
2. Employment—Individuals who work for a period of less than three months may request an exemption, although in practice such requests are usually not granted.
3. Acting as a director of a company established in the Netherlands Antilles.
4. Immovable property (within the Netherlands Antilles).
5. A mortgage on immovable property.
6. Under certain circumstances, income from a Netherlands Antilles Company in which a substantial interest is held.

Substantial interest

Dividends and interest from shares belonging to a substantial interest as well as capital gains upon the sale of such shares received by a nonresident shareholder within 10 years after migration from the Netherlands Antilles are subject to income tax. With respect to the determination of the amount of the capital gains derived from a substantial interest, the acquisition price for shares and profit sharing certificates in a resident company is established at the historic acquisition price.

With regard to the acquisition price of shares and profit-sharing certificates in a nonresident company of an individual who immigrates to the Netherlands Antilles the acquisition price is, as a general rule, established at the fair market value.

Capital gains and investment income/Capital gains and losses arising from the sale or exchange of private assets are exempt from taxation. If private assets are employed as capital of a business, the capital gains and losses form part of personal taxable income. Also, capital gains realized on the sale of shares are taxed if the seller has a "substantial interest" (that is, at least a 5% shareholding) in the company. Shares held by a spouse will be taken into consideration in determining whether the 5% shareholding criterion has been met. If the seller does not have a "substantial interest," but a (grand)child or (grand)parent has a "substantial interest," the seller's shares are considered to constitute a "substantial interest." The gain is subject to a reduced rate of tax applicable to nonrecurring items of income. Liquidating dividends are taxable to the extent that they exceed paid-in capital.

Where a person has a "substantial interest" or is considered to have one, then a receivable on the company is also considered a substantial interest.

Deductions

Business deductions/To the extent they are business-related and not reimbursed, an individual can deduct such items as moving expenses, travel expenses, entertainment expenses, and automobile expenses.

Expatriate exemptions/The Netherlands Antilles have regulations in place for expatriate income taxes. Fringe benefits (wages in kind) are tax exempt insofar as they are less than NAf15,000 per year. Expatriate status can under certain conditions be granted for five years, and renewed for a second period of five years.

Expatriates in the Netherlands Antilles are those employees who prior to the employment in the Netherlands Antilles resided for a period of at least five years in a foreign country, who are working in the offshore financial, tourism, telecommunications, airline, or oil industry, or at universities, and who are staying in the Netherlands Antilles on a temporary basis. The employee must contribute specific expertise to the company. This expertise can be proven in two ways.

1. The employee must have completed studies at an institution of higher education or academic institution and have at least three years' working experience.
2. The employee must have at least five years' working experience and have a salary of at least NAf100,000. In order to qualify, the "specific expertise" should not be readily available in the local labor market.

The following salary elements are, among others, not included in the taxable salary.

1. Compensation for educational costs at the international or Dutch school on Curaçao or an equivalent school abroad, up to a maximum of NAf25,000 per child annually.
2. Social security premiums paid abroad if they are intended as an old-age provision.
3. Travel and moving expenses in relation to the immigration and repatriation of the employee and family, including hotel room costs, with a certain maximum.
4. Settling-in allowance of the lesser of two months' salary or NAf12,000.
5. Car rental expenses during the first two months after the arrival, up to a maximum of NAf2,700.

Nonbusiness expenses/Subject to limitations, a resident taxpayer can deduct charitable contributions, medical expenses, life insurance premiums, and savings plan payments. In addition, a resident taxpayer can deduct interest, pension plan contributions, social security premiums, and alimony.

Personal tax credits/Personal allowances take the form of tax credits. The personal tax credits are granted at the following amounts:

	NAf
Basic tax credit for every taxpayer	1,462.50
Additional credits:	
For married taxpayer with nonworking spouse	975.00
For aged 60 years and over	390.00
For children, depending on age, study, place of residence	104.00 – 1,040.00

Tax credits

Tax credits are generally not allowed unless provided for by a specific tax treaty. Foreign taxes can be deducted from gross income.

Other taxes

Social security taxes/As of 2002 (income year 2002) the employee's share of taxes for old-age pension, widows and orphans is 5% of a maximum of US$25,337 gross wages. The employer contributes 6%. Amounts over this are not charged. Expatriates may be exempt from this tax.

Coverage for workers earning up to US$25,337 is compulsory. Contributions are 2.1% for the employee, 8.3% for the employer.

Contributions for accident insurance amount to 0.5% to 5%, depending on employment on a maximum salary of US$25,337.

AVBZ, a national social insurance from which the entire population of the Netherlands Antilles can derive rights, guarantees, among other benefits, medical care to persons suffering from a chronic disease or a mental or physical disorder. The premium charged amounts to, in general, 2% of taxable income, with a maximum charge of US$3,784 per year. The employer's share amounts to 0.5% of the employee's income, with a maximum of US$946 per year. Individuals qualifying for minimum income of US$2,921 (unmarried) or US$3,314 are charged at the rate of 1%.

Old-age pensioners are taxed at a rate of 1.5%.

Dividend withholding tax/As from January 1, 2000 a dividend withholding tax has been introduced. The withholding tax amounts to 10% on profit distributions from N.A. companies. However, the provisions will become applicable for profit distributions that have been distributed on or after a date that is still to be announced in a separate ordinance. This will likely not happen in the near future.

When dividend withholding tax becomes applicable, it may be deducted from income tax due.

Inheritance and gift taxes/Gifts and receipts from an estate of an Antillean resident are taxable. Nonresidents owning real estate in the Netherlands Antilles also are subject to these taxes. The rates (from 2% up to 24%) depend on the amounts received and the relationship of the beneficiary to the deceased or the donor. Gifts and receipts from estates of a nonresident shareholder of a N.A. company are not subject to Antilles estate and gift taxes.

Land and property taxes/The transfer of N.A.-located immovable property is subject to a 4% transfer duty. A land tax is levied on real estate located in the Netherlands Antilles at an annual rate of 0.5% on the value of undeveloped land and 0.6% of the value of built-up land. The 15% island surcharge also is applicable.

Tax treaties

As part of the Kingdom of The Netherlands, the Netherlands Antilles is party to a federal tax agreement with The Netherlands and Aruba (TAK). Subject to this treaty, dividends, interest, and royalties paid out to a N.A. recipient may qualify for reduced rates of withholding taxes in the subject countries. For an individual recipient, the Dutch withholding tax amounts to 15%.

Effective January 1, 1997 the TAK was amended. The major changes are that the conditions under which the agreement applies have been enhanced and a regulation has been added to prepare the way for the application of Dutch anti-abuse legislation. Also, the existing pensionado arrangement (see "Retirees") no longer qualifies for application of the federal tax agreement. However, a transitional arrangement applies for persons who became resident in the Netherlands Antilles before January 1, 1997 and have been resident in one of the parts of the Kingdom within the previous five years. For these people, certain new anti-abuse provisions will not apply to their regular income until January 1, 2002.

Tax administration

Returns/Tax returns are filed on a calendar-year basis. Each spouse is taxed individually on his or her personal income (e.g., income derived from a business, a profession or employment). Nonpersonalized income is, in principle, included in the taxable income of the spouse with the higher personal income.

Payment of tax/The Netherlands Antilles employs the pay-as-you-earn (PAYE) system, so tax is withheld from salaries.

Tax rates

Progressive rates are levied on taxable income. In addition, an island surcharge is levied on the amount of tax due. The maximum rate amounts to 57.2%.

Special reduced rates apply to certain nonrecurring items of income, for example, liquidation proceeds from a company at a maximum of 39% and dividends from or capital gains on the sale of "substantial share interests" at 32.5%.

A dividend withholding tax was introduced as of January 1, 2000. The provisions will become effective at a later date, but that is not likely to happen in the near future. Salaries and wages are subject to tax withholding at source. Provisional assessments can be issued during a fiscal year. Any additional tax is payable upon receipt of an assessment. Netherlands Antilles tax relief may be obtained for specific sources of foreign income.

Tax rates effective for the year 2002 are as follows.

Taxable income		Tax on	Percentage
Over	Not over	Column 1	on excess
(Column 1)			
0	NAf 23,950	—	15.6
NAf 23,950	34,450	NAf 3,736.20	23.4
34,450	45,550	6,193.20	32.5
45,550	60,450	9,800.70	39.0
60,450	102,000	15,611.70	46.8
102,000		35,057.10	57.2

INDIVIDUAL TAX CALCULATION

Calendar year 2002

Assumptions

Resident married taxpayer with two children (under 16 years old).

Tax computation

Gross income:		
Salary		NAf 160,000.00
Interest		14,000.00
Capital gain		5,000.00
Total gross income		179,000.00
Less—Tax-exempt capital gain		5,000.00
Adjusted gross income		174,000.00
Less—Itemized deductions:		
Interest	10,000.00	
Social security	2,500.00	
Alimony	8,000.00	20,500.00
Taxable income		NAf 153,500.00
Income tax before credits		NAf 64.515.00
Tax credits:		
Basic tax credit	1,462.50	
For nonworking spouse	975.00	
Two children's credits (2 x 208)	416.00	(2,853.50)
Income tax payable		NAf 61,661.50

Note:

Exchange rate of the Netherlands Antilles guilder at December 31, 2001:
US$1 = NAf1.78.

PwC contact

For additional information on taxation in New Caledonia, contact:

Laurence Pedamon
Société d'Avocats JurisCal*
B.P. 3745
98846 Nouméa Cedex
New Caledonia
Telephone: (687) 27 16 88
Fax: (687) 27 30 23
e-mail: laurencepedamon@offratel.nc

*A correspondent firm of PricewaterhouseCoopers.

Significant developments

There have been no significant taxation or regulatory developments as regards individual taxation in the last year.

Territoriality and residence

Resident individuals are subject to New Caledonian income tax on their worldwide income except as indicated in the provisions of the tax treaty between France and New Caledonia.

Nonresident individuals are subject to New Caledonian income tax on their local-source income. A 25% notional tax rate is applied to these revenues.

In accordance with the Territorial Tax Code, the following persons would be considered resident.

1. Individuals who have established their home or are present for more than 183 days each year in the territory.
2. Individuals who exercise their profession in New Caledonia, unless they demonstrate it is only on a limited basis.
3. Individuals who maintain the center of their economic interests in New Caledonia.

Gross income

Employee gross income/Income from personal services (cashed income) includes salaries, commissions and allowances of all types, including those for housing, living expenses and tax reimbursements, as well as cashed participations of employees in profits.

Benefits are free of tax except for benefits derived from the use of company housing or a company car. For these benefits, valuation is not challenged if it is equal to at least the following.

1. 12% of gross salary, for housing.
2. XPF12,000 to XPF51,000 monthly for a company car, depending on the car tax classification.
3. Airline fares paid by the company are not considered benefits.

No concessions are available for short-term residents.

Capital gains and investment income/Capital gains are generally tax exempt for individuals unless they result from the sale of a personal business or practice.

Net dividends received from New Caledonian companies are subject to withholding at source of 13.25%. This is a final tax. Net interest income received from deposits with local banks or from shareholders' loans in local companies, at up to an officially published rate, is also exempt from income tax.

All other investment income, including capital gains on capitalization bonds held for less than eight years, is subject to tax. The withholding tax collected locally or in France (double taxation treaty) gives the right to a tax rebate.

Deductions

Business deductions/Individuals are allowed to deduct an amount equal to 10% of their net salary (within an XPF600,000 limit) as a standard business deduction. However, they may elect to justify actual costs.

Other deductions/There is a standard deduction of 20% of salary revenue net of the business deduction (i.e., only 80% of salary revenue net of business deduction is retained for purposes of calculating income tax). This deduction is limited to XPF1,800,000.

In addition, the following expenses are deductible.

1. Social security contributions.
2. Life insurance premiums, within an annual XPF275,000 limit.
3. Mortgage interest for a principal home, limited XPF500,000 limit, or with no limit, depending on the date of the loan.
4. Certain investment incentives, within an annual XPF1 million or XPF1.5 million limit.
5. Alimony (no limit) paid to a divorced spouse.
6. Superannuation contributions, within an annual limit of approximately XPF2.9 million (employer and employee contributions).
7. Salaries and related charges paid for domestic help, within a limit of XPF800,000.

Personal allowances/Tax is calculated on a family basis. The family includes self, spouse and dependents. All income earned by the family is aggregated and then divided by the following, according to the status of the individual shown.

1. Bachelor, divorced or widowed, without dependents—1.0.
2. Married with no dependents—2.0.
3. Widowed with one or more dependents—1.5.

This number is then increased by the following.

1. 1.0 per disabled child or child completing studies in France or abroad.
2. 0.5 per any other dependent child.
3. 0.5 per dependent parent.

The divided revenue is used for the scale calculation. The income tax charge determined is then multiplied by the number.

Tax credits

A standard rebate of 10% of tax, up to a limit of XPF100,000, is granted to resident taxpayers. No specific credits are available to short-term residents.

Other taxes

Social security taxes/Compulsory social security taxes are levied; the employee contribution equals 8.09% of gross salary within an approximate XPF290,300 monthly limit. A compulsory additional retirement fund contribution also applies.

Local taxes on income/There are no local income taxes payable in addition to central government taxes.

Tax administration

Returns/The tax year is the calendar year. Joint filing for prior-year revenue of husband and wife must be completed by April 1 each year. An additional month is allowed for individuals declaring business revenues on a nonstandard basis.

Payment of tax/There is no payroll withholding of income tax. Tax is payable by three installments: the first and second installments for year n tax are payable by March 31 of year $n + 1$ and July 31 of year $n + 1$ and are each equal to one-third of the year $n - 1$ income tax charge. The balance is generally claimed in October of year $n + 1$.

Tax rates

The tax rates applicable to the share of taxable income are as follows.

Taxable income*		Tax on	Percentage
Over (Column 1)	Not over	Column 1	on excess
0	XPF 1,000,000	—	0
XPF 1,000,000	1,300,000	—	5
1,300,000	1,600,000	XPF 15,000	10
1,600,000	2,200,000	45,000	15
2,200,000	2,800,000	135,000	20
2,800,000	4,500,000	255,000	30
4,500,000		765,000	40

*Total assessable income less deductions divided by the number that is a function of the number of dependents and of marital status.

INDIVIDUAL TAX CALCULATION

Based on the law and tax rates in effect at December 31, 2001

Assumptions

1. Resident who earns a salary, with wife and two children (number of shares: 2 + 0.5 + 0.5 = 3).
2. Wife and children have no income.
3. Husband's income is as follows.

	XPF
Net salary, allowances and bonuses (after compulsory contributions and superannuation contributions within the limits allowed by the Tax Code)	8,000,000
Housing benefit (12% of salary)	960,000
Investment income from abroad (not France), on which a 30% foreign tax (XPF150,000) was paid to the foreign country	500,000
	9,460,000

4. Allowable deductions include the following.

	XPF
Domestic help	400,000
Mortgage interest of XPF1,000,000, limited to	500,000
	900,000

Tax computation

Determination of taxable income

Salary, allowances and bonuses		XPF 8,000,000
Fringe benefits		960,000
		8,960,000
Less:		
Business deduction	600,000	
Standard deduction	1,792,000	2,392,000
		6,568,000
Add—Investment income from abroad		350,000
		6,918,000
Deduct:		
Salaries paid to domestic help	400,000	
Mortgage interest	500,000	900,000
Taxable income		XPF 6,018,000
Income per share—(6,018,000 ÷ 3)		XPF 2,006,000

Determination of tax per share

On the first 1,600,000	XPF 45,000
On the remaining 406,000 at 15%	60,900
	XPF 105,900

Determination of total tax payable

Tax per share (105,900) x 3	XPF 317,700
Less—10% standard tax rebate	(31,770)
Tax payable	XPF 285,930
Rounded to	XPF 285,900

Note:

Exchange rate (selling) of the Pacific franc at December 31, 2001: US$1 = XPF133.95. The Pacific franc is pegged to the Euro at €1 = XPF119.33.

New Zealand

PwC contacts

For additional information on taxation in New Zealand, contact:

Julia C. Hoare or Stewart J. McCulloch
Tax Partners
PricewaterhouseCoopers
P.O. Box 243
Wellington, New Zealand
Telephone: (64) (4) 462 7000
Fax: (64) (4) 462 7001
e-mail: julia.hoare@nz.pwcglobal.com
stewart.j.mcculloch@nz.pwcglobal.com

Significant developments

The government has implemented a regime that prevents individuals diverting income through trusts to related minors, and has recharacterized certain services that were previously not assessable as related payments so that they now are part of gross income. However, restrictive covenant payments in connection with the sale of a business are specifically excluded from gross income.

Territoriality and residence

A resident of New Zealand is subject to tax on worldwide income. A nonresident is subject to tax only on income from sources in New Zealand.

Residence is determined by the following tests.

1. Permanent place of abode:
   Persons are deemed residents of New Zealand if they have a permanent place of abode in New Zealand, notwithstanding that they may also have a permanent place of abode outside New Zealand.
2. 183 days' presence:
   Persons are deemed residents of New Zealand from the date of their arrival in New Zealand if they are personally present in New Zealand for a period or periods exceeding in total 183 days in any 12 month period.

Employment and self-employed income earned in New Zealand by nonresidents is taxable unless the nonresidents' exemption or a double taxation agreement exemption applies.

Nonresidents' exemption/A nonresident's personal services income earned in New Zealand is exempt from New Zealand tax if all the following conditions apply:

1. The visit (or visits) of the nonresident do not exceed a period or periods of 92 days in total in the income year.
2. The nonresident is liable for income tax on New Zealand-sourced income in their country of residence.
3. The services are performed on behalf of a person who is not resident in New Zealand.

This exemption does not apply to public entertainers, such as performing artists and professional athletes. They are subject to a maximum 20% withholding tax.

Double taxation agreements/Although the terms of treaty articles vary, generally, remuneration derived by a nonresident employee from personal services performed in New Zealand is not taxable in New Zealand if all the following conditions apply.

1. Recipient is present in New Zealand for not more than 183 days in any 12-month period.
2. Remuneration is paid by or on behalf of a nonresident employer.
3. Remuneration is not borne by a permanent establishment (branch) or a fixed base that the employer has or is deemed to have in New Zealand.

Gross income

Employee gross income/A resident is taxed on salary, wages, bonuses, tax reimbursements, allowances, and retirement gratuities received in cash, regardless of where payment is made. Nonresidents are taxed only to the extent their employment income is earned in New Zealand (i.e., services are performed in New Zealand), regardless of where payment is made and whether it is remitted to New Zealand. Allowances paid in cash that are no more than a reimbursement of expenses incurred within employment are generally not taxable. The benefit arising from the use of an employer-provided automobile, a low-interest loan or discounted goods or services is not taxable to the employee, but the value of a benefit from the provision of shares or options, lodging or housing by an employer is taxable to the employee. Other benefits provided to an employee in a non-monetary form are generally not taxable in the employee's hands (see "Fringe benefit tax").

Resident individuals are subject to New Zealand tax on their overseas income. A credit is available for foreign tax paid on that income up to the level of New Zealand tax payable.

Capital gains and investment income/There is no capital gains tax. However, the income tax legislation specifically includes various forms of gain that would otherwise be considered a capital gain within the definition of "income." Gross income includes gains on the sale of real estate in certain circumstances and on personal property where the taxpayer acquired the property for resale, or deals in such property, or where a profit-making purpose or scheme can be deemed or imputed. Gains on financial instruments are taxable when realized or when the instruments are deemed to have been disposed of. Above certain threshold limits, such gains are taxable on an accrual (yield-to-maturity) basis, which may include unrealized gains.

Rent derived from property is gross income. Deductions are allowed for expenses incurred in deriving the rental income.

New Zealand residents holding a 10% or greater interest in a controlled foreign company (CFC) include in their taxable income the income (calculated under New Zealand tax rules) of the CFC multiplied by the percentage their interest represents in the company.

A foreign investment fund (FIF) regime applies to nonexcepted interests in foreign investment funds. Resident holders of such interests are taxed on the change in value of the interest over the income year, together with distributions received. Generally, income from interests in CFCs and FIFs resident in the following countries is excluded: Australia, Canada, Germany, Japan, Norway, the United Kingdom, and the United States. No distinction is made between passive and business income.

Investment income derived by a nonresident from a New Zealand source is taxable in New Zealand, but where that person is a resident of a country that has a double taxation agreement with New Zealand, the tax on dividends and interest income is generally limited to 15% or 10% of that gross income under the provisions of the treaty. The foreign investor tax credit (FITC) regime effectively eliminates nonresident withholding tax (NRWT) on fully imputed dividends paid by a New Zealand company to a nonresident. The FITC regime provides that total New Zealand tax paid on a nonresident investor's earnings through a New Zealand company can be limited to 33% (the company tax rate). It does not operate by exemption from NRWT. Rather, where a dividend is imputed, the paying company qualifies for a reduction in its income tax if it pays a supplementary dividend. The combination of reduced income tax plus NRWT on both dividends can result in a total New Zealand tax on the earnings of only 33%.

Deductions

Business deductions/No deduction is allowed for expenditure to gain income from employment. Deductions are available for expenditure incurred in deriving gross income (other than employment income) or in carrying on a business. Subject to certain exemptions, entertainment expenditure is only 50% deductible.

Nonbusiness expenses/No deduction is permitted for medical, superannuation or insurance contributions.

Personal allowances/Common rebates include the following.

	Maximum rebate
	NZ$
Child taxpayer rebate	156
Charitable donation rebate	500
Housekeeper rebate	310

In addition, tax credits for family assistance are available. These credits are aimed at low- and middle-income families. They are generally paid in fortnightly installments with any under or overpayment being calculated annually. Amounts received are not taxable.

Tax credits

Tax credits are available for the following.

1. Tax withheld at source:
   a. Deduction from employee wages;
   b. Installments (provisional tax) paid by business taxpayers;
   c. Resident withholding tax (RWT) on interest and dividends paid to residents;
   d. Nonresident withholding tax on interest, dividends and royalties where the withholding tax is not a final tax.
2. Tax paid by a CFC on the income that is attributed to New Zealand shareholders.
3. Foreign tax paid on foreign-sourced income derived by a resident (up to the level of New Zealand tax payable).
4. Imputation credits. To avoid double taxation of income derived by a corporation, the tax it pays on its income is imputed to the shareholder. Where a dividend is accompanied by an imputation credit, tax is payable on the gross dividend

(dividend received plus imputation credits), with the imputation credits available to offset the tax. Imputation credits cannot be utilized by nonresident shareholders. However, dividend withholding payment credits, which arise from a withholding tax on foreign dividends received by resident corporations, can be utilized by nonresidents.

5. See also "Personal allowances" for permitted rebates.

Other taxes

A statutory-based scheme of accident insurance is funded in part by premiums payable by employers and employees. Premiums paid by employers (including the self-employed) fund insurance for work-related accidents. Premiums are payable at a rate set for the industrial category on leviable earnings up to a maximum of NZ$85,795 per employee.

Nonwork accident insurance is funded by premiums paid by employees and the self-employed. The premium is a flat NZ$1.10 per NZ$100, including goods and services tax (GST), on taxable earnings up to a maximum of NZ$85,795. The maximum levy is therefore NZ$943.75.

Fringe benefit tax/Employers are subject to a tax-deductible fringe benefit tax (FBT) on the value of noncash fringe benefits provided to their employees. Employers can elect to pay FBT at flat rates (64% on attributed benefits, 49% on pool benefits, that is, those benefits that cannot be attributed to a particular employee) applied against the value of the benefit, or can attribute fringe benefits to individual employees and pay FBT based on each employee's marginal tax rate. Under the attribution option, the applicable FBT rate depends on the net remuneration (including fringe benefits) paid to the employee. The attribution calculation treats the fringe benefit as if it was paid in cash and calculates FBT as the notional increase in income that otherwise would have arisen. The multi-rates areas follows.

Net remuneration	FBT Rate %
NZ$8,071 or less	17.65
NZ$8,076 – NZ$30,590	26.58
NZ$30,591 – NZ$45,330	49.25
More than NZ$45,331	63.93

Fringe benefits include cars available for private use, loans at below prescribed interest rates, contributions to medical insurance schemes and contributions to foreign superannuation schemes. Employers' contributions to an approved superannuation fund (excludes foreign schemes) are subject to a withholding tax of 33%. Fringe benefit tax is also applicable to benefits received by an employee from a third party where there is an arrangement between the employer and the third party, and where the benefit would be subject to fringe benefit tax if it had been provided by the employer.

Goods and services tax (GST)/A form of value-added tax, GST, applies to most supplies of goods and services. The narrow category of exempt supplies includes financial services. The rate applied to taxable supplies is 12.5% or 0%. The 0% rate applies to only a few supplies, including exports.

Superannuation fund withdrawal tax/An effective tax of 5% applies to amounts withdrawn from superannuation funds, to the extent the withdrawals include the return of superannuation contributions made by an employer on an employee's behalf after

April 1, 2000. The tax also applies to withdrawals of earnings derived after April 1, 2000 on employer contributions.

Tax administration

Returns/The New Zealand tax year ends on March 31. Returns (if required) must be filed by July 7 each year, depending on the income type and/or the country of source. Individuals file separate returns. There is no provision for joint returns for husband and wife. Failure to file a return (if required) may result in prosecution with penalty. There is no requirement to file a return for most individuals who earn only employment income, or income where tax is deducted at source at the appropriate rate.

Payment of tax/With the exception of employee shares/options income, employment income (source deduction income) is subject to income tax under a pay-as-you-earn (PAYE) system. If tax on non-source deduction income exceeded NZ$2,500 in the prior year, provisional tax payments are required during the year, generally on the basis of the prior year's tax uplifted by 5%. Provisional tax is generally paid in advance in 3 installments. Any balance of tax (terminal tax) payable arising from the filing of a return to March 31 is generally not due for payment until the following February 7 (For those linked to a tax agent, terminal tax is due on April 7). From April 1, 2001, tax not paid by the due date is subject to an initial late payment penalty of 5%, plus an incremental penalty of 1% per month until the tax is paid (prior to April 1, 2001, the incremental penalty was 2%). From April 1, 2002, the initial late payment penalty is staggered so that 1% will apply on the day after due date and a further 4% applies if the tax is still outstanding after seven days.

Where provisional tax paid is less than the amount of income tax deemed due on that installment date, interest is imposed. Where provisional tax is overpaid, interest is payable to the taxpayer. The interest expense is deductible for tax purposes to business taxpayers, and interest earned on overpaid terminal tax is gross income for tax purposes. Interest rates effective from November 8, 2001 are 11.93% on underpayments and 4.83% on overpayments.

Tax rates

Year ending March 31, 2002

Taxable income		Tax on	Percentage
Over	Not over	Column 1	on excess
(Column 1)			
0	NZ$ 38,000	—	19.5
NZ$ 38,001	60,000	NZ$ 7,410	33.0
60,001		14,670	39.0

INDIVIDUAL TAX CALCULATION

Income year 2002 (year ending March 31, 2002)

Although this summary states the law and practice at January 1, 2002, the calculation is for the income year ending March 31, 2002.

Assumptions

Salary earner (resident) plus spouse and two dependents.

Tax computation

Gross salary		NZ$ 153,000
Add:		
Housing benefit (1)	5,000	
Stock options exercised—Benefit	10,000	
Cost-of-living allowance (1)	5,000	
Taxable reimbursement	5,000	
Foreign-source interest	3,100	28,100
Taxable income		NZ$ 181,100
Tax thereon		NZ$ 61,899
Plus ACC (accident compensation) levy		944
		62,843
Less—Rebates:		
Deductible donations to New Zealand charities (33%)		(500)
		62,343
Less:		
Tax withheld from salary and taxable income	63,268	
Foreign tax credit	310	(63,578)
Refund due		NZ$ 1,235

Notes:

1. Depending on the individual's specific circumstances, housing and other allowances may be able to be paid tax free.
2. Exchange rate of the New Zealand dollar at December 31, 2001: US$1 = NZ$2 415.

Nicaragua

PwC contact

For additional information on taxation in Nicaragua, contact:

Oscar S. Cuadra
PricewaterhouseCoopers
Centro FINARCA
Managua, Nicaragua
Telephone: (505) (2) 270-9639
Fax: (505) (2) 270-9665
e-mail: oscar.cuadra@ni.pwcglobal.com

General note

This entry is repeated from the 2001/2002 edition. For more up-to-date information, consult the contact listed above or Mark Friedlich at mark.friedlich@us.pwcglobal.com.

Significant developments

There have been no significant tax or regulatory developments in the past year.

Territoriality and residence

Nicaragua taxes its citizens and all residents and nonresidents on their income originating in Nicaragua. Taxable income that originates in Nicaragua obtained by nonresidents or nondomiciled persons is determined as a percentage of gross income, depending on the nature of the income.

Gross income

Employee gross income/The taxable compensation of employees, resident or nonresident, includes all types of income (salary, bonuses, overtime, paid vacations, housing and car allowances, reimbursement for tax and children's educational expenses, benefits-in-kind, etc.). There are no concessions of any kind to foreigners. Total personal gross income can be estimated ex officio by the fiscal establishment.

Capital gains and investment income/Capital gains on the sale of property and real estate or shares of other companies are taxable as ordinary income. Investment income earned in Nicaragua is taxable. Interest income from savings and time deposits is not taxable. Dividends paid to Nicaraguan citizens are exempt from income tax.

Deductions

Business deductions/Personal business-related expenses are deductible if properly documented and accounted for and if accepted by the fiscal authorities as proportional to income originated by the business activities. Total business expenses can be determined ex officio by the fiscal authorities as a percentage of gross income.

Nonbusiness expenses/Such expenses are not recognized as deductible expenses.

Tax credits

Tax credits are not permitted.

Other taxes

Social security taxes/Tax approximates 6.25% of salaries and wages with no maximum limit for employees; 15.00% is payable by the employer.

Tax administration

Returns/A corporation has the obligation to withhold monthly the income tax applicable to the employees that earn more than C$50,000 and must prepare and present at the end of August an annual report to the fiscal authorities indicating the total income and the withheld tax. No income tax return is required by the employee. An employee that received other income provided by other activities is obligated to file an income tax return. The tax year for individuals that are not employees ends June 30; this return must be filed within 90 days of this date.

Payment of tax/There is income tax withholding from salaries. All other income is subject to 1% withholding tax.

Tax rates

A partial tax rate table is as follows.

Taxable income			
Over	Not over	Tax on Column 1	Percentage on excess
(Column 1)			
0	C$ 50,000	—	—
C$ 50,000	100,000	—	10
100,000	200,000	C$ 5,000	15
200,000	300,000	20,000	20
300,000	400,000	40,000	25

INDIVIDUAL TAX CALCULATION

Assumptions

Resident employee with wife and two children; one spouse earns income.

Tax computation

Gross income:		
Salary and personal business activities		C$ 400,000
Interest income from savings and time deposits		30,000
Dividends received		10,000
Total gross income		440,000
Less:		
Interest income from savings and time deposits	30,000	
Personal business expenses properly documented	75,000	
Dividends received	10,000	115,000
		C$ 325,000
Tax thereon:		
On the first 300,000		C$ 40,000
25% on the remaining 25,000		6,250
		C$ 46,250

Note:

Exchange rate of the Cordoba Oro at June 30, 2000: US$1 = C$12.6804.

PwC contacts

For additional information on taxation in Nigeria, contact:

Ken U. Igbokwe
Bimpe Balogun
Lasisi Faseun
PricewaterhouseCoopers
26 Ajani Olujare Street
Alaka Estate, Surulere
Lagos, Nigeria
Telephone: (234) (1) 580 2140/2, 583 6940 (direct)
Fax: (234) (1) 583 0594, 269 4607
e-mail: ken.igbokwe@ng.pwcglobal.com
bimpe.balogun@ng.pwcglobal.com
lasisi.faseun@ng.pwcglobal.com

General note

This entry is repeated from the 2001/2002 edition. For more up-to-date information, consult the contact listed above or Mark Friedlich at mark.friedlich@us.pwcglobal.com.

Significant developments

Refer to the contacts listed above for any significant developments affecting personal taxation.

Territoriality and residence

Any person who resides in Nigeria for 183 days within 12 months is liable to pay tax to the relevant tax authority in Nigeria. There are no concessions for foreigners.

Gross income

Employee gross income/Employers can provide, among other items, basic salaries, housing allowance, transport allowance, utilities, lunch allowance, leave allowance, club subscriptions, clothing allowance, leave passage, insurance premiums, and tax reimbursements to their employees. Basic salary, utility allowance, insurance premiums, tax reimbursements, leave allowance, clothing allowance, and club subscriptions are fully taxable in the hands of an individual, except as provided by the Finance Miscellaneous Taxation Provisions Decree No. 30 of 1999, which took effect from January 1, 1999. The 2001 fiscal policy provides that the following allowances paid by an employer to employees are not taxable.

1. Rent allowance: NGN150,000.
2. Transport allowance: NGN20,000.
3. Meal allowance: NGN5,000.
4. Utility allowance: NGN10,000.
5. Entertainment allowance: NGN6,000.
6. Leave grant: Maximum of 10% of basic salary.

Apart from the above, employers also provide cars and accommodation for their staff. If a company provides accommodation for an employee, the employee would be taxed on the ratable value of the accommodation. The employer deducts withholding tax at the rate of 10% at source. If a car is allocated for an employee's use, 5% of the cost of the car would be treated as benefit-in-kind that would form part of the employee's taxable income. Leave passage supported with travel documents is tax exempt. Also, the provision of any uniform, overall, or other protective clothing by an employer would not be treated as part of the employee's taxable income. Provision of canteen meals for staff is generally not treated as part of the employee's taxable income.

Capital gains and investment income/Capital gains are taxable.

The cost of the chargeable asset and the associated cost of disposal are deducted from the sales proceeds to determine the chargeable gains. The chargeable gains are taxed at 10%.

Chargeable gains accruing from a disposal of assets situated outside Nigeria by an individual who resides in Nigeria for 183 days within 12 months are liable to capital gains tax.

Dividends, interest, rents, or royalties derived and brought to Nigeria in convertible currency through government-approved channels and paid into a local account in an approved bank are exempt from Nigerian tax.

There is no favorable rate for capital gains tax.

Deductions

Business deductions/Allowable deductions are expenses incurred wholly, exclusively, necessarily, and reasonably in the production of the income, including, but not limited to, the following.

1. Interest on money borrowed and employed as capital in acquiring the income.
2. Motor vehicle expenses, travel expenses, entertainment, office rent, and service charges.
3. Repairs of premises, plant, machinery, equipment, and fixtures used in generating the income.
4. Bad debts and contributions to a pension and provident or other retirement benefit scheme approved by the Joint Tax Board.

There are no blanket or standard deductions. Deductions are granted on condition that the items concerned meet the criteria for allowable expenses.

Nonbusiness expenses/Other types of deductible expenses include the following.

1. Interest on loans for developing owner-occupied residential houses in Nigeria: This does not include mortgage interest on an expatriate's foreign home or other building not located in Nigeria. Other interest is not allowable for deduction.
2. Medical expenses incurred that are supported with authentic receipts from medical centers.
3. Social security contributions such as Nigerian Social Insurance Trust Fund (NSITF): The maximum contribution per individual is NGN18,480 per annum. The government has amended NSITF contributions. The details of the amendments are stated in the subsequent page.
4. Life insurance premiums: The amount allowable is the actual amount of premium paid for self and spouse.

There are no standard deductions. Charitable contributions are not allowable expenses.

Personal allowances/Personal and other allowances available to a taxpayer include the following.

Personal allowance	NGN5,000 and 20% of earned income
Child allowance	NGN2,500 per child, up to a maximum of four children
Dependent relatives	NGN2,000, maximum of two
Spouse	Canceled
Nigerian Social Insurance Trust Fund (NSITF)	3.5% of gross salary, subject to a maximum of NGN18,480 per annum*

*Per the amendment that took effect from January 1, 2001.

The allowances are in the form of deductions and not credits. An expatriate who spends 183 days within 12 months in Nigeria is entitled to personal, child, and dependent relative allowances.

Tax credits

Foreign tax payable in respect of an income in a country with which Nigeria has double taxation arrangements is allowed as a credit against tax payable in respect of that income in Nigeria.

Other taxes

Social security taxes/Contributions to the Nigerian Social Insurance Trust Fund are made by Nigerian employees and their employers.

The employee contributes 3.5% of annual gross salary to the fund, up to a maximum of NGN18,480, while the employer contributes 6.5% of the employee's gross salary, up to a maximum of NGN34,320. Consequently, the total contribution per annum is not more than NGN52,800.

The NSITF scheme applies for Nigerian citizens only. Those who have not been employed in Nigeria for six years, and who participate in a similar scheme outside Nigeria, do not contribute.

Apart from NSITF, Nigerian workers contribute to pension schemes set up by their employers. If the schemes are approved by the Joint Tax Board, the contributions are tax deductible.

Local taxes on income/The relevant State Board of Internal Revenue is empowered by law to collect taxes on income of individuals, except the following persons, who are assessed to tax by the Federal Board of Inland Revenue.

1. Persons employed by the Nigerian Army, Navy, Air Force, and Police Force, other than in a civilian capacity, and officers of the Nigerian Foreign Service.
2. Every resident of the federal capital territory.
3. Persons not resident in Nigeria who derive income or profit from Nigeria.

Apart from the above, no tier of government has legal authority to impose tax on the income of individuals.

Tax administration

Returns/There is no joint filing (income splitting) for husband and wife in Nigeria.

The taxable year is the calendar year. Other tax years are not permitted.

Payment of tax/Income tax is withheld from payroll under the pay-as-you-earn (PAYE) system.

Tax rates

Tax rates for 2001 are as follows.

Taxable income		Tax on	Percentage
Over	Not over	Column 1	on excess
(Column 1)			
0	NGN 30,000	—	5
NGN 30,000	60,000	NGN 1,500	10
60,000	110,000	4,500	15
110,000	160,000	12,000	20
160,000		22,000	25

INDIVIDUAL TAX CALCULATION

Year of assessment 2001

Assumptions

Expatriate with no children and two dependent relatives. The employee was provided with accommodation and car for personal use by the company. Salary is US$80,000 at NGN103 = NGN8,240,000.

Tax computation

Salary		NGN 8,240,000
Add—Ratable value of:		
Occupied accommodation	12,500	
Benefit-in-kind on motor vehicle (5% of 2,000,000)	100,000	112,500
		8,352,500
Less:		
Personal allowance (5,000 + [20% x 8,352,500])	16,705,000	
Dependent relative (2)	4,000	1,674,500
Taxable income		NGN 6,678,000
Tax thereon:		
On first 160,000	22,000	
On remainder—25% of 6,169,000	1,629,500	
Tax payable		NGN 1,651,500

Notes:

1. Income on which tax credit could be claimed, such as fees and commissions, is not part of the calculation.
2. Exchange rate of the naira at December 31, 2000: US$1 = NGN103.

PwC contact

For additional information on taxation in Norway, contact:

Tore Østebrød
Advokatfirmaet PricewaterhouseCoopers DA
Karenslyst allé 12
0245 Oslo, Norway
Telephone: (47) 23 16 06 76
Fax: (47) 24 06 26 76
e-mail: tore.ostebrod@no.pwcglobal.com

Significant developments

There have been no significant tax or regulatory developments regarding individual taxation in the past year.

Territoriality and residence

Norway taxes its residents on their worldwide income and capital. Nonresidents working in Norway are taxed on their compensation attributable to Norwegian sources. Resident status is obtained when an alien intends to reside in Norway other than temporarily. A stay of more than six months is always considered to be residence.

Gross income

Employee gross income/Nonresident aliens are taxed on salary earned for work performed in Norway, irrespective of where payment is made or whether it is remitted. Compensation relating to work performed outside Norway is not taxed. All benefits paid by the employer (e.g., living allowances, housing allowances, tax reimbursements, paid vacation, travel costs for nonbusiness visits to the employee's country of origin) are subject to tax.

Capital gains and investment income/Capital gains on portfolio investments are taxed at a flat rate of 28%. A nonresident alien is taxed on Norwegian-source capital gains received during a stay in Norway, irrespective of the period of the stay. Norwegian real estate capital gains are always taxable, regardless of residence.

Dividends received by domestic shareholders from domestic companies are subject to income tax at the rate of 28%. Such shareholders are, however, given a credit for tax paid by the distributing company, with the effect that they pay zero tax.

Foreign-source dividends received by a domestic shareholder are taxed as ordinary income unless otherwise decreed in the relevant tax treaty. Foreign withholding tax is credited against Norwegian tax.

A withholding tax of 25% is levied on dividends paid by a Norwegian company to nonresident aliens. The withholding tax can be reduced by the relevant tax treaty.

Deductions

Business deductions/If not reimbursed, an alien (resident or nonresident) can deduct all business-connected expenses. These expenses comprise such items as moving expenses, traveling expenses and automobile expenses. Entertainment expenses will not be allowed as a deduction. In practice, this will apply only to individuals who are not employed, e.g., consultants.

Nonbusiness expenses/An alien (resident or nonresident) can deduct mortgage and other interest expenses (limitations may exist for interest on foreign loans, for nonresidents etc.), expenses incurred in producing income, private pension premiums (maximum NOK40,000), alimony, and commuting expenses in excess of NOK9,200. In addition, an allowance (minimum, NOK4,000; maximum, NOK43,000) can be claimed as a deduction. An alien who intends to be in Norway for less than four years can elect to take a standard deduction instead of itemized deductions. The standard deduction is calculated as 15% of gross taxable income (earned income only). If the standard deduction is elected, only the minimum allowance with a maximum NOK43,000 and contributions to company pension schemes may be deducted.

Personal allowances/No personal allowances can be claimed when calculating net income subject to tax.

Tax credits

Resident aliens can take income taxes paid to a foreign country as a credit against their tax liability (subject to limitations and tax treaty conditions). In practice, this applies only to income earned in non–tax-treaty countries and to dividends. A nonresident alien would not be entitled to a foreign tax credit.

Other taxes

Social security taxes/The taxpayer contributes to the social security system through a social security tax, which is calculated on gross salary income (including benefits-in-kind) at a rate of 7.8%. The employer pays an additional 14.1% of the employee's gross income as a contribution to the social security scheme. A solidarity tax of 12.5% on gross income is payable on income (salary-related) in excess of 16G (one G is at present NOK51,360).

Local taxes on income/See "Tax rates."

Tax administration

Returns/Joint filing with income splitting is not permitted. If both spouses have earned income, each files a separate return and is taxed in Class 1 as a single taxpayer. Otherwise, they file one return and are taxed in Class 2 as a married couple. Tax returns must be filed on a calendar-year basis. A tax return (PSA) is to be completed by the end of April. In the PSA, all available details have been imposed by the tax authorities, and the taxpayer must check the return carefully and delete or add items in accordance with the facts.

Payment of tax/There is income tax withholding from salaries. Generally, if taxpayers have sizable income not subject to withholding, they will be required to make quarterly payments of estimated taxes.

Tax rates

Local taxes on income/All municipalities are separate taxing authorities and impose a local tax at an aggregate rate of 28% on taxable income in excess of NOK60,200 for a married person whose spouse is not working (Tax Class 2). This band is NOK30,100 for a single person or married couple where both are working (Tax Class 1).

Top tax/An additional tax (state tax) on salary income, including benefits-in-kind, is assessed. For Class 2 taxpayers, top tax is 13.5% of earned income between NOK342,200 and NOK830,000 and 19.5 % in excess of NOK830,000. For Class 1 taxpayers the tax free ban is NOK320,000 and increasing to 19,5% on income in excess of NOK830,000.

INDIVIDUAL TAX CALCULATION

Fiscal 2002

Assumptions

Resident alien husband and wife, two children; one spouse earns all of the income.

Tax computation

Gross income:		
Salary		NOK 600,000
Interest		60,000
Dividends from abroad		10,000
Gain on sale of shares		30,000
Total gross income		700,000
Less (choosing the 15% standard deduction):		
Minimum allowance	43,000	
15% standard deduction on 600,000	90,000	
Contribution to pension scheme (paid by employer)	18,900	151,900
Taxable income		NOK 548,100
Income tax:		
Local tax (municipal tax)—28% of (548,100 – 60,200)		NOK 136,612
Social security		46,800
Top tax—13.5% of (600,000 – 342,200)		34,803
		218,215
Less—Withholding tax on foreign dividend (25%)		(2,500)
Income tax for married couple		NOK 215,715

Note:

Exchange rate of the krone at December 28, 2001: US$1 = NOK9.0225.

Oman

PwC contact

For additional information on Oman, contact:

Jeffrey Todd
PricewaterhouseCoopers
Hatat House, Suites 205–210
(P.O. Box 3075, PC112)
Ruwi, Sultanate of Oman
Telephone: (968) 56 37 17
Fax: (968) 56 44 08
e-mail: jeff.todd@om.pwcglobal.com

Absence of taxation

Income tax is not imposed on individuals in Oman.

Note

Exchange rate of the Omani rial at December 31, 2001: US$1 = RO0.385.

PwC contact

For additional information on taxation in Pakistan, contact:

Syed Shabbar Zaidi
A.F. Ferguson & Co.
State Life Building 1-C
I.I. Chundrigar Road
Karachi 74000 Pakistan
Telephone: (92) (21) 242 6682-6, 2426711-5
Fax: (92) (21) 241 5007, 242 7938
e-mail: s.m.shabbar.zaidi@pk.pwcglobal.com

Significant developments

A new tax law, the Income Tax Ordinance, 2001, has been promulgated in Pakistan, and takes from July 1, 2002. The following information on taxation in Pakistan is according to that new law and is accurate as of March 1, 2002.

Territoriality and residence

Liability to tax varies according to the tax residential status of the individual in the tax year (July to June). Individuals are resident in Pakistan in a tax year if they are in Pakistan for a period amounting in all to 182 days or more, or for periods amounting in all to 90 days or more in that year and have, within the four years preceding that year, been in Pakistan for a period of or for periods amounting in all to 365 days or more. Individuals who do not qualify as resident are assessed as nonresidents.

Residents are taxed on worldwide income. except where under a double taxation treaty the income earned outside Pakistan is not taxable in Pakistan. A foreign tax credit is allowed in Pakistan for tax paid abroad on foreign-source income. This relief is allowed at the lower of tax at the average rate of tax in Pakistan and the foreign income tax paid. Foreign-source income of a resident who is not a citizen of Pakistan is exempt if the individual is resident only by virtue of employment, and presence in Pakistan does not exceed three years. This exemption does not apply in the case of income from a business established in Pakistan and foreign-source income that is brought into or received in Pakistan.

A nonresident is taxed only on Pakistan-source income, including income received in or deemed to be received in Pakistan or deemed to accrue or arise in Pakistan.

Gross income

Employee gross income/Salary is Pakistan-source income and therefore taxable in Pakistan if it results from employment exercised in Pakistan or if it is paid by or on behalf of the federal government, a provincial government or a local authority. Salary is the amount received by an employee from employment, whether of a revenue or capital nature. It can include leave pay, payment in lieu of leave, overtime, bonuses, commissions, fees, gratuities, work condition supplements, monetary and nonmonetary perquisites, any allowance except that solely expended in the performance of employee's duties of employment, profits in lieu of or in addition to salary, pensions, annuities, and tax reimbursements. In addition, amounts or perquisites paid or provided by an associate of the employer, a third-party under an arrangement with the employer or associate of the employer, a past employer or a prospective employer, or payments to an associate of the employee are also to be considered as salary. The extent of taxability and exclusions from income of some perquisites are discussed under "Deductions" below.

Capital gains and investment income/Capital gains on the sale, exchange or transfer of movable capital assets are taxable. However, exemptions apply to personal effects, including wearing apparel, jewelry and furniture, and shares of Pakistan public companies (modaraba certificates). Capital gains tax does not apply to stock in trade. Capital gains, other than on statutorily depreciable assets, realized within one year of acquisition are fully taxed; after one year, 75% of such gains are taxed and 25% are exempt.

All cash dividends are to be taxed at the rate of 10% as a separate block of income. Stock splits are taxed as normal income.

Capital gains and investment income earned outside Pakistan are not taxable in the case of nonresidents.

Employees share scheme/The value of a right or option to acquire shares under an employees share scheme is not chargable to tax. However, when an employee is issued shares under the scheme, the value of resulting benefit is taxed as "salary" income.

Deductions

As shown below.

1. Utilities—Reimbursement for utilities or a utilities allowance is exempt from tax up to 10% of basic salary.
2. Medical allowance or reimbursement is exempt up to 10% of the basic salary. Reimbursements in excess of that threshold are allowed to be carried forward to the next year, subject to a maximum limit of 10% of the basic salary.
3. A rebate at the average rate of tax is allowed on donations made to approved nonprofit organizations on the lower of donation value and 30% of the individual's taxable income.
4. Personal expenditure on medical services incurred by a resident individual are allowed as a deduction from total income, provided the expenditure is supported by documentary evidence. The allowance, however, is not to exceed lower of PRs30,000 and 10% of the basic salary.

Tax credits

Foreign tax credit is granted for foreign tax paid on income accrued outside Pakistan, as outlined under "Territoriality and residence."

Other taxes

Social security taxes/No social security tax is payable in Pakistan.

Local taxes on income/The only significant tax on salaries is federal income tax.

Tax administration

Returns/All taxpayers must file returns separately. Joint returns cannot be filed. Employees are required to file their returns only on a fiscal-year basis (July to June). Every resident taxpayer is required to file a wealth statement along with the return of income. Besides, commissioner can also require any person to furnish the said statement.

Payment of tax/There is income tax withholding from salaries. The amount to be withheld is arrived at by applying to the salary paid the average rate of tax on the estimated income of the employee for the fiscal year.

Tax rates

Where agricultural income is nil or comprises up to PRs80,000 of total income

Taxable income		Tax on	Percentage
Over (Column 1)	Not over	Column 1	on excess
0	PRs 60,000	—	—
PRs 60,000	150,000	—	7.5
150,000	300,000	PRs 6,750	12.5
300,000	400,000	25,500	20.0
400,000	700,000	45,500	25.0
700,000		120,500	35.0

Where agricultural income comprises more than PRs80,000 of total income

Taxable income		Tax on	Percentage
Over (Column 1)	Not over	Column 1	on excess
0	PRs 150,000	—	7.5
PRs 150,000	300,000	PRs 11,250	12.5
300,000	400,000	30,000	20.0
400,000	700,000	50,000	25.0
700,000		125,000	35.0

A rebate, based on the amount of income tax liability calculated before the rebate, is allowable. The amount ranges from 5% of income (on salary in excess of PRs1,000,000) to 70% (where salary is below PRs80,000 but more than PRs60,000).

INDIVIDUAL TAX CALCULATION

Income year ended June 30, 2003

Assumptions

An expatriate considered resident for Pakistan tax purposes earns the income. There are no special exemptions for marital status or children.

Tax computation

Basic salary		PRs 2,400,000
Rent paid by the employer in respect of accommodation provided to the employee		120,000
Utility allowance	300,000	
Less—Exempt up to 10% of basic salary	(240,000)	60,000
Addition for company-maintained car (1)		60,000
Adjusted salary income		2,640,000
Additional income:		
Dividends	5,000	
Long-term capital gain	50,000	
Less—Exempt up to 10% of basic salary	(240,000)	60,000
Taxable income		PRs 2,682,500
Tax on dividend income PRs5,000 @ 10%		PRs 500
On balance of PRs2,677,500		812,625
		813,125
Less—Rebate @ 5%		(40,656)
Total tax payable		PRs 772,469

Notes:

1. 7.5% of the employer's cost of acquiring car less payment made by the employee for the use of the motor vehicle or for its running costs (partly used for business purposes and partly for private).
2. Exchange rate of the Pakistan rupee at January 1, 2002: US$1 = PRs63.0020.

PwC contact

For additional information on taxation in Panama, contact:

Antonio E. Latorraca
PricewaterhouseCoopers
Samuel Lewis Avenue & 55 East Street
Obarrio, Panama
P.O. Box 6-4493
El Dorado, Panama)
Telephone: (507) 223-1313
Fax: (507) 264-5627
e-mail: antonio.latorraca@pa.pwcglobal.com

General note

This entry is repeated from the 2001/2002 edition. For more up-to-date information, consult the contact listed above or Mark Friedlich at mark.friedlich@us.pwcglobal.com.

Territoriality and residence

Panama's tax system is based on a territorial concept of income. Citizens and residents are taxed on income earned from Panama sources. Nonresidents are taxed only on income from Panama sources, and the tax on any type of income paid to a nonresident must be withheld by the payer. Citizens, residents, and nonresidents are not taxed on exempt income (i.e., interest on Panamanian government securities and interest on savings accounts and time deposits maintained with banks established in Panama).

According to this territorial principle of taxation, compensation received in respect of duties performed wholly overseas will not be subject to Panama individual income tax. The system for determining this exempt income is to consider income related to the days spent outside Panama on job-related duties as foreign source, so that it is not liable to tax.

Gross income

Employee gross income*/*An employee is taxed on compensation earned for work done in Panama, regardless of where payment is made or received.

Compensation includes salary, premiums, profit distributions, living allowances, housing allowances, tax reimbursements, benefits-in-kind, house, car, retirement benefits, and any other compensation-in-kind. There is no concession to a foreign employee.

Capital gains and investment income*/*Capital gains on the sale of real estate located in Panama and on securities not registered with the National Securities Commission are taxable.

Capital gains arising from the sale of real estate are subject to a specific tax rule. Capital gains from the sale of shares, bonds, and other securities represent an integral part of the taxpayer's gross income, unless these securities are exempt.

Investment income from a Panama source, such as dividends, is subject to a 10% withholding tax. However, dividends on bearer shares are subject to 20% withholding tax.

Deductions

Business deductions/Unreimbursed items such as moving expenses, business-connected travel expenses, and business entertainment expenses are not deductible against the employee's compensation income.

A fixed allowance (representation expenses) can be given to employees as a part of salary. This allowance is considered to be gross taxable income, and the taxpayer may deduct 25% of this allowance as expenses up to a maximum of B/. 6,000 per year. Representation expenses are not subject to social security and educational insurance taxes for either the employee or the employer.

Nonbusiness expenses/Interest paid on mortgage loans for homes or for home improvements on residences located in Panama is deductible; the maximum deduction allowed is B/. 15,000 annually, provided the interest payment does not classify as preferential interest for new homes. Interest paid on loans for financing education is deductible if duly documented. The educational insurance tax (see below) is deductible. Medical expenses are deductible, provided they were incurred in Panama and are duly documented. Donations to local educational and charitable institutions are deductible, provided the deductions are authorized by the law establishing such institutions or by the Income Tax Department. Dues paid to nonprofit associations or organizations in Panama are also deductible expenses.

Personal allowances/An individual who is not married is entitled to a personal exemption of B/. 800; married couples filing a joint return are entitled to an exemption of B/. 1,600. An additional exemption of B/. 250 is granted for each dependent. These exemptions are applicable in determining taxable income.

Tax credits

No tax credits are allowed for income taxes paid to foreign countries.

Other taxes

Social security taxes/Social security tax is assessed at a rate of 7.25% on wages and other compensation paid, including compensation-in-kind. However, compensation-in-kind from the employer is subject to social security tax. There is no maximum limit on the taxable amount.

Educational insurance tax/Educational insurance tax is assessed at the rate of 1.25% on salaries and wages paid. There is no maximum limit on the taxable amount.

Local taxes on income/There are no local taxes on income.

Tax administration

Returns/Husbands and wives can file joint returns. Joint filing is not advantageous if both spouses earn separate income, because the tax rates are graduated. The only advantage of filing a joint return for a couple with a single source of taxable income is that in a joint return, there is an exemption of B/. 1,600, while in a single return, the exemption is B/. 800.

All taxpayers, except employees having only one source of income from wages, salary, or other remuneration for personal services and whose monthly income tax is deducted by the employer, must file a tax return on a calendar-year basis.

Employees having only one source of income from personal services who want to take advantage of nonbusiness expenses must file a tax return. Employees who receive representation expenses are also required to file a tax return.

Tax returns and estimated income for the current year must be filed on forms prescribed and supplied by the Income Tax Department.

Payment of tax/There is income tax withholding from wages, salaries, and other remuneration for personal services.

The total amount of the taxpayer's estimated income tax is payable annually in three equal installments on June 30, September 30, and December 31. If the estimated amount paid exceeds the actual amount computed at the end of the year, the excess is applied against the current year's estimated income tax or against taxes due in subsequent years. If there is still an overpayment after applying the excess to the estimate for the current year, a refund may be obtained, provided the tax authorities determine that no additional tax is due.

Tax rates

Taxable income		Tax on	Percentage
Over (Column 1)	Not over	Column 1	on excess
B/. 3,000	B/. 3,250	—	2.0
3,250	4,000	B/. 130	4.0
4,000	6,000	160	6.5
6,000	10,000	290	11.0
10,000	15,000	730	16.5
15,000	20,000	1,555	19.0
20,000	30,000	2,505	22.0
30,000	40,000	4,705	27.0
40,000	50,000	7,405	30.0
50,000	200,000	10,405	33.0
200,000		59,905	30.0

INDIVIDUAL TAX CALCULATION

Calendar year 2000

Assumptions

Resident married taxpayer with four children.

Tax computation

Salary		B/. 80,000
Less—Deductions:		
Interest on mortgage	15,000	
Charitable contributions	500	
Educational insurance tax (80,000 x 1.25%)	1,000	16,500
		63,500
Less—Personal exemptions:		
Joint return	1,600	
Children (250 x 4)	1,000	2,600
Taxable income		B/. 60,900
Tax thereon:		
On first 50,000		B/. 10,405
On remaining 10,900 at 33%		3,597
Tax payable		B/. 14,002

Note:

Exchange rate of the balboa at December 31, 2000: US$1 = B/. 1.00.

PwC contacts

For additional information on taxation in Papua New Guinea, contact:

Chris Eastwood/John Leahy
PricewaterhouseCoopers
P.O. Box 484
Port Moresby, Papua New Guinea
Telephone: (675) 321 1500
Fax: (675) 321 1428
e-mail: chris.eastwood@pg.pwcglobal.com
john.leahy@pg.pwcglobal.com
Web site: www.pwc.com.pg

Significant developments

The government has embarked on a course of privatization of public enterprises, with most being offered for sale. To date, only the Papua New Guinea Banking Corporation has been sold.

The government's new Superannuation Act is expected to come into force during 2002. This is the result of a major overhaul of the country's superannuation system and will result in the end of the virtual monopoly currently enjoyed by the National Provident Fund.

Territoriality and residence

Residents of Papua New Guinea are taxable on their worldwide income. However, a deduction for losses incurred by residents from a source outside Papua New Guinea is allowed only against foreign-source income and not against Papua New Guinea-source income.

Residents of Papua New Guinea are persons who reside in Papua New Guinea and satisfy either of two conditions.

1. Their domicile is in Papua New Guinea, unless the Commissioner General is satisfied that their permanent place of abode is outside Papua New Guinea;

   or

2. They have actually been in Papua New Guinea, continuously or intermittently, during more than one-half of the year of income, unless the Commissioner General is satisfied that their usual place of abode is outside Papua New Guinea and that they do not intend taking up residence in Papua New Guinea.

Nonresidents of Papua New Guinea are subject to tax only on their income from sources in Papua New Guinea.

Persons coming to Papua New Guinea to take up a contract of employment would be regarded as residents even if they are to be in the country for a short term of, say, two to four years. Citizenship does not determine liability to Papua New Guinea income tax. Under Papua New Guinea law, the source of remuneration is generally considered to be the place where the services are performed, although this is not necessarily the sole test. Thus, remuneration for services rendered in Papua New Guinea would be taxable to both residents and nonresidents, wherever received.

Double taxation treaties have been effected with Australia, Canada, the People's Republic of China, Fiji, the Republic of Korea, Malaysia, Singapore, and the United

Kingdom. In certain circumstances, these treaties exempt remuneration for services rendered in Papua New Guinea by nonresidents from PNG tax.

Gross income

Employee gross income/Tax is payable by salary or wage earners on salary or wage income on a fortnightly basis; it is a first and final tax. Gross income of an employee subject to the fortnightly salary or wages tax includes cash remuneration, commissions, bonus remuneration of any kind, and allowances (whether paid in cash or otherwise).

Employee benefits are generally taxable in the hands of the employee. Benefits or allowances for housing and motor vehicles are taxed according to prescribed taxable values. In general, all other allowances or benefits paid to employees are taxed in full. Airfares from the place of engagement to Papua New Guinea for the taxpayer and family, as well as annual-leave return airfares from Papua New Guinea to the place of engagement, are not taxed, provided they are not paid as a cash allowance or converted to cash. When an employee is provided with additional leave fares in a year, the cost is taxable as an employee benefit.

Capital gains and investment income/The types of capital-gain-related income subject to tax are listed below.

1. Profit on sale of property acquired for the purpose of profit making by sale or from the carrying out of any profit-making undertaking or scheme.
2. Dividends, other than certain types of stock dividends, received from a company out of capital profits are taxable in the shareholder's hands.

Residents are subject to tax on investment income from all sources, including interest, dividends, rents, royalties, and annuities.

Nonresident individuals are subject to withholding tax on dividends at the rate of 17% (15% for treaty country residents with the exception of Australia and U.K. residents). Dividends paid by mining companies attract a rate of 10%. Royalties are subject to withholding tax at 10% or, where the recipient is associated with the payer, at 30%. A withholding tax of 15% is payable on interest (subject to certain exceptions). The withholding tax applies whether the recipient is a resident or a nonresident. Most of PNG's double taxation agreements limit the rate of withholding tax on interest to 10%.

Deductions

Business deductions/In calculating the tax payable on salary or wage income for a fortnight period, allowance is made for tax rebates for dependents and for an assumed (automatic) deduction from gross salary or wage income of K200 per annum for expenditures incurred by employees in the course of employment. Employees who incur revenue expenditure in a calendar year in the course of deriving salary or wage income are entitled to apply to the Commissioner General for a rebate of tax with respect to that expenditure for the calendar year. The tax rebate is equivalent to 25% of expenditure incurred. Outgoings and losses of a private, domestic or capital nature do not qualify for the rebate.

Individuals are allowed a rebate for tuition fees paid to primary and secondary schools, whether within or outside Papua New Guinea subject to a maximum of K750 per dependent child. Tax-deductible donations may be made to prescribed charitable organizations and sporting bodies, with a minimum donation of K50. Other examples of rebatable expenditure include travel and automobile expenses incurred by employees in deriving their salary or wage.

Losses and outgoings incurred by employed persons in deriving nonsalary or nonwage income are deductible to the extent they represent revenue expenditure incurred in deriving that income.

Nonbusiness expenses/Nonbusiness expenses, such as home mortgage interest, are not deductible or rebatable.

Personal allowances/Resident taxpayers are entitled to a rebate of 15% of tax assessed or K450, whichever is less, for the first wholly maintained dependent and 10% of tax assessed or K300, whichever is less, for each of the second, third and fourth dependents.

The tax rebate for dependents is incorporated in the fortnightly tax scale by which the salary or wage tax payable by an employed person is calculated.

Tax credits

A tax credit is available to a resident individual for foreign tax paid on income included in the individual's Papua New Guinea income tax return. The credit is limited to the lesser of the foreign tax paid or the Papua New Guinea tax that would otherwise have been payable on the foreign income.

Residents are also entitled to a credit for tax withheld from dividends and interest received from resident companies.

Personal allowances (see above) take the form of tax rebates.

Other taxes

Social security taxes/There are no social security taxes payable by expatriates.

Local taxes on income/No local taxes are payable on income.

Tax administration

Returns/Salary or wage earners who have had salary or wages tax deducted from their salary are generally not required to file annual tax returns, unless they derive gross income from other sources in excess of K100 per year.

Resident individuals whose gross income, including salary or wages, does not exceed K6,000 are exempt from filing tax returns.

Where a return is required, it covers the year ended December 31 and must be filed by the following February 28. There is no joint filing of returns.

Payment of tax/As indicated above, tax is deducted on a fortnightly basis from salary or wages. No refund of tax withheld from an employee's salary or wage is allowed where the tax payable by the employee on salary or wages income for the year (calculated by reference to the annual progressive tax rates scale) is less than the amount of the tax withheld from the employee's salary or wages because, for example, the employee has been employed in Papua New Guinea for only part of the year of income.

Tax is payable on nonsalary and nonwage income usually one month after an assessment is issued. Such income is also subject to advance payments of tax based on the prior year's taxable income.

Tax rates

Resident individuals

Taxable income Over (Column 1)	Not over	Tax on Column 1	Percentage on excess
0	K 6,000	—	0
K 6,000	16,000	—	25
16,000	70,000	K 2,500	35
70,000	95,000	21,400	40
95,000		31,400	47

Nonresident individuals

Taxable income Over (Column 1)	Not over	Tax on Column 1	Percentage on excess
0	K 16,000	—	25
K 16,000	70,000	K 4,000	35
70,000	95,000	22,900	40
95,000		32,900	47

INDIVIDUAL TAX CALCULATION

Calendar year 2002

Assumptions

Resident husband and wife, two children; one spouse earns all the income. High-cost apartment (weekly rental of K700 or more) and motor vehicle with fuel are provided by the employer.

Tax computation

Gross income:		
Salary		K 80,000
Employee taxable benefits (220 x 26 fortnights; 220 = 75 for car + 145 (maximum) for house)		5,720
Interest (from a PNG financial institution—gross)		2,000
Interest (foreign-source—gross)		7,000
Long-term capital gain		4,000
Total gross income		98,720
Long-term capital gain		4,000
Income subject to tax		K 94,720
Tax thereon		K 31,288
Less—Gross tax on salary or wage income of 85,720 per tax rates (1)		(26,558)
Tax payable on nonsalary income		4,730
Less:		
Rebate for business expense (1,040 x 25%)	260	
Credit for domestic interest withholding tax	300	
Credit for foreign tax paid on interest income	700	(1,260)
Net tax payable		3,470
Salary or wage tax payable on a fortnightly basis during the year on 85,720		26,558
Total tax		K 30,028

Notes:

1. Salary and wage tax payable of K26,558 is after allowing for the automatic deduction from gross salary of K200 and dependents' rebates of K1,050.
2. Exchange rate of the kina at December 30, 2001: US$1 = K3.8241.

Paraguay

PwC contacts

For additional information on taxation in Paraguay, contact:

Daniel O. Elicetche
E. Rubén Taboada
Price Waterhouse
(Member Firm of PricewaterhouseCoopers)
General Díaz 521
6 Piso, Edificio Internacional Faro
Asunción, Paraguay
Telephone: (595) (21) 445 003
Fax: (595) (21) 444 893
e-mail: daniel.o.elicetche@py.pwcglobal.com
ruben.taboada@py.pwcglobal.com

Note

The following information on taxation in Paraguay is accurate as of December 31, 2001. For subsequent developments, refer to the contact above.

Absence of taxation on income or earnings

Income tax is not imposed on individuals in Paraguay.

Exchange rate

The free market exchange rate (applicable for any kind of transaction) of the guaraní at December 31, 2001: US$1 = PYG4.650.

PwC contacts

For additional information on taxation in Peru, contact:

Rudolf Röder
Monica Nieva
Walter Aguirre
PricewaterhouseCoopers
Canaval y Moreyra 380, Floor 19
Lima 27, Peru
Telephone: (511) 2116500
Fax: (511) 4422073
e-mail: rudolf.roeder@pe.pwcglobal.com
monica.nieva@pe.pwcglobal.com
walter.aguirre@pe.pwcglobal.com

Significant developments

There have been no significant tax or regulatory developments regarding individual taxation in the past year.

Territoriality and residence

For income tax purposes, individuals are classified as domiciled and nondomiciled. The former are individuals of Peruvian nationality residing permanently in Peru and foreign individuals who have resided in Peru for a continuous period of two or more years. Temporary absences of up to 90 days in the taxable year do not interrupt the continuity of such residence. Domicile is lost after two years of residency abroad or when the individual obtains a resident visa in another country or has a labor contract to work abroad for a period of no less than one year.

In general, changes in the domiciled or nondomiciled status of an individual become effective for tax purposes only as from the next calendar year. A domiciled individual is liable for Peruvian tax with respect to worldwide income, whereas a nondomiciled individual is liable only with respect to Peruvian income.

Gross income

Employee gross income/Gross income from employment consists of salaries, bonuses, housing and school allowances, and, in general, any payment in cash or in kind earned by an employee in Peru, regardless of nationality, length of residence in Peru and whether the remuneration is earned or paid outside Peru. Houses and cars owned by the company and furnished to employees do not generate taxable income for the latter. Such houses are normally furnished to employees when they work in mining, petroleum and other non-urban production centers.

Foreigners are given the same tax treatment as Peruvians, without any special concessions; however, mobilization costs and accommodation expenses during the first three months after arrival in Peru, as well as the cost of home-leave fares, are not deemed taxable income. Severance indemnities in the amounts provided by law and indemnities for vacations not taken that are paid to terminated employees are excluded from income tax.

Capital gains and investment income/Eventual (occasional) capital gains are not subject to the general income tax. Peruvian-source interest, rentals and royalties are subject to general income tax and must be computed to determine the individual's taxable income.

Dividends are no taxable.

Deductions

Business deductions/Peruvian legislation allows companies to pay directly or to reimburse business expenses incurred by executives. Consequently, deductions for moving, travel, automobile, and other expenses are not permitted to individuals.

Nonbusiness expenses/Individuals with income other than remuneration are entitled to certain deductions in accordance with the type of income obtained. In the case of rentals, they can deduct 20% of the income. In the case of royalty payments, they can deduct 10% of gross royalties received. Independent professionals can deduct 20% of gross revenues, up to a limit of 24 tax units (UIT), plus an annual amount of seven tax units.

Personal allowances/Domiciled individuals who receive income from employment or professional income are entitled to a total deduction equivalent to seven tax units (S/.21,700 for 2002) from their gross income.

Tax credits

Donations to universities, educational institutions and qualified cultural institutions, up to a maximum of 10% of taxable income, generate a tax credit equivalent to the average income tax of the donor applied to the amount donated.

Taxpayers may claim a credit for income taxes paid abroad (subject to limitations).

Other taxes

Social security taxes/The social welfare fund comprises the Pension Fund (National Pension Fund or Private Pension Fund) and the Health System. With regard to the Pension Fund, the employee must choose between the National and Private Funds.

Extraordinary solidarity tax (EST)/This tax has replaced the housing fund as from September 1, 1998. The EST must be paid by the employer, applying a 2% rate on remuneration. Employees are not required to pay this tax. Independent professionals are also liable for the EST at the 2% rate.

The rates to be applied to the employee's monthly salary are as follows.

	Employer %	Employee %
National Pension Fund	—	13
Private Pension Fund	—	8*
Health System	9	—
Extraordinary Solidarity tax	2	—

*Each pension fund will charge an insurance rate and commission, resulting in a total approximate 12% rate.

The employee's contributions are not deductible in determining taxable income.

Local taxes on income/Income tax is the only tax assessable on income. There are no state or municipal income taxes.

Tax administration

Returns/Income tax returns must be generally filed by the first week of April. Late filing is subject to fines; late payment is subject to moratorium interest. Individuals earning only income from employment are not obliged to file tax returns.

Payment of tax/Income tax on remuneration must be withheld. It must be paid on account on a monthly basis. Any balance due must be paid by individuals according to the rules established by the tax administration.

Tax rates

Income tax rates are as shown below.

Taxable amount	Tax rate %
Less than 7 UIT (S/.21,700)	0
Up to 27 UIT(S/.83,700)	15
From 27 to 54 UIT (S/.167,400)	21
Over 54 UIT (S/.167,401)	27

Note:

One tax unit (UIT) for year 2002 has been fixed at S/.3,100.

INDIVIDUAL TAX CALCULATION

Calendar year 2002

Assumptions

1. Resident Individual domiciled taxpayer.
2. Salary: US$100,000.
3. Exchange rate of the nuevo sol: US$1= S/.3.50.

Tax computation

Gross income		S/. 350,000
Actual deduction (7 UIT) (1)		21,700
Taxable income:		S/. 328,300
Income tax thereon		
15% on first 27 UIT	12,555	
21% on 27 to 54 UIT	17,577	
27% on income over 54 UIT	43,443	
		S/. 73,575

Notes:

1. There are no deductions or allowances for marital status and children.
2. Exchange rate of the nuevo sol at December 31, 2001: US$1 = S/.3.5908.

PwC contact

For additional information on taxation in the Philippines, contact:

Tammy H. Lipana
PricewaterhouseCoopers Philippines
29th Floor Philamlife Tower
8767 Paseo de Roxas
1226 Makati City, Philippines
Telephone: (63) (2) 845 27 28, (63) (2) 459 2001 (direct)
Fax: (63) (2) 845 28 06
e-mail: tammy.lipana@ph.pwcglobal.com

Significant developments

A program for electronic filing of tax returns has been initiated by the Bureau of Internal Revenue (BIR). Taxpayers may chose to use the Electronic Filing and Payment System (EFPS) to file their returns, including any attachments, and pay the taxes due thereon through the Internet. Returns that may be filed electronically are those for withholding taxes, income tax, value-added tax, percentage tax, and excise tax.

Beginning in tax year 2001, nonresident citizens, overseas contract workers and seamen who are exempt from tax with respect to income derived from sources outside the Philippines are no longer required to file Annual Income Information Returns (BIR Form 1703) on their income derived from sources outside the Philippines.

The rates of withholding taxes on certain income payments as well as the deadlines for the filing of returns and payments for withholding taxes, value-added tax and document stamp tax have been revised. Further, subcontractors engaged in petroleum operations per Presidential Decree 87 and nonresident cinematographic film owners, lessors, or distributors have been added to the list of taxpayers subject to final withholding tax. These persons are subject to withholding tax at 8% on gross income from contracts and 25% on gross income from all sources within the Philippines, respectively. The new withholding tax regulations took effect for remittances in November 2001 with respect to money/income payments that are paid or payable or accrued/recorded as expenses/assets in the books of account for October 2001. Henceforth, monthly withholding tax on compensation is due on the 10th of the following month for manual filers and the 15th for those using the EFPS, except for withholding tax for the month of December, which is due on January 15 for manual filers and January 20 for those filing under the EFPS.

The income tax rates applicable to aliens and Filipinos occupying managerial and technical positions in representative offices had been clarified to be the graduated rates of 5% to 32% and not the flat rate of 15% that applies to executives of regional headquarters or regional operating headquarters. The graduated rates took effect in January 2002.

Tax treaties with Switzerland and with China came into force effective January 2002.

Territoriality and residence

The Philippines taxes its resident citizens on their worldwide income. Nonresident citizens and aliens, whether or not resident in the Philippines, are taxed only on income from sources within the Philippines.

A nonresident alien individual who comes to the Philippines and stays there for more than 180 days during any calendar year will be deemed a nonresident alien engaged in trade or business in the Philippines. If the aggregate stay in the Philippines during any calendar year does not exceed 180 days, the individual is deemed a nonresident alien not engaged in trade or business in the Philippines.

Expatriates assigned in the Philippines for a definite period are generally regarded as nonresidents engaged in trade or business in the Philippines.

Gross income

Employee gross income/An alien, whether resident or not, is taxed on compensation income earned from services rendered in the Philippines regardless of where payment is made and whether it is remitted into the Philippines. The nonresident alien is not taxed on compensation income from services performed outside the Philippines. Employee gross income, from the point of view of a nonresident alien engaged in trade or business in the Philippines, includes all payments for services rendered in the Philippines, such as salaries and bonuses.

Social security contributions and union dues paid by employees are not included in gross income and are exempt from taxation.

Fringe benefits tax/Fringe benefits furnished to managerial and supervisory-level employees by the employer are subject to a final fringe benefits tax (FBT) of 32% on the grossed-up monetary value of the benefits. Managerial employees are those who may lay down and execute management policies to hire, transfer, suspend, lay off, recall, discharge, assign, or discipline employees. Supervisory employees are those who effectively recommend such managerial actions if the exercise of authority on behalf of the employer is not merely routine or clerical in nature but requires the use of independent judgment. The FBT is a final tax payable on a calendar quarterly basis by the employer and deductible as part of fringe benefit expense. Benefits subject to FBT are no longer included in employees' taxable income.

The grossed-up monetary value of a fringe benefit is determined by dividing the actual monetary value of the benefit by 68%. It represents the whole amount of the income realized by the employee, which includes the net amount that has been received plus the amount of fringe benefit tax due from the employee but paid by the employer.

"Fringe benefits" are defined as any goods, services or other benefits furnished or granted in cash or in kind by an employer to an individual employee, except rank and file employees such as, but not limited to, the following.

1. Housing.
2. Expense account.
3. Vehicles of any kind.
4. Household personnel, (e.g., maid, driver).
5. Interest on a loan at less than the market rate (currently set at 12%) to the extent of the difference between the market rate and the actual rate granted.
6. Membership fees, dues and other expenses borne by the employer for the employee in social and athletic clubs and similar organizations.
7. Expenses for foreign travel.
8. Holiday and vacation expenses.
9. Educational assistance to the employee and dependents.

10. Premiums for life insurance, health and other non-life insurance, and similar amounts in excess of what the law allows.

As regards housing and motor vehicles, the monetary value of the benefit is equal to 50% of the lease payment or the depreciation value of the property, whichever is applicable.

However, if the housing unit is situated in or adjacent (within 50 meters) to the business premises, the benefit is not taxable.

The following fringe benefits are not taxable.

1. Fringe benefits required by the nature of or necessary to the trade, business or profession or for the convenience or advantage of the employer.
2. Benefits authorized by and exempted from tax under special laws.
3. Employer contributions for the benefit of the employee to retirement, insurance and hospitalization benefit plans.
4. Benefits given to rank and file employees, whether or not granted under a collective bargaining agreement. However, these are subject to withholding tax on compensation, unless otherwise tax exempt.
5. De minimis (small value) benefits as defined in the rules and regulations.

Valuation of fringe benefits/In general, if a fringe benefit is granted in money or directly paid for by the employer, the value of the fringe benefit is the amount granted or paid for. If furnished in property and ownership thereof is transferred to the employee, the value of the fringe benefit is the fair market value of the property as determined by the Commissioner of Internal Revenue, pursuant to his power to prescribe real property values. If the fringe benefit is granted or furnished by the employer in property but ownership is not transferred to the employee, the value of the fringe benefit is equal to the depreciation value of the property.

Taxation of expatriates/Expatriates assigned in certain industries enjoy certain tax concessions. These expatriates include alien executives of offshore banking units, service contractors and subcontractors engaged in oil exploration activities, and regional headquarters and regional operating headquarters of multinational companies. They are taxed at 15% on their gross compensation income. The applicable FBT rate is also 15%. The grossed-up monetary value is determined by dividing the actual value of the benefit by 85%.

The FBT imposed on fringe benefits enjoyed by nonresident aliens not engaged in trade or business within the Philippines is 25% of the grossed-up monetary value of the fringe benefit. The grossed-up monetary value is determined by dividing the actual value of the benefit by 75%.

Capital gains and investment income/Nonresident aliens are taxed on Philippine-source capital gains, irrespective of their period of stay in the Philippines. The rates are 0.5% of the gross sales for those shares of stocks listed and traded in the stock exchange; 5% on the first PHP100,000 and 10% on the excess of the net capital gains for unlisted shares of stock; and 6% of the higher of the gross sales price or fair market value of real property sold. Capital losses are deductible only from capital gains. In computing net capital gains or losses from other capital assets, only 50% of the gain or loss is to be taken into account if the capital asset has been held for more than 12 months; otherwise, 100% of the gain or loss is to be considered.

A nonresident alien is also taxed on Philippine-source investment income such as interest, dividends and royalties at the rate of 20% (for those engaged in trade or business in the Philippines) or 25% (for those not engaged in trade or business in the Philippines) final tax (or a lower treaty rate). The tax is withheld at source, and the income is no longer subject to the graduated rates.

Resident aliens are taxed on their Philippine-source income at graduated rates. However, Philippine-source interest and royalties are taxed at 20%. Interest on residents' deposits under the expanded foreign currency deposit system (FCDU accounts) is taxed at 7.5%, while interest on long-term deposits or investment in the form of savings, common or individual trust funds and other investments evidenced by certificates, and so on, is exempt from tax, subject to certain conditions. Interest income on FCDU accounts of nonresidents is tax exempt. Royalties on literary works and musical compositions are subject to a final tax of 10%. Dividend income received from a domestic corporation is taxed at 10%.Tax rates for capital gains from shares of stock and real property are the same as those for nonresident aliens.

Deductions

Business deductions/Aliens, whether residents or not, who are receiving only salary or compensation income are not allowed any deduction against such income.

In the case of individuals engaged in business or the practice of a profession, the following expenses are allowed as deductions from gross income.

1. All ordinary and necessary expenses paid or incurred during the taxable year in connection with the trade, business or profession, including raw materials, supplies and direct labor.
2. Wages and other forms of compensation for personal services actually rendered, including the grossed-up monetary value of fringe benefits and travel expenses incurred in the pursuit of the trade or profession.
3. Business rentals.
4. Interest paid or incurred within a taxable year in connection with the conduct of a taxpayer's profession, trade or business, less an amount equal to a certain percentage of the interest income subject to final tax.
5. Entertainment, amusement and recreation expenses, not to exceed ceilings prescribed by the Secretary of Finance (none yet as of this writing).
6. Taxes.
7. Losses.
8. Bad debts.
9. Depreciation.
10. Charitable and other contributions, subject to certain limitations.
11. Research and development expenditures.

In lieu of these allowable deductions, an individual other than a nonresident alien may elect a standard deduction not exceeding 10% of gross income.

Nonbusiness expenses/Home mortgage interest, medical expenses, contributions, and other personal expenses cannot be claimed as deductions for income tax purposes. However, social security contributions are excluded from gross income.

Personal allowances/Resident aliens and, subject to certain conditions, nonresident aliens engaged in trade or business in the Philippines, are allowed a personal exemption of PHP20,000 if single, PHP25,000 if head of the family and PHP32,000 if married. An additional exemption of PHP8,000 for each dependent child (not to exceed four dependents) is allowed to married individuals. These personal and additional exemptions take the form of deductions instead of tax credits.

A family with gross income of not more than PHP250,000 for the year may deduct premium payments for health/hospitalization insurance up to a maximum of PHP2,400.

Tax credits

Aliens deriving income from foreign sources are not allowed a tax credit for foreign income taxes against Philippine income tax.

Other taxes

Social security taxes/The maximum annual social security and Philhealth contribution payable by a taxpayer for 2002 is PHP7,500.

Local taxes on income/The local governments are not authorized to impose any tax on income.

Tax administration

Returns/For tax purposes, a husband and wife must file one consolidated income tax return, but the tax is computed separately. Income that cannot be definitely attributed or identified as exclusive income of either spouse is divided equally between them. Generally, this results in lower combined tax liability than when the tax is jointly computed.

All individual taxpayers are required to file their returns on a calendar-year basis. The return must be filed on or before April 15 of the succeeding year.

Payment of tax/Generally, the income tax withheld from the salaries or compensation of aliens, resident or not, is equal to their final tax liability on such compensation. If not, the balance must be paid at the time the return is filed. In certain cases, income tax liability may be paid in two equal installments.

Tax rates

Rates of tax on income of aliens, resident or not, depend on the nature of their income—i.e., compensation income, income subject to final tax or other income (see below).

Compensation/For resident aliens and nonresident aliens doing business (as earlier defined) and receiving compensation income, the tax rates are as follows.

Taxable income		Tax on	Percentage
Over	Not over	Column 1	on excess
(Column 1)			
0	PHP 10,000	—	5
PHP 10,000	30,000	PHP 500	10
30,000	70,000	2,500	15
70,000	140,000	8,500	20
140,000	250,000	22,500	25
250,000	500,000	50,000	30
500,000		125,000	32

For example, the tax due on a taxable compensation income of US$25,000 (PHP1,285,100) is US$7,319 (PHP376,232).

Business income/For an individual, whether citizen or resident alien, who is self-employed or practices a profession, the tax rates are the same as above. An individual with a taxable compensation income of US$25,000 and a taxable business or professional income of US$25,000 will have a total taxable income of US$50,000 (PHP2,570,200) and will pay a total individual income tax of US$15,319 (PHP787,464).

In the case of nonresident aliens not doing business in the Philippines, the tax rate is a flat 25% of the gross income received from all sources within the Philippines.

Income subject to final tax/This is usually on passive investment income. For resident and nonresident aliens engaged in trade or business in the Philippines, the maximum rate is 20%; for nonresident aliens not engaged in trade or business in the Philippines, the rate is a flat 25%. (See also discussions under "Capital gains and investment income.")

INDIVIDUAL TAX CALCULATION

Calendar year 2002

Assumptions

1. Resident alien husband and wife with two dependent children.
2. Salary and allowances of husband arising from employment: salary of PHP600,000; living allowances of PHP100,000; housing benefits (100%) of PHP300,000.
3. Teaching salary of wife: PHP50,000.
4. Gross dividend income from investment in shares of stock of a domestic corporation of PHP10,000 (from 2001 profits).
5. Interest of PHP20,000 on peso bank account.
6. Capital gain on sale of shares of PHP5,000.
7. Taxes withheld by employer of husband at PHP173,640 and by employer of wife at PHP1,300.

Income tax computation

	Husband	Wife
Gross income (1):		
Salary	PHP 600,000	PHP 50,000
Living allowances	100,000	—
Housing benefits (300,000) (2)	—	—
	700,000	50,000
Deductions:		
Personal exemption	32,000	32,000
Additional exemption for dependent children (3)	16,000	—
	48,000	32,000
Net taxable income	PHP 652,000	PHP 18,000
Tax due:		
On first 500,000	PHP 125,000	
On remainder of 152,000 at 32%	48,640	
On first 10,000		PHP 500
On remainder of 8,000 at 10%		800
	173,640	1,300
Less—Tax withheld by employer per Form 2316 (4)	(173,640)	(1,300)
Net tax due	PHP 0	PHP 0

Notes:

1. The following items were not included in the income tax return because they are subject to final tax.

	PHP
Interest on peso bank account	20,000
Capital gain on sale of shares	5,000
Dividend income	10,000
Housing benefits	300,000

A final tax of 10% on dividend applies to income earned on or after January 1, 1998. Income that is part of retained earnings as of December 31, 1997, even if declared or distributed as dividends on or after January 1, 1998, is not subject to final tax.

2. Housing benefits are subject to FBT, payable by the employer. Under the revenue regulations governing the application of the fringe benefits tax, such benefits are taxable to the extent of 50% of the rentals for the house or living quarters used by the employee and paid by the employer if the lease contract is in the name of the employer.

   To compute the fringe benefits tax due, 50% of the rental payment is grossed-up before applying the 32% tax. Thus, the grossed-up value of PHP150,000 is PHP220,588, and the tax payable is PHP70,588.

3. The additional exemption for dependent children is to be claimed by the husband unless he explicitly waives his right in favor of his wife.
4. For individuals receiving salary and other allowances from one employer only, the tax due is usually equal to tax withheld, since the employer is required to compute and withhold the total tax due on the employee's compensation earned during the year, using the annual graduated income tax table, before paying the last payroll for the year.

5. The above individual tax calculation also applies to nonresident aliens engaged in trade or business in the Philippines for their Philippine-source income, except that personal exemptions are allowed only under certain conditions.
6. Exchange rate of the Philippine peso at December 28, 2001: US$1 = PHP51.404.

PwC contact

For additional information on taxation in Poland, contact:

Piotr Kowalski, Managing Partner
PricewaterhouseCoopers Warsaw
ul. Nowogrodzka 68
02-014 Warsaw, Poland
Telephone: (48) (22) 523 4000
Fax: (48) (22) 523 4040
e-mail: piotr.kowalski@pl.pwcglobal.com

Significant developments

As of March 1, 2002 the following capital gains are taxed at 20% flat tax rate: interest paid on current account, saving account, long-term deposits, bonds (including Treasury Bonds), and profits from investment funds. The new regulation applies to savings interest and capital gains paid out on or after March 1, 2002 and based on the agreements concluded on or after December 1, 2001.

In the period from January 1, 2002 to December 31, 2003 capital transfers abroad (as defined by the foreign exchange law) will be subject to 2% flat tax rate.

Territoriality and residence

An individual who is a resident of Poland or whose temporary stay in Poland is longer than 183 days in a given tax year is liable to tax on worldwide income, irrespective of the origin of the income. A nonresident who stays in Poland for less than 184 days in a given tax year is liable to tax only on income from work performed in the territory of Poland on the basis of a service agreement or an employment contract, irrespective of the place of payment or of other income arising in the territory of Poland.

Irrespective of the length of stay in Poland, a nonresident individual who has arrived in Poland for a temporary stay in order to take employment in a foreign small business enterprise, a company established with foreign participation, or a branch or representative office of a foreign company or bank is liable to tax only on income from work performed in the territory of Poland on the basis of a service agreement or an employment contract, irrespective of where this is paid, and other income arising in the territory of Poland.

Gross income

Employee gross income/Employee gross income includes basic pay, overtime pay, supplemental pay, awards and bonuses, compensation for unused holiday or vacation time, all other monetary amounts, and benefits in kind, as well as all other services obtained without payment.

Income from each source is defined as the surplus generated in a tax year of revenue over the costs of obtaining that revenue. If, in a given tax year, losses from any source of income (with a few exceptions) exceed the taxpayer's total income from all sources, the taxpayer has the right to carry forward each source's loss by deducting this loss over the next five years from income derived from the same source. Such deduction shall not exceed 50% of total amount of loss in any of the given five years. For individuals liable to Polish tax only on Polish-source income, earnings from some sources are taxed at a flat rate of 20% unless a bilateral tax treaty between Poland

and the individual's country of residence states otherwise. These types of earnings are the following.

1. Earnings from copyrights and other intellectual property rights such as trademarks, patents and designs, including proceeds of sale.
2. Income from the transfer of technology.
3. Income received from another party for the use of industrial, commercial or scientific equipment.
4. Income received from another party for information and expertise in the fields of industry, commerce or science.
5. Income from work in the fields of art, literature, science, education, journalism, and athletic activities, including income from participation in artistic, scientific and cultural competitions (independent work).
6. Income from work commissioned by national or local government authorities or administrative bodies or by the courts or the prosecutor's office (in particular, that of expert witnesses in all types of legal and administrative proceedings) and income received as a fee for participation in commissions established by local government bodies.
7. Income received as fees for membership on boards of directors, supervisory boards, committees, and other decision-making bodies of legal entities.
8. Income from rendering personal services on the basis of a specific work contract or self-employment contract concluded with a legal entity, an entity without legal personality or a business, as long as these services are not business services offered by the individual contractor to the public.
9. Income received from activities performed personally under management or similar contracts.

Capital gains and investment income/Income from the sale of real property is taxed separately at the rate of 10% if the sale is not carried out within the scope of regular economic activity and occurs within five years from the end of the tax year in which the purchase of the property took place (with certain exceptions, for example, when revenue from the sale of real property is spent for living accommodation of the taxpayer) or if a special tax relief was claimed, the sale occurs within ten years.

Income from the sale of objects (i.e., chattels) is taxed at the progressive tax rates if the sale occurs within six months from the date of acquisition of the object.

Income from the sale of State Treasury bonds (issued after 1989) and of bonds issued by self-governed territorial units (after 1997) is exempt from taxation until the end of 2003. Also part of income gained from sale of shares of companies formed to lease privatized property is exempt from income tax (per annum to the amount equal to half of the average monthly remuneration in the national economy).

Interest income from the granting of a loan is taxed at 20%, except where the granting of loans is the object of regular economic activity. Dividends from joint stock companies and shares in profits of limited liability companies are distributed from the net after-tax profit of a company. Dividends and these shares, as well as undistributable retained earnings, are not aggregated with income from other sources. This type of income is taxed at 15%.

Tax-exempt income/More than 100 types of income are tax exempt. The most important are as follows.

1. Monetary damages received on the basis of administrative law, civil law and other legal acts.
2. Receipts from property insurance and personal insurance claims (with certain exceptions).
3. Interest on State Treasury bonds as described above.
4. Money won in legally registered games of chance and lotteries.
5. Income of individuals if that income derives from funds established by international financial institutions or from resources allocated by other countries on the basis of agreements concluded between the Council of Ministers of Poland (or a Ministry with the consent of the Council of Ministers) and those institutions or countries.
6. Cash equivalents provided to employees when they need to use their own tools, goods and equipment to perform work.
7. Reimbursement of an employee's costs for relocation to another place of employment and reimbursement for the costs of settling in the new place (up to 200% of the monthly salary due to the employee in the month of transfer).
8. Limited daily allowances and other amounts due to employees for the duration of business trips.
9. Additional pay granted to employees temporarily transferred to work away from home and other benefits granted according to the principles and limits outlined in the rules for state employees.
10. Value of expenses covered by an employer for employees staying in hotels for employees and in quarters rented from private persons for the purpose of collective lodging of employees.
11. Limited payments to employees who use their private cars for company business.
12. Income originating outside Polish territory if an agreement for the avoidance of double taxation signed by Poland and the foreign country provides for such exemptions.

Deductions

Business deductions/There is a standard annual deduction for employees equal to 0.25% of the income ceiling of the first tax bracket (PLZ1,155.20 for 2002, or PLZ96.26 per month). If an employee derives income from several sources, the sum of deductions in a given tax year cannot exceed 4.5% of the above amount. An individual doing Independent work may claim various allowances, depending on the type of activities performed.

Nonbusiness expenses/The employee's portion of social security contributions is deductible from gross income before tax. Other expenses that may be deducted from gross income are membership fees of organizations that the taxpayer must join certain rehabilitation expenses (limited) and donations (for legal persons only, up to the limit of 10% or, in some cases, 15% of gross income). Starting from 2002 expenses borne for interest payments due on loans granted to the taxpayer for private accommodation purposes are also deductible.

Other major deductions include 19% of expenses incurred for, the purchase of professional equipment and education/self-training (both subject to limitations) and health insurance contributions.

Personal allowances/For 2002 there is a personal allowance of PLZ518.16 for all taxpayers.

Tax credits

A taxpayer's income originating abroad, if subject to Polish taxation (not exempt from taxation in Poland under an agreement for the avoidance of double taxation), is accumulated with income earned from work in Poland, and the tax is calculated on this sum according to the tax table. Income tax is then reduced by the amount of tax paid outside Poland. This tax credit may not exceed the tax calculated on total income multiplied by the proportion of income arising outside Poland to total income (unless a relevant double tax treaty provides otherwise).

Other taxes

Social security taxes/Until the end of 1998 the employer was subject to the entire obligation for Polish social insurance. From January 1, 1999, following the reform of the Polish social security system, the obligatory social security contribution has been divided between the employer and the employee.

Contributions to pensions and disability insurance are paid by employer and employee on total gross compensation until such cumulated compensation exceeds the contribution cap, which is set at 30 times the national average monthly salary estimated for a particular year (for 2002 the cap is set at PLZ64,620—approximately US$15,500).

When the individual's cumulative income reaches the cap limit, contributions are no longer paid to pensions and disability insurance either by the employee or the employer. Contributions to sickness (employee) and accident insurance (employer) as well as the Labor Fund and Guaranteed Benefits Fund (employer) are paid without a cap limit on total gross salary.

The contribution rates are as follows.

	Contribution amount	Paid by
Pensions and disability insurance	16.26% of total gross salary (up to the cap)	Employer
	16.26% of total gross salary (up to the cap)	Employee
Sickness insurance	2.45% of total gross salary	Employee
Accident insurance	1.62% of total gross salary	Employer
Labor Fund	2.45% of total gross salary	Employer
Guaranteed Benefits Fund	0.08% of total gross salary	Employer

The amount of the contribution paid by the individual is deductible from gross income before tax unless the income on which the social security contributions were calculated is exempt form personal taxation.

Foreign individuals engaged with a Polish entity under an employment contract are generally subject to security contributions, unless an exemption is provided under an applicable totalization agreement. However, according to the law there are some social security exemptions, including those listed below.

1. Service contracts if the individual is already subject to mandatory social security contribution from another source and the service contract is concluded with

another entity than the regular contract of employment and work under service contract is not provided for the former employer.

2. Management board fees.
3. Some benefits set out in the decree of the Minister of Labor and Social Policy of December 18, 1998 concerning "detailed rules of setting the assessment base for pensions contributions."

Health insurance/Polish nationals who are subject to social security insurance are mandatorily subject to national health insurance; alternatively, they can voluntarily participate in the state health insurance scheme. Foreign individuals are subject to obligatory health insurance only if they are subject to Polish social insurance and if they are residing in Poland on the basis of a visa with work permit or residence card or temporary residence card. Foreign individuals not referred to above are neither obliged nor entitled to participate (i.e., voluntarily) in the national health insurance system, unless an appropriate international agreement provides otherwise.

The monthly contribution rate for health insurance is 7.75% of the assessment base. In the case of obligatory participation, this is equal to the individual's gross income diminished by the social security contributions. In the case of voluntary participation, the amount of the assessment base is declared by the insured individual but cannot be lower than the average national salary as published from time to time. The contribution to health insurance is deducted from the individual's Personal Income Tax (PIT) and paid directly to the Polish Social Security Institution (ZUS).

Tax administration

Returns/Annual tax returns are to be prepared before the end of March and submitted to the proper tax office by April 15 of the year following a given tax year if the annual tax is assessed by the employer. If the annual tax return is self-assessed by the taxpayer, it is filed before the end of April of the year following a given tax year. The tax year is the calendar year.

Husbands and wives are treated as individual taxpayers unless they apply to have their incomes combined. This is permitted only when the spouses are married throughout the given tax year, are subject to the marital property law and are liable to Polish tax on their worldwide income.

Payment of tax/Individuals whose income derives from an employment contract, a commission contract or a retirement or disability pension will have tax withheld from sums due to them. The standard procedure is to withhold the full amount of tax due (at 19%, 30% or 40%) from an employee's monthly income. 19% is withheld monthly if income does not exceed PLZ37,024; 30% if income is between PLZ37,024 and PLZ74,048; and 40% thereafter (for 2002). The rate of withholding depends on the cumulative income earned from the start of the year to the month preceding the month for which the tax is withheld. Income is understood to include all revenues obtained by an employee in a given month less PLZ96,26 (standard monthly deduction from earnings in 2002).

Employers are obliged to prepare an annual tax reconciliation for most employees. Excess withholdings will be credited against the taxpayer's March advance tax payment.

Some taxpayers (e.g., those exercising a profession or receiving remuneration outside Poland) must file tax returns with the tax office, stating income earned in the given year. The tax returns must be filed before April 30 following the close of the fiscal year for which they are made, and differences between advance payments and the taxpayer's actual tax liability must be settled by this deadline.

Tax rates

Annual taxable income		Tax on Column 1	Percentage on excess
Over (Column 1)	Not over		
0	PLZ 37,024	—	19
PLZ 37,024	74,048	PLZ 6,516.40*	30
74,048		17,623.60	40

*The personal allowance of PLZ518.16 has been deducted.

A flat-rate income tax is payable by individuals performing business activities and partnerships with turnover below PLZ470,745 for the previous year (2001). The tax rates in 2002 are 8.5% for services, 5.5% for manufacturing and construction, and 3.0% for trade.

INDIVIDUAL TAX CALCULATION

Calendar year 2002

Assumptions

The taxpayer is nonresident and arrived in Poland for a temporary stay (over 183 days in a given tax year) in order to take employment in a company with foreign participation.

Tax computation

Annual salary		PLZ 234,400.00
Interest on savings		2,200.00
Benefit in kind—Accommodation		46,800.00
Income originating abroad		43,500.00
Long-term capital gain (originating abroad)		5,900.00
		332,800.00
Less—Income taxed at the flat rate:		
Interest on savings (1)	2,200.00	
Income originating abroad	43,500.00	
Long-term capital gain	5,900.00	51,600.00
Annual gross income		281,200.00
Less:		
Pension and disability insurance contribution (16.26%, up to the cap)	10,507.21	
Sickness insurance contribution (2.45% of gross income)	6,889.40	
Standard deduction	1,155.20	
Donation to a hospital	105.60	18,657.41
Annual taxable income		PLZ 262,542.59

Total annual tax due, taking account of personal allowance	PLZ 93,021.44
Less—Health insurance contribution (7.75% of gross income)	(20,444.76)
Less—Tax advances paid during year (2)	(58,000.00)
Additional tax payment to be made by April 30 of the following year	PLZ 14,576.68

Notes:

1. However, the taxpayer would have to pay 20% flat rate tax on interest on savings: Interest on savings = PLZ2,200.00; flat 20% = PLZ440.00.
2. Tax advances do not include the health insurance contribution to be paid monthly.
3. Exchange rate of the zloty at January 1, 2002: US$1 = PLZ3.98200.

Portugal

PwC contact

For additional information on taxation in Portugal, contact:

John Duggan
PricewaterhouseCoopers
Edificio Caravelas
Rua Dr. Eduardo Neves, 9 - 5°
1069- 053 Lisbon, Portugal
Telephone: (351) 21 791 4247
Fax: (351) 21 791 4289
e-mail: john.duggan@pt.pwcglobal.com

General note

The information below is current as of January 2002. For subsequent developments consult the contact listed above.

Significant developments

Portugal has introduced a new regime for the taxation of capital gains arising from the disposal of shares, which will only be in force as from January 1, 2003. Up to that date, the "old" regime, in force as of December 31, 2000, will apply.

The definition of residence in Portugal has been expanded to include transfer of residence of Portuguese nationals to territories with a more favorable tax regime, unless justifiable reasons can be demonstrated.

Territoriality and residence

For tax purposes, residents in Portugal are taxed on their worldwide income at progressive rates varying from 12% to 40%, while nonresidents are liable to income tax only on their Portuguese-source income, which includes not only the portion of the remuneration that can be allocated to the activity carried out in Portugal but also the remuneration that is borne by a Portuguese company or permanent establishment. Nonresidents are taxed at a flat rate of 25% on the above remuneration.

A person is considered to be resident who spends more than 183 days in aggregate in Portugal during the calendar year; or, although spending fewer than 183 days in Portugal during a calendar year, maintains a residence in Portugal that suggests habitual residence as of December 31 in that year.

The definition of "residence" in Portugal has been expanded to include the transfer of residence by a Portuguese national to territories with a more favorable tax regime, unless it is proved that the relocation is for a relevant reason, namely an assignment from a company domiciled in Portugal to that territory for a specific period of time. Should this condition apply, the individual is deemed to be tax-resident in Portugal, not only for the tax year of transfer, but also for the following four years.

It should be noted that residence status applies for an entire tax year, which is the calendar year. Split-year residence is not possible under domestic law.

Married couples are deemed to be resident taxpayers if one spouse is resident for tax purposes in Portugal.

Taxable income

Employment income/Employment income/remuneration is specifically defined in the personal income tax code and covers all payments in connection with work carried out in Portugal, such as salary, bonuses, commissions, tax reimbursements, redundancy payments, pensions, allowances (such as cost-of-living and housing allowances) and benefits in kind (such as company cars), regardless of from where the payment is made.

Domestic and foreign travel allowances in excess of those permitted to employees of state departments are also taxable as employment income.

Mileage and lunch allowances are not taxable within the thresholds established for employees of state departments.

Benefits in kind/In general, benefits in kind provided by an employer are subject to income tax at the employee level. There are specific provisions regarding taxation of employer-provided housing or housing allowances and company cars.

The taxable benefit from the use of a company car is 0.75% of the acquisition cost of that car, multiplied by the number of months of use of the car. If the company car is then acquired by the employee, a further benefit in kind will correspond to the difference (if positive) between the average market price of the car and the price paid by the employee to acquire the car plus the total amount already taxed to the employee as a benefit in kind as result of using the car.

Pensions/The first €7,805.60 of pension income is tax exempt, unless the taxpayer's total income exceeds a certain limit (approximately €72,000 for 2002), in which case, the exemption is reduced by the above excess.

Termination of employment/Redundancy payments are taxable on the portion that exceeds one and a half the average remuneration paid during the last 12 months of service, multiplied by the number of years of service, except if a new employment contract or service contract is made with the employer or a related person within 24 months from the date of termination of the employment contract.

Capital gains/Portugal has introduced a new regime for taxation of capital gains arising from the disposal of shares, which will only be in force as from January 1, 2003. Up to that date, the "old" regime, in force as of December 31, 2000, will apply.

Further to the above, in accordance with the Budget Law for 2002, shares acquired up to December 31, 2002 that are held for more than 12 months are exempt from personal income taxes. A special rate of 10% will apply to capital gains on the disposal of these shares if they are held for less than the specified 12 months.

For shares acquired as from January 1, 2003, 50% of the capital gains arising from the disposal of those shares is liable to income tax progressive rates in force for 2003. Capital gains amounting up to €2,500 will be exempt from income tax, but should be disclosed on the annual tax return for the purposes of determining the tax rate applicable to total taxable income.

If, as from January 1, 2003, shares are disposed of through a financial institution in Portugal, any capital gains exceeding the above limit are liable to withholding tax at a rate of 10%.

Fifty percent of capital gains on real estate are taxed as regular income unless the property sold is the taxpayer's primary residence and the sale proceeds, reduced by the value of any outstanding loans relating to the purchase of the first property, are reinvested in another residence in Portugal within two years of the sale, or during the 12 months before the sale.

Capital gains on the disposal of shares or a property located in Portugal by nonresidents, which are not borne by a permanent establishment in Portugal, are fully taxable at a flat rate of 25%.

Fifty percent of dividends paid by companies that have a permanent establishment in Portugal to resident individuals are liable to Portuguese personal income tax and must be disclosed on the annual tax return.

A 15% withholding tax applies to dividends paid by resident entities. This tax can be set off against the individual's tax liability. A further 5% inheritance tax is also leviable on dividends paid by companies that are tax resident in Portugal.

Dividends paid by companies that are not resident in Portugal are liable to income tax and should be fully disclosed on the annual tax return. A credit against the tax liability in Portugal is available for the lower of a) the tax paid in the foreign country on those dividends; or b) the amount of tax payable in Portugal on that income.

For dividends paid by countries with which Portugal has signed a double taxation treaty, the tax credit should not exceed the percentage established in the treaty.

Should these dividends be paid through a paying agent in Portugal, a 20% final tax will be deducted on those dividends, unless the dividends are paid to an investment fund in Portugal.

Interest income arising from current or saving accounts on Portuguese banks is taxed at 20% for both residents and nonresidents.

Business and professional income/Income from commercial, industrial and agricultural activity; a sole trader; or intellectual rights (when earned by the original owner) may be taxed either in accordance with a new simplified regime or based on the taxpayer's accounts. The simplified regime will apply only to taxpayers who, not having opted for organized accounts, have a turnover lower than €149,739.37 or a gross business and employment income lower than €99,759.58. Under this simplified regime the above income is taxed on 0.20 of sales of products or 0.65 of income arising from other business and professional services.

Deductions

Rental income/Maintenance and repair expenses may be deducted from rental income, to the extent that they are dully documented. Municipal property tax paid with regard to the rented property may also be deducted against the rental income.

Pension income/Union fees (in the part that does not constitute a direct contribution for health, education, elderly support, home, insurance, or social security benefits) may be deducted against pension income up to a limit of 1% of the taxpayer's gross employment or pension income. This deduction is equivalent to the union fees increased by 50%.

Tax credits

The following tax credits are available for 2002 against the amount of tax due by an individual.

1. Personal tax credits:
    a. Single person: €208.80;

b. Married couple (husband and wife): €348;
c. Per dependent child: €139.20;
d. Per ascendant: €174;
e. Single parents: €278.40.

The above tax credits are increased by 50% for individuals with proven disabilities, with an exception to ascendants.

2. Health expenses:

   A tax credit of 30% of the nonreimbursed health expenses, if properly documented, including health expenses (exempt from value-added tax (VAT), or subject to VAT at a rate of 5%) incurred by the taxpayer and his/her spouse and dependants, expenses incurred by the taxpayer's ascendants with an income lower than the national minimum wage (€348 per month) and interest on loans made to bear the mentioned expenses.

   A tax credit of 30% of all other health expenses resulting from a medical prescription is also available, with a limit of €53.81 or 2.5% of those expenses (whichever is higher).

3. Education expenses:

   30% of all education expenses up to a limit of €556.80. This limit is increased by €104.40 for each dependent, provided the number of dependent children studying is three or more.

4. Housing interest or rent:

   30% of interest or capital repayments on loans made for the acquisition of principal private residences or the rental of a permanent house, limited to €517.64. This tax credit is not available when the loans were granted by entities which are resident in territories with a more favorable tax regime (as defined by the Portuguese tax authorities) and that do not have a permanent establishment in Portugal to which that income may be recharged.

5. Life insurance premiums and contributions to complementary social security schemes:

   25% of premiums with a limit of €53.81 for single person and €107.63 for married couples.

6. Health insurance premiums:

   25% of premiums with the limit a €71.75 for a single person and €143,50 for married couples. These limits are increased on €35.88 for each dependent child.

7. Contributions to individual retirement saving plans (PPR), educational plans (PPE), or individual retirement/educational plans (PPR/E):

   25% of the above contributions with a limit of €648.44, per taxpayer, or 5% of the total taxable income, if lower.

   These limits may be increased in 5%, for taxpayers between 35 and 50 years old, and 10%, for taxpayers younger than 35 years old.

8. Payments to *Planos Poupança em Acções* (special saving plans in shares):

   7.5% of the above payments limited to €498.80 per taxpayer, on the basis that no reimbursements are made within six months after the payments.

9. Acquisition of shares at public offerings made by the Portuguese State:

   5% of the acquisition cost of shares of companies being privatized until December 2002, up to a maximum of €170.09, for a single person, and €340.18, for married couples. For employees of the company being privatized, a tax credit of 7.5% of the acquisition cost with a limit of €256.38 for a single person and €512.76 for married couples, will be allowed.

10. Annual deposits in *Contas Poupança-Habitação* (savings accounts used to fund housing acquisition and maintenance):

    A tax credit of 25%, limited to €564.28 is allowed.

11. Acquisition of new equipment for the utilization of renewable energy or natural gas consumption:

    30% of the total costs of acquisition of the above-mentioned equipment or other complementary equipments, limited to €700.

12. Acquisition of personal computers, hardware or software:

    25% on the acquisition expenses limited to €179.38.

13. Expenses of lawyers and other legal services:

    20% of the above expenses, limited to €134.28.

14. Fees and expenses paid to retirement homes in respect of parents and grandparents whose income does not exceed the national minimum salary (€348 per month):

    25% with a limit of €303.41.

    The combined amount of credits for education and retirement home expenses is limited to €697.03.

15. Donations to the central or local government or any government agency or body:

    Donations to a church, religious institution, charity, museum, school, library or other recognized social welfare or cultural entity: tax credit of 25%, limited to 15% of the individual's income tax liability.

16. International double taxation:

    Tax credits are available on foreign source of income.

Alimony payments or other amounts defined by court order are deductible up to the amount of the individual's taxable income.

Other taxes

Social security

1. Employee contributions:

   Individuals are subject to social security contributions on their gross income at 11%. These contributions cover family, pension and unemployment benefits.

   Foreign residents may be exempt from social security in Portugal if they contribute to a compulsory social security system in a European Union (EU) country or a country with a bilateral social security agreement with Portugal.

   An employed individual is entitled to an earned income deduction of 72% of the annual national minimum salary (€3,006.72), or of the actual social security contributions, whichever is higher.

2. Employer contributions:

   In addition to social security contributions at a general rate of 23.75%, employers must make contributions to an insurance fund for occupational accidents. These contributions vary according to work and risk classification.

   Please note that members of statutory boards of companies are subject to different social security rates (10%, with respect to contributions due by the employee, and 21.25% regarding contributions due by the employer). The contributions of members of statutory boards are based on their effective remuneration but subject to a monthly minimum and maximum income level of €348 and €4,176, respectively (at 2002 value).

3. Self-employed individuals are subject to a social security scheme that enables them to choose between two available schemes and the level of income on which contributions are paid:
   a. Compulsory contribution scheme, subject to a 25.4% rate;
   b. Extended contribution scheme, subject to a 32% rate.

   Self-employed individuals are entitled to select the monthly income level on which social security contributions are paid, which may vary between €348 (national minimum salary for 2002) and €4,176 (12 times the national minimum wage). The selected level of income must be communicated to the Social Security authorities. Upon default, it will be based on the minimum level of income or on the last reported level under the earlier scheme.

Local taxes/Municipal property tax is charged on the registered value of real estate.

Tax administration

Tax returns/Tax returns must be filed by March 15 of the year following the tax year in question, for individuals that have only earned employment income and/or pensions, or April 30 of that following year, in all other cases. The tax year is the calendar year.

Married couples file joint returns. Income is divided by two to determine the tax rate. The resulting tax liability is then doubled, regardless of the earnings ratio. The same procedure applies to nonmarried couples living together for two years or more who opt to be taxed as married couples.

Payment of tax/Portugal uses a PAYE (pay-as-you-earn) system, adjusted by tax return filing. Additional payments or refunds are made based on the tax returns filed.

Tax rates

Resident income tax rates

Taxable income		Tax rates	Deductible amount
From	To	%	
0	€ 4,100.12	12	0
€ 4,100.13	6,201.42	14	€ 82.00
6,201.43	15,375.45	24	702.14
15,375.46	35,363.52	34	2,239.69
35,363.53	51,251.48	38	3,654.23
51,251.48		40	4,679.26

As mentioned above, special rates apply to capital gains and investment income.

INDIVIDUAL TAX CALCULATION

Calendar year 2002

Assumptions

1. Resident foreigner and spouse, with two dependant children under 18.
2. One spouse without income.
3. The proceeds on the sale of a property are not reinvested in another private residence in Portugal.
4. Election to waive Portuguese social security contributions.

Tax computation

	€	€
Earned income:		
Salary		70,000.00
Tax withheld (assume 28.5%)	19,950.00	
Capital gain on sale of house (reduced price index because owned for more than two years)		10,000.00
Interest on saving account (1)		2,000.00
Tax withheld at 20%	400.00	
		82,000.00

	Option A (1)	Option B (1)
Taxable income:		
Salary	70,000.00	70,000.00
Capital gains (2)	5,000.00	5,000.00
Interest on saving account (1)	2,000.00	—
Deductions:		
Social security	3,006.72	3,006.72
	73,993.28	71,993.28
Split income (coefficient to be used: 2)	36,996.64	35,996.64
Tax rate	38%	38%
Deductible amount	3,654.23	3,654.23
Tax on declared income	20,808.99	20,048.99
Tax credits:		
Married personal credit	348.00	348.00
Children personal credit (3)	278.40	278.40
School expenses (4)	556.80	556.80
Health expenses (5)	150.00	150.00
Tax withheld on interest on saving account (1)	400.00	—
Tax withheld on account on salary	19,950.00	19,950.00
Refund on tax paid	874.21	1,234.21
Tax payable		
Net income (6)	€ 57,924.21	€ 56,284.21

Notes:

1. Taxpayers may opt to declare the interest on saving accounts and, therefore, to consider the tax withheld on that interest, at a 20% tax rate, as a payment on account. Options A and B reflect both scenarios.
2. As mentioned, on the basis that the proceeds on the sale of the property were not reinvested in another private residence in Portugal, only 50% of the capital gains on the sale are taxed as regular income.
3. €139.20 per dependent child, for 2002.
4. Limit for 2002: €556.80.
5. 30% on the assumed amount of health expenses (€500).
6. (Total income – tax withheld + refund on tax paid).
7. Exchange rate of the Euro at January 3, 2002: US$1 = €1.106.

Puerto Rico

PwC contact

For additional information on taxation in Puerto Rico, contact:

Marta Acevedo
PricewaterhouseCoopers LLP
Banco Bilbao Vizcaya Tower, Suite 900
254 Muñoz Rivera Avenue
Hato Rey, Puerto Rico 00918
Telephone: (1) (787) 772-7929
Fax: (1) (787) 766-1094
e-mail: marta.acevedo@us.pwcglobal.com

General note

This entry is repeated from the 2001/2002 edition. For more up-to-date information, consult the contact listed above or Mark Friedlich at mark.friedlich@us.pwcglobal.com.

Significant developments

There have been significant tax and regulatory developments in the last year.

Territoriality and residence

All bona fide residents of Puerto Rico (regardless of citizenship) are subject to Puerto Rico income tax on their worldwide income at graduated rates. Generally, a bona fide resident for income tax purposes is a person residing in a "bona fide" dwelling in Puerto Rico for a period of 183 days or more. Nonresident individuals are taxable only on their income from sources within Puerto Rico and on gross income effectively connected with the operation of a trade or business within Puerto Rico.

Gross income

Employee gross income/In general, all compensation for personal services rendered within Puerto Rico, of whatever kind and in whatever form or place paid, is includable in gross income. If services are paid for with property other than money, the fair market value of the property is included in gross income. Other compensation, such as housing allowances, school allowances, cost-of-living allowances, and tax reimbursements, is also generally includable.

Capital gains and investment income/Resident individuals are subject to tax at the graduated rates on net income from capital gains, interest, dividends, rents, and distributions of partnership profits from sources within and without Puerto Rico. Puerto Rico's tax laws accord favorable tax treatment to long-term capital gains versus ordinary income by allowing the excess of net long-term capital gains over net short-term capital losses to be taxed at a fixed 20% rate. Otherwise, the taxpayer may opt to include this gain as part of gross income in the income tax return for the year in which the gain is recognized and pay a tax in accordance with normal tax rates.

Interest income received from banks and thrift institutions in Puerto Rico, to the extent it exceeds an annual exclusion amount of US$2,000, is eligible for a flat 17% tax in lieu of taxation at graduated rates, provided the payer is authorized in advance to withhold the 17% at source.

Dividends received from Puerto Rican corporations, as well as from foreign corporations that have derived 80% or more of their gross income during the preceding three-year period from Puerto Rican sources, other than dividends paid from certain tax-exempt income, are eligible for a flat 10% tax in lieu of taxation at graduated rates, provided the tax is withheld at source, as generally required by law.

Nonresidents engaged in a trade or business in Puerto Rico (i.e., performing services within Puerto Rico) are taxed on their net income from Puerto Rican–source capital gains and investment income at the same rates as resident individuals.

Nonresident U.S. citizens not engaged in a trade or business in Puerto Rico are subject to Puerto Rican taxes on net income from Puerto Rican–source capital gains, interest, dividends, rents, and distributions of partnership profits at the same rates as resident individuals. Nonresident aliens not engaged in a trade or business within Puerto Rico are subject to Puerto Rican taxes on the gross income from such sources at a flat rate of 29%, or at a higher graduated rate if that rate exceeds the flat rate of 29%, except that the flat 10% tax rate is applicable to certain dividends, as described above for resident individuals.

Deductions

Business deductions/Resident individuals can deduct, to the extent not reimbursed, ordinary and necessary business expenses in connection with a trade or business, subject to a limitation of US$1,500 or 3% of adjusted gross income (AGI) from salaries, whichever is less. In the case of married persons living together who opt to file separate returns, the limitation would be US$750 or 3% of AGI from salaries, whichever is less, for each. Nonresident individuals can deduct such expenses to the extent they are connected with income that is effectively connected with the operation of a trade or business within Puerto Rico.

Nonbusiness expenses/The law provides an option to itemize deductions or to claim a standard deduction. The standard deduction for 2000 is US$3,000 for married individuals filing a joint return, US$2,000 for single individuals and married individuals living separately, US$2,600 for heads of households, or US$1,500 for married individuals filing separate returns.

Resident individuals can deduct as itemized deductions property tax on residential property, fees paid on automobile license plates, casualty losses to the taxpayer's principal residence, and, subject to limitations, mortgage interest, rent paid on a house constituting the taxpayer's principal residence, certain costs for the education of dependents in elementary or secondary schools (including interest paid on student loans at university level), medical expenses, charitable contributions, interest paid on student loans, and childcare expenses.

Additional deductions (that can be claimed even if the taxpayer elects to claim the standard deduction) include, subject to certain limitations, interest on an automobile loan, contributions to IRA accounts, contributions to government pension plans, two wage earners' deductions, and deductions for veterans, young people who work, and ordinary and necessary expenses.

Nonresident U.S. citizens are allowed to deduct most of the nonbusiness deductions in the same proportion that Puerto Rican–source AGI bears to total AGI from all sources.

Nonresident aliens are generally not allowed any of the nonbusiness deductions listed above.

Personal allowances/Resident individuals and nonresident U.S. citizens are allowed as a deduction a personal allowance of US$1,300 if single or married not living with spouse, US$3,000 (per couple) if married and filing a joint return or head of household, or US$1,500 if married and filing a separate return. In addition, a US$1,600 allowance is allowed for each dependent who is a university student (not over 26 years of age). A US$1,300 allowance is allowed to all other dependents.

No personal allowances are granted to nonresident alien individuals.

Tax credits

A foreign tax credit is available to all individuals (both U.S. citizens and aliens) resident in Puerto Rico. However, for aliens, there is a requirement that the foreign country of citizenship must grant a similar credit to U.S. citizens residing in that country.

Other taxes

Social security taxes/The U.S. social security combined tax rate of 7.65% applies in Puerto Rico in the same manner and uses the same wage base and tax rates as in the United States. For 2000, the old-age, survivors, and disability insurance (OASDI) rate of tax is 6.2% of the taxable wage base of US$76,200. The Medicare rate of 1.45% applies to all wages paid. For self-employed individuals, the rates are 12.4% of self-employment income up to the base of US$76,200 and 2.9% on total self-employment income, respectively. (No deduction of this amount is permitted in determining AGI for Puerto Rico income tax purposes.)

Local taxes on income/Other than the municipal license tax on gross business income of a sole proprietor, there are no local taxes on individual income.

Tax administration

Returns/Husbands and wives living together may elect to file separate or joint returns. There are different tax rate schedules for each case. Taxpayers may file their returns on a calendar- or fiscal-year basis.

Resident individuals must file a Puerto Rico return if gross income for the taxable year exceeds the personal exemptions and standard deductions allowed. Nonresident U.S. citizens must file a Puerto Rico return if their Puerto Rican-source income exceeds the personal exemptions, unless the tax has been fully paid at source. Nonresident aliens must file a Puerto Rico return for their Puerto Rican-source income regardless of the amount, unless the tax on such income has been fully paid at source.

Tax returns are due by the 15th day of the fourth month following the close of the taxable year in the case of residents and nonresident U.S. citizens, and by the 15th day of the sixth month following the close of the taxable year for nonresident aliens.

Payment of tax/Wages and salaries of resident individuals are subject to withholding tax. Generally, if taxpayers have sizable income not subject to withholding tax, they will be required to make quarterly payments of estimated tax. Any income taxes due after estimated payments are to be paid in full on or before the 15th day of the fourth month following the close of the taxable year (April 15 for calendar-year individual taxpayers).

Tax rates

Rates in effect for taxable year 2000 are as follows.

1. Married person living with spouse and filing a joint return, married person not living with spouse, single person, head of household, estate, or trust:

Taxable income Over (Column 1)	Not over	Tax on Column 1	Percentage on excess
0	US$ 2,000	—	7.5
US$ 2,000	17,000	US$ 150	11.0
17,000	30,000	1,800	16.5
30,000	50,000	3,945	29.5
50,000		9,845	33.0

2. Married person living with spouse and filing separate return:

Taxable income Over (Column 1)	Not over	Tax on Column 1	Percentage on excess
0	US$ 1,000	—	7.5
US$ 1,000	8,500	US$ 75	11.0
8,500	15,000	900	16.5
15,000	25,000	1,972	29.5
25,000		4,922	33.0

Alternative minimum tax/Taxpayers with AGI of US$75,000 or more are subject to an alternative minimum tax at the following rates: over US$75,000 but not over US$125,000—10%; over US$125,000 but not over US$175,000—15%; over US$175,000—20%.

Additional tax/Taxpayers with taxable income in excess of US$75,000 are subject to a 5% additional tax on the excess; for married individuals living with their spouse and filing separate returns, the additional tax will be 5% on the excess over $37,500. This additional tax is limited in 2000 to $6,655 plus 33% of the taxpayer's personal exemption and credits for dependents.

INDIVIDUAL TAX CALCULATION

Year ending December 31, 2000

Assumptions

The taxpayer is a resident of Puerto Rico for the entire year 2000, married and living with spouse and two children, filing a joint return, and electing the optional 17% withholding tax on certain interest income.

Tax computation

Gross income:		
Salary		$ 80,000
Interest from Puerto Rican banks	8,000	
Less—Annual exclusion	(2,000)	
	6,000	
Less—Amount subject to optional 17% withholding tax (see below)	(6,000)	—
Gain on sale of stock (held more than six months)		5,000
Total gross income		85,000
Less—100% of capital gain		5,000
Adjusted gross income		80,000
Deductions (itemized):		
Mortgage interest	5,500	
Real estate tax on personal residence	500	
Charitable contributions (excess over 3% of AGI)	700	6,700
		73,300
Personal allowances:		
Married, living with spouse	3,000	
One university student	1,600	
One nonuniversity student	1,300	5,900
Taxable income		$ 67,400
Income tax:		
On first 50,000		$ 9,845
On remainder (17,400) at 33%		5,742
Tentative regular tax liability		$ 15,587
Alternative minimum tax (10% of AGI)		$ 8,000
Regular tax liability		15,587
Optional 17% withholding tax on interest (17% of 6,000)		1,020
Alternative tax on long-term capital gain (20% of 5,000)		1,000
Total tax liability		$ 17,607

Note:

The monetary unit is the U.S. dollar.

PwC contacts

For additional information on Qatar, contact:

Abbas M Alradhi, Country Senior Partner
Tony Mukbel, Resident Senior Manager
PricewaterhouseCoopers
HSBC building, 4th floor
P.O.Box 6689
Doha, State of Qatar
Telephone: (974) 415700
Fax: (974) 416040
e-mail: abbas.m.alradhi@bh.pwcglobal.com
tony.s.mukbel@qa.pwcglobal.com

Absence of taxation

Income tax is not imposed on individuals in Qatar.

Note

Exchange rate (selling) of the Qatari Riyal at January 1, 2002: US$1 = QR3.64.

PwC contacts

For additional information on taxation in Romania, contact:

Ron Barden
Joe Kerrane
PricewaterhouseCoopers Romania
Opera Center
1–5 Costache Negri Street
Sector 5 Bucharest
Romania
Telephone: (40) (1) 202 8500
Fax: (40) (1) 202 8700
e-mail: ron.barden@ro.pwcglobal.com
joe.kerrane@ro.pwcglobal.com

Significant developments

As of January 1, 2002, Government Ordinance 73/1999 was replaced by Government Ordinance 7/2001. From January 1, 2002 the maximum marginal rate of 40% is applied to monthly income in excess of ROL10,200,000 (approximately US$312).

Equivalents in this entry assume the March 2002 exchange rate.

Territoriality and residence

New global income tax legislation entered into force on January 1, 2002. It applies to the following individuals.

1. Romanian individuals domiciled in Romania are liable to tax on revenues arising either in Romania or abroad (the methodological norms have not yet been published, thus it has not yet been clarified whether income received from abroad is simply to be declared as part of global income or if it will be taxed separately from Romania-source income).
2. Romanian individuals without Romanian domicile are taxed on income obtained from Romania through a fixed base in Romania or during a period of presence in Romania of more than 183 days in any 12-month period.
3. Foreign individuals are taxed on their income obtained from Romania through a fixed base in Romania or during a period of presence in Romania of more than 183 days in any 12-month interval.

Income is considered as deriving from a Romanian source if the place of origin of the income of the natural person or the place where the income is earned is situated in the Romanian territory, irrespective of where it is paid.

Individuals may be exempt from individual income taxation under the regulations of the international conventions for the avoidance of double taxation between Romania and their country of residence.

Work permits/A number of important changes to the work permit legislation have been introduced as of March 1, 2000.

1. Work visas and work permits are issued for foreign individuals who intend to be employed in Romania based on a Romanian employment contract.
2. A work visa is granted by the Romanian diplomatic offices in the countries where the foreign individual is domiciled, based on a certificate that can be obtained from the Romanian Ministry of Labor.

3. A work permit is granted by the Romanian Ministry of Labor, based on the work visa and an extensive set of documents to be provided by the foreign individual.
4. No work permits are required for foreign individuals who perform some specifically mentioned activities for less than 30 days or for the sole shareholders of Romanian companies.
5. Work permits are generally issued for six months with the possibility for six months extensions, and they are kept by the employer.
6. Foreign individuals who have arrived in Romania to be employed before March 1, 2000, do not need a work visa (and respectively a certificate for the citizens of Republic of Moldova) in order to obtain/extend the work permit. The Ministry of Labor should receive a confirmation from the Passport Office or Consular Department within the Ministry of Foreign Affairs that the Romanian entrance visa was granted for the purpose of employment.

Work visas are not required in order to obtain a work permit in the following cases.

1. Citizens of states with which Romanian has concluded mutual agreements for the elimination of visas at border crossing (e.g., citizens of Republic of Moldova).
2. Foreign citizens studying or graduating in Romania.
3. Foreign citizens entering the country for business purposes.
4. Family members of foreigners who already have work permits.
5. Family members of Romanian citizens.

EU (European Union) citizens are allowed to enter Romania without a visa.

Gross income

Employee gross income/Employee gross income includes basic pay, overtime pay, supplemental pay, awards and bonuses, compensation for unused holiday or vacation time, and all other monetary amounts and benefits in kind, as well as other services obtained without payment. The income from each source is defined as the total amount of revenues received during a month, irrespective of the period in which it was generated.

Salary tax continues to apply to salary income (at a marginal rate of 40% for amounts exceeding approximately US$312 per month).

Income tax applies to income resulting from salaries; a freelance profession; rental of real estate; copyrights; agricultural activities (in agricultural associations without legal personality); independently organized art, entertainment or sports; prizes; and pensions. Individual income taxes also apply to any gains, interest and other earnings of a permanent or casual nature.

Certain sources of income are exempt from individual income tax, for example income obtained by foreign consultants from programs approved by the Romanian government with other governments or international government or non-government organizations.

Benefits in kind are basically taxable only if the costs of providing them are considered as deductible expenses; the private use if company cars is generally taxable at 1.7% on a monthly basis of vehicle value proportionately divided by the private mileage covered. Other benefits in kind are taxed at their market value.

The value of in-kind benefits is assessed and is taxed in the month they are received. Tax settlement is made at the same time with payment of last salary rights pertaining to the respective month.

According to Romanian law, there are no concessions for short-term residents.

Capital gains and investment income/Capital gains are taxed at 1%. The 1% tax is a withholding tax and is considered a final tax. According to the Romanian legislation, the capital gain represents the positive difference between the selling price and the purchase price per types of securities, less applicable commissions and the difference between the selling price and the nominal value on the case of social shares. Tax is to be withheld by the buyer.

Certain capital investment income is exempt from tax, such as income from interest on demand accounts (except from bank accounts operated for business purposes), interest on state treasury bonds and the withdrawal of funds from trust funds. Dividends from joint stock companies are distributed from the net after-tax profit of a company. Dividends and shares in profits, as well as undistributable retained earnings, are not aggregated with income from other sources. The dividends are subject to a 5% withholding tax when paid by the company. No income tax is levied at this stage.

Individual income tax of 1% will be calculated on interest and withheld by the bank at the moment it is registered in the current account or in the deposit account (when capitalized) or at repurchase of deposit certificates.

Nonresidents/Nonresidents are subject to the following withholding taxes unless a bilateral tax treaty between Romania and the individual's country of residence states otherwise.

1. 10% on interest.
2. 10% on commissions on commercial transactions.
3. 15% on revenues from technical assistance, expertise, training, and other services.
4. 15% on royalties obtained through concession of patents, licenses, trademarks, and other intellectual rights.

Tax-exempt income/The most important types of tax-exempt income are specified below.

1. Income from the sale of movable and immovable assets.
2. Income from trading securities.
3. Interest on bank deposits, certificate of deposits and interest on state treasury bonds.
4. Reimbursement of an employee's relocation expenses, according to specific legislation, if the transfer is in the company's interest.
5. Limited daily allowances due to employees for the duration of business trips.
6. A personal deduction of ROL1,600,000 (approximately US$49) per month. A related professional deduction is available, but only where the recipient's principal employment is under a permanent labor contract. The professional deduction amounts to 15% of the personal deduction, currently ROL240,000 (approximately US$7.3). Only Romanian individuals are entitled to benefit from these deductions.
7. Payments during the period of notice to quit.
8. Income originating outside Romanian territory.
9. Pensions up to ROL5,000,000 (US$153) monthly.

Deductions

Business expenses/Taxpayers are not entitled to standard annual deductions.

Nonbusiness expenses/There are no allowable nonbusiness expenses.

Personal allowances/There is a personal and professional deduction of ROL1,840,000 (approximately US$56) per month (see above).

Other taxes

Social security taxes/From April 1, 2001, employers must pay social security contributions, etc., calculated on gross salary, as follows.

Social Security	23.33% (applied to a maximum of three average national salaries)
Health Fund	7% (not capped)
Unemployment Fund	5% (not capped)
Solidarity Fund	2% (not capped)
Chamber of Labor Commission	0.75%, 0.25% or Labor Office Commission (5% on gross salary plus social security) for local employees of representative offices, embassies and airline agencies

From April 1, 2001, an employee makes the following contributions.

Social Security	11.67% (applied to a maximum of three average national salaries)
Health Fund	7% (not capped)
Unemployment Fund	1% (not capped)
Payroll tax	According to applicable tax bands

The average gross national salary for 2002 is estimated at ROL5,582,000 (approximately US$171).

As of March 1, 2002, a new law regarding the Unemployment Fund became effective. According to the new provisions, foreign citizens performing services in Romania based on a local employment agreement are obliged to pay the Unemployment Fund contribution.

The persons covered by social security are Romanian citizens, as well as citizens of other states or stateless persons for the period of time they are domiciled or have their residence in Romania.

The benefits provided include old age pension, disability pension, widow's and orphan's pension, sick leave, and maternity leave allowances, among others.

The law also stipulates the change to be introduced in the computation of state social security contributions (the quotas being annually determined by the law on the state social security budget).

The method of computation of social security benefits has also changed for medical leave, maternity leave, leave for childcare for infants up to 2 years of age, and old age pension, among others.

Foreign citizens working in Romania on the basis of a work permit and a labor contract registered with the Labor Office are considered Romanian employees (whether or not they are deemed to be resident in Romania) and are liable for Romanian social security contributions.

A foreign citizen who is not resident in Romania and is not employed or paid by an employer who has a permanent establishment in Romania has no liability to pay social security contributions and no requirement to prove payment of social security contributions in another territory.

Local taxes on income/There are no local taxes on income.

Tax administration

Returns/The income tax is deducted from an employee's salary and paid by the local employer through a bank payment order at the time monthly salaries are paid. There is no requirement for individuals to submit tax returns if they are receiving only salary income form the same employer during the year. For these individuals the employer has the obligation to register with the Romanian Tax Authorities (RTA) a fiscal form.

For Romanian individuals receiving income other then salary a global individual income tax return must be submitted to the RTA by March 31 of the following year (it is expected that for the year 2002 the RTA extended the deadline to April 30, 2002).

The following individuals domiciled in Romania are among those who must submit individual income tax returns.

1. Romanians working or seconded abroad.
2. Romanians who have two jobs at any one time.
3. Romanians who receive interest and/or dividends and/or rental income from abroad.
4. Independent consultants.
5. Collaborators.

A foreign citizen working in Romania on a foreign employment contract must file a tax declaration letter within 15 days following the month to which the payment relates. The Romanian beneficiary of the foreign employee's services must file a monthly notification letter within the above period. The expatriate has to appoint a fiscal representative to observe the tax compliance rules for the period(s) the expatriate is not in the country. The fiscal representative and the expatriate can be held jointly responsible for failure to observe the tax compliance rules.

Husbands and wives are treated as individual taxpayers; the concept of income splitting does not exist in the Romanian legal system.

Penalties for late submission of tax declarations amount to 10% for a delay of up to 30 days, 30% for a delay of up to 60 days and 50% for a delay exceeding 60 days.

In addition to the global individual income tax declaration, taxpayers must submit special declarations for income obtained from abroad, income obtained from independent activities, incomes obtained from ceding the usage of goods (for example leasing of property or machinery), and so on.

For income that has borne final tax at source (i.e., from dividends, transfer of shares, interest, other income, and pensions), the payer of the income and therefore of the tax (by withholding) must submit an informative declaration. The payers of such income who are making payments for more than 20 beneficiaries must use computer-generated forms.

Tax registration/The following classes of individuals and legal entities obtaining income from activities rendered in Romania must register with the Romanian Tax Authorities to obtain a tax number (fiscal code) and a tax certificate.

1. Romanian individuals without domicile in Romania and foreign individuals who obtain income from activities carried out in Romania must submit a tax registration declaration within 15 days of crossing the Romanian border.
2. Individuals who carry out commission, mandate, representation, royalty, or other similar contracts must register within 15 days from the beginning of the activity.

The Romanian Tax Authorities must be informed within 15 days of any change in the data.

Payment of tax/Individuals whose income derives from an employment contract, a commission contract or a retirement or disability pension will have tax withheld from the sums due them. The standard procedure for a local employment contract is to withhold the full amount of tax due (at the levels shown below) from the employee's monthly income.

In the case of a foreign employee who is paid in hard currency, the calculation of tax due is made by translating the monthly gross income into lei at the official exchange rate of the last day of said month, and the taxes will be calculated and paid from this amount.

As of January 1, 2001, the entire individual income tax is to be paid to the State Budget.

Excess withholdings will be given back to the employee within 60 days after the reconciliation.

Late payment penalties currently amount to 0.1% per day, with an additional 0.5% for each month of delay.

Tax rates

Annual rates/For the year 2002 the maximum marginal rate of 40% is applied to annual income in excess of ROL122,400,000 (approximately US$3,743).

Annual income		Tax on	Percentage
Over (Column 1)	Not over	Column 1	on excess
0	ROL 21,600,000	—	18
ROL 21,600,000	55,200,000	ROL 3,888,000	23
55,200,000	87,600,000	11,616,000	28
87,600,000	122,400,000	20,688,000	34
122,400,000		32,520,000	40

Monthly rates/For the year 2002, the maximum marginal rate of 40% is applied to monthly income in excess of ROL10,200,000 (approximately US$312).

Monthly income				
Over	Not over		Tax on Column 1	Percentage on excess
(Column 1)				
0	ROL 1,800,000	....	—	18
ROL 1,800,000	4,600,000	....	ROL 324,000	23
4,600,000	7,300,000	....	968,000	28
7,300,000	10,200,000	....	1,724,000	34
10,200,000		....	2,710,000	40

INDIVIDUAL TAX CALCULATION

Assumptions

The taxpayer is nonresident, arrived in Romania for a temporary stays (over 183 days in any 12-month period) and is employed by a foreign employer.

Tax computation

Monthly basis (assuming the expatriate has only a foreign employment agreement)

	ROL
Monthly gross income	73,000,000
Tax on salary	27,830,000
Net monthly income	45,170,000

Annual income

	ROL
Annual gross income	876,000,000
Tax on salary	333,960,000
Net monthly income	542,040,000

Note:

The exchange rate of the lei (National Bank of Romania rate) on March 11, 2002: US$1 = ROL32,698.

PwC contact

For additional information on taxation in the Russian Federation, contact:

Lionel Endsley
PricewaterhouseCoopers
Kosmodamianskaya Nab. 52, Bld. 5
113054 Moscow, Russia
Telephone: (7) (095) 967 6000
Fax: (7) (095) 967 6001
e-mail: lionel.endsley@ru.pwcglobal.com

General note

This entry is repeated from the 2001/2002 edition. For more up-to-date information, consult the contact listed above or Mark Friedlich at mark.friedlich@us.pwcglobal.com.

Significant developments

Starting January 1, 2001, Part II of the Russian Tax Code came into force, abolishing the personal income tax and social security legislation previously in effect.

The following information on individual taxation in the Russian Federation is accurate as of January 1, 2001. For subsequent developments, refer to the contact above.

Territoriality and residence

For both Russian and foreign individuals, tax residence in Russia is determined by the number of days in the calendar year in which a person is present in Russia. For personal income tax purposes, an individual is considered resident if physically present in Russia for 183 or more days in a calendar year (days of arrival and departure are counted as one day).

Russian residents are liable to tax on their total worldwide income received in a calendar year. Nonresidents are taxed on income received from sources in Russia. Income tax on Russian-source payments to nonresidents will usually be withheld at source.

Some tax treaties provide for longer periods of exemption from Russian taxation on the Russian-source income of foreign residents. Consequently, the details of any applicable tax treaty should always be examined before any period of work in Russia.

Income from Russian sources is determined as income received from property located in Russia, remuneration for activity performed in the Russian territory, dividends received from the Russian legal entities, etc. The most important change in the definition of the Russian-source income provides that income received for work in the Russian territory is subject to Russian personal income tax even if it is paid by a foreign legal entity from abroad.

Gross income

Employee gross income/All income received in the course of a calendar year from employment is subject to personal income tax. This includes all earnings, bonuses, and other forms of payment or remuneration. For expatriates, taxable income includes allowances paid to employees living in Russia and compensation for school fees, food, travel by the employee's family on holiday, and other nonbusiness purposes. Benefits-in-kind are taxed at their monetary equivalent (market price).

Capital gains and investment income/There is no separate capital gains tax. Instead, gains from the disposal of property and assets are subject to income tax at the normal rate. The taxable amount is calculated as the difference between sale proceeds and historical cost or statutory exemption. The statutory exemption is provided for all property sold during a calendar year and is limited to RUB1,000,000 in the case of real estate and RUB125,000 for other property, as set by the Russian government. Proceeds received from the sale of property are fully excluded from taxation if the property is owned for five years (immovable) and three years (other). This statutory exemption does not apply to gains on assets disposed of in the course of entrepreneurial activities.

The following types of income are taxable.

1. Interest income from deposits outside Russia.
2. Dividends on shares and income from other financial assets.
3. Income from leasing property, both in Russia and abroad.
4. Royalties from the creation, publication, performance, and use of works of literature, art, and science, as well as from inventions, discoveries, and industrial prototypes.
5. Interest and gains from deposits in banks and other credit institutions in Russia (above set limits).

The following income is not taxable.

1. Reimbursement by an employer for expenses arising from a work-related change of domicile and relocation allowances within set limits.
2. Payments by an employer in compensation for injury or damage to health incurred in the performance of employment duties.
3. Severance gratuities payable upon dismissal (limits may be applicable).
4. Business travel expenses within limits.

Deductions

Nonbusiness expenses/Donations to qualifying charities are deductible from taxable income (within limit of 25% of the individual's income).

Expenditures incurred by an individual on the acquisition or construction of an apartment or house and payment of interest on bank loans obtained for these purposes are allowed as a deduction of up to RUB600,000 plus amount of interest. This is a once-in-a-lifetime exemption.

Personal allowances/Individuals are granted a deduction of RUB400 per month for the taxpayer and RUB300 per month for a child. These deductions are provided until the individual's cumulative annual income reaches RUB20,000.

Individuals can also deduct from taxable income costs of education of themselves and their children (in Russian-licensed institutions), medical services (for themselves and relatives), and medicine. The limit on each type of deduction is RUB25,000.

Tax credits

Residents of Russia are entitled to a credit against their Russian tax equal to the amount of foreign tax paid on income taxable in Russia. The credit applies if this foreign tax credit exemption is provided by a relevant double taxation treaty. The credit cannot exceed the amount of tax payable in Russia on income received outside of Russia.

Other taxes

Social security taxes/All Russian and resident foreign legal entities employing Russian citizens are required to make Unified Social Tax (UST) payments with respect to their employees. The maximum amount of the UST is 35.6%. Regressive tax rates are applied if certain requirements are fulfilled. Thus, the minimum UST rate is RUB105,600 plus a 2% (5% in the year 2001) contribution to the Pension Fund on income exceeding RUB600,000. Russian pension contributions are not mandatory for foreign employees under Russian law; thus, the major part of the UST may not be payable with respect of income of foreign nationals. The UST is the liability of the employer only; employees are not liable to make any social security contributions.

Employers are also obliged to pay an obligatory contribution of insurance against accidents at work and professional diseases. The rate of this contribution varies from 0.2% to 8.5% of the wage fund, depending on the type of activity of the employer.

Gift and inheritance tax/Gift and inheritance tax is payable by Russian and foreign citizens on transfers of assets situated in Russia, whether the transfer is by way of gift or inheritance. Rates vary from 5% to 40%, depending on the value of the transfer and the relationship of the transferor and transferee. Transfers from one spouse to another are exempt.

Property tax/Property tax is imposed on property situated in Russia and owned by foreign citizens. The tax applies to buildings, houses, and apartments and is levied at the rate of 0.1% to 2% of the value of the property. Private helicopters, yachts, and boats are liable to this tax, and the amount varies according to the horsepower of the engine. Private cars are subject to vehicle-owner's tax, which applies to local and foreign corporate and individual vehicle owners. It is payable annually (no later than August 1 in Moscow and St. Petersburg) at rates per horsepower, depending on the vehicle's engine capacity; for vans, the tax rate varies per horsepower.

Tax administration

Returns and payment/Tax in respect of employment earnings and certain other payments must be deducted at source by the entity making the payment. This includes tax on income from the performance of labor under civil law contracts. Individuals receiving income from foreign sources and some other types of income from which tax is not withheld at source are responsible for the declaration of taxable income and payment of Russian tax. The procedure of tax returns submission and tax payment for such individuals is described below.

Declarations of income must be submitted no later than April 30 following the reporting year. The tax payment is generally due by July 15 of the year following the reporting year. Tax overpaid may, at the taxpayer's request, be either refunded or applied against future liabilities.

A declaration of actual income received during the period of stay in Russia must also be made one month prior to departure from Russia. Joint returns for a husband and wife are not permitted. There is no provision for a taxable year other than the calendar year.

Tax rates

Income tax is payable in rubles at the rates applicable to certain income categories. Earnings in foreign currency are converted into rubles at the exchange rate of the

Central Bank of the Russian Federation on each date income is received. The tax rate is 13% for all types of income, except that listed below.

The tax rate of 35% is established in respect of the following income.

1. Winnings paid by the organizers of lotteries, totes, and other risk-based games (including slot machines).
2. The value of any winnings and prizes received during contests, games, and other events conducted for the purpose of advertising goods, work, and services, in excess of the limits.
3. Insurance payments under voluntary insurance agreements in excess of the limits.
4. Interest income on bank deposits in excess of the amount calculated, based on three-quarters of the Central Bank current interest rate on ruble deposits during the period for which the interest is accrued and 9% annual interest on foreign currency deposits.
5. Saved amounts of interest on the taxpayer's borrowed funds in excess of the limits.

The tax rate is established at 30% in respect of dividends and any income received by individuals that are not residents of the Russian Federation for tax purposes.

Exchange rate issues

Foreign income is convertible into rubles for tax calculation purposes at the exchange rate quoted by the Central Bank of the Russian Federation, effective on the date of receipt of the income. Tax payments are to be made in rubles only.

Exchange rate of the ruble at April 2001: US$1 = RUB28.86.

PwC contact

For additional information on taxation in St. Lucia, contact:

Richard N. C. Peterkin
PricewaterhouseCoopers
PricewaterhouseCoopers Centre
Pointe Seraphine
P.O. Box 195
Castries, St. Lucia, W.I.
Telephone: (1) (758) 452 2511
Fax: (1) (758) 452 1061

Significant developments

The government of St. Lucia circulated a draft new Income Tax Act in 1999 that contained a number of new proposals to simplify the tax legislation, consolidate amendments over the last ten years, and introduce a number of new measures. After considerable public discussion on the new proposals, the draft was withdrawn for further study, and a Tax Committee was established to review any future proposals. It is unlikely that any new omnibus tax act will be introduced in 2000, and no major changes are expected to the existing legislation.

Amendments made to the Act in 1999 in respect of resident individuals included the following items.

1. Provisions for the deduction of a maximum of EC$3,000 of interest paid on student loans for tertiary education.
2. Provisions for the deduction of qualifying registered pension annuity plans up to a limit of one-tenth of assessable income or EC$8,000.
3. Provisions for the deduction of up to a maximum of EC$6,000 per annum invested in Registered Home Ownership Savings Plans to be used wholly for the acquisition or construction of an owner-occupied house.

Territoriality and residence

St. Lucia income tax is imposed on the following.

1. Income of an individual ordinarily resident in St. Lucia that accrues to the individual directly or indirectly from all sources whether in or outside St. Lucia.
2. Income of an individual resident but not ordinarily resident in St. Lucia that accrues to the individual directly or indirectly from all sources in St. Lucia and income accrued from sources outside St. Lucia to the extent that the income is remitted to St. Lucia.
3. Income arising in St. Lucia to a nonresident, and income accrued from sources outside St. Lucia to the extent that the income is received in St. Lucia.

An individual is regarded as resident in St. Lucia if one of the following applies.

1. The individual's permanent place of abode is in St. Lucia and the individual is physically present for some period of time in the income year.
2. The individual is physically present in St. Lucia for not less than 183 days in the income year.

3. The individual is physically present in St. Lucia for a continuous period of less than 183 days in the year of income but is resident in the immediately preceding or succeeding year of income.

Gross income

Employee gross income/Employees resident in St. Lucia are taxed on their salary and on the value of any allowances or benefits, whether in cash or otherwise, received from an employer. Taxable benefits include employer-provided automobile and housing (except where representative occupation can be established) but do not include travel and entertainment allowances where the employee substantiates expenditure in the performance of duties to the extent of the allowances.

Capital gains and investment income/Capital gains are not taxable to individuals ordinarily resident in St. Lucia. Investment income in the form of dividends and bank interest from corporations or banks in St. Lucia is exempt from income tax. For individuals not ordinarily resident in St. Lucia (i.e., those present for a short term), such income, if arising outside St. Lucia, is taxable only to the extent that it is remitted to St. Lucia.

Deductions

Business deductions/Employees may deduct expenses incurred wholly and exclusively in the performance of the duties of their employment, but only to the extent that these expenses are not reimbursed by the employer.

Nonbusiness expenses/Nonbusiness expenses are not deductible.

Personal allowances/In determining chargeable income, a resident individual, upon due claim, is allowed the following deductions.

	EC$
Personal allowance	12,000
Spouse allowance	1,500 (Note 1)
Maintenance or alimony (under court order)	Full amount
Child allowances	1,000–2,000
Deduction for higher education	5,000
Deduction for life insurance, other retirement benefits:	
Premiums paid in St. Lucia (maximum)	8,000
Premiums paid outside St. Lucia (maximum)	3,000
Owner-occupied property:	
Mortgage interest (maximum)	15,000
Property taxes	Actual
Insurance premiums	Actual
Upkeep and maintenance	Actual
Donations to charitable, religious, educational institutions (under deed of covenant for at least three years)	(Note 2)
Medical expenses	Actual
Purchase of shares in building or cooperative societies	Up to 3,600

Notes:

1. Reduced dollar-for-dollar to the extent the spouse's assessable income exceeds EC$1,500.
2. Actual, but may not exceed 25% of assessable income.

Tax credits

A tax credit for foreign tax paid is granted where income accrues to a resident in St. Lucia when that income has been taxed in another country with which there is no treaty or where the income is not covered by the applicable treaty. This credit is the lesser of the tax payable in the other country or the tax charged in St. Lucia.

Other taxes

Social security taxes/The individual's share of National Insurance Scheme contributions (for retirement, sickness and disability benefits) is 5% of gross salary up to a maximum contribution of EC$150 per month (i.e., on a monthly salary of EC$3,000).

Local taxes on income/There are no other taxes on income.

Tax administration

Returns/Separate returns are required from married persons where the other spouse has income in that spouse's own name. For employed persons, the taxable year is the calendar year.

Payment of tax/There is withholding of tax from salaries. Employed persons must file returns within three months of the end of the income year, and any additional tax assessed is payable upon filing.

Tax rates

Tax rates on chargeable income from January 1, 2000 are as follows.

Taxable income			
Over (Column 1)	**Not over**	**Tax on Column 1**	**Percentage on excess**
0	EC$ 10,000	—	10
EC$ 10,000	20,000	EC$ 1,000	15
20,000	30,000	2,500	20
30,000		4,500	30

INDIVIDUAL TAX CALCULATION

Assumptions

1. Married person resident in St. Lucia with two children; one child attends a university overseas; Spouse has no assessable income.
2. Employment income: EC$150,000, net of National Insurance contributions.
3. Director's fees: EC$6,000.
4. Bank interest received: EC$12,000 (bank in St. Lucia).
5. Dividend income received: EC$8,000.
6. Mortgage interest paid: EC$18,000.
7. Life insurance premiums: EC$9,000. (Insured amount: EC$250,000).
8. Capital gain on sale of investments: EC$60,000.

Tax computation

Gross income:		
Income from employment		EC$ 150,000
Director's fees		6,000
Bank interest received		12,000
Dividends received		8,000
Capital gain on sale of investments		60,000
		236,000
Deduct—Tax-exempt income:		
Bank interest	12,000	
Dividends	8,000	
Capital gain	60,000	80,000
		156,000
Less—Allowances:		
Personal allowance	12,000	
Spouse allowance	1,500	
Child allowance (1 x 1,000)	1,000	
Child higher education allowance (1 x 5,000)	5,000	
Life insurance premiums (restricted)	8,000	27,500
		128,500
Less—Owner-occupied property expenses:		
Mortgage interest (maximum)	15,000	
Property taxes (say)	2,000	
Insurance premium (say)	1,500	
Upkeep and maintenance (say)	1,000	19,500
Chargeable income		EC$ 109,000
Tax thereon:		
On the first 30,000		EC$ 4,500
On the remaining 79,000 at 30%		23,700
		EC$ 28,200

Note:
Exchange rate of the Eastern Caribbean dollar at January 1, 2002: US$1 = EC$2.670.

PwC contact

For additional information on taxation in Saudi Arabia, contact:

Sami B. Al Sarraj, Managing Partner
Al Juraid & Company
10th Floor, North Tower
King Faisal Foundation Bldg.
P.O. Box 8282
Riyadh 11482, Saudi Arabia
Telephone: (966) (1) 465 4240
Fax: (966) (1) 465 1663
e-mail: salsarraj@aljuraid.com

Absence of taxation

Income tax is not imposed on individuals in Saudi Arabia.

Note

Exchange rate of the Saudi Riyal at January 1, 2002: US$1 = SR3.75.

Senegal

PwC contact

For additional information on taxation in Senegal, contact:

Aziz Dièye
Coopers & Lybrand Dièye
2 Place de l'Indépendence
Immeuble SDIH (BP 188)
Dakar, Senegal
Telephone: (221) 821 85 88, 821 86 71, 822 30 24
Fax: (221) 821 75 94

General note

This entry is repeated from the 2001/2002 edition. For more up-to-date information, consult the contact listed above or Mark Friedlich at mark.friedlich@us.pwcglobal.com.

General note

The information in this entry is current as of January 1998. For subsequent developments, consult the contact listed above.

Territoriality and residence

Senegal taxes its citizens and residents on their worldwide income from whatever source, unless it is explicitly excluded by tax treaty. Individuals who do not have their tax domicile in Senegal (nonresidents) are subject to tax only on their income arising from Senegal.

Individuals are deemed to be domiciled in Senegal if Senegal is the place of their permanent home or if they stay in Senegal for six months.

Gross income

Employee gross income/All compensation paid to an employee is taxable, as is the income from business and the exercise of professional activities. Compensation includes, but is not limited to, salaries, wages, and allowances.

Capital gains and investment income/Gains and income from investments are taxable as ordinary income. The gains on disposals of fixed assets are tax free if they are reinvested within three years; otherwise, they are taxable as ordinary income.

Dividend and interest income is first subject to the withholding tax on personal property (movable capital). It is then categorized as investment income for individual income tax purposes, except for interest income from *bons de caisse* issued by banks, which is taxed at 20% and is exempt from all other taxes. Taxable investment income consists of net income after application of the withholding tax mentioned above. This withholding tax will be deductible from individual tax.

Deductions

Business deductions/The deductions allowed are as follows.

1. Pension contribution—up to 10% of total remuneration.
2. Transportation—CFAF11,910 per month.
3. Allowance of up to 15% on graduated tax for income salary solely.

Nonbusiness expenses/The deductions allowed are as follows.

1. Life insurance premiums—up to 5% of net taxable income.
2. Charitable contributions listed by *Arrêté du Ministère des Finances*—up to 2% of net income.
3. Interest on loans for acquisition of, maintenance of, or repairs to a principal residence.

Personal allowances/There are no personal allowances.

Tax credits

Generally, individuals are not entitled to a foreign tax credit.

Other taxes

Social security taxes/Contributions to the social security fund are made at the rate of 7% of gross salary, with a maximum of CFAF60,000 per employee. The contribution is paid only by the employer.

Local taxes on income/There are no local taxes on income.

Tax administration

Returns/Husbands and wives can file joint returns. These joint returns are optional. Taxable years other than the calendar year are not permitted.

Payment of tax/For employees domiciled in Senegal, Senegalese employers are required to withhold from the taxpayer's monthly salary a sum representing tax liability, calculated from the official printed table.

Individuals who are not subject to this requirement must pay their current year's tax in two provisional installments and a final payment.

Tax rates

Income tax/Income tax is composed of two elements: a proportional rate and a graduated rate.

Proportional rate/A proportional rate is due on the net result of each category of income (salaries and wages of employees, real property income, noncommercial activities income or corporate income tax, income from movable capital). Net income is determined by deducting allowable expenses.

The following rates are in effect.

	%
Salaries and wages over CFAF600,000	14
Real property income	20
Corporate income or BNC tax on excess over CFAF330,000	28
Income from movable capital	8 to 16

Graduated rate/A graduated rate is applicable to net total taxable income, which is determined by aggregating net income of each category of income and deducting common allowable expenses.

To calculate the graduated rate, the following procedure is used.

1. The net total taxable income is divided by the number of shares to obtain the income per share.
2. Tax rates from the tax schedule below are then applied to a share of income.
3. The tax corresponding to the share of income is then multiplied by the number of shares and aggregated in order to calculate total tax payable.

The tax rates are as follows.

Taxable income		Tax on	Percentage
Over (Column 1)	Not over	Column 1	on excess
0	CFAF 600,000	—	0
CFAF 600,000	890,000	—	18
890,000	1,010,000	CFAF 52,200	22
1,010,000	1,410,000	78,600	25
1,410,000	2,475,000	178,600	28
2,475,000	3,540,000	476,800	30
3,540,000	7,650,000	796,300	35
7,650,000	9,650,000	2,234,800	40
9,650,000	12,650,000	3,034,800	45
12,650,000		4,384,800	50

Minimum tax/Minimum tax is payable by all persons earning salaries and wages who are resident in Senegal, provided their employers are resident or established in Senegal. The yearly tax payable is as follows. Taxpayers are divided into classes according to their actual income. The tax liability is graduated: CFAF18,000, CFAF6,000, CFAF4,800, CFAF3,600, and CFAF900. The tax is assessed on both heads of household and on their spouses, whether the spouse is an employee or not.

INDIVIDUAL TAX CALCULATION

Calendar year 1997; Income year 1996

Assumptions

Resident alien husband and wife with two children; number of dependents supported by taxpayer—three.

Tax computations

Computation of proportional rate

Salary		CFAF 40,000,000
Less:		
Pension fund (at 10%)	4,000,000	
Transportation	142,920	4,142,920
Net taxable income		35,857,080
Add:		
Capital gains (interest income)	800,000	
Noncommercial activities income	500,000	1,300,000
Total net taxable income		CFAF 37,157,080
Salary tax payable: (35,857,080 – 600,000) x 14%		CFAF 4,935,991
Interest income tax payable: 800,000 x 16%		CFAF 128,000
Long-term capital gain tax payable: (500,000 – 330,000) at 28%		CFAF 47,600

Computation of graduated rate

Total net taxable income		CFAF 37,157,080
3 shares; income per share (37,157,080 ÷ 3)		CFAF 12,385,693
Income tax payable:		
On the first 9,650,000	3,034,800	
On the remaining 2,735,693 at 45%	1,231,061	CFAF 4,265,861
On 3 shares		CFAF 12,797,583

Tax payable

Proportional rate on salary	CFAF 4,935,991
Proportional rate on capital gain	128,000
Proportional rate on noncommercial activities income	47,600
Graduated rate	12,797,583
Minimum tax	36,000
Total income tax payable	CFAF 17,945,174

Note:

Exchange rate of the CFA franc at December 31, 1998: US$1 = CFAF563.00.

Parity remains fixed between the CFA franc, used in 14 French-speaking African countries, and the French franc. The rate is CFAF100 = FF1. The convertibility of the CFA franc continues to be assured, as long as transfers are made through banking channels.

PwC contact

For additional information on taxation in Singapore, contact:

Jenny Goh
PricewaterhouseCoopers Services Pte Ltd.
8 Cross Street
#17-00 PWC Building
Singapore 048424
Telephone: (65) 6236 3388
Fax: (65) 6236 3715
e-mail: jenny.goh@sg.pwcglobal.com

Significant developments

Details of the Supplementary Retirement Scheme (SRS) were released. These include conditions whereby a contributor can qualify for 50% exemption from tax on the amount withdrawn. In addition, although the amounts withdrawn by foreigners and Singapore permanent residents are subject to withholding tax at the prevailing corporate tax rate, resident individuals may file a tax return to claim the excess of withholding tax paid over the tax applicable on the contributions withdrawn based on resident rates. Nonresident individuals may also file a tax return to claim the excess of the withholding tax paid over the higher tax that is applicable by applying 15% or by applying resident rates on the taxable amount of SRS contributions. Amounts contributed would qualify for tax relief but would be subject to capping rules similar to Central Provident Fund (CPF) capping rules. This scheme was implemented on April 1, 2001.

Two new stock option plans were introduced—the Entrepreneurial Employee Stock Option and the Company Stock Option Plans. Qualifying stock option gains under either plan would be exempt from tax, but the amount of exemption differs in each plan.

All bands of personal tax rates (for tax residents only) have been reduced; the reduction ranges from 2% to 5% with effect from year of assessment 2002.

Territoriality and residence

Income is taxable when it accrues in or is derived from Singapore, whether or not the individual is resident in Singapore. Income derived from sources outside Singapore is taxable only if it is received in Singapore by a resident individual.

Individuals are resident in Singapore if they reside there except for such temporary absence therefrom as may be reasonable and not inconsistent with a claim to be resident in Singapore. Individuals who are physically present or who exercise an employment (other than as a director of a company) in Singapore for 183 days or more during the year preceding the year of assessment are treated as resident for that year of assessment. As a concession, an expatriate who stays in Singapore for a consecutive period spanning three calendar years (not necessarily three complete calendar years) is considered a resident.

Resident individuals are entitled to certain personal allowances and are subject to graduated tax rates ranging from 0% to 26%. Nonresident individuals are not entitled to any personal allowances and are subject to tax at the corporate rate of 24.5%. As a concession, their employment income is taxed at the higher of 15% or the graduated resident rates. This concession does not apply to nonresident directors.

Gross income

Employee gross income*/*If the employment is exercised in Singapore, employment income is treated as earned there and is therefore taxable in Singapore. The countries of the employer, of payment and of the beneficiary of the services are irrelevant in determining the country of source of employment income.

Employment income includes salaries, bonuses, allowances, perquisites, and benefits in kind. Certain benefits in kind are accorded preferential rates, which are less than the actual cost to the employer. The benefit of rent-free housing is normally calculated as the lesser of 10% of the assessable emoluments (including gains from stock options) and the annual (rental) value of the property. By concession, only 20% of the cost of home-leave passage is assessed on the expatriate employee. The amount of tax borne by the employer is treated as additional income of the employee.

Short-term visiting employees are not subject to tax on income from an employment exercised in Singapore if the employment does not exceed 60 days. This exemption, however, does not apply to a public entertainer or to a company director.

Area representatives of nonresident companies who reside in and use Singapore as a base for activities extending to other countries are assessed on the remuneration relating to the time actually spent in Singapore or on the remuneration received in Singapore, whichever is greater.

All retirement benefits other than CPF benefits, including gratuities and pensions, are taxable. CPF is the national pension scheme in Singapore. The scheme is only available to Singapore citizens and permanent residents and it provides a lump sum at the normal retirement age, consisting of past contributions made at prescribed rates by the employee and the employer, as well as interest thereon. However, CPF contributions made under certain circumstances are deemed to be part of employment income, which is taxable.

With effect from April 1, 2001, the new SRS scheme was implemented. Withdrawals from this scheme may be fully taxable or 50% taxable, depending on whether certain predetermined conditions have been fulfilled.

Capital gains and investment income*/*There is no capital gains tax in Singapore. Where an individual enters into a series of capital transactions, however, the tax authorities may take the view that the individual is carrying on a business and assess that person to income tax accordingly.

Although there is no tax on capital gains, as part of the antispeculation measures introduced by the Singapore government in May 1996, profits from properties sold within three years of their purchase are taxable as income. The taxable proportion decreases by one-third with each year added to the holding period. Besides real property, the tax also applies to short-term gains from the sale of shares in a private company holding 75% or more of its assets in the form of real property or shares in property companies. These special rules apply only to properties located in Singapore. With effect from October 13, 2001 (i.e., for sales contracted on or after this date), the antispeculation measures were abolished, with the result that such gains will no longer be subject to income tax, except those which are considered revenue in nature under the general tax principles.

Income from interest, dividends, rents, royalties, etc., derived from Singapore is taxable whether or not the individual is resident in Singapore. However, certain types of interest received by a nonresident individual are exempt from income tax, such as interest on deposits with banks and on qualifying debt securities. Investment income derived from sources outside Singapore is taxable in the hands of resident individuals only if it is received in Singapore. Statutory provisions govern the basis of treating foreign income as received in Singapore.

Deductions

Business deductions/Where an individual carries on a trade, business, profession, or vocation, deductions are allowed for all outgoings and expenses incurred wholly and exclusively in the production of the income being assessed, including capital allowances (fiscal depreciation) on most fixed assets except for land and nonindustrial buildings.

Nonbusiness expenses/An individual can deduct annual subscriptions paid to professional institutes or societies in which membership is generally required as a condition of employment. A deduction may also be claimed for donations to approved charities. Interest expense may be deductible, provided it is incurred wholly and exclusively in the production of income. Mortgage interest is, therefore, deductible only where the property concerned yields income. With effect from January 1, 2001, deductions can also be claimed for donations made in the form of shares that are listed on the Singapore Exchange and unit trusts readily marketable in Singapore.

No deductions are allowed for medical expenses or for any other personal or household expenditure.

Singapore citizens and permanent residents are allowed deductions against their taxable income for contributions made to the CPF or an approved pension/provident fund but subject to the following limits.

1. Contributions made up to the limit prescribed in the CPF Act.
2. For a self-employed individual, the deduction for contributions made is restricted to the lesser of S$25,920 or 36% of assessable business income, whichever is lower.

Any life insurance premium is deductible, but the total deduction (i.e., contributions to the CPF and life insurance premium) is restricted S$5,000. For Singapore citizens and permanent residents, their CPF contributions must be less than S$5,000 before they can claim this deduction.

With effect from April 1, 2001, a deduction for SRS contributions of up to 15% (for Singapore citizens and permanent residents) and up to 35% (for foreigners) of income can be claimed against the income earned in the year in which the contributions are made (subject to income capping rules similar to CPF income capping rules).

Personal allowances/For year of assessment 2002 (income year 2001) the following amounts are deductible from the assessable income of a resident individual to arrive at the income subject to tax.

1. Personal allowance—S$3,000.
2. Wife allowance—S$2,000.
3. Handicapped spouse allowance—S$3,500 for the maintenance of a handicapped spouse whose income does not exceed S$2,000 for the year.
4. Earned income allowance—Lesser of actual earned income or S$1,000 if age is under 55; increased for individuals who are 55 and over or are handicapped.

5. Child allowance:
   a. Individuals having up to four children (under the age of 16 years)—First, second and third child S$2,000 each; fourth child S$2,000 only if born after 1987;
   b. Handicapped child—S$3,500;
   c. Where a child is undergoing university or similar education abroad—Allowance up to twice the amount of the normal deduction for that child may be allowed, subject to certain conditions;
   d. Increased child allowances for better-educated working mothers—The child relief for each of the first four children is equal to the normal child relief plus a percentage of the mother's earned income, subject to a maximum. For a child 12 years and above on January 1, 2001, the percentages applicable for the first, second, third, and fourth child are 5%, 10%, 15%, and 15%, respectively, with a maximum for each child of S$10,000. For a child under 12 years of age on January 1, 2001, the respective percentages for the first, second, third, and fourth child are 5%, 15%, 20%, and 25%, with a maximum for each child of S$15,000. Relief is available for a fourth child only if born after 1986. As a fourth child born in 1987 does not qualify for normal child relief, the increased or enhanced child relief is given at S$1,500 plus the applicable percentage of the mother's earned income.

      A working mother has the option to claim the enhanced child relief in full, or to claim the relief on the basis of the applicable percentage of her earned income with the husband claiming the normal child relief. The total relief claimed by husband and wife must not exceed the maximum claim available for each child. This option of a split claim is not available for the fourth child if born in 1987;
   e. A S$20,000 one-time tax rebate against either or both parents' tax liability plus a tax rebate at 15% of the mother's earned income against her tax liability is available for a third child born after 1986 and a fourth child born after 1987 if the child and the elder siblings are all Singapore citizens. The 15% tax rebate is restricted to S$20,000 in respect of the third child and S$40,000 in respect of the fourth child born on or after April 1, 2001.

      For a second Singaporean child born after 1989 to a mother under 31 years of age, a one-time special rebate against either or both parents' tax liability, depending on the mother's age, is available as follows.

Age of mother	**Tax Rebate**
	S$
Below 28 years	20,000
Below 29 years	15,000
Below 30 years	10,000
Below 31 years	5,000

      The special tax rebates must generally be used up within seven or nine years.
6. Aged dependent relief:
   a. Aged parent or grandparent maintained by taxpayer—$3,500.
   b. Aged parent or grandparent living with taxpayer—$5,000.
   c. Aged dependent's income must not exceed $2,000 per annum.

7. Delivery and hospitalization expenses—The amount not exceeding S$3,000 for a fourth child born after 1987.
8. Educational expenses—Course fees (including tuition and examination fees) not exceeding S$2,500 relating to approved academic, professional or vocational qualifications.
9. Foreign maid levy—Twice the amount of levy imposed on one maid is deductible against the earned income of a married woman or of a divorced or separated woman with dependent children living with her in the same household.
10. Reservists—S$1,000 or S$2,000 for those who have completed or performed national service. A relief of S$500 each will also be given to Singaporean parents and wives of reservists against their own income.

Additional allowances are granted for dependent great-grandparents and handicapped siblings, as well as for topping up parents' CPF accounts.

Tax credits

For treaty countries, credit for all or part of the foreign tax against the tax assessed on the foreign income in Singapore may be granted. For nontreaty countries, unilateral tax credits are given for foreign tax paid on dividend income, employment income and director's fees derived therefrom, and prescribed service fees received from certain countries. The tax deducted at source from a Singapore dividend is available as a credit against any Singapore tax payable or, if no tax is payable, as a refund.

Other taxes

Social security taxes/CPF contributions are payable. With effect from January 1, 2001, the employer contributes 16% (previously 12% from April 1, 2000). The employee contributes 20% of ordinary wages paid in cash, up to a maximum contribution of S$1,200 per month, and 20% of additional wages (e.g., year-end bonus), up to a maximum contribution on 40% of annual ordinary wages if total wages exceed S$100,000 and annual ordinary wages exceed S$72,000. If total wages exceed S$100,000 but annual ordinary wages do not exceed S$72,000, the maximum contribution on additional wages will be limited to the amount payable on the difference between S$100,000 and annual ordinary wages. A foreign national is exempted from contributing to CPF. See also "Employee gross income" and "Nonbusiness expenses."

As for contributions made to the new SRS scheme, the contribution rate caps are as follows.

	%
Singapore citizens or permanent residents	15
Foreigners	35

Unlike CPF, this is a voluntary scheme and employers are not allowed to contribute. The maximum amount to be contributed is subject to income capping rules that are similar to CPF income capping rules.

Local taxes on income/There are no other taxes on income in Singapore.

Tax administration

Returns/Each taxpayer is required to make an annual return of income and of such particulars as may be required to determine the personal allowances due. A wife can elect to be separately assessed on her income. In such a case, she can choose to file a return separate from her husband's. The tax return must be filed on a calendar-year basis and must be submitted by April 15.

Payment of tax/The tax assessed is payable within one month of the date of the assessment whether or not a notice of objection to the assessment has been lodged with the tax authorities. The notice of objection must be lodged within 30 days of the date of the notice of assessment, failing which the assessment will be treated as final.

In the case of an employee, the tax authorities will upon application generally allow the payment of tax by monthly installments with no interest, using the GIRO system.

Tax rates

Residents/A resident individual's taxable income (after setoff of personal allowances) is subject to income tax at progressive rates. Current rates for year of assessment 2002 (income year 2001) are shown below for taxable income of S$35,000 and above.

Taxable income		Tax on	Percentage
Over (Column 1)	Not over	Column 1	on excess
S$ 35,000	S$ 50,000	S$ 1,275	9
50,000	75,000	2,625	12
75,000	100,000	5,625	15
100,000	150,000	9,375	18
150,000	200,000	18,375	21
200,000	400,000	28,875	24
400,000		76,875	26

Note:

Resident individuals are entitled to a fixed-sum GST rebate of S$250 and an additional rebate of 10% for year of assessment 2002.

Nonresidents/Nonresident individuals are normally taxed at 24.5%, except that Singapore employment income is taxed at a flat rate of 15% or at resident rates, whichever yields a higher tax. A nonresident director's remuneration does not qualify for the reduced rate, and tax at 24.5% must be deducted from remuneration paid to a nonresident director.

INDIVIDUAL TAX CALCULATION

2002 tax liability (based on 2001 income)

Assumptions

The employee is a foreign national resident in Singapore, his wife does not earn any income and they have two children under the age of 16.

Tax computation

Salary and allowances		S$ 150,000
School fees		15,000
Benefits in kind:		
Home-leave passage—20% of 11,500	2,300	
Furniture, refrigerator, air conditioners, stove, and fans at nominal rates, plus (estimated) utilities	6,900	9,200
		174,200
Value of unfurnished accommodation—Lesser of annual rent paid by employer (say 72,000) and 10% of assessable emoluments (174,200)		17,420
		191,620
Investment income:		
Bank interest income	500	
Dividends—Gross (Singapore)	6,000	6,500
Assessable income		198,120
Deduct—Personal allowances:		
Personal	3,000	
Earned income	1,000	
Wife	2,000	
Children	4,000	(10,000)
Taxable income		S$ 188,120
Tax thereon:		
Tax on first 150,000		S$ 18,375
Tax on balance—38,120 at 21%		8,005
Total tax payable		26,380
Less:		
10% tax rebate (10% of 26,380)	2,638	
Tax deducted at source from dividend (24.5% of 6,000)	1,470	
GST tax rebate for year of assessment 2002	250	(4,358)
Net tax payable		S$ 22,022

Note:

Exchange rate of the Singapore dollar at December 31, 2001: US$1 = S$1.7937.

PwC contact

For additional information on taxation in the Slovak Republic, contact:

Paul Barnes, Tax Partner
PricewaterhouseCoopers Tax, k.s.
Hviezdoslavovo namestie 20
815 32 Bratislava
Slovak Republic
Telephone: (421) (2) 5441 41 01
Fax: (421) (2) 5441 41 02
e-mail: paul.barnes@sk.pwcglobal.com

Significant developments

New tax legislation was introduced in the Slovak Republic on January 1, 2002. The legislation may be subject to frequent amendments and official interpretation as the market economy develops. It is therefore advisable to contact PwC Bratislava for up-to-date information.

Territoriality and residence

A resident of the Slovak Republic is subject to tax on worldwide income, irrespective of whether the income is remitted to the Slovak Republic.

An individual who spends more than 183 days in a calendar year or holds a residence permit or has a permanent place of abode in the Slovak Republic is resident for tax purposes.

A nonresident is liable to tax on Slovak-source income only, subject to an applicable double taxation treaty. Slovak-source income includes income from work performed in the territory of the Slovak Republic. This includes income for work of even one day's duration. It is also irrespective of the place of payment, if the employer is a Slovak resident or has a permanent establishment in the Slovak Republic.

Gross income

Employee gross income/The gross income of employees includes all wages, salaries and bonuses paid and any benefits in kind (subject to minor exceptions) received as a result of employment. In principle, benefits in kind are valued at open-market values, although a fixed rate of 12% per annum of the purchase price is applied to cars provided by the employer, unless the employee has no private use of the car. The reimbursement of travel expenses in excess of fairly low statutory limits is also a taxable benefit to the employee.

Fees payable to non resident members of other statutory bodies of Slovak companies, to tax residents and to members of other statutory bodies of Slovak companies are taxed under the payroll administration using progressive tax rates. Employers must keep Slovak payroll records.

Capital gains and investment income/Capital gains form part of total income and are therefore subject to income tax at the taxpayer's marginal rate. Exemptions are available for gains that arise on the disposal of assets that have not been used for commercial purposes and have been held for specified minimum periods, as follows.

1. Securities held for more than 36 months.
2. Cars and other movable assets held for more than 12 months.
3. Real estate held for more than five years.

Subject to certain conditions, a gain on the sale of an apartment or a house, provided that it has been owned by the taxpayer and has been the taxpayer's residence for at least two years before the sale, as well as a gain on the sale of property by the first owner after restitution are also exempt from personal income tax.

Interest earned on Slovak savings deposits is subject to a final withholding tax of 15%. Dividends received from Slovak companies are also subject to final withholding tax at the rate of 15%.

Interest, dividends and other investment income received from foreign sources are added to total taxable income and taxed at a progressive rate. Credit relief is available for foreign taxes paid on such income (see "Tax credits").

Foreigners who are not tax residents in the Slovak Republic are not liable to tax on investment income received from foreign sources.

Deductions

Business deductions/No deductions are available from income from employment. Sums received by way of reimbursement of expenses incurred in connection with employment are exempt from tax, provided they do not exceed the statutory limits. Private entrepreneurs may deduct ordinary business expenses.

Nonbusiness deductions/In certain cases necessary expenses incurred in the earning of income from nonbusiness sources can be deducted from the income earned (i.e., rental income). There are no standard deductions. For certain categories of income, a fixed percentage of gross income can be claimed as a deduction instead of actual expenditures. Employees' social and health insurance contributions are deductible from employment income. Donations to Slovak organizations for the purpose of, for example, financing science and education are deductible up to a maximum of 10% of total taxable income, provided the total value of the donations is at least SKK500. From January 1, 2002, it is possible to donate 1% of the taxpayer's personal tax liability to eligible organizations by request to the tax authorities.

Personal allowances/A basic allowance of SKK38,760 per annum is available to all individuals. A further SKK12,000 per annum is available to taxpayers supporting a spouse in a joint home, provided the spouse's income does not exceed SKK38,760 per annum. An allowance of SKK16,800 per dependent child is available, and further allowances are available for disabled dependents. The allowances are deducted from the tax base. Spouse and child allowances are not available to individuals who do not have a permanent abode in the Slovak Republic.

Tax credits

A credit for foreign tax paid on foreign-source income taxable in the Slovak Republic is available up to the amount of tax that would be payable on that income in the Slovak Republic.

Other taxes

Social security taxes/Individuals employed by a Slovak entity must pay social and health insurance contributions totaling 12% of gross salary, up to a maximum of SKK24,000 for health insurance and SKK32,000 for social security contributions. Employers must pay corresponding contributions totaling 38% of gross salary. The employees' contributions are deductible from salary for income tax purposes. Neither foreign individuals nor their employers are required to make contributions if they are employed by a foreign company under foreign law.

Private entrepreneurs must contribute to social security and health insurance at the rate of 50% of half of the prorated monthly tax base from their business activities. This half cannot be lower than SKK3,000 and should not exceed SKK24,000.

Local taxes on income/There are no local taxes on income.

Tax administration

Returns/If annual income is in excess of SKK10,000, a return must be filed by March 31 following the calendar year-end. A request to extend the filing deadline to June 30 may be submitted at the latest by March 31. The deadline may be extended to June 30 if the personal income tax return is prepared by a registered Slovak tax adviser under a power of attorney. There is also a possibility to file a request for an extension of the tax return filing date with the tax authorities, but in this case the extension is based on decision of the tax authority and the tax authority has 30 days to notify the taxpayer of the actual decision.

Husbands and wives must file separate income tax returns.

A tax return does not have to be filed if all income received has been subject to tax at source in the Slovak Republic. This also applies if the employment income paid by a Slovak employer is the only source of income of an individual and the individual did not change its employer or was not employed by two entities during the year.

Payment of tax/Income tax is withheld monthly at source from employment income for employees of a Slovak company or branch, for employees of a foreign company assigned to work in a Slovak branch or permanent establishment of that foreign company, as well as for employees assigned to work in a Slovak company.

For income from all sources that has not been liable to Slovak tax at source, individuals are responsible for making advance tax payments on the basis of their previous year's tax liability, unless their only Slovak-source income is from a dependent activity, in which case the taxation is administered through a Slovak payroll.

Tax rates

Personal income tax

Taxable income		Tax on	Percentage
Over (Column 1)	Not over	Column 1	on excess
0	SKK 90,000	—	10
SKK 90,000	180,000	SKK 9,000	20
180,000	396,000	27,000	28
396,000	564,000	87,480	35
564,000		146,280	38

INDIVIDUAL TAX CALCULATION

Calendar year ending December 31, 2002

Assumptions

The individual is a foreigner who is employed by a non–Slovak-resident employer and assigned to work in the Slovak Republic for a period of more than 183 days in a calendar year. The individual is married, supports a spouse and two children. No social security liability arises. Accommodation is directly provided by the employer. The individual was resident in the Slovak Republic for the financial year.

Tax computation

Income from employment:		
Salary	2,000,000	
Accommodation	245,000	
Company car (1)	96,000	SKK 2,341,000
Less—Personal allowance		38,760
Taxable income		SKK 2,302,240
Rounding		SKK 2,302,200
Tax due (146,280 + 38% of 1,738,200)		SKK 806,796

Notes:

1. 12% of purchase price (including value-added-tax (VAT)) of SKK800,000.
2. Exchange rate of the Slovak koruna as of December 31, 2001: US$1 = SKK48.467.

PwC contact

For additional information on taxation in Slovenia, contact:

Nada Drobnic
PricewaterhouseCoopers
Parmova 53
1000 Ljubljana
Telephone: (386) (1) 475 01 00
Fax: (386) (1) 475 01 09
e-mail: nada.drobnic@si.pwcglobal.com

Significant developments

There have been no significant tax or regulatory developments as regards individual taxation in the past year.

Territoriality and residence

Both resident and nonresident persons are liable to individual income tax.

Residents, that is, individuals with permanent residence in Slovenia, are liable for tax on their Slovenian-source income as well as—in certain cases—on their worldwide income (e.g., income from property, dividends, interest).

Nonresident individuals who have a temporary domicile in Slovenia are also subject to tax, but only on their Slovenian-source income. Income may arise from payments for an activity performed in Slovenia or from payments made in Slovenia for an activity performed abroad. Nonresidents are exempt from tax on income if so stipulated by an international treaty ratified by the Republic of Slovenia. Nonresidents are obliged to submit annual tax return if they are present in Slovenia for at least six consecutive months in a calendar year.

Taxable income

Individuals are subject to tax under the Law on Personal Income Tax, which entered into force on January 1994.

Individuals are taxed at progressive rates on their income received in one calendar year, which is classified into the following six categories.

1. Income from employment, pensions and other receipts.
2. Income from agriculture.
3. Income from private business or professional activity.
4. Capital gains.
5. Income from property.
6. Income from property rights (royalties).

The annual taxable base is the aggregate of the taxable bases of these different types of income.

Income from employment, pensions and other receipts/The first category of income includes salaries, salary compensation and other income from employment, income in the form of incentive and benefits (compensation for work-related expenses are exempt from the tax base up to a certain level as determined by the government regulations) less social security contributions; pensions; gross income earned under contracts for temporary work or for the execution of services and jobs on other bases reduced by expenses in a lump-sum amount (10% of the income) or actual expenses; and other receipts, including prizes.

The taxable benefits that form a part of the personal income tax base include the following items:

1. Payments made by the employer for noncompulsory old-age pension and health insurance, other personal insurance, lodging expenses; and educational expenses unrelated to employment.
2. The value of any gifts provided by the employer if, in the month in which the gifts are received, their value exceeds 5% of the average salary of all employees in the Republic of Slovenia in the previous month.
3. The difference between the interest charged on the basis of growth of retail prices and the lower interest charged by the employer on a loan given to an employee.
4. Cars provided by an employer for the personal use of an employee. Two percent of the vehicle's net book value is included in the employee's monthly tax base, taking into consideration the straight-line depreciation method and an annual depreciation rate of 15%.
5. The amount of the discount granted to the employee on products, commercial goods and services of the employer.

Income from agriculture/Cadastral income of farmland and woodland under the regulations on ascertainment such income.

Income from private business or professional activity/This income refers to the profit derived by a sole proprietor whose sole activity is the independent performance of a profit-making activity and the profit derived from the professional activity of writers, painters, sportsmen, and so on. The profit is determined by deducting expenditures from income for a given calendar year.

Capital gains/Capital gains are defined as the gain achieved by selling real estate and/or securities and other shares in capital.

Taxes paid by the taxpayer in connection with real estate are deducted from the taxable base.

Income from property/Income from property is defined as income from participation in profits; interest from loans; and income from renting land and buildings.

Income from participation in the profits of legal persons, i.e., dividends, is subject to a lump-sum deduction of 40%. Income from participation in profits of partnerships, i.e., income received by a limited partner, is not subject to this 40% deduction.

Income from interest on loans is determined by subtracting the interest calculated on the basis of the growth of retail prices from the interest received.

Income derived from rental property (except land) is subject to either a lump-sum deduction or the actual expenses incurred. The lump-sum deductions that may be claimed are as follows.

1. For renting accommodation, buildings for business purposes and garages—40%.
2. For renting furnished accommodations with equipment—60%.

If a lump-sum deduction is claimed, no other expenses may be deducted.

Allowable deductions from income derived from renting land are those expenses actually incurred, including any taxes.

The taxable base for income derived from the renting of equipment and other property is arrived at after deduction of the actual expenses for investment and current maintenance.

Income from property rights/Income from property rights is defined as income from copyrights; income from inventions, trademarks and technical innovations; and income from inherited intellectual and industrial property rights, whether or not they are protected by relevant legislation.

Income from property rights is subject to lump-sum deduction (40% of the income) unless the taxpayer chooses to calculate actual expenses.

Deductions

The consolidated taxable base can be decreased by allowable deductions, which are as follows.

1. General allowance:
   11% of the annual average wage in Slovenia for all taxpayers.
2. Disabled person's allowance:
   Full annual average wage in Slovenia if the taxpayer is a 100% disabled person (one deduction per year).
3. Student allowance:
   40% of the average wage if the taxpayer is a student (only when he derives income from his work as a student).
4. Seniority allowance:
   8% of the annual average wage if the taxpayer is above 65 years of age.
5. Special deductions:
   Certain expenses may be deducted from the aggregate taxable base up to a limit of 3% of the taxable base for the purposes specified in the law.
6. Family allowances:
   These are granted to taxpayers who are supporting their children, as follows:
   a. 10% of the annual average wage for the first child or any other dependent family member;
   b. 15% of the annual average wage for the second child;
   c. 20% of the annual average wage for the third child, etc.; and
   d. 50% of the annual average wage for a disabled child.

Tax credits

Payments of foreign tax may be credited against the Slovenian tax liability.

Other taxes

Special tax for certain receipts/The payer is obliged to pay the special tax at a rate of 25% of the amount payable to individuals who are employed by the payer (legal entity or natural person) on temporary contracts. The tax payment should be made within three days of the payment to the individuals.

Payroll tax/The Law on Tax on Payroll entered into force on July 1, 1996. The taxpayers are all legal entities and individuals who are obliged to pay social security contributions, usually those employing people on a permanent basis and are paying out salaries. The taxable base is gross salary.

The taxable base is taxed as follows.

Taxable base (In Slovenian tolars)	Tax %
Up to 110,000	0
110,001–130,000	2
130,001–400,000	4
400,001–750,000	8
Over 750,000	15

Social security contributions/Contributions for pensions, health insurance and unemployment are paid by employers and by employees. In both cases, the payment of the contributions is administered by the employer, on its own behalf and on behalf of its employees. The contributions amount to 38% (15.90% paid by employer and 22.10% by employee) and are as follows.

1. Pension and disability insurance—paid to the Pension Fund at 24.35%.
2. Health care—paid to the Health Fund at 12.72%.
3. Unemployment insurance—paid to the state budget at 0.20%.
4. Maternity benefit—paid to the state budget at 0.20%.
5. Injury and illness—0.53%.

The tax base is the amount of the gross salary. The contributions are deducted monthly from the employee's salary.

Tax administration

Returns/The tax year is the calendar year. All income received must be included in the annual tax return, as well as all compulsory contributions and advanced taxes paid during the tax year.

All taxpayers must submit the annual tax return in the prescribed form to the Ministry of Finance by March 31 of the following year.

Payment of annual tax/Tax due (calculated as the difference between the total tax payable and the total amount of advance payments) must be paid within 30 days from the day the written order is submitted. When the total sum of advance payments exceeds the tax payable, a refund can be requested.

Advance tax rates/There are two tax schedules (one for income from employment and pensions, one for income from private business or professional activity) containing income brackets and progressive tax rates, which are revalued each period according to the movement of the average wage in Slovenia in the relevant previous period and different flat advance tax rates depending on the category of income.

With respect to employment income, income of professional activities (if the taxpayer is a registered person) and royalty income, the employer or the payer is required to calculate and withhold tax from the gross payment and remit the tax withheld to the tax administration office.

The amount of advance payment of income tax, which is automatically withheld from salaries by the employer, is as follows.

Taxable income		
More than	Up to	Advance tax
(AMW)	(AMW)	
0	50%	17%
50%	100%	50% AMW x 17% + 35% over 50% AMW
100%	150%	50% AMW x 52% + 37% over 100% AMW
150%	200%	50% AMW x 89% + 40% over 150% AMW
200%	300%	50% AMW x 129% + 45% over 200% AMW
300%		50% AMW x 219% + 50% over 300% AMW

Note:

"AMW" is the average monthly salary of employees in the Republic of Slovenia in the month before last.

1. The rate of advance tax on income earned under contracts for temporary work or for the execution of services and on other receipts, including prizes, is 25%.
2. The rate of advance tax payment on income from property and income from property rights is 25%.
3. The rate of advance tax payment on capital gains is 30%.
4. In the case of income from agriculture, the rates of advance tax are as follows:
   a. 0% of taxable base below 30% of the average annual wage in Slovenia in the preceding year;
   b. 8% of taxable base exceeding 30% of the annual wage in Slovenia in the preceding year;
   c. 17% for nonresidents.

Annual tax rates

An individual's annual income is aggregated and the total amount is taxed according to the special annual tax schedule, containing six income tax brackets and the following progressive tax rates: 17%, 35%, 37%, 40%, 45%, and 50%.

Note

Exchange rate of the Slovenian tolar at December 31, 2001: US$1 = SIT250.9450.

Solomon Islands

PwC contact

For additional information on taxation in the Solomon Islands, contact:

Wayne Morris
PricewaterhouseCoopers
City Centre, First Floor
Mendana Avenue
P.O. Box 70
Honiara, Solomon Islands
Telephone: (677) 21851
Fax: (677) 23342
e-mail: wayne.f.morris@sb.pwcglobal.com

Significant developments

There have been no changes to the Income Tax Act during the last two years.

Territoriality and residence

An individual who was present in the Solomon Islands for a period or periods exceeding in the aggregate six months of the tax year is deemed to reside in the Solomon Islands for income tax purposes.

Gross income

Employee gross income/Employee gross income includes wages, salary, leave pay, sick pay, payment in lieu of leave, fees, commissions, bonus, gratuity, or any other allowances or perquisites or other benefits. Most benefits in kind are taxable, including the value of free or subsidized housing, vehicles supplied by employers, and education allowances paid by employers. There are no concessions for short-term residents.

Capital gains and investment income/There is no capital gains tax. Short-term residents are not subject to tax on capital gains and investment income from outside the country.

Deductions

Business deductions/Individuals are allowed work-related deductions for transport, entertaining or other expenditure where the Commissioner is satisfied it was necessarily incurred in gaining income.

Nonbusiness expenses/Interest on maximum borrowings of SBD20,000 for a principal residence in the Solomon Islands can be deducted.

Personal allowances/Individuals are allowed a basic exemption of SBD7,800 regardless of whether they are single or married.

Tax credits/Tax credits are given to resident individuals for withholding tax deducted. The basis of assessment of foreign income and the calculation of available tax credits is the same as for corporations. The Solomon Islands tax payable is computed as the average rate applicable to total income.

Other taxes

Social security taxes/A National Provident fund provides social security benefits to residents on retirement. Employers are required to contribute 7.5% of employees' salaries or wages; employees are required to contribute 5% (minimum). Income tax deductions apply to these contributions (within limits), and proceeds on retirements are tax-free. Expatriate employees are required to contribute unless approval to contribute to a nonresident scheme has been granted. Benefits withdrawn on final departure from the Solomon Islands are tax-free.

Local income taxes/There are no local income taxes, but local Councils are permitted to charge a head tax on individuals, which is known as the basic rate. Employers are required to withhold this tax from employees' salaries and wages and to account to the Council by June 30.

Tax administration

Returns/December 31 is the standard year-end, but an alternative date may be adopted by business taxpayers. Provisions do exist to aggregate the income of married individuals in certain circumstances.

Payment of tax/A pay-as-you-earn (PAYE) system of taxation applies to all income from employment or services rendered.

Tax rates

Resident individuals are subject to tax only on taxable income accruing in, derived from, or received in the Solomon Islands. Income tax rates are the same for residents and nonresidents.

A PAYE system of taxation applies to all income from employment or service rendered.

The tax payable on total income less personal exemptions and deductions is as follows.

Taxable income		Tax on	Marginal
Over (Column 1)	Not over	Column 1	Rate
SBD 0	SBD 15,000	SBD 0	11
15,000	30,000	1,650	23
30,000	60,000	5,100	35
60,000		15,600	40

INDIVIDUAL TAX CALCULATION

Salary	SBD 410,250
Interest income	10,000
	420,250
Less—Basic deduction	7,800
Taxable income	SBD 412,450
Tax payable	SBD 156,580

Note:

Exchange rate of the Solomon Island dollar at December 31, 2001: US$1 = SBD5.6306.

South Africa

PwC contact

For additional information on taxation in South Africa, contact:

Koos van Wyk
PricewaterhouseCoopers
P.O. Box 168
Bellville 7535, South Africa
Telephone: (27) (21) 940-4100,
Fax: (27) (21) 948-6817
e-mail: koos.van.wyk@za.pwcglobal.com

Significant developments

The tax system changed from mainly being source based, to being residence based. In addition, capital gains tax was introduced on October 1, 2001.

Territoriality and residence

South African (SA) residents are taxed on their worldwide income. Credit is granted in SA for foreign taxes paid. Nonresidents are taxed on their SA-source income. The same rates of tax are applicable to both. Although residence has not historically been a major factor in the SA tax system, it is becoming more so as exchange controls are relaxed. Residence of less than 183 days in a fiscal year may give rise to exemption from tax under double taxation agreements. In addition, nonresidents who are physically absent from SA for at least 183 days in aggregate during the year are exempt from tax on interest earned in SA in certain circumstances.

Gross income

Employee gross income/Taxable remuneration includes all cash amounts received for services rendered, including bonuses, allowances, tax reimbursements, and most benefits in kind, such as the use of assets and soft loans. There are no special concessions for short-term residents, except under double taxation agreements.

Capital gains and investment income/25% of net capital gains realized are taxed at the normal income tax rates. However, a gain may be treated as noncapital income, and subject to income tax, if it arises from a profit-making scheme. Following the recent replacement of the source basis of taxation with a residence basis, all foreign income of a SA resident is included in the SA tax net.

Local dividends are exempt from tax, but foreign dividends of SA residents are subject to tax. This applies for dividends accrued to or received by SA residents on or after February 23, 2000, as well as dividends that accrued to a SA resident before that date but were received after it. The first R4,000 of taxable interest and foreign dividend income is exempt from tax (R5,000 for taxpayers over 65).

Deductions

Business deductions/A taxpayer may deduct expenses not of a capital nature incurred in the production of income, such as business-related travel, automobile and entertainment expenses. There are no blanket or standard business expense deductions.

Nonbusiness expenses/A taxpayer may deduct certain expenses, including pension fund and retirement annuity fund contributions where such funds are registered in SA (subject to certain maximum limits) and donations to certain approved public benefit organizations involved in education- and AIDS-related activities (up to a maximum of the greater of R1,000 or 5% of taxable income). Taxpayers over the age of 65 may deduct all their medical expenses, handicap medical expense in excess of R500 are deductible while there are fairly limited deductions for medical expenses incurred by other taxpayers. Mortgage and other personal interest expenses are not deductible.

Personal allowances/A taxpayer is entitled to personal allowances in the form of tax rebates, which are deducted from tax payable.

1. Primary rebate—R4,140 for all natural persons.
2. Additional rebate—R3,000 if the taxpayer is age 65 or over.

Tax credits

A rebate is allowed for taxes paid on foreign income that is taxable in SA. Personal allowances (see above) take the form of tax rebates.

Other taxes

Donations tax/Donations tax is payable by SA-resident individuals. Exempt donations include those between spouses. Donations, to the extent they exceed R25,000 in aggregate per tax year, are subject to donations tax at a flat rate of 20% of the value of the property donated.

Estate duty/Estate duty is levied on the "dutiable" amount of a deceased person's estate. An abatement of R1,000,000 is deducted from the net value of the estate in order to determine the dutiable amount, on which estate duty at a flat rate of 20% is calculated. Only assets of nonresidents located in South Africa are subject to estate duty.

Regional services levies/Individuals who trade in their own names or practice a profession are liable to regional services levies comprising a payroll levy at the rate varying between 0.25% to 0.38% of remuneration paid to employees and a regional establishment levy varying between 0.1% and 0.2% of turnover (plus 14% value-added tax (VAT) on both). Partners' drawings are regarded as remuneration for purposes of the payroll levy.

Employers are obliged to make contributions for employees earning less than R8,099 per month or R97,188 per year to a State Unemployment Insurance Fund at the rate of 1% of gross remuneration.

Skills Development Levy/A compulsory levy to fund in-house education and training is also levied on an employer's payroll. The Skills Development Levy consists of 1% of an employer's payroll per month.

There are no other social security taxes.

Tax administration

Returns/The tax year for individuals ends at the end of February or, in few exceptional cases, June. Spouses are taxed separately and must submit separate returns.

The date for the filing of returns is fixed each year, which usually in May or June. Reasonable extensions may be obtained upon request.

Payment of tax/Pay-as-you-earn (PAYE) withholding tax is withheld on salaries. Standard Income Tax on Employees (SITE) is an alternative method for determining liability for normal tax of persons earning net remuneration not exceeding R60,000. Where PAYE deductions are made from remuneration, these deductions constitute nothing more than advance payments toward liability for normal tax. The main objective of SITE is to ensure that taxpayers who earn salaries of less than R60,000 per tax year need not file tax returns; for them, SITE represents the full and final amount of income tax they will pay. For other taxpayers, SITE constitutes the minimum amount of income tax to be paid.

Tax rates

Natural persons/Taxable income is taxed at progressive rates. Taxable income in excess of R215,000 per annum is taxed at R72,660 plus 42% of the excess.

Taxpayers other than natural persons and companies (e.g., trusts)/taxable income is taxed at progressive rates. The tax rates on the taxable income of trusts other than special trusts (for example, a trust created solely for a person who suffers from a "mental illness") are 32% on taxable income not exceeding R100,000 and 42% on the taxable income exceeding this amount. They do not qualify for the tax rebates referred to above.

Tax payable/The formula for calculating the tax payable is as follows.

Gross income (Total receipts and accruals less receipts and accruals of a capital nature)	XXX
Less—Exempt income	(XXX)
Less—Deductions and allowances	(XXX)
Add—Taxable capital gains (effective October 1, 2001)	XXX
Taxable income	XX
Tax thereon calculated per tables	XX
Less—Rebates	(X)
Tax payable	X

INDIVIDUAL TAX CALCULATION

Year of assessment 2001/2002 (based on year ending February 28, 2002)

Assumptions

Husband and wife, one spouse earns all the income; number of children irrelevant.

Tax computation

Receipts:		
Salary		R 269,800
Interest income		5,000
Long-term capital gain		30,000
Total receipts		304,800
Less:		
Capital Item—Long-term capital gain	30,000	
Exempt income—Standard interest exemption (limited to 4,000)	4,000	34,000
		270,800
Less—Deductions:		
Donation to an approved public benefit organizations	1,000	
Pension fund contribution (maximum 7.5% of income from employment)	20,235	21,235
Taxable income before taxable capital gains		249,565
Add—Taxable capital gain		5,000
Total taxable income		R 254,565
Tax thereon:		
On 215,000		R 72,660
On 39,565 at 42%		16,617
		89,277
Less—Primary rebate		(4,140)
Tax payable		R 85,137

Notes:

1. Capital gains tax calculation:

	R
Proceeds	50,000
Less—Base cost	20,000
Gain	30,000
Less—Annual exclusion	10,000
Gain	20,000
Taxable gain (at 25% inclusion rate)	5,000

2. Exchange rate of the rand at January 31, 2002: US$1 = R11.60.

Spain

PwC contact

For additional information on taxation in Spain, contact:

Jose Félix Gálvez
PricewaterhouseCoopers
Paseo de la Castellana, 53
28046 Madrid
Telephone: 00 34 91 568 45 30
Fax: 00 34 91 568 46 72
e-mail: jose.felix.galvez@es.pwcglobal.com

Significant developments

Personal income tax is levied only on available income, calculated as income received reduced by personal and family minimum figures. The Personal Income Tax Act attempts to bring taxation into line with the taxpayer's actual capacity with respect to the taxable base, rather than through deductions from tax payable. This has given rise to major changes in the overall structure of the tax.

General note

This entry also covers the Canary Islands.

Territoriality and residence

Personal income tax is regulated by two laws, one for residents and another for nonresidents, and persons are liable to Spanish income tax either as residents and nonresidents.

1. Resident—Persons who reside in Spain for more than 183 days in a calendar year or have Spain as their center of economic interest are considered to be resident for tax purposes. A person can also be liable to tax whose family unit is in Spain and the members opt for the joint taxation system. In such cases, worldwide income, capital gains and wealth are subject to tax. Joint taxation is maintained as the basic system for the taxation of the members of the family unit. However, this system is no longer compulsory, and it is possible for each individual to file separately.
2. Nonresident—Persons who do not reside in Spain for more than 183 days in a calendar year or do not have Spain as their center of economic interest are not considered to be resident for tax purposes. In such cases, Spanish-source income and capital gains and wealth in Spain are subject to tax.

For the purpose of calculating the period of residence, temporary absences abroad are taken into consideration unless it can be proved that the taxpayer has been resident or domiciled in another country.

In determining the permanence period of more than 183 days in the Spanish territory, those temporary visits to Spain that derive from contractual obligations under cultural and humanitarian collaboration agreements with the Spanish Public Administration without remuneration will not be computed.

Gross income

Employee gross income/Taxable income includes all types of remuneration, such as salary, living allowances, housing allowances, bonuses, tax reimbursements, and remuneration in kind (e.g., schooling and rent-free housing). Withholdings and advanced payments on account are required on wages and salaries and on benefits. Leaving indemnities, as stipulated by law, are not taxable. Income derived from the delivery of courses, conferences, seminars, and the like is regarded as gross earned income, as is income from literary, artistic, or scientific works when the rights to the exploitation thereof have been transferred. Income from involvement in humanitarian or welfare activities organized by not-for-profit entities is also regarded as gross earned income.

Capital gains and investment income/Capital gains can arise on all transfers inter vivos, but not mortis causa. The new law has eliminated the updating ratios that were applicable under the previous legislation with regard to capital gains. These are retained only for transactions involving real property.

Short-term capital gains (i.e., generated in under one year) are included with other ordinary income in the "general part" of the taxable base and are taxed at the general rate. In contrast, capital gains from assets held for more than one year are included in the "special part" of the taxable base and are taxed at 18%.

The capital gains bases arising in 2002 from transfers of assets or rights acquired before December 31, 1994 are reduced by 14.28%, 25.00% or 11.11%, depending on the type of assets, for each year the assets or rights have been held between the acquisition date and December 31, 1996 for more than two years. The law provides that no tax is due if these assets have been held for more than 8, 5, and 10 years, respectively.

Capital gains or losses arising on inheritance are not taxed under the personal income tax regime.

Profits or losses deriving from the transfer of assets used in the taxpayer's business activity are now subject to personal income tax. However, the taxpayer may choose between paying tax under personal income tax legislation or applying the provision contemplated under corporate income tax legislation, in which taxation may be deferred if the income is reinvested. The capital gain obtained from the sale of a taxpayer's home is exempt in the same proportion as the amount that is reinvested in a new home, provided the new home is purchased within two years.

Disposal by a nonresident of a property located in Spain is subject to capital gains tax. The purchaser is required to deduct and pay to the local authorities 5% of the actual consideration if the property has been held for less than 10 years. This withholding is treated as an advance payment of capital gains tax for the vendor. The nonresident vendor must be formally represented through a lawyer or legal representative.

The following investment income items are taxable: dividends, interest, pensions, notional rent, royalties, fees, actual rent, annuities, alimony and income deriving from insurance contracts. The amount declared is generally the gross amount received. Any withholding at source is available as a tax credit against the final tax liability.

When urban property is rented or subleased by the taxpayer, the amounts actually received from the tenant or subtenant are included in taxable income. With regard to the taxpayer's real property, no tax is paid as a "profit" obtained from the taxpayer's habitual dwelling, but tax is paid in respect of other nonhabitual dwellings owned by the taxpayer that have not been let. The tax payable in this case is 1.1% or 2% of the ratable value.

Capital losses/Capital losses arising from the transfer of assets held for more than one year can be offset only against capital gains generated in more than one year. If the result of the offset is negative, it may be offset only against capital gains generated in more than one year, arising in the following four years. Capital losses arising from the transfer of assets held for no more than one year can be offset only against capital gains generated in no more than one year. The excess losses can be offset against other types of regular income, limited to 10% of such income. Further unused losses may be carried forward four years.

Deductions

Business deductions/Only expenses that are necessary to obtain income are deductible.

Nonbusiness expenses/The nonbusiness expenses listed below are deductible.

1. Social security contributions.
2. Legal defense expenses, up to a maximum of €300.51, in relation to earned income.
3. In relation to investment income, the expenses necessary to obtain the income and deterioration suffered due to use or the passage of time.

Legal reductions/As follows.

1. Personal minimum figure, which in general amounts to €3,305.57 and which increases to €3,906.58 when the taxpayer is over 65, and to €51,08.60 or €6,911.64 when the taxpayer is disabled. For joint filing, the personal minimum is €6,611.13.
2. A family minimum figure of:
   a. €601.01 per annum for each ascendant over 65 forming part of the taxpayer's household who is dependent on the taxpayer and whose annual income does not exceed the official minimum wage;
   b. €1,202.02 for each of the first two single descendents under 25 forming part of the taxpayer's household;
   c. €1,803.04 for any more such descendents;
   d. Additional €300.51 for any descendent under 3 years of age;
   e. Additional €150.25 for any descendent between the age of 3 and 16.
3. Taxpayers annual contributions to pension plans up to a maximum of €7,212.15 per annum. If the employer makes contributions to a pension plan on behalf of the employee, this limit will increase by another €7,212.15.
4. Alimony or maintenance payments under court order.
5. Reduction in the taxable base when income has been generated over more than two years or in a clearly inconsistent manner over time. This reduction is applied to the gross income and may be 30%, 40%, 60%, or 70%, depending on the kind of income involved and the length of time over which it was generated. Nevertheless, the gross income from employment that could benefit from the reduction of 30% has a limit. This limit is the result of applying 30% on the result of multiplying the taxpayer's median annual salary by the number of years in which the income has been generated. In the case of income obtained over notably irregular time periods, the number of years will be five. The average annual salary for 2001 was €17,400.

Personal allowances/Under the new Act, the number of deductions has been reduced in favor of the personal and family minima referred to above.

Corporate tax incentives/Such incentives will be applicable to individuals who carry on business, professional and artistic activities, with the same rates and limits.

Tax credits

Withholding taxes and payments on account are credited against total tax due.

Credits are granted for the following expenditures.

1. Acquisition of main residence—15% to 25% to 20% of expenses, as follows:
   a. Without loan—15%, up to a limit of invested amount of €9,015.18.
   b. With loan—For the first two years of investment 25% and 15% of the amounts paid, up to a limit of invested amount of €9,015.18. The 25% is credited on the first €4,507.59 and 15% on the excess up to €9,015.18.

      For subsequent years of investment credits amount to 20% rates 15% of the amounts paid, up to a limit of invested amount of €9,015.18. The 20% is applied on the first €4,507.59 and the15% on the excess up to €9,015.18.
2. Donations—10% or 20% of the amount, depending on the type of the donation.
3. Dividends received on which corporate tax has been paid—40% of dividends received.

Nonresidents with a permanent establishment in Spain can claim the credits for taxes withheld, dividends received and corporate tax incentives when applicable.

In addition to the credits listed above, credits are available for foreign income tax paid, provided it is not greater than the Spanish tax on the income.

Other taxes

Social security taxes/Social security contribution rates are applied on basic salaries ranging from €516.00 to a maximum of €2,574.90 per month, depending on the individual's category. The general percentage contribution rates as from January 2002 are 6.35% or 6.4% for employees, depending on the type of contract and 30.6% for employers.

Local taxes on income/For residents in Spain, income regional taxes are levied at rates varying from 5.94% to 15.84% of the taxable earned income. These rates, together with the central tax rates, will constitute the total personal income tax rates applicable to taxpayer.

Wealth tax/Resident individuals are subject to wealth tax on worldwide wealth; nonresident individuals are subject to this tax on wealth in Spain only. Wealth of individuals is computed by adding all assets and deducting liabilities. A tax-free allowance of €108,182,18 is available for residents. Additionally, the habitual dwelling is tax exempt up to €150,253.03. Nonresidents do not receive tax-free allowances.

Wealth tax rates are as follows.

Taxable base			Tax on Column 1	Percentage on excess
Over (Column 1)	Not over			
0	€ 167,129.45	....	0	0.2
€ 167,129.45	334,252.88	....	€ 334.26	0.3
334,252.88	668,499.75	....	835,63	0.5
668,499.75	1,336,999.51	....	2,506.86	0.9
1,336,999.51	2,673,999.01	....	8,523.36	1.3
2,673,999.01	5,347,998.03	....	25,904.35	1.7
5,347,998.03	10,695,996.06	....	71,362.33	2.1
10,695,996.06		....	183,670.29	2.5

Tax administration

Returns/Returns must be filed and tax paid before July 1. The tax period is the calendar year.

Payment of tax/Withholding taxes are imposed on investment income at the rate of 18%. Capital gains generated from the transfer or redemption of equity shareholdings or holdings in collective investment institutions are subject to an 18%% withholding. For the letting and subletting of property, the Act lays down a withholding rate of 18%.

Withholding taxes are credited against total tax due.

Tax rates

The following rates apply for 2002.

Central tax

Taxable base			Tax on Column 1	Percentage on excess
Over (Column 1)	Not over			
0	€ 3,678.19	....	0	12.060
€ 3,678.19	12,873.68	....	€ 443.59	16.080
12,873.68	25,134.33	....	1,922.22	18.961
25,134.33	40,460.13	....	4,246.96	24.924
40,460.13	67,433.56	....	8,066.76	30.150
67,433.56		....	16,199.25	32.160

Regional tax

Taxable base			Tax on Column 1	Percentage on excess
Over	Not over			
(Column 1)				
0	€ 3,678.19	.....	0	5.940
€ 3,678.19	12,873.68	.....	€ 218.48	7.920
12,873.68	25,134.33	.....	946.76	9.339
25,134.33	40,460.13	.....	2,091.78	12.276
40,460.13	67,433.56	.....	3,973.18	14.850
67,433.56		.....	7,978.73	15.840

Notes:

1. For the tax year beginning January 1, 2002 the taxpayer's income deriving from joint and individual returns must be declared, and it will be divided into two parts. From the total taxable income, 67% goes to the central government, while 33% is allocated to the regional government of the area in which the taxpayer resides. The tables above give the details.
2. For residents, the 2002 rate is restricted to a maximum of 70% cumulative when considered together with the wealth tax.
3. For nonresidents, general income is subject to a flat rate of 25%; capital gains are subject to a flat rate of 35%, and dividends and interests at a flat rate of 18%.
4. Exchange rate of the Euro at January 3, 2002: US$1 = €1.106.

Sri Lanka

PwC contact

For additional information on taxation in Sri Lanka, contact:

Daya Weeraratne, Head of Tax and Legal Services
PricewaterhouseCoopers
100, Braybrooke Place
Colombo 2
Sri Lanka
Telephone: (94) (1) 304282
Fax: (94) (1) 304286
E-mail: daya@pwc.lanka.net

Copies of all inquiries regarding entry advice and related tax issues in Sri Lanka should be sent to the above address.

Significant developments

A concessionary tax rate of 10% is applicable to income earned in foreign currency by individuals or partnerships in respect of services rendered by such individuals or partnerships to persons outside Sri Lanka in the course of carrying on any profession or any vocation in the field of literature or fine arts.

Territoriality and residence

Individuals physically present in Sri Lanka for 183 days or more during any tax year are treated as resident in Sri Lanka throughout that year. Those persons treated as resident for two or more consecutive tax years are treated as resident until absent from Sri Lanka for an unbroken period of 365 days; when so absent, they are treated as nonresident from the commencement of the tax year in which the absence commences. Where a person is deemed nonresident, any presence in Sri Lanka for 30 days or less will be treated as spent outside the country.

Upon being employed in Sri Lanka, an individual who is not a citizen of Sri Lanka is treated as nonresident for a period of three years, calculated from the date on which employment commences in Sri Lanka. However, if the individual is employed by a company in which the foreign investment is not less than US$50 million or its equivalent in any other foreign currency, the employee is treated as nonresident for five years from commencement of employment. Resident individuals are subject to income tax on their worldwide income. Nonresident individuals are taxed on Sri Lanka-source income only.

Gross income

Employee gross income*/*Employment income is computed gross and comprises all items of remuneration received in the course of employment; the value of any benefits to the employee and to the employee's spouse, child or parent; and payments to third parties for the benefit of the employee, spouse, child, or parent. Also included in gross employment income are payments made upon termination of employment, such as retirement gratuities, monies accumulated to the credit of the employee in an approved provident fund and compensation for loss of employment, as well as the rental value of a residence provided rent free by the employer and the benefit from use of an employer-provided automobile.

The rules for determining the statutory income from a trade, business, profession, or vocation are the same as those described for a company. (See the Sri Lanka entry in

Corporate Taxes—A Worldwide Summary). Deductions are given only for remuneration accrued but not paid (treated as bad debts) and for contributions made to an approved provident fund by an employer on the employee's behalf.

Exempt income/Certain items of income are exempt in the hands of an individual. Some notable exemptions are as follows.

1. Emoluments paid to persons serving the public sector.
2. Non–Sri Lanka-source income and official emoluments of certain residents, such as foreign diplomats and members of their staff who are citizens of the countries represented by these diplomats; experts, advisers, technicians, or officials who are brought to Sri Lanka by the government through the United Nations Organization (UNO) but are not paid by the government; foreign trainees sent to Sri Lanka under the aegis of the UNO or the Colombo Plan Organization; and officials of the UNO who are not citizens of Sri Lanka.
3. Official emoluments of resident Sri Lanka citizens employed by the UNO or any of its specialized agencies.
4. Travel warrants and passages granted to expatriates serving in Sri Lanka or to their spouses and children to enable them to travel between their home countries and Sri Lanka.
5. Travel, subsistence and lodging allowances granted to employees for travel abroad in connection with their employment.
6. Emoluments and pensions earned in foreign currency and paid in Sri Lanka or remitted to residents or their spouses for employment services, past or present, that they have rendered outside Sri Lanka.
7. Emoluments of residents earned in foreign currency and remitted to Sri Lanka for professional or vocational services exercised outside Sri Lanka.
8. Capital sums paid as gratuities or compensation for death or injuries.
9. Sums paid to informants as rewards by the government.
10. Income from scholarships, exhibitions or bursaries enjoyed by students in educational establishments.

Capital gains and investment income/Capital gains are taxed as part of ordinary income, but not at more than 25% if the gain is other than from a change of ownership of property. Where the gain is from the change of ownership of property, special rates apply if the property has been held for more than two years since its acquisition (for special rates, see the Sri Lanka entry in *Corporate Taxes*). If the property changes ownership within two years, the gain is taxed at the normal tax rates applicable to the individual.

In computing a capital gain, deductions are allowed for expenses incurred solely on the acquisition of the property (other than its purchase price), expenses incurred on improvements to the property and expenses incurred solely on the transaction that results in the gain. Capital gains from the transfer of quoted public company shares or profits from trading in quoted public company shares and capital gains from transfer of shares of a company that has entered into an agreement with the Board of Investment of Sri Lanka (BOI) are exempt from income tax. Capital gains from the sales of units held in a mutual fund or unit trust made after one year from the date of acquisition are also exempt.

Capital losses can be relieved only against capital gains; any unrelieved excess of a capital loss can be carried forward for deduction from future capital gains. When a person dies, any unrelieved balance of capital loss available for the last tax year can be deducted from the total income of that year, and the unrelieved balance of that loss (if any) can be carried back for deduction from the total income of each of the three immediately preceding tax years taken in due order.

Rental income from land and improvements is computed on the gross rent received or receivable. Deductions are allowed for rates and for 25% of the balance for repairs, to the extent the owner bears their costs.

Dividends, interest, annuities, and royalties are computed gross without deductions. Interest or royalty payable to a nonresident is taxed at 15%, but this rate will be lower (generally 10%) if the taxpayer is a resident in a country with which a double tax avoidance treaty is in force.

Dividends are grossed up for assessment in the hands of the shareholder so as to include the gross dividend distributed and the advance corporate tax (ACT) paid on the dividend. The shareholder is entitled to deduct any withholding tax and ACT (if included in the total dividend) from the overall income tax payable. Where the shareholder is resident in a country with which a double taxation treaty is in force, the treaty withholding tax is the final income tax due. ACT is not payable on dividends paid by a company to nonresident shareholders.

The law provides for the assessment of either interest accrued or interest received, with appropriate adjustments for either interest not received or accruals received in excess of the receipts assessed, as the case may be. Where income tax has been withheld on interest or royalties, this tax is deductible from the overall income tax payable. Where the shareholder is resident in a country with which Sri Lanka has a double taxation treaty, the tax withheld on interest or royalties is the final income tax due.

Deductions

A deduction is allowed for interest paid in business borrowings and certain loans. In computing taxable income, a deduction is allowed for a tax-free allowance of Rs144,000 (resident individuals only), for unrecouped investments in shares of companies approved by the BOI after November 6, 1997 and purchased between November 6, 1997 and April 1, 2000; donations to approved charities; and contributions in cash or kind to the government. Furthermore, an employee can deduct any annual contributions to an approved provident fund. However, the total deduction for investments, donations (except donations to the government) and contributions to an approved provident fund cannot exceed one-third of assessable income or Rs25,000, whichever is lower. An additional deduction is allowed in respect of premiums paid on a life or medical insurance policy subject to one-third of the assessable income or Rs25,000, whichever is lower. Donations to the government can be deducted without limit, and any unrelieved excess can be carried forward indefinitely.

Tax credits

If a double taxation treaty applies, residents with foreign-source income are entitled to a credit equal to the income tax levied on that income in the foreign country. This credit cannot exceed the Sri Lanka income tax imposed on that income.

If no tax treaty is in force, the foreign tax paid is allowed as a deduction in computing the profits from the applicable source for Sri Lanka income tax purposes.

Other taxes

Local taxes/Taxes (commonly called "rates") are currently assessed and collected annually from the owners of land and premises by the local authorities of the areas in which the properties are located. These authorities also impose and collect annual license fees from certain businesses as well as "taxes" based on the annual gross takings of certain businesses such as hotels.

Employees Provident Fund/Employers and employees are required to contribute specified percentages (employer, 12%; employee, 8%) of each employee's monthly emoluments to the Employees Provident Fund (EPF) established by the government. Alternatively, employers and employees must contribute to certain private provident funds approved by the labor authority.

Employees Trust Fund/Employers are also required to contribute a specified percentage (currently 3%) of each employee's monthly emoluments to the Employees Trust Fund established by the government.

Tax administration

Returns/A tax year is any period of 12 consecutive months commencing on April 1 and ending on the March 31 following. An individual is required to file an income tax return in a prescribed format (with financial statements and supporting schedules, if applicable) on or before November 30 immediately following the end of the tax year.

Spouses are taxed separately on their individual incomes. The statutory income of a child (under 18 years of age, unmarried, not illegitimate), whether natural or legally adopted, is aggregated with the father's income if the marriage subsists. If the parents are living separately, either under a court decree or in circumstances that are likely to be permanent, the income is aggregated with the income of the parent who maintains the child.

Payment of tax/Under the pay-as-you-earn (PAYE) tax system, employers are required to deduct from the monthly emoluments of each employee income tax computed on the basis of statutory tables provided by the tax authority. In general, where employment is an individual's only source of income, the tax deducted by the employer and paid to the tax authority is the final income tax due from the employee. Individuals with high employment income or income from other sources are entitled to set off the annual income tax deducted by the employer from the overall income tax payable.

Under Sri Lanka's pay-and-file system, individuals other than employees are required to pay tax in installments on or before August 15, November 15 and February 15 of the tax year and the May 15 immediately following its end. If each installment is not less than one-quarter of the income tax payable for the immediately preceding tax year, the balance of any income tax payable may be paid without incurring penalties on or before September 30 immediately following the end of the tax year.

Tax rates

Tax rates are as follows:

Taxable income	Rate
Rs	%
First 100,000	10
Next 100,000	15
Next 100,000	25
Remainder	35

Concessionary tax rates apply to sums paid to an employee on cessation of employment, by way of compensation, commuted pension, retirement gratuity, accumulated employers contribution to an approved or regulated provident fund, and contributions to the Employees Trust Fund. Compensation paid under a uniform scheme of voluntary retirement approved by the tax authorities or under a scheme of retrenchment approved by the labour authority is exempt from tax. Income from agriculture, nontraditional exports, fisheries, tourism, livestock, and construction activities qualifies for a rate of not more than 15%. A concessionary rate of 10% is accorded to emoluments and fees earned in foreign currency by an individual or partnership in respect of services rendered by such individual or partnership to persons outside Sri Lanka in the course of carrying on any profession or any vocation in the field of literature or fine arts.

Where the taxable income includes a capital gain, the gain will be separately taxed, subject to the special rate ceilings (see under "Capital gains and investment" income above). An expatriate who commences employment in Sri Lanka is taxed on Sri Lanka-source income at a flat 15% for a period of three consecutive years from the commencement of employment and at 15% of Sri Lanka employment income for the next two years. However, if employed in an enterprise with a total investment of not less than US$50 million or its foreign currency equivalent and for which a tax holiday has been approved by the BOI, the tax rate is 15% for the duration of the expatriate's employment within the tax holiday period, even if it exceeds five years.

INDIVIDUAL TAX CALCULATION

Assumptions

Resident and nonresident individuals; nonresident resides in treaty country.

Tax computation

	Resident individual	Nonresident individual
Employment income	Rs 6,000,000	
Quoted company dividends (1)	154,000	Rs 100,000
Fixed deposit interest	100,000	—
Loan interest		100,000
Royalties	100,000	100,000
Capital gains:		
Sale of land held six years	100,000	—
Sale of quoted company shares	25,000	25,000
Total statutory income	6,479,000	325,000
Less:		
Exemptions—Capital gain on quoted company shares	25,000	25,000
Tax-free allowance	144,000	—
Contribution to Employees Provident Fund	25,000	—
	6,285,000	300,000
Less (items treated separately):		
Capital gain on sale of land (2)	100,000	—
Loan interest		100,000
Royalties	—	100,000
Balance of taxable income	Rs 6,185,000	Rs 100,000
Income tax (excluding capital gains)	Rs 2,109,750	Rs 10,000
Tax on capital gain, royalty, loan interest	17,500	20,000
	2,127,250	30,000
Less—Tax credits:		
Employment income—Tax deducted	(1,985,831)	—
Tax deducted on dividends		(15,000)
Advance corporate tax	(54,000)	—
Tax deducted on:		
Fixed deposit interest	(10,000)	—
Loan interest (3)		(10,000)
Royalties (3)	—	(10,000)
Balance of income tax payable/(repayable)	Rs 77,419	Rs (5,000)

Notes:

1. Includes ACT of Rs54,000.
2. Taxed at 17.5%.
3. Taxed at no more than 10% under presumed treaty.
4. Average exchange rate (buying/selling) of the Sri Lanka rupee at December 31, 1999: US$1 = Rs71.94.

Swaziland

PwC contact

For additional information on taxation in Swaziland, contact:

Theo Mason
PricewaterhouseCoopers
MTN Office Park
Smuts Street
P.O. Box 569 or 2513
Mbabane, Swaziland
Telephone: (268) 40-43143, 40-40658, 40-42861
Fax: (268) 40-45015, 40-43142
e-mail: theo.mason@sz.pwcglobal.com

General note

This entry is repeated from the 2001/2002 edition. For more up-to-date information, consult the contact listed above or Mark Friedlich at mark.friedlich@us.pwcglobal.com.

Significant developments

Swaziland is in the process of adopting a new taxation bill. The Bill is expected to be enacted with effect from July 1, 2001. The draft Bill has now been published. No new legislation has been drafted since 1994.

Territoriality and residence

Residence is not specifically defined, but effectively anyone in employment or business in Swaziland will be regarded as resident for tax purposes. Work permits are required for noncitizens to take up employment in Swaziland, and, as such, expatriates who work under a permit held by their employers or who are self-employed are deemed to be resident for tax purposes.

Gross income

Employee gross income/Income tax, as for companies, is levied on all income derived from a source within or deemed to be within the country, irrespective of whether the recipient of the income is actually resident in Swaziland.

Standard valuations apply for various benefits-in-kind and are included in the taxpayer's gross income for tax purposes. These include the following.

1. Free and subsidized housing: Valuation depends on the size and location of the house and ranges from E4,294 to E8,588 per annum in the main centers.
2. Private use of motor vehicles: Valuation depends on the cubic capacity or value of the vehicle and ranges from E5,153 to E15,459 per annum.
3. Entertainment and travel expenses: The benefit is the amount paid by the employer, less justifiable expenses incurred by the employee.
4. Free or subsidized fuel supplied by the employer for the employee's transport.
5. Provision of personal services:
    a. Electricity and telephone: E763 per annum for each service;
    b. Gas, coal, water, etcetera: E381 per annum for each service.
6. Children's educational benefits: 80% of school fees and other related costs actually paid.

7. Domestic servants:
   a. Household (cooks, maids, etc.): E954 per annum per servant;
   b. Gardeners: E476 per annum per servant.

A gratuity or bonus received by or accrued to an employee upon bona fide termination of employment by reason of a written agreement of employment is exempt from normal tax. This exemption is subject to the condition that the gratuity or bonus is not more than 25% of the total amount of actual salary received from the date of commencement of employment in respect of the written agreement of employment, which must be for a period of at least two years.

A tax directive must be obtained before a gratuity can be paid out to an employee.

Income from farming on traditional land is exempt from tax.

Capital gains and investment income/There are no capital gains or estate taxes.

The first E2,000 of dividend income is tax exempt. A rate of 10% applies to dividends in excess of E2,000 received by or accrued to or in favor of an individual from a company listed with the Swaziland Stock Exchange, and a rate of 20% applies to dividends in excess of E2,000 received by or accrued to or in favor of an individual from a company not so listed.

Income from the following sources is exempt from tax.

1. First E2,000 of interest received from a Swaziland-licensed financial institution.
2. Maximum of E10,000 received from permanent or fixed-period shares in the Swaziland Building Society.
3. Maximum of E10,000 received from deposits in the Swaziland Development and Savings Bank.

Deductions

Business deductions/For the purpose of ascertaining the taxable income of any person, the following may be deducted from the income of that person.

1. Expenditure and losses actually incurred in Swaziland by the taxpayer in the production of income, as well as such expenses incurred outside Swaziland in the production of taxable income as the Commissioner may allow, provided the expenditure or losses are not of a capital nature.
2. Expenditure actually incurred by the taxpayer during the year of assessment for repairs of property occupied for the purpose of trade or in respect of which income is receivable and sums so expended for the repair of machinery, implements, utensils, and articles employed by the taxpayer for the purposes of the taxpayer's trade.
3. Such sum as the Commissioner may think just and reasonable as representing the diminished value by reason of wear and tear during the year of assessment of any plant, machinery, implements, utensils, and articles used by the taxpayer for the purposes of the taxpayer's trade.

Nonbusiness expenses/The following maximum deductions apply for the tax year to June 30, 2001.

1. Pension fund contributions: Up to E1,750 per annum by persons holding appointed office or employment.

2. Retirement annuity fund contributions: Contributions during the year of assessment by members of the fund, with the sum of these contributions not to exceed:
   a. 15% of the taxable income accruing to the taxpayer from the trade carried out by the taxpayer, provided the allowable deductions do not exceed E5,000;
   b. E3,000, less contributions made by the taxpayer to a pension fund; or
   c. E1,750.
3. Mortgage interest paid to an approved financial institution at commercial rates (self or spouse):
   a. Where the gross income of the taxpayer or spouse does not exceed E15,000—200% of the interest paid during that year of assessment;
   b. Where such gross income exceeds E15,000 but not E60,000—100% interest paid during that year of assessment;
   c. Where such gross income exceeds E60,000—50% of the interest paid during that year of assessment.

However, the interest for the purposes of this subsection is limited to the lower of (1) interest payable on that portion of the amount of the loan, mortgage, or similar financial arrangement that does not exceed E60,000 or (2) E9,000.

No deduction is allowed for medical expenses.

Personal allowances/rebates/General rebates for married and unmarried persons are incorporated into the marginal tax rates.

Tax credits

See "Personal allowances/rebates" above.

Other taxes

There are no social security taxes or local taxes on income. There is a graded tax (poll tax) of E1.50 per month for all employed persons.

Stamp tax on a sliding scale rising to 6% is payable on transfers of real estate, mortgages, leases, and transfers of shares.

Tax administration

Returns/The tax year runs from July 1 to June 30. All persons liable to taxation, whether personally or in a representative capacity, are required to file returns within 30 days of June 30. The Commissioner may allow an extension of time as deemed appropriate.

A married woman with income in excess of E13,000 per annum is required to register as a taxpayer, and her income is subject to the rates of taxation applicable to individuals, except for income from the following sources.

1. A partnership in which her husband is a partner; her husband; or a company whose voting power is held by her, by her husband, or by both jointly, either directly or through nominees, to the extent of 12.5% or more during any time of the year of assessment. (Income from the above three sources is aggregated with her husband's gross income.)
2. Any other person, where such income is in excess of an amount considered reasonable by the Commissioner, under which circumstances it is also aggregated with her husband's gross income.

Payment of tax /Individuals in paid employment are subject to pay-as-you-earn (PAYE).

Every provisional taxpayer is required to submit to the Commissioner on the prescribed form an estimate of the total tax payable for the year of assessment. The estimate of taxable income for provisional tax purposes should not be less than the taxable income assessed for the latest preceding year of assessment for which an assessment has been issued not less than 21 days before the date the current estimate is made, unless the taxpayer can satisfy the Commissioner of Taxes that the taxable income for the current year will be less than that for that preceding year.

A provisional taxpayer is rendered liable to a penalty if the estimate of taxable income for the purposes of the second payment of provisional tax is found to be less than 90% of the taxable income as finally determined and is also less than the taxable income as assessed for the immediately preceding tax year.

For individuals, the first payment must be made by December 31 and the second payment by June 30, and if a third top-up payment is required, this should be paid by December 31 of the following year, that is, one year after the first provisional tax payment.

Tax rates

The following rates apply for the tax year to June 30, 2001.

Taxable income		Tax on	Percentage
Over	Not over	Column 1	on excess
(Column 1)			
0	E 13,000	—	0
E 13,000	16,000	—	12
16,000	20,000	E 360	16
20,000	24,000	1,000	20
24,000	28,000	1,800	24
28,000	32,000	2,760	28
32,000	36,000	3,880	32
36,000	40,000	5,160	36
40,000		6,600	39

INDIVIDUAL TAX CALCULATION

For year ending June 30, 2001

Tax computation

Salary		E 200,000
Benefits-in-kind (1):		
House	8,588	
Car	15,459	24,047
Bank interest		13,000
		237,047
Deduct:		
Bank interest allowance—General	2,000	
Mortgage interest of 9,000 per annum (restricted) (2)	4,500	
Pension contributions (maximum)	1,750	8,250
Taxable income		E 228,797
Tax payable (3)		E 80,230.33
Graded tax (poll tax) payable		E 18.00

Notes:

1. Benefits-in-kind are based on a four-bedroom executive house in Mbabane (capital) and a 2,500-cc engine capacity car costing E100,000.
2. Mortgage interest relief is restricted to the lower of 50% of interest on a maximum mortgage amount of E60,000 or E9,000.
3. In practice, the salary could include a 25% tax-free gratuity element to reduce the effective rate of taxation.
4. Exchange rate of the emalangeni at December 31, 2000: US$1 = E7.86.

PwC contact

For additional information on taxation in Sweden, contact:

Claes Elinder
Öhrlings PricewaterhouseCoopers
Kungsgatan 18
S–113 97 Stockholm, Sweden
Telephone: (46) (8) 555 33 000
Fax: (46) (8) 555 33 002
e-mail: claes.elinder@se.pwcglobal.com

Significant developments

There have been no significant tax or regulatory developments as regards individual taxation in the past year.

Territoriality and residence

The amount of income subject to national and municipal income taxes depends on the individual's residence status. Persons staying in Sweden continuously for more than six months are deemed to have gained taxable residence and become liable to pay income taxes on income from all sources worldwide. Individuals present in Sweden for less than six months are usually liable to pay taxes only on Swedish-source income.

Residence status at year-end determines whether an individual is liable to net wealth tax on all taxable property worldwide or only on taxable property in Sweden. However, foreign citizens who are staying temporarily (for no more than three years) in Sweden have limited tax liability.

Five-year rule/Citizenship affects the residence status of Swedes only. Swedish citizens, as well as foreigners who have been resident in Sweden for ten years, are deemed resident in Sweden for tax purposes until they can prove that all important ties with Sweden have been broken. Five years after a taxpayer leaves Sweden, the burden of proof is reversed and the tax authorities must prove that ties still exist between the individual and Sweden.

Six-month and one-year rule/Swedish residents who have been assigned to work abroad or who have taken up employment abroad with a planned duration of not less than six months are not liable to Swedish income taxes on income from this employment, provided the income is taxed in the country of employment and you do not spend more than six days per month or maximum 72 days per 12-month period in Sweden. If no tax is payable in that country because of exemptions under domestic legislation, the income is tax exempt in Sweden only if the assignment or employment is intended to last for at least one year.

Gross income

Employee gross income/All remuneration from employment, whether in cash or in kind, is treated as taxable income, including directors' fees, bonuses, commissions, pensions, annuities, and all kinds of allowances. Tax equalization payments are taxable. The rental value of free housing, the estimated value of free automobiles and the value of free meals are the major taxable benefits-in-kind.

Reimbursement from a Swedish employer to a nonresident individual is taxed at a flat rate of 25% at source, i.e., foreign citizens temporarily in Sweden without attaining tax residence are taxed at the flat rate of 25% on their salary. The same rate applies when a pension is paid by a Swedish source to a person not tax-resident in Sweden.

Foreign experts and key personnel are only liable to tax on 75% of the income earned during their first three years in Sweden. Some benefits, like school fees, moving allowances and home travel allowances, are tax exempt. These regulations apply to foreign personnel employed by a Swedish company with a permanent establishment in Sweden. The employment and residence in Sweden must be limited in time (not exceeding five years), and the employee cannot have been a resident in Sweden prior to the employment. To qualify for this exemption, the employee must obtain a ruling from the National Tax Board.

Loans from an employer to an employee at low or no interest are deemed to generate a taxable benefit. However, the taxable benefit is deductible as ordinary interest paid.

Capital gains and investment income/Individuals resident in Sweden are taxed on capital gains realized during the period of residence.

Nonresident individuals are not taxed on Swedish-source capital gains, except for capital gains on Swedish situs real estate. For private real property and tenant owner's apartments, the maximum taxable profit is two-thirds of the profit. However, it is possible to roll the tax payment over when buying new private real property.

The taxable gain on the sale of shares is the net profit, that is, the sales price less the average purchase price for all shares of the same kind. Only 70% of the calculated loss may normally be deducted.

Special rules apply to the taxation of capital gains from the sale of shares of small companies. Those rules are very complicated, and it is therefore recommended that Öhrlings PricewaterhouseCoopers be contacted if consideration is to be given to selling such shares.

Gains on the sale of personal assets are taxable only if they exceed SEK50,000 per year. The acquisition cost of personal assets is either the real purchase price or, optionally, 25% of the sales price. Other assets are taxed on the net profit without the mentioned limitations.

The taxable portion of the capital gains is taxed as capital income.

All current income from bank savings, financial instruments, claims of different kinds, and dividends received by a resident person is taxable as capital income.

Deductions

Business deductions/In principle, all expenses incurred during the fulfillment of the employment agreement are deductible, e.g., travel expenses, automobile expenses, living allowances on business trips, necessary literature, and tools of the trade. The deduction related to cost-of-living allowances is, however, limited.

Nonbusiness expenses/The most common deductions are listed below.

1. Under certain conditions, expenses for travel between home and place of work, based on the cheapest means of public transport or, if a private car or a company car is used, on a fixed amount per kilometer. Only the part of the cost exceeding SEK7,000 is deductible.
2. Interest paid, when calculating capital income.

3. Management costs for the administration of investments, to the extent the costs exceed SEK1,000.
4. Personal pension insurance premiums and contributions to restricted pension savings, to a limited extent.

Personal allowances/From the aggregate taxable income, a basic allowance of SEK11,200 to SEK20,900 (for 2002) or one-twelfth of SEK11,200 per month or part of a month the person has been resident in Sweden is granted.

Treatment of losses/Losses from earned income and business may be set off against future earned income and business profits without time limitation. This will be done only within each individual source of income. For losses incurred on income from capital, a tax credit of 30% of the loss is granted against tax on earned income for losses not exceeding SEK100,000 and 21% for losses in excess thereof. However, when calculating the final loss, losses from the sale of private real property, securities, etc., are in general deductible only up to 50% or 70%. The tax credit may not be carried forward.

Tax credits

Foreign tax credits are available.

Other taxes

Social security taxes/Social security charges of 32.82% (2002) of total remuneration in cash and in kind are levied on the employer. A pension fee of 7% of gross earned income up to SEK313,100 (i.e., a maximum fee of SEK21,900) for 2002, is payable by the employee, 25% of which is deductible for income tax purposes.

Local taxes on income/Municipal income taxes are assessed together with the national income tax and vary between 27% and 34% according to municipality (Stockholm—30%). They are not deductible for national tax purposes.

Wealth tax/Wealth tax is paid by individuals owning assets with a net value in excess of SEK,1,500,000 and (SEK2,000,000 for families) at December 31. The 2002 tax rate is 1.5%.

Real estate tax/Real estate tax is paid by the owner. The tax rate is 1% of the taxable value of the real estate for houses and for a block of flats. For persons resident in Sweden, real estate tax is payable for real estate (as well as flats) situated abroad if the property is held for private purposes.

Tax administration

Returns/Individuals file a tax return for the calendar year. For most individuals, the filing date is May 2 (simplified returns). However, some individuals (for example, owners of closely held companies) must file their return by April 2. The tax authorities assess income taxes by applying the appropriate tax rates to the aggregate taxable income from the various sources. Spouses are taxed separately, except on wealth.

Payment of tax/Preliminary taxes must be withheld by a resident employer. In the case of a nonresident employer, tax payment must be submitted to the tax authority by the employees themselves. A final tax bill will be issued to the individual in August (simplified returns) or December in the year after the income year. Income taxes not covered by the preliminary taxes withheld must be paid by the individual 90 days after the final tax bill is issued.

Tax rates

Income year 2002

Employment income tax/As follows, on rounded taxable income amounts.

Taxable income	National income tax	Municipal income tax*
	SEK	%
From 0 to SEK273,800	200	31
From SEK273,800 to SEK414,100	200 + 20%	31
Over SEK414,200	200 + 25%	31

*This rate equals the average municipal tax rate.

Capital tax/Flat rate of 30% (2002).

Wealth tax/Flat rate of 1.5% on net wealth in excess of SEK1,500,000 for single taxpayers and SEK2,000,000 for families.

INDIVIDUAL TAX CALCULATION

Income year 2002

Assumptions

The taxpayer is resident in Sweden and does not own real estate in Sweden or abroad.

	SEK
Salary	680,000
Capital income:	
Interest received on bank deposit	10,000
Dividends received	25,000
Interest paid	150,000
Loss on sale of shares	20,000

Tax calculations

Income from employment (earned income) taxation

Salary for year		SEK 680,000
Add:		
Sickness allowance received under the National Insurance Act	8,000	
Travel allowance granted by employer	8,800	
Other remuneration in cash or kind:		
Telephone	3,000	
Newspaper	1,600	21,400
		701,400
Deduct:		
Business travel expenses	4,400	
Travel costs from home to office (8,000 – 7,000)	1,000	5,400
Net income from employment		696,000
Deduct:		
Private pension insurance premium	34,800	
Pension fee (7%) of which 25 % is deductible	5,500	40,300
		655,700
Less—Basic allowance		11,200
Taxable income for national and municipal tax (1)		SEK 644,550
National income tax		SEK 85,655
Municipal income tax		193,550
Pension fee		21,900
Less—Tax reduction, 75% of pension fee (rounded down)		(16,400)
Total tax on income from employment		SEK 284,705

Income from capital (unearned income) taxation

Interest received on bank deposit	SEK 10,000
Dividends received	25,000
Interest paid	(150,000)
Loss on shares (70% x 20,000)	(14,000)
Total loss	SEK (129,000)
Tax credit:	
(30% x 100,000)	SEK 30,000
(21% x 29,000)	6,090
Total tax reduction	SEK 36,090

Total tax

On income from employment	SEK 284,705
Less—Tax credit on unearned income	(36,090)
	SEK 248,615

Notes:

1. Swedish income taxes are always computed on the taxable income rounded off to the next lowest SEK100.
2. Exchange rate of the krona at December 31, 2001: US$1 = SEK10.6675.

PwC contact

For additional information on taxation in Switzerland, contact:

Georg Ladner
PricewaterhouseCoopers AG
Stampfenbachstrasse 52
8035 Zurich, Switzerland
Telephone: (41) (1) 630 11 11
Fax: (41) (1) 630 45 15
e-mail: georg.ladner@ch.pwcglobal.com

Significant developments

There have been no significant tax or regulatory developments in the past year.

Territoriality and residence

Switzerland taxes its residents on their worldwide income, with the exception of income from foreign permanent establishments and real estate situated abroad. Individuals are regarded as resident if they are residing within Switzerland with the intention of staying there permanently.

Nonresidents are treated as residents for tax purposes if they are residing in Switzerland and/or are performing a gainful activity (employed or self-employed). Nonresidents staying in Switzerland but not performing a gainful activity are also treated as residents after they have been in Switzerland for a certain period.

Taxes are governed by federal law and 26 cantonal tax laws. As of January 1, 2001, all cantonal tax laws are required to comply with the Federal Tax Harmonization Act. Therefore, the general principles of taxation now are the same in all cantons. However, the amount of deductions and the tax rates are not subject to the Harmonization Act, so taxation will still vary considerably in the various cantons. Additionally, in most cantons communal taxes are levied as a percentage of cantonal taxes, and each commune independently determines its own percentage. Therefore, the choice of location between canton and, to a lesser degree, commune is of some importance for taxpayers provided movement is not limited by the holding of a work permit/residence permit issued by the canton where the employing company is based. The share of the total tax burden attributable to federal, cantonal and communal taxes may be estimated at one-third each. The following outline is based on the tax laws of the cantons of Zurich and Geneva and the federal tax law.

Gross income

Employee gross income/An employee resident in Switzerland for tax purposes is taxed on any salary and any other monetary benefits (including reimbursements of living expenses, etc.) received from the employer and based on the employment contract. This holds true regardless of the length of the employment, where the work has been performed, where payment is made, and whether it is remitted.

Any income of the spouse and dependent children is included in the employee's taxable income.

There are some special concessions for expatriates in many cantons such as Zurich and Geneva, which allow special deductions for expatriates, and Basle (Land and City), which allows a "tax holiday" for certain benefits. Many cantons allow educational expenses for children as a tax-free benefit if the company enters into a cooperation agreement with the school. As per January 1, 2001 new expatriate concessions were implemented also on the federal level. As a general rule, it should be possible to claim the following concessions in all cantons:

Transportation
Moving costs to Switzerland (e.g. transportation of household) as well as the moving costs upon return to their home country are deductible for expatriates. The same applies for travel expenses for the expatriate and his family at the beginning and at the end of the assignment.

Housing
If an expatriate maintains his foreign apartment or house during the period of his assignment in Switzerland, the costs of additional housing in Switzerland are deductible, provided such costs do not exceed a reasonable amount.

School fees
Children of expatriates often attend international rather than national schools. Expenses incurred to send school aged children to foreign language private schools, where the public school do not provide adequate instruction, are tax deductible.

Capital gains and investment income/Capital gains on movable property realized by employees are normally tax-exempt. Capital gains on disposal of Swiss real estate are subject to separate taxation for cantonal but exempt for federal tax purposes (unless they are qualified as being "professional").

Investment income, such as dividends, interest and royalties, is subject to income tax on a worldwide basis, subject to treaty based tax credit relief. Rental income from real estate situated abroad is basically tax-exempt. However, this income is to be taken into account in the determination of the tax rate applicable on Swiss taxable income.

Deductions

Business deductions/An individual may deduct any expenses necessary for earning employment income to the extent they are not reimbursed, such as business-related travel expenses, business-related automobile expenses, travel costs to and from work, business entertainment expenses (subject to restrictions), additional costs for outside meals, professional literature and continuing education. Moving expenses may not be deductible. Tax regulations provide for basic standard deductions, but actual costs are normally deductible if they are higher than standard deductions.

Nonbusiness expenses/A wide variety of deductions is allowed and generally includes any interest charges on mortgages or other borrowings (limited to the total private investment income, hypothetical or actual rental value plus CHF50,000), as well as any contributions to compulsory federal social security and pension fund schemes. Certain donations to recognized charitable organizations in Switzerland are deductible up to a certain percentage of net income. Other deductions may be claimed up to the maximums set forth below.

	Direct federal tax CHF	Zurich cantonal tax CHF	Geneva cantonal tax CHF
Premiums for personal insurance (1) and interest on savings accounts:			
Married taxpayer	3,100	4,600	3,000
Single taxpayer	1,500	2,300	2,000
Single, divorced or widowed taxpayer living with dependent children or other dependents	—	—	2,000
For each dependent child	700	700	750
Medical bills:			
Married taxpayer (2)	—	—	4,500
Single taxpayer (2)	—	—	3,000
For each dependent child or other dependent	—	—	750
Deduction from wife's employment Income (if any): 20% (Zurich), (Geneva) (3), up to	7,000	5,200	3,500
Deduction for Swiss social security pension	(4)	(4)	(4)

Notes:

1. Geneva—Deduction limits apply only to life insurance premiums. Sickness and accident insurance premiums are fully deductible.
2. Only the part exceeding the 1% of the net taxable income.
3. To be taken into account separately in the computation of the tax discount introduced further to the Federal Tax Harmonization Act as of January 1, 2001.
4. Computed accordingly to the type of pension received and to the gross income excluding the pension.

Personal allowances/Personal allowances are granted according to individual circumstances, as shown below.

	Direct federal tax	Zurich cantonal tax	Geneva (Note 1) cantonal tax
	CHF	CHF	CHF
Married taxpayer	—	—	27,500
Single taxpayer	—	—	15,000
Single, divorced or widowed taxpayer living with dependent children or other dependents	—	—	27,500
For each dependent child	5,600	5,400	4,500
For each additional dependent child	—	—	6,500
For each dependent other than wife or child	5,600	2,400	4,500
For each additional dependent	—	—	6,500
Childminder expenses (2)			2,500

Notes:

1. Geneva: these deductions are to be taken into account in the separate computation of the tax discount introduced further to the Federal Tax Harmonization Act as of January 1, 2001.
2. For a dependent child of less than 12 years old. The same amount is to be taken into account whether the taxpayer has one or several dependent children fulfilling the condition.

An authorized lump-sum 'foreign service residence' tax deduction (commonly called "Residency allowance" deduction) from Geneva cantonal tax may be negotiated for expatriates, provided certain conditions are fulfilled. As from the 1999 tax year, the deduction has been of 10% of the base compensation, limited to the total of expatriate allowances paid (in practice, this deduction also applies for federal taxes assessed in Geneva because the calculation and levying are delegated to the cantonal authorities). However, based on the new Swiss federal tax Ordinance relating to expatriates, the practice will change in Geneva, probably by 2004, towards a specific, but sometimes limited, exemption of the Transportations moving costs, as well as of the housing on school fees of expatriate and specialist hires working/residing in Switzerland for a limited period of time (see "Gross income" section above).

Tax credits

A credit may be claimed for unrelieved foreign withholding taxes on dividends, interest and royalties derived from most countries with which Switzerland has concluded a double taxation convention.

When the tax payable by an employed individual has possibly been computed based on an ordinary tax return, the tax liability is reduced by the tax already paid by wage tax (if any) and any Swiss anticipatory tax on dividends and interest (if any) withheld at source.

Other taxes

Social security tax/For 2002 the taxpayer's share of social security contributions (old-age and dependent pension schemes, disability insurance and military service compensation schemes) is 5.05% with no upper limit (9.5% for self-employment income) and 1.5% for unemployment insurance on the first CHF106,800 and an additional 1% from CHF106,800 up to CHF267,000. In Geneva, as from July 1, 2001 an additional compulsory maternity insurance contribution of 0,2%, with no ceiling, is also perceived. The same rate of contribution applies to the employer. See also "Nonbusiness expenses" above.

Health insurance is compulsory and must be organized privately by each individual.

Cantonal and communal taxes/As outlined above, in most cantons a communal tax on income is levied, mainly as a percentage of cantonal taxes.

In addition, most of the cantons levy a surcharge on their tax (parish or church tax) to support the three recognized churches (Protestant, Roman Catholic and Christian Catholic), if applicable. For individuals who belong to another faith or who are not a member of any faith, the tax is not levied. In the canton of Zurich, it is important to indicate religious denomination clearly on the registration form at the town hall when first entering Switzerland, as this will serve as the basis for assessing parish tax. In the canton of Geneva, payment of the parish or church tax is not compulsory.

Wealth tax/All cantons levy a wealth tax based on net owned assets. The direct federal tax is not imposed on private property. Net assets include all assets (real estate property, net business assets, securities, receivables, deposits, surrender value of life and similar insurance policies, movable property and loans, advances, mortgages and private borrowings). To arrive at the taxable wealth, standard allowances prescribed by the law according to personal circumstances may be deducted.

Personal tax of CHF24 (CHF48 for joint filing) in Zurich and CHF25 in Geneva is levied on each return.

Tax administration

Returns/Normally, income and net wealth items are added together to determine the joint taxable income of wife and husband for Swiss tax purposes. However, special rates apply for married couples. Furthermore, the concept of income splitting between spouses is being heavily debated at the moment. There might be changes in the future as some cantons already apply this system.

For direct federal tax purposes, tax returns must be filed annually or biannually (only applicable for the cantons of Vaud, Ticino and Wallis), starting with an odd year, (i.e., 2001/2002). In the other cantons, tax returns must be filed annually. Employed persons are required to enclose a certificate of remuneration issued by their employers. Taxpayers must file their returns on a calendar-year basis. The tax administration may request further evidence, particularly in respect of deductions, and may interview the taxpayer. For federal tax and cantonal tax purposes (except from the cantons of Vaud, Ticino and Wallis that will probably change their timing system in 2003), the tax period is the current year. Upon receipt of notification of final assessment, the period for filing an appeal commences.

Foreign employees with no permit to settle permanently in Switzerland and whose employer is resident in Switzerland are usually taxed at source. However, they are obliged to file a tax return if their gross annual income exceeds CHF120,000 (for the canton of Geneva, CHF 500,000 but 4 other conditions exist in Geneva). There are some exceptions to taxation at source, e.g., when the salary is paid directly by a non-Swiss company with no charge-back of costs to Switzerland.

Payment of tax/Under the system of taxation at source, income tax is withheld from salaries if the employee has no permit to settle permanently in Switzerland. Otherwise, payment of tax is based on the tax bills (issued based on the tax returns filed) received, and it basically must be settled in three installments for Zurich cantonal tax purposes, in ten installments for Geneva cantonal tax purposes and by the end of March each year for federal tax purposes.

Tax rates

Direct federal tax on income

I—Spouses Living Together (prior year)—only valid for the cantons of Vaud, Ticino and Wallis

Taxable income		Tax on	Percentage
Over	Not over	Column 1	on excess
(Column 1)			
CHF 0	CHF 22,600	—	—
22,600	40,600	—	1
40,600	46,600	CHF 180	2
46,600	60,100	300	3
60,100	72,100	705	4
72,100	82,600	1,185	5
82,600	91,700	1,710	6
91,700	99,200	2,256	7
99,200	105,200	2,781	8
105,200	109,700	3,261	9
109,700	112,800	3,666	10
112,800	114,300	3,976	11
114,300	115,800	4,141	12
115,800	715,500	4,321	13
715,500		82,282	
715,600		82,294*	

*11.5% of total income (11.5% being the maximum rate applicable).

II—Other Taxpayers (prior year) Vaud, Ticino and Wallis

Taxable income		Tax on Column 1	Percentage on excess
Over (Column 1)	Not over		
CHF 0	CHF 11,600	—	—
11,600	25,300	—	0.77
25,300	33,100	CHF 105.45	0.88
33,100	44,100	174.05	2.64
44,100	57,900	464.45	2.97
57,900	62,400	874.30	5.94
62,400	82,700	1,141.60	6.60
82,700	107,500	2,481.40	8.80
107,500	140,500	4,663.80	11.00
140,500	603,000	8,293.80	13.20
603,000		69,343.80	
603,100		69,356.50*	

*11.5% of total income (11.5% being the maximum rate applicable).

III—Spouses Living Together (current year)

Taxable income		Tax on Column 1	Percentage on excess
Over (Column 1)	Not over		
CHF 0	CHF 24,900	—	—
24,900	44,700	—	1
44,700	51,300	CHF 198	2
51,300	66,200	330	3
66,200	79,400	777	4
79,400	91,000	1,305	5
91,000	101,000	1,885	6
101,000	109,300	2,485	7
109,300	115,900	3,066	8
115,900	120,900	3,594	9
120,900	124,300	4,044	10
124,300	126,000	4,384	11
126,000	127,700	4,571	12
127,700	788,400	4,775	13
788,400		90,666	
788,500		90,678*	

*11.5% of total income (11.5% being the maximum rate applicable).

IV—Other Taxpayers (current year)

Taxable income Over (Column 1)	Not over		Tax on Column 1	Percentage on excess
CHF 0	CHF 12,800		—	—
12,800	27,900		—	0.77
27,900	36,500		CHF 116.25	0.88
36,500	48,600		191.90	2.64
48,600	63,800		511.30	2.97
63,800	68,800		962.70	5.94
68,800	91,100		1,259.70	6.60
91,100	118,400		2,731.50	8.80
118,400	154,700		5,133.90	11.00
154,700	664,300		9,126.90	13.20
664,300			76,394.10	
664,400			76,406.00*	

*11.5% of total income (11.5% being the maximum rate applicable).

Zurich cantonal tax

V—Income Tax

Table A—Married Taxpayers/Taxpayers Living with Children in Own Household

Taxable income Over (Column 1)	Not over		Basic tax on Column 1	Percentage on excess
CHF 0	CHF 11,000		—	0
11,000	16,400		—	2
16,400	23,200		CHF 108	3
23,200	31,400		312	4
31,400	40,900		640	5
40,900	53,100		1,115	6
53,100	80,300		1,847	7
80,300	107,500		3,751	8
107,500	148,300		5,927	9
148,300	197,200		9,599	10
197,200	250,200		14,489	11
250,200	311,400		20,319	12
311,400			27,663	13

Table B—Other Taxpayers

Taxable income				
Over	Not over		Basic tax on Column 1	Percentage on excess
(Column 1)				
CHF 0	CHF 5,500	....	—	0
5,500	9,600	....	—	2
9,600	13,700	....	CHF 82	3
13,700	20,400	....	205	4
20,400	28,600	....	473	5
28,600	38,100	....	883	6
38,100	49,000	....	1,453	7
49,000	63,900	....	2,216	8
63,900	92,500	....	3,408	9
92,500	121,000	....	5,982	10
121,000	165,900	....	8,832	11
165,900	224,300	....	13,771	12
224,300		....	20,779	13

VI—Wealth Tax

Table A—Married Taxpayers/Taxpayers Living with Children in Own Household

Taxable wealth				
Over	Not over		Basic tax on Column 1	Percentage on excess
(Column 1)				
CHF 0	CHF 136,000	....	—	0
136,000	340,000	....	—	0.05
340,000	680,000	....	CHF 102	0.10
680,000	1,223,000	....	442	0.15
1,223,000	2,039,000	....	1,256.50	0.20
2,039,000	2,854,000	....	2,888.50	0.25
2,854,000		....	4,926.00	0.30

Table B—Other Taxpayers

Taxable wealth				
Over	Not over		Basic tax on Column 1	Percentage on excess
(Column 1)				
CHF 0	CHF 68,000	....	—	0
68,000	272,000	....	—	0.05
272,000	612,000	....	CHF 102	0.10
612,000	1,155,000	....	442	0.15
1,155,000	1,971,000	....	1,256.50	0.20
1,971,000	2,786,000	....	2,888.50	0.25
2,786,000		....	4,926.00	0.30

Effective cantonal income and wealth tax is determined by multiplying the basic tax by the multiplier applicable for the tax (calendar) year in question. For Zurich for 2002, effective cantonal tax is 105% of basic tax.

Zurich communal tax/Each commune levies its taxes as a percentage of basic cantonal tax. For 2002 the effective communal tax of the city of Zurich is 122% of basic tax.

Parish tax/Parish tax is levied as a percentage of basic cantonal tax. For 2002 the following percentages are applicable in the city of Zurich.

	%
Protestant	10
Roman Catholic	12
Christian Catholic	14

Geneva cantonal tax

Preliminary note:

The Geneva (cantonal/communal tax estimates shown hereafter are **still based on the 2001 tax scales,** as the 2002 tax scales had not yet been issued on June 21, 2002.

VII—Income Tax

Table A—Married Taxpayers and Taxpayers Living with Children in Own Household

Taxable income	**Base cantonal (1) tax**	**Tax rate before tax discount**
CHF	CHF	%
20,000	1,082.10	5.41
30,000	2,083.45	6.94
40,000	3,230.40	8.08
50,000	4,471.65	8.94
75,000	8,028.65	10.70
100,000	11,822.20	11.82
150,000	19,807.60	13.21
200,000	28,201.70	14.10
300,000	45,803.75	15.27
500,000	82,658.05	16.53
1,000,000	177,217.85	17.72

(1) Before cantonal /communal multiplicators, personal tax discount and 12% communal taxes rebate.

Table B—Other Taxpayers

Taxable income	Base cantonal (1) tax	Tax rate before tax discount
CHF	CHF	%
20,000	1,615.20	8.08
30,000	2,879.65	9.60
40,000	4,226.35	10.57
50,000	5,620.40	11.24
75,000	9,248.65	12.33
100,000	13,042.55	13.04
150,000	21,027.95	14.02
200,000	29,422.05	14.71
300,000	47,024.15	15.67
500,000	83,878.45	16.78
1,000,000	178,438.20	17.84

(1) Before cantonal/communal multiplicators, personal tax discount and 12% communal taxes rebate.

VIII—Wealth Tax

Table A—Basic Tax

Taxable wealth			Maximum tax for the band	Percentage
Over	Not over			
CHF 1	CHF 101,418	....	CHF 177.50	0.175
101,419	202,836	....	228.20	0.225
202,837	304,253	....	278.90	0.275
304,254	405,671	....	304.25	0.300
405,672	608,507	....	659.20	0.325
608,508	811,342	....	709.90	0.350
811,343	1,014,178	....	760.65	0.375
1,014,179	1,217,013	....	811.35	0.400
1,217,014	1,521,267	....	1,293.10	0.425
1,521,267		....		0.450

Table B—Supplementary Tax on Basic Tax

Taxable wealth			Maximum tax for the band	Percentage
Over	Not over			
CHF 1	CHF 101,418	....	CHF 0	0
101,419	202,836	....	11.40	0.01125
202,837	304,253	....	13.95	0.01375
304,254	405,671	....	30.45	0.03000
405,672	608,507	....	65.90	0.03250
608,508	811,342	....	106.50	0.05250
811,343	1,014,178	....	114.10	0.05625
1,014,179	1,217,013	....	162.25	0.08000
1,217,014	1,521,267	....	258.60	0.08500
1,521,268	3,042,533	....	1,711.40	0.11250
3,042,533		....		0.13500

The above tax rates are basically applicable to taxpayers filing a tax return. Effective cantonal income and wealth tax is determined by multiplying the basic tax by the multiplier applicable for the tax (calendar) year in question, which is 148.5% for tax year 2001, and then by adding the supplementary tax on wealth.

Geneva communal tax/Each commune levies its taxes as a percentage of the above tax. For 2001 the effective communal tax of the city of Geneva is 45.5% of basic tax.

INDIVIDUAL TAX CALCULATION— CANTON AND CITY OF ZURICH

Calculation for direct federal tax and cantonal and communal taxes, canton and city of Zurich 2000.

Assumptions

1. Married couple with two children, member of the Protestant Church, living in Zurich.
2. Employment income CHF175,000 for 2002, net of social security taxes and pension fund contributions.
3. Compensation as director CHF3,200.
4. Securities and savings accounts total CHF140,000; income thereon CHF4,000 (including interest on savings accounts of CHF2,200).
5. Living in own apartment; assessed value CHF180,000, estimated net rental income of personally used real estate property CHF12,500; mortgage CHF100,000; mortgage interest CHF5,000.
6. Income-related expenses CHF7,000 per annum (travel to and from work, external boarding, etc.).
7. Insurance premiums CHF2,300 per annum; surrender value of life and annuity insurance total CHF5,000.
8. Motorcar with market value of CHF25,000.

Determination of taxable income

	Direct federal tax—2002	Zurich tax—2002
	Income of 2002	Income of 2002
	CHF	CHF
Determination of net income		
Gross income:		
Income from employment	175,000	175,000
Secondary income—Director's fees	3,200	3,200
Net income from real estate property	12,500	12,500
Income from securities and receivables	4,000	4,000
Total	194,700	194,700
Deductions:		
Income-related expenses	7,000	7,000
Insurance premiums and interest on savings accounts:		
Direct federal tax—Maximum for married couples 3,100 plus 700 for each minor child	4,500	—
Cantonal tax—Maximum for married couples 4,600 plus 700 for each minor child	—	6,000
Interest on mortgage	5,000	5,000
Other interest on debts	—	—
Charitable donations	300	300
Total	16,800	18,300
Net income:		
Total of gross income	194,700	194,700
Total of deductions	16,800	18,300
	177,900	176,400

	Direct federal tax—2002	Zurich tax—2002
	CHF	CHF
Determination of taxable income		
Net income	177,900	176,400
Tax-free amounts (social allowances):		
Direct federal tax:		
For each child—5,600	(11,200)	—
Cantonal tax:		
Deduction for each minor child—5,400	—	(10,800)
Taxable income	166,700	165,600

Determination of taxable wealth

	(Zurich tax, December 31, 2002)
	CHF
Determination of net assets	
Assets:	
Real estate property	180,000
Securities and receivables	140,000
Surrender value of life and annuity insurance	5,000
Motorcar	25,000
Other assets	?
Total	350,000
Liabilities:	
Mortgage	100,000
Other debts	?
Total	100,000
Net assets:	
Total assets	350,000
Total liabilities	(100,000)
	250,000
Taxable wealth	
Taxable wealth	250,000

Tax computation

Direct federal tax		
Income tax on taxable income of 166,700 per year (rounded off)		CHF 9,845
Cantonal, communal and parish tax		
Computation of basic tax:		
Income tax on taxable income of 165,600	11,329	
Wealth tax on taxable wealth of 250,000	57	
Basic tax	11,386	
Total tax liability		
Cantonal tax—105% of basic tax	11,955	
Communal tax—122% of basic tax	13,891	
Parish tax (Protestant Church)—10% of basic tax	1,139	
Personal tax	48	26,033
Total of taxes payable in canton of Zurich		CHF 35,878

INDIVIDUAL TAX CALCULATION— CANTON AND CITY OF GENEVA

Calculation for direct federal tax 2001 and cantonal and communal taxes, canton and city of Geneva 2001.

Assumptions

1. Foreign executive transferred by an international group to Switzerland for a maximum period of five years; married with two children (aged more than 12); one spouse earns all the income.
2. Employment income, net of social security taxes and pension fund contributions.

	2001
	CHF
Base salary	153,000
Residency allowances	22,000
Total	175,000

3. Compensation as director: CHF3,200.
4. Securities and savings accounts total CHF140,000; income thereon, CHF4,000 (including interest on savings accounts of CHF 2,200).
5. Living in own apartment, assessed value of CHF180,000; estimated net deemed rental income of personally used real estate property: CHF12,500 for Geneva cantonal and federal tax purposes; mortgage: CHF100,000; mortgage interest: CHF5,000.
6. Income-related expenses: CHF7,000 per annum (travel to and from work, external boarding).
7. Sickness and accident insurance premiums: CHF2,000 per annum. Life insurance premiums: CHF300 per annum; surrender value of life insurance: CHF5,000.
8. Medical bills: CHF3,000.
9. Deposits on children's savings accounts: CHF600 per child.
10. Charitable donations: CHF3,500.
11. Car market value: CHF25,000.

Determination of taxable income

	Direct federal tax 2001	Geneva tax 2001
	Income of 2001	Income of 2001
	CHF	CHF
Determination of net income		
Gross income:		
Income from employment	175,000	175,000
Secondary income—Director's fee	3,200	3,200
Net income from real estate property	12,500	12,500
Income from securities and receivables	4,000	4,000
Total	194,700	194,700
Deductions:		
Income-connected expenses, lump-sum representation expenses	8,750	8,750
Travel to and from work: Federal tax—Depending on distance	840	—
Authorized tax deduction: Lower of 10% of gross employment income or residency allowances (1)	17,500	17,500
Sickness and accident insurance premiums	2,000	2,000
Life insurance premiums and interest on savings accounts	2,500	2,500
Medical bills (Note 2 for Geneva tax and Note 3 for direct federal tax)	—	1,410
Interest on mortgage	5,000	5,000
Total	35,750	37,160
Net income:		
Total of gross income	194,700	194,700
Total of deductions	(35,750)	(37,160)
Less—Portion of charitable donations deductible (Note 4 for Geneva tax; Note 5 for direct federal tax)	(3,500)	(3,500)
	155,450	154,040

Notes:

1. As per 2002 practice. Changes to come, probably by 2004.
2. Only the part exceeding the 1% of the net taxable income.
3. Only the part exceeding the 5% of the net taxable income.
4. Cash donations to charities up to 5% of the net taxable income.
5. Cash donation to charities up to 10% of the net taxable income.

	Direct federal tax 2001	Geneva tax 2001
	Income of 2001	Income of 2001
	CHF	CHF
Determination of taxable income		
Net income	155,450	154,040
Tax-free amounts (social allowances):		
For married persons	—	
For dependent children	(11,200)	
Taxable income	144,250	154,040

Determination of taxable wealth

	(Geneva tax, December 31, 2001)
Determination of net assets	
	CHF
Assets:	
Real estate property	180,000
Securities and receivables	140,000
Surrender value of life insurance	5,000
Car	25,000
Total	350,000
Liabilities:	
Mortgage	100,000
Total	100,000
Net assets:	
Total assets	350,000
Total liabilities	(100,000)
	250,000
Taxable wealth	
Net assets	250,000
Tax-free amount (social allowance):	
For married persons with two children	(150,000)
Taxable wealth	100,000

Tax computation

Direct federal tax		
Income tax on taxable income of 144,250 (rounded off)		CHF 8,383
Cantonal and communal tax		
Computation of basic tax:		
Income tax on taxable income of 154,040	17,420.75	
Wealth tax on taxable wealth of 100,000	175	
Basic tax	17,595.75	
Total tax liability		
Cantonal tax—147.5% of basic tax (rounded off)	25,953.75	
Less—Reduction of initiative 111 – 12 % of cantonal tax (CHF25,695.60, see note 1)	(3,083.45)	
Supplementary cantonal tax – 1% of basic tax	174.20	
Communal tax—45.5% of basic tax	8,006.05	
Supplementary wealth tax on 100,000	—	
Personal tax	25	
Real estate cantonal tax (0.1% of CHF180,000)	180	31,257.30
Total of taxes payable in canton of Geneva		CHF 39,639.80

Notes:

1. Discount on income cantonal tax only.
2. Exchange rate of the Swiss franc at December 31, 2001: US$1 = CHF1.63.

PwC contact

For additional information on Tahiti and French Polynesia, contact:

Christophe Parion
PricewaterhouseCoopers–Fitec
Centre Vaima
BP 608 – Papeete
Tahiti
Telephone: (689) 50 86 00
Fax: (689) 43 99 31
e-mail: coopers@mail.pf
Att: Christophe Parion

Absence of taxation

Income tax is not imposed on individuals in Tahiti or French Polynesia.

Note

Exchange rate (selling) of the Pacific franc at December 31, 2001: US$1 = XPF133.95. The Pacific franc is pegged to the Euro at €1 = XPF119.33.

PwC contact

For additional information on taxation in Taiwan, contact:

Wen-Horng Kao, Tax Partner
PricewaterhouseCoopers
Hsin-Ji Building, 12th Floor
460 Hsin Yi Road, Sec. 4
Taipei 110, Taiwan, ROC
Telephone: (886) (2) 2729 5209
Fax: (886) (2) 8789-1937 (Tax)
e-mail: wen-horng.kao@tw.pwcglobal.com

Significant developments

The tax return filing period has been changed from between February 20 and March 31 to between May 1 to May 31. No extension is allowed.

Territoriality and residence

Taiwan taxes its citizens, as well as aliens whose period of stay in Taiwan is more than 90 days in a calendar year, on compensation attributable to Taiwan situs services and other Taiwan-source income. An alien whose period of stay is not more than 90 days is taxed only on income paid in Taiwan.

Aliens who reside in Taiwan for 183 days or more in a calendar year are considered residents. Those who were resident in the previous year and continue to reside in Taiwan are also considered residents in the current year, regardless of their period of residence during this year. An alien who resides in Taiwan for less than 183 days is considered a nonresident.

Gross income

Employee gross income/An alien who is present in Taiwan for more than 90 days is taxed on salary, bonuses and commissions earned for work done in Taiwan, regardless of where payment is made, but is not taxed to the extent that the compensation relates to services performed outside Taiwan. Such an individual is also taxed on fringe benefit reimbursements, such as housing, living, education, and transportation allowances. However, many major fringe benefits, such as housing, rent and utilities, automobile purchase and operating costs, and compensation for servants, are not taxed if provided directly by the employer without cash payment to the employee.

Income tax concessions to expatriates/If a nonresident individual holding the position of director, manager or technician of an enterprise that invests in Taiwan in accordance with the Statute for Investment by Foreigners/Overseas Chinese stays in Taiwan to perform investment, plant construction or market survey operations for a period of less than 183 days in a taxable year, the salary for such work paid by the overseas employers will not be deemed to be Taiwan-source income.

Capital gains and investment income/Gains from the disposal of capital assets are included in an individual's taxable income with the exceptions listed below.

1. Gains from the sale of land and household furniture.
2. Gains from the sale of marketable securities (for both listed and unlisted securities) are liable to securities transaction tax at a rate of 0.3% on the gross

proceeds from sale of stocks and 0.1% on the gross proceeds from sale of debentures and government-approved bonds.

3. Income tax on gains from the sale of an owner-occupied house may be refundable if the taxpayer purchases another house for occupation (at an amount greater than the selling price of the old house) within two years from the date of sale. The income tax on the gain can be refunded up to the amount by which the cost of the new house exceeds the sale price of the old house. The tax reduction is also available if the new house is purchased before sale of the old house.

Capital losses are deductible expenses only against capital gains; unused losses may be carried forward for three years.

Imputation tax system/The main purpose of the imputation tax system is to eliminate double taxation on earnings of a corporation. Corporations are taxed at 25% on profits (an additional 10% tax is imposed on any undistributed current earnings). This tax can be distributed to the domestic individual shareholders to offset their individual income tax. Any excess tax credits will be refundable to the resident individual shareholders.

As for foreign shareholders, only the 10% tax on undistributed retained earnings can be claimed by foreign corporate shareholder as tax credit to offset the 20% withholding income tax on dividend distribution. No refund would be available to foreign shareholders.

Income on investments outside Taiwan is not taxed. Investment income earned in Taiwan is taxable. The first TWD270,000 of certain types of interest income is exempt from tax.

Deductions

Business deductions/No deduction of business expenses is allowed to individuals.

Nonbusiness expenses/Taxpayers have the option to claim either a standard deduction or itemized deductions for their income deduction purpose. These deductions are as follows.

1. Standard deduction:

   The deduction for single taxpayers is TWD44,000. A husband and a wife filing a joint return are eligible for a standard deduction of TWD67,000.

2. Itemized deductions:

   Itemized deductions include charitable contributions, insurance premiums (maximum TWD24,000 per person), medical expenses, calamity and losses, interest paid on loans for the purchase of an owner-occupied house in Taiwan (maximum TWD300,000), and rental payment (maximum TWD120,000) for the lease of a self-use residence in Taiwan. There is no ceiling on the itemized deduction total.

Nonresident aliens are not eligible for any deductions.

Personal allowances/A resident alien is eligible for a personal exemption of TWD74,000. Additional exemptions of TWD74,000 are available for a spouse and for each dependent, and an exemption of TWD111,000 applies to a dependent over 70 years of age. In addition, taxpayers may deduct TWD75,000 of their income from salaries or wages and a maximum amount of TWD270,000 of their interest income.

The following allowances are also available.

1. A handicapped person is eligible for a deduction of TWD74,000.
2. Tuition for children attending college can be deducted up to TWD25,000 per family.
3. Losses from disposal of properties can be deducted to the extent of gains resulting from the disposal of properties in the same tax year.

The amounts for exemptions, the standard deduction, the special deduction of income from salaries or wages, and the special deduction for handicapped persons are to be revised triennially to reflect the inflation rate.

A nonresident alien is not eligible for any personal allowances.

Tax credits

According to the Statute for Promotion of Industries Upgrading, aliens may be entitled to an investment credit. Individuals subscribing to or underwriting important high-tech enterprises or venture capital enterprises may claim 10% of the investment amount as a tax credit.

Other taxes

There are no social security or local income taxes in Taiwan.

Tax administration

Returns/Husbands and wives must file joint returns if either the husband or wife has resided in Taiwan for more than 90 days in a calendar year. A spouse has the option to calculate the taxes due on that spouse's salaries or wages separately. Total tax liability for the joint return consists of the taxes due on the spouse's salaries or wages and the taxes due on all other joint income.

Nonresidents who are in Taiwan for not more than 90 days are not required to file an income tax return, since tax is withheld by the employer on compensation paid in Taiwan.

Income tax returns must be filed on a calendar-year basis between Mary 1 and May 31 of the following year.

Payment of tax/There is income tax withholding on locally paid salaries. Additional tax due must be paid at the time of filing. Unless they have a local tax guarantor, aliens resident for more than 90 days will not be permitted to leave Taiwan until they have paid taxes due through the exit date.

Tax rates

Tax rates are as follows.

1. A nonresident alien residing in Taiwan for not more than 90 days is subject to 20% withholding tax on remuneration received from a Taiwan-registered entity. Remuneration received from an entity registered outside of Taiwan is not taxable.
2. A nonresident alien residing in Taiwan for more than 90 days but less than 183 days is subject to a 20% income tax rate on Taiwan taxable income, regardless of where paid.
3. A resident alien is subject to progressive tax rates as shown below.

Taxable income		Rate of tax	Less progressive difference
Over	Not over		
		%	
0	TWD 370,000	6	0
TWD 370,000	990,000	13	TWD 25,900
990,000	1,980,000	21	105,100
1,980,000	3,720,000	30	283,300
3,720,000		40	655,300

Note:

The progressive difference is subtracted from taxable income times the tax rate to determine income tax due.

INDIVIDUAL TAX CALCULATION

Assumptions

Resident alien husband and wife, two children; one spouse earns all the income.

Tax computation

Gross income:		
Salary		TWD 2,700,000
Dividend income		100,000
Interest income		400,000
Total gross income		3,200,000
Less—Qualifying interest income up to 270,000		270,000
Adjusted gross income		2,930,000
Less—Itemized deductions:		
Insurance premiums (maximum deduction—24,000 per person)	96,000	
Medical expenses	42,000	
Charitable contributions	8,000	
Calamity	10,000	156,000
		2,774,000
Less:		
Personal exemptions (74,000 x 4)	296,000	
Salary exemption	75,000	371,000
Taxable income		TWD 2,403,000
Income tax		TWD 437,600
Less—Tax credits derived from dividend received (1)		(25,000)
Net income tax payable		TWD 412,600

Notes:

1. Tax imputation system (investee corporation), calculated as follows.

	TWD
Income before tax	100,000
Income tax of 25%	25,000
Net income	75,000
Distributable earnings	75,000
Tax credits distributable to shareholders	25,000

   The investee corporation can distribute TWD75,000 of dividend and TWD25,000 of tax credit to the shareholders under the new tax imputation system.

2. Exchange rate of the Taiwan dollar at January 1, 2002: US$1 = TWD35.09150.

PwC contacts

For additional information on taxation in Tanzania, contact:

Vinoo Somaiya or David Tarimo
PricewaterhouseCoopers
International House
Garden Avenue
PO Box 45
Dar-es-Salaam, Tanzania
Telephone: (255) (22) 2133100
Fax: (255) (22) 2133200
e-mail: vinoo.somaiya@tz.pwcglobal.com
david.tarimo@tz.pwcglobal.com

Significant developments

There have been no significant developments regarding individual taxation in the past year.

Territoriality and residence

Residents, including short-term residents, are taxed on their worldwide income. Nonresidents are taxed on their income accrued in or derived solely from sources within Tanzania.

An individual who fulfills one of the following criteria is considered resident.

1. Has a permanent home in Tanzania and is present in Tanzania during any part of a tax year;
2. Spends more than 183 days in Tanzania in any one tax year;
   or
3. Spends an average of more than 122 days per year over three tax years.

Gross income

Employee gross income/Income from employment or services rendered includes salaries, wages, leave pay, sick pay, payment in lieu of leave, fees, commissions, bonuses, gratuities, and any allowances (excluding those expended wholly and exclusively in the production of income from employment or services rendered), as well as benefits-in-kind, for example, the value of residential accommodation provided by employer; furniture; private use of a car provided by employer; school fees; and gas, electricity and water supplied at the expense of the employer.

Capital gains and investment income/Capital gains tax was reintroduced at a rate of 10% as of July 1, 1999. Interest income exceeding the first TShs150,000 on monies saved in any bank operating in Tanzania and dividend income are taxed only at the appropriate resident withholding tax rates for such income.

Investment income derived by residents from sources outside Tanzania is taxable.

Deductions

Business deductions/Business expenses that are deductible from income derived from employment or services rendered are not specifically listed, but an individual may claim a deduction for expenses incurred wholly and exclusively in the production of such income. No blanket or standard deductions are available.

Nonbusiness expenses/No deductions are allowed for mortgage or other interest, social security contributions, taxes, or charitable contributions. There are no standard deductions.

Tax credits

The following tax credits are available to resident individuals, including short-term residents.

1. Any tax paid in another country in respect of income derived from that country.
2. Any tax paid in a country, with which Tanzania has concluded a treaty for relief from double taxation, in respect of income derived from that country.

Other taxes

Social security taxes/Every employer must contribute to the National Social Security Fund. The contribution is 20% of the employee's gross employment earnings. The employer is entitled to recover up to half of this from the employee.

Local taxes on income/Employees are normally subject to a development levy. In Dar es Salaam every employee is required to pay a development levy equal to 1% of his or her annual income through deductions from salary.

Tax administration

Returns/Taxpayers file both provisional and final returns, as follows.

1. Provisional return:

   Individuals are required to furnish a provisional return, containing an estimate of their chargeable income. Tax is payable thereon in four quarterly installments from the beginning of the year of income or the accounting period to which the return relates.
2. Final return:

   Individuals are also required to file a final return of income containing a statement of their income from all sources chargeable to individual income tax in Tanzania within 30 days from the date of service of the notice requiring them to furnish this return. In case of a person carrying on business who has made a provisional return of income, the return is due for submission within six months from the end of the year of income or the accounting date to which the return relates.

An individual whose income is derived solely from employment and whose employment income has been fully subjected to pay-as-you-earn (PAYE) deduction is not obliged to furnish a provisional or final return of income.

Joint filing of returns applies only where the wife derives income from any employment in any business carried on by her husband or with any partnership firm in which her husband is a partner. Otherwise, spouses file separate returns and are liable to tax on their respective incomes.

Tax years not coinciding with the calendar year are permitted in relation to income from any source other than employment or services rendered.

Payment of tax/Payroll withholding of individual income tax operates under the PAYE scheme.

Tax rates

Tanzania/The following table is applicable to residents of Tanzania.

Annual taxable income			
Over	**Not over**	**Tax on Column 1**	**Percentage on excess**
(Column 1)			
0	TShs 540,000	—	—
TShs 540,000	2,160,000	—	17.5
2,160,000	4,320,000	TShs 283,500	20
4,320,000	6,480,000	715,500	25
6,480,000		1,255,500	30

Zanzibar/Individuals who are ordinarily resident in Zanzibar and whose income is accrued in or derived from Zanzibar are liable to tax at the rates given below.

Monthly taxable income			
Over	**Not over**	**Tax on column 1**	**Percentage on excess**
(Column 1)			
0	TShs 20,000	—	—
TShs 20,000	40,000	—	7.5
40,000	60,000	TShs 1,500	10.0
60,000	80,000	3,500	12.5
80,000	100,000	6,000	15.0
100,000	120,000	9,000	17.5
120,000	140,000	12,500	20.0
140,000	170,000	16,500	22.5
170,000	210,000	23,250	25.0
210,000	260,000	33,250	27.5
260,000		47,000	35.0

INDIVIDUAL TAX CALCULATION

Tanzania resident

Assumptions

1. Resident employee, gross income TShs64,000,000 per annum.
2. Housing provided by the employer.
3. Benefits provided by employer:
   a. Car.
   b. Payment of electricity, telephone and water bills aggregating to TShs3,000,000.
   c. Domestic servant with annual salary of TShs500,000.
4. Bank deposit interest: TShs3,000,000.
5. Mortgage interest: TShs1,000,000 (no deduction permitted).
6. Capital gain: TShs3,000,000.
7. Dividend income: TShs2,000,000. (Assumption: not listed on Stock Exchange).

Tax computation

Salary income		TShs 64,000,000
Benefits in kind:		
Utilities	3,000,000	
Domestic servant	500,000	3,500,000
		67,500,000
Housing benefit (15% of salary plus benefits)		10,125,000
		TShs 77,625,000
Tax thereon:		
On the first 6,480,000	1,255,500	
On the remainder (71,145,000) at 30%	21,343,500	TShs 22,599,000
Tax on dividend income of 2,000,000 at 10% (resident withholding tax rate) (1)		TShs 200,000
Tax on bank interest income (3,000,000 – 150,000) at 15% (resident withholding tax rate) (1)		TShs 427,500
Capital gains tax on 3,000,000 at 10%		TShs 300,000

Zanzibar resident

Assumptions

1. An employee, married with two children, gross income TShs64,000,000.
2. Benefits provided by employer: car; payment of electricity, telephone and water bills aggregating to TShs300,000; and domestic servant annual salary TShs360,000.
3. Bank deposit interest: TShs300,000.
4. Mortgage interest: TShs84,000 (no deduction permitted).

Tax computation

Salary income		TShs 64,000,000
Benefits in kind:		
Utilities	300,000	
Domestic servant	360,000	660,000
Chargeable income		TShs 64,660,000
Tax thereon:		
On the first 3,120,000	564,000	
On the remainder (61,540,000) at 35%	21,539,000	TShs 22,103,000
Tax on bank interest income (300,000 – 150,000) at 15% withholding tax rate (1)		TShs 22,500

Notes:

1. Taxed at withholding tax rate. Withholding tax is final tax.
2. Exchange rate of the Tanzanian shilling at December 31, 2001: US$1 = TShs916.

PwC contact

For additional information on taxation in Thailand, contact:

Janist Aphornratana, Knowledge Management Manager
PricewaterhouseCoopers Legal & Tax Consultants Ltd.
Bangkok City Tower, 15th Floor
179 South Sathorn Road
Bangkok 10120, Thailand
Telephone: (66) (2) 286 9999
Fax: (66) (2) 286 2666
e-mail: janist.aphornratana@th.pwcglobal.com

Significant developments

There have been no significant tax or regulatory developments in the past year.

Territoriality and residence

Thailand taxes its residents and nonresidents on their assessable income derived from employment or business carried on in Thailand, regardless of whether such income is paid in or outside Thailand. Residents, defined as persons residing in Thailand at one or more times for an aggregate period of 180 days or more in any tax year (calendar year), who derive income from abroad are taxable on that income if remitted into Thailand in the year in which it is received. Short-term residence is not defined under Thai tax regulations.

Gross income

Employee gross income/Both resident and nonresident individuals who receive assessable income by virtue of hire of service performed in Thailand, including salary, bonuses, gratuities, pensions, the monetary value of rent-free housing, the employer's payment of income tax, or any other money, property or benefits derived by virtue of hire of service, are subject to tax in Thailand, regardless of whether the income is paid within or outside Thailand. There are no concessions to foreigners or short-term residents.

Capital gains and investment income/Most types of capital gains are taxable as ordinary income, except that (1) capital gains from the sale of shares in a company listed on the Securities Exchange of Thailand and from the sale of investment units in a mutual fund are exempt and (2) in respect of gains from the sale of government bonds, debentures, bills, or certificates of indebtedness issued by a corporate entity, an individual may elect to bear only withholding tax at a flat rate of 15% and exclude the gains from assessable income in the computation of personal income tax at the end of the year.

Capital losses may not be offset against capital gains.

Capital gains and investment income earned by a resident from sources outside Thailand are not taxable unless remitted to Thailand.

Interest received from bank deposits, loans made to finance companies, government bonds, debentures, and bills issued by a corporate entity is subject to withholding tax at a flat rate of 15%. Individuals may choose to exclude such interest income from other income, in which case they pay the 15% withholding tax, or they may choose to include such interest income with other income and pay tax according to the personal income tax rates, in which case the tax withheld at source is credited against the tax liability.

A dividend received from a company incorporated in Thailand is subject to withholding tax at a flat rate of 10%. A resident who receives dividend income from a company incorporated in Thailand may elect to exclude this income from the computation of income tax and waive the tax credit mentioned below.

Deductions

Business deductions/There are no business deductions.

Nonbusiness expenses/Donations to specified charities are deductible up to 10% of taxable income after all other allowances are deducted. Life insurance premiums paid by a taxpayer or spouse to a Thai insurer are deductible up to a maximum of Bht10,000 each. Contributions to an approved provident fund in Thailand may be deducted up to a maximum of Bht300,000. Mortgage interest incurred for the purpose of purchase or construction of a residential building in Thailand may be deducted up to a maximum of Bht50,000. Contributions to the Social Security Fund (see below) may be deducted.

If the acquisition is made from September 7, 2001 to September 6, 2002, the actual interest paid on the purchase of a building, a building and surrounding land, a condominium unit, or land with a construction hire may be deducted up to a maximum of Bht200,000. The exemption will be given to such interest paid for two consecutive tax years, by deducting half the amount in each year. However, if the property purchased is mortgaged as collateral, the exemption granted will not exceed Bht100,000 and will apply for only one-year.

Personal allowances/A standard deduction of 40% with a limit of Bht60,000 is permitted in respect of income from employment. In addition, there is a personal allowance of Bht30,000 each for the taxpayer and the taxpayer's spouse, Bht15,000 for each child and an additional Bht2,000 for children studying in government-recognized institutions. A nonresident is allowed deductions for spouse and children only if they are resident in Thailand.

Tax credits

Persons domiciled and residing in Thailand can elect to take income tax withheld at source from dividends received from Thai-incorporated companies as a credit against their tax liability. In this case, a credit to take into account the underlying corporate income tax paid on the profit being distributed is added to dividend income, which is then aggregated with other types of income. Tax at the personal income tax rates is calculated on the total taxable income; the value of the tax credit is then deducted from the tax so calculated.

Foreign taxes cannot be taken as a credit against Thai taxes unless permitted by treaty.

Other taxes

Social security taxes/All employers are required to contribute an amount equal to 3% of each employee's salary (maximum of Bht450 per employee per month) to a social security fund. The government and employees are also required to contribute an equal amount of 3%. However, until the end of 2002, the government portion of the contribution has been reduced to 2% (maximum of Bht300 per employee per month).

Other taxes on income/No other taxes are levied on income.

Tax administration

Returns/There is no reduced tax rate for a joint return filed by husband and wife. Where a joint return is filed, all income is attributed to the husband. Separate returns may be filed for income in the form of salaries and wages only, but, in this event, special rules apply concerning the allocation of income allowances and deductions between husband and wife.

The taxable year is the calendar year. All persons liable to taxation are required to file a return no later than March 31 of the following year.

Payment of tax/There is income tax withholding from salaries and other benefits and some other categories of income. The balance of any tax due for a calendar year is paid at the time of filing the annual tax return. Individual tax rates are shown below.

Tax rates

Individual tax rates are shown below:

Taxable net income			
Over (Column 1)	**Not over**	**Tax on Column 1**	**Percentage on excess**
0	Bht 50,000	—	0
Bht 50,001	100,000	—	5
100,000	500,000	Bht 2,500	10
500,000	1,000,000	42,500	20
1,000,000	4,000,000	142,500	30
4,000,000		1,042,500	37

INDIVIDUAL TAX CALCULATION

Calendar year 2001

Assumptions

Tax computation

Salary		Bht 3,750,000
House rent paid by employer		960,000
Tax paid by employer on house rent		517,409
Total assessable income		5,227,409
Less—Deductions:		
40% standard deduction, but not exceeding 60,000	60,000	
Personal allowances:		
Self	30,000	
Spouse	30,000	
Two children in school	34,000	
Charitable contributions	10,000	
Social security contribution	2,700	166,700
Total taxable income		Bht 5,060,709
Income tax thereon		Bht 1,434,962
Payable by employee		Bht 917,553
Payable by employer		Bht 517,409

Note:

Exchange rate of the Baht at December 31, 2001: US$1 = Bht43.27.

Trinidad and Tobago

PwC contact

For additional information on taxation in Trinidad and Tobago, contact:

Peter R. Inglefield
PricewaterhouseCoopers
11–13 Victoria Avenue
Port-of-Spain, Trinidad
Telephone: (1) (868) 623 1361
Fax: (1) (868) 623 1512
LN domain: Peter Inglefield@Price Waterhouse-CARIB
e-mail: peter.inglefield@tt.pwcglobal.com

Significant developments

The 2002 Budget changed the dates for the payment of quarterly tax installments form the last day of each of the quarters of March, June, September, and December to the 25th day of March, June and September and the 22nd day of December. A general election was called immediately after the presentation of the Budget. No Act of Parliament has as yet been called to give effect to this change.

Territoriality and residence

Citizens of Trinidad and Tobago who are also resident therein are taxed on their worldwide income whether or not such earnings are remitted to Trinidad and Tobago. A nonresident alien is taxed on income arising from employment in Trinidad and Tobago, subject, where applicable, to the provisions of double taxation treaties. Aliens are considered temporarily resident for tax purposes if they are in Trinidad and Tobago for more than 183 days in any calendar year.

Gross income

Employee gross income/An alien is taxed on income received for services performed in Trinidad and Tobago whether or not such income is received in Trinidad and Tobago. For tax purposes, the term "income" includes all benefits and allowances derived from employment, including the value of board and lodging provided by the employer.

Sole traders and self-employed individuals are also subject to a business levy on income exceeding certain levels.

Capital gains and investment income/Only gains on the disposal of an asset within 12 months of its acquisition are taxable. Excluded are gains on the disposal of any security in Trinidad and Tobago; also excluded are gains on motorcars and household goods disposed of for TT$5,000 or under. Taxable gains are included with other income and are not separately taxed. Capital gains realized outside Trinidad and Tobago by resident aliens are not taxable.

See "Other taxes" below for the taxation of interest and dividends.

Income arising outside Trinidad and Tobago paid to a resident alien is taxable in Trinidad and Tobago only to the extent that such income is received in Trinidad and Tobago.

Deductions

Business deductions/An employed individual is not entitled to any blanket or standard deductions. Such an individual may claim a deduction only for unreimbursed travel expenses incurred wholly, exclusively and necessarily in the course of employment. Where the individual is self-employed and is carrying on a trade, business, profession, or vocation, the expenses incurred wholly and exclusively in the production of the income are deductible, as are capital allowances.

Promotional expenses incurred by sole traders or persons employed in agriculture in the expansion of existing markets or the creation of new markets for the export of locally produced goods are tax deductible as an expense at150% of the actual outlay. Other tax allowances available include the Training Allowance of 150%; Apprenticeship Allowance of 200%; and a Local Entertainment and Education Production Allowance of 100%.

Nonbusiness expenses/A deduction in respect of mortgage interest for owner-occupied property is granted up to an amount of TT$18,000. This allowance may also be used in respect of expenses incurred for tertiary education of the taxpayer or the taxpayer's spouse or children.

Income received on an annuity purchased by an individual over 60 years of age is exempt from tax.

From 2002 child maintenance and alimony are exempt from tax in the hands of a recipient when received under a deed of covenant or court order.

Personal allowances/A personal allowance of TT$25,000 per taxpayer is granted. For persons aged 60 years and older the personal allowance is TT$36,000.

Tax credits

Credit is granted to residents for taxes paid in foreign countries and to nonresidents for doubly taxed income on the bases set out in existing double taxation treaties for the particular type of income.

Other taxes

Tax on interest/Interest received by a resident individual on all classes of savings or other accounts with banks, financial institutions or other forms of deposit-taking institutions is exempt from tax.

Tax on dividends/Dividends, excluding preference dividends, received from investments in resident companies are now exempt from tax in the hands of resident individuals. Distributions other than interest received from a mutual fund established in Trinidad and Tobago are also exempt from tax in the hands of a resident individual.

Tax on insurance premiums/A tax on general insurance premiums at the rate of 6% is imposed. Excluded are long-term (life) insurance business, commercial insurance relating to ships and aircraft, loss of or damage to goods in international transit, risks arising outside Trinidad and Tobago, and reinsurance. The 6% tax is collected from policyholders and paid over to the Board of Inland Revenue by the insurance company.

Social security taxes/There is a social security tax, referred to as National Insurance, which is deducted at source at varying rates. The maximum rate is TT$6.45 per week for monthly income over TT$1,000. Seventy percent of such contributions may be deductible in arriving at taxable income.

Health surcharge/A health surcharge is deductible at source for all employees, in accordance with the income tax regulations. The maximum rate is TT$8.25 per week for monthly income over TT$470.

Business levy/As of January 1, 2001 a business levy of 0.20% is applicable to sole traders and self-employed individuals having gross income or receipts in excess of TT$200,000 per annum.

Tax administration

Returns/Tax returns must be filed by April 30 of the year following the calendar or accounting year-end. A six-month grace period is allowed, following which a penalty of TT$100 for every six months or part thereof accrues. Tax returns are filed for income earned in a calendar year (which coincides with the tax year) except in the case of a sole trader or partnership, where filing is done according to the accounting terminal date.

Each individual must file a separate tax return. There is no provision for joint filing by husband and wife.

Payment of tax/Income tax is deducted at source on all employment income under the pay-as-you-earn (PAYE) system. Any shortfall of taxes deducted at source should be settled by the due date, that is, April 30 following the year of income.

Tax rates

The tax rates currently in force for 2002 are listed below.

Taxable income		Tax on	Percentage
Over (Column 1)	Not over	Column 1	on excess
0	TT$ 50,000	—	28
TT$ 50,000		TT$ 14,000	35

INDIVIDUAL TAX CALCULATION

Year of income 1999

Assumptions

1. Individual alien with salary of TT$340,000, with a nonworking spouse and two children attending school.
2. Alien is resident for more than 183 days in a calendar year and therefore is able to claim personal allowance.
3. Alien owns a residential property and is able to secure a mortgage in Trinidad and Tobago.

Tax computation

Salary		TT$ 340,000
Deduct:		
Mortgage interest (25,000, but restricted)	18,000	
National insurance contributions (335 x 70%)	234	18,234
Subtotal		321,766
Deduct—Personal allowance		25,000
Taxable income		TT$ 296,766
Income tax thereon:		
On first 50,000	14,000	
On remainder 246 766) at 35%	86,368	TT$ 100,368
Less—PAYE withholding		(100,000)
Balance payable		TT$ 368

Note:

Exchange rate of the Trinidad and Tobago dollar at January 1, 2002 US$1 = TT$6.3.

Turkey

PwC contact

For additional information on taxation in Turkey, contact:

Adnan Nas; Chairman, Senior Tax Partner
PricewaterhouseCoopers
Basaran Nas Yeminli Mali Müsavirlik A.S.
BJK Plaza, Spor Caddesi, No. 92
B Blok, Kat 9 Akaretler
Besiktas 80680
Istanbul, Turkey
Telephone: (90) (212) 259 49 80
Fax: (90) (212) 259 49 02
e-mail: adnan.nas@tr.pwcglobal.com

Significant developments

During 1998, the definition of income was broadened to include revenues from all sources. As of January 1, 2000 the former article, under which any income not listed in the law does not constitute taxable income, has been restored to replace the revised definition until the end of 2002.

The one-year holding requirement for the capital gains exemption on disposal of shares was reduced to three months until December 31, 2002.

The Income Tax Law article 63/3 was amended in July 2001. According to the new regulations, employee contributions to private pension companies established in compliance with the Turkey's private pension law, and employees' payments on their own behalf or on behalf of a spouse and/or children to insurance companies whose legal residences are in Turkey are deductible in determination of the taxable income.

Until December 12, 2004, the interest and capital gains of individuals derived from the government bonds and treasury bills issued between July 26, 2001, and December 12, 2002, are exempt from income tax, subject to a threshold (TL50 billion in 2001).

Territoriality and residence

Turkey taxes its residents on their worldwide income, whereas nonresidents are taxed on Turkish-source earnings only. Residents are persons with legal residences in Turkey or who intend to settle in the country. Persons with uncertain residence status are considered to be resident if they have lived in Turkey uninterruptedly for more than six months in one calendar year.

Residents are treated as full taxpayers. Individuals who do not have a residence in Turkey or do not reside in Turkey for more than six months in a calendar year are treated as limited taxpayers. In general, those who stay in Turkey for more than six continuous months exclusively for the fulfillment of specific and temporary assignments are not considered as resident, and they will still be treated as limited taxpayers.

Gross income

Employee gross income/Taxable income includes all amounts, whether in cash or in kind, arising from an office or employment in Turkey. In addition to salary, any bonuses and commissions, overseas adjustments, cost-of-living allowances, housing allowances, education payments, and home leave payments are also considered as employment income.

Resident individuals are taxed on salary earned for work performed anywhere in the world, regardless of where payment is made and regardless of whether it is remitted. Nonresidents are taxable on remuneration for work performed in Turkey but may be exempted under double tax treaty provisions.

Capital gains and investment income/Until December 31, 2002, gains on shares that have been held for at least three months are exempt from tax. Additionally, both residents and nonresidents are exempt from tax on the first TL3,500 million of their capital gains in a calendar year. The three-month holding period will increase to one year with effect from January 1, 2003. Additionally, effective until the end of 2002, individuals are not required to file tax returns for the following investment income generated in Turkey, which is taxed at source through withholding.

1. Interest on bank deposits.
2. Dividends paid by marketable securities investment funds.
3. Repo (repurchase order) income.
4. Interest from government bonds and treasury bills and dividends (including tax credit amounting to one-fifth of the dividend) not exceeding in the aggregate TL6,650 million in 2002.

Until December 31, 2004 the interest and capital gains of individuals derived from government bonds and treasury bills issued between July 26, 2001 and December 31, 2002 are exempt from income tax subject to a threshold (TL50 billion in 2001).

Capital gains, interest income and dividends on capital invested abroad are not taxed on nonresidents. Both residents and nonresidents are taxed on investment income at the same rates.

Indexation of cost and inflation allowance/Alternative adjustment mechanisms are available to find the real base for capital gains and other investment income meeting certain conditions. For goods and rights sales, the purchase price is increased according to the WPI (wholesale price index). Alternatively, income from the sale is reduced by the discount ratio announced by the Ministry of Finance (50.7% for 2001 earnings). Discount ratio also applies on interest from government bonds and treasury bills.

Deductions

Business deductions/For individual employees, no business deductions are permitted

Nonbusiness expenses/Nonbusiness deductions are possible within defined limits for donations to specific institutions. Personal insurance premiums (for self, spouse and/or children) and pension contributions are deductible. However, the deduction cannot exceed 10% for pension contributions, and 5% for insurance premiums, of the individual's monthly gross income. Furthermore, the annual cumulative deduction cannot exceed the annual minimum gross wage. Contributions to social security may also be deducted.

Additionally, there is a special deduction regime for employees. According to Turkish Income Tax Law Article 63/5, it is possible to deduct one-third (limited to 35% of the annual cumulative tax base) of the education, food, health, clothing, and residential rent expenses of the employee, spouse and children from the employee's income tax base. After the deduction is made, the income tax withheld previously is adjusted and the difference is offset against the income tax liability of the employee in the coming months or refunded in cash if the employee is no longer working. In the absence of a local employer, related expenses are directly offset against the income tax base shown on the annual tax return.

Personal allowances/If the resident alien is earning a salary, a specified amount per year (TL360,000,000 for 2002) is allowed.

Tax credits

Residents may deduct from their income tax liability foreign taxes assessed on foreign income. However, the deductions may not exceed the rate of tax assessed for similar income earned in Turkey.

Other taxes

Social security taxes/Social security premiums, which are calculated on salary limits of a minimum of TL7,000,000 and a maximum of TL35,000,000 per day (to be revised in April 2002), must be paid by the employer and the employee at rates defined according to labor categories. For Turkish nationals, the general rates are 19.5% for the employer and 14% for the employee.

A foreign national who remains covered under the social security system of his home country is not required to pay Turkish social security premiums, provided proof of foreign coverage is filed with the local social security office. If the employee is not subject to foreign social security, full contributions would generally be imposed in Turkey. However, for nationals of countries with which Turkey does not have a social security agreement, the rates would respectively reduce to 8.5% and 5%, since the premiums for disability, old age and death are not due, unless a written application is filed with the local authorities to make full contributions.

The employee's portion of the social security contributions is deductible in determining taxable income.

Unemployment insurance/Unemployment insurance premiums are calculated over an upper earnings level of TL35,000,000 per day. The premiums are paid by the employee, employer and the state at the following rates.

	%
Employee	1
Employer	2
State	1

Foreign nationals qualify for this insurance on condition of reciprocity between Turkey and their home countries.

Local taxes/There are no local taxes or national wealth taxes apart from some minor transaction charges and immovable property tax imposed and collected by municipalities.

Tax administration

Returns/The annual tax return for the year has to be filed by the end of January of the following year if income is derived exclusively from immovable property, by the end of February if it is derived exclusively from trade activities subject to the simple method of taxation and by the end of March in all other cases. No extensions are available.

Payment of tax/Income tax is withheld every month from salaries paid through a Turkish payroll under the pay-as-you-earn system (PAYE). Except for taxable remuneration received directly from abroad, no further declaration is necessary for employment income.

The tax, when a return is filed for any outstanding liability under the aforementioned principles, is paid in three equal installments; by the time of filing and in the 3rd and 6th months thereafter. Nonresidents leaving Turkey have to settle full liability within 15 days before departure.

Taxpayers filing income tax returns for their commercial or professional income must pay advance income tax (under the title of "temporary tax"), calculated as 15% of their cumulative income as at the end of each quarter during the calendar year. This tax must be paid by the 15th of the second month following the end of related quarter. Tax paid in advance is credited to income tax computed on the annual tax return for the same year.

Tax rates

The following rates apply from January 1 through December 31, 2002.

Individual income tax—On employment income*

(In TL '000s)

Taxable income			
Over (Column 1)	Not over	Tax on Column 1	Percentage on excess
0	TL 3,800,000	—	15
TL 3,800,000	9,500,000	TL 570,000	20
9,500,000	19,000,000	1,710,000	25
19,000,000	47,500,000	4,085,000	30
47,500,000	95,000,000	12,635,000	35
95,000,000		29,260,000	40

Individual income tax—On all other income*

(In TL '000s)

Taxable income			
Over (Column 1)	Not over	Tax on Column 1	Percentage on excess
0	TL 3,800,000	—	20
TL 3,800,000	9,500,000	TL 760,000	25
9,500,000	19,000,000	2,185,000	30
19,000,000	47,500,000	5,035,000	35
47,500,000	95,000,000	15,010,000	40
95,000,000		34,010,000	45

*Except for employment income, a 10% fund levy applies on the income tax.

INDIVIDUAL TAX CALCULATION

Calendar year 2002, income year 2002

Assumptions

Resident alien on a local company's payroll. Total compensation is TL65,000,000,000 per annum.

Tax computation

		(In TL '000s)
Base salary		TL 53,000,000
Add:		
Housing allowance	7,700 ,000,000	
Tuition for dependents	1,000,000,000	
Year-end bonus	3,300,000,000	12,000,000
Total employment benefits		65,000,000
Less:		
Personal allowance	360,000,000	
Social security premiums (1,050,000,000 x 14% x 12) (1)	1,764,000,000	
Unemployment insurance premiums (1,050,000,000 x 1% x 12) (1)	126,000,000	2,250,000
Taxable income		TL 62,750,000
Tax thereon:		
On first 47,500,000,000		TL 12,635,000
On remainder (15,250,000,000 x 35%)		5,337,500
		TL 17,972,500
Fund surcharge (10%) (2)		0
Stamp duty (0.6%) (3)		TL 390,000

Notes:

1. Employee is assumed to be a national of a country with which Turkey has a social security agreement, without social security coverage in his home country.
2. Fund surcharge will not be applied on income tax attributed to salary income.
3. 0.6% stamp duty applies on gross income paid through a local payroll.
4. Exchange rate of the Turkish lira at December 31, 2001: US$1 = TL1,439,567.

PwC contact

For additional information on taxation in Uganda, contact:

Simon Kagugube
PricewaterhouseCoopers
Communications House
1 Colville Street
(P.O. Box 8053)
Kampala, Uganda
Telephone: (256) (41) 236018
Fax: (256) (41) 230153
e-mail: simon.kagugube@ug.pwcglobal.com

Significant developments

There have been no significant tax or regulatory developments regarding individual taxation in the past year.

Territoriality and residence

Individuals are taxed on worldwide income. A resident individual is a person who meets the following criteria.

1. Has a permanent home in Uganda;

   or

2. Is present in Uganda for 183 days in any 12-month period that commences or ends during the year of income or has been present for an average of 122 days per year of income for the current and the two preceding years of income.

Gross income

Employee gross income/For pay-as-you-earn (PAYE) purposes, the Income Tax Act 1997 is applied with effect from January 1, 1998, that is, the middle of the fiscal year. All information set out below is based on the new act.

Gross income of an employee includes wages, salary, leave pay, fees, commissions, bonuses, gratuities, compensation for the termination of a contract, all allowances except security, and any other income derived by an employee from employment. Where housing is provided by the employer, the benefit is calculated as the lower of the market rent or 15% of employment income including the market rent.

Major exclusions from employment income are the following.

1. Cost of passages on appointment and termination of contract for noncitizens recruited or engaged outside Uganda;
2. Cost of any medical services provided by the employer;
3. Allowances for accommodation, travel and subsistence when traveling, provided the allowances do not exceed actual cost;

   and

4. Meals provided in staff canteens if all full-time employees have access to the canteen on equal terms;
5. Any contribution or similar payment by the employer made to a retirement fund for the benefit of the employee or any of his or her dependents.

Capital gains and investment income/All income not included in employment income is taxable except for capital gains.

Rental income/Rental income is taxed separately from other income at the rate of 20% on 80% of the gross rental income, provided it exceeds UGS1,560,000.

Deductions

Business deductions/No business deductions are available.

Personal allowances/None.

Nonbusiness deductions/Graduated tax (see below) is an allowable deduction. A limited possibility to make allowable donations to eligible organizations is available.

Tax credits

Foreign tax paid is creditable up to the average Ugandan tax rate.

Other taxes

Social security taxes/Employers are required to contribute 15% of salaries and are entitled to recover 5% from the employees. Employees are entitled to a refund of the total contributions upon retirement.

Graduated tax/Graduated tax is payable by every individual over the age of 18 with income from farming, business or employment. The rate is progressive, with a maximum of UGS80,000 per annum. The tax is an allowable deduction for income tax purposes.

Tax administration

Returns/Resident individuals are required to submit provisional estimates and final returns, except those who have no income other than from employment and who believe that the whole of the tax payable will be recovered by deduction by the employer.

Unincorporated businesses may apply to be taxed on the income of their accounting period ending with another date than 30 June, which is the normal tax year. It is no longer necessary to obtain the Commissioner's written permission before a "small" taxpayer (with gross turnover of less than UGS50 million) can make a normal return of income. A provisional estimate is due within three months from the commencement of the accounting period. A final return is due four months after the end of the tax year.

Payment of tax/Employers are required to deduct tax on a monthly basis from any taxable emoluments paid to an employee.

Tax, as per the provisional estimate, is payable in four equal installments due three, six, nine, and twelve months after the commencement of the accounting period. If the final tax charge exceeds the provisional estimate, the excess is payable within 45 days from the service of the notice of assessment.

Tax rates

Resident individual tax rates

Taxable income			Tax on Column 1	Percentage on excess
Over (Column 1)	Not over			
0	UGS 1,560,000	....	—	—
UGS 1,560,000	2,820,000	....	—	10
2,820,000	4,920,000	....	UGS 126,000	20
4,920,000		....	546,000	30

Nonresident individual tax rates

Taxable income			Tax on Column 1	Percentage on excess
Over (Column 1)	Not over			
0	UGS 2,820,000	....	—	10
UGS 2,820,000	4,920,000	....	UGS 282,000	20
4,920,000		....	702,000	30

Rental income tax rate/Rental income is taxed at the rate of 20% on 80% of the gross income, provided it exceeds UGS1,560,000.

INDIVIDUAL TAX CALCULATION

Year ending June 30, 2002

Assumptions

The taxpayer is a resident individual.

Tax computation

Gross income:		
Salary		UGS 120,400,000
Interest		2,000,000
Dividends		1,000,000
		123,400,000
Less—Deductions:		
Dividends, interest	3,000,000	
Charitable donations	500,000	
Graduated tax paid	80,000	3,580,000
Taxable income		UGS 119,820,000
Tax payable:		
On first 4,920,000		UGS 546,000
On balance of 114,900,000 at 30%		34,470,000
		UGS 35,016,000

Note:

Exchange rate of the Uganda shilling at December 31, 2001: US$1 = UGS1,720.

PwC contact

For additional information on taxation in Ukraine, contact:

Jorge E. Intriago, Tax Partner
PricewaterhouseCoopers
5th Floor, 38 Turgenevska
Kyiv 01054
Ukraine
Telephone: (380) (44) 490 6777
Fax: (380) (44) 216 4558/244 5571
e-mail: jorge.e.intriago@ua.pwcglobal.com

General note

Ukraine's tax system is undergoing reform. The new Tax Code, which is expected to be adopted in 2002, will significantly change the Ukrainian legislation governing taxation of individuals.

The following information on individual taxation in Ukraine is accurate as of February 1, 2002. For subsequent developments, refer to the contact above.

Significant developments

The following significant developments in Ukrainian legislation governing individual taxation took place during 2001.

1. Due dates for filing personal income tax returns have been changed, as have penalties for noncompliance.
2. Rates of contributions to the Social Security Fund and the Unemployment Insurance Fund were decreased from 5.5% to 5% for employers and increased from 0.5% to 1% for employees.
3. As of March 22, 2001, the cap on the taxable base for social contributions (both employer's and employee's) has been increased from UAH1,000 to UAH1,600 per individual per month.
4. As of April 1, 2001, a new payroll tax was introduced. The tax is payable by employers to the Fund for Social Insurance Regarding Accidents. The tax rate ranges from 0.2% to 13.8% of the gross payroll, depending on the level of risk of accident in the enterprise's industry sector.

Territoriality and residence

The tax status of individuals is defined according to their residence status. Tax residents are defined as those individuals physically present in Ukraine for 183 days or more in a calendar year. Nonresidents are those present in Ukraine for less than 183 days in a calendar year.

Residents are liable to Ukrainian income tax on their total worldwide income received during a calendar year unless protection under a double taxation treaty is available. Nonresidents are taxed on their Ukrainian-source income. The notion of Ukrainian-source income is not well defined in legislation, but in practice it normally includes only income from the use or granting the right to use property located in the territory of Ukraine as well as income paid by a Ukrainian entity or organization.

In general, payment of Ukrainian-source income to nonresidents is subject to withholding tax at a flat rate of 20% unless otherwise provided by the relevant tax treaties.

Gross income

Employee gross income/All income received from employment in monetary form or in kind during a calendar year is subject to personal income tax. This includes all basic pay, overtime pay, supplemental pay, awards and bonuses, compensation for unused vacation, all other monetary amounts, and benefits in kind, as well as all other services obtained without payment received as a result of employment. In general, benefits in kind are taxed at their cost to the employer or at their monetary equivalent valued at market value.

Taxable income of foreign nationals who are residents of Ukraine is determined in the same order as for Ukrainians. Taxable income of foreign nationals also includes any type of allowances for living in Ukraine (e.g., hardship, cost-of-living allowances, etc.), as well as compensation for school fees, food, travel by the employee's family on holiday, and other nonbusiness expenses.

Capital gains and investment income/There is no separate capital gains tax. Instead, gains from the disposal of property and assets are subject to income tax at the general rates. The taxable amount is calculated as the difference between sale proceeds and historical cost. However, if a stamp duty is paid in respect of property sale, income received as a result of this sale is tax-exempt, except for sale of goods or property in course of entrepreneurial activity.

The following types of income are generally taxable in Ukraine.

1. Interest income from deposits outside Ukraine. Credit relief is available for foreign taxes paid on such income (see "Tax credits" below).
2. Dividends on shares and other financial assets.
3. Income from leasing property, both in Ukraine and abroad.
4. Royalties from the creation, publication, performance, and use of works of literature, art and science, as well as from inventions, discoveries and industrial prototypes.

Tax-exempt income/There are several types of tax-exempt income. The main are as follows.

1. Reimbursement by an employer for actual expenses arising from a work-related change of abode and relocation allowances in amount of up to 100% (plus 25% in respect of each relocated family member) of average monthly salary at the new place of work.
2. Vouchers for health treatment and vacations at sanatoriums and children's recreation centers, with the exception of tourist and international facilities.
3. Payments received by an employee in compensation for injury or damage to health while performing employment duties.
4. Redundancy payments, within statutory limits.
5. Income received from sale of an individual's car once per calendar year.
6. Income received from sale of personal property (including real estate), provided the stamp duty is paid on the sales transaction.

7. Interest, discounts and premiums earned on Ukrainian government bonds and registered saving certificates, premiums on Ukrainian state treasury bills.
8. Prizes from state lotteries.
9. Income from Ukrainian bank deposits in both local and foreign currency.
10. Dividends on shares of stock and other corporate ownership interests, provided Ukrainian corporate profits tax has been paid on this income. In other cases, dividends are taxed at the general rates, subject to foreign tax credit relief, if applicable.
11. Income inherited or received as a gift from other individuals, provided the stamp duty is paid.

Social security contributions (see below) made by the employer per Ukrainian tax legislation are not included in the taxable income of the individual.

In addition to the above, the following exemptions are available for foreigners, provided certain conditions are met.

1. Contributions by an employer to state social security and pension funds.
2. Compensation paid to reimburse accommodation costs.
3. Payment for the maintenance of a car for business purposes.
4. Business travel expenses.

Deductions

Business expenses/In general, bona fide expenses incurred by individuals in the course of business or trade can be deducted from taxable income. Individual entrepreneurs may deduct business expenses and depreciation charges subject to the rules established by the Corporate Profits Tax Law. If actual expenses of an individual entrepreneur cannot be documented, then a specific standard deduction may be applied.

Nonbusiness deductions/Donations made by individuals to charity institutions are deductible up to an amount equal to 4% of the total taxable income of the individual for the respective calendar year, provided documents confirming the transfer of funds to such institutions are available.

Employees' pension and social security contributions are, in general, not deductible from employment income.

Personal allowances/All taxpayers are entitled to a deduction equal to the minimum monthly nontaxable income (currently UAH17—approximately US$3). In addition, one parent may deduct an amount equal to the minimum monthly nontaxable income for expenses of maintaining a child under the age of 16, provided that the total taxable monthly income of the taxpayer does not exceed ten times the minimum monthly wages (as of January 1, 2002 the minimum monthly wage is UAH140—approximately US$26).

A 50% reduction of personal income tax liability is available to individuals who have three or more children under the age of 16. Adequate documentation is required.

Child allowances are not available to individuals who are not tax residents.

Tax credits

A credit is allowed for foreign income tax paid on income received abroad by residents of Ukraine, provided there is a double taxation treaty in place between

Ukraine and the respective country. However, this credit is limited to the amount of Ukrainian tax liability that would arise from equivalent income in Ukraine.

Other taxes

Social security taxes/Employers (including representative offices of foreign companies in Ukraine) are required to pay the following social security taxes in respect of their employees based on gross salary.

1. Pension Fund—32%.
2. Social Security Fund—2.5%.
3. Unemployment Insurance Fund—2.5%.
4. Accidents at Work Insurance Fund—From 0.2% to 13.8%. (The rate should be determined by Fund's authorities specifically for each entity and depends on the level of accident risk of the entity's industry sector.)

Employees' contributions (withholding requirement applies) are as follows.

1. State Pension Fund—2% (1% if the monthly salary is up to UAH150).
2. Social Security Fund—0.5% (0.25% if the monthly salary is up to UAH150).
3. Unemployment Insurance Fund—0.5% (for Ukrainian national employees only).

Social contributions (both employee's and employer's) are not due on the income that is not subject to personal income tax. The taxable base subject to such contributions, both employer's and employee's, is currently capped at UAH1,600 per individual per month.

Employee's contributions, in general, are not deductible for personal income tax purposes.

Foreign nationals temporary employed by a Ukrainian entity are not subject to unemployment insurance in Ukraine. Therefore, they are not required to contribute to the Unemployment Insurance Fund. However, the employer should pay contributions to the Fund in respect of such employees.

Foreign nationals remaining on the foreign payroll are not liable to pay social contributions in Ukraine.

Individual entrepreneurs, except for those paying taxes under the "unified tax" regime, must contribute 32% of the annual tax base to the Pension Fund. In order to have right to enjoy social security benefits, individual entrepreneurs may contribute voluntarily 3% of the annual tax base to the Social Security Fund and 3% to the Unemployment Insurance Fund. The tax base is determined as gross income less deductions. The tax base is currently capped at UAH1,600 per month.

Gift and inheritance tax/There is no gift or inheritance tax in Ukraine. However, stamp duty is payable by individuals, both Ukrainian and foreign nationals, on transfers of certain properties (e.g., real estate, cars) situated on the territory of Ukraine, whether the transfer is by way of gift or inheritance. Rates vary from 0.1% to 5%, based on the value of the transfer and depending on the relationship of the transferor and transferee.

Tax administration

Returns/Ukrainian nationals who have worked for more than one employer or received income from nonemployment sources during a calendar year are required to file a year-end tax return by April 1 of the next calendar year. A tax return should not be filed if an individual received income from "main" employment only. "Main" employment means an employer who is authorized to maintain an individual's labor book.

Each individual is taxed on his/her own income. There is no aggregation of income for spouses (except for spouses and other family members jointly involved in the same entrepreneurial activity conducted as a proprietorship), and returns are to be filed separately by married persons.

Ukrainian nationals engaged in entrepreneurial activities are generally required to file quarterly tax returns within 40 days following the reporting quarter and file a year-end tax return before April 1 of the next calendar year. Private entrepreneurs who pay tax under the "unified tax" regime are required to file quarterly reports by April 5, July 5 and October 5 of the current year and January 5 of the year following the reporting one.

Foreign nationals who qualify as residents of Ukraine should file their income tax returns with the Ukrainian local tax authorities where the individual's activities are carried out. Foreign nationals who expect to be tax resident in Ukraine are required to file, within one month of arrival, a preliminary tax return specifying total taxable income they expect to receive during the current calendar year. Quarterly tax returns are then due within 40 days following the end of the reporting quarter, that is, by May 10, August 9, and November 9. The final tax return specifying annual worldwide income actually received by the individual during the calendar year is due by February 9 of the following calendar year. A final (departure) tax return should be filed one month prior to the individual's departure.

Payment of tax/Tax in respect of employment income must be withheld at source by the entity making the payment.

Individual entrepreneurs, as well as foreign nationals—residents of Ukraine for tax purposes—are required to make quarterly advance payments of the estimated liability for the year before March 15, May 15, August 15, and November 15. Payments of the "unified tax" by private entrepreneurs are due in advance, generally on a monthly basis.

Final settlement of any tax liability must be executed within one month after receipt by the individual of the assessment issued by the tax authorities.

Tax rates

Income tax is payable in Ukrainian Hryvnia (UAH) according to a progressive scale of rates, as shown below. Earnings in foreign currency are converted to Hryvnia at the exchange rate of the National Bank of Ukraine (NBU) on the date income was received.

The tax rates for 2002 are as follows.

Annual taxable income			
Over (Column 1)	Not over	Tax on Column 1	Percentage on excess
0	UAH 204	—	0
UAH 204	1,020	—	10
1,020	2,040	UAH 81.60	15
2,040	12,240	234.60	20
12,240	20,400	2,274.60	30
20,400		4,722.60	40

Nonresidents pay tax at source on Ukrainian income at a flat rate of 20%.

Under the "unified tax" regime, fixed monthly amounts of tax are established by local authorities. The monthly amounts of tax may range from UAH20 to UAH200, depending on the type of business activity.

INDIVIDUAL TAX CALCULATION

For the calendar year ended December 31, 2001

Assumptions

The following assumptions are made in the tax computation below.

1. Individual is a foreigner employed by a non-Ukrainian resident employer and assigned to work in Ukraine for a period of more than 183 days in a calendar year.
2. Individual is married and supports a wife and three children under the age of 16, who remain in their home country.
3. The employee receives an annual salary of US$120,000, a reimbursement of school expenses for his children in the amount of US$24,000 and a monthly accommodation allowance in the amount of US$4,000, but, based on the rental agreement, pays monthly rent in the amount of US$3,000.
4. No social security contribution liability arises in Ukraine.

Tax computation

	US$	UAH
Income from employment:		
Salary	120,000	
School expenses	24,000	
Accommodation allowance (1)	12,000	
Taxable income (2)	156,000	826,566.00
Tax liability (4,722.60 + 40% of 806,166.00)		327,189.00
Less—Parent relief (50%)		(163,594.50)
Tax due		163,594.50

Notes:

1. The difference between the allowance and the actual expenses incurred is taxable (i.e., [US$4,000 – US$3,000] x 12).
2. Exchange rate of the Hryvnia as of December 31, 2001: US$1 = UAH5.2985.

PwC contact

For additional information on taxation in the United Arab Emirates, contact:

Sanjay Manchanda
PricewaterhouseCoopers
Level 40 Emirates Towers Offices
Sheikh Zayed Road
P.O. Box 11987
Dubai, United Arab Emirates
Telephone: (971) (4) 3043100
Fax: (971) (4) 3304100
e-mail: sanjay.manchanda@ae.pwcglobal.com

Absence of taxation

Income tax is not imposed on individuals in the United Arab Emirates.

Note

Exchange rate of the dirham at December 31, 2001: US$1 = AED3.673.

United Kingdom

PwC contacts

For additional information on taxation in the United Kingdom, contact:

Personal taxation

Clive Mackintosh
PricewaterhouseCoopers
No 1 London Bridge
London SE1 9QL, England
Telephone: (44) (20) 7804 3000,
804 5614 (direct)
Fax: (44) (20) 7403 5265
e-mail: clive.mackintosh@
gb.pwcglobal.com

Expatriate taxation

Stephanie Phizackerley
PricewaterhouseCoopers
Southwark Towers
32 London Bridge Street
London SE1 9SY, England
Telephone: (44) (20) 7804 3000,
804 1765 (direct)
Fax: (44) (20) 7378 0647
e-mail: stephanie.phizackerley@
gb.pwcglobal.com

Significant developments

1. National insurance contributions by employees, employers and the self-employed are to be increased by 1% with effect from April 6, 2003. Earnings above the upper thresholds beyond which employees and self-employed contributions were previously not charged will attract a 1% charge from the same date.
2. The qualifying holding period for business assets to attract a 10% capital gains tax rate has been reduced from four years of ownership to only two years.

Territoriality and residence

The United Kingdom taxes its residents on their worldwide income and capital gains and taxes nonresidents on their U.K. income (but not generally on capital gains). The non-U.K. investment income and capital gains of a person resident but not domiciled in the United Kingdom are generally taxed only if they are received in the United Kingdom.

The domicile of individuals is generally the country or state in which they have their permanent homes. However, for inheritance tax purposes only, individuals are also regarded as domiciled in the United Kingdom at any time if they have been resident in the United Kingdom for tax purposes for not less than 17 out of the 20 tax years before that time or were domiciled in the United Kingdom during the three years before that time.

Persons are resident in the United Kingdom for a particular tax year if they are present for more than 183 days in that year or have made, or intend to make, regular and extended visits over a period of years.

However, persons who come to the United Kingdom for at least two years are treated as resident from the day of arrival to the day of departure. If they come for less than two years or do not know the length of their time of stay, they will be treated as resident for the year only if the normal conditions dealt with above apply.

Similarly, a person who leaves the United Kingdom to work full time abroad under a contract of employment or for self-employment is treated as not resident and not ordinarily resident in the United Kingdom from the day after departure until the day before returning to the United Kingdom at the end of the period of overseas employment/self-employment, provided that certain conditions apply.

1. The absence from the United Kingdom and the employment/self-employment abroad last for at least a whole tax year;

   and

2. During the absence, visits to the United Kingdom are less than 183 days in any tax year and less than 91 days on average (the average is calculated over a maximum period of four years).

In his Budget speech, the Chancellor of the Exchequer indicated his intention to begin a consultative exercise on the rules relating to residence and domicile.

Gross income

Employee gross income/A non–U.K.-domiciled but U.K.-resident individual is taxable on worldwide emoluments (salary, personal expense allowances and reimbursements, and benefits), except in the instances noted below.

1. A short-term resident is taxable on emoluments for work performed outside the United Kingdom only if they are received in the United Kingdom.
2. Other residents are taxable on the emoluments of a separate employment carried on wholly outside the United Kingdom for a nonresident employer only if the emoluments are received in the United Kingdom.

A non–U.K.-domiciled person who is not resident in the United Kingdom is taxable only on emoluments for work performed in the United Kingdom but may be exempted by a double taxation treaty.

Capital gains and investment income/Capital gains are taxable on persons resident in the United Kingdom and on nonresidents if the gains are realized on U.K. trading assets. Generally, gains realized on non-U.K. assets by a U.K.-resident but non–U.K.-domiciled person are taxable only if the gains are received in the United Kingdom. Gains realized in the tax year of arrival in or departure from the United Kingdom may, in certain circumstances, be taxable even if realized before arrival or after departure. From March 17, 1998, an individual who leaves the United Kingdom for a period of nonresidence of less than five tax years and has been resident for at least four of the seven tax years prior to the departure is taxed on the disposal, while nonresident, of any assets that were acquired before ceasing to be resident. The assets are treated as disposed of in the year of return to the United Kingdom.

Capital gains are taxed at rates equivalent to the rates of income tax that would apply if gains were treated as the top slice of the individual's "savings" income, but there are numerous reliefs available, including an allowance for inflation (up to April 5, 1998), annual exemptions, exemptions for certain assets (including a principal private residence), and deferrals for certain types of gifts.

The amount of gain that is taxable (after reliefs and the offset of losses but before the annual exemption) is reduced by a "taper" factor based on the length of ownership after April 5, 1998. For business assets held for two or more years after April 5, 2000, and disposed of after April 5, 2002, only 25% of the gain is subject to tax, the taper factor being 75%. For assets held for less than two years, the taper factor is 50% after one year of ownership. For nonbusiness assets, the taper is less generous. There is no reduction for assets held for less than three full years after April 5, 1998; thereafter, the taper factor is 5% per full year until the asset has been held for 10 or more years, only 60% of the gain then being taxable. Where the nonbusiness asset was owned on March 17, 1998, the ownership period for taper purposes is increased by one full year.

Gains and losses arising on the disposal of assets held on March 31, 1982, are computed as if the assets were acquired at their market value on that date. The costs to be deducted from gross proceeds on the disposal of an asset are the market value of the asset on March 31, 1982, and the costs of any improvements made after that date, or the costs of acquisition and subsequent improvements if the asset was purchased after March 31, 1982, plus indexation. Indexation represents an uplift in the above costs based on the percentage rise (if any) in the U.K. retail prices index (RPI) over the relevant period, that is, from March 31, 1982, the date of acquisition, or the dates the improvements were carried out, as appropriate, to the date of disposal or April 5, 1998, whichever is earlier. See the computation under "Capital gains tax." There are various exceptions to these rules, in particular where using market value produces a greater gain or a greater loss than that arising from using historical cost and insofar as indexation cannot create or increase a capital loss.

A non–U.K.-domiciled individual resident in the United Kingdom is taxable on all U.K. interest, dividends, rents, and royalties and on any overseas investment income received in the United Kingdom. The tax liability on U.K. investment income of a non-U.K. resident is often reduced or eliminated by a double taxation treaty. Even where there is no such treaty relief, the U.K. tax liability of a nonresident on certain "excluded income" cannot exceed the tax (if any) withheld or deducted at source or treated as deducted at source. "Excluded income" includes dividends from U.K. companies, interest income, and certain social security benefits.

Deductions

Business deductions/Necessary business expenses (restrictively defined) can be deducted from employment income and are not taxable if paid for or reimbursed by the employer. Travel to and from work is not regarded as a business expense.

Reimbursements for business entertainment and for removal and relocation expenses of up to £8,000 are not normally taxable.

Nonbusiness expenses/Contributions to qualifying employee pension schemes of up to 15% of total earnings are eligible for tax relief. However, for these purposes, where a scheme was set up on or after March 14, 1989, or a new member joins an existing scheme after May 31, 1989, earnings in excess of a permitted maximum are disregarded so that there is no relief for contributions in excess of 15% of the limit. For the year ending April 5, 2003, the permitted maximum is £97,200. (The maximum is generally increased annually in line with the retail prices index.) For those not in pensionable employment and who contracted a qualifying retirement annuity policy prior to July 1, 1988, tax relief is available for premiums up to a limit of 17.5% of total earnings (higher limits apply for those over 50 years of age). Whether or not they are in pensionable employment, from June 30, 1988, individuals may alternatively make contributions to personal pension schemes for which, generally, contributions up to a limit of 17.5% of total earnings are eligible for tax relief; higher limits apply for contributions made by those over 35, but in all cases, tax relief for contributions made to personal pension schemes is subject to the permitted maximum of earnings of £97,200 for the year ending April 5, 2003. Tax relief at the basic rate is given at source, and for higher-rate taxpayers, a claim for further relief can be made through their self-assessments (see below).

With effect from April 6, 2001, the earnings "cap" will apply to individuals who contribute to a stakeholder pension. Stakeholder pensions are available to any U.K. resident who is under 75, in receipt of U.K. taxable earnings, and not a member of an occupational scheme. Contributions of up to £3,600 can be made without any reference to the individual's earnings. Tax relief at the basic rate is given at source. Higher-rate taxpayers can claim further relief through their self-assessments.

Relief is available for gifts to U.K. charities under approved payroll deduction schemes and also by way of outright money gifts and charitable payments made under deeds of covenant. No relief is available for medical expenses, social security contributions, council tax, other U.K. taxes, or insurance premiums (except for qualifying life insurance premiums on policies issued before March 14, 1984).

Personal allowances/Apart from the married couple's and other linked allowances, personal allowances are fully deductible in determining taxable income. Every individual who is under 65 throughout the year of assessment ending April 5, 2003, is entitled to a tax allowance of £4,615. This allowance will be frozen at that rate for the year of assessment ending April 5 2004.

Those over 65 but under 75 at any time during that tax year, £6,100; and those 75 and over at any time during that tax year, £6,370. Married couples are also entitled to a married couple's allowance of £5,465 where either member of the couple is 65 or older but under 75; the allowance is £5,535 where either is 75 or older. The increased age-related allowances are reduced by £1 for every £2 of income in excess of £17,900. Relief for the married couple's allowance is given at a rate of 10%. The couple may elect to divide the married couple's allowance between them equally or to allocate it wholly to either one.

Children are taxable in their own right unless their income derives from gifts by the parent.

From April 6, 2001, single parents, married couples, and unmarried couples living together as husband and wife can claim a children's tax credit if they have one or more children under the age of 16 living with them. The credit will be £5,290 at 10% but will be reduced by £2 for every £3 of taxable income above £29,400. For a year in which a child is born, the amount of children's tax credit is increased to £10,490.

Tax credits

Either by double taxation treaty or by U.K. unilateral relief, U.K. residents are entitled to a credit for foreign taxes paid against the U.K. income tax or capital gains tax payable on overseas income or gains. Alternatively, the taxpayer may elect for the foreign tax to be deducted from the taxable amount rather than be taken as a credit.

Other taxes

Social security taxes/National insurance contributions apply to salary (excluding benefits) up to £585 per week. On the first £89 per week, no contributions are payable; thereafter, between £89 and £585 per week, contributions amount to 10%. In situations where the employees are in contracted-out employment (broadly, where they are not entirely covered by the state pension scheme), an abatement is given. Persons not domiciled but resident in the United Kingdom are in some circumstances exempt from contributions during the first year of their stay if they are employed by a non-U.K.-resident employer.

Self-employed persons pay a flat-rate contribution of £2.00 per week. There is an additional contribution on earnings between £4,615 and £30,420 per annum of 7% of the excess over £4,535 (therefore, the maximum additional contribution is £1,775.55 on earnings of more than £29,900 per annum).

All the rates quoted above are for the year ending April 5, 2003. For the year ending April 5, 2004, rates of national insurance will increase. For employees, earnings between £89 and £585 per week (subject to a further inflationary increase in these limits) will be taxable at 11%, with a further 1% levy applicable to earnings in excess of that figure.

Self-employed persons' contributions will also increase, from 7% to 8% on profits between £4,615 and £30,420, with an additional 1% charge on profits in excess of that figure.

As noted, relief against income tax is not available for social security contributions.

The United Kingdom has treaties with many countries with regard to social security.

Other taxes on income/There are no other taxes on income. Other taxes are raised in the form of customs and excise duties on certain goods and on air travel, value added tax on the purchase of most goods and services, inheritance tax on certain gifts and on estates, and insurance premium tax.

Local taxes on income/There are no local taxes on income as such. Local authorities are financed partly by the imposition of council tax, a property-based tax levied on the occupier of a domestic dwelling at a flat rate per dwelling. Unoccupied dwellings are also taxed on the property's owner. The remainder of local authority finance comes from the imposition of the uniform business rate on business property and from central government grants.

Tax administration

Returns/Returns must be filed for each tax year ending April 5, but only a quarter to a third of taxpayers are required to file a return, since most liabilities are collected by withholding at source. Married couples are independently responsible for their own affairs, and each spouse files his or her own return. The taxable year for individuals is always the year commencing April 6 and ending on the following April 5.

The United Kingdom has a self-assessment tax system. Returns for 2002/2003 will be due by January 31, 2004, if the taxpayer self-assesses and pays the balance of tax due with the return. Alternatively, the taxpayer may elect to have the Inland Revenue compute the liability, in which case the return must be filed by September 30, 2003, the tax still being due by January 31, 2004. If a tax return has not been issued, the taxpayer must notify the Inland Revenue of significant capital gains and new sources of income by October 5 following the end of the tax year.

Payment of tax/Income tax is normally withheld from salaries under the pay-as-you-earn (PAYE) system. Income from most other U.K. sources is received after the savings-rate tax has been deducted. Under the new self-assessment regime, any tax not collected through withholding is paid through payments on account on January 31 in the tax year and July 31 after the end of the tax year, with any final balance due at the latest by January 31 after the end of the tax year.

Employers are required to notify the revenue authorities of total pay, benefits, and expenses paid or reimbursed, and the employee then makes a claim for allowable business expenses.

Tax rates

Tax rates for the tax year ending April 5, 2003 are as follows.

Income tax

Taxable income			Other income	Dividends	Savings income
Over	Not over				
			%	%	%
0	£ 1,920	....	10	10	10
£ 1,920	29,900	....	22	10	20
29,900		....	40	32.5	40

Dividends are treated as the top slice of income (and carry a tax credit that covers the 10% rate), "savings income" as the next slice, and other income as the lowest slice. The most common form of "savings income" is interest, but certain other forms of income are also included.

Capital gains tax

Taxable gains			Tax on Column 1	Percentage on excess
Over (Column 1)	Not over			
0	£ 7,700	....	Nil	—
£ 7,700		....	—	—*

*Gains are taxed as the highest part of income and gains.

INDIVIDUAL TAX CALCULATION

I—Income tax

Assumptions

Non–U.K.-domiciled married man; husband and wife under 65, with U.K.-resident employers; tax computation based on income in the year to April 5, 2003.

Tax computation

	Husband	Wife
	£	£
Salary	50,000	12,000
Car benefit (based on carbon dioxide emissions)	5,250	—
Gasoline benefit (scale rate)	3,620	—
Total earned income	58,870	12,000
Dividends from U.K. companies (Husband, 2,700 plus tax credit of 300; wife, 900 plus tax credit of 100)	3,000	1,000
Loan interest received—Husband, net 800 plus 200 tax withheld; wife, net 160 plus 40 tax withheld	1,000	200
Total income	62,870	13,200
Less:		
Mortgage interest paid (2,600)	—	—
Personal allowance:		
Husband	4,615	—
Wife	—	4,615
Taxable income	58,255	8,585
Income tax thereon:		
Husband:		
On first 1,920 at 10%	192	
On next 27,980 at 22%	6,156	
On dividends—3,000 at 32.5%	975	
On remaining 25,355 at 40%	10,142	
Wife:		
On dividends—1,000 at 10% (1)		100.00
On interest—200 at 20% (2)		40.00
On first 1,920 of other income at 10% (1)		192.00
On remaining 5,465 at 22%		1,202.30
Total tax liability (3)	17,465	1,534.30
Less—Credits/withholding on dividends and interest	(500)	(140.00)
	16,965	1,394.30

Notes:

1. Dividend income is taxed only at 10%, except for taxpayers who pay tax at the highest rate. This 10% liability is satisfied by the tax credit for such income, although the credit cannot be repaid to nontaxpayers. Dividend income that is taxable in any event at 10% will not be treated as using part of the general 10% rate band.
2. Savings income—normally interest—is taxed at only 10% or 20%, except for taxpayers who pay tax at the 40% rate. Tax is normally deducted at source at a rate of 20% and can be repaid to nontaxpayers.

3. The total liabilities as calculated above are discharged partly by withholding at source and partly by direct tax payments.

II—Capital gains tax

Assumptions

In September 2002, a non–U.K.-domiciled but U.K.-resident individual disposes of a non-U.K. asset acquired in April 1994 and realizes a capital gain (net of indexation allowance—see above) of £4,000. Of £10,000 proceeds of sale, £2,000 is received in the United Kingdom. The individual also sells a taxable U.K. business asset for £200,000 in September 2002 that cost £25,000 in July 1980. As at March 31, 1982, the asset had a market value of £35,000. The individual is liable to U.K. income tax at the higher (40%) rate.

Tax computation

1. U.K. business asset:

Proceeds of sale		£ 200,000.00
Market value at March 31, 1982		35,000.00
Total gain		165,000.00
Indexation allowance:		
RPI March 1982	79.44	
RPI April 1998	162.60	
Value at March 31, 1982 (35,000 x 1.047)		(36,645.00)
Taxable gain before taper		128,355.00
Taper—Disposal of business asset owned for two complete years—Business asset taper of 75%		(96,266.25)
Taxable gain		£ 32,088.75

2. Overseas asset:

Taxable gain = (Proceeds received in U.K. ÷ Net proceeds) x Total gain

Gain	£ 4,000.00
Less—Taper relief (four complete years owned since April 5, 1998, but treated as five years' ownership since held before March 17, 1998. Nonbusiness asset taper of 15% is available)	(600.00)
Total gain	£ 3,400.00
Taxable gain—(2,000 ÷ 10,000) x 3,400	£ 680.00

3. Total taxable gains	£ 32,768.75
Less—Annual exemption	(7,700.00)
Taxable amount	£ 25,068.75
Capital gains tax payable January 31, 2003 at 40%	£ 10,027.50

Note:

Exchange rate of the pound sterling at December 31, 2001: US$1 = £0.6905.

United States

PwC contact

For additional information on taxation in the United States, contact:

Michael Budnick
PricewaterhouseCoopers
1177 Avenue of the Americas
New York, NY 10036
Telephone: (1) (646) 471-8740
Fax: (1) (646) 471-8845
e-mail: michael.budnick@pwcglobal.com

Significant developments

Legislation was passed in 2001 to reduce tax rates and provide additional relief in the areas of education, retirement savings, and transfer taxes (among others). Many of the provisions phase in over a number of years, and several sunset in the year 2010.

Territoriality and residence

The United States taxes its citizens and resident aliens on their worldwide income. Nonresident aliens are taxed on their U.S.-source income, as discussed below. The determination of an alien's residence status is subject to a set of relatively objective tests. These rules generally treat the following individuals as residents.

1. All lawful permanent residents for immigration purposes ("green card" holders).
2. Those who meet a "substantial presence test." (Present in the United States for at least 31 days in the current year and a total of 183 equivalent days during the current year and prior two years. For the purposes of this 183-equivalent-day requirement, each day present in the United States during the current calendar year counts as a full day, each day in the first preceding year as one-third of a day and each day in the second preceding year as one-sixth of a day.)

Special rules apply to the determination of the portion of the year an individual will be treated as a resident or nonresident in the first and last years of residency.

Gross income

Employee gross income/Nonresident aliens are taxed on compensation earned for work performed in the United States, regardless of when or where payments are made, absent a treaty or Internal Revenue Code provision to the contrary.

Resident and nonresident alien employees are generally not taxed on reimbursements for either personal living expenses (i.e., food and housing) or for travel expenses while on "travel status." However, reimbursements for similar expenses of a spouse or dependent are taxable. Unlike the tests for determining U.S. residence status described above, being in travel status requires a temporary absence from an individual's tax home. Assignments for more than one year in a single work location are not considered to be temporary, regardless of any other facts and circumstances.

Capital gains and investment income/Capital gains of a resident alien are included in worldwide income and subject to U.S. taxation. Investment income of a resident alien is treated in the same manner.

Nonresident aliens are taxed at 30% on U.S.-source net capital gains if they are in the United States 183 days or more during the taxable year in which the gain occurs.

The operation of this provision is limited to situations where an alien is not otherwise taxed as a resident under the substantial presence test above. Capital gains from U.S. real property interests are taxable regardless of U.S. presence.

Nonresident aliens' U.S.-source interest, dividends, rents, and royalties are generally subject to a flat 30% tax rate (or lower treaty rate), usually withheld at source. However, a nonresident alien can elect to report real property rental income net of expenses, subject to tax at graduated rates. In addition, certain "portfolio interest" earned by a nonresident alien is generally exempt from tax.

Deductions

Business deductions/Resident and nonresident aliens can generally deduct, to the extent not reimbursed, travel or personal living expenses while on "travel status"; ordinary and necessary business expenses, including those for business-connected moving; and travel and entertainment expenses, subject to certain limitations. The deductible amount for meals and entertainment expenses is limited to 50% of actual costs. Additionally, all business expenses are deductible only to the extent that, when added to other miscellaneous itemized deductions, they exceed 2% of adjusted gross income (AGI). Unreimbursed moving expenses are not subject to this 2% floor and are deductible in arriving at AGI. Reimbursements for moving expenses may be eligible for exclusion from an employee's income; if reimbursement of moving expenses is so excluded, the expenses are not deductible by the employee. Nonresident aliens in travel status may deduct commuting expenses; however, resident aliens generally may not, because they are typically not in travel status.

Nonbusiness expenses/Resident aliens can deduct as itemized deductions qualified residence interest; most state and local income and property taxes; expenses incurred in producing income to the extent that they and other miscellaneous itemized deductions exceed 2% of AGI; and, subject to limitations, medical expenses, casualty and theft losses, and charitable contributions. No deduction is allowed for personal interest.

There is a limitation on these otherwise deductible itemized deductions (other than medical expenses, casualty and theft losses, and investment interest) for taxpayers with an AGI exceeding certain thresholds. In 2001 these thresholds are $132,950 for married taxpayers filing jointly, single taxpayers and head of household taxpayers and $66,475 for married taxpayers filing separately. These amounts are adjusted annually for inflation.

Such otherwise allowable itemized deductions are reduced by an amount equal to 3% of the amount of AGI in excess of the threshold amounts. In no event is the total of these otherwise allowable deductions reduced by more than 80%.

Interest paid on investment debt is deductible, but only to the extent there is net investment income (i.e., investment income net of investment expenses other than interest). Disallowed excess investment interest expense may be claimed as a deduction in subsequent years, to the extent of investment income.

Nonresident aliens may deduct, subject to limitations, casualty and theft losses incurred in the United States, contributions to U.S. charitable organizations, and state and local income taxes.

Instead of itemizing deductions, resident aliens may claim a standard deduction. The standard deduction for 2001 is $7,600 for married individuals filing a joint return, $4,550 for single individuals, $6,650 for heads of households, and $3,800 for married individuals filing separate returns. These amounts are adjusted annually for inflation. Nonresident aliens may not claim a standard deduction.

Taxpayers who are blind or age 65 or over, including resident aliens, are entitled to a higher standard deduction. For 2001 they may increase it by $900 if they are married or by $1,100 if they are single. If they are blind *and* age 65 or over, they may increase their standard deduction twice.

Personal allowances/Resident aliens are allowed a personal deduction (exemption) for themselves, for their spouse (subject to exceptions) and for each of their dependents (who must be citizens or residents of the United States, Canada or Mexico).

Nonresident aliens are entitled to only one personal exemption (except for those from Canada, Japan, the Republic of Korea, or Mexico).

For 2001 the personal exemption amount is $2,900. The personal exemption is adjusted annually for inflation.

The deduction for personal exemptions is phased out by 2% for each $2,500 or fraction thereof ($1,250 for married persons filing separate returns) by which a taxpayer's AGI exceeds a certain threshold. For 2001 these thresholds, which are adjusted annually for inflation, are $199,450 for joint return filers, $166,200 for head-of-household filers, $132,950 for single filers, and $99,725 for married persons filing separately.

Tax shelters/Tax reform has limited the use of tax losses derived from tax shelters ("passive" losses) to offset other taxable income. No longer can tax shelter losses offset income from other sources, such as earned income and portfolio (i.e., interest and dividend) income. Such losses can be used to offset passive income only. Similarly, credits from such investments can be used only to offset tax on net income from these investments. Disallowed losses can be carried forward to offset income from tax shelters in future years and, when the investment is sold or ceases operation, income from other sources.

Tax credits

Resident aliens may claim a credit against their tax liability (subject to limitations) for income taxes paid to foreign countries or foreign governmental units. Alternatively, foreign taxes may be deducted from taxable income. Nonresident aliens are generally not entitled to a deduction or credit for foreign taxes. Resident aliens may claim a child credit if the child is a resident of the United States.

Other taxes

Social security and Medicare hospital insurance taxes/For 2001 a resident or nonresident employee's share of social security taxes is 6.2% of the first $80,400 of salary ($84,900 for 2002), plus Medicare hospital insurance taxes of 1.45% on all wages. The social security tax for self-employed individuals is equal to 12.4% of the first $80,400 of net self-employment income plus Medicare hospital insurance tax of 2.9% on all net self-employment income. Self-employment tax (i.e., social security and Medicare hospital insurance tax) is imposed on residents. Nonresidents are not subject to self-employment tax. Social security and Medicare hospital insurance taxes are not deductible in determining an employee's taxable income. However, a deduction is allowed for an amount equal to one-half of the combined self-employment social security and Medicare hospital insurance tax imposed.

State and local income taxes/Most states and a number of municipal authorities impose income taxes on individuals working or residing within their jurisdictions.

California

The 2001 California personal income tax rates range from 1% to 9.3%. The top marginal rate of 9.3% applies to California taxable income in excess of $75,450 for married individuals filing joint returns and $37,725 for single individuals and for married individuals filing separate returns.

New York State

The New York State personal income tax rates range from 4.00% to 6.85% for 2001 returns. The top marginal rate of 6.85% applies to New York State taxable income exceeding $40,000 for married individuals filing joint returns and $20,000 for single individuals or married individuals filing separate returns. When New York State taxable income exceeds $150,000, the tax rate is a flat 6.85% on total taxable income.

In addition, New York City imposes a tax on its residents in 2001 at graduated rates from 2.683875% to 3.592%. The top marginal rate of 3.592% applies to New York City taxable income exceeding $90,000 for married individuals filing joint returns and $50,000 for single individuals or married individuals filing separate returns.

Tax administration

Returns/Husbands and wives may generally file a joint return only if each is either a citizen or a resident. However, where only one spouse is a full-year or part-year citizen or resident, a joint return may be filed if both spouses agree to be taxed as full-year residents on their combined worldwide income.

Generally, joint filing will result in a lower tax liability than separate filing. However, with the phase-out of the personal exemptions and the limitation imposed on the deductibility of itemized deductions, this determination can be made with certainty only after a thorough review of the taxpayers' facts and circumstances. Married nonresident aliens (i.e., where both spouses are nonresident aliens such that an election to file jointly is not available) may not file joint returns and must use the tax table for married persons filing separate returns. Nonresident aliens may not file as heads of household.

Payment of tax/Income tax is withheld from employee compensation. Resident and nonresident taxpayers with significant income not subject to withholding (e.g., self-employment income, interest, dividends) must generally make quarterly payments of estimated tax due April 15, June 15, September 15, and January 15. Nonresident aliens who do not have any income subject to payroll withholding tax make three estimated tax payments (rather than four) due June 15, September 15 and January 15, with 50% due with the first payment.

Tax rates

Effective 2001

Married taxpayers

Joint return (Notes 1, 2, and 3)

Taxable income		Tax on Column 1	Percentage on excess
Over	Not over		
(Column 1)			
	$ 45,200	—	15.0
$ 45,200	109,250	$ 6,780.00	27.5
109,250	166,500	24,393.75	30.5
166,500	297,350	41,855.00	35.5
297,350		88,306.75	39.1

Separate return (Note 1)

Taxable income		Tax on Column 1	Percentage over
Over	Not over		
(Column 1)			
0	$ 22,600	0	15.0
$ 22,600	54,625	$ 3,390.00	27.5
54,625	83,250	12,196.88	30.5
83,250	148,675	20,927.50	35.5
148,675		44,153.38	39.1

Unmarried taxpayers

Single (Note 1)

Taxable income		Tax on Column 1	Percentage over
Over	Not over		
(Column 1)			
0	$ 27,050	0	15.0
$ 27,050	65,550	$ 4,057.50	27.5
65,550	136,750	14,645.00	30.5
136,750	297,350	36,361.00	35.5
297,350		93,374.00	39.1

Head of household (Notes 1 and 3)

Taxable income			
Over (Column 1)	Not over	Tax on Column 1	Percentage over
0	$ 36,250	0	15.0
$ 36,250	93,650	$ 5,437.50	27.5
93,650	151,650	21,222.50	30.5
151,650	297,350	38,912.50	35.5
297,350		90,636.00	39.1

Notes:

1. The maximum federal tax rate on capital gains is 20% for assets held for more than 12 months. The graduated rates of tax apply to capital gains from assets held for 12 months or less.
2. Joint return rates may be used by a qualifying widow(er).
3. As noted, nonresident aliens may not take advantage of head of household status or joint return rates.

Alternative Minimum Tax/In lieu of the tax computed using the above rates, the Alternative Minimum Tax (AMT) may be imposed under a two-tier rate structure of 26% and 28%. The 26% rate applies to the first $175,000 ($87,500 for married individuals filing separate returns) of a taxpayer's alternative minimum taxable income (AMTI) in excess of an exemption amount; thereafter, the 28% rate applies. The exemption amount for 2001 is $49,000 for a joint return or qualifying widow(er), $24,500 for married filing separate returns, and $35,750 for other taxpayers. If, however, AMTI exceeds $150,000 for married taxpayers filing jointly ($75,000 for married filing separate returns and $112,500 for other taxpayers), the exemption is reduced by 25% of the excess amount.

Alternative Minimum Tax is payable only to the extent it exceeds the regular net tax liability. The foreign tax credit is available for determining AMT liability to the extent of the foreign tax on the foreign-source AMTI, subject to certain limitations. No more than 90% of AMT liability may be offset by foreign tax credits.

Alternative minimum taxable income is generally computed by starting with regular taxable income and adding tax preference deductions (claimed in the computation of regular taxable income) and making special adjustments to some of the tax items that were used to calculate taxable income. For example, the taxpayer must add back all state and local income taxes claimed in computing regular taxable income.

For nonresident aliens with a net gain from the sale of U.S. real property interests, the Alternative Minimum Tax is calculated on the lesser of their alternative minimum taxable income (before the exemption) or the net gain from the sale of the U.S. real property interest.

INDIVIDUAL FEDERAL TAX CALCULATION

Calendar year 2001

Assumptions

Resident alien husband and wife with two children; one spouse earns all the income, none of which is foreign-source income. A joint return is filed. AMT liability is less than regular tax liability.

Tax computation

Gross income:		
Salary		$ 120,000
Interest		16,200
Long-term capital gain (on assets held for more than one year)		1,250
Total gross income		137,450
Adjustments		0
Adjusted gross income		137,450
Less—Itemized deductions:		
State and local taxes	8,000	
Charitable contributions	1,000	
Unreimbursed business expenses (exclusive of 50% of meals and entertainment costs)—1,500 (1)	0	
Phaseout of itemized deductions (2)	(135)	8,865
		128,585
Less—Personal exemptions: 4 x 2,900 (3)		11,600
Taxable income		$ 116,985
Tax thereon:		
On taxable income of 115,735 (116,985 less capital gain of 1,250) at joint return rates		$ 26,371
On 1,250 capital gain at 20%		250
Total tax		$ 26,621

Notes:

1. Must exceed 2% of AGI ($137,450), or $2,749, to be deductible.
2. Reduced by 3% of AGI ($137,450) over $132,950.
3. Phaseout begins when AGI ($137,450) exceeds $199,450.

PwC contacts

For additional information on individual taxation in Uruguay, contact:

Leonardo Decarlini
Patricia Marques
PricewaterhouseCoopers
Cerrito 461, Piso 5
11000 Montevideo, Uruguay
Telephone: (598) (2) 916 0463
Fax: (598) (2) 916 0605, 916 0653
e-mail: leonardo.decarlini@uy.pwcglobal.com
patricia.marques@uy.pwc.global.com

Significant developments

There have been no significant regulatory or tax developments in the past year.

Absence of income tax

Income tax is not imposed on individuals in Uruguay.

Other taxes

Social security taxes/The Uruguayan social security system is comprehensive, covering retirement pensions, health insurance, sick pay, and unemployment insurance. Social security contributions are compulsory, based on the salary earned, including bonuses and commissions, and are borne by the employer and the employee.

The employer contributes an amount equivalent to 18.625% and withholds 19.125%, 20.125% or 24.125% from the employee, as follows.

	Employer contributions	Employee contributions
	%	%
Retirement contributions	12.5 or 0 (1)	15
Health insurance	5 or 2,5 (2)	3 (2)
Payroll tax	1	0, 2 or 6 (3)
Labor restructuring	0.125	0.125

Notes:

1. The 0% rate is applied to salaries earned by workers of industrial plants.
2. There is no health insurance contribution for corporate directors. The 2.5% rate is applied to salaries earned by workers of industrial plants.
3. The rate depends on the amount of the employee's salary. For salaries up to three National Minimum Salaries (SMN) the rate is 0%; between 3 SMN and 6 SMN the rate is 2% (since May 1, 1998); and for salaries exceeding 6 SMN, the rate is 6%. The SMN is currently UYP1,110 (equivalent to US$75).

Salaries above UYP31,158 (approximately US$2,100) are not subject to the retirement contribution on the excess of the referred amount. Health insurance and payroll tax are applicable on the whole salary.

Capital tax/Individuals that own capital not related to industrial and commercial activities exceeding UYP992,000 (equivalent to US$67,170) are subject to capital tax, which is applied on net worth (assets located in the country less certain liabilities) at progressive rates, which vary between 0.7% and 3%.

Note

Exchange rate of the peso at December 31, 2001: US$1 = UYP14.768.

PwC contact

For additional information on taxation in Uzbekistan, contact:

Abdulkhamid Muminov, Senior Tax Manager
PricewaterhouseCoopers
Akademik Boymukhamedov kochasi, 4
Makhallya Darkhan 3
Tashkent 700052, Uzbekistan
Telephone: 998 71 120 6101
Fax: 998 71 120 6645
e-mail: abdulkhamid.muminov@uz.pwcglobal.com

Significant developments

Legislation in the Republic of Uzbekistan is constantly evolving during the period of economic transition from the pre-independence socialist economy. The information presented below is based on laws, regulations, and practices as of February 18, 2002.

Significant changes in the tax and regulatory legislation are effective from January 1, 2002 and include the reduction of the top personal income tax rate 33% (down from 45% to 40% in 2000, further to 36% in 200).

Territoriality and residence

Both residents and nonresidents are subject to tax in Uzbekistan. Residents are taxed on their worldwide income, whereas nonresidents are taxed on income from their activities in Uzbekistan. An individual is a resident if one of the following two tests is met.

1. The individual resides in Uzbekistan on a permanent basis.
2. The individual is present in Uzbekistan for 183 days and more during any 12-month period beginning or ending in a calendar year.

Gross income

Gross income of an individual includes the following items.

1. Income from employment, including:
   a. Salary and other payments for work performed, as envisaged by labor or civil contracts;
   b. Negative difference between the prices at which goods (work, services) are provided to employees and the costs of acquisition of these goods (work, services);
   c. Reimbursement of employee's expenses not related to business activity;
   d. Employee's debts to an employer forgiven by the employer;
   e. Employer's expenses in relation to nonobligatory life and health insurance;
   f. Amounts subject to withholding from an employee, but paid by an employer;
   g. Other expenses of an employer constituting, directly or indirectly, income of an employee.
2. Income from property (interest, dividends and rent income).
3. Income from entrepreneurial activity.

Capital gains taxes/Capital gains generated from entrepreneurial activity are subject to income tax.

There are no specific concessions offered to foreigners in the personal income tax legislation with the exception of diplomats.

Exempt income/The following income items are not subject to personal income tax.

1. Statutory social security allowances, unemployment allowances, dismissal payments, maternity payments, aid payments received from charity and ecology funds (sick leave allowances are not exempt).
2. Child support received.
3. Scholarships within statutory limits.
4. Statutory pensions.
5. Income from disposal of personal property (if the disposal is in the course of entrepreneurial activity, the income is taxable).
6. Gifts from legal entities valued at less than six times the statutory minimum monthly wage during a year (approximately US$30 per year).
7. Money and property received in the course of inheritance.
8. Insurance proceeds.
9. Bank interest from Uzbek banks.
10. Material support (if related to natural disaster—exempt in full; in other cases—limited to 12 times the statutory minimum monthly wage during a year (approximately $60 per year).
11. Dividends used for the purchase of shares of a company from which the dividends were received.
12. Income from intellectual property.
13. Reimbursement of business expenses (business trips), within statutory norms.

Deductions

There are no standard deductions under Uzbek law. Effective January 1, 2001, the right to a monthly deduction of one statutory minimum monthly wage was abolished. The only deductions available relate to income derived from entrepreneurial activities and represent expenses and mandatory payments and charges associated with such activities.

Certain categories of individuals are also either fully exempt from personal income tax (for example, diplomats) or provided with an additional monthly deduction of four amounts of the statutory minimum monthly wage (approximately US$20 per month), including veterans, disabled people, widows/widowers with children, and women with many children, among others.

Local income taxes

There are no local income taxes.

Tax credits

According to the tax code, a credit is provided for foreign taxes paid to countries with which Uzbekistan has a double taxation treaty. However, in practice, the state tax authorities allow credit for any foreign income taxes paid on income that is also subject to Uzbek taxation.

Tax administration

The tax period is the calendar year. A tax return must be submitted by the individual to the tax authorities at the location of the individual's registration in Uzbekistan on or before April 1 of the year following the reported year.

Tax rates

The tax rates are as follows.

Taxable income	Tax rate
	%
Up to 4 times the minimum annual wage	13
From 4 to 8 times the minimum annual wage	23
More than 8 times the minimum annual wage	33

The minimum annual wage is UZS60. As mentioned above, the annual wage deduction has been abolished.

INDIVIDUAL TAX CALCULATION

As of January 1, 2002 (1)

	US$	UZS
Salary	80,000	55,040,000
Interest from a foreign bank	5,000	3,440,000
Taxable income	85,000	58,480,000
Tax base	85,000	58,480,000
Tax thereon:		
4 x MMW at 13%	31	21,403
4 x MMW at 23%	55	37,867
Balance at 33%	27,892	19,189,738
Subtotal	27,978	19,249,008
Foreign tax paid (2)	(10,000)	(6,880,000)
Tax due	17,978	12,369,008

Notes:

1. Assumes an average exchange rate of Soum UZS688 per US$1 (actual rate as of January 1, 2002).
2. In theory, only foreign tax paid in a country with which Uzbekistan has a double taxation treaty can be credited against Uzbek tax.
3. Capital gains from the disposal of nonbusiness property are not included to taxable income (e.g., sale of premises, cars, etc.).
4. Official exchange rate of the Soum at January 1, 2002: US$1 = UZS688. Over the past few years, the exchange rate of the soum has undergone many revisions. At January 1, 2000 the rate was US$1 = UZS140.00 and during the year changed rapidly. With effect from May 1, 2000, official exchange rate of US$1 = UZS149.38 was eliminated in favor of the commercial rate of US$1 = UZS231. The next change was even more substantive, introducing a “free market exchange rate,” which would be defined by banks based on demand and supply of the foreign currency. Thus, by January 1, 2001, Uzbekistan had two effective rates for accounting/taxation/reporting purposes and operations at the over-the-counter market. These two rates were merged into one single rate to be used for accounting and reporting purpose.

PwC contacts

For additional information related in Venezuela, contact:

Luis Fernando Miranda, PwC Tax Partner
Robert de Liefde, International Tax Manager
Espiñeira, Sheldon y Asociados
Edificio Del Rio
Avenida Principal de Chuao
Caracas 1061-A, Venezuela
Telephone (58) (0212) 9026124, 9026194
Fax (58) (0212) 9915210
e-mail: fernando.miranda@ve.pwcglobal.com

Mailing address:
Espiñeira, Sheldon y Asociados
c/o Jet International-M347
P.O. Box 020010
Miami, Florida 33102-0010
U.S.A.

Significant developments

The following information is updated at March 5, 2002.

Changes to the Income Tax Law entered into effect as of January 1, 2001, and include the following.

1. The broadening of the territoriality regime by establishing a system based on taxation of worldwide income.
2. Creation of a dividend tax.
3. A regime of international fiscal transparency has been created for the purpose of establishing special standards of fiscal control governing capital investments in countries classified as jurisdictions with low fiscal taxation (JLFTs, tax havens). Venezuelan tax residents who own or economically speaking control a tax-haven company may become subject to Venezuelan income tax on an accrual basis as of 2001.

Territoriality and residence

Changes to the Income Tax Law, effective as of January 1, 2001 have broadened the territoriality regime, establishing a system based on taxation of worldwide income, as follows.

1. Resident individuals are subject to tax on their total worldwide income.
2. Individuals domiciled abroad with a permanent establishment in Venezuela must pay taxes on their income of national or foreign source attributable to said establishment.
3. Nonresident individuals will pay taxes on their income whenever the cause or origin of such income lies within Venezuela.
4. Resident individuals, as well as individuals domiciled abroad with a permanent establishment in Venezuela, may credit the income tax paid abroad for income of extraterritorial source.

Individuals are considered to be residents in Venezuela for tax purposes when they spend more than 183 days in Venezuela in aggregate during a fiscal year or if they have spent more than 183 days in Venezuela in the preceding year. Thus, an individual who spends 184 days in Venezuela will be deemed to be a resident for tax purposes.

Gross income

Employee gross income/Resident and nonresident individuals are taxed on salaries and wages and on any other remuneration for personal services such as meal allowances, pensions, profit sharing, and other similar remunerations, regardless of the place of payment or currency used. Employees are not taxed on pensions and termination benefits as set forth in the Labor Law or collective contracts (employer/union) and interest thereon, or income from trusts established to administer employer contributions to the related funds.

Until December 31, 2000 foreign-source income was not taxable in Venezuela. Thereafter, foreign-source income will be taxable unless an exemption or tax treaty applies.

Tax units/The 1994 amendment to the Income Tax Law established the concept of a tax unit (TU) to reduce the negative effect of inflation on the determination of the tax rates. The Tax Code established the initial TU at Bs. 1,000 with annual basis adjustment based on the variation of the consumer price index (CPI) from the previous year. In March of each year, the tax unit value is adjusted for inflation that occurred in the preceding fiscal year.

For the 2002 the tax unit value will be close to Bs14,800.

Capital gains and investment income/Capital gains are taxable as ordinary income. Individuals are taxed on any Venezuelan source income, including income derived from industrial and commercial activities, earnings derived from the sale of personal property or services, and royalties and interest.

Income earned by individuals investing in the local stock exchange (sale of shares) are subject to a flat tax of 1% (via withholding). Profits and losses related to the same activity can not be taxable or deductible against ordinary taxable income.

Effective January 1, 2001, a dividend tax has been established. The tax is levied at a flat rate of 34% on the positive difference between book income and fiscal income generated after 2001. To determine this difference, the last in first out (LIFO) method applies. The 34% (domestic) rate can be mitigated under tax treaties to 10%, 5% or even 0%. The withholdings are to be made at the moment a dividend is declared or credited (to an account of the recipient).

Dividends obtained from companies incorporated or domiciled abroad or incorporated abroad and domiciled in Venezuela are excluded from the dividend tax system. However, these dividends will be taxed at 34% flat tax income tax rate.

Income received in the form of interest, royalties or proceeds from the sale of real estate is taxable when paid. Interest earned from Venezuelan saving deposits or saving funds is tax exempt.

Deductions

Business deductions/Resident individuals who are not employees can deduct expenses allowed by law, using the same guidelines applicable for corporations. Taxable income does not include travel expense reimbursements and limited representation allowances. Business deductions from salary income are not allowed.

Nonbusiness expenses/In determining taxable income, Venezuela residents can deduct the following expenses.

1. Educational payments made in Venezuela for the taxpayer and for the dependent children under 25 years of age.
2. Life, surgery, hospitalization, and maternity insurance premium payments.
3. Medical, dental and hospitalization payments.
4. Rent or interest payments on loans granted for the acquisition or enlargement of the taxpayer's home. The authorized disencumbrance might not exceed 1,000 TU for the fiscal year in the case of interest on loans, or 800 TU for the fiscal year in the case of payments associated with the leasing of main or permanent housing.

Taxpayers should attach the invoices, with the RIF (taxpayer) number, to the tax return.

Special deductions/Taxpayers have the option to claim a special (single) deduction of 774 TU. No documentation is necessary. Taxpayers who choose the special deduction cannot claim the deductions indicated above.

Personal allowances/Residents receive a personal tax credit of 10 TU for the taxpayer, spouse, and any dependent.

Tax credits

Resident Individuals may take credit for income tax paid abroad in regard to extraterritorial source income.

Other taxes

Social security taxes/Social security taxes are 4% of salary, up to a maximum salary of Bs90,000 per month.

Unemployment benefit program/Funds to finance this program are obtained from contributions paid by both the employers and the employees. The rate is 2.2% of the salaries earned by employees, of which 1.7% must be paid by the employer and 0.5% by the employee through monthly withholdings.

Mandatory housing savings plan/Special legislation aimed at creating funds for financing construction for low to medium-priced housing, requires employers and employees/workers to make a monthly contribution to personal accounts opened by employers on behalf of their employees. The employer must contribute 2% and the employee/worker 1% of salary.

Other taxes on income/Municipal tax authorities impose taxes on commercial activities conducted by individuals within their jurisdiction. An individual carrying out business activities can deduct these taxes in determining their Venezuelan income tax.

Tax administration

Returns/Spouses must, in principle, file joint returns even if they have personal income arising from their own activities. They will be considered as a single taxpayer. Husbands and wives can file separate tax returns only when the following conditions apply.

1. There was a mutual agreement for separation of property.
2. They both are reporting salaries, wages and professional fees.

Individual taxpayers must file their returns on a calendar-year basis. Exceptions are permitted (for instance, when an individual leaves Venezuela or ceases all business).

Payment of tax/Income tax is withheld from salaries, professional fees, royalties paid to nonresidents, and certain other payments received by nonresidents.

Individuals other than employees must file estimated returns only if, during the year immediately preceding fiscal year, they received income exceeding 1,500 TU from commercial, credit, leasing, or subleasing activities involving movable or real property or salaries exceeding 1,000 TU.

The estimated tax is based on 75% of the tax that would result from applying full rates to the estimated income declared (80%). The prepaid tax resulting from the estimated returns must be paid in either a single installment or in three equal installments.

Final tax returns must be filed within three months following the end of the tax year. Tax resulting from the filing of the final tax returns must be paid in a single installment or in three equal installments.

Tax rates

Resident individuals are subject to tax using graduated rates, with the marginal rate reaching 34% on annual income above approximately US$105,000 in 2001 (using an exchange rate of US$1 = Bs750).

Income for nonresident individuals arising from nonbusiness professional activities is subject to tax of 34% on 90% of the gross payments. Salary and other income received by nonresidents for services performed in Venezuela are subject to a flat 34% tax, withheld at source.

The annual income tax, before credits, is calculated using the following tax rate table (Tariff No. 1).

Range of taxable income (in TU)		Tax rate	Deduction
Over	Not over	%	TU
0	1,000	6	0
1,001	1,500	9	30
1,501	2,000	12	75
2,001	2,500	16	155
2,501	3,000	20	255
3,001	4,000	24	375
4,001	6,000	29	575
6,001		34	875

Note:

Exchange rate of the Bolivar at January 1, 2002: US$1 = Bs769.000.

PwC contacts

For additional information on taxation in Vietnam, contact:

Tim Finlayson
Richard Irwin
Tax and Consulting
PricewaterhouseCoopers (Vietnam) Ltd.
4th Floor, Saigon Tower
29 Le Duan, District 1
Ho Chi Minh City, Vietnam
Telephone: (84) (8) 823 0796
Fax: (84) (8) 825 1947
e-mail: tim.j.finlayson@vn.pwcglobal.com
r.irwin@vn.pwcglobal.com

Significant developments

Under new tax regulations, contributions to Social Insurance and the Health Insurance Fund from employees' salaries and wages are not taxable.

Taxpayers can elect to pay tax themselves or have their employers withhold and pay tax.

The personal income tax (PIT) rates reflected in this summary are effective for the 2002 year for foreigners only. For other tax (including personal tax on Vietnamese employees) or regulatory developments, please refer to the contact above.

Territoriality and residence

Residence is determined as follows.

1. Foreigners are considered to be resident in Vietnam and are taxable on their worldwide income if they live and work in Vietnam for an aggregate of 183 days or more within a period of 12 months. Tax is computed at progressive rates (see "Tax rates" below).
2. Nonresident foreigners who spend between 30 days and 182 days working in Vietnam are taxed only on Vietnam-source income, and the tax rate is a flat 25% in the first year. In subsequent years "a nonresident foreigner" must pay PIT at progressive tax rates on their Vietnamese sourced income. Individuals who are tax resident of countries which have a double taxation agreement with Vietnam can obtain a tax exemption if they are nonresident for Vietnam tax purposes and certain additional conditions are met.
3. Nonresident foreigners who spend less than 30 days working in Vietnam are exempt from PIT.

Gross income

Employee gross income/In general, tax applies not only to employment income but to all forms of income received by an individual. Regular income includes salaries, wages, directors' fees, allowances, and bonuses. Employer-provided housing, electricity and water are taxed.

Technically, all noncash benefits are taxable. However exceptions to this include school fees for expatriates' children, home leave for expatriates, and education/training fees for employees, provided that these payments are paid directly by the employer to the suppliers.

The value attributed to housing which is added to taxable income is limited to 15% of gross wages or salary if this is less than the actual housing cost.

Where an employee is remunerated on a net basis (i.e., net of tax) this net income is required to be grossed-up to determine gross income subject to PIT.

Irregular income (e.g., gifts from overseas; lottery prizes; fees or commissions for technology transfer, industrial design or technical construction design; and royalties from cultural works, conducting technical seminars or scientific research) is taxed separately on each transaction at rates different from those applicable to regular income. Business income would normally be subject to business income tax and not personal income tax.

Capital gains and investment income/Under the tax regulations, certain capital gains and investment income are temporarily not taxable, including: interest on bank deposits, bank savings and loans; profits from purchases of bonds and shares; income derived from investment in stocks and gains from purchases and sales of stocks.

Deductions

Business deductions/Business income and deductions are dealt with under the rules for business income tax, not personal income tax.

Nonbusiness expenses/No deductions are allowable.

Personal allowances/There are certain types of allowances that are treated as nontaxable, these include specific hardship, night-shift and fixed meal allowances. There are no personal allowances.

Tax credits

Vietnam has no unilateral tax credit relief for foreigners or Vietnamese nationals, however relief or exemption is available where tax treaties apply.

Other taxes

Social security taxes/Employers contribute 15% and employees 5% of the employee's total wages for social insurance purposes every month. Expatriates are exempt.

Health insurance/Health insurance is payable by employers at the rate of 2% of the employee's wages. The employee contributes an additional 1%. Expatriates are exempt.

Under new tax regulations, contributions to Social Insurance and the Health Insurance Fund from employees' salaries and wages are not taxable.

Tax administration

Returns/Personal income tax (PIT) returns can be filed on an individual or company basis. Tax on regular income is finalized annually or upon termination of the employment contract. Employers or employees are required to file monthly provisional PIT returns. The tax year is the calendar year, and annual tax returns of employees are to be finalized with the tax authorities by February 28 or within 30 days of the termination of the contract.

Payment of tax/There are two options: the employee can pay the tax personally each month or the employer can withhold tax monthly and pay it to the authorities on behalf of the employees within 15 days of beginning of the following month. An employer that withholds the PIT and remits to the tax authorities receives a commission (0.5% of tax payable) for being the withholding agent.

The monthly payments are provisional and will be finalized at the end of the year.

Tax rates

Regular income/Rates for resident foreigners are as follows. Note that even for finalization of annual PIT returns the employee's income is converted to a monthly basis and tax is calculated accordingly.

Rates applicable from July 1,1999

Monthly income		Tax on	Percentage
Over (Column 1)	Not over	Column 1	on excess
0	VND 8,000,000	—	—
VND 8,000,000	20,000,000	—	10
20,000,000	50,000,000	VND 1,200,000	20
50,000,000	80,000,000	7,200,000	30
80,000,000	120,000,000	16,200,000	40
120,000,000		32,200,000	50

The rate for nonresident foreigners is a flat 25% in the first year on the Vietnam-source income. In subsequent years the provisional tax rates for foreign residents apply, but only on the Vietnam-source income.

Irregular income/Rates on such income, applied to each individual transaction, are as follows.

Monthly income		Tax on	Percentage
Over (Column 1)	Not over	Column 1	on excess
0	VND 2,000,000	—	—
VND 2,000,000	4,000,000	—	5
4,000,000	10,000,000	VND 100,000	10
10,000,000	20,000,000	700,000	15
20,000,000	30,000,000	2,200,000	20
30,000,000		4,200,000	30

In the case of fee income from technology transfers, the rate is a flat 5% per transaction (nil for income of less than VND2,000,000).

For lottery winnings, the rate is a flat 10% per event (nil for winnings of less than VND12,500,000).

In the case of gifts from overseas, the rate is a flat 5% (nil for items less than VND2,000,000).

INDIVIDUAL TAX CALCULATION

For regular income earned by foreigners, for the calendar year 2002.

Assumptions

Annual gross income is VND1.08 billion (VND90 million per month), that is, annual income of US$71,933 and monthly income of US$5,994.

No housing is provided by the employer.

Tax computation

Gross monthly taxable income	VND	90,000,000
Income tax thereon:		
On first 80,000,000	VND	16,200,000
On remainder (10,000,000) at 40%		4,000,000
	VND	20,200,000
Annual equivalent (12 x 20,200,000)	VND	242,400,000

Note:

Exchange rate of the Vietnamese Dong at January 1, 2002: US$1 = VND15,014.

PwC contact

For additional information on taxation in Zambia, contact:

Eileen Duncan
PricewaterhouseCoopers
National Savings and Credit Bank Building
Seventh Floor
North End, Cairo Road
(P.O. Box 30942)
Lusaka, Zambia
Telephone: (260) (1) 228809-10, 220782, 220778
Fax: (260) (1) 220768
Internet: pwclsk@zamnet.zm
e-mail: Eileen.duncan@zm.pwcglobal.com

Significant developments

The information in this entry is current as of January 2002. For subsequent developments consult the contact listed above.

Territoriality and residence

Zambia taxes income received by individuals from a source within Zambia and foreign interest and dividends received by citizens and residents (including expatriates). For the purposes of Zambian taxation, individuals are not treated as resident if they are visitors with no intention of establishing residence in Zambia and have not actually been resident for a total of 183 days in any tax year. An alien person taking up employment in Zambia under contract enters Zambia on a work permit and is classified as an "expatriate."

Gross income

Employee gross income/An employee is taxed on total emoluments and benefits (other than those detailed below), regardless of where payment is made and regardless of whether it is remitted. Inducement allowances to expatriates are subject to tax in their hands. The cost of inducement allowances is allowed as a deduction in determining the employer's taxable income.

The gratuity up to 25% of the basic salary or inducement allowance for a minimum period of two years under a written contract of employment is taxed separately. Any amount in excess of 25% is added to the salary and other emoluments and taxed normally.

An employee is not taxed on the following items.

1. Accommodation provided by the employer directly or for which rent is paid by the employer to the landlord. However, the housing benefit to be disallowed in the employer's tax computation is 30% of the taxable income paid to an employee per annum, regardless of whether the housing is employer-owned or rented.
2. Mortgage interest paid by an owner/occupier of a residential property.
3. Car benefit. However, the Commissioner of Taxes has determined that the value of noncash fringe benefits for cars that are also used personally by the holder is disallowed in the employer's tax computation. For this purpose, two categories have been set up:

a. Luxury cars—Those with an engine capacity of 1,800 cc and above. The fringe benefit for these cars is assessed at ZK200,000 per month.

b. Other cars—Cars with an engine capacity that is below 1,800 cc. The fringe benefit for these cars is assessed at ZK120,000 per month.

4. Terminal benefits paid by way of ex gratia payments or compensation for loss of office. The first ZK3,000,000 is exempt, and the balance is taxed at a flat rate of 10%. Any ex gratia payment in respect of a deceased employee or payment for termination of employment on medical grounds are exempt from tax.

In addition to the above, an expatriate is not taxed on the following items.

1. Economy-class commencement and terminal passages made by the individual.
2. An education passage for each child for each consecutive period of four months.

Capital gains and investment income/Currently, capital gains are not taxable. Dividends received by an expatriate outside Zambia are aggregated with Zambian income. Relief for any tax withheld by the foreign country is subject to the provisions of any tax treaty between the two countries. Rental income received from outside Zambia is exempt from Zambian tax.

Interest earned by a resident on any sum deposited in Zambia is exempt from tax up to a maximum of ZK300,000. The excess is taxed at a flat rate of 25%. Foreign bank interest received by a resident in Zambia is taxed at the normal rate for individuals, currently 30%.

Deductions

Business deductions/Every person can deduct pension contributions to an approved fund (subject to limitations) and, to the extent not reimbursed, subscription fees for membership in technical/professional associations.

Nonbusiness expenses/An expatriate can deduct premiums paid under an approved annuity contract (not exceeding ZK180,000) and approved charitable contributions (restricted to 15% of assessable income). Alimony and maintenance payments are not deductible and are not subject to tax in the hands of the recipient. Insurance premium payments are not allowable as deductions. No other standard deductions are available.

Individual tax credit/The individual tax credit for every individual taxpayer is ZK144,000 per annum, which is deductible from the total tax due. The individual tax credit has replaced the primary allowance. This means that an individual with an annual income of ZK1,440,000 or less is not liable to tax for the year in question.

The tax credit for handicapped persons is ZK1,200 per annum.

Tax credits

Resident taxpayers can take income taxes paid to foreign countries as a credit against their Zambian tax liability, subject to the provisions of a tax treaty.

See also "Individual tax credit."

Other taxes

Social security taxes/Social security contributions are deductible for a resident taxpayer. Expatriates are not eligible to contribute to the Social Security Fund.

Local taxes on income/Apart from the personal levy, which is negligible, there are no local taxes on income.

Tax administration

Returns/For all persons, annual self-assessment returns are required to be filed by September 30 of each year for the previous fiscal year ended March 31. Outstanding tax liabilities should be settled by that date. There is a penalty for failure to submit tax returns on or before any specified due date.

Husbands and wives can file separate returns even if both are resident in Zambia. The earned and investment income of the wife is taxed on her separately. As a result of a change in the tax law with effect from April 1, 1996, the wife's investment income is no longer assessable on the husband.

Payment of tax/Income tax is withheld from salaries (pay-as-you-earn (PAYE)). A taxpayer who has a sizable income not subject to PAYE is required to make quarterly payments of estimated tax on a current-year basis. All unsettled income tax liabilities must be paid by September 30 of each year (i.e., within six months of the March 31 fiscal year-end).

Tax rates

Expatriate employees may be paid remuneration in two parts, a local salary and an inducement allowance, which are both liable to income tax at unified rates (however, see "Gross income" above).

With effect from April 1, 2001, tax rates are as follows.

Taxable income		Tax on Column 1	Percentage on excess
Over (Column 1)	Not over		
0	ZK 1,600,000	—	10
ZK 1,600,000	2,200,000	ZK 160,000	20
2,200,000		280,000	30

INDIVIDUAL TAX CALCULATION

For fiscal year ending March 31, 2002

Assumptions

Resident husband and wife, two children; husband earns all the income.

Tax computation

Salary (including inducement allowance)		ZK 10,000,000
Add:		
Zambian-source bank interest	100,000	
U.K.-source bank interest	50,000	
Cash allowances	400,000	550,000
		10,550,000
Less—Deductions:		
U.K. National Insurance contributions (social security)	5,000	
Charitable contributions	50,000	
Exempt bank interest	100,000	155,000
Taxable income		ZK 10,395,000
Tax liability		ZK 2,738,500
Less—Tax credit		(144,000)
Tax due (1)		ZK 2,594,500

Notes:

1. Normally, tax amounting to ZK2,594,000 (net of ZK144,000 tax credit) on the salary and cash allowances would have been deducted by the employer under the PAYE system.
2. Exchange rate of the kwacha at December 31, 2001: US$1 = ZK3,950.

PwC contact

For additional information on taxation in Zimbabwe, contact:

Josephine Matambo
Price Waterhouse
P.O. Box 453
Harare, Zimbabwe
Telephone: (263) (4) 307213-19
Fax: (263) (4) 332724/332495
e-mail: josephine.matambo@zw.pwcglobal.com

Significant developments

There have been no significant tax or regulatory developments as regards individual taxation in the past year.

Territoriality and residence

The Zimbabwean income tax system operates mainly on a territorial basis, and income is as a general rule taxable in Zimbabwe if the source is within Zimbabwe. Individuals who are not ordinarily resident are taxable only on income from sources in Zimbabwe. Individuals who are regarded as being ordinarily resident in Zimbabwe are subject to tax on employment income earned during temporary absences from Zimbabwe (up to 183 days in a tax year) and on foreign investment income. Income for services performed outside Zimbabwe is deemed to be from a Zimbabwean source if the services are incidental to employment in Zimbabwe.

There is no definition of "ordinarily resident" in the legislation, and no hard and fast rules apply for determining whether a person is ordinarily resident in Zimbabwe. The question must be decided on the particular circumstances of each case. A foreign employee who has been present in Zimbabwe for two years or more and who has been joined there by spouse and family would be regarded as being ordinarily resident in Zimbabwe for the period of stay. On the other hand, employees who were there for six months to a year and who left their families at home would probably not be treated as ordinarily resident.

Gross income

Employee gross income/Expatriate employees are taxable on salary and on any overseas allowances, irrespective of the place of payment and whether or not they are remitted to Zimbabwe. Living and housing allowances, tax reimbursements and the value of benefits such as free accommodation and the use of motor vehicles, as well as the deemed value of interest-free or low-interest loans, are included in taxable income. There are no tax concessions in favor of short-term residents, and all income relating to services rendered in Zimbabwe is taxable.

Any bonus received by an employee (to the extent that it does not exceed Z$10,000 or 10% of annual remuneration after excluding the amount of the bonus, whichever is lower) is exempt from income tax.

A foreign employee who was present in Zimbabwe on a short-term contract for a very limited period (one year or less) and who was not ordinarily resident would have a reasonable chance of successfully claiming that the provision of accommodation did not constitute a taxable benefit. This would be on the basis that the accommodation was for the purpose of the employer's business and that the foreign employee continued to maintain the family establishment in the home country. As with ordinary residence, there are no strict rules, and taxability of benefits must be decided on the basis of individual circumstances.

Capital gains and investment income/Zimbabwe-source capital gains are taxable at the rate of 20%. Tax is levied on the gain after deduction of acquisition costs and a 30% annual allowance on these costs. The tax is confined to disposals of immovable property (real estate) and marketable securities, which include, as the most important items, stocks and shares. (Shares quoted on the Zimbabwe Stock Exchange are exempt.) The intent is to exclude gains on foreign real estate and foreign stocks and shares from Zimbabwean capital gains tax. Residence in and of itself has no bearing on liability for capital gains tax.

Dividends payable to resident individuals by Zimbabwean corporations are subject to a 20% withholding tax but are exempt from income tax. Dividends from corporations quoted on the Zimbabwe Stock Exchange are subject to a reduced rate of 15% withholding tax.

Withholding tax at a rate of 20% applies to interest (including discount instruments and treasury bills) payable by a Zimbabwean bank, discount house, financial institution, or building society to a resident. The interest is exempt from normal income tax and the 20% withholding tax is final. Interest from local foreign-currency-denominated accounts is exempt. All other taxable interest from Zimbabwean sources is taxed at normal tax rates. Interest and dividend income on foreign investments is taxable in Zimbabwe if the recipient was ordinarily resident in Zimbabwe at the time of accrual of the income.

Short-term residents regarded as ordinarily resident in Zimbabwe are taxable on such income. Interest is taxable as ordinary income, but foreign dividends are taxed at a special flat rate of 20%. Foreign rents and royalties are not taxable in Zimbabwe except for royalties paid for the use of the property or rights in question in Zimbabwe. Zimbabwe-source interest and dividends (other than dividends from shares listed on the Zimbabwe Stock Exchange) payable to nonresident individuals are subject to withholding taxes of 10% and 20%, respectively, unless reduced by a double taxation treaty. Dividends from shares listed on the Zimbabwe Stock Exchange are subject to a withholding tax of 15%, again subject to the provisions of any double taxation treaty.

Deductions

Business deductions/No business-related expenses are deductible unless they are incurred as a condition of employment or for the purpose of producing the employee's income, such as in circumstances where the expenditure can be shown to influence the level of the employee's income. An employee remunerated on a commission basis could be in this position. Moving and travel expenses are not deductible. Entertainment expenses are prohibited as a deduction, and business entertainment and travel allowances provided by an employer are taxable to the extent that they are not expended for the purpose of the employer's business. There are no standard or blanket deductions except a nominal deduction for tradesmen's tools where the tools are provided by the employee. Subscriptions to business, trade, technical, or professional associations are deductible.

Nonbusiness expenses/Contributions to approved pension funds (to a maximum of Z$45,000) are deductible, including contributions to approved social security schemes of other countries. Credits are allowable on medical expenses (if the taxpayer is ordinarily resident in Zimbabwe).

No allowances are available for mortgage and other interest payments, taxes and charitable donations (except to a few specified institutions). There are no standard deductions for nonbusiness expenses.

Personal allowances/No personal credits are available.

Tax credits

Unilateral relief from double taxation is available where income from foreign sources is deemed to be from a Zimbabwean source. The relief takes the form of a foreign tax credit up to the amount of the tax brought about by inclusion of the foreign income in the Zimbabwean assessment.

Other taxes

National Social Security contributions are payable by all employees (to a maximum of Z$2,520 per annum). No local income tax is payable in addition to central government taxes.

Tax administration

Returns/Married taxpayers file tax returns separately. Filing of joint returns is not permitted. Taxpayers must adhere to a calendar year.

Payment of tax/A pay-as-you-earn (PAYE) system, under which income tax is withheld from remuneration payable to employees, is in operation. From the year ending December 31, 2002 this will be the final tax for employees who are employed by the same employer throughout the year and who have no other source of income. Such employees will not be required to file tax returns.

Tax rates

Income tax/In the case of income from employment, with effect from January 1, 2002, there are graduated taxes of tax up to Z$840,000 of taxable income. The tax on this amount is Z$271,500. Thereafter, the maximum rate of 45% applies. In addition there is an AIDS levy of 3% of the tax chargeable, giving an effective rate of 46.35%. The income tax on remuneration of Z$1,000,000 is Z$353,805, including the levy.

Any taxable income accruing to an individual from any trade, investment or other activity (excluding employment or pension) is taxed at a flat rate of 30% plus an AIDS levy of 3% of tax chargeable, giving an effective rate of 30.9%.

INDIVIDUAL TAX CALCULATION

Assumptions

A foreign national is on a three-year contract and is regarded as ordinarily resident in Zimbabwe. Income and deductions for the year ending December 31, 2002 are as shown below.

	Z$
Salary	1,350,000
Overseas allowance	40,000
Net local bank interest (withholding tax, Z$1,800) (1)	840
Proceeds from sale of private residence in Zimbabwe (purchased in February 1999 for Z$800,000)	1,700,000
PAYE deductions from salary	590,000
Contributions to company pension fund	67,000

Tax computation

Income tax computation

Salary	Z$ 1,350,000
Overseas allowance	40,000
	1,390,000
Less—Pension fund contributions (maximum)	45,000
Taxable income	Z$ 1,345,000
Income tax on 1,330,000 (rounded)	Z$ 513,713
Less—PAYE	(590,000)
Net income tax refundable	Z$ 76,287

Capital gains tax computation

Proceeds from sale of residence		Z$ 1,700,000
Less:		
Cost of acquisition	800,000	
30% on acquisition costs for each tax year involved = 90%	720,000	1,520,000
Capital gain		Z$ 180,000
Capital gains tax payable at 20%		Z$ 36,000

Notes:

1. Bank interest from which tax has been withheld at source does not figure in the income tax determination.
2. Exchange rate of the Zimbabwe dollar at January 1, 2002: US$1 = Z$55.